Poverty, Gender and Migration

Other volumes in the series

Volume 1: *Transnational Migration and the Politics of Identity*
Editor: Meenakshi Thapan

Volume 3: *Gender, Conflict and Migration*
Editor: Navnita Chadha Behera

Volume 4: *Exploring Migrant Women and Work*
Editor: Anuja Agrawal

Volume 5: *Marriage and Migration*
Editors: Patricia Uberoi and Rajni Palriwala

Women and Migration in Asia, Volume 2

SERIES EDITOR: MEENAKSHI THAPAN

Poverty, Gender and Migration

Editors
Sadhna Arya
Anupama Roy

SAGE Publications
New Delhi/Thousand Oaks/London

First published in 2006 by

Sage Publications India Pvt Ltd
B-42, Panchsheel Enclave
New Delhi 110 017
www.indiasage.com

Sage Publications Inc.
2455 Teller Road
Thousand Oaks, California 91320

Sage Publications Ltd
1 Oliver's Yard, 55 City Road
London EC1Y 1SP

Published by Tejeshwar Singh for Sage Publications India Pvt Ltd, phototypeset 10/12 Aldine401BT by Siva Math Setters, Chennai and printed at Chaman Enterprises, New Delhi.

Library of Congress Cataloging-in-Publication Data

Poverty, gender, and migration / editors, Sadhna Arya, Anupama Roy.
    p. cm. — (Women and migration in Asia ; v. 2)
    Includes bibliographical references and index.
    1. Women immigrants—Asia—Social conditions. 2. Women migrant labour—Asia. 3. Sex discrimination against women—Asia. 4. Poverty—Asia. 5. Asia—Emigration and immigration—Social aspects. I. Arya, Sadhna. II. Roy, Anupama. III. Series.

JV6347.P68   331.4086'24—dc22   2006   2005034718

ISBN: 0–7619–3458–8 (HB)   81–7829–608–X (India-HB)
         0–7619–3459–6 (PB)   81–7829–609–8 (India-PB)

Sage Production Team: Ankush Saikia, Anindita Pandey, Girish Sharma and Santosh Rawat

Contents

SERIES INTRODUCTION 7
Acknowledgements 18

1 When Poor Women Migrate: Unravelling
Issues and Concerns 19
Sadhna Arya and Anupama Roy

2 Bringing Home the Money: Migration and
Poverty in Gender Politics in Sri Lanka 49
Sepali Kottegoda

3 Leaving Home: Filipino Women Surviving Migration 72
Maureen C. Pagaduan

4 Poverty, Globalisation and Gendered Labour
Migration in Nepal 87
Jagannath Adhikari

5 Migration, Gender, Poverty: Family as
the Missing Link? 107
Arjan de Haan

6 Power, Culture and Resources in Gendered
Seasonal Migration from Santal Parganas 129
Nitya Rao

7 Adivasis, Gender and Migrations: Re-situating
Women of Jharkhand 151
Shashank Shekhar Sinha

8 Just Surviving or Finding Space to Thrive?
The Complexity of Internal Migration of
Women in Bangladesh 171
**Janet Seeley, Sheila Ryan, Iqbal Alam Khan and
Munshi Israil Hossain**

9 Migrating for Work: Rewriting Gender Relations 192
Ravinder Kaur

10   Sex Work, Poverty and Migration in Eastern India   214
     Geetanjali Gangoli

11   Solicitation, Migration and Day Wage Labour:
     Gender, Sexuality and Negotiating Work in the City   236
     Svati P. Shah

About the Editors and Contributors   251
Index   255

Series Introduction

Migration and the movement it entails has always accompanied civilisation in every stage of its development. Historically, people have moved from one place to another either by force in terms of slavery, or for reasons of colonisation. Towards the late 19th and early 20th centuries, international migrations began to be prompted by industrialisation and urbanisation. A shift in base and settlement, prompted by varied reasons and sponsored by different agents, is thus not a new concept. Unlike the early migrations, which were largely directed towards the north and the west, migration today cannot be understood in linear terms but rather in terms of fluid movement, within structural constraints and continuities, the movements being marked by turbulence and change, and undertaken in multiple directions. In the contemporary context of globalisation, as has often been noted, the world is in a constant state of flux. People are presented with multiple worlds, images, things, persons, knowledge and information at the same time and at an ever-increasing pace. Moreover, the life cycle of each of these has been drastically shortened, such that the world we encounter is perceived and consumed largely in temporary terms. Change is then the only constant and the changes that characterise this external world we inhabit are internalised by us and have a significant impact on our lives and our perceptions about time and space. Individuals are forced in one way or the other to respond to the larger forces operating on them, since no one remains completely removed from the turmoil that surrounds them; the world having come closer, globalisation has facilitated the process of migration considering the forces of demand and supply, needs and gratifications, and the increased and easier possibility of movement and communication.

In this process of movement, one undoubtedly leaves behind a familiar world to explore one's chances in an alien land. The process of migration may thus have a constraining effect on us not only in structural terms, of the choices made available, or cultural terms, but also in the sense in which it may include abuse and exploitation, and emotional and psychological distress. However, migration is largely undertaken with the positive hope of a better life in an unseen world. There is therefore a need to investigate the nuances and complexities entailed in this process and the way in which it impacts the lives and identities of the individual migrants in a world which is in constant flux and movement.

Migration has earlier been explained in dual terms of the push and pull factors, i.e., the voluntarist perspective. It has also been understood from a structuralist perspective, whereby migration is mapped in dichotomous terms of centre–periphery, industrialised–peasant based, west and north–east and south. However, both perspectives have limitations since the former has understood it in simplistic terms of an individual's rationally calculated decision while the latter ended in economic determinism. In order to understand the phenomenon in all its complexity, a more holistic approach is required. Any theory of migration must account for it in terms of race, religion, nationality, sense of belonging and nostalgia. More significantly, much of the early literature on migration has been silent on the issue of 'gender' and there is thus a need to analyse the migration process and the differential experience of women and men in the context of a gendered world. Migration no doubt constitutes a complex subject of study, and an understanding based on the gender dimension serves to further enhance the complexity when we consider the multiple and heterogeneous backgrounds and experience of migrant women and the very complex category of 'woman' herself.

Within this framework, the initiative to publish the five volumes on aspects of 'Women and Migration in Asia' emerged from the ongoing programme on Gender Perspectives on Asia located at the Developing Countries Research Centre, University of Delhi. The first activity of this programme was the international conference on Women and Migration in Asia in December 2003. The conference was attended by participants from all over the world including representatives from Canada, Australia, Pakistan, Nepal, China, Singapore, France, Italy, Bangladesh, the UK, Israel, Netherlands, Philippines, Japan, Korea, Taiwan, Trinidad and from within India.

The five volumes are based on themes that emerged from the conference. It was proposed that the publication of these volumes would disseminate the deliberations, and their publication is a collective enterprise aimed at understanding the gender implications of migration processes, for women, within and across Asian societies and globally.

Women and Migration in Asia

Essentially, the endeavour to publish these five volumes is a critical response to migration theories that have failed to take into consideration the gender aspect thereby failing to account for the complex experience of migrant women. Migration is often perceived as being mainly a male movement, with women either being left behind or following their men folk as dependents. However, figures suggest that women have migrated in almost the same numbers as men, i.e., in the year 2000, there were 85 million female migrants as compared to the 90 million male migrants (Zlotnik as quoted in Jolly, Bell and Narayanswamy 2003: 6). Women account for 46 per cent of the overall international migration from developing countries (ibid.).

In addition, as compared to other continental regions, Asia has the maximum number of international migrants. There exist, however, disparities within the region in the sense that countries in South East Asia allow greater mobility for women owing to relatively more liberal attitudes than other South Asian and Arab countries. While men still form the majority of international migrants in Asia, there is an ever increasing number of women migrating in the region, as shown in Table 1:

Table 1   Proportion of Female Migrants as a Percentage of Total International Migrants by the Region

	1990	2000
South Asia	44.4	44.4
East and South East Asia	48.5	50.1
West Asia	47.9	48.3

Source: Zlotnik in Jolly, Bell and Narayanswamy 2003.

Despite the rising number of female migrants, women are not given equal importance as compared to men in migration, since they are still not perceived as equal actors worthy of being accounted for. According to the official records, the majority of women migrate legally merely as a part of family reunions. Those who migrate for employment purposes, thus find themselves doing so illegally, considering the rigid cultural and state ideologies and limiting visa policies and work permits regarding the movement of women especially in countries like Bangladesh and

Pakistan. Thus, while viewing women migrants as dependents, we may often ignore their individual economic contributions, and an analysis based solely on official figures would give an inadequate account of the actual migration flows pertaining to women.

Women may migrate alone or along with their families or community. Their migration may be associational (for example, through marriage) or women may be independent migrants. Women may be compelled to migrate owing to their economic condition, in search of better work opportunities, or they may opt to migrate as an escape from an oppressive marriage and the traditional patriarchal norms. They may be driven by individual needs and aspirations which most often coincide with those of the family, or migration may be structured and facilitated by the state. Whichever the case may be, migration has undeniably become a prominent reality in the modern world and the feminisation of migration is an even more significant although less explored aspect of this reality.

Poverty and a search for employment have been the predominant propellants of the migration of people, which affords them the opportunity to explore their life chances. The decisions of women to migrate are informed by the twin forces of opportunities and constraints and are taken primarily by the family and, when taken independently, familial and cultural considerations have a great influence. Apart from the cultural and societal restrictions, structural factors like the demand for female labour and the trends in industry and agriculture, also affect their decision to migrate. In migration, women, owing to their structural position in society, have limited access to information and resources which determines the differential experience of men and women, on transit and entry. Women are more vulnerable to physical and sexual abuse, lower wages and other forms of exploitation. Migration is thus undertaken with the aim of betterment, in terms of employment and economic gains, and as an escape from cultural and societal constraints in terms of achieving greater autonomy and independence. However, while it may afford them material gains, whether migration enables women to completely break away from the binding patriarchal and traditional norms remains questionable.

Migration: Themes and the Volumes

The volumes in the present series bring out the extent to which a gender perspective makes a contribution to migration theory and the manner in which it aids a comprehensive understanding of women's experience of migration, and how in the process, migration simultaneously emphasises certain gender related aspects pertaining to the specific contexts addressed by each volume. It is the migration flow of women in South Asia around which most of the papers in the five volumes are centred. At the same time, the comparative dimension is present in all the volumes that are essentially concerned with the Asian region but provide cross-cultural and regional diversity in their understanding of the issues under consideration. The five volumes are clearly also the result of an attempt to address the issues in an interdisciplinary perspective while being rooted in their particular disciplinary domains. This has in fact resulted in the volumes using very eclectic theoretical approaches as well as a focus on particular issues in their complexity and variety. It is also the case that the subject of study is rather complex and cannot be wholly dealt with in terms of a single volume. In order to understand and encompass the multiple realities and identities of migrant women, analyses from different perspectives and vantage points become important and necessary. All the volumes are held together around a set of common themes and each volume must be viewed as providing a significant insight into the larger picture and the series should be seen as a coherent whole.

While migration viewed along the axis of gender is the overall focus of this series, the aim is to address the issue in terms of particular contexts like conflict, family and marriage, transnationalism, work, poverty, and to do justice to each. Thus while all the volumes are interconnected owing to the common issues they address, within the larger framework, however, each volume makes a valuable contribution in terms of their particular vantage point and the specific context they aim to address and emphasise.

Situated in the larger context of globalisation and the ever increasing rate of cross-border movements thereof, the volumes serve to analyse the varied motivations that propel a woman to migrate, discovering the gap between the migrant woman's aspirations and expectations and the resulting reality. Most of the papers in the volumes point to the fact that the migrant woman's experience cannot be understood merely in terms of the material benefits that may accrue as a result of migration. The social structures and relations that inform the migrant's experience to a great extent also need to be considered for a holistic understanding of the complex experience of such women.

The volumes find common ground in examining the difference between forced and voluntary migration in general (common to men and women), and serve to highlight the voluntary and independent aspect of women's migration, exploring the element of 'choice' and the extent of agency they have in framing their own experience. Woman's agency in different contexts is in fact a critical component of the analyses across the volumes. The notion of 'agency' is thus problematised and examined in terms of personal experience and in relation to the state and legal systems.

The focus is on women on the move. Through their papers, the volumes question the assumption that women essentially migrate as dependents, their migration being seen as largely associational. Women even in the most empathetic discourse are thus at best represented as victims. The indifference towards or denial of the independent aspect of migration of women, in the dominant discourses, as has been argued across the five volumes, serves to ignore the dialectics between these women and the larger social structures and gender relations both in the home and host countries in terms of the reciprocal impact that each has on the other. It is this dominant, official discourse which has predominated in various disciplinary approaches to migration within which women are inadequately represented and assumed to form one homogeneous category characterised, in traditional terms, as being submissive, dependent and largely confined to the household sphere. The volumes in this series provide an insight into the gap between the dominant narratives and those of the women themselves, attempting to reach reality as closely as possible.

The collection of papers on 'Transnational Migration and the Politics of Identity' highlights the fact that migration today does not imply a complete break from the past; rather the migrant must be understood as inhabiting two worlds simultaneously. It explores the ways in which a migrant woman constructs her identity in an alien land, the problems she confronts and the strategies she deploys in making life in the host country more liveable. There is not only fluidity in the experience and construction of identity but also in the manifold ways in which there is a 'back-linking' with the past, the country of origin, whether this is in terms of rituals, practices and values, relationships and family ties, or even in the 'idea' of the country that is carried to the new lands. At the same time, however, the migrant woman is constrained by the structures of the host country, its regulatory regimes and practices, and the limits imposed on her. The volume thus brings out the significance of the fluid nature of a migrant's identity without, however, ignoring the fact that this fluidity itself and her identity is regulated and structured to a certain extent by the state and other social institutions. Moreover, it examines the manner in which she negotiates with the larger structures and institutions such as the state, patriarchy, family, welfare institutions, etc., which impinge on her everyday personal experience and how this struggle helps in defining and re-constructing her identity in different ways.

In the context of internal migration, and even more in terms of transnational migration, the impact of state policies on the experience of the migrant becomes crucial and has been examined in most of the volumes in terms of the motives of the state in facilitating or curtailing migration out-flow and in-flow respectively, and the extent to which the state carries out its responsibilities. The volume on 'Poverty, Gender and Migration' focuses on the relationship between state policies and poverty, and the manner in which shifts in state policies bring about corresponding changes in patterns of migration. It explores how transnational migration has unfolded as a continuing process of exclusion and deprivation, whereby state policies have promoted migration, but on the other hand withdrawn from assuring protective support. Internal migrations too, in the light of the shifts and continuities, show a similar link between state policies, poverty and migration. The volume further argues that the experiences of poor women in migration are informed not only by poverty but also by the ideological dimensions of work which is visible in their concentration in jobs in the informal sector that are characterised by a sexual division of labour. The volume thus highlights the common theme that the larger structures affect the personal experience of migrants, and that there is a strong social, cultural and political context to migration by women. In the transnational context, not only do the social and structural categories of the recipient country affect the migrant's experience, the culture, tradition and customs of the home societies and the dominant familial discourse grounded in patriarchy also continue to inform the construction of the migrant woman's identity and experience.

The volume on 'Conflict, Gender and Migration' attempts to break through the homogeneous 'victimhood' image, presented in the dominant discourse, of women migrants affected by war and conflict and seeks to explore the space for women's agency in these situations. It simultaneously highlights the suffering that women are subjected to in a conflict situation as well as the survival strategies adopted by them. The volume thus attempts to break the homogeneity of state discourses by bringing in women's experiences, which make it more complex. It raises a methodological issue in questioning the extent to which recording women's testimonies empowers them, or whether it is a traumatising experience, since it rips open the memories of their 'traumatic pasts'. Further, the volume also examines the ethical dilemma of the researcher's subjective involvement in the 'manipulation of their memories' to serve their own ends and its impact on the researchers themselves. The volume seeks to contribute to the literature on migration in terms of the 'cyclical' character of most 'conflict' and 'peace' situations, the phenomenon of 'internally displaced persons' and to some extent, forced migrants as well.

Migration may thus be either voluntary or forced, may involve individuals or families and even whole communities. One therefore needs to consider the life choices and circumstances of all categories of migrant women while simultaneously addressing the range of gender-specific types of work and their impact on women. Feminisation of the labour force gained momentum after the Second World War when immigration became a state sponsored project, undertaken in response to the labour shortage in the developing and industrialising countries which was to be filled by the Third World countries supplying labour. Women thus migrated to work in export processing zones in the Asian region, as domestic labour, and in the entertainment and sex industries. This highlights the ways in which women in different circumstances and owing to different reasons cross the boundaries of home and community to engage in work in completely different surroundings.

The volume on 'Women, Work and Migration', by focusing upon women who migrate for work, provides indicators to the patterns that are discernible in the migration of women. The volume highlights the specific conditions under which they migrate, the preponderance of women in certain sectors of the labour market, specifically the reproductive and the care sector, the social, economic and political discrimination that particular groups of women are confronted with and the strategies they adopt to cope with such circumstances. It also makes an important contribution to the literature on migration in terms of studying gender and migration in the significant context of women who migrate alone or are the primary migrants, citing case studies of women who are 'solo' migrants. The volume also puts forth the idea that the structural ramifications of women's migration extend beyond the lives of migrant women themselves insofar as the labour of such women is an important factor in shaping the gender relations found in the societies of both, the migrants and their hosts, thereby suggesting new ways of looking at issues such as gender equality, household division of labour and the state policies regarding welfare provisions.

The collection of papers on 'Marriage and Migration' focuses on several aspects of marriage and migration in intra- and transnational contexts. It poses questions as to how the institution of marriage in and of itself may often effectively imply women's migration through the operation of 'kinship' rules of marriage and (post-marital) residence; how marriage can become a strategy to enable individuals and their families to migrate; the dynamics of match-making and marriage negotiations in the context of migration, including the transfer of resources through marriage payments; and, more broadly, how intra- and international migration affects the institution of marriage and wider relations within the family in the Asian context.

The papers in this volume contend that marriage in new contexts of migration may unravel euphemised and gendered practices and relationships. Migration may also impinge on the institution of marriage and transform familial relationships in a variety of ways. It may introduce new considerations into the process of match-making, reinforce or amplify traditional patterns of family and marriage and, in many cases, put the conjugal relationship and relationships between the generations under particularly severe strain, resulting in domestic violence and international custodial disputes. This raises the important question of policy orientations and commitments, in an international dimension, towards women migrants.

Policy Implications

Migration and the focus on women demands that the policies of the sending and receiving countries regarding migration be reviewed and restructured keeping in mind the migrant's interest. While there do exist laws aimed at safeguarding the interest of migrant women and their protection, they are either inadequate or lack effective implementation. In this light, the conference proposed that the distinction between voluntary and forced migration be emphasised such that the policies for each are based on the specific considerations of their particular context. Further, in order to effectively protect the rights and ensure the well-being of specific groups, their particular motivations for migration must be assessed.

The complexity of the process, the multiple and heterogeneous backgrounds of the migrants, and the differential experiences of women and men make policy analysis difficult in this area. Moreover, the countries involved may have different policy goals, the concerns of one may not concern the other. While, one country may encourage migration for the positive economic benefits in terms of remittances, the other may do so for acquiring cheap labour. In this sense both the sending and receiving countries have their regulatory mechanisms to protect and enhance worker welfare. Women, like men, contribute through their labour and remittances; however, the restrictions on migration imposed by the two countries limit the benefits that migration may accrue both to the migrant as well as to the involved countries.

Migration has been institutionalised to an extent in terms of the employment brokers managing the entire process for the migrants; however, by curtailing movement, these governments, in a sense, serve to strengthen and perpetuate the exploitation and abuse of women. These women in turn migrate illegally, in search of work, and are thus left to the whims and fancies of these middlemen in transit and employers on arrival. In order to make migration beneficial for the two countries as well as the migrant woman, there is a need to rid the existing laws of their restrictive features and to incorporate in the policies protective measures that would ensure women their rights and welfare. Further, to reduce the power of the mediating agencies, the governments of these countries must devise policies to regulate and standardise the recruitment procedure so that these agencies can not harass potential migrants (Labour Watch in Jolly, Bell and Narayanswamy 2003).

Considering the increased movement in the region, the sending and receiving states may be called upon to build networks between them and share the relevant information with each other and with the women, so as to ensure that migrants move in a well planned environment whereby their experience is not left to fate and chance and they are aware of the migration channels in the receiving country. The governments of the host regions must endeavour to assist migrants in adjusting to the new world, by creating conditions approximate to those in their home nations. In order to help them cope with the social/psychological consequences of migration, the sense of dislocation, alienation and loss of a sense of belonging, the governments in both regions must have policies regarding certain provisions of skill training, for instance in the language of the destination country, that would equip these women to find their way about in the new situation.

The heterogeneous aspect of the migrant population and their backgrounds highlights the need for a group specific and country specific approach, as that would view the migrant woman's problems more realistically, accounting for her particularities. A holistic approach towards migration is called for that would include apart from the lower classes the situation of the middle class migrant as well. The analysis must be based on a complete consideration of the specific context within which the migrant is located, in order to effectively formulate policies. Moreover, there is a need to focus attention on the manner in which women migrants are represented in the official discourse, their movement having been rendered invisible by law. These women in reality engage in negotiations with the larger institutions and the state; however, the latter by silencing them makes their agency negligible. While formulating policy, there is a need to therefore ensure a just and visible representation of women.

Meenakshi Thapan
Series Editor
Women and Migration in Asia

Reference

Jolly, Susie, Emma Bell and Lata Narayanswamy. 2003. *Gender and Migration in Asia: Overview and Annotated Bibliography*. No. 13. Bridge, Institute of Development Studies, UK.

Acknowledgements

During the course of the conference on *Gender and Migration in Asia* of which the panel on 'Poverty, Gender and Migration' was a part, and in the process of bringing together this volume, we experienced enormous goodwill and encouragement. We are grateful to Manoranjan Mohanty whose infectious enthusiasm and optimism kept us going, and to Meenakshi Thapan, who conceived and steered the programme with indomitable zeal. Our numerous discussions with Uma Chakravarti helped us identify issues and potential speakers. We are grateful to her for giving us time, for her assuring presence, and for being there when we needed her. Patricia Uberoi, Rajni Palriwala, Navnita Chadha Behera and Anuja Agrawal—the other panel organisers, editors and fellow travellers in our journey—we thank for their *camaraderie* and support. Neera Chandhoke was a source of strength and Ashish Ghosh calm and composed when the going got tough. We thank the paper writers for their patience and cooperation. Friedrich Ebert Stiftung (FES), we thank for funding our panel, and Sushila Zetlyn of the Department for International Development (DFID) for showing particular interest in our panel. We thank the University of Delhi which gave the initial financial support, around which more substantial contributions from DFID, the British High Commission, the Japan Foundation, the Planning Commission (Government of India), and Indian Council for Social Science Research, accumulated. At Sage, Omita Goyal showed unwavering interest and faith in the project, and Ritu Vajpeyi saw it through. We thank the library staff at CWDS, Teen Murti and Ratan Tata Library, Delhi University for their help, and Deo Nath Pathak for providing research assistance.

1

WHEN POOR WOMEN MIGRATE: UNRAVELLING ISSUES AND CONCERNS

Sadhna Arya and Anupama Roy

While movement has always been an inseparable aspect of human existence, modern practices of rule and strategies of development have shown an overriding concern with 'fixity', by enumerating populations, identifying communities or marking nation-state boundaries. There has simultaneously been a general discomfort with what cannot be slotted or placed in a defined category. The paradox of modernity has been that political practices and development strategies have also generated anomalies and ambivalences defying or complicating the process of categorisation. For long, then, state practices have resorted to edging out anomalies to sustain the dominant patterns, whether ideological, economic or cultural. Thus, the displaced, the vagrant, the footloose migrant, the stateless person, etc., have all led a precarious existence, criminalised at certain times and subjected to perpetual relocations and rejections at others.

This volume explores the large-scale movement of populations, internal as well as transnational, for its impact on gender, by giving centrality to poverty. All the papers in their distinctive ways concern themselves with poverty and the attendant issues of powerlessness that mediate experiences of migration. While gender has provided the conceptual tools whereby differential experiences of social reality can be mapped, by identifying migration and poverty as the axes around which social relations and processes can be mapped, the volume attempts to unravel specific layers of this complexity. Women's experiences of migration when seen along these axes present a broad spectrum rather than homogeneity of responses.

This work, moreover, adheres to a perspective that seeks to understand poverty as a process of social exclusion, rather than as a condition that can be captured through a set of statistical indicators. A social exclusion perspective allows an understanding of poverty through an integrated and dynamic analytical framework that reveals the 'process, agency and multidimensionality of disadvantage'.[1] It moreover allows the broadening of the notion of deprivation by bringing together diverse manifestations and multiple causes in the form of historically emergent patterns of disadvantage, viz., political, social, cultural and economic. This historical analytical framework is especially useful for exploring the gender dimensions of poverty since it incorporates the various aspects of exclusion and the diverse ways in which it makes itself manifest. Such an approach is especially important for our purpose since it enables us to see the relationship between migration and poverty in terms of multidimensional and multilinear historically emergent processes.

We have attempted to enrich our understanding of these processes by transcending an India-centric approach. By bringing in shared experiences from other countries in the Asian region, both in terms of migration within the region and outward migration, we hope to identify patterns of sameness and differences within a broader framework of relationships, viz., the capitalist world economy and changing patterns of labour relations. While making sense of these patterns we hope to further our understanding by exploring the relationship in a lateral timeframe as well as changes over time, comparing patterns of migration both in terms of space and temporality, raising new issues and revisiting old ones.

Citizen Outsider: New Migratory Flows and the Racialisation of Gender

The unprecedented large-scale movement of populations across borders is frequently identified as a significant change marking a movement towards global interdependence and porousness of borders among nations. The idea of world citizenship and human rights, free from the confines of nation-state boundaries, is espoused as an accompanying intellectual shift in the idea of the political community and the norms that govern its membership. What needs to be noted, however, is that much of the discourse on transnational movement of populations is exclusionary, occluding class and gender specificities, and the contexts within which the movement of populations is generated and experienced, both in the home country and the country of destination. Much of this movement is likely to be trapped in a web of illegalities, the whorls of illegality progressing from the village to the city, and further to the nation-state, ossifying in each case the geographical and cultural boundaries. We may, therefore, identify two mutually contradictory strands in social and political theory pertaining to the rights and plight of people forced to leave their homes in search of safety and economic security across borders. Referring to the large-scale transnational movements of workers and refugees, one of these strands argues that nation-states are losing their sanctity. Rights, therefore, cannot be seen as being guaranteed solely on the basis of membership in the nation-state, and that human rights and world citizenship reflect more appropriately the realities of contemporary times (Vogel and Moran 1991; Turner 1986, 1993; Habermas 1992). The talk of human rights and the world citizen, directed towards a supposedly more humane 'world order', where respect for human dignity goes beyond the confines of national boundaries is, however, counterbalanced by a simultaneous lament of a 'crisis in citizenship'. Citizenship itself is defined in exclusionary terms and emerges as the bastion on which the nation-state asserts its sovereignty and fortifies itself against the 'hordes of starving people'.[2] Far from making them permeable, a direct outcome of the movement of populations has therefore been the fortification of national-cultural-political boundaries against the inflow of people (Anupama Roy 2005: 246).

It follows from the foregoing discussion that transnational migrations when uncritically acknowledged as a distinctive aspect of globalisation disregard the uneven and hierarchical relationships within the international system which inform population flows. The processes of uneven development set in motion by colonisation continue to unfold with the integration of post-colonial societies into the world economy as dependent and subordinate partners. The presence of multinational companies, the burden of external debts and dependence on export-led growth has assured their continued dependence.

The nature, volume and direction of migratory flows have closely corresponded with these patterns of uneven development. While forced migration in the form of slavery and indentured labour that characterised migration flows in the initial phases of the emergence of the capitalist world system has petered out, the forms that compulsions take have changed, reflecting the responses of state policies to changes in the global economy. Significant about the new migratory flows, apart from the fact that women have become a consistent and significant/visible part of this flow (Campani 1995: 547), is that much of it takes place in a context of demands in the international labour market in specific sectors. Moreover, the flows are of a temporal nature in the sense that movement includes circulation back to the countries of origin. The International Labour Organisation data shows that large numbers of women who move out either to other Asian countries like Japan, Singapore and Hong Kong or European countries are from the Philippines, Indonesia and Sri Lanka. The Sri Lankan Bureau of Foreign Employment (SLBFE), as pointed out by Sepali Kottegoda in the second chapter of this volume, has recorded that the demand for women migrant workers almost doubled in the mid-1990s. Sixty-five per cent of an estimated total of almost a quarter-of-a-million workers who left for employment overseas in 2002 were women. Significantly, of the total number of women migrant workers 108,514 or 82 per cent went overseas to work as housemaids (SLBFE 2003).

The importance of women in the new migration flows manifests changes in the international labour market that has witnessed a growing demand for traditionally female jobs in the domestic sector, e.g., maids, nurses and entertainers (women working in the sex industry, dance bars, etc.), and labour intensive sectors in the garment and textile industries. The development of demand in the domestic, entertainment and labour intensive sectors, and the employment of immigrant women in them, reveals one of the main aspects of the new migratory process: a shift in the economic insertion of immigrants from the industrial to the service sectors and to the informal economy. In other words, there are areas in the international labour market that demand immigrant labour, and the specificity of this demand primarily concerns the female labour force (Lim 1989).

In both developed and developing societies, the transformations in the global economy have brought in policies that nurture and protect 'capital', with a commensurate neglect of labour and a progressive violation and erosion of labour laws. In many economically developed countries the pressures to have a competitive advantage in the global economy has resulted in the cutting of social expenses and labour downsizing. For the developing countries, surviving international competition has meant dispensing with the rights of workers, especially labour standards, and the insistence that labour standards be de-linked from trade issues (Symonides 1998: 268–69). A related development has been the emergence of a vast global assembly line of casualised and feminised labour around a predominantly male core of skilled workers, prompting the expression 'labour made cheap' (Cynthia Enloe 1992).[3] Not all poor women, therefore, migrate overseas to work. A large number of them become part of the hierarchised, racialised and gendered global labour market through employment in the export processing zones (EPZs) in their own countries. Many women have entered the workforce through jobs in EPZs which, along with domestic work, are jobs created largely by globalisation.[4]

The fact that a large number of poor Asian women have engaged in specific kinds of work in developed countries, or in EPZs, on low wages has led to a hierarchising of women on the axes of class, region, ethnicity and colour, resulting in what has been termed the 'racial division of labour'. Globalisation has thus reconfigured state hierarchies, and a state's positioning within this hierarchy determines the support that a state's citizen's claims may receive in another state. Thus some states like Sri Lanka, Indonesia and Philippines may get branded as 'nations of servants', and the claims of their citizens for dignity and protection may go unheeded, resulting in a sexualised hierarchy of women. At the same time, the presumed suitability of these women to the work they are employed for, it may be argued, has led to the 'racialisation of gender'.

Transnational migration has, moreover, unfolded as a continuing process of exclusion and deprivation, whereby state policies have promoted migration but withdrawn from assuring protective support. Moreover, the fact that women in the process of migration are being pushed into highly privatised work in unfamiliar environments not only renders their work invisible and outside the purview of laws, but also makes them vulnerable to exploitation and to physical and sexual abuse. In the case of sex workers in particular, the vulnerability of the women involved accrues from the fact that the profession continues to be seen as degrading and disruptive both by the law and by society.

The three chapters in the volume that concern themselves with the transnational migration of women from Sri Lanka, Nepal and Philippines, by Kottegoda, Adhikari and Pagaduan respectively, show a relationship between state policies and poverty, as well as the manner in which shifts in state policies bring about corresponding changes in patterns of migration. Structural adjustment programmes undertaken by the Nepal government since the 1980s and the subsequent weakening of the agricultural sector, especially hill agriculture, compelled the poor, especially poor women from the hills, to migrate in search of work either to the cities, or to countries of South Asia, South-East Asia and West Asia. Experiences of Nepali, Sri Lankan and Filipino women migrating abroad in search of work show that migration is largely a means of negotiating with poverty or as an exit route compelled by entrenched socioeconomic hierarchies and conditions of powerlessness. At the same time, however, it is not the poorest who migrate, but those who have some means to invest, or an available network enabling them to migrate. Moreover, the growing demand of traditionally female jobs in the domestic sector, e.g., maids, nurses and entertainers, and in labour intensive sectors like the garment factories also prompted some governments, like in the Philippines and Sri Lanka, both of which had previous experience of labour migration to West Asia, and to an extent Nepal, to promote overseas migration of women for remittances to the home country.

Both Sri Lanka and Philippines had a history of overseas migration for employment. After the opening up of labour markets in West Asian countries in the late 1970s, both responded to the new demands for migrant labour in Europe, West Asia and South-East Asia with state policies promoting migration. The Sri Lankan government 'institutionalised the procedure of employment migration' in 1985 with the setting up of the SLBFE to promote and develop employment opportunities outside Sri Lanka. In an interesting formulation, Sepali Kottegoda explores the process of women's migration overseas for employment in terms of a double paradox. While the policies and schemes of the state recognise the significance of women 'bringing home the money', yet they remain paradoxical to women not only because they are deeply gendered but also because the policies work with the notion of the household as a nuclear family, while social relations, particularly those on which migration is dependent, are deeply embedded in the extended family structure and in social practices.

The question why women migrate leads once more to a paradoxical situation, where development programmes undertaken by the Sri Lankan government in consonance with the International Monetary Fund (IMF) and the World Bank (WB), also include poverty alleviation programmes, ironically, for those who are edged out by these development programmes. In Sri Lanka most of the women who migrate are from the poverty-stricken regions and districts in the west and north-west of the country. Sepali Kottegoda's study in this volume points out that poverty and lack of employment in Sri Lanka, which would bring in wages comparable to the earnings from overseas jobs, coupled with the demand overseas for domestic workers, has led to large numbers of women becoming the 'absentee income earner for the family based household'. Kottegoda shows that 82 per cent of the total number of women migrants in the year 2002 went overseas as housemaids, primarily to four countries in West Asia—Saudi Arabia, Kuwait, the Lebanon and the United Arab Emirates—who employ maids from Sri Lanka. Significantly, the preference in these countries for Muslim women for their familiarity with the sociocultural contexts in the employing country has had an impact on the mobility of Muslim women in Sri Lanka. There is also a preference for married women for the skills required in the jobs. Thus about 75 per cent of the women who are employed as housemaids are in the 25–44 years age category. Here again, the paradoxical relationship between state policies that envisage nuclear families, and women in this age group who are likely to be away from home for a period ranging between 2–5 years, and more likely therefore to require familial support, becomes evident. Not only do migrant women remain embedded, therefore, in extensive familial networks, the latter play an active role in the decision to migrate, and participate therefore, in the process of migration, through their initial concurrence and subsequent support.

In the Philippines, as Maureen Pagaduan points out in chapter three of this volume, overseas work in the 1970s was primarily for males, and regarded as an 'interim response to unemployment and balance of payment difficulties'. In a manifestation of the 'increasing permanence of the temporary', under what she calls conditions of 'unabated poverty and globalisation', the Philippines, along with Indonesia and Sri Lanka, now sends the largest number of workers overseas. These overseas workers are primarily women, the majority of whom are concentrated in reproductive work in countries in West Asia and in Japan. The number of overseas Filipino workers legally deployed in 2002 was 891,908, a 2.8 per cent rise from the previous year. Moreover, out of 288,155 new overseas recruits in 2002, 73 per cent were women. When these overseas women workers 'remit their earnings to their families, it brings about a pseudo-economic boost that the government encourages'. Viewing labour migration in terms of remittances has been an aspect of the government's approach towards women overseas workers not just in the Philippines, but also in Sri Lanka and Nepal. There is, however, a significant difference between the outflow of women workers from the Philippines and Sri Lanka to the countries of West Asia, reflecting perhaps the sociocultural contexts in which migrations take place. Unlike the Sri Lankan case, the women who migrate from the Philippines are young—between the ages 20 and 29—unmarried, fairly educated, under the direct authority of their parents, and a value system that views daughters as more consistent and assured sources of financial support.

In Nepal, as Jagannath Adhikari's study in chapter four of this volume shows, the crumbling base of its national economy and a declining agricultural economy manifest themselves in unemployment and increased poverty as irresolvable problems. Perhaps more than any other paper in the volume, this paper shows the differential effects of poverty on women's capacity to leave home for work. Thus while the very poor among Nepali women migrate, their migration is more likely to be either seasonal or short-term; to the city to work on 'development sites', in carpet and garment factories, or as household maids, or cleaners and waitresses in restaurants. They may, however, also be trafficked to brothels in India, or to the Gulf countries to work as domestic help. Like the Sri Lankan and Philippine governments, the Nepal government has realised the potential of remittances from the migration of women to contribute to the national economy, a fact made manifest in the thrust of the Tenth Plan (2002–2007). The shift to a democratic government in Nepal in the 1990s saw, albeit under pressure from donor agencies, the setting up of several training programmes, especially nursing, to equip prospective migrants with the necessary skills. Unlike the Sri Lankan and Philippine experience, government policies while promoting migration for remittances have also hedged it with conditions. Illegality and its correlate, vulnerability for women in migration, are, however, built into the national laws, particularly those that pertain to migration, which are premised on perpetual dependence for women. The Foreign Employment Act 1985 (amended in 1989 and 1998) and the Labour Act 1992 prohibit women from working under certain conditions, and the former allows women to leave for foreign employment only upon permission from their guardians. Moreover, women need the permission of their guardians—their fathers or husbands—to obtain a passport. Migration to the West Asian countries has been prohibited since the Cabinet decision that was taken in March 1998 after an incident of sexual abuse and subsequent death of a Nepali woman worker in the Gulf.

Participation in the overseas labour market for women in all three countries may well be described, following Maureen Pagaduan, as a double-edged opportunity for women. While women migrants emerge more confident in their productive roles as workers, paradoxically, the nature of their work is such that they remain embedded in the reproductive roles of caring and nurturing. The cycle is reinforced when on their return home they are entrusted once again with the reproductive roles that they had in the perception of their immediate and extended families relinquished for productive work. Again, despite the fact that women acquire greater coping skills in the process of migrating for work, their vulnerability as women gets greatly augmented in unfamiliar surroundings. In Sri Lanka, for example, of the total number of complaints of exploitation and violation of employment conditions received from migrant workers by the SLBFE, the highest numbers come from the housemaids.

The experiences of 'coming back home' in all three countries show a broad range in the sense that in some cases the long absence from home causes problems for the women relocating themselves within the family. Some women on their return are confronted with marital discord, separation, indifference or alienation with their children, or generally dysfunctional families. For others, migration may bring in a degree of empowerment accruing not only from their own experiences of independence, but also from their economic worth which also translates into relative material well-being.

Internal Migration: From Rural Marginalisation to Urban Vulnerabilities

Transnational and internal migrations cannot be studied independently of one another since both unfold within the larger framework of development practices and economic policies, structures of inequality, and the social and cultural practices that inform them. Internal migrations, in their historically emergent patterns of shifts and continuities, show a similar link between state policies, poverty and migration. Development practices followed by the state in colonial as well as independent India have simultaneously resulted in dispossessions, displacements, landlessness, unemployment and impoverishment of people. Village communities have petered out as a result of the destruction of their environment and life-world, restrictions on access to forests, and depletion of livelihood resources—their fields, rivers and common lands. Moreover, nothing substantial seems to have been done by the government on the poverty alleviation front even as the rural poor bear the brunt of liberalisation policies. Moreover, government policies in the 1980s and 1990s aggravated conditions of poverty by forced closures of factories and mills that affected both rural and urban economies. In many states wasteland and common grazing lands are now leased out to corporate houses, rather than being distributed to the rural poor to strengthen their livelihood base.

The issue of shrinking space for livelihoods in the countryside and lack of other local employment, with survival becoming more precarious due to the privatisation of common property resources, driving the rural population out of their homes, has been brought out in some of the recent studies on migration. The access to uncultivated fields in villages for grazing, for gathering firewood needed for fuel or an opportunity for earning a little extra income by sale of forest produce (work that is normally done by women), is no more available to landless households, accentuating the exclusion of rural and tribal communities. Most studies also point to the implication of the state in the informalisation process (Ananya Roy 2003; Breman 1996). The depletion of rural economies coupled with the downsizing of the public sector in industries have led to large-scale unemployment in villages and cities, and a flow of population from the rural areas to the cities for absorption in the vast and exploitative informal economy.

In a series of articles in *The Hindu*, P. Sainath (2003, 2004a, 2004b) argues that long before drought hit parts of Andhra Pradesh, the new policies unleashed by the state government in the 1980s and 1990s had already eroded the regional economy by breaking the links between workers, farming and industry.[5] Writing of Anantapur district, perhaps the worst affected in the region, Sainath says that the process of erosion began in the late 1980s with the closure of the Guntakal Spinning Mills, one of the largest in Asia, resulting in the loss of 3,000 jobs. Then came the rapid closures and lockouts in both public and private units in the 1990s. Hundreds of workers were thrown out when the government-owned Nizam Sugar Factory Limited (NSFL) was sold and shut down. Since the NSFL used local produce, it also hit the peasants—the cane farmers who sold their crop to the factory. Allwyn, the Bharat Gold Mining Ltd., A.P. Oilfed, Pattabhi Forge and Anantapur Cotton Mills were also among those that folded up, apart from about 70 per cent of oil mills. The huge retrenchments and fall in employment growth in rural Andhra Pradesh to 0.29 per cent were followed by a significant rise in child labour, large-scale migration for work, and a search for alternative livelihood sources. While some workers set up small *bidi* and cigarette stalls, large numbers took to plying autorickshaws. Subsequently, as the number of autorickshaws shot up four-fold from the late 1980s to the late 1990s, the earnings of the autorickshaw drivers dipped to less than half of what they were earlier (Sainath 2004b).

A large number of the rural poor hit by drought as well as huge power tariffs, soaring input costs, fake pesticides and corruption in food-for-work programmes, migrated to the cities, heading primarily for Mumbai, Pune, Hyderabad, and other cities in Gujarat, Rajasthan and Orissa, to work in some of the toughest construction projects in the cities. The meagre work available in their own district was concentrated in the hands of contractors who grabbed all government projects and preferred to bring labourers from outside so that they could be kept in submission.[6]

Most of those who left their villages in busloads were small farmers and landless workers, Lambada Adivasis, and poor Dalits, who just locked up their houses, or in some cases left behind the oldest member of the family. 'Without Mumbai and Pune', they said, 'we cannot survive. Our households are deep in debt. Our children (are) starving. Any chance of agriculture here is finished. The costs are simply too high. If you are a labourer, it's worse. In a month you cannot find more than three or four days of work. All this makes life too hard. And now there is no water either'.[7]

The relationship between state policies and migration decisions resonates in all papers in the volume. An underlying theme that weaves together the papers that focus on internal migration is the shift in cultivation patterns, and the manner in which it affects people's access to, or ownership and relation with, land. The changing pattern of land use and ownership, erosion of resources in rural areas, increased dependence of rural households on agricultural wage labour, privatisation of common property resources, shrinking spaces for landless livelihoods and its differential impact on people's lives and livelihood become focal in the migration process. Clearly, the growing structural inequalities in rural and tribal belts and the concentration of wealth in the hands of a few along with mechanisation, deforestation and various development projects have forced women and men to move out in search of work for sheer survival. This movement may take the form of temporary or permanent, or short-distance or long-distance, migration; studies including the ones in this volume point to the fact that in the case of women their initial disadvantage emanating from their class, caste and gender position continues through these migratory processes (Schenk-Sandbergen 1995).

The relationship between livelihood choices and access to and control over resources, particularly land, and the manner in which it fashions migration is brought out in Nitya Rao's study in chapter six of this volume. The process of land alienation in the Santhal Parganas started in the colonial period, with an interventionist colonial state standardising Adivasi law into a technically precise lexicon. The process of disinheritance of Santhali women was simultaneously set off. Despite the widespread practice of women cultivating land, societal norms, prevalent patriarchal ideologies and state interventions worked towards truncating the ownership rights of Santhali women. Alongside the changing pattern of land ownership with its implications for gender, the process of deforestation and restriction on the use of forestland led to debt bondage and mortgage of land, and then migration. Dealing with seasonal and rural-to-rural migration of women, Rao shows how the decisions and experiences of migration are gendered. The state's support to a more technical interpretation of the Adivasi law of inheritance, according to which only males could inherit land, led to the shrinkage in a range of flexible and informal rights of women in land and assertion of male power in controlling land as a productive resource. Access to land mediated by gender, seniority and kinship relations ultimately determine who migrate and who do not, as well as the position from which they migrate. In this gender hierarchy, widows and separated women without the 'protective support' of men in the family are perhaps the worse off.

The impact of economic activities of the state on people's lives and livelihoods has been brought out in Shashank Shekhar Sinha's study of Chotanagpur Adivasis in chapter seven of this volume. Sinha points out that the development policies initiated in the Chotanagpur region under colonial rule, and continued by the state in independent India, were characterised by new agrarian and land relations, and the concurrent and subsequent development of mines and industries. These developments triggered out-migration of the dispossessed and landless tribal population and the in-migration of populations to the region. These movements not only changed the demographic profile of the region, but also gender relations at the interface of conflicting cultural codes and shifting patterns of livelihood. The 'contact zones' created under the impact of colonialism not only dismantled the limited rights of women in land—'outside values' destroyed the traditional safeguards women had, especially widows and single women. The increasing use of violence in the form of witch-hunting to dispossess women from their land became significant reasons for pushing women to take recourse to migration as a survival strategy. In the emerging economic and demographic configuration, leading to substantial restructuring of traditional division of labour and relocation of women's economic roles from self-supporting agricultural labourers to migrant wage workers and casual labourers, women have been absorbed at the lowest levels as cheap labour, earning less than men and being sexually exploited by managers, supervisors and fellow male workers.

Svati Shah's study in chapter eleven of this volume analyses the process of migration against the backdrop of depleted water tables, arable land being subject to frequent droughts and earthquakes, and inadequate rural development schemes. Shah's study of migration from rural communities of lower castes and 'untouchable' agricultural labourers to Mumbai in the 1980s and 1990s, sees migration as a direct outcome of the erosion of resources linked with changing patterns of land use. With the area becoming drought prone owing to land being used increasingly for water intensive cash crops like sugar, the search for economic sustainability by people who had limited or no access to education, land and a steady income triggered off out-migration.

The experiences of poor women in migration are informed not only by poverty but also by the ideological dimensions of work. While for men migration and dissociation from land, in some cases from owner-ship of land, may indicate a process of emasculation, for women it means a reinforcement of 'womanly' work. This is visible in their con-centration in the jobs that are not only located in the informal sector but are characterised also by a sexual division of labour. Migration, there-fore, unfolds as a process that transports migrants from one situation of deprivation and dispossession to another. The migrants into Mumbai, as Shah points out, are unlike those from the earlier periods of migra-tory flows, which saw them find work in the textile and real estate development industry. The downturn in the industries has seen the rural poor get sucked into a vast and expanding urban informal wage economy—doing construction work, selling or trading sexual services, piece work, factory work, or any day wage labour, leading a precarious existence amidst insecure and exploitative work conditions. Day wage labour, bought and sold from numerous public spaces, constitutes the most visible aspect of the city's vast informal economy. Shah uses the term *naka* to denote the market space where the sale of labour takes place, which in the case of women migrants is also the space where women's labour is made visible and simultaneously regulated through the surveillance mechanisms of society and the state. For women as day wage labourers the *naka* is a place which gives them access to the public, for 'legitimate' socialisation, and at the same time it holds for them promise as a potential income generating space. As a space for legitimate socialising, the *naka* is, however, governed by the same norms that define and determine the appropriateness of spaces for women. The promise for 'work' that the space holds for women makes the boundaries between legitimate and illegitimate fortuitous, as women use the *naka* for garnering daily wages, both from construction work and sex work. Yet, societal norms and regulation of the public space through anti-trafficking legislation and laws that govern the public solicitation of clients by women for sex work heightens their vulnerabilities.

While providing a vantage point from which to look at the intersection between migration, sex work and sexuality, the paper also provides a framework for examining the ideology of work—its class and gender components—as well as the flexibility and fluidity that notions of work are attributed in India's urban informal economies. The debate on agency and compulsion vis-à-vis solicitation in the cities, when read in the context of migration and public solicitation conducted by poor women in urban areas, acquires significance not merely as particularities of the experience of migrants in urban settings. A powerful and influential discursive relationship between the 'city' and (its) 'legitimate inhabitants' on the one hand, and between 'migrants' and 'danger' on the other prepares the ground for the internal and external regulation of migrants from poverty stricken areas. This regulation elides the city's need for a supply of cheap, unskilled workers to build and maintain its rapidly growing infrastructure and service sectors.

The complexity of defining work gets accentuated when one sees it in the context of migration driven by poverty, and the large number of female migrants concentrated in the sex-related entertainment industry that has grown alongside global restructuring of capitalist production and investment. While sexual labour of women has increasingly become important to national economies (Kempadoo 2003), prostitution continues to be viewed as degrading and destructive both in law and at the social levels. In chapter ten of this volume Geetanjali Gangoli provides significant insights into the relationship between poverty and migration into sex work, and then proceeds to complicate this relationship by bringing in the intervening and contested variables of 'choice' and 'agency'. While the stigma attached to 'prostitution' may compel women to define themselves as 'innocent victims', in their personal narratives they are more likely to 'recast' themselves as agents. Examining the range of issues woven into the debate on 'work' vs. 'coercion' and 'work' vs. 'morality', in the context of women migrants and sex work, Gangoli feels that the definitive stances of the state and civil society groups do not capture the wide range of experiences of women in prostitution. Moreover, by feeding into the patriarchal views on prostitution, they silence women's experiences, especially those of violence, which ironically reinforce positions that subscribe to prostitution being 'inherently harmful' and coerced. What gets obfuscated in the process is that as in the case of domestic work, particularly in international labour migration, where control over the worker remains in the hands of employers because of state regulations with regard to permit systems, immigration, deportation, etc., constituting the legality or illegality of the worker's status, in the case of sex workers the laws prohibiting or regulating prostitution and migration combine to create highly complex and oppressive situations for women in sex work.

Choosing to Survive: Family in Migration

As stated at the outset, migration is a complex process that manifests the diverse ways in which structural conditions, viz., capitalist economy or feudal society, are experienced, and negotiated, and class, race and gender ultimately provide both specificity and diversity to these patterns. The focus on structural and ideological factors forming the contexts of migration is matched, therefore, by an equal concern among scholars with the diversity of ways in which the structures are experienced and negotiated with. In this context the issue of 'voluntariness' of migration is repeatedly interrogated. Yet, perspectives that provide a determining role to economic structures reducing migration to a passive response are constantly engaged with, and the complex layers of needs, networks and choices that are available in poverty driven migration closely examined. For a broad spectrum of the poor, it is argued, migration may be a livelihood strategy arising not from choice but from compulsions of survival. The question of making a choice, it is argued, may not exist for many, particularly women from landless and marginal families and certain occupation based castes who may be moving from one subsistence situation to the other.

Quite like transnational migrations, women have formed a substantial component of internal migration flows. Large numbers of women migrate with their families, and sometimes alone, to flee the destitution and poverty they face in their immediate surroundings. When the issue of voluntariness is taken up in the context of the gendered nature of migration, it assumes further complexities. Studies on rural-urban migration in India, for example, have sounded a note of caution, emphasising that the concept of 'autonomous' migration needs to be looked into critically. While migration of women individually or in groups to work as domestic maids, nurses or workers in small factories may appear to indicate autonomy, to term these migrations as autonomous would be erroneous. Women may have taken these decisions on their own to better their own or their families' conditions, but these may actually be decisions forced by circumstances (Karlekar 1995). Here the role of family and kin group in arriving at this decision is crucial and the initial motivation may be survival.

The interplay of autonomy and compulsion, the relative and changing significance of the two in specific contexts, and the manner in which it is gendered, is perhaps best brought out in works on seasonal migration. These works show that migration, particularly seasonal, is not only gendered, but also shows differentiation along the lines of status, as well as differential outcome, for different categories of the poor. Thus as Nitya Rao points out in chapter six of this volume, for the poorest it may be a forced livelihood and survival response, arising from a complex set of social relations including those of debt and dependency, while for others it may be a 'positive opportunity' to earn, save or accumulate capital. The latter of course is contingent on the status and prestige of the migrant, including the networks of migration that may be accessed and availed. For the poorest among the poor, not only are the networks not available, they are often of a nature that places them in the lowest paid and the hardest unskilled jobs, where they are more likely to 'sink further into debt'.

Seasonal migration, as some studies point out, is one of the strategies which are chosen when all the household sources of income, including child labour, are insufficient for survival (Listen et al. 1989; Schenk-Sandbergen 1988). In his study of three villages in the Burdwan district, Narayan Banerjee concludes that for the Santhals 'seasonal migration has become a traditional practice' (Banerjee 1987: 206). Other studies have sought to show that seasonal migration has different outcomes for different regions. Seasonal migration into the south of West Bengal for rice cultivation has shown that, unlike in the former south-east of Bihar (now Jharkhand) region, migrants may have relatively more power since employers were not collusive, and lead to a different pattern of social change (Rogaly et al. 2001).

Since gender relations in tribal communities are usually assumed to be more equal, egalitarian and symmetrical than in Hindu culture (Fernandes and Menon 1987), several scholars have emphasised the importance of studying seasonal migration among tribal women, not only to study the gendered impact of state policies, but also the impact of 'survial migration' on the unequal relation between women and men, and the effect of migration on women's productive and reproductive roles (Schenk-Sandbergen 1995: 12). In her study of migration patterns in the Santhal Parganas, Rao points out that while women are primarily engaged in short-term seasonal migration to West Bengal for paddy cultivation four times during a year, the men prefer longer term migration, often to construction sites, which fetch higher wages and is more likely to be associated with notions of 'adventure' and not considered emasculating. Even when women *and* men migrate seasonally for the short-term, as from Dumka to Bardhman district in West Bengal, paddy transplantation, which is seen as primarily women's work, is also done by the men, who justify their presence alongside women engaged in 'womanly work' for the 'protection' of the women. The precipitating factor for 'feminisation of internal migration', especially in tribal communities, as discussed in the earlier section, has been state policies that have truncated women's land ownership and curtailed their property rights. For most women then, migration is not only seasonal, it is also primarily for survival and sustaining the household. For men, on the other hand, migration is seen more in terms of earning money to reclaim land, or making investments and improving assets. As far as gender relations and ideology are concerned, studies focusing on household migration have found that a deterioration in gender relations following household migration may be seen, manifested not only in a widening gap in the world views of men and women, with the men seeing themselves as more 'modern', but also in the change in values among women themselves about their role in labour participation. The influence of dominant Hindu cultural ideals prompts them into adopting reproductive roles as mother and housewife, thereby bringing about their increased dependence on the wage labour of their husbands (Menon 1995).

Significantly, the migration of women, though dependent on family decisions, is not secondary, nor is its economic imperative incidental. Most papers in this volume, however, also argue that women's migration cannot be analysed *only* within a framework of 'rational choices' or in terms of the economic imperative of costs and benefits. Apart from the outer framework of state policies, development strategies and ideologies of work that inform migration decisions in general and women's experience of migration in particular, the negotiations that take place at the micro-level of the family, informed by its own hierarchies of decision-making and need perception, are seen as being equally relevant.

The manner in which the family itself gets redefined in the process of migration, reinforcing the interlocking relationships with the extended kinship and community networks and simultaneously the ideologies of ethnicity and gender, of power, status and relative valuation of work, is also significant. Arjan de Haan in chapter five of this volume seeks to reinsert the 'missing link' of the family to emphasise the fact that there is a strong social context to migration by women. His paper emphasises that in order to clearly understand the links between poverty and migration, it must be understood that migration is not merely driven by economic motives, that its mechanisms are not just economic and that its impact stretches beyond economic costs and benefits. There is a strong sense of intermix in de Haan's analytical framework in that he sees the extended family and the kinship groups as permitting or shaping migration decisions as an investment for potential monetary benefits in the future. Moreover, drawing comparisons from migration patterns in Africa and different regions in India, de Haan feels that there may not in fact be a single or generally applicable pattern. While labour migration, still predominantly male, may include women, and women's migration may not only be life-cycle migration, there is a North-South divide in so far as women's migration is concerned. But again, though the divide may suggest region specific patterns, each pattern may hold its own complexity and diversity of strands. Generally, however, migrant women have restricted access to employment, or choice of employment, get lower wages for the same work and suffer additional disadvantages in terms of sexual harassment and the double burden of domestic work.

Recent works that look at the gendered nature of migration often prefer not to focus attention on the continuing constraints on decision-making, or on women's relative marginality in the migration process. They would rather look for changes, and would focus on women's migration as neither degradation nor improvement in women's social marginality, but as a process of restructuring of gender relations (Tienda and Booth 1991). This restructuring may take place through the assertion of autonomy in social life, through relations within the family of origin or through participation in various networks and formal associations (Campani 1995: 548). The reverberations of such restructuring may, however, also be felt as a sense of crisis in the traditional community, village and family structures in the country of origin. This sense of crisis may get aggravated as more and more women move across state boundaries in search of work, and are placed beyond the protection/control of the community, increasingly being seen as 'out of place' or 'transgressors of other places'. The sense of crisis results in a renewed subjection to familial roles, surveillance and control. Moreover, in the context of rise of particularist identity movements, especially in migrant-receiving countries, migrants or racialised/ethnic minorities may come to be seen as competition or a threat. Amidst a rise in identity politics, women become vulnerable to boundary policing by both in-group and other men and women, as markers of community boundaries, signifiers of cultural difference and as reproducers both physically and culturally (Yuval-Davis and Anthias 1989).

While the image of transgression and the subsequent community policing may bring in its wake violence and restrictions on mobility, women's testimonies have also shown that moving away from the village releases them from the constraints of the immediate social structure. The anonymity of the city frees them from the strangleholds of caste and village hierarchies and weakens patriarchal norms. In chapter nine of this volume, Ravinder Kaur suggests that the 'habitus' of the woman migrant is composed of a complex mental map that encompasses her rural as well as urban life. While she relishes the conditions that the urban setting provides to disengage from the norms that bind, she does not disengage herself completely from the values and responsibilities of her rural roots, and the subsequent ambiguities that arise from her embeddedness in the urban-present. Kaur's paper lists a range of reasons both in terms of demand and supply for poor rural women migrating to the urban metropolis of Delhi, a large majority of whom are pulled into the domestic labour sector of the urban informal economy. This large scale and perceptible absorption into the domestic labour sector lends a measure of autonomy to women's migration, which had so far been seen mainly as male dependent.

Kaur points to the broader canvas of understanding migratory decisions beyond pull and push factors to include various sociocultural, political and economic dimensions adding importance to the questions of mobility and agency. Yet, the decision to migrate may emerge from larger household livelihood assessments and not just as an individual decision. Most papers in this volume have tried to transcend the contest over voluntariness and located the migration of women within the broader framework of social relations in which structures of access to resources as well as deprivation are embedded. The process of migration, from the stage of making a decision to leave, through the process of relocating in new surroundings, to 'sending home the money', or returning to the fold, is largely embedded in a complex network of community and social relations. Often there can be seen a gendered hierarchy of decision-making, attributing little or no autonomy to women. On the other hand, as has been seen in the preceding section, the demand for female labour in the new (segmented and hierarchised) global economy in EPZs or as migrant domestic workers has given women a more significant role in the migration process. While the latter may inject an element of ambivalence in the traditional hierarchies of decision-making, decisions for migration may, however, still continue to be taken as a family-income earning strategy. Yet contributing to the family income may give a sense of freedom and autonomy to women.

These issues resonate in chapter eight of this volume, on women's internal migration in Bangladesh. The paper by Janet Seeley, Sheila Ryan, Iqbal Alam Khan and Munshi Israil Hossain argues that women's migration into urban areas, often as independent migrants, to work in the readymade garments industry that has come up in the context of the liberalisation of the Bangladeshi economy, represents in many ways a 'quiet revolution'. The experience of migration by itself may have a liberating effect insofar as life in the city may mean freedom from oppressive socioeconomic structures. Apart from the fact that independent migration by itself signifies a weakening of immediate familial bonds and male guardianship, as also the inversion of the sanctity of women's status in the family accruing from seclusion and family care, at a more fundamental level it also signifies a breaking free from the prescriptive social and cultural practices of seclusion in an Islamic society. Again, however, the authors do not see notions of autonomy or of rational choice applying in entirety to independent migration by women, as more often than not, the well-being of the entire family, as also survival and chances to improve their lives, figure in competing measures in the various migration decisions. While women may gain confidence over time and earn enough to gain some control over family decisions, the initial visibility of women may to a large extent be a result of poverty. Thus a large number of women may migrate because of destitution and the gradual erosion of the familial support system, or be prompted by factors such as the need to earn a dowry or to escape from difficult economic circumstances. Thus questions focusing on whether women are subordinate to men in the migratory process, confined to reproductive functions and a marginal position in the labour market, or, conversely, are active and independent participants in decision-making, become crucial. In the latter case, the issue of the implications of women's participation becomes important, in terms of the transformations it makes in social relations and also the manner in which women as workers and women's work comes to be perceived in society and state policies.

Protection and Inclusion: Policy Implications

The discussion so far has made it evident that women's experiences of migration are fashioned and often circumscribed by state policies. In the case of transnational labour migration, state policies promoting migration show an overriding concern with the encouragement and management of flow of remittances and maximising potential benefits for the economy. Facilitation of migration has amounted to limiting the monitoring of outflows and standardisation of procedures that are designed more to regulate migration flows than to strengthen the bargaining power of migrants. While both the migrant sending and receiving countries benefit from women's labour, efforts to improve their conditions of work, choice of livelihood, emotional and physical well-being, and the amelioration of the social and familial disruptions and dislocations that follow migration, have been few and half-hearted. Migrant women are excluded from social welfare provisions relating to health, housing or care services in the receiving countries, owing to their non-citizen status. Most sending countries too do not go beyond promoting migration, to provide even rudimentary knowledge to migrant women about regulations pertaining to migrant aliens in receiving countries, or helping them develop the skills required for their jobs. Issues pertaining to the needs of migrants, the nature of support networks available in civil society, or provided by the state, and the gaps that remain, therefore, become exceedingly important.

The processes of internal migration too have shown that the scale, nature and direction of migration are closely linked to the development patterns and social and economic policies adopted by the state. This means that the larger issues of landlessness, land alienation, land degradation and shrinking livelihood opportunities in rural and tribal areas, owing to deforestation, ecological degradation, development projects leading to large-scale displacement of populations and appropriation of rural and tribal livelihood resources by economically and politically powerful forces, need to be addressed. Moreover, the kind of deprivations and repression faced in the course of migration and at various and constantly shifting end points, which have been brought out by the papers in the volume, also need to be addressed.

There persists, therefore, the need to pin down state responsibility, as well as identify areas of civil society initiatives and cooperation like capacity building, training programmes, learning new skills and legislative initiatives to systematise the migration process from a labour rights perspective. A crucial starting point in this context can be, as de Haan has suggested in his paper, to accept the existence of migration and the futility of trying to stem it. Instead of advocating, therefore, a 'right to stay', which comes to be interpreted in a manner that focuses predominantly and often exclusively on creating conditions that stem migration, it is important that the right to stay be made more dynamic and multilayered. The right to stay interpreted as staying back in one's own village or native place with dignity, raises significant issues pertaining to the development process, and makes claims on the state to withdraw policies that encroach on the livelihood resources of people, and provide opportunities for livelihood and sustenance that protects them from sliding into an impoverished existence. On the other hand, considering that the history of modernity is inextricably imbued with processes of population flows, manifesting strands of coercion and volition to different degrees, it is also important that a dynamic approach to a right to stay be adopted. This approach would enable that the right be interpreted in a way so as to extend simultaneously and in an equal measure to support the rights of migrants to a dignified and safe life and security of livelihood, in the entire process of migration. In this context information networks, sensitivity to cultural differences, the provision of enabling conditions and moral obligations of the political community and civil society become crucial.

A significant area of concern is the specificity of women's experiences of migration that accentuates their vulnerability in the migration process. This vulnerability emanates from the initial position of disadvantage from which they embark. In the process of international migration women are especially debilitated owing to their location in a hierarchised global economy. A number of discriminatory rules apart from social practices, manifested in restrictive racially discriminatory immigration laws, or patriarchal practices of the sending and receiving countries, push women into conditions that augment their vulnerability. A situation of illegality of status in the receiving country, for example, not only constrains women migrants but also renders them vulnerable to physical and sexual abuse, exploitative practices and conditions of work that approximate that of bonded labour.[8] Moreover, the highly privatised nature of the work of women migrants also makes it invisible, taking it out of the purview of laws.

There has been a general unwillingness on the part of the governments to address these issues in the 'rights' context. Thus although new legal arrangements have been established to deal with and facilitate the cross-border movement of capital, there has not been a simultaneous effort to deal with the concomitant cross-border movement of people and labour through legal processes. Instead, states have sought refuge in traditional notions of nation-state identity and sovereignty to resist cross-border traffic. The kind of legal intervention that is made in the lives of transnational subjects thus does not take into account the economic factors that precipitate migration of women. Moreover, they also render invisible the productive and reproductive labour of women migrants, which, significantly, subsidises the economic costs in the provision of care services etc., of the host country (Anderson 2000). Ironically, while migrant domestic workers provide social welfare services and contribute directly to the state, enabling the provision of social rights to the citizens of the country, the same rights are mostly denied to migrant workers. Again, reminiscent of a racialised hierarchy among women, migrant women, whose labour relieves women in the receiving country for participation in the public sphere, are denied the right to be mothers or bring their children along with them.

In the context of women, the issue of the value of reproductive labour and its relationship with capitalism has been debated mainly around the issue of productivity of housework. The feminisation of migrant labour and the concentration of this labour in domestic and sex work has once again opened up the need to re-centre the issue of reproductive labour of women and critically examine as to what is it that women reproduce. The reproductive labour both in terms of domestic work and sexual services by women performed both inside their own home and as paid labour has generally been viewed in terms of the reproduction of gender relations that supports and reinforces patriarchal power. In the context of female migrant workers, particularly, reproduction of relations of power in terms of class, nationality, ethnicity, etc., occupy an equally important position.

As far as internal migration is concerned, the migrant labour placed in the larger context of the processes of globalisation and the development agenda adopted by the states, the emphasis on privatisation and unregulated market forces and resultant mechanisation, deforestation, landlessness, drought, floods, displacement due to major development projects like big dams etc., have adversely affected the living conditions of masses of people, pushing them into seeking recourse to migration for survival. On the other hand, the curtailment in labour rights has led to the disempowering of the labouring poor. The flexibilisation of labour by the dismantling of social legislation governing labour, and the denigration of organised labour as a major obstacle to efficiency and growth, has been accompanied by an expanding informal economy which is associated with casual, contract and piece-rate type work with lower wages and highly insecure and exploitative conditions of work (Chen 2003).

The issues of identity and citizenship rights are equally relevant in case of intranational migrations. Poor rural and tribal migrants who move to cities face problems of illegality of their status as they use up government land for housing purposes in the absence of other alternatives. They might otherwise have documents that give them identity, but the state machinery refuses to recognise their rights on that basis. Both within the state and society they continue to be looked upon as the 'other', encroachers, job stealers or the ones making the city dirty (Ananya Roy 2003; JAGORI 2004; Janwadi Adhikar Manch 1998, 2001a, 2001b). Within India, the only legislation available to migrant workers is the Inter-State Migrant Workmen (Regulation of Employment and Conditions of Service) Act 1979 that has fairly substantial possibilities of safeguarding the rights of migrant labour. In addition, there is a range of labour laws for those working in the informal and unorganised sector of the economy.[9] Many studies, including those in this volume, indicate, however, the 'incapacitating debility' of the migrant labour that inhibits access to these laws. These conditions of debility are constituted by their socioeconomic deprivation, absence of alternative employment prospects, lack of information about labour laws and mechanisms of redressal, difficulties of organising themselves, the state's apathy towards the implementation of its own laws, and its collusion in truncating the provisions of laws.

Apart from the responsibility of the state to ensure the access of people to protective laws, it is also important that people organise and mobilise not only to ensure government accountability, but also to continually widen the scope of these laws by pushing at their frontiers to incorporate new needs and aspirations. Despite the difficulties of organising because of the mobile and diverse nature of migrants, and high insecurity associated with their illegal status, several efforts to network and lobby have given visibility to the issues and struggles of migrant women workers both in internal and international migration. The issues relating to living conditions, better wages and human rights are being raised at various fora, international and local (Dutt et al. 1997).

At the level of the United Nations, the Convention on the Protection of the Rights of All Migrant Workers and Members of their Families was adopted in 1990. The Convention applies to both men and women workers and their families and has no special provisions for women. There are several ILO (International Labour Organisation) conventions and recommendations that concern migrant workers, but they have received very few ratifications (Symonides 1998: 278–79). While rigid positions of nation-state sovereignty hamper ratification in most cases, even when such instruments are ratified, their implementation remains an area of concern. To assure that discourses of state sovereignty do not hamper the implementation of international guidelines on migrants' rights, and more importantly to keep enhancing the contents and frontiers of these rights, it is important that civil society groups, both NGOs and voluntary civil rights organisations, keep up the pressure. The latter is particularly important since despite a plethora of research in the past decade on issues of migrant labour, including women migrants, the women's movements have not included these concerns in their agendas in a substantially effective way. But the networks that have come up over the years mainly through the efforts of migrant women themselves have been able to raise their issues at the Fourth UN World Conference on Women in Beijing.[10]

Looking at internal migration, in the past two decades various movements have taken up issues that touch upon the rights of the migrants tangentially but address the conditions that push them to resort to migration as a survival need. Most recently, state responses have been in the form of policies directed towards ensuring rural employment[11] and protecting the traditional rights of tribal populations to the use of forest resources.[12] More often than not, however, as several studies have pointed out, actually existing ameliorative and welfare schemes are not available to migrants either due to the high levels of unawareness about them or owing to the disinterest in the issues of migrants in the bureaucratic machinery. A study of seasonal migrants from the Dumka district of West Bengal, for example, showed that migrant workers were excluded from house building grants earmarked for poor families under the Indira Awas Yojana, because they were deemed likely to be absent during the stipulated period for building. Similarly in the destination areas, the study showed, pregnant and neonatal seasonally migrant women did not gain access to Integrated Child Development Scheme facilities (Rogaly et al. 2001: 4556).

Rogaly emphasises, and one agrees with him here, that while more protective policies and solidarity with migrants and their inclusion in welfare schemes when they are away from home is needed, the latter cannot be a matter for bureaucratic edict alone. A more *political approach to migrant's rights*, which requires a framework of protection against exclusion as well as breaking new grounds of inclusion, through a consolidation of the interests of migrants, and their expression politically in terms of rights, is therefore required. A space to assemble peacefully for negotiation of the terms of work contracts is an important aspect of this right, which may in most cases be denied, since workers meetings are more likely to be repressed through intimidation by employers in collusion with the police. In many cases, as in the case of workers in the EPZs, this right may be denied altogether. Equally important are rights that ensure safe travel, treatment for ill-health which is most likely to be neglected because of fear of loss of wages and jobs, education of children, which is worst affected in the context of seasonal migration which is dictated by agricultural cycles, and access of infants and pregnant and post-natal migrant women to care in the Integrated Child Development Scheme-funded anganwadis (ibid.). These measures, however, will have to unfold simultaneously with measures directed at structural transformations that protect people from exclusion.[13] Ultimately, therefore, migration has to be seen as mentioned at the outset, in terms of 'the process, agency, and multidimensionality' of exclusion, and the countervailing processes would similarly unfold at the specific layers of exclusion. The policy frameworks of the state, to be truly responsive and democratic, have to take into account these specificities, as well as the overarching frameworks of disadvantage and exclusion.

Notes

1   In her study of women and poverty in Morocco, Loubna H. Skali (2001) confirms that the notion of social exclusion is more pertinent as a conceptual tool precisely because it offers a way of integrating loosely connected notions such as poverty, deprivation, lack of access to goods, services and assets, and precariousness of social rights. The concept of social exclusion enables a better understanding of poverty as a process that involves multiple agents as well as institutions. Focusing on the 'processes of impoverishment' rather than on the poor, facilitates the 'causal analysis' of the phenomenon as well as a perception of the interplay between its material and non-material dimensions. The approach, she points out, is especially important in a country where the different levels of gender-related exclusions are only beginning to be explored and the inadequacies of past paradigms of addressing women's poverty recognised.

2   The situation is well illustrated by relatively recent writing on 'global constitutionalism' which suggests that human rights, with the exception of political ones, were always proclaimed to be universal, from the declaration of the Rights of Man of 1789 onwards. It suggests, however, that these rights were proclaimed universal 'when the distinction between man and citizen did not create any problems, it being neither likely or foreseeable that the men and women of the Third World would arrive in Europe and these statements of principle might be taken literally (Ferrajoli 1996: 151–54).

3   A large number of young women are employed in export processing zones or EPZs. Maria Mies points out that women in the First and the Third World have become part of a globalised feminised working class, using this to argue against the limited view of cultural relativism—which claims that women are divided by culture worldwide—whereas in fact women are both divided and connected by commodity relations, by their positioning within the global economy (1986: 3).

4   Variously termed as 'free zones', 'special economic zones' and 'maquiladoras', EPZs are free trade enclaves where foreign manufacturing firms produce mainly for export and benefit from a number of fiscal and financial incentives and protections that are given by the host country. At least 70 countries (mainly developing countries) have such zones. Low labour costs are one of the important incentives for government decisions to establish EPZs, since entrepreneurs may produce goods for export with the cheap labour of the developing country minus onerous customs and fiscal constraints. Textiles, clothing, footwear and electronics are the main goods produced in these zones (Symonides 1998: 272).

5   P. Sainath (2004a) recounts the 'frightening struggle for survival' of farmers in the Ananthpur district of Andhra Pradesh where there have been four successive crop failures.

6   Sainath (2003) illustrates the rising trend of outward movement with the help of the massive rise in the number of weekly buses from the region to Mumbai, which rose from one in 1993 to about 34 in 2004. About 65 per cent of the villagers had reportedly gone out to work on the buses. Interestingly a large part of the Andhra Pradesh State Road Corporation's revenue comes from the Mumbai route. There are often more then a hundred passengers on the 58-seat buses, which mean that a substantial number keeps standing over a large part of the 18-hour journey.

7   Ibid.

8   Migrant labour as part of this informal economy is further handicapped because of its position of illegality in terms of citizenship status and stringent immigration laws, and is therefore constantly viewed as the 'other'. The middlemen and agencies that mediate migration make use of laws that are completely against the interests of those migrating and rather become the means of their exploitation and vulnerability both at the hands of these recruiting agencies as well as their employers. This cannot be viewed as a simple arrangement between the recruiting agencies, employers and the migrants in search of jobs where if certain redressal mechanisms are put into force, the situation can be taken care of. In both situations—of the presence of an anti-migrant law or the absence of a law protecting the interests of migrants—employers and recruiting agencies act on behalf of the state. Each one is benefiting from these arrangements 'by jointly criminalising them and by constructing them as a particularly right-less people' (Das Gupta 2003, JAGORI 2004). Studies in this volume and otherwise have pointed to the 'bonded labour' or slavery type conditions that result with the use of such state regulations and laws.

9   Some of these are, Plantation Labour Act 1951, The Mines Act 1952, The Beedi and Cigar Workers Act 1966, The Equal Remuneration Act 1976, Contract Labour (Regulation and Abolition) Act 1970, Bonded Labour Abolition Act 1976, Equal Remuneration Act 1976, Dock Workers Act 1986, Contract Labour (Regulation and Abolition) Act 1996, and Building and Construction Workers Act 1996.

10 The document titled 'Platform for Action' released at the Beijing Conference initially did not have a single reference to immigrant women and women migrant workers, but finally included the concerns of these women only because of the presence, lobbying and persistence of migrant women's organisations and other NGO advocates. While the economic value of migrant women's work both for the sending and receiving countries was recognised and an admission was made that 'migrant female workers remain the least protected by labour and immigration laws', the document still lacked a clearly stated commitment to protect the rights of migrant women, immigrants, refuges and other displaced women to work in a safe environment free of violence, exploitation, slavery-like conditions and sexual harassment. Still, the inclusion of their concerns in the document has to be seen as a first important step towards their efforts in mainstreaming their issues, though it remains to be seen how they are going to achieve their goals of equality and justice.

11 The UPA government came up with a National Rural Employment Guarantee Bill 2004 with a view to provide for at least 100 days of employment to begin with on asset creating public works programmes every year at minimum wages for at least one able bodied person in every rural household. The Bill ostensibly takes note of the need for some employment alternatives in the rural areas and intends to provide some relief to families affected by the agrarian crises. Since the Bill contains no special provisions for women, women's organisations and others concerned with women's interests have pointed it out to the government that non-inclusion of specific measures for women would amount to excluding women from the benefits of this Bill. The Bill was passed in September 2005.

12 The draft Scheduled Tribes (Recognition of Forest Rights) Bill 2005 aims at providing tribals rights to forest resources with the objective of compensating for the 'historical injustice' done to forest dwelling tribes that were denied their traditional right to forest lands and resources in the past 200 years, with the declaration of the lands they had been dwelling on as 'forest land' or 'protected areas' and reserves for

wildlife and environment conservation. The recognition of their rights restores their right to basic livelihood sources. At the same time, the Bill also recognises the concerns of conservation of forests and their non-human dwellers, bringing with it responsibilities of forest protection to the users. For a discussion of the Bill and the debates surrounding it see Ashish Kothari and Neema Pathak (2005: 88–89).

13 This requires public investment in source areas to counter the unevenness of development and economic opportunities. Such development could be most effective if tailored to the specific potential of different sub-regions, and might include irrigation investments in water-scarce areas or initiation of non-agricultural enterprises where land is scarce (Rogaly et al. 2001).

References and Further Readings

Anderson, Bridget. 2000. *Doing the Dirty Work? The Global Politics of Domestic Labour.* Zed Books: London.

Banerjee, Narayan. 1987. Women's Work and Family Strategies: A Case Study from Bankura, West Bengal. Unpublished report, New Delhi: Centre for Women's Development Studies.

Breman, J. 1996. *Footloose Labour: Working in India's Informal Economy.* New York: Cambridge University Press.

Batistella, Graziano. 1993. *Human Rights of Migrant Workers, An Agenda for NGOs.* Quezon City: Philippines.

Campani, Giovanna. 1995. 'Women Migrants: From Marginal Subjects to Social Actors', in Robin Cohen (ed.), *The Cambridge Survey of World Migration.* Cambridge: Cambridge University Press.

Chen, Martha Alter. 2003. 'Rethinking the Informal Economy', *Seminar,* 531, November.

Das Gupta, Monisha. 2003. 'The Neoliberal State and the Domestic Workers Movement in New York City', *Canadian Women Studies,* 22(3&4).

Dutt, Mullika, Leni Martin and Helen Zia (eds). 1997. *Migrant Women's Human Rights in G-7 Countries: Organising Strategies.* Brockington: Family Violence Prevention Fund and Centre for Women's Global Leadership.

Enloe, Cynthia. 1992. 'Silicon Trick and the Two Dollar Women', *New Internationalist,* 227, January, http://www.newint.org/issue227/silicon.htm.

Fernandes, Walter and Geeta Menon. 1987. *Tribal Women and Forest Economy: Deforestation, Exploitation and Status Change.* Delhi: Indian Social Institute.

Ferrajoli, L. 1996. 'Beyond Sovereignty and Citizenship: A Global Citizenship', in Richard Bellamy (ed.), *Constitutionalism, Democracy and Sovereignty: American and European Perspectives.* Avebury: Ashgate.

Habermas, J. 1992. 'Citizenship and National Identity: Some Reflections on the Future of Europe', *Praxis International,* 12(1), April.

JAGORI. 2004. *Rights and Vulnerabilities: A Research Study of Migrant Women Workers in the Informal Sector in Delhi.* Delhi: JAGORI.

Janwadi Adhikar Manch. 1998. *Things Fall Apart.* Delhi: Janwadi Adhikar Manch, March.

———. 2001a. *How Many Errors Does Time Have Patience For?* Delhi: Janwadi Adhikar Manch, April.

———. 2001b. *Always on the Run.* Delhi: Janwadi Adhikar Manch, May.

Karlekar, Malvika. 1995. 'Gender Dimensions in Labour Migration', in Loes Schenk-Sandbergen (ed.), *Women and Seasonal Labour Migration*. New Delhi: Sage Publications.

Kempadoo, Kamala. 2003. 'Globalising Sex Workers Rights', *Canadian Women Studies*, 22(3&4), Spring/Summer: 143–50.

Kothari, Ashish and Neema Pathak. 2005. 'Forests and Tribal Rights', *Frontline*, 3 June.

'Kyoto Statement on the Worker's Human Rights in the APEC Region.' 1995. Quebec: International Centre for Human Rights and Democratic Development.

Lim, L.L. 1989. 'The Status of Women in International Migration: Background Paper for the Meeting on International Migration Policies and the Status of Female Migrants', United Nations.

Listen, G.K., Olga Nieuwenhuys and Loes Schenk-Sandbergen (eds). 1989. *Women, Migrants and Tribals: Survival Strategies in Asia*. New Delhi: Manohar.

Menon, G. 1995. 'The Impact of Migration on the Work and Status of Tribal Women in Orissa', in L. Schenk-Sandbergen (ed.), *Women and Seasonal Labour Migration*. New Delhi: Sage Publications.

Mies, Maria. 1986. *Patriarchy and Accumulation on a World Scale: Women in the International Division of Labour*. London: Zed.

Rogaly, B., J. Biswas, D. Coppard, A. Rafique, K. Rana and A. Sengupta. 2001. 'Seasonal Migration, Social Change, and Migrants' Rights: Lessons from West Bengal', *Economic and Political Weekly*, 8 December.

Romero, Ana Teresa. 1995. 'Labour Standards and Export Processing Zones: Situations and Pressures for Change', *Development Policy Review*, 13(3): 247–76.

Roy, Ananya. 2003. *City Requiem Calcutta: Gender and the Politics of Poverty*. Minnesota: University of Minnesota Press.

Roy, Anupama. 2005. *Gendered Citizenship: Historical and Conceptual Explorations*. Delhi: Orient Longman.

Sainath, P. 2004a. 'Dreaming of Water, Drowning in Debt', *The Hindu*, 17 July.

———. 2004b. 'Job Drought Preceded Farm Crisis', *The Hindu*, 29 July.

———. 2003. 'The Bus to Mumbai', *The Hindu*, 1 June.

Schenk-Sandbergen, Loes (ed.). 1995. *Women and Seasonal Labour Migration, Indo-Dutch Studies on Development Alternatives*. New Delhi: Sage Publications.

———. 1988. *Poverty and Survival: Kudumbi Female Domestic Servants and their Households in Alleppey (Kerala)*. New Delhi: Manohar.

Skali, Loubna H. 2001. 'Women and Poverty in Morocco: The Many Faces of Social Exclusions', *Feminist Review*, 69, Winter.

Sri Lanka Bureau of Foreign Employment. 2003. *Statistical Handbook on Migration 2002*. Colombo.

Symonides, Janusz. 1998. *Human Rights: New Dimensions and Challenges*. Ashgate: Dartmouth.

Tienda, M. and K. Booth. 1991. 'Gender Migration and Social Change', *International Sociology*, 6(1): 51–72.

Turner, Bryan. 1986. *Citizenship and Capitalism: The Debate Over Capitalism*. London: Allen and Unwin.

———. 1993. *Citizenship and Social Theory*. London: Sage Publications.

Vogel, Ursula and Michael Moran. 1991. *The Frontiers of Citizenship*. New York: St. Martin's Press.

Yuval-Davis, Nira and Flora Anthias. 1989. *Women-Nation-State*. Basingstoke: Macmillan.

2

BRINGING HOME THE MONEY: MIGRATION AND POVERTY IN GENDER POLITICS IN SRI LANKA

Sepali Kottegoda

In Sri Lanka, 'migration', or *medaperadiga yaama*, is inextricably linked with Sri Lankan housemaids in West Asian countries, along with images of women from mainly working class or rural areas departing from or arriving at the airport, and of women from low income households who wear gold jewellery. Their mobility and attire 'conspicuously' sets them apart from others in the neighbourhood. The phrase also elicits a certain degree of dissatisfaction and unease among the general public as it connotes several other socially 'troubling' images: victims of violence, broken families, unfaithful wives/husbands, children who are subject to incest and rape within the family and of women losing their sense of family obligations.

The emergence of the woman from the poor household as the main income earner for her household and the 'exhibition' of her income seriously challenge prevailing notions of gender roles within society. The general social unease does not acknowledge the fact that remittance from migrants working in West Asia has formed the second highest source of foreign exchange for the country for more than two decades, nor that the strategic role these women play within their households demands acknowledgement and positive recognition. This paper addresses several of these concerns that have arisen with the phenomenon of women's migration for overseas employment as housemaids.

The paper will explore three aspects related to women's migration overseas for employment. First, it will examine the impact of this phenomenon of female migration on changing forms of the family-based household and the gender relations within them. Historically, Sri Lanka, as with other South Asian countries, has viewed the extended family as the basic unit of social relations. The notion of the extended family remains strong and forms the basis of much of the arrangements that prospective women migrants make when taking the decision to migrate.

Second, the paper will discuss the clear paradox between state policy and prevailing social practice. This paradox can be seen in relation to key gender-related socioeconomic areas (housing, poverty alleviation strategies, access to credit from lending institutions, etc.) that are clearly premised on the concept of the nuclear family on the one hand, and social practice in extended family structures (for example intense use of family ties routinely resorted to by prospective women migrants) on the other.

Third, the paper will examine how these social dynamics of female migration are reflected in efforts to respond to the basic issues of gender: women's empowerment, status in the family and general rights issues, etc.

Poverty in Sri Lanka

The population of Sri Lanka at the last census in 2001 stood at 18.73 million. Successive governments have over the past three decades implemented development programmes in line with the structural adjustment policies advocated by the International Monetary Fund (IMF) and the World Bank. Strengthening targeted poverty alleviation programmes to 'protect' those who are unable to benefit from these policies has been a major concern of these policies. The Sri Lankan government has had in place measures to address the problem of poverty through the Janasaviya Poverty Alleviation Programme in the 1980s and then the Samurdhi Poverty Alleviation programme from 1994 till the present day. The Ministry of Samurdhi, the main agency for poverty alleviation in Sri Lanka, currently uses Rs 1,500 (approximately US$ 15) per month as the poverty line and estimates that 2 million households in the country (excluding representative samples from the Northern and Eastern Provinces) were beneficiaries of this programme in 2001.

The analysis of the distribution of poverty reveals that it is concentrated in certain provinces and districts in the country. The Uva, North-Western and Sabaragamuwa Provinces have the highest population in poverty.[1] Correspondingly the Sri Lanka Bureau of Foreign Employment (SLBFE) records the most number of female migrants overseas are from the districts of Colombo (Western Province), Kurunegala (North Western Province) and Gampaha (Western Province) (SLBFE 2003: 29;

op. cit. pp. 116–19). The SLBFE also notes that in 2002, approximately 10 per cent of the total number of women migrants were from the north and east of the country, specifically from the Ampara, Trincomalee and Batticaloa districts.[2]

Women's Employment and Unemployment

The major foreign exchange earning employment opportunities in Sri Lanka since 1977 have been highly gendered with women's labour in the Free Trade Zones (FTZs), in the plantations and in West Asia forming the backbone of this income structure. Women employed in the FTZs and in sweatshops around the FTZs and Colombo are mostly between the ages of 18 and 25, single and have nimble fingers; the women workers in the plantation sector that was set up over 150 years ago (near bonded labour conditions) have traditionally ranged from 16 to 45 years. While the former generally come from mainly the Sinhalese and the Tamil communities, the latter are descendents of Tamil labourers brought over by the British colonisers.

The female labour force participation rate increased from 19.41 per cent in 1981 to 32.2 per cent in the first quarter of 2003, and also reflects a shift in the employment status of women (Central Bank of Sri Lanka 1999: 51, 2003: 161; Department of Census and Statistics 2003a, this computation includes data from the Eastern Province for the first time since the 1981 Census). A downward shift in the category 'unpaid family labour', which comprises mostly women, from 26.5 per cent in 2000 to 21.7 per cent in 2002 shows that women are more aware of their potential as wage earners and are moving out of the traditional 'unpaid worker' sector to avenues of employment which bring them a direct income (Department of Census and Statistics 2002, 2003b). This trend is also found in the North Western, North Central and Central Provinces which have a high concentration of unpaid family workers and also record some of the highest outflows of women as migrant workers (housemaids) to West Asian countries (Department of Census and Statistics 2002, op. cit. p. 18; SLBFE 2003, op. cit. p. 30).

The unemployment rate for women has remained more than twice that of men for over two decades. Despite equal access to free education for girls and boys, there is greater educated unemployment among women as compared to men (Central Bank of Sri Lanka 1999, op. cit. p. 63;

Department of Census and Statistics 2003a, Tables 4 and 5). On the other hand, unemployment rates are relatively lower among the less educated women. Many of the women seeking employment in the FTZs or as migrant workers come from among those who have secondary or lower levels of education.

In Sri Lanka, housework is not defined as economically productive work but as an activity that does not require any skill. The gendered nature of housework, the subordinate position of women who are socially expected to fulfil household chores which are based on more than eight hours of physical labour on a daily basis, are not issues that engage policy-makers. Where women do housework in the homes of others and are paid for their labour, such activity is defined as economically productive; the fact that the work is what women are *expected* to perform, seems to be sufficient to categorise it as 'unskilled' work.

Migrant Workers to Overseas Labour Markets: The Institutional Mechanisms

In the late 1970s, responding to the opening of labour markets in West Asian countries following the oil crisis, the Sri Lankan government initiated several policies to facilitate overseas migration for employment. This strategic policy move not only secured a regular and much needed avenue of foreign exchange earnings, but also changed the contours and profile of Sri Lankan migrants seeking income earning avenues outside the country. By 2002, there were an estimated 970,000 Sri Lankans employed as migrant workers overseas, out of which 87 per cent were employed in Saudi Arabia, Kuwait, the United Arab Emirates (UAE) and Lebanon (SLBFE 2002).

The Sri Lankan government institutionalised the procedure of employment migration in 1985 with the setting up of SLBFE to promote and develop employment opportunities outside Sri Lanka and, among other objectives, to assist and support foreign employment agencies in their growth and development. Sri Lanka is party to the seventh basic human rights instrument of the United Nations, the International Convention on the Protection of the Rights of All Migrant Workers and Members of Their Families, which came into force on 1 July 2003.

The SLBFE has also put into operation a system of model contracts between migrant workers and employers through a series of Memorandums of Understandings or MoUs signed between itself and recruitment agencies in Kuwait, Saudi Arabia, Oman, Qatar, the UAE, Lebanon, Bahrain, Jordan, Cyprus and Singapore (ibid.: 17).

The system of migration advocated by the SLBFE is through foreign employment agencies registered with them. In 2002, the SLBFE recorded 538 such registered private recruitment agencies which played a key role in finding employment opportunities and placements overseas (Dias and Jayasundera 2000: 14). While these procedures have increased the registration of migrant women workers with the SLBFE from 40 per cent in 1994 to 70 per cent in 1999, 30 per cent of prospective migrants find employment overseas through unlicensed employment agencies or through personal contacts in other countries (ibid.). It is these women who are most vulnerable to exploitation while working overseas.

The SLBFE in collaboration with the Ministries of Foreign Affairs and of Labour has instituted several initiatives to address complaints of violation of employment conditions of overseas workers.[3] Labour attaches and welfare offices have been appointed in the country missions in the UAE, Saudi Arabia, Kuwait, Oman, Qatar, Lebanon, Jordan and Singapore to provide assistance to Sri Lankan workers in these countries. Notwithstanding these measures, assistance to migrant workers whose contracts have been violated still remains confined to those who establish contacts with the Sri Lankan Embassy in the receiving countries (Dias and Jayasundera 2000: 19).

Of the total number of complaints received by the SLBFE from migrant workers overseas, those by housemaids comprise the highest. The percentage of complaints has, over the period 1998 to 2002, stayed around 5.2 per cent (approximately 6,000 individuals) of all migrant housemaids (SLBFE 2003: 27; see also Samuel 1999). The most frequent violations reported range from non-payment of agreed wages to harassment; there are also reports of deaths overseas. The most number of complaints have been received by the SLBFE from women working in Saudi Arabia, Kuwait, Lebanon and the UAE.

Officially, the salary for a Sri Lankan housemaid in most West Asian countries as negotiated by the Sri Lanka Foreign Employment Bureau is US$ 130 (approximately 13,000 Sri Lankan rupees) a month. In reality, a woman may earn between Rs 8,000–10,000 depending on the deal made by the foreign employment agency through whom her placement and travel was arranged in Sri Lanka and the recruiting agency in the receiving country. The amount of wages paid is considerably higher than what most housemaids receive in the local labour market.

The Gendered Overseas Labour Market

By 1988, the shift in the profile of migrant workers from males to females clearly indicated that Sri Lanka had found a niche in the overseas employment market. While the demand for women migrant workers almost doubled in the mid-1990s, 65 per cent of an estimated total of almost 250,000 migrant workers who left for employment overseas in 2002 were women. Significantly, the SLBFE recorded that of the total number of female migrants, 108,514 or 82 per cent went overseas to work as housemaids (SLBFE 2003, op. cit. p. 23).

The Sri Lankan female migrant worker is between the ages of 25 and 44 years of age; 75 per cent of 108,514 women who find employment as housemaids were within this age category (ibid.: 38; Dias and Jayasundera 2000, op. cit.; INSTRAW 2000: 118). In West Asian countries preference is given to married women who are perceived to be more familiar with the tasks entailed in housekeeping and also more responsible.

Most studies indicate that close to 50 per cent women who seek employment overseas have at least a secondary level education; the proportion of women with no formal education is placed at less than 3 per cent (INSTRAW 2000; Dias and Jayasundera 2000, op. cit. p. 4; Cenwor 2002, op. cit.).

Major Female Labour Importing Countries

The primary employers of housemaids from Sri Lanka are four countries in West Asia, Saudi Arabia, Kuwait, Lebanon and the United Arab Emirates, which absorbed 87 per cent of migrant workers. The periodic tensions in the West Asian region or reports of ill-treatment or even death appear to have little impact on either the demand for Sri Lankan housemaids or the numbers of women seeking employment overseas. The SLBFE notes a 5.5 per cent increase in growth rate in 2002 compared to 2001 with the highest increase in demand recorded from Saudi Arabia (SLBFE 2003, op. cit. p. 22). Non-West Asian countries which also employ Sri Lankan housemaids such as Singapore, Hong Kong and Cyprus account for less than 3 per cent of migration (ibid.).

Occupational Specifications

In the initial phase of migration of Sri Lankan women, the overwhelming demand from West Asian countries was for Muslim (ethnic Moor/Malay) women who were perceived to have the capacity to blend in with the sociocultural framework of the receiving countries (Kottegoda 1991). This changed the relative mobility of Muslim women who are traditionally largely confined to their immediate domestic sphere. There is careful attention to ensuring that their work overseas does not deviate from their own domestic environment in Sri Lanka. The Muslim woman now plays a more visible role as a substantial income earner for their households, while remaining within the cultural and religious boundaries of their community (Kottegoda 1991; Cenwor 2002). The demand for women workers from specific ethnic groups has however, changed over the past two decades, with significant numbers of non-Muslim women (ethnic Sinhala and Tamil) also migrating for employment to West Asian countries (Cenwor 2002: 43).

Muslim and Christian women have a high demand in West Asian countries followed by non-Muslim women and those who can generally work as a housemaid. Although the demand for Muslim women is marginally higher than for non-Muslim women, on the supply side, there is a higher proportion of non-Muslim women who seek and obtain employment as housemaids (SLBFE 2003: Table 43).

Foreign Exchange Earnings from Remittances

In the year 2002, private remittances of foreign exchange comprised 29 per cent of total foreign exchange earnings in the country (SLBFE 2003: 40). Over the period 1991–2002, remittances from West Asia as a percentage of total remittances from overseas rose from 52 per cent to 61.3 per cent. Most importantly, despite the fact that housemaids, categorised as unskilled workers, earn lower wages than skilled workers (most of whom are male), the fact of them being the significant majority of overseas workers is sufficient to place them as the main source of *foreign exchange remittances* to Sri Lanka (ibid.: 39).

This discussion on the demand for women migrant workers and the profile of women who migrate to countries primarily in West Asia sets out the basic proposition of this paper: to argue that the increased role that women play as income earners for the family-based household as well as for the state squarely places them as key to the development process. Within the framework of the discourse of women's rights and of social mobilisation nationally, the changing role of women as economic actors raises several areas of interest in relation to women's ability to negotiate the boundaries of gender roles and being able to draw out at the societal and policy level recognition and acknowledgement of their contributions at the household and national levels.

Woman as Absentee Income Earner for the Family-Based Household

Poverty and lack of employment in Sri Lanka that would bring in wages commensurate with the potential earnings overseas are the fundamental push factors in women's decision to migrate. Almost all women migrants express the desire first to improve the economic status of their families, especially to build a permanent home, educate their children better and overcome economic difficulties such as their constant state of indebtedness as the priority reasons for seeking the wages offered in overseas labour market for housemaids (Kottegoda 1991; Yapa 1995; Cenwor 2002; INSTRAW 2000; Gamburd 2002; Dias and Jayasundera 2000). The desire to get away from abusive relationships at home was a subsidiary factor in some instances that motivated women to migrate overseas for extended periods of time (Yapa 1995). Overall, one of the driving forces for women to migrate overseas for employment has been the need to better their households and themselves, economically as well as socially.

Historically, Sri Lanka, as with other South Asian countries, has viewed the extended family as the basic unit of social relations. One of the most enduring features of women's strategies to utilise increased earnings overseas has been the consistent resort to their extended families as support bases for ensuring that the family she leaves behind is cared for and the monies that she remits are carefully managed. Despite the fact that the state has over the past several decades sought to 'restructure' the family as a nuclear unit, the notion of the extended family remains strong in Sri Lanka and forms the basis of much of the arrangements that prospective women migrants make when taking the decision to migrate.

Migration overseas for employment carries with it the prospect of the migrant being away from her home for periods ranging from two to five years. Hence, it is not a decision that is taken lightly by the women. In the majority of cases, the prospective woman migrant explores the possibility of finding employment overseas through discussion with immediate family members, women returnee migrants and extended family members.

For married women the process of decision-making begins with discussions with their spouses. Often, the initial reaction of spouses is one of reluctance to assume household and family responsibilities (INSTRAW 2000: 133–34). In general, women's endeavours are supported by their families, most commonly by her own and also by the extended family including her in-laws. Most often initial travel investments are heavily dependent on resources obtained through the extended family networks. This strategy carries with it an element of self-interest by both parties. As Yapa points out:

> In this process (of deciding to migrate) the extended family of the migrant plays an equally important role as that of the immediate family of the migrant. The migrant worker depends heavily on the family networks for emotional support and care of children. The family has an interest in the migration of one of its members and hence lends a helping hand to the migrant to overcome the constraints of childcare (1995: 111).

Referring to some researchers who had anticipated that the extended family would collapse under the strain of extending their support to families where the woman had migrated overseas, Gamburd notes that:

> ... the extended family played a crucial role in facilitating migration by providing childcare, financing agency fees, finding jobs in the Middle East (West Asia) for female migrants and seeing the family through crises at home ... in general migration seemed to strengthen extended family relationships, not weaken or endanger them (2002: 237).

Once the woman is assured that she has the support either of her spouse and/or her own natal family, she proceeds with finding a foreign employment agency.[4] The monies for processing her application are generally found through borrowing and/or pawning personal jewellery; the urgency of finding suitable work overseas and ensuring that remittances are managed efficiently becomes an even more critical issue in the face of debts incurred (Yapa 1995: 95; INSTRAW 2000; Cenwor 2002: 13).

Unlike in the initial phases of migration where women tended to send all their remittances back home to their spouses, women are now more strategic in their planning for management of their earnings. The reliance on their own family members or in-laws to manage their remittances from overseas has increasingly been the strategy of most women migrants. While consultations are held with most family members regarding the decision to migrate, the prospective migrants make their own assessment as to whom they remit their earnings to. Mostly, they decide to remit either the whole or part of their earnings overseas to their own mothers, sisters or even in-laws (mother or sister); this is particularly the case where remittances from an initial stint of working overseas do not bring the expected financial benefits (INSTRAW 2000: 136; Gamburd 2002: 181; Yapa 1995: 111–12). There is also a growing tendency for migrant women to open bank accounts in their own names and remit monies directly so that they have an assured sum of money waiting for them on their return.

The challenges women face in these endeavours arise in the arena of the politics of gender roles in the institutional structures (public arena) and within the family-based household (private arena). The strategies employed by women to obtain employment overseas clearly demonstrates that the 'family' the migrant relates to is overwhelmingly that of the extended family.

Head of Household: Law, Policy and Reality

The legal framework of the country which applies to roles and responsibilities within marriage poses additional challenges to the woman who is struggling to win social and formal recognition as main income provider for her family-based household. While the Constitution of Sri Lanka (Article 12) guarantees non-discrimination in the area of gender this assurance is not played out in critical areas of legislation.

The operation of the General Law (founded on the Roman Dutch Law) together with the Special Laws functions to place the father with a greater role and responsibility than the mother in relation to household decisions.[5] While under the Kandyan Law and the Muslim Law a married woman can deal with her own property, under the Thesavalame a married woman is required to obtain her husband's consent to dispose of or deal with her immovable property. In relation to rights and responsibilities within the family, de Soysa (1998) points out:

> In Roman Dutch Law it is the husband who has a decisive say in all matters relating to the common life of the spouses and it is he who determines where the parties ought to live and in what style. It is well accepted now that these decisions ought to be reasonable but there is running through the General Law, a continued recognition of the principle that the husband has a decisive say in matters relating to the common life of the spouses. This runs counter to accepted international standards which require the State to take measures to eliminate discrimination against women in all matters relating to marriage and family relations (de Soysa 1998: 87).

While the Sri Lankan law does not state explicitly that it is the male who is the head of the household, and the Special Laws separately or together with the General Law refers to specific situations where women have clearly set out rights, the patriarchal framework within which women are perceived implicitly places them in a secondary position within the family-based household (Scharenguivel 2003).

Legally, the status of a woman as head of her household, i.e., responsible for supporting her household, is recognised only in situations where the spouse is unable to maintain himself or where she has become a widow. This is reflected in the formulation of state policy in relation to distribution of welfare benefits through household units deemed to be in poverty.

State intervention has conceptualised and targeted the household as the unit that receives the handouts given by these poverty alleviation programmes. The household continues to be viewed as the centre of harmonious family relations where gender inequities and differences in power and access to resources between women and men found everywhere else in society apparently do not exist (Kottegoda 2003). While debate and discussion on the conceptual construction of the household and that of the family is ongoing, definitions that are used in mainstream development policy in Sri Lanka largely overlook different forms of family (one-parent families, female-headed families, extended families) while defining eligibility criteria for participation in such programmes (Chakraborthy 2002; Kottegoda 1991b, 1995).

The focus at the policy level is on the nuclear family as the primary family form in development.

The Samurdhi Scheme continues to target 'poor' (primarily male-headed) households as beneficiaries. The savings and membership of the scheme lists as eligible the male 'head' of the household while the woman (spouse) is confined to membership of the women's *samithi*. The entitlement card is given under Samurdhi only to the chief member (the husband) to make any claims every six months. If the card is not collected by him the household is unable to make any claims. Most importantly, the husband is able to claim the entitlement card only if the wife has been regularly attending the women's *samithi* meetings every fortnight.[6] Women's participation at the ground level is a compulsory condition for the household to claim entitlement to the benefits of the programme. The husband does not have any such requirement (except to ensure that the spouse attends the compulsory meetings). Although there are undisputed records that 80 per cent or more of the participants in the Samurdhi schemes at the household level are women, the official policy focus is on the husband as the beneficiary.

Allocation of state land is similarly framed to reflect the superior position given to the male as the head of the household and rightful owner/heir of lands allocated. State lands, particularly in irrigation projects or major 'colonisation' schemes, have been premised on the assumption that the male has priority in ownership of land over the woman. Gunaratne (2001) observes:

> Given the fact that permit holders are generally male and therefore the spouse is female, these provisions appear to be based on the assumption that the land is merely given to him for economic reasons. If she remarries there is a further assumption that her second husband will provide her with economic support and therefore she will not require land anymore.

In any event, on the death of the owner, priority is given to the son/s as next in line to permit/holder (ownership) of the property.

Another development policy of interest to this discussion is the construction of housing, sponsored by the state in particular but also promoted by private sector home development companies, of dwellings that are designed to accommodate the standard nuclear family. The

Urban Development Authority of the 1980s, which was transformed in the 1990s to the National Housing Development Authority as the main state agency for the promotion and development of housing facilities in the country, has been from its early years constructing houses designed for nuclear families.

Women Workers or Just Housewives?

The earnings overseas of approximately 100,000 women opens up the space within the prevailing gender-based social norms of conduct for women to exert a degree of power and control which they otherwise would not have been able to enjoy. Their own substantial monetary income and the opportunity to openly display items of wealth compels household members, and indeed the community, to consider them as economic assets. This tendency for patriarchal social structures and institutions to recognise women's worth only when it is perceived in terms of monetary value is not new in Sri Lanka (Hospes et al. 2001; Kottegoda 2003). In the case of migrants, the financial contributions are considerably high and often utilisation of these funds is very much in the public sphere, in most cases deliberately so—for example, in the husbands' ability to purchase liquor for friends and relatives from remittances sent by the wives, women's ability to buy land and/or build homes, their children having access to better quality food, etc. This in turn effectively poses a challenge to re-examine the gender roles and responsibilities that are the 'norms' in society.

Success of the strategy of migration is primarily assessed within a narrow economic framework and generally does not accommodate or acknowledge its impact on enabling women to recognise in the public sphere the value of their own contributions to their households (Amarasuriya 2000). There appears to be strong resistance to recognising women as *the* primary income earner and main source of support in the migrant's household. Women migrants are repeatedly classified as housewives. Gunatilleke notes that:

The majority of migrants, approximately 60 per cent, were *housewives* (author's emphasis) for whom the outcome of the migration was not directly related to their own future income-earning capacity. Most of them expected to return home to their position as housewives and homemakers after earning a substantial sum from their employment abroad. The *primary income earner for the household was the husband* (author's emphasis) who normally continued in employment (Gunatilleke 1992: 228).

This perception that women migrants are primarily housewives while their spouses are the primary income earners is also reflected in other studies that insist on the woman income earner's secondary status as provider for her family. Household financial management (as different from earning income) and childcare are socially not seen as primary duties of the husband.

The wife/mother becoming the principal income earner can also lead to situations where the challenge to perceived gender duties and obligations are critically laid at the feet of the woman migrant.

The changes taken place in the ideological plane have an impact on the relationship patterns within the family and community. The man-focused or man-centred relationships that were there in these families are now turning into a different set-up with replacement of woman-focused relationships. The man loses his position as the disciplinarian in most families, and as a result the children go astray, and get used to a new consumerism.... The father who has lost his traditional authority has also got addicted to alcohol or drugs or both. In many families where the wife is gone abroad, the husbands do not attempt to get employed (de Silva 1997: 65).

In this frame of analysis, the changing roles of women within the household places an unacceptable burden on the status of men in family and in society:

In this context ... the traditional authority of the husband is under challenge. The new situation created in most of the households has altered the behaviours of the husband ... to a person confronting directly with the wife ... has made the husband a drunkard and/or a drug addict. Very few have resolved the situation by accepting the changes and authority of the wife. In a few cases, however, particularly when the wife is feeble or a woman with some understanding, the couple has worked out alternative systems where both roles are mutually accepted with some division of responsibilities (ibid.).

Institutional Mechanisms for Recognition of Women as Workers

The institutional recognition of women's issues as national policy saw the setting up in 1978 of the Women's Bureau, followed by the Ministry of Women's Affairs in 1981. In 1993 Parliament passed the Women's Charter drafted by NGOs and government representatives, which sets out the government policy framework on women. In 1996, a National Committee on Women (NCW) was appointed mandated with the preparation of a 'National Plan of Action on Women'. The recognition of women's economic contributions forms a key focus in these policy directives.

Strong lobbying by women's groups and the legal community saw the Penal Code Reforms carried out in 1995 which recognised sexual harassment as a crime and increased the maximum penalty for rape to 20 years. The non-inclusion of drafted new legislation that would have recognise marital rape as a crime, however, exemplified the patriarchal refusal to acknowledge women's equal rights within marriage. As Goonesekere and Gunaratne observe: 'While there has always been male interest in protecting women from rape, there has also been a corresponding interest in protecting men from accusations of the offence' (Goonesekere and Gunaratne 1998: 21).

Since independence over 50 years ago, there has been only one formal attempt to incorporate paternity leave as a necessary regulation within the sphere of employment in the formal sector. The Ministry of Women's Affairs anticipated policy changes through this initiative in 2002: however, discussions with employers elicited more suspicion and reluctance than an understanding of the long-term benefits in terms of social and economic productivity. The focus continues to be singularly on the woman's maternal responsibility and the negative impact of her absence on her children (Resources Development Centre 1997).

The Ministry of Labour articulates women's economic participation through the framework of maternity and gendered responsibility (National Committee on Women 2001). The Draft National Employment Policy for Sri Lanka (2002) sets out the role for women in the labour market as follows:

Women's employability is perceived to be seriously constrained by existing gender-based attitudes and stereotypes in society.... Whilst improving women's employability in the labour market, adequate attention would also be paid to *their* (author's emphasis) commitment to fulfil their maternal responsibilities.... *Consideration will be given to women's maternity functions and awareness to be created amongst women that maternity would not become a hindrance to their careers* [author's emphasis] (Sri Lanka Ministry of Employment and Labour 2002: 47).

The emphasis here is on ensuring that women understand and perform their maternal roles as a priority; men's paternal roles and responsibilities essential for the formation of the desired heterosexual 'stable' family are not addressed similarly. According to the Government of Sri Lanka, 'Women working in the Middle East (West Asia), as domestics and nannies risk mal-treatment, are exposed to the threat of sexually transmitted diseases and are vulnerable to the breakdown of traditional family arrangements in their absence' (GoSL 2003: 120). The narrow focus on women's role in the breakdown of marriages is given special mention as a serious problem in the discussion on migrant workers. Their critical role as income contributors to their families and the country remains subsumed under the patriarchal 'protective' language (Fernando 2001).

Household Responsibility

The phenomenon of women's employment overseas continues to be one of intense debate. While the state actively pursues means to enhance opportunities for foreign exchange remittances through the export of Sri Lankan workers overseas, the market still remains open for the 'unskilled' lower paid housemaids. Sri Lankan women from low-income or poor households have in effect made the move from the local/national informal sector to the international informal sector, and their earnings overseas have become essential for the survival of most of their households on the one hand, and to replenish the national coffers on the other (Kottegoda 2000).

Social- and class-based resistance to recognising the economic contributions of these women can be seen in marked criticism of the women from other 'better off' classes in society; such attitudes can be clearly noted in interactions with migrants on their return at the airport as well as in interactions in residential areas where poorer households are located amid middle or upper class households (Amarasuriya 2000).

One of the most serious challenges faced by women migrants and mostly ignored by society in general and the family in particular is the fact that for such a strategy to 'succeed' financially and economically, it is imperative that the spouse and family take on his/their responsibilities in managing the remittances sent by the woman. Kottegoda (1991) notes that

> By migrating to West Asia, women often become the main income contributor to their households for at least the duration of their stay abroad. However, the fact by itself does not give a woman control over her earnings, particularly where remittances have been misused by the spouse or other family members. The only way in which a woman can maintain control over her income is either by sending only a part of her earnings back, or opening a savings account in her own name which cannot be handled by anyone else (Kottegoda 1991: chapter 7).

In a similar vein, the INSTRAW Study (2000) points out that the success or failure of a woman's strategy of migration overseas for better income is closely associated with the level of careful management and involvement in childcare by her spouse: 'The success of migration has depended to a great extent on the capacity of both sexes to adapt, and change their respective socially-assigned roles' (INSTRAW 2000: 140).

Where the strategy of female migration has had an impact on gender-based domestic arrangements, the INSTRAW Study found that fewer men were ready to take over household chores as they considered these burdensome. The extended family is expected to move in to take over the role of looking into the domestic needs such as childcare and nutrition of the 'mother-less' family (ibid.: 141). The reported increase in cases of incest and child abuse nationally is often attributed and blamed on the decision by women to migrate overseas. There is no serious public questioning or discussion of shared 'morally correct' parental responsibilities towards children (Yapa 1995; Gamburd 2002; INSTRAW 2000).

Women as Primary Income Earners:
Room for Negotiation?

The opening up of the West Asian labour market for women and the role that women play in Sri Lanka's economy and society are compelling reason to re-examine gender roles and responsibilities in society and in policy formulation. Within the international definitions of economically productive/non-productive work the 'army of migrant housemaids' offers compelling evidence that women *do* in fact have skills to sell, for which *there is* a labour market. The mere fact that for over 20 years Sri Lankan women have shown their ability to obtain paid work as house-maids in their thousands challenges 'accepted' norms of what is 'valued' work. It is the skill of housewifery which gender-based socialisation imparts to women that the West Asian labour markets have turned into an economically productive activity at the international level for women from Sri Lanka. What continues to be categorised as 'unskilled' work is one of the most significant and influential factors relating to the role of women as wage workers in the international labour market and as a major income contributor in her own family-based household.

The increased visible participation of women in the labour force, and in particular in activities such as migration overseas for employment in turn poses a challenge to notions of the male breadwinner of the family-based household. It also poses what is perceived as a challenge to class-based notions of entitlement to enjoy the privileges of 'luxury' items such as televisions, radio/cassette players, fans and other symbols of wealth. State policy encourages women to migrate overseas and depends on the earnings of the migrant workers. However, there is widespread criticism of women who migrate for apparently abrogating their primary roles as wives and mothers and for paving the way to undermine and even destroy the family. This is evident in periodical calls by both state and non-state actors to prohibit the migration overseas of women as a means to 'save' the 'endangered' family.

However, this examination of the phenomenon of migration over-seas for employment shows that women have actively strategised on the opportunities available to them to become income earners. It is not simply that women have been 'enabled' by state policy to go to West Asia. The rapid increase in the numbers of women migrating overseas, which within less than a decade overshadowed male migration over-seas, strongly indicates that women have been proactive in realising the potential for their own and their families' economic and social advancement. Women have actively seized the opportunity to migrate very quickly and vigorously. The rising incidents of exploitation and abuse of these women workers compels the state to focus on improv-ing institutionalised procedures for more secure terms of employment. Although there is still no such absolute guarantee for migrant workers, reports of gross violations are better monitored and mechanisms are periodically reviewed to address shortcomings.

Reports of an average 6,000 cases of ill-treatment, physical and sexual abuse, or in some cases death, does not appear to have stemmed the tide of women searching for employment overseas. This strong interest indicates that the push factors, primarily poverty, remain compelling; equally significantly, in terms of women's interventions in the economic and social status of their households, it also demonstrates women's determination and conviction that *they* have the ability to make a difference. The uninterrupted flow each year of over 100,000 prospective women migrants to West Asia illustrates that over the past two decades, there has emerged a shared acknowledgement among these women of their enhanced capacities to make decisions relating to their own lives and those of their families. Migration to West Asia has served as a means of enhancing women's economic independence and enabled most women to become the principal decision-maker in the family even *before* they actually leave; for example, the decision to leave, whether encouraged or not by the larger family, is ultimately the woman's. She attains the status of chief income earner and therefore principal economic manager of her household (even though many decisions may be mediated by males and elders) and, in becoming all of the above, is able to be a key economic actor in family and society.

Women have recognised and utilised the extended family support networks as an essential component for the success of the strategy to migrate overseas for employment. The analysis of the intensity of extended family participation points to the fact that women play a critical role in sustaining social institutions, particularly in the face of the challenges of modernisation. The strategic utilisation of family networks in a variety of ways as clearly demonstrated by women shows that not only has the extended family not gone away, but also that the nuclear family is as yet unable to provide the type of support, both emotional and physical, which is provided by the extended family. Despite an emphasis in state policy on promoting the nuclear family, there has not been a corresponding effort to institutionalise those support services that the extended family provides, such as childcare facilities.

In the recent past, there have been a number of notable civil society interventions that encompass the demand for recognition of workers' rights, especially where the significant majority of the workers are women. Since the late 1990s, women's groups have campaigned and lobbied for legislation on domestic violence, which led, in October 2003, to the Ministry of Justice formulating the Draft Bill on the Prevention of Domestic Violence. This Bill was passed by Parliament in August 2005.

Women's participation in decision-making processes within the political arena has been another concern for many years with its potential to bring into public discourse the right of women to be decisively involved in national policy. In 2003, women's groups successfully utilised the avenues for public expression by presenting their arguments at the Parliamentary Sub-Committee on Electoral Reforms for reservation of a percentage of nominations for political elections at all levels.

The Migrant Services Centre initiated the campaign in 2001 to win voting rights for migrant workers who are denied this right according to prevailing electoral regulations. Women's groups lobbied the Electoral Reforms Committee on this issue. While these endeavours are gradually pushing women's rights on to the mainstream legal and policy frameworks, it is important that such interventions by both civil and state actors focus on developing *policy and practice* that would publicly highlight the determined engagement women migrant workers together with other women workers have in the social, political and economic arenas in the country. The demonstration by women migrant workers of their ability to support their families, and upon their return to meet social/family challenges, are in themselves synonymous with 'mobilisation of women'. The need now is to see how these masses of economically mobilised women can become a social and political force for change within the current patriarchal family-based household and the wider polity.

Notes

1   Abeyratne (2001: 7) observes that though the Western Province ranks low in terms of the incidence of consumption poverty (head count index) relative to other provinces, it has the largest share of the country's population, and hence more poor people (a fifth of the total poor) live in this Province than elsewhere.

2   Since the signing of a 'ceasefire' (temporary suspension of active military engagement) in February 2002, the protracted ethnic conflict in the country moved up to a level of negotiations for sustainable peace in the country and broadened employment avenues for the population in the north-east of the country.

3   Report in Sri Lanka Daily News. 2 January 2003. Associated Newspapers. Colombo.

4   Women are increasingly going for overseas employment through foreign employment agencies registered with the SLBFE, which assures substantial support in terms of insurance and scholarships to dependent school children, etc. (SLBFE 2003: 50–51).

5　The Kandyan law for the Sinhalese of hill country domicile, the Thesavalame for the Tamils of Jaffna domicile and the Muslim Marriage Law operate along with the General Law of the country.

6　Each member of the women's *samithi* has to contribute Rs 5 per week for seven months in order to become a member of the Samurdhi women's bank. On membership, women are entitled to obtain an initial loan of Rs 250, upto Rs 100,000, for housing and/or enterprise development.

References and Further Readings

Abeyratne, Senake. 2001. 'Sri Lanka: Regional Approaches for Poverty Measurement', Second Annual Symposium on Poverty Research in Sri Lanka. Centre for Poverty Analysis, Programme to Improve Capacities for Poverty Research (IMCAP) and the Sri Lanka Association for the Advancement of Science (SLAAS). Colombo.

Amarasuriya, H. 2000. 'An Army of Housemaids: Representation and Construction of Sri Lankan Female Migrant Workers'. M.A. thesis, Department of Anthropology, Marcquarie University.

ACTFORM. 2002. 'Report of ACTFORM', prepared for the Migrant Forum in Asia and the Asian Migrant Centre Conference in Bangladesh. Colombo.

Asian Migrant Centre. 2000. Asian Migrant Yearbook 1999. Asian Migrant Centre, Migrant Forum Asia. Hong Kong.

———. 2001. Asian Migrant Yearbook 2000. Asian Migrant Centre, Migrant Forum Asia. Hong Kong.

Central Bank of Sri Lanka. 1999. Report on Consumer Finance and Socio Economic Survey, Sri Lanka, 1996/97, Part 1. Colombo.

———. 2003. Annual Report 2002. Colombo.

Cenwor. 2001. 'Channelling and Utilisation of Remittances of Migrant Women Domestic Workers', Report of Discussion Meeting. Document Series No. 69. Colombo.

———. 2002. 'Returnee Migrant Women in Two Locations in Sri Lanka'. Colombo.

Chakraborthy, K. 2002. *Family in India*. Delhi: Rawat Publications.

Department of Census and Statistics. 2002. 'Annual Report of the Sri Lanka Labour Force Survey—2000'. Colombo.

———. 2003a. 'Bulletin of Labour Force Statistics of Sri Lanka', Issue No. 25. Ministry of Interior, Colombo.

———. 2003b. 'Quarterly Report of the Sri Lanka Labour Force Survey—Third Quarter 2002'. Colombo.

———. 2003c. 'Sectoral and Provincial Poverty Lines for Sri Lanka', S.V. Vidyaratne and K.G. Tilakaratne, Ministry of Interior. Colombo.

Dias, M. and R. Jayasundera. 2000. 'Sri Lanka: Good Practices to Prevent Women Migrant Workers going into Exploitative Forms of Labour', ILO Genprom Working Paper No. 9, Geneva.

Fernando. N. 2001. 'Pre-Departure Reintegration Policy Advocacy in the Migration Process'. IMADR, Asia Committee Office. Colombo.

Gamburd, M.R. 2002. *Transnationalism and Sri Lanka's Migrant Housemaids: The Kitchen Spoon's Handle*. Colombo: Vijitha Yapa Publications.

Goonesekere, S.W.E. and C. Gunaratne. 1998. 'Women, Sexual Violence and the Legal Process in Sri Lanka: A Study on Rape', Centre for Women's Research. Colombo.

GoSL (Government of Sri Lanka). 2003. 'Regaining Sri Lanka: Vision and Strategy for Accelerated Development, Part II'. Colombo: GoSL.

Gunaratne, C. 2001. 'Land Ownership Rights of Women in Irrigation Settlements in Sri Lanka', Study conducted for the World Food Programme, Sri Lanka.

Gunatilleke, G. 1992. 'Sri Lanka', in 'The Impact of Labour Migration on Households: A Comparative Study in Seven Asian Countries'. UNU: Japan.

Hospes, O., K. Athukorale, I. Wijesiriwardena and S. Kottegoda. 2001. 'An Evaluation of Micro-Finance Programmes in Sri Lanka as Supported Through the Dutch Co-Financing Programme: With a Focus on SEEDS', Steering Committee for the Evaluation of the Netherlands' Co-Financing Programme. Wageningen Universiteit.

INSTRAW. 2000. 'Temporary Labour Migration of Women: Case Studies of Bangladesh and Sri Lanka'. United Nations: Santo Domingo.

Kottegoda, S. 1991. 'Survival Strategies of Women in Urban Low income Households: A Case Study from Sri Lanka', Unpublished D.Phil thesis, Institute of Development Studies, University of Sussex, UK.

―――. 1991b. 'Intra-Household Resource Distribution and Women's Survival', Centre for Women's Research. Colombo.

―――. 1995. 'Finding the Household: Some Experiences from Sri Lanka', *The Economic Review*. March. Colombo: People's Bank Economics Division Publication.

―――. 2000. 'Economic Activities and Poverty', in 'Sri Lanka: Shadow Report to the CEDAW Committee', Centre for Women's Research. Colombo.

―――. 2003. 'Interventions in Poverty Alleviation: Women Recovering from Poverty or Women Recovering the Family from Poverty?' in 'Poverty in Sri Lanka: Towards New Empirical Insights', Centre for Poverty Analysis (CEPA), Programme for Improving Capacities for Poverty Research (IMCAP) at the University of Colombo, Sri Lanka, Association for the Advancement of Science (SLAAS). Colombo.

Migrant Service Centre. 2002. 'Report of the National Consultation of Stake Holders on Migrant Domestic Workers', conducted by the Sri Lanka Foundation Institute and the Migrant Services Centre. Colombo.

Ministry of Women's Affairs. 2003. 'Sri Lanka Country Paper: National Machinery for Gender Equality', Paper presented at the 'Regional Meeting of National Machineries for Gender Equality in Asia and The Pacific: Towards a Forward Looking Agenda', The Ministry of Gender Equality, Korea.

National Committee on Women. 2001. 'National Plan of Action on Women', Ministry of Women's Affairs. Colombo.

Resources Development Centre. 1997. 'Study on Migrant Workers: A Literature Survey and Identification of Data Needs and Policy Action', Employment Policy Planning Unit, Department of National Planning, Ministry of Finance and Planning. Colombo.

Samuel, K. 1999. 'Women's Rights Watch'. The Women and Media Collective. Colombo.

Scharenguivel, S. 2003. 'Women and the Civil Law: An Agenda for Reform', Paper presented at the 'National Committee on Women' lecture series, August. Colombo.

de Silva, A., W.D. Lakshman and M.D.A.L. Ranasinghe. 1995. 'Migrant Remittances as a Source of Development Funding: A Study of Sri Lanka'. US-ISS Working Paper Series, Working Paper No. GE9502. Faculty of Graduate Studies, University of Colombo.

de Silva, M.W. A. 1997. 'Women in Conflict Situations', SRI/97/206.

SLBFE (Sri Lanka Bureau of Foreign Employment). 2002. *Statistical Handbook on Migration 2001.* Colombo: GoSL.

———. 2003. *Statistical Handbook on Migration 2002.* Colombo: GoSL.

de Soysa, S. 1998. 'Transformation of the Family, An Agenda for Reform: The Sri Lankan Experience', *Sri Lanka Journal of Social Sciences,* 21(1&2).

Sri Lanka Ministry of Employment and Labour. 2002. 'Draft National Employment Policy for Sri Lanka', Ministry of Employment and Labour. Colombo.

Yapa, L.A. 1995. 'Decision-Making Process of International Labour Migration with Special Reference to the Sri Lankan Housemaid', unpublished M.A. thesis, Women's Studies, University of Colombo.

3
LEAVING HOME: FILIPINO WOMEN SURVIVING MIGRATION

Maureen C. Pagaduan

At the time of writing this paper, around the Christmas of 2003, a significant event was happening in my home country. An 'economic boost' through the infusion of hard earned dollars from the remittances of the overseas Filipino workers (OFWs) had once again lifted the economy of the Philippines afloat. Credence and salute was given to our modern day heroes. Their remittances provided an opportunity to turn the bleakness of Christmas celebrations to one of hope, and added more festivity around the Christmas meals of people, more so in the absence of their loved ones, the Filipina overseas domestics. Culturally, Filipinos are known for their extravagance during this festive season, and the government encourages 'balikbayans' to spend their dollars through various discounted packages, from tourism and housing to outright product purchases.[1] When OFWs remit their annual earnings to their families, it brings about a pseudo-economic boost that the government encourages, as it persistently views labour migration merely in terms of remittances. The Philippine government, as a policy, aggressively rallies the promotion of overseas employment through labour migration to address unemployment and poverty while resolutely pursuing debt servicing, running into billions of dollars.[2] The Department of Foreign Affairs estimated that 5,488,167 OFWs and overseas Filipinos were spread in 193 countries throughout the world as of June 2002.

As with previous critical studies on migration, this paper will examine issues and concerns related to migration in the context of the so-called 'push and pull' factors for migrating under conditions of unabated poverty and globalisation. It will focus on the most accessible employment abroad for poor women, that is domestic work, which continues to be seen as an alternative, notwithstanding dramatic tales of persecution and abuse told by returning overseas workers. It will discuss how the Philippine government props up this situation by promoting overseas work through the establishment of agencies and programmes tasked with the welfare and delivery of efficient services to applicants, who ultimately are significant sources of additional government revenues. Further, it will look at the efforts of the state to legislate measures seeking to protect migrant workers programmes and services while supporting advocacy work towards international regulation. It will describe efforts of NGOs working with migrant groups, specifically their advocacy agenda, including their programmes and services for migrant workers, those abroad and those returning and their families.

Finally, the paper will look at how domestic work, the private, unpaid and reproductive work of women, has been reconfigured by the phenomenon of foreign domestic work. Women in large numbers leave their homes in order to secure them. Their efforts and sacrifices draw recognition from a government that gains political and economic capital from their remittances. Though nationally their status has been raised, overseas their work is the reserve of those without much free choice for employment and dignity of work. Women migrant domestic workers liberate housework, whether paid or unpaid, from its devaluing connotations of being (unwanted) at home, and the meaning of housework changes to something that can put food on the table, provide education to children, care for sick and elderly relatives and even hold the promise of a better life abroad. It is not surprising, therefore, to see how challenges have also confronted gender roles and relationships in the home countries as well as in receiving countries. Male and female identities and masculinities and femininities have been radically altered with both positive and negative effects.

The Increasing Permanence of a Temporary, Interim Strategy

The Philippines, unable to shed the historical vestiges of colonialism, has not been able to develop its productive forces adequately to answer the growing demand for jobs and incomes by a population leaping to 84 million in just a couple of years. English-speaking Filipino professionals and other college graduates have joined the ranks of the out-of-school that have poured into the job markets, both locally and globally. The labour they offer is abundant, flexible and cheap. A long history of labour migration where Filipinos from the northern parts of the country left for plantations in Hawaii added the quality of mobility to Filipino labour, which made the route easy to formal official policy. The early years of President Ferdinand Marcos' rule in the 1970s saw the sanctioning of the first arrivals of the overseas contract workers (OCWs). Overseas work was then seen as an interim response to unemployment and balance of payment difficulties, which the government explained was a temporary condition. Many of those who left during those years were Filipino male workers bound for the Middle East.

In this era of globalisation, the Northern capitals of the world and the more affluent Asian countries have pushed for the pursuit of dual careers in households, made possible by higher education and techno-logical developments. Management and maintenance of western households have become increasingly mechanised, making housework more routine and requiring less skill. These changes in the organisa-tion of reproductive work and the lack of state support to household management made it increasingly attractive for Western and wealthier homemakers to prefer to pay for cheap domestic work. The qualities of Filipino labour, especially female labour, fit this demand.

Along with Indonesia and Sri Lanka, the Philippines is one of the three countries in the Asian region where women comprise the major-ity of migrant workers. From a trickle in the 1970s, the numbers grew in the 1980s, and by the 1990s women came to comprise the majority—accounting for as much as 60 per cent—of the annual deployment of new hires from the Philippines. Like Indonesia and Sri Lanka, the majority of Filipino women migrant workers are concentrated in repro-ductive work, i.e., the work of caregiving and nurturing that has tradi-tionally been assigned to women (Guerrero et al. 2001).

Philippine NGOs working with migrant groups have foreseen the outflow of more Filipinas abroad, mostly to Japan. The ongoing eco-nomic and political crises plaguing the country make Philippine society and its citizens pessimistic and desperate as to their chances for jobs and incomes. The peso–dollar exchange has peaked, reaching its highest rate in the 1990s, and is now set at 55 pesos to the dollar. The political situation is as dire, given the unpredictability and instability caused by the presidential elections of May 2004. In response, many Filipinos, mostly women, will grab the first chance to pack their bags to seek better opportunities abroad for survival, thus solidly affirming the trend of forced labour migration and the phenomenon of feminisation in migration.

The Philippine government and the country as a whole was critically positioned to respond to the demand-given experiences gained in the 1970s with large-scale overseas employment, mainly to the Middle East. A total of 891,908 OFWs were legally deployed in 2002, posting a 2.8 per cent rise from 2001. Daily deployment was pegged at 2,444, an increase by 2.7 per cent from 2002's 2,377. Government figures reveal that out of 288,155 new hires for overseas jobs in 2002, 210,353 or 73 per cent were women. The number of women workers in Japan was higher at 95 per cent (73,494 out of 77,870).[3]

Professional and technical workers (35 per cent), service workers (34 per cent) and production workers (24 per cent) continue to form a huge bulk of total OCWs, accounting for an overwhelming 93 per cent of the total. Professional and technical workers posted an 11-year high of 100,585, the largest group of newly hired OCWs for the second straight year. Service workers reached an 11-year high with 98,007, marking the third straight year this category posted more than 90,000 workers. Service workers were either the first or second largest group. Of the newly hired OCWs, women comprised 73 per cent (209,822), a slight increase compared to 72 per cent (186,018) in 2002. Newly hired women dominated the service (90 per cent) and professional (80 per cent) occupations in 2002, while the men dominated the production sector at 71 per cent. Domestic workers and related household workers continued to be the largest group under the service category, reaching a total of 63,434, constituting 65 per cent of deployed service workers. Entertainers made up 73 per cent of 100,585 professional and technical workers. Composers, musicians and singers numbered 40,770, while dancers and choreographers totalled 32,724. Nurses, under the professional and technical category, fall third at 11,867. The deployed entertainers in Japan nearly make up the entire documented Filipino labour force there (73,062 out of 73,477, or 99.4 per cent).

At present, labour migration contributes to keeping the Philippine economy afloat; in 2002 OFWs remitted a total of US$ 6.9 billion, broken down into US$ 5.7 billion from land-based workers and US$ 1.2 billion from sea-based workers respectively (*Philippines Star*, 16 May 2003). In the first three months of 2003 remittances reached US$ 1.78 billion, reflecting in part the increase in the number of Filipinos leaving for work abroad. This was noted by the Philippine Overseas

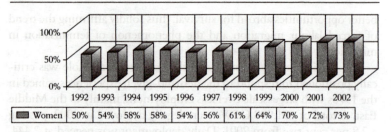

Figure 3.1 Deployment of Women OFWs (1992–2002)

Table 3.1 Male and Female Land-based Workers by Type of Occupation (2002)

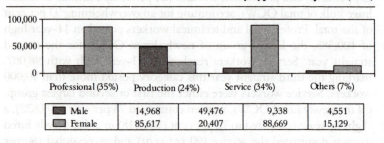

Table 3.2 Deployment of OFWs (1998–2002)

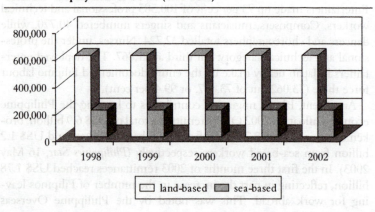

Employment Administration (POEA) when it declared a marginal growth of 0.4 per cent on the statistics of hires and rehired workers for the period January–February 2003 alone. Most of the OFWs are in the field of services, medical care and entertainment (*Trends, News and Tidbits* 2003).

The broader macro-economic context of migration shows the Philippine economy's performance as being unable to provide any hope for workers who do not wish to leave, but who fear the consequences of poverty. The Philippine economy registered a GDP growth of 3.9 per cent in 2000, higher than other South-east Asian countries, but from a comparatively lower base growth. The agricultural sector grew at 3.4 per cent, pushing many rural workers into the cities. The services sector rose 4.4 per cent, registering the highest growth of all sectors, and filling employment demands for relatively lower paying jobs. The industrial sector registered a 3.6 per cent increase while the corporate sector, which has not yet fully recovered from the Asian financial crisis, indicated a high rate of non-performing loans in the banking system pegged at 16.2 per cent at the end of November 2002.

The unemployment rate rose to 9.3 per cent at the beginning of 2002 and peaked at 10.1 per cent by the end of October 2002. On an annual basis, it is higher at 11.1 per cent in 2002. Although the inflation rate declined a little, at 3 per cent in 2000, it continues to increase with the rise in world oil prices, the depreciation of the peso and the adjustment of wages. The government's fiscal deficit in 2000 was Philippine peso (Php) 136.1 billion. These figures did not improve in 2003 even as the government prioritised efforts to augment macroeconomic stability, improve tax collections, expedite the privatisation process, rationalise expenditures and improve cash management through good governance and acceleration of structural reforms, while promoting private sector participation and rural development (Asian Migrant Yearbook 2001).

Gendered Dimensions of Migration: Double-Edged Opportunities

While poverty is an important push factor for large-scale overseas employment, gender construction reveals other important facets of the phenomena of migrant work as well. The profiles of documented Filipino women migrant workers during 1992–93 show them to be young, around 20 to 29 years of age and unmarried. Sarah Balabagan, the Filipina domestic imprisoned in Saudi Arabia after killing her employer who attempted to rape her, was only 14 when she was recruited. Those who are older are fairly educated, with college degrees or with some college education. This segment of the female population appears to be more subject to parental authority, giving into subtle pressure to migrate in order to provide means for their families to afford better lives. Studies also show that daughters more than sons tend to provide more consistent financial support, sending money regularly to their households. Past studies reveal patterns of local migration from rural to urban areas in the 1960s that were predominantly composed of women as well and which are similar to overseas migration of women. Rural women migrated to the cities mainly as a household survival and mobility strategy.

Female migration has long been undertaken not so much for individual interests as for the family's collective welfare and solidarity. This is consistent with a gender ideology that socialises women to fulfil roles to nurture and provide care to their families even at the risk of self-sacrifice in order to satisfy such obligations. In turn, families do their best to makeover household arrangements to be more supportive to women overseas workers. Mothers or mothers-in-law take over childcaring and household work for families of married overseas workers. They also facilitate de-stigmatisation by communities of any overseas worker whether engaged in domestic or entertainment work, by drawing on the economic benefits of such work rather than its moral costs, much like the government strategy.

The role of personal and social networks appears to also be the key to facilitating female migrant work. 'As the ones responsible for much of kin work, women are likely to have more access to information and support that is exchanged between family members. The chain migration that develops among the relatives and friends of migrant workers reflects the function of the networks' (Guerrero et al. 2001). These networks are also formed or joined by women while abroad and continue to provide them with significant support and a sense of community that alleviates loneliness and a longing to be home. In fact more positive experiences have been reported by women domestic workers in countries with active and strong visibility of either a non-governmental organisation, an organisation of resident Filipinos or migrant Filipino communities, and a proactive and responsive consular office (Guerrero et al. 2001).

Moreover, women themselves acknowledge the actual contribution that their overseas stint has had on their self-confidence, their adaptability and flexibility to apply themselves to unknown situations and unfamiliar surroundings. To some, work abroad has provided the opportunity to escape from oppressive personal and cultural circumstances that might have otherwise trapped them forever in lives of subordination and subjugation. Living abroad and exposure to different cultures has immensely widened women workers' worldviews. They have learned to live independently and developed skills in interacting with people, with some even forming organisations.

But this is only one side of a double-edged advantage, also referred to as the 'comparative advantage of women's disadvantage'. As pointed out by Cox (1997), 'the vulnerabilities of women migrant workers—practically for those in domestic services—derive from their being women, their being domestic workers, the fact that they come from developing countries, the lack of interest on the part of governments, employers, and other parties to protect their interests, the nature of domestic work overseas and the role of social networks in promoting this type of migration'. Women migrant workers are more vulnerable to abuse and violence, even sexual violence. Many are exposed to health risks such as HIV-AIDS and may experience mental breakdowns. The social construction of reproductive work as private and of little value has rendered women workers invisible, isolated and unprotected by labour laws. These social consequences make evaluation of gains and benefits of female overseas domestic work more contentious.

At the macro level, concerns have been raised with regard to the erosion of nationalism, the attacks on national dignity, the rise of consumerism and materialism, and the disharmony and break-up of families. Though profiles show that single women dominate migrant work, questions persist as to what happens when wives and mothers leave. What challenges are thrown to gender stereotypes to radically affect families without any social protection and support?

Domestic Work: Challenging Stereotypes in Labour and Gender Constructs

Domestic work by challenging stereotypes in labour and gender constructs explore the status of women inside and outside the home country.

Domestic work, traditionally equated with unpaid work, housework by wives, sisters, aunts, mothers and grandmothers, is now the number two dollar earner of a country overwhelmed by one crisis after another. Thus, women domestics are held in high regard, even called new-day heroes. The year 2000 was even proclaimed by the Philippine government as the 'Year of Overseas Filipino Workers (OFWs)' and 2002 to be the 'Year of Service Providers'.

Moreover, domestic work, which was traditionally low-paid housework of unschooled women from rural areas in upper class or professional-headed households, is now work that employs college graduates, professionals, even those formerly working as secretaries and personnel of private corporations in their home country in foreign middle class to upper class households. The participation of an educated sector of the population in domestic work renders this kind of work a credible status to the majority of the less affluent middle class population.

Domestic work, traditionally regarded as limiting women's development and personal growth, now contributes to women's public exposure, their economic autonomy, an increase in knowledge in cross-cultural matters and a newfound personal drive for fulfilment and better lives. They have also gained status at home in some families, de facto becoming the family income provider and household head. These situations lead to a greater influence exercised over decisions in matters such as marriage, family finances, number of children and their education, social obligations, etc.

Domestic work, traditionally, was the sole responsibility of wives and other women relatives. Now, in the absence of wives turned overseas domestic workers, some men or husbands left behind take on the role and responsibilities of caregiving or childcare and housework as part of the sacrifices for the sake of the family and the future of their children. To many, the kinship system in Filipino culture functions to transfer domestic responsibilities to other women relatives as these are traditionally relegated to women. These relatives also function as a watchdog of their migrant relatives to ensure that husbands remain faithful, and finances wisely spent and invested. In turn, these relatives may benefit from the remittances, given the inclusion of responsible extended families in Philippine culture, and share of 'blessings' from the migrant worker upon her return home.

Domestic work, once viewed as contributions of wives and women to household harmony and long-lasting marriage, now threatens many families with disunity and insecurity. Marital separations, child delinquencies and dysfunctional families, the psycho-social stresses on the families left behind as well as the migrant worker herself, are still the unvalued and neglected costs of overseas work. Traditionally regarded as reproductive private work, domestic work that comes with marriage and commitment to serve one's loved ones must now be subject to regulation, nationally and globally, just like in most industries, to protect the rights of women workers employed who are often subject to abuse abroad.

On the other hand, overseas or foreign domestic work continues to be low-paid and lowly regarded work by the societies of receiving countries. It is still routine, relatively unskilled and unchallenging work to women of these societies that they simply would pay another to do. A dollar is 55 times more the peso, enough to drive a lot of women to work abroad even if it means creating their own vacuum in the families they leave behind.

It is thus ironic that globalised labour, in this instance domestic work, produces an unceasing modernising process where cultural and traditional social forms are disembedded while re-embedding the same in another culture and society. In a doctoral study on the consequences to male identities of migrant work conducted by Pingol (2001), a three-fold model of the structure of gender was posed to assess impact of migrant work on gender relations. This model distinguishes relations of power, production and cathexis.

Power relations refer to the dominant position of men over women, or patriarchy in the Western context. Production relations refer to a division of labour where certain tasks are male while others are female. Cathexis or emotional attachment refers to practices, which generate sexual desire and may include questions on relationships—consensual or coercive.... The spouses' positions in productive and sexual relations reflect power relations. In other words, the relation of husbands and wives in the productive and reproductive arenas necessarily connote power relations. The production arena covers the provision of material needs of the family, while the reproductive arena refers to sexual practices, childbirth and infant care, taking charge of the emotional needs of the members of the family, or the nurturing role. While power in the productive arena coincides with power in the sexual or reproductive realm when men are the providers, it is not necessarily so when women assume the provider role. Norms guiding the relations of power in the reproductive realm may prevent the translation of economic power to power in the reproductive sphere (Pingol 2001).

The migration of women, while shifting their reproductive role to productive ones as income providers, does not necessarily shift powers to them from their male spouses or male kin. Their overseas work only widens spheres of power negotiations between wives and husbands or men and women in general. Thus, it may not be at all surprising that when women return home, their roles before they left are handed over back to them essentially unchanged. Such a possibility strengthens the position that economic change can provide an opportunity for cultural change, specifically to gender relations, if other actors in society like the women's movement and a gender aware and gender fair government promote and support such change with a policy agenda, institutionalised programmes, structures and mechanisms.

Government and Non-Government Action: Restriction, Regulation and Recognition

Indeed, problems attendant to female migration surfaced even in the early years of the phenomenon. Like male migration, women migrant workers are subjected to such problems as illegal recruitment, illegal or exorbitant placement fees, contract substitution, withholding of passports and non-payment or delay in salaries. Owing to the vast economic benefits the country gains from migrant work, the government has tended to balance restriction, regulation and recognition strategies in addressing the many issues and concerns of migrant work. This 'balancing act' often comes under criticism from the many NGOs, women's organisations and politicians eager to remake themselves as saviours of the Philippines' modern day heroes. Private organisations such as recruitment agencies and trade unions alike throw in their own criticisms, especially in government regulations involving fees, accreditation and processing of migrant workers' permits and papers.

Compared to other countries, the Philippines has, in fact, instituted various measures to ensure the protection of women migrant workers. Several times the 'government had instituted several bans on the deployment of domestic workers (1982 for Saudi Arabia, which did not push through, a general ban in 1987 and the gradual lifting of the ban as better conditions obtain in the receiving countries; a ban for Singapore in 1995) and in the deployment of entertainers to Japan in 1991, in the hopes of stopping the migration of women migrant workers' (Guerrero et al. 2001).

The Migrant Workers and Overseas Filipinos Act of 1995 provided for the eventual phase-out of unskilled workers (including domestic workers) in light of the vulnerabilities of such workers' experiences. The law, though, is currently under review. The Law on Absentee Voting has also been recently passed as well as the Anti-Trafficking in Persons Act. Since migration cannot be stopped, and in the absence of other options, the government has instead attempted to empower migrant workers by providing them with information and training. There are two principal government agencies tasked with handling OFWs. These are the Philippine Overseas Employment Agency (POEA) and the Overseas Workers Welfare Administration (OWWA). Other departments like the Department of Foreign Affairs and the Department of Labour and Employment have other units and offices specifically dealing with OFW matters, such as the Office of the Undersecretary for Migrant Workers' Affairs under the former and the Office of the Undersecretary on OFW Reintegration under the latter. The government has also established an Office of Legal Assistance for Migrant Worker Affairs (OLAMWA), Migrant Workers and Overseas Filipino Resource Centres, as well as various replacement and monitoring centres. For women migrant workers (particularly household workers), for example, the mandatory pre-departure orientation seminars have been provided by NGOs since the 1990s instead of recruitment agencies. RA 8042[4] recognises NGOs as partners in protecting migrant workers. Many NGOs serve OFWs, although some destination countries do not welcome NGOs.

The Philippines has ratified the International Convention on the rights of Migrants and Members of Their Families, one of 12 countries that have ratified the convention as of 1999. It has also signed other UN conventions related to human rights, including those of migrant workers such as the UN Economic and Social Rights, Civil and Political Rights, Elimination of Racial Discrimination, CEDAW, Traffic in Persons, Rights of the Child, and Status of Refugees. Further, it has ratified ILO Resolutions 87 (Freedom of Association and the Right to Organise Convention), 118 (Equality of Treatment, Social and Security Convention) and 157 (Maintenance of Social Security Right Convention).

NGOs have different types of programmes and activities that address the research, training, organising, welfare, and information and advocacy needs of the migrant labour sector of the Philippine economy. Invariably, these organisations provide free legal assistance, provision of reproductive healthcare services, feminist counselling services and shelter, livelihood assistance and cooperatives organising, transportation assistance, policy advocacy and lobbying. There are coalitions, nationally and regionally, such as the Alliance of Migrant Workers and Advocates, that push, for example, for the passing of amendments to the 1995 Magna Carta for Migrant Workers and the RA 8042. There is as well Migrante and NOVA (Network Opposed to Violence Against Migrant Women). Most are funded by foreign donors and relatively smaller non-governmental networks based in the United States, Canada and Europe.

Though heavily relying on these funds, the NGOs working on the issues of migrants in the Philippines are a vital and vibrant group that lead in the theorising and activism on national and global migrant concerns, and have chalked up some significant successes in their struggles.

In general, while the institutional framework for many of these programmes has been set in place, there is a need to review how they are actually implemented and their impact in improving the conditions of women migrant workers. Unwavering commitment of receiving countries to promote migrant rights while they work overseas must be built to ensure comprehensive protection. In Asian countries where migrant work is temporary, restricted and highly regulated, women migrant workers cannot simply change occupations even if they are qualified for other jobs. There is very little chance of social mobility and women migrant workers become stuck in domestic work.

Policies that seek to improve the protection of women indeed need to be enhanced but through approaches that accommodate to, rather than those that restrict population flows. Emphasis should be placed on the promotion of equality of treatment and access to opportunities rather than just protection. A consideration of policy intervention in the region should be that policies to be effective must be tailored to specific needs in specific areas. It is unlikely that any region-wide blanket policies can truly address the very real needs of women in the region. Certain specific areas are identified for urgent attention, particularly those where the trafficking of women and the intensification of abuse may result owing to the current economic crisis. There is a concern as well for policies and programmes that address the reintegration needs and problems of returning migrants. Lastly, policies must lead to more international cooperation and collaboration, mindful of the rapid changes brought about by globalisation. These changes carry with it risks as well as enhance the overall environment for local and global action.

At the end, this paper agrees with the position taken by some migrant group advocates that globalisation must free borders to legitimate workers as it frees the flow of products globally. One imagines that in the future no worker can be declared illegal and women's domestic work will be recognised as a model of indispensable work that nurtures and cares for the lives of children and families.

Notes

1 There are two terms for designating migrant workers in the Philippines: balikbayan, or immigrant Filipinos primarily from North America who periodically visit their home country, and OCWs, or overseas contract workers who are employed on a contractual basis in such places as the Middle East, Europe, East and South-east Asia. See Vicente L. Rafael, 'Ugly Balikbayans and Heroic OCWs', http://www.bibingka.com/phg/Balikbayan/default.htm (accessed on 7 November 2005).

2 The House Joint Resolution No. 002 introduced in the House of Representatives of the Philippines creating a congressional commission to review and assess the debt policies, strategies and programmes of the Philippines, and conduct a public audit of all debts acquired and the payments made thereon, gave the following figures for the Philippines' total debts and debt service payments: the outstanding debt stock of the government increased from 700 billion pesos in 1997 to 2.8 trillion pesos in 2002, and to 3 trillion pesos in 2003. In 2004, the outstanding debt stock was projected to hit 3.2 trillion pesos. The government has been paying enormous amounts to service these debts, shelling out in 2002, 185.9 billion pesos in interest payments and 172.1 billion pesos in principal payments for a total debt-servicing amount of 358 billion pesos. For 2003, the government allocated 425.6 billion pesos for debt service, and for 2004 the proposed amount was 542.2 billion pesos. See http://www.freedomfromdebtcoalition.org/main/pages/lagman.pdf.

3 Figure 3.1 and Tables 3.1 and 3.2 are based on official overseas employment statistics available at www.poea.gov.ph/html/statistics.html, www.poea.gov.ph being the official website of the Philippines Overseas Employment Administration under the Department of Labour and Employment, The Republic of Philippines.

4 RA 8042 or Republic Act No. 8042 or the Migrant Workers and Overseas Filipinos Act of 1995 is an Act to institute the policies of overseas employment and establish a higher standard of protection and promotion of the welfare of migrant workers, their families and overseas Filipinos in distress.

References

Cox, David. 1997. 'The Vulnerability of Asian Women Migrant Workers to a Lack of Protection and to Violence', *Asian & Pacific Migration Journal*, 6: 59–76.

Guerrero, Sylvia, Mariya M.B. Asis, Agnes Españo, Teresita Ibarra-Taberdo, Helen Dayo, Raymundo Rovillos and Thelma Kintanar. 2001. *Women and Gender in Population and Development*. Quezon City: University Centre for Women's Studies.

Pingol, A.T. 2001. *Remaking Masculinities*. Quezon City: University Centre for Women's Studies.

Santos, Nida. 2002. *Women in the International Migration Process Report*. Pattern, Profiles and Health Consequences of Sexual Exploitation: The Philippine Report. San Juan: Coalition against Trafficking in Women.

Fast Facts on Filipino Labour Migration, 2000 & 2002. Quezon City: Kanlungan Centre Foundation, Inc.

Skeldon, Ronald. 'The Migration of Women in the Context of Globalisation in the Asian and Pacific Region', unpublished discussion paper available at http://www.unescap.org/esid/GAD/Publication/DiscussionPapers/02/series2.pdf.

Asian Migrant Yearbook. 2001. Hong Kong: Asian Migrant Centre Ltd./Migrant Forum in Asia.

Trends, News and Tidbits. 2003. Quarterly Publication of the Kanlungan Centre Foundation, Inc. 11(13), Quezon City, January to June.

4

POVERTY, GLOBALISATION AND
GENDERED LABOUR MIGRATION IN NEPAL

Jagannath Adhikari

Foreign labour migration is not a recent phenomenon in Nepal. Both men and women have been leaving the country, mostly temporarily, over the past 200 years. It is generally believed, however, that migration in the past was predominantly by men. Information and data are not readily available to prove that migrants consisted of women as well. In most permanent migrations women accompanied their husbands or family members. Various folk songs still sung in villages in Nepal recount the pains as well as benefits of these migrations. The history of migration is also associated with the recruitment of Nepali people in the British armies since 1816, and later in the Indian Army since 1949. As this type of foreign labour migration was of a special nature, there was (and still is) no participation of women. These practices led to the belief that migration, especially to foreign countries, was exclusively a male domain. Therefore, the concept of migration was generally associated with male migration.

There were many factors in the past that restricted women from migrating on their own volition. This was especially so for foreign labour migration. Patriarchal attitudes dominant in society restricted women's mobility. Moreover, foreign migration also required money and networks, which were not available to most women. A large majority of women in Nepal do not have ownership of property, making it difficult for them to move away from home.

Women's migration was, therefore, limited to nearby villages or cities. Village studies (Adhikari 1996; Seddon et al. 2001) conducted have revealed that poor women had been migrating to other villages, and nearby towns and cities where development work was being carried out. Daily commuting was most common. Poor women from lower castes were seen migrating from village to village or to urban areas in search of work. Poor women from the higher castes were generally found to commute to cities and development sites. Seasonal migration of Dalit women and others to the city, or to a place where development projects were being implemented or labour jobs were available, was also common. In the winter season, after the harvest of paddy, both men and women would become free and use this time for earning some income in cash or kind.

Since the 1990s, the tendency of women to migrate has grown. This was partly facilitated by the establishment of a democratic government, which by relaxing restrictions on obtaining a passport imposed by the previous political regime made it easier for people to go to a foreign country. The earlier regime also publicly discouraged people from migrating for employment in menial work (as mostly the uneducated migrants would do), considering this practice as bringing shame to the 'nation'. During the 1990s the impact of globalisation was also being strongly felt, and cheaper and unorganised labour—both male and female—was in demand in developed and newly industrialising countries. While the restriction on movement is now relaxed, women continue to be discriminated against, since they need the consent of their guardians (preferably husbands or fathers) to obtain a passport and to migrate.

While globalisation and the subsequent creation of job opportunities is thought, even by those who have participated in labour migration, to be a practice of employing cheaper, unorganised and illegal labour, thereby serving the interest of the capitalists, it was also considered as an opportunity to improve living conditions. This explains not only the attraction among people for these jobs, but also the investment of large sums of money by them to get such an opportunity. Women, as will be discussed later, have also shown a great ability to bypass various obstacles created by society and the state to avail such opportunities. But these barriers have also meant that the poorest of the poor have not been able to make much of these opportunities. Moreover, even those who have been able to avail such opportunities have suffered a lot.

The increased migration of Nepali women to foreign countries in the 1990s and early 2000s cannot be understood without referring to the changes that have taken place in the national economy. The agriculture base of the national economy, particularly hill agriculture, has weakened. Agricultural production and productivity have declined significantly and people are now opting for non-farm income sources rather than farm work. The availability of cheap cereal grains (because of hidden subsidies and the like), often imported from India and other countries, means that it is unwise to carry out the subsistence type of agriculture practised in the hills. Only those not able to find employment in the non-farm sector are still carrying it out, but on a diminished scale. Accordingly, a large number of poor households now need to seek alternative employment. This compulsion has forced many poorer households to move to urban areas in search of work. Various studies (Adhikari 1996; Seddon et al. 2001) also suggest that out-migration is markedly higher from the hills as compared to the plain Tarai, a relatively better agricultural area.

In urban areas too employment opportunities are scarce and fluctuating. Because of structural adjustment programmes implemented since the mid-1980s, employment opportunities have become scarcer. Some sectors like the army which employ relatively large numbers of people are not accessible to women. Other government and civil jobs are also not available for a large majority of women, as they do not qualify for them because of their low educational qualifications. A few educated women are, however, better placed, primarily because under the pressure of donor agencies the practice of gender balancing is followed in the expanding NGO sector. A large majority of poor women are in desperate need of jobs because of a general reduction in food security status of poorer migrant households in the urban areas (see Adhikari and Bohle 1999). Because of the existing dominant thinking among women that food security is their domain, many women have been compelled to seek alternative employment and income generating activities. In the face of such crises, women have taken to foreign labour migration (particularly in the jobs traditionally regarded as women's jobs, created due to globalisation) despite many hurdles created by society and the state.

Even though migration of women has increased, there is still lack of information as to the total volume of migration to different countries and their contributions to the total remittances that enter Nepal. There is also a large gap in the knowledge about how women have been able to migrate and what specific problems they face in Nepal and abroad. Various data available about foreign labour migration and remittances are not segregated on gender basis. This has created difficulty in analysing the role of women in foreign labour migration and remittances, and in the formulation of policies to improve the status and scope of foreign labour employment for women.

Women in Migration: Disadvantages and Discriminations

As women generally have less access to information and resources, they have difficulty moving independently. In addition to this, the money they require in order to move makes them dependent on a host of people within the family and outside. As of now only 10.83 per cent of households have women who own land, and altogether women own only 4.4 per cent of the agricultural land in the country. Of the women who own land, 81 per cent have less than 1 hectare land holding (NPC 2003: 443). Even though the role of land and agriculture has been declining in recent times, land is still a main source of property, especially in rural Nepal, where about 86 per cent of the country's population resides. In a few cases, it is also seen that women, who are not supported by their family members, have gained some financial support for out-migration through their own (women's) associations. But these cases are rare. Lack of information, low education levels, lack of confidence and difficulty in undertaking independent movement are other factors that make it difficult for them to undertake migration and earn money for themselves and their families.

There are a considerable number of discriminatory laws, policies and procedures in relation to women's migration (FWLD 2000), but many of them have also arisen from cultural traditions. As the cultural traditions relating to women's access to resources and property and the freedom to move independently are different in different cultures, the cultural background of women can also be a factor affecting as to who participates in foreign labour migration. Moreover, the process of reintegration is also influenced by these traditions.

The other discriminations faced by women have been the outcome of the general perception that women are weaker and need greater protection than men. Women in Nepal cannot get a passport and citizenship on their own account. They need to take their guardians, especially father or husband, with them to the concerned office. The whole state machinery runs on this mind-set. The Foreign Employment Act 1985 (amended in 1989 and 1998) and the Labour Act 1992 prohibit women from working under certain conditions. These prohibitions are said to be in the interest of women protecting them from health hazards, sexual and other forms of abuse and exploitation. The Foreign Employment Act 1985 allows recruiting agencies to send women for foreign employment only upon obtaining permission from the government and the guardians of women (see also Singh 2000).

The issue of migrant workers in general and migrant women workers in particular became very visible as well as contentious during the past few years. The alleged sexual abuse and death of a migrant woman worker (Kanu Sherpa) in the Gulf created a big hue and cry nationally. The issue became so controversial that on March 1998, with a Cabinet decision, women's migration for work in the Gulf countries was banned. The ban was lifted on January 2003, but only for the organised sector. It continued to apply on the informal sector/domestic work where the majority of women had been employed in the past. On the other hand, while male workers have also died while working abroad, it has rarely been taken as an excuse to change policy.

Migrant women were also found to face various forms of discrimination in the destination countries. Since a significant proportion of migrant women work in countries (like Gulf countries) where gender equity and women's treatment are far from satisfactory, migrant women are also found to face discrimination and problems there. In other countries too Nepali women are employed mainly as domestic helps and are responsible for care of children and the elderly, kitchen work and housekeeping. Only a few are employed in factories, where women's patience is required in doing repetitive work. There is a high demand in Nepal for 'nurses' to work in the Gulf countries. In 2002, there was a demand for about 50,000 nurses, despite the fact that Nepal is not a country known to have such skilled labour. This actually led to a great rush to nursing schools in Nepal. Similarly, training institutes to help potential migrant women learn domestic work skills relevant in the destination countries have increased in recent times. The whole process of globalisation has thus led to the creation of new set of relationships between men and women. Therefore, even foreign labour employment opportunities have reinforced the division of work based on gender. Since poor women are not in a position to take such training courses, efforts have been made by the government as well as donor agencies to help them receive such training and make them capable of taking up jobs in foreign countries. This has also been one of the aims of the Tenth Plan (2002–07), though it has not yet materialised fully.

Magnitude of Migration and Changing Government Attitude

As has been pointed out earlier, it is difficult to get data on women's migration. Given the fact that migration of women to foreign countries has visibly increased, there has been pressure from women's groups and donor agencies upon the government to collect gender-segregated data on migration. The efforts of the government in this regard have been quite inadequate. For example, the governmental records show that only 161 women went abroad for work from 1985 to 2001. But informal sources reveal that there are at least 12,000 Nepali women working as domestic servants in foreign countries, excluding India (SAMANATA 2003). Various estimates reveal that they earn about 10 billion Nepalese rupees a year, which constitutes about 12 per cent of the total remittances entering Nepal. The 2001 Census records 762,118 as the absentee population, of which 10.8 per cent were women. About 83 per cent of the women absentee population was in India, and only 17 per cent of them went to other countries. This means that about 14,000 women have gone to countries other than India (CBS 2000). Furthermore it is estimated that 5,000 to 7,000 girls are trafficked from Nepal to India and other neighbouring countries every year, and that about 200,000 Nepali girls and women are currently working in the sex industry in India (ILO 2001).

A recent study has revealed that altogether about 35,000 Nepali women have been working abroad (excluding India) in 2002 (NIDS 2003), of which 67 per cent worked in Asia, mainly in South East and East Asia (57 per cent). In that year they sent about 10.8 billion rupees to Nepal as remittances. It is extremely difficult to estimate the number of Nepali women working in India, but the Census report of 2001 indicates that about 170,000 may be working there (CBS 2002). It is possible that these women remit about two billion rupees annually.

Poverty and Migration: Government's Perspective

Poverty reduction and improvement of livelihood of marginal families is the greatest need of the country. The thrust of the whole Tenth Five

Year Plan (2002–07) is in this direction. The Plan also recognises the importance of female labour migration in poverty reduction. This implicitly assumes that it is poverty that forces women to migrate. According to the Plan, about 10.85 per cent of the total foreign labour migrants are women. While in the Plan document the reproductive role of women has been pointed out as a major hurdle for women in taking the decision to migrate, the suggested strategies of the Tenth Plan with regard to foreign labour migration of women emphasise only skill upgrading, monitoring of migrant women and safe remitting processes. The following objectives of the Plan are indicative of this:

- To improve the skill and work capacity of women so that women's employment in foreign countries increases.
- To monitor those women who have been to foreign countries for work.
- To make bilateral agreements with female labour employing countries regarding minimum pay and security arrangements.
- To arrange for safe money remitting process.
- To constantly monitor and evaluate foreign employment companies.

Even though government assumes that by promoting migration of women poverty reduction can be partly realised, it is now proven that the poorest of the poor women are unable to migrate for employment. This fact is also established from various research studies, and is true for both men and women migrants (Seddon et al. 2001; NIDS 2003). Poor women were also found to migrate, but they resort to different forms of migration. As explained earlier, seasonal or very short-term migration, often to a town or city, is a common form of migration for poor women. Some of them are lured by agents to work in carpet and garment factories in the urban areas, or to work as household maids, cleaners or waitresses in restaurants. Later these women are moved by agents to brothels within Nepal or are trafficked to brothels in India.

Due to lack of skills, education and networks, poor Nepali women were not found to be migrating through formal channels, but were lured by unscrupulous agents who pushed them into sex industry or made them work in extremely difficult jobs in foreign countries. For a period of time (from 1998 to 2003), the Government of Nepal did not permit Nepali women to go to the Gulf countries. The recruitment agents took them to India and Bangladesh for migration to the Gulf illegally. Now the government allows women to go for work in the Gulf, but only those who are skilled and to work only in the organised sector and not as domestic help. Often the poor women who are lured to jobs in the Gulf countries are first taken to India or Bangladesh and then are forced to work in brothels. As the little money they could generate from various means is wasted, they do whatever work is available to them. It is difficult to get information about this process and contact women facing such problems. But media reports reveal that this is indeed taking place (Ghimire 2003; Giri 2003; Shrestha 2003; *Post Reporter* 2003). There is also a tendency on the part of the government to use these reports as a pretext to impose restrictions on women's mobility.

Gender and Methodological Problems

A study[1] carried out in 2003 to map the foreign labour migration of Nepali women was to identify the migration patterns of different types of women, motivating factors, decision-making with regard to migration, the process of migration, problems and discrimination faced at each stage of migration (at home, society, government offices, recruitment agents, immigration offices, at the workplace, and while reintegrating into society). The experiences of women while abroad and while reintegrating into society and family and the changes in relationships within households with husbands and other members of society were also studied.

While conducting the study, the survey team found it extremely difficult to interview returnee migrant women workers. It was not so much because the research team consisted of men (all enumerators were women) as because the women did not want to be known in society as migrant women. This was especially so with women who returned from the Gulf countries. Migrant women having stayed alone in India would not venture to go back to their original villages, and this stigma is also attached to women working in the Gulf countries. This made it hard for us to interview women from the lower economic brackets who often end up in Gulf countries. Even though we had planned to interview at least a 100 migrant women, we ended up with only 86 interviews. Some of the respondents answered questions and participated in the focus group discussions because of their personal acquaintance with the study team. Other women who were not hesitant to talk with the study team and participate in the focus group discussions were those who worked in better paying countries like Japan, Taiwan, South Korea and Hong Kong. These women rather are respected in society, mainly because they are relatively better off economically. The social stigma attached to women who have worked in the Gulf countries is revealed in the following letter to a national weekly written by a woman migrant who found the situation extremely distressing:

> Women working in Gulf countries are looked down upon by the society, but those women working in Japan, Singapore, Korea, Hong Kong, UK and USA are very much respected even though it is the fact they also have to stay away from the family for a long time. So it is the society that recognises money as an important factor for social status. Moreover, high status women who spend time in developed countries for work, study or training are also respected in the society. Because of the societal practice to look down upon women working in the Gulf, their psychological and moral willpower is eroding. If they are also given some social respect (like to those who have been working in developed countries), it would boost their morale and they will be able to contribute to family and society. (Letter from *Drishti Vernacular Weekly*, 3 June 2003, written by Saru Rai, a returnee migrant woman worker from Saudi Arabia. Author's translation).

It should also be emphasised that women working in the Gulf countries belong mainly to the lower economic and social strata of society. As the initial investment required for going to the Gulf countries is less (about Rs 50,000–70,000) than that for going to other advanced countries (about Rs 300,000–900,000), the lower middle class women have also been going to the Gulf countries. This is also established from our study. As is seen later, one of the main reasons for their migration was to solve immediate financial problems in the family like paying debts, sickness of family members or due to some personal problems like difficulty in coping with the husband and his family members. But again these women face another kind of stigma after their migration.

Another problem faced during research was about gaining information about the relationships with family members after migration to foreign countries. In various focus group discussions, though men left the discussion and went out of the room to facilitate discussion on changes in relationships between husbands and wives, or within the family, after the latter migrated for work, not much information could be gained. The probable reason could be that migrant women think differently from the women who are educated and live in the city. Communication between them was also not straightforward.

Society, Ethnicity and Class

The biographical information of the women migrants surveyed reveals that social milieu, ethnicity and class are important in peculiar ways. It should be noted that out-migration is quite high from the hill areas, and with certain ethnic groups because of historical reasons and also due to the marginal nature of their economy.

- Hill ethnic groups from which proportionately more women migrants have come are known to have less restriction on women. In such families women's position within the household and society is generally higher, and they do not have strict concepts of purity or impurity in daily lives. Freedom of mobility is also significantly higher in these groups and taboos associated with mobility are also lower.
- Women undertaking migration also have a prior exposure to the phenomenon of migration because their fathers, brothers and neighbours have/had been to a foreign country.

Out-migration of Dalit women is another aspect that links poverty and migration. In the survey, it was seen that about 14 per cent of the out-migrants are Dalit women, who mainly go to the Gulf countries where incomes are less and possible problems are many. Among the Dalits also, only those who are slightly well off have been able to do so because migration to foreign countries (except India) requires some investment. Exploitation within the family and society, poverty, and relative freedom from concepts of purity/impurity push Dalit women into foreign migration. Within the country, it is seen that Dalit women are free to move to urban areas for employment on a seasonal basis, something which they have been doing.

Respondents were also asked to state their socioeconomic position. While a large proportion (47.7 per cent) stated that they were from the 'lower middle class', 34.8 per cent of the respondents stated that they were from the 'low class'. Only 17.4 per cent regarded themselves as from the 'upper middle class', while none reported that they came from a wealthier (upper class) group. The survey data also showed that about 78 per cent of the women participating in foreign labour migration had low education levels, i.e., they had not completed high school. Recently, the United Arab Emirates (UAE) developed a policy to seek workers with at least an SLC (School Leaving Certificate, i.e., high school) qualification. Given that only about 10–15 per cent girl students pass the SLC examination in Nepal, conditions like those imposed by the UAE government might further limit the opportunities for poor women to out-migrate for jobs.

Process of Migration: Motivations and Decisions

The following analysis reveals the centrality of family and friends in making decisions to migrate. Generally unmarried women were found to be discouraged from migration by their families. About 63 per cent of the foreign migrant women were married before going to work in foreign countries, and only about one-third of them were unmarried. Those who migrated before marriage were not allowed to go back after getting married and having children. Usually husbands do not let their wives to go because of the dominant attitude that it is the man's responsibility to go out. There was only a single widow among the 86 interviewees. Similarly, 4.6 per cent of women were separated from their husbands before migrating abroad.

For most migrants, their migration was the outcome of a joint decision within the family. Only a few said that individual circumstances (like discrimination within the household, souring of relationships with husbands, separation, and the like) forced them to migrate. As much as 52 per cent said that they had obtained information about migration from their family members and friends. Other important sources of information on migration were neighbours (20 per cent) and relatives (16.5 per cent). Only about 10 per cent of the respondents said they had obtained information from recruiting agents.

The main reason for migration, as reported by the respondents, was to alleviate family problems related to lack of income, poverty and sickness. For a majority of women migrants, lack of income opportunities in Nepal and sicknesses within the family were major reasons for migration. This is illustrated by five different case studies.

CASE 1

Rima Thapa, 36, of Shree Tole Dharan, had an unemployed husband who was a heavy drinker. Her husband did not earn anything for the family and spent the little they had on drinking. Due to this she was left with no option but to venture to a foreign country to improve her family's financial status. She was greatly encouraged when her neighbour and close friend agreed to come along with her.

CASE 2

Meena Dhital, 26, a mother of three children and a resident of Dharan, was having a hard time trying to make ends meet. Her daughter contracted tuberculosis and Meena took loans for her daughter's treatment. Besides, due to poor health her husband was unable to earn for the family. With no one to earn at home, she was in deep trouble and was very worried about repaying back the loans. Looking at the condition at home, she decided to leave for foreign employment. Fearing that her husband and family might stop her from taking employment abroad, she disclosed her decision only at the last hour. Meena worked in Saudi Arabia for three years as a domestic help.

CASE 3

Pabitra Rai, 24, a resident of Shree Tole Dharan, returned from Saudi Arabia after working there for four years. Pabitra had an inter-caste marriage and was not accepted by her in-laws. Therefore the couple were deprived of family property, and as both she and her husband were unemployed they were in deep financial need. When she learnt about foreign employment, she saw this as the only way out of their financial problem. Seeing her determination to go abroad to work, her husband did not object to it. Finally, she borrowed money from her relatives and went to Saudi Arabia for employment.

CASE 4

Devi Bika, 32, of Bajpatan, Pokhara, was unemployed, and so was her husband. Having no permanent source of income it was becoming difficult for them to shoulder the responsibility of their household. Besides leading a hand-to-mouth existence, the most worrying part for them was paying back loans. Actually, Devi wanted her husband to go abroad for work, but as he was unwilling to go she decided to go instead. She borrowed money for her journey, took help from an agent and went to Saudi Arabia.

CASE 5

(Focus group discussions in Pokhara). The main reason to go out is to earn money. In Nepal we had to be unemployed. We wanted to improve our economic conditions. It was difficult to improve economic conditions from jobs in Nepal. We wanted to be independent and self-standing in economic matters. Even a staff nurse had been to Korea. She used to get only Rs 3,000 salary in Nepal, but when she went to Korea her salary increased to Rs 40,000. Moreover, we wanted to know the foreign culture and experience their life. In Korea, we opened up the Nepal Contact Society. The aim was to help the migrant Nepalis.

As far as destinations were concerned, it seems that most of the respondents had gone to Kuwait, followed by Hong Kong and Saudi Arabia. A direct relationship between education and the destination country was also discernible. Illiterate and marginally literate migrants had gone to Saudi Arabia and Kuwait. These women were also generally the poorer ones as compared to others. Those relatively better off and better educated went to other advanced countries like Japan, the UK and the USA. The destination country is an indicator of the income also. Accordingly, it seems that wealthier and educated women are able to go for work in better paying countries, whereas those with low education and less money end up in badly paying countries. In the latter countries human rights records are also extremely poor.

Difficulties and Discrimination at the Workplace

A large majority (66 per cent) of migrant workers had undertaken 'domestic work' after their migration to foreign countries. Even though Nepali law does not permit women to work as 'domestic help', it is the main employment undertaken by Nepali women. Other important jobs that were undertaken were 'work in factory', 'restaurant work' and 'office work'. Educational status of women migrants is found to directly correlate with the type of work done in the destination countries. About three-quarters of respondents reported that they had no prior experience of the work that they did in overseas countries. The problems faced by migrants included: language difficulties, difficulties in handling electronic goods, lack of proper work skills, cultural shock, taxing work and strict employers, and lack of food, holidays and resting time. Generally, poor women with no education were not able to communicate effectively or handle electronic goods, which they had hardly seen at home. These women faced particularly severe problems. Harassment was also reported by a large majority of respondents. But most women bore these hardships, and their circumstances at home including economic problems compelled them to stay on. The problem of paying back loans also kept them there even when they found the place unsuitable. These are the problems generally reported by the poor women who migrated to work as domestic help. One of the reasons for their vulnerability was that they were not aware of various rights available to them (see also Malla 2003; GFONT/ILO 2000). Their illegal position in some cases also hindered them from exercising these rights.

Most migrant women say that they receive no support from government agencies in solving the problems they face at work. The only support they have is from a few friends working in the same locality. The Nepali Embassy too has not taken any initiative to help migrant women. Apart from the fact that the staff do not have enough resources to deal with and solve the problems of migrant workers, the attitude of the Nepal Embassy staff was also found to be unsupportive. They would try to avoid coming in contact with the migrant persons. Migrant women also reported that the attitude of the staff was not favourable towards them. It is a common fact that the Nepal Embassy staff anywhere are generally from the elite background, and who would cater only to the needs of the elite and powerful. The Nepali diplomatic corps, therefore, were not supportive of women's migration, because the common problems faced by poor women migrants failed to arouse their sympathy. This is perhaps also the reason for imposing a ban on women's migration from time to time.

Income and Empowerment of Women from Migration

The survey revealed that, on an average, a migrant woman working in a foreign country (other than India) would earn a monthly income of Rs 43,500, of which they could save about Rs 26,400 (see Table 4.1). This indicates that women could save about 61 per cent of their income. In general, the saving rate of women migrants was higher than that of men. It is also seen that all the money saved by women is not sent home, and part of the income is used to buy goods and valuable items when they return. On an average, it is seen that only about 47 per cent of the total income is sent home in cash. How much money is brought in terms of

Table 4.1 Average Monthly Income, Savings and Duration of Stay of Women Migrants from Different Socioeconomic Status in Foreign Jobs, and their Departure Expenses and Income in Nepal (2003)

Income/savings	Upper middle class (n = 15)	Lower middle class (n = 41)	Lower class (n = 30)	All (n = 86)
Monthly income (Rs)	132,440	31,463	14,916	43,303
Monthly savings (Rs)	80,185	19,137	9,408	26,391
Duration of stay (years)	4.47	3.71	3.17	3.65
Total savings (Rs)	4,301,123	851,979	357,880	1,155,926
Departure expenses	243,333	71,631	389,000	97,914
Income in Nepal/month	4,856	2,092	4,241	3,324
Income in Nepal/year	58,266	25,109	50,900	39,889

Source: A study 'mapping foreign migrant women workers from Nepal' conducted for UNIFEM, Nepal in 2003 (Field survey July–December 2002)

goods and valuables was difficult to estimate (Table 4.1). Table 4.1 also shows that a woman belonging to the 'upper middle' class earned Rs 1.32 lakh per month, as compared to Rs 31,500 for the 'lower middle' class. Respondents belonging to the 'lower economic class' reported that their average monthly income was about Rs 15,000.

A woman from the 'upper middle' class would save Rs 4.3 million as compared to Rs 0.85 million for a 'middle class' woman and Rs 0.36 million for a 'lower class' woman. The higher savings of a woman from a higher economic class can be attributed not only to her higher income (due to a combination of education and social networks), but also to the longer duration of her stay in foreign countries. In fact the duration of stay seems directly and positively related to the economic position of women (Table 4.1).

As is evident from Table 4.1, the change in income of women before and after migration is quite significant, especially for women belonging to the higher economic group. The Table shows that the income of an upper middle class migrant woman increased 27 times, that of a lower middle class woman 15 times, and that of a lower class woman 3.5 times during the period of migration. This shows that even though the income of all women increases from foreign labour employment for all migrants cutting across class lines, the disparity in incomes also increases substantially.

As compared to their average monthly income in foreign countries (Rs 43,500), income for the women from job in Nepal was just a small fraction (7.6 per cent), as evident from the Table. On an average, a woman would earn 13 times more if she were successful in getting a job in a foreign country. The survey also reveals that income in Nepal of a migrant woman from the higher class was higher (Rs 4,855 per month) in comparison to the income of a migrant woman from the lower class (Rs 4,242 per month). The income in Nepal of a migrant woman from the lower middle class was only (Rs 2,092), which is less than that of the lower class. The most probable reason for this income pattern in Nepal is that usually women from upper and middle classes go for income-earning activities only if they are white-collar jobs. But a lower class woman would perform whatever job she got to survive. But in foreign countries the income drastically differs.

The money saved by women migrants was found to have been later spent on a variety of items. A large proportion of respondents expressed that they spent money on buying daily necessities of the household. Another important response was that they spent money on sending their children to good schools. Constructing a house, paying back loans and lending out money were some other uses to which they put their money. It is generally seen that women were able to acquire property in their names from these savings. This also contributed to the enhancement of their status within the family. In some cases the money/property also helped them improve their marriage prospects. Exposure to the outside world was also found to have made them more confident, particularly in managing their families independently. Some women returned home to become successful entrepreneurs and were also involved in social work.

Reintegration into Society

Upon their return women migrants faced a variety of problems in settling back with their families, and the claims made on the money that they brought with them. Perhaps the greatest problem faced by many women migrants on their return was that people tried to rob them of their hard-earned money. About 51 per cent of the women reported this as a major problem faced immediately after returning to Nepal. With the expectation that they had money, people came to them to borrow, without intending to return it. They also carried out other pretences for extracting money from the women.

Family-related problems were also found to be severe. About 14 per cent of them found their husbands living with other women, while

6 per cent of them found their husbands suffering from problems related to loneliness and an increased workload at home. About 5 per cent of the women also faced problems with their children who felt distanced from their mother. About 25 per cent of the respondents reported that they faced other family problems.

Another serious problem faced by women is related to Nepali culture, which does not permit mobility to women. Absence from home for a long time makes women vulnerable to charges of being of a 'loose character'. Migrant women, especially those who had been to the Gulf countries, were more likely to be labelled as such. These women, therefore, had a tendency of not returning to the place of their origin, but staying permanently in another town or city. But as discussed above, there was a difference in the treatment of women according to where they had gone to work. Those women who had stayed in high-paying advanced countries were respected by society.

In the absence of government support, migrant women reported facing problems putting their money to use productively. Many successful returnees said that they do not get support from banks and government agencies to get a loan to complement the money that they bring home, and thus the money could not be used appropriately.

Conclusion

Changes in national economic conditions like decline in agricultural production and food security and existence of various traditional barriers against women obtaining domestic non-farm work have been the main reasons for increased out-migration of Nepali women to foreign countries. On the other hand, globalisation and changes in the economic structure of the destination countries, especially in the 1990s, created a certain niche for the women of Nepal to go out in search of work. In general, the process of globalisation has resulted in increasing the influence of global capitalists with the weakening of labour power through employment of cheap and unorganised labour. In the case of migrant women, their illegal position further weakens their power to bargain. In spite of that these jobs are attractive to Nepali women, as out-migration into these jobs is the only way for them to escape their impoverished economic conditions.

The increase in job opportunities for women in foreign countries, however, has not helped poor women derive much benefit in comparison to educated women from higher classes. The various barriers created by existing gender-based regulations with regard to mobility of women are also found to affect poor women adversely. Even the successful poor women migrants do not benefit much. Their income in destination countries increases by only 3.5 times their earnings in their home country. Moreover, the expenses are high in the destination countries. Despite this, for poor women, migration is clearly a survival strategy by which they are able to solve their day-to-day problems of food security, medical treatment of sick family members and sending their children to schools. But educated women have managed to earn good incomes. Economic disparity seems to have thus augmented with foreign labour migration.

The economic prospects that migration provided led to an enhancement in the position of women in their families because the earnings of these women helped families to get over their economic crises and sometimes even helped to raise their standard of living. Yet, this improvement is not uniformly experienced and is conditioned by women's earnings. In general, women working in countries like India and in the Gulf countries, where incomes are low, are not accorded the same respect and social prestige as women who have worked in advanced and developed countries.

With regard to who participates in foreign labour migration, it is largely determined by location, family and the community's history of migration, caste/ethnicity and economic position. Women from hill ethnic groups (like the Gurung, Magar, Rai and Limbu) have proportionately large participation in foreign labour migration. The probable reason could be that their culture does not restrict mobility and no stigma is attached to these women. Moreover, as the hill economy is characterised by a decline in agriculture and a lack of other employment opportunities, proportionately more women migrants come from this area.

Foreign migration was also found to have some consequences on gender relations in society. Men were found to have been involved in looking after the children and the domestic work in the absence of women. The enhancement in the ownership of property of women from remittances they earned also resulted in women having a greater say in family decision-making. But the joint family system still acts as a barrier for greater changes in gender relationships. While foreign labour migration of women has opened up the possibility of changes in gender relations within the family, it has not brought about any major transformation. Moreover, due to their employment in the destination country in what is considered women's work, the traditional divisions of work between men and women has persisted. Discrimination and harassment were also common among women domestic workers (the main type of employment), but they coped with it, considering the fact that the situation at home was not any better and problems were more pressing. Even a few reported cases of separation on their return have not deterred women from going abroad for employment. Increase in incomes seems to have given women a considerable degree of independence and security.

With the growing migration of women, the state considered it a new opportunity to earn revenues and solve the problem of poverty. This can be discerned from the changes that have been made in state policy since the 1990s with regard to migration of women. Accordingly, the state has started looking at migration on a gender basis, announcing policies and programmes for enhancing the migration of women to foreign countries. But the main emphasis in these policies is to facilitate the migration of women by removing certain restrictions. Yet there is a lack of commensurate effort on the part of the state in assisting migrating women, especially the poor and uneducated, to acquire the necessary skills and knowledge about legal and other matters in the destination countries which would help them to get over difficult situations in a foreign land.

Note

1 The study 'Mapping foreign migrant women workers from Nepal', on which this paper is based, was sponsored by UNIFEM Nepal. The study was conducted in three major cities of Nepal—Pokhara, Kathmandu and Dharan—and was based primarily on participatory research methods, mainly on focus group discussions with migrant women and other stakeholders. Individual interviews were also conducted with 86 returnee women migrant workers.

References

Adhikari, Jagannath and Hans-Gorge Bohle. 1999. 'Urbanisation, government policies and growing food insecurity in Kathmandu metropolis', *Studies in Nepali History and Society*, 4(1): 191–246.

Adhikari, Jagannath. 1996. *The Beginnings of Agrarian Change: A Case Study in Central Nepal*. Kathmandu: TM Publications.

Central Bureau of Statistics (CBS). 2000. *Statistical Yearbook*. Kathmandu: CBS, and His Majesty's Government of Nepal (HMG/N).

———. 2002. *Census Report 2001*. Kathmandu: CBS and HMG/N.

Forum for Women, Law and Development (FWLD). 2000. *Discriminatory Laws in Nepal and Their Impact on Women: A Review of the Current Situation and Proposals for Change*. Kathmandu: FWLD.

General Federation of Nepalese Trade Unions (GFONT)/ILO. 2000. *Rights of female labourers*. Kathmandu: GFONT.

Ghimire, Bhim. 2003. 'Housewives and women labourers fall in the trap of *dalals*' (in Nepali), *Kantipur* 25 August, p. 4.

Giri, Girish. 2003. 'Nepali Women are Also Sold in Gulf' (in Nepali), *Kantipur*, 25 August, p. 1.

International Labour Organisation (ILO). 2001. *Women Trafficking in Nepal*. Kathmandu: ILO.

Malla, S. Pradahan. 2003. 'Role of Civil Society in Protecting the Rights of Foreign Migrant Workers'. Paper presented at a workshop on 'Role of the Civil Society for Empowering Migrant Women Workers of Nepal', Kathmandu, 9 May.

NIDS. 2003. 'Mapping Women's Migration to Foreign Countries'. Unpublished report submitted to UNIFEM, Nepal.

National Planning Commission (NPC). 2003. The Tenth Five Year Plan 2002–2007. Kathmandu: NPC and HMG/Nepal.

Post Reporter. 2003. 'Lured With Bait of Gulf Jobs, Young Girls Wind Up in Indian Brothels', *The Kathmandu Post*, 25 August, p. 1.

SAMANATA. 2003. *Policies, Service Mechanisms and Issues of Nepali Migrant Women Workers*. Kathmandu: Nepal.

Seddon, David, Jagannath Adhikari and Ganesh Gurung. 2001. *The new Lahures. Foreign employment and remittances economy of Nepal*. Kathmandu: NIDS.

Shrestha, Rekha. 2003. 'How unskilled tag helps artful traffickers beat law', *The Himalayan Times*, 25 August, p. 1.

Singh, M.S. 2000. 'Study report on different aspects of the phenomenon of women migrant workers and its impact on Nepalese economy'. Report submitted to UNIFEM Regional Office, New Delhi.

5

MIGRATION, GENDER, POVERTY: FAMILY AS THE MISSING LINK?

Arjan de Haan[1]

Much has been written on the links between migration and poverty—though opinions continue to differ—and increasingly a gender perspective has informed studies on migration. The *family dynamics* of migration seem to have received less attention. This is surprising as the household or family seems to be key to decision-making processes around migration, and family dynamics are key to the way different individuals benefit or suffer from engagement in labour markets and employment.[2]

This paper is rather introspective, and does not present new empirical research on migration. It reflects on earlier research and secondary material, scanning the literature on how well this does in terms of helping to understand social relations, particularly those relating to family dynamics, that structure labour migration, its outcomes and policy approaches. A key question in this respect is whether theoretical approaches allow, particularly gender analysis, for understanding diversity, as within the Asian context the differences in terms of gendered patterns of migration are as striking as the similarities.

This paper explores whether there is a missing link in the literature on migration, with a focus on South Asia and on labour migration. This starts from the premise that looking at the family is an important (though by no means the only) gender perspective, that rather than looking at women it is important to focus on the social relations in which structures of access and deprivation are embedded. This is done partly from a historical perspective, based on earlier research on long-term trends in Indian industry that suggest how women's access to employment and migration have changed during the 20th (and some argue 19th) century (de Haan 1994b). Building on this historical perspective, it will also shed light on the reasons for very diverse gendered patterns of migration across Asia, and even across India.

In doing so, the paper will not be much concerned with the numbers of migrants and gendered patterns among these[3]—though this is clearly a key issue which was dealt with in other papers at the conference. The paper is written on the assumption that, internationally, the majority of migrants are men, but that women are by no means absent. Trends in this composition are diverse, with, for example, recent globalised production processes relying heavily on female labour (for example in South East Asia), but on the other hand post-colonial history in India (as will be described) showed declining participation of women, at least in some industries like jute manufacturing. Furthermore, and this will also be discussed, segmentation of migration streams—and its positive and negative impacts—often has a gendered nature, calling for insights into the processes that provide access to or exclude from specific opportunities.

The next section of the paper sets the scene with reference to my research in Kolkata, West Bengal, focusing on family dynamics and processes showing how migration and its outcomes are gendered. The subsequent section reviews the South Asian literature, summarises knowledge regarding the migration-poverty links and identifies the gaps in knowledge and data (as in the Indian National Sample Survey). Section 3 revolves around approaches to incorporate better understanding of the social processes and relations—which are necessarily context-specific—that structure migration and gender-specific outcomes, and policy implications. Sections 4 and 5 extend this emphasis on social processes, with ideas regarding linkages between family forms and dynamics and structuration of migration, drawing on research from outside the continent in Section 4 and focusing on India/South Asia in Section 5. Section 6 concludes the paper.

A Gendered Migration Perspective: Setting the Scene

This section of the paper focuses on family dynamics and processes showing how migration and its outcomes are gendered, in the context of labour migration in Eastern India.[4] During my Ph.D. research among labour migrants in Kolkata, I was struck by the differences in patterns of migration across social, regional and income groups.[5] Key differences appeared to exist between a pattern of predominantly male migration leaving the family at home, migration with the entire family, and migration by single women.

The majority of the men I interviewed in an industrial neighbour-hood in Kolkata said that their wives did not work outside the house-hold, and many stated that this had been so in the past as well. For many of the men it was clear *why* women should not work in factories (or more generally outside the household), although the reasons given were formulated differently. They did not give permission to do so. A concept of honour was of central importance in this urban context with mostly unskilled work,[6] even though often such gender ideolo-gies were not practised, or could not be practised, and particularly women from poorer families did work outside the household.

But women were, of course, not absent from the workforce,[7] and female workers came from all communities. However, rather different ideologies regarding female employment existed. For example, it was often claimed—on both official contemporary reports, and in oral histories[8]—that no Bengali woman would work in the factories unless she was truly unfortunate. People from north India, from Bihar, Uttar Pradesh and northern Orissa, generally said that women should not work. Muslims were most outspoken about not 'permitting' women to work outside the house (although this also can vary across West Bengal, as will be discussed). In contrast, women from south India, from south Orissa and Andhra Pradesh, generally migrated and worked outside the home, and objections against this were much fewer. I concluded from my research that there was indeed a north-south divide in patterns and perceptions of female labour, and that the divide that could not be explained by different economic backgrounds or recruitment policies of management.

Practices and ideologies of female migration and employment have changed over time. In the 1990s there were almost no women left working in the jute industry. The decline in female labour was caused by a combination of factors: female-specific legislative measures which made women less attractive to employers, the disappearance of a labour shortage that made women dispensable, and a change in perceptions about female labour. I also found some, though by no means complete, convergence across different communities regarding perceptions of female labour (as there was regarding dowry for example), that women should not work outside the household unless driven by extreme need.

A second key finding of my research, and many other studies too, relates to the pattern of circular migration. Particularly when men migrated by themselves 'leaving women behind', but also in cases of migration of entire families, links with villages of origin remained very strong, and continued over generations.[9] Family strategies, thus, continue to straddle rural and urban areas (or different rural areas, or countries, or 'tradition' and 'modernity')[10], in an economic as well as social-cultural sense. In a recent article Mukherjee (2001) describes comparable dynamics for female migrants in Delhi; earlier political-economy analysis has emphasised the function of such circular migration for capitalist development (e.g., Mukherji 1985), and a recent book by Markovits et al. (2003) focuses entirely on 'circulation' during the colonial period in South Asia. These and many other studies provide enough evidence that movement of people is the rule rather than an exception, and that such movements in many cases are not one-way. In most cases, such movements are structured around gender, as well as other factors.

Thus while I would accept that the explanations for differences and trends in migration patterns need further scrutiny, my own research clearly confirmed that migration movements are strongly gendered, and that the nature of this varies across social and economic groups (variously defined), and is subject to change over time. To understand these differences, we need to understand the macro-economic factors that impinge on gender-division of labour (such as increasing or decreasing demand for female labour), commonalities and differences in terms of groups' definitions of proper divisions of labour, and ways in which these are embedded and negotiated within households or family relations. The next section explores how these gendered patterns of migration relate to links between migration and poverty, while sections 3 and 4 come back to these differences across groups, and emphasise the social relations and processes of contestation in which they are embedded.

Migration, Poverty, and Gaps in Knowledge

This section reviews some of the literature, particularly from South Asia, that has looked at the relationship between migration and poverty,[11] identifies gaps in knowledge and data, and argues the importance of strengthening gender analysis in this context.

Much of the debate has been driven by a controversy—with much deeper origins than just differences regarding who migrates and why[12]—between individualistic-economistic and structuralist approaches. The Todaro model emphasises how prospective migrants make individual decisions weighing differences between earnings in the village and expected earnings from urban employment.[13] On the other hand, structuralist or political-economy approaches emphasise the structural nature of migration, not just in the context of permanent rural-urban migration, but also with respect to the temporary migration of workers between rural areas. This challenges the individualistic emphasis in the analyses of Todaro and others, and sees labour migration as inevitable in the transition to capitalism, rather than as a choice for poor people. Stark (1991) has extended the Todaro model, in which the household rather than the individual is the unit of analyses; this is often referred to as the 'new economics of migration', though it does not move away from the emphasis on individual units as agents of decision-making to include analysis of social and other structures in which decisions and actions are embedded.

Predictably, findings regarding links between migration and poverty differ.[14] Simplified, some authors emphasise the deprivation of migration, whereas a second category emphasises migration by the better off, whereas a third strand focuses on the diversity of migrants. According to a survey in India in the 1980s, the landless (and poor) in Bihar were *more* prone to out-migrate, though the differences were small.[15] Breman's (1985) research in western India showed that Harijans are over-represented among circular migrants, while in a book review in the *Economic and Political Weekly* he emphasises how poorer migrants without connections tend to end up in the worst slums of Calcutta (Breman 2003). Most recently, Chaganti (2004) emphasises a link between the creation of cheap labour economies in the Third World and in the First World, including a pattern of feminisation of migration.

A second strand of analysis disputes the strong (statistical) link between deprivation and migration. As emphasised by Lipton and others, it is often not the poorest who migrate.[16] Recent research in Madhya Pradesh and Andhra Pradesh also concludes that the poorest rarely migrate, possibly because of availability of labour in the household and the minimal resources required for undertaking the move (Deshingkar and Start 2003). Yadava et al. (1996/97) conclude on the basis of primary and secondary data that migrant households in India are socio-economically and educationally better placed than others, and that there is a positive relationship between landholding and migration. My own simple analysis of 1983–84 NSS data for Indian urban migrants suggested that migrants have a higher average per capita consumption than non-migrants (de Haan 1997); this pattern was confirmed by more detailed analysis of NSS data with Amaresh Dubey (de Haan and Dubey 2002).

Third, many studies also emphasise the diversity of migration patterns. Studies exist—including my own—that show migrants come from all sections of the population. For example, indentured migrants from northern India appear to have come from an average, broad-middle sample of India's rural population, and during the 20th century as well there are indications that, for example, from Bihar all socioeconomic groups have had large numbers of out-migrants (de Haan 1994a, 2002; Skiba 2003). While generally international migration opportunities—particularly of the modern variety, and not of course in the colonial indentured system—cannot be accessed by poorer migrants, research on migration from the Punjab emphasised that even the lower-castes and worse-off migrated as well, sponsored by the better-off and early migrants (Pettigrew 1977). The study by Oberai et al. quoted above emphasised that links between migration and poverty varied across states: in Kerala for example higher migration by the middle peasantry was found (Oberai et al. 1989). Mosse et al. (2002) describe highly differentiated patterns of migration even among very poor tribal migrants (in western India): the poorest migrants have no choice but to move with whole families, and as a result women migrants tend to be among the poorest; while households with some food security send family members in turn, and migration provides a means to manage risk, and build assets. Research in Palanpur, Uttar Pradesh (Lanjouw and Stern 1989) showed changes in such dynamics over time: higher castes were more prominently represented among migrants in 1983–84, but lower castes had seized the opportunity for outside jobs in earlier years. Probing the findings from NSS data that migrants were *on average* better off than non-migrants, and marginalised groups on average had lower mobility than others, de Haan and Dubey (2002) found that differences within the group of migrants (measured by Gini coefficient) are larger than within the group of non-migrants.

A key conclusion, thus, ought to be that one cannot generalise regarding links between poverty and migration, neither at the macro-level, nor at the level of individuals and groups (which the above has focused on). Similar variations can be encountered when one looks at the impact of migration on poverty. The complexity is compounded by the fact that migrants may be among the poorest in areas of destination, but among the better off in their areas of origin, and even low-status jobs may help to increase their economic position back home (or their status, as migrants may hide facts regarding status of their jobs). Moreover, and this is the subject of the next section, patterns of migration are closely intertwined with social identities, and social networks play a key role in structuring patterns of migration.

Migration: Social Processes and Relations

As perhaps with other students of migration processes, I have often been surprised, probably naively, by the difficulty regarding generalisations about causes and consequences of migration. While the basics of the Harriss–Todaro model seems hard to refute, and in my view not inconsistent with political-economy approaches, a broader view of migration tends to negate any possibility of generalisation. For example, in my research in Kolkata I had assumed that poverty and deprivation would be the main driver behind migration; but the geographic as well as the gendered patterns of migration proved to be much more complex, and personal views regarding migration, its causes and consequences often not in sync with outsiders' observations. This section, as an introduction to the following section focusing on family, describes a number of elements around the theme of social relations, and how they impact on processes of migration.

It may be helpful to start with some notes on geographic patterns of migration. While migration of course almost by definition involves the kind of move predicted in the Harriss–Todaro model, migration *patterns* are much more complex. In our respective researches in West Bengal, Rogaly and this author found streams of migration leapfrogging each other: while migrants from the areas on the border of West Bengal and Bihar moved to green revolution agricultural occupations in central West Bengal, migrants from further away western Bihar moved to Kolkata and urban jobs (de Haan and Rogaly 1996). Historical studies on population movements in eastern India similarly shows highly segmented labour markets or streams of migration, some of which were institutionalised by a highly interventionist colonial state (cf de Haan 1995 and references there). My own research, including investigation of factory records, showed that over time the percentage of workers from one particular district in one factory had increased, and that even departments within factories showed clustering of workers with a particular regional or ethnic background (de Haan 1994a). Most studies on migration, I believe, show segmentation of migration and clustering of social groups.[17]

The crucial issue for the argument here is not the existing of these segmented patterns of migration, which has been well documented, but the explanation for the phenomenon. It has often been argued that such segmentation is the result of employers' strategies, for example to exclude local labour because they would be too expensive or likely to start forming trade unions and other forms of protest.[18] But other factors play a role as well. One of them is history: certain patterns come into existence—for whatever reasons—and continue to exist and reinforce themselves. This is reflected in migrants' answers regarding reasons for coming to a specific place: often, this is related to the presence of a relative, friend or simply somebody else from the village of origin.

Social networks are key in providing access to opportunities for migration and employment; conversely, of course, migration creates new networks.[19] As all social networks, these provide opportunities as well as limitations, perhaps for women in particular as described in the next section. My own research in Kolkata found, as indicated, how important social networks are in accessing employment opportunities in West Bengal's industry. Interestingly, over time while conditions and availability of jobs changed significantly, this predominantly personalistic character of the labour market did not seem to have changed significantly. Research by Kuhn (2003) on rural-urban migration in Bangladesh emphasises how the power through networks of the established patrons over newcomers may decline over time (as well as the fact that some have no access to such networks). Mosse et al. (2002) describe the close interrelationship of migration with the servicing of debt—and hence a poverty trap for the poorest among the migrants—as well as social relations among poor migrants in tribal western India.

With social networks, identity is key for the structuration of migration movements, and vice versa, and migration processes can involve changes in and negotiation over identities.[20] Rogaly et al. (2002) who researched four distinct streams of seasonal migration in West Bengal emphasise how caste and religion, as well as class, structure patterns of migration in rural West Bengal. These streams of migration have been formed over long periods of time, in some cases labour markets being at the centre and in other cases labour recruiters. Rogaly et al. (ibid.) found that migrants often choose their employer on the basis of religious identity, and refuse to work for people of another religion. Muslim migrants maintain their identities, for example, through insisting on being paid in cooked food as well as cash—food that is cooked by women in employer households. In a subsequent article they emphasise how the process of labour migration itself is shaped by, and influences, ethnic identities related to religion, caste, region and (scheduled) tribe. Migration itself influences how people think of themselves, influenced by processes of familiarisation and 'othering'.

Individual motives also are formed by a combination of economic and non-economic factors. To start with, and discussed in more detail below, decisions of migration *of* individuals are often made *by* families or senior members of households. In some cases, for young men[21] migration forms a *rite de passage*, and the move of young men a normal part of the life-cycle of many village families. The expected returns from migration, while predominantly economic (particularly for the poorest), can include status, escape from social control, and even exploration of the world outside.[22] Finally, the impacts of migration on areas and lives can be extremely complex, and unexpected.

Thus, a key reason why we cannot get a clear grasp of the links between poverty and migration lies in the social nature of migration: it is not just driven by economic motives, its mechanics are not just economic, and its impact can stretch beyond economic costs and benefits. To understand migration patterns, one has to take into account complexity. Migrants contain as much diversity as a group as society does as a whole, and migration movements similarly cannot be reduced to simple equations and explanations. This section has emphasised that against the background of wider structures of political-economy, and while personal motives regarding betterment do play a role, migration movements operate within the context of social networks and cultural structures, which both enable and constrain individuals' actions, and change over time. Gender and family are among the key social institutions that impinge on migration, as the next two sections will show.

Migration, Gender, Family: Insights from Elsewhere

This paper is primarily about South Asia, and India in particular. But for my argument, it may be helpful to refer to insights regarding migration processes elsewhere. While working on a review of African literature to summarise links between migration and poverty,[23] I realised that the diversity of household or family patterns made it extremely difficult to generalise about patterns of migration and impacts on the well-being of migrants and those staying behind. Across the African continent, family and household patterns are extremely diverse; my limited understanding of the literature in this area suggests that each of these household forms are constitutive for patterns of migration (as well as the potential for migration to contribute to socio-economic improvement), and in turn that migration patterns contribute to what constitutes households.[24] Such diversity cannot be observed within the South Asian continent, but the reference may be helpful as a reminder regarding the importance of differences—across space and time—in gender and family relations, and how they may impinge on patterns of migration.

The first type of household structure is the nuclear type of peasant household common in Kenya and Ethiopia, for example (areas with high population density and possibly low fertility, and relatively great degrees of commercialisation), or in Sudan as described in the comparative research by David (1995), and comparable to household forms in South Asia. Particularly with high population density, small households like larger ones need to send out migrants. Research has shown that nuclear households have been able to develop effective livelihood strategies that straddle different rural areas, as well as urban and rural areas. But a comparison with more extended households—see below—suggests that migration strategies are limited by this form of household. As research in Mali shows, the effects of young men being absent may be particularly harsh on the smallest households, and the receipt of remittances is considered a poor substitute for the young man's contribution to filling the family granary.[25]

A second type of household is marked by a fluid family structure, as in Zambia, Botswana or Lesotho. In such households, labour and food are commonly shared. Matrilineality is combined with male out-migration. Fieldwork in a village west of Gaborone in Botswana—where men tend to establish their own household only when they are around forty years of age—showed multiple forms of co-habitation, overlapping social units that characterise social organisation, and varying and conflicting claims on men, which change over their lifetime. Social arrangements are fluid, links between households and individuals multiple, with an intricate networks of roles, responsibilities and reciprocities (Townsend 1997). Research in these areas has questioned the notion of household as a residential unit from which people depart, and return back to; movement of people between residential units is the norm rather than the exception (see also de Haan, Kirsten and Rwelamira 2002). Members may be residing elsewhere, may have another dwelling on agricultural land, may be residing in the compound or at the agricultural land, at the cattle post—often far from the village—in town, or in South Africa. In this case, one might argue that migration rather than being a disruption to normal household life and composition constitutes the very form of households. Perhaps central for the understanding of poverty, it is actually hard to conceive of a basic unit (household) from which people depart and return to.

In the third case, of the extended households in West Africa, for example, migration dynamics are determined in yet another way. Research by the Institute of Development Studies, Sussex (IDS) in south Mali quoted earlier focused on Senoufou households with small production units in Cote d'Ivoire, who have traditionally organised themselves in complex, extended households, related by patrilineal kinship, and headed by its oldest male member. Members of the same household cultivate a common field and eat from a single granary, and individual wealth is rare. Migration decisions are household decisions. Heads of households decide about the migration of their sons or nephews—and their wives. This is an economic investment, but also has a social function, alleviating the frustration of young men and allowing them some independence within the household structure. Migration may lead to greater independence, and there is always a risk associated with migration, but the households overall remained unified (and some regarded migration as less of a threat to this unity than, for example, diversification of economic activities in the village itself).[26]

Significantly, this research in Mali put little emphasis on migration as an economic household strategy, and emphasised household management and hence the social functions of migration. It sheds light on the relationship between household size and poverty, and the role of migration in this. As other West African research suggests, large households are better off. Large households offer opportunities for the head of the households to devise efficient strategies, including diversification of livelihood sources, and can more easily adapt to the absence of migrants.

Emphasising these very different household forms may help improve our understanding of migration and poverty in at least two ways.[27] First, household composition can be a crucial determinant for both motivations and possibilities of migration. For example, men may be forced to migrate if they are single income earners, but at the same time may be held back by household responsibilities or (other) demands for labour. In the extreme, households that need migration most because of the composition of the household may not be in a position to send away household members for income opportunities elsewhere. Each of these types of households have gendered norms regarding the desirability of migration, and for example regarding inheritance/property rights of household members who leave.[28] The household form also influences the impact of migration, in terms, for example, of changing household responsibilities and work burden after migration, with large extended households being much better able to absorb the absence of household members without significant changes in gendered division of labour and responsibilities.

Second, and conversely, migration—the movement of people away from the residential unit and back—is in itself a key constituent of households, or household types themselves. Particularly in the case of the more fluid household structures of the second type described above, the movement of people in and out of the residential unit is not a one-off or exceptional phenomenon, but the regular movements define what this household is, and how it relates to the wider environment. Migration movements are similarly core elements of what constitute large households as described for Mali, and contribute to the economic and social cohesion of such households. Migration crucially affects household structure, and can play both a unifying and dis-unifying role.

Finally, it is not the intention here to suggest that such patterns of households or migration are fixed and unchanging. As indicated, migration itself poses challenges to household unity. Over time, predominant household forms change, as the case of the secular decline of extended households seems to illustrate, and the relationships and norms surrounding employment and migration are constantly subject to interpretation and negotiation.[29]

Migration and the Family in South Asia

This last section aims to bring out how important family or household structure is in understanding migration, and its links with poverty, in South Asia. To start with, it may be helpful to remind ourselves of the predominant patterns of movement of people, as reflected in India's national Census and National Sample Survey. Both show that overall migration is dominated by women, for marriage purposes, and hence the key role of migration in the life-cycle of households. But the emphasis here is on labour migration, which tends to be dominated by men.

There is substantial literature regarding the vulnerability of women in the migration process (many contributions in the conference showed this as well). For example, Mehra and Gammage (1999) show that for migrants, employment in the urban 'informal sector' does not provide a stepping stone to other forms of employment, but their participation reflects lack of occupational mobility and access to markets. My own research (de Haan 1994b) on industrial (jute) labour shows how women lost access to employment when the conditions of employment were improving. In rural areas, the vulnerability of migrants has been described, for example, in western India by Teerink (1989) and for Santhal women in south Bihar by Rao (1998); common issues include vulnerability of female migrants, restricted access to types of employment, lower pay for the same work, sexual harassment, etc.

Some research has also stressed the importance of family structure and composition. In the research by Deshingkar and Start (2003), availability of labour within the household is cited as a possible reason why the poorest do not migrate.[30] This was reflected in my own research in Kolkata (de Haan 1994a), where many male migrants stated they could only leave when there were other people to take care of the rest of the family; hence, I concluded, those with small families or households, despite being poor, may not be able to migrate, or their migration strategies may be less effective.

The literature on international migration has generally—and more than studies on national migration, though my own research suggests similarities—stressed the key role of family and other networks in the process of migration. Migrants remain closely linked to family and village affairs back home, they continue for a long time to identify themselves with areas of origin, gift exchanges become extremely important, and migrants often wish to return home after retirement, or be buried at home after they pass away.[31] Migration, one may argue, strengthens family networks, and extended families in the sense of non-residential units.

I am not aware of research that looks at the role migration plays in the life-cycles of family or households.[32] On the one hand, similar to the research in Mali discussed above, migration by young men—or young women as shown in the research by Elmhirst (2002) in a trans-migration area in Indonesia—is sometimes seen as allowing youngsters to explore the world, for a relatively short period, before assuming household responsibilities. Of course, the timing of migration depends on the push of family circumstances and the pull of labour market opportunities (also determining, for example, whether men or women will migrate), but in my own research I was struck by the number of stories regarding young men 'wandering' for some time before choosing settlement. For young women in South Asia this is of course much more restricted.

A key contribution to debates about the gendered nature of migration was Andrea Menefee Singh's article in the 1984 volume *Women in the Cities of Asia*. According to her, macro- and micro-level studies consistently showed contrasting patterns of female rural-to-urban migration in northern and southern India, with the south having higher rates of female migration. She relates this to Boserup's famous 1970 study of women's role in economic development, and notes that the pattern of female participation in northern India resembles that of women in West Asia and North African countries, whereas the pattern in southern India resemble those of South East Asia, and 'West Asian culture never penetrated to the same degree as in the north' (Singh 1984: 96). Her analysis emphasises cultural norms, in particular northern Indian practices related to seclusion of women, that affect female migration and employment.[33]

Such patterns are by no means fixed or simple. While the predominance of male migration from northern parts of South Asia, and the relatively large numbers of women from Kerala and Sri Lanka moving to the Gulf seem to fit this pattern, the fairly sudden increase of female migrants to industrial jobs in Bangladesh does not. Moreover, within regions, differences may be as large as similarities. This is illustrated for example by research by Rogaly et al. in West Bengal, in differences in patterns of migration between Muslims from Murshidabad, and Santhals from Santhal Parganas.[34]

Earlier I referred to research by Mosse et al. (2002) in western India, showing differentiated patterns (and impacts) of migration among very poor tribal migrants, with the poorest having no choice but to move with whole families, while households with some food security send family members. However, the differences in patterns of migration between 'tribals' and non-tribals, while being related to poverty (as tribals are on average are poorer than others), may help to reflect on the cultural and social differences in norms regarding family responsibilities and gendered norms regarding divisions of labour.

What these different pieces of research suggest, and what needs to be further explored in further research, is the importance of differences in migration patterns across the continent, and how these are related to family structures and norms. The type and composition of household or family influences the needs as well as possibilities of migration, and how migration impacts on the families (including strengthened extended networks with members living away from home). Research among different social-cultural groups indicate that norms regarding family responsibility influence migration patterns, and these may change over time,[35] and are subject to negotiation. Some of the variations found in the literature relate to norms within Muslim families that restrict women's migration, differences perhaps between lower and higher castes, the processes of Sanskritisation that may tend to extend restrictions to a wider segment of the population, and the relatively greater mobility among tribal women. These differences do overlap to some extent with poverty and different needs to obtain an income, but the importance of culturally determined motivations—including beliefs of others regarding group identities, and the role played by sociocultural norms surrounding women's participation in the labour market—cannot be ruled out. Finally, migration itself, and the extent to which this leads to physical separation of residential units, determines the very form that households take.

Conclusion

The key argument of this paper relates to the need for a better understanding of family dynamics while studying processes of migration, and vice versa. Across India, it appears that there is not a very large variety in household forms, not as large as in Africa as described in Section 4. However, the norms governing families do show significant differences, and the argument of this paper is to emphasise these in our understanding of migration; how household forms and norms influence migration, how migration influences these forms and norms, and how these household forms mediate the links between migration and poverty.

The argument here is not one of causality, regarding links between migration and poverty or well-being. Household forms do not entirely preclude migration options, or determine directly the kinds of effect they have. But different household forms may lead to different migration strategies. Linking migration to poverty is not impossible, but this needs to be sensitive to the social dynamics of which migration is a part, in this case the forms of households, and the meaning 'migration' has within the context of norms about household forms and formation.

Policy implications follow from this. While we have emphasised before (de Haan and Rogaly 2002) the need for policies, first, to accept the existence of migration movements (and the failure of policies to try and stem migration), and, second, to aim to support the rights and for example information networks of migrants, the key policy implication of the argument here relates to the need for policies to be sensitive to such cultural differences. Policy responses should take into account, for example, differences across migrants in terms of their networks with and obligation to (extended) family back home, differences across social groups in labour market participation of different household members, the exploitative relations in which particularly migration of women can be embedded, and processes of identity formation and changes as a result of migration. Better policies for migration are essential from a rights perspective, and also as enabling factors that can make the difference between migration strategies that fail or succeed.

Notes

1 Arjan de Haan is social development adviser at the Department for International Development (DFID), and was posted in New Delhi at the time of the conference where this paper was first presented. He is currently on special leave from the Department, and Visiting Professor at the University of Guelph, Ontario, Canada. This paper has greatly benefited from comments by participants at the conference, particularly Rafique Abdur and Ben Rogaly.

2 The title of this article was formulated before a debate regarding renaming of Indian centres for women's/gender studies began in 2003; after that I would probably not have included reference to the 'family'. I have kept it in to underline a key argument that I hope to support in the paper, regarding the need for a better understanding of family dynamics while studying processes of migration, and vice versa (see also de Haan 1999b). This builds on a social science perspective that emphasises the need to study people's purposive and reasoning behaviour as well as the societal structures that constrain and enable that behaviour. Key texts which have informed my understanding of gender analysis in migration studies include Chant and Radcliffe (1992) and Wright (1995); for a discussion on the use of the theoretical framework of Giddens (1979, 1984) see de Haan (1994a).

3 Figures on the percentage of women among international Asian migrants (often around 45 per cent or more) are reproduced in Jolly et al. (2003).

4 This builds on de Haan and Rogaly (2002) and acknowledges the contribution made by Ben Rogaly and other contributors to that volume for informing my views on this.

5 de Haan (1994a, 1994b); the history of female labour in the industry, including ideologies around female labour, have been described very well in Sen (1992, 1999); see also Banerjee (1989).

6 The nature of work, conditions of work and pay are important for what is considered 'honourable'; I thank Rafique Abdur for pointing out this complexity and the inter-actions, as well as emphasising different practices among ethnic or religious groups, and changes over time (sometimes very sudden) in perceptions regarding acceptabil-ity of work and migration.

7 At the turn of the century, women constituted a considerable part of the jute indus-try's labour-force (about 15 per cent). Managers' reports and enquiries on employ-ing women or not gave contradictory statements; see de Haan 1994b.

8 The two sources often showed remarkable convergence, though the reasons for this and possible 'distortions' introduced over time and biases in memories may need further investigation.

9 In the case of Calcutta, and the industrial area Titagarh in particular, this is reflected in an initially extremely unbalanced sex ratio, and a slow increase in the number of women compared to men.

10 This theme has been extensively discussed in the special issue of *Contributions to Indian Sociology* 37(1&2) edited by Osella and Gardner.

11 This builds on Arjan de Haan (1999a) and de Haan and Rogaly (2002); a recent overview of the debate is presented in Skeldon (2002); Skeldon (2003) summarises a series of national case studies commissioned by the DFID.

12 Interestingly, explanations tend to revolve around why people migrate, and not why they stay; authors who have taken up the last question include Kothari (2002) and Racine (1990).

13 Todaro (1969) presents the original model, and Ghatak (1996) an application for India; but see also a contrasting perspective in Thadani and Todaro (1984).

14 The following focuses on the individual level, but this could also be extended to the macro-level. In particular, while it is generally assumed that migration is from poorer to richer areas, these links tend to be complex as well. Punjab has high levels of out-migration, but is not among the poorer states in India. James (2000) shows that inter-district migration patterns in Andhra Pradesh were not in confor-mity with dominant migration theories, as people moved from the relatively developed Godaveri-Krishna zone into Telangana district where land was available, possibly mainly in 'tribal areas'.

15 Oberai et al. (1989); in Bihar, 15 per cent of out-migrants belonged to the lowest income class, while 7 per cent of the total sample population belonged to this income group—but these figures exclude remittances, which are particularly important for the poorest groups.

16 Connell et al. (1976); see also a study on the basis of census data by M. Dev and Evenson, quoted in *The Times of India*, 3 August 2003. In fact the village studies emphasised the bipolar nature of migration, as does a study of rural-urban migra-tion in Bangladesh (Afsar n.d.).

17 See for example the studies on Mali (where it is argued that the migration of young women occurs within large extended kinship networks, in turn reinforcing those), or Indonesia (where these networks rapidly involve after initial migration by young women) in the edited volume by de Haan and Rogaly (2002); for migration in and from Nepal, see Seddon (1997); see also Skeldon (2003).

18 The role of contractors (mukadams, sardars) and control over migration movements have been described by a range of authors; e.g., Breman (1985), and with emphasis on exploitation of women, Teerink (1989).

19 de Neve (2003) emphasises that, while networks are often defined in terms of kinship, among migrants in Tirupur, Tamil Nadu he found many such networks but based on friendships formed at the workplace; see also the introduction to this special CIS issue, Gardner and Osella (2003), particularly pp. xix–xxii.

20 In research among the Fulani in Sahel, Hampshire (2002) emphasises that *exode* is part of a social process, and meaning and acceptability of migration to different groups is heavily influenced by identity, based on ethnic group, gender and generation.

21 Or young women from villages in southern Mali, for whom migration within closely defined extended family networks (called *namadé*), is a core strategy to obtain their trousseau (de Haan et al. 2002).

22 The impact of migration is usually gendered, perhaps particularly where a shortage of labour exists or develops because of migration. If most agricultural activities are carried out by hand, the absence of able-bodied men can be keenly felt, leading to a labour gap and further over-burdening women, particularly if remittances are too low to hire in labour (Findley 1997: 126).

23 de Haan (1999a); similar issues emphasising the complexity caused for understanding migration by different household forms came out in the comparative EU-funded research project on rural inequality, fertility and migration in Botswana, India and South Africa. See also, for example, Adepoju and Mbugua (1997).

24 Findley (1997: 118 ff.) stresses the complexity of family-migration interactions, and describes how African family structure conditions migration patterns, and vice versa, including how the extended family structure facilitates migration and male-female segregation of roles, how dominance of lineage over conjugal relations helps migration decisions to be made in the wider household or clan context, the impact of polygamy on the need to earn cash for bride price and maintain the larger family, and how dominance by elders may make youth migrate to escape their control.

25 Research in central Mali by Toulmin, quoted in Brock and Coulibaly (1999).

26 See also the research by David (1995) in four African countries: the extended family structure in three West African cases (Diourbel in Senegal, Bankass in Mali, Passoré in Burkina Faso) meant that most migrants' wives continue to live in their husbands' compound, or in the care of his extended family, while in El Ain in Sudan in much smaller conjugal units, women became heads of household, and more vulnerable after migration—though tight-knit village relationships provided for a great deal of inter-household support.

27 It can also shed light on the relationship between household size and poverty. As some West African research suggests, large households are better off. This is partly a normative issue, since large households are the norm. But the migration strategies indicate the economic advantages of such large households: large households offer opportunities for the head of the households to devise efficient strategies, and the absence of migrants can be more easily adapted to.

28 Hart argues that forms of migration in West Africa are strongly linked with maintenance of property rights in the countryside: some groups reserve a place at home for all migrants, but in Hausa states those who migrate lose their land immediately; quoted in Eades (1987).

29 While the migration of young women in Mali indicates accepted patterns of migration by women before marriage, Elmhirst's (2002) research in Indonesia provides detailed evidence on changing gendered ideologies of work due to the action of young women seeking factory work away from home.

30 The debate regarding links between family size and poverty is of relevance here, though insights from migration research emphasise the importance of a close look at household composition as well as mere size.

31 See for example research by Werbner (1990) in Pakistan, Gardner (1995) in Bangladesh, Pettigrew (1977) for the Indian Punjab; Racine (1990) emphasises the consequences of male migration on sociocultural patterns governing family life in India.

32 The research in Mali as summarised in de Haan et al. (2002) showed how young women's migration was related to attempts to obtain a trousseau, and thus the importance of timing of migration in household cycles.

33 See also Bina Agarwal (1994) regarding regional differences in female labour participation.

34 Rogaly et al. (2002) describe arguments between an elder man and woman about whether a young woman with a child should migrate for work. Through migrating women may be asserting different ideas about what is proper work for them, and identity is thus directly linked with ideologies of work, and related to gender, age and position in the family hierarchy.

35 Kapadia (2000) shows in south India, and Sen (1999) in her historical study of labour in colonial Bengal, that ideologies of work change with the changing rewards to that work and how they are valued by people in positions of power in a household.

References and Further Readings

Adepoju, A. and W. Mbugua. 1997. 'The African Family: An Overview of Changing Forms', in A. Adepoju (ed.), *Family, Population and Development in Africa*. London: Zed Books.

Afsar, R. 2002. 'Migration and Rural Livelihoods'. Mimeo, BIDS (Bangladesh Institute of Development Studies): Dhaka.

Agarwal, Bina. 1994. *A Field of One's Own. Gender and Land Rights in South Asia*. Cambridge: Cambridge University Press.

Banerjee, N. 1989. 'Working Women in Colonial Bengal: Modernisation and Marginalisation', in Kum Kum Sangari and Sudesh Vaid (eds), *Recasting Women: Essays in Colonial History*. New Delhi: Kali for Women.

Breman, Jan. 1985. *Of Peasants, Migrants and Paupers: Rural Labour Circulation and Capitalist Production in West India*. Oxford: Oxford University Press.

———. 2003. 'At the Bottom of the Urban Economy. A review of A. Roy's *City Requiem, Calcutta: Gender and the Politics of Poverty*', *Economic and Political Weekly*, 27 September.

Brock, K., and N. Coulibaly. 1999. 'Sustainable Rural Livelihoods in Mali', Institute of Development Studies, Research Report 35, Brighton.

Chaganti, S. 2004. 'Creation of a Third World in the First. Economics of Labour Migration', *Economic and Political Weekly*, 39(22), 29 May: 2220–226.

Chant, S. and S.A. Radcliffe. 1992. 'Migration and Development: The Importance of Gender', in S. Chant (ed.), *Gender and Migration in Developing Countries*, pp. 1–29. London, etc.: Belhaven Press.

Connell, J., B. Dasgupta, R. Laishley and M. Lipton. 1976. *Migration from Rural Areas: The Evidence from Village Studies*. Delhi: Oxford University Press.

David, R. 1995. *Changing Places: Women, Resource Management and Migration in the Sahel*. London: SOS Sahel.

Deshingkar, P. and D. Start. 2003. 'Seasonal Migration for Livelihoods in India: Coping, Accumulation and Exclusion'. ODI Draft Working Paper 220, London.

Eades, J. 1987. *Migrant Workers and the Social Order*. London: Tavistock.

Elmhirst, B. 2002. 'Daughters and Displacement: Migration Dynamics in an Indonesian Transmigration Area', in A. de Haan and B. Rogaly (eds), *Labour Mobility and Rural Society*. London: Frank Cass.

Findley, S. 1997. 'Migration and Family Interactions in Africa', in A. Adepoju (ed.), *Family, Population and Development in Africa*, pp. 109–38. London: Zed Books.

Gardner, Katy. 1995. *Global Migrants, Local Lives. Travel and Transformation in Rural Bangladesh*. Oxford: Clarendon Press.

Gardner, K. and F. Osella. 2003. 'Migration, Modernity and Social Transformation in Asia: An Overview', *Contributions to Indian Sociology*, 37(1&2).

Ghatak, A. 1996. 'Labour Migration in the Indian States and the Todarian Hypothesis', *Asian Economic Review*, 38(2): 212–28.

Giddens, A. 1979. *Central Problems in Social Theory. Action, Structure and Contradiction in Social Analysis*. London: Macmillan.

———. 1984. *The Constitution of Society. Outline of the Theory of Structuration*. Cambridge: Polity Press.

de Haan, A. 1994a. *Unsettled Settlers. Migrant Workers and Industrial Capitalism in Calcutta*. Hilversum: Verloren (and 1996, Kolkata: K.P. Bagchi).

———. 1994b. 'Towards a Single Male Earner: Decline of Child and Female Employment in an Indian Industry', *Economic and Social History in the Netherlands*, 6: 145–67.

———. 1995. 'Migration in Eastern India: A Segmented Labour Market', *Indian Economic and Social History Review*, 32(1).

———. 1997. 'Rural-Urban Migration and Poverty. The Case of India', *IDS Bulletin*, 28(2).

———. 1999a. 'Livelihoods and Poverty: The Role of Migration. A Critical Review of Migration', *Journal of Development Studies*, 36(2): 1–47.

———. 1999b. 'Migration and Poverty in Africa: Is There a Link?', Background Paper for the 1999 World Bank SPA Status Report on Poverty: University of Sussex.

———. 2002. 'Migration and Livelihoods in Historical Perspective: A Case Study of Bihar, India', *Journal of Development Studies*, 38(5) June: 115–42.

de Haan, A., K. Brock and N. Coulibaly. 2002. 'Migration, Livelihoods and Institutions: Contrasting Patterns of Migration in Mali', in A. de Haan and B. Rogaly (eds), *Labour Mobility and Rural Society*. London: Frank Cass.

de Haan, A. and A. Dubey. 2002. 'Are Migrants Worse or Better-Off? Asking the Right Questions', Paper for conference at NEHU, Shillong, November.

de Haan, A. and B. Rogaly. 1996. 'Eastward Ho! Leapfrogging and Seasonal Migration in Eastern India', in G. Rodgers et al. (eds), *The Institutional Approach to Labour and Development*. London: Frank Cass.

——— (eds). 2002. *Labour Mobility and Rural Society*. London: Frank Cass.

de Haan, A., J. Kirsten and J. Rwelamira. 2002. 'Migration and Rural Assets: Evidence from Surveys in Three Semi-arid Regions in South Africa, India and Botswana'. Poverty Research Unit, University of Sussex. www.sussex.ac.uk/Units/PRU/demography. html.

Hampshire, K. 2002. 'Fulani on the Move: Seasonal Economic Migration in the Sahel as a Social Process', in A. de Haan and B. Rogaly (eds), *Labour Mobility and Rural Society*. London: Frank Cass.

James, K.S. 2000. 'Internal Migration in Andhra Pradesh. A Quantitative Analysis', Working Paper No. 38, Centre for Economic and Social Studies: Hyderabad.

Jolly, S. et al. 2003. 'Gender and Migration in Asia: Overview and Annotated Bibliography', prepared for DFID by BRIDGE, IDS, Sussex.

Kapadia, K. 2000. 'Gender Ideologies and the Formation of Rural Industrial Classes in South India Today', in J.P. Parry, J. Breman and K. Kapadia (eds), *The Worlds of Industrial Labour*. New Delhi: Sage Publications.

Kothari, A. 2002. Migration and Chronic Poverty. Mimeo, IDPM (Institute of Development Policy and Management): University of Manchester.

Kuhn, R. 2003. 'Identities in Motion: Social Exchange Networks and Rural-urban Migration in Bangladesh', *Contributions to Indian Sociology*, 37(1&2): 311–38.

Lanjouw, P. and N. Stern. 1989. 'Agricultural Changes and Inequality in Palanpur, 1957–1984', DEP No. 24, Development Economics Research Programme: London School of Economics.

Markovits, C., J. Pouchepadass and S. Subrahmanyam (eds). 2003. *Society and Circulation. Mobile People and the Itinerant Cultures in South Asia, 1750–1950*. Delhi: Permanent Black.

Mehra, R. and S. Gammage. 1999. 'Trends, Countertrends, and Gaps in Women's Employment', *World Development*, 27(3): 533–50.

Mosse, D., S. Gupta, M. Mehta, V. Shah and J. Rees. 2002. 'Brokered Livelihoods: Debt, Labour Migration and Development in Tribal Western India', in A. de Haan and B. Rogaly (eds), *Labour Mobility and Rural Society*. London: Frank Cass.

Mukherjee, N. 2001. 'Migrant Women from West Bengal: Ill-Being and Well-Being', *Economic and Political Weekly*, 30 June 2001.

Mukherji, Shekhar. 1985. 'The Process of Wage Labour Circulation in Northern India,' in G. Standing (ed.), *Labour Circulation and the Labour Process*. London: Croom Helm, 252–89.

de Neve, G. 2003. 'Expectations and Rewards of Modernity: Commitment and Mobility among Rural Migrants in Tirupur, Tamil Nadu', *Contributions to Indian Sociology*, 37(1&2): 251–80.

Oberai, A.S., P.H. Prasad and M.G. Sardana. 1989. *Determinants and Consequences of Internal Migration in India. Studies in Bihar, Kerala and Uttar Pradesh*. Delhi: Oxford University Press.

Pettigrew, J. 1977. Socio-economic Background to the Emigration of Sikhs from Doaba, *Punjab Journal of Politics*, 1(1): 48–81.

Racine, J. 1990. 'To Migrate or to Stay? Mobility and Retention of Rural Population in South India', Pondy Papers in Social Sciences, Pondicherry.

Rao, N. 1998. 'Alienated Land, Declining Forests: Gendered Implications for Migration amongst the Santhals of South Bihar'. Mimeo, University of East Anglia.

Rogaly, B., D. Coppard, A. Rafique, K. Rana, A. Sengupta and J. Biswas. 2002. 'Seasonal Migration and Welfare/Illfare in Eastern India: A Social Analysis', in A. de Haan and B. Rogaly (eds), *Labour Mobility and Rural Society*. London: Frank Cass.

Seddon, D. 1997. 'Foreign Labour Migration and Sustainable Rural Livelihoods in Nepal'. Mimeo, University of East Anglia.

Sen, Samita. 1992. 'Women Workers in the Bengal Jute Industry, 1890–1940: Migration, Motherhood and Militancy'. Ph.D. thesis, University of Cambridge.

———. 1999. *Women and Labour in Late Colonial India*. Cambridge: Cambridge University Press.

Singh, Andrea Menefee. 1984. 'Rural-to-Urban Migration of Women in India: Patterns and Implications', in J.T. Fawcett et al. (eds), *Women in the Cities of Asia. Migration and Urban Adaption*, pp. 81–107. Boulder: Westview Press.

Skeldon, R. 2002. 'Migration and Poverty', *Asia-Pacific Population Journal*, December: 67–82.

———. 2003. 'On Migration and Migration Policy in Asia: A Synthesis of Selected Cases'. Mimeo, University of Sussex.

Skiba, K. 2003. 'Migration in Bihar: A Case Study of the History and Economics of Affour'. Mimeo, University of Virginia.

Stark, Oded. 1991. *The Migration of Labour*. Cambridge, Mass.: Harvard University Press.

Teerink, R. 1989. 'Women and Seasonal Labour Migration in India, research report, IDPAD (Indo-Dutch Project Alternatives in Development), Amsterdam.

Thadani, V.N. and M.P. Todaro. 1984. 'Female Migration: A Conceptual Framework', in J.T. Fawcett et al. (eds), *Women in the Cities of Asia. Migration and Urban Adaption*. Boulder: Westview Press.

Tinker, H. 1974. *A New System of Slavery: The Export of Indian Labour Overseas, 1830–1920*. London: Oxford University Press.

Todaro, M.P. 1969. 'A Model of Labour Migration and Urban Unemployment in Less Developed Countries,' *The American Economic Review*, 59: 138–49.

Townsend, N.W. 1997. 'Men, Migration, and Households in Botswana: An Exploration of Connections Over Time and Space', *Journal of Southern African Studies*, 23(3).

Werbner, Pnina. 1990. *The Migration Process. Capital, Gifts and Offerings among British Pakistanis*. Oxford: Berg.

Wright, C. 1995. 'Gender Awareness in Migration Theory: Synthesising Actor and Structure in Southern Africa', *Development and Change*, 26: 771–91.

Yadava, K.N.S., S.S. Yadava and R.K. Sinha. 1996/97. Rural Out-migration and its Economic Implications on Migrant Households in India. A Review, *The Indian Economic Journal*, 44(2): 21–38.

6

POWER, CULTURE AND RESOURCES IN GENDERED SEASONAL MIGRATION FROM SANTAL PARGANAS

Nitya Rao

Migration as an important part of the livelihood strategies of poor people is not a new phenomenon. Such processes are strongly gendered, and rooted in the valuations of roles and responsibilities of different members of the household. Early discourses on migration in the colonial period were linked to the forced movements of labour as slaves or indentured workers. Land revenue settlement reports from the Santal Parganas, the focus of my present paper, record large-scale migration of Santals to Assam in the late 19th century, to clear the land and establish tea plantations for British settlers. While migration decisions may no longer be forced, the conceptual categories need to be questioned. What indeed does forced or voluntary really mean? If people are on the brink of starvation, for instance, or then looking at the living and working conditions of many migrant workers, is the term 'voluntary' really significant?

Authors like Standing (1985) and Breman (1985, 1996) emphasise that migration is not really a choice for the poor, based on economic trade-offs (Todaro 1969), but their only option for survival following alienation from their land.

Several studies in India[1] have explored the motivation and reasons behind migration of different groups—the elements of choice or compulsions of survival involved, the segmentation of the labour market, its implications in terms of security and status, both in source and destination areas. Mosse et al. (2002) illustrate the diversity of causes and effects of migration on the Bhils in western India. While for the poorest it is a forced livelihood response, arising from complex sets of social relations including those of debt and dependency, for others it is a positive opportunity to save, accumulate capital or invest in assets.[2] Wealth and social standing, prestige and position in village-based networks, and links to recruiting agents are found to influence outcomes, with the better off appearing to gain more from migration than the poorest.[3] The latter often end up in the lowest paid and hardest unskilled jobs, working long hours in poor working conditions, often sinking further into debt than previously.

This emerges from my own work in the Santal Parganas too. While women are primarily engaged in short-term seasonal migration to West Bengal, four times a year, for paddy cultivation, men prefer longer-term migration, linked as it is to higher wages and notions of adventure. Fifty-year-old Badku Soren of Dumka block, after many years of working as a migrant labourer, primarily as a paddy harvester and thresher in West Bengal's Bardhaman district, rose to be a recruiting agent, and was thus gradually able to earn more, build up his assets and lease in more land in his home village.[4] He is now considered a 'village elder'. Another migrant labourer from the same village, Chutki Tudu, a widowed woman with two daughters to support, could not save anything, spending whatever she earned on food and healthcare for her girls. While the men mostly migrate to reclaim their alienated land or make investments to improve it, for women, access to land itself being increasingly challenged, the purpose seems to be survival and household maintenance. In a good season they may be able to make marginal improvements in their living conditions. Younger widows and separated women are the most vulnerable and gain little from migration. Preliminary evidence leads me to suggest that this is related to the growing challenge to their property rights in their home villages,[5] as well as lack of male kin support.

Lipton (1983) identified the causal linkage between casual wage labour, lack of assets and poverty, but the notions of power, as well as the cultural categorisations in constructing ideology and appropriate work roles, was largely left unexplored. Recent sociological and anthropological approaches, including gender analyses, portray more complex pictures of migration, incorporating not just individual motives and structural factors, but also the sociocultural underpinnings of gendered work that shape gender division of roles and responsibilities within households. With shifts in external factors as well as life-cycle changes among members, this would change.[6] All these contribute to determining who migrates and who stays behind, the gainers and the losers from the migration process. Does it contribute to the renegotiation of gender roles and identities, or to a move out of poverty?

It is recognised now that women too migrate for economic reasons, a departure from relegating female migration to the private sphere by talking of 'marriage migration' only.[7] But women rarely have the 'autonomy' to take decisions regarding migration. An entire gamut of domestic and household responsibilities—the care of children and the elderly, small livestock and homestead plots—have to be adequately arranged for first. This constrains both choice and the spontaneity of movement. Patriarchal relations however manifest themselves differently: amongst the Saoras of Orissa, the men migrate, while in Kerala the women, especially from poor fishing communities, do so (Schenk-Sandbergen 1995).

In the next section, I examine the data on Santal livelihoods, particularly changes in land relations and control, and the linkages with migration decisions of both men and women. Does the challenge to their land-holding status in the village, particularly for widowed and separated women, affect their ability to benefit from migration? I then discuss the differentiated patterns of male and female migration, in terms of who goes for what work and for how long? How far are these patterns structured by underlying gender, ethnic and class relations, as well as by systemic, structural and individual reasons such as domestic obligations and responsibilities, access to networks, skill levels and social status? And finally, what are the implications for poverty, well-being and autonomy?

This paper is based on fieldwork conducted in 1997 in the Dumka district of the Santal Parganas, Jharkhand, with support from a local women's group, followed by my own in-depth research in two villages between 1999–2000, and briefly in 2003.[8] The larger purpose of the research was to understand the gendered nature of livelihood choices amongst the Santals, and its relationship to access and control over resources, particularly land.

Livelihood Contexts and Choices

The population of Dumka is primarily rural and comprises more than 40 per cent scheduled tribes, mostly Santals. Low literacy rates and poor health status characterise the district in a region considered one of the poorest and most food insecure in India.[9] The district

Table 6.1 Population Characteristics of Dumka District (Census of India, 1991)

Block	Total population	Total ST population	Per cent ST to total population	Per cent female literacy	Per cent female of total main workers
Saraiyahat	101,862	20,024	20	29	29
Jarmundi	117,204	33,243	28	24	29
Jama	104,245	54,715	52	27	38
Ramgarh	113,705	58,141	51	23	37
Gopikandar	32,095	27,628	86	35	50
Kathikund	52,801	36,042	68	32	27
Dumka	108,732	54,656	50	41	37
Shikaripara	95,536	61,291	64	40	39
Ranishwar	79,797	36,680	46	47	34
Masalia	95,121	58,368	61	31	55
Kundahit	101,463	35,928	35	39	31
Nala	136,306	52,593	39	29	22
Jamtara	143,304	55,248	39	26	20
Narayanpur	122,623	31,892	26	19	27
District (1991)	1,404,794	616,449	44	31	36
District (2001)	1,759,602	701,903	40	26.4	23
District (2001: STs)				18	30

Source: Census of India, 1991.

average of women's workforce participation is 36 per cent. Block-wise analysis reveals considerable variation—from 50 per cent in the forested Gopikandar block to 29 per cent in the Hindu-dominated agricultural plains of Jarmundi, and falling to a low of 20 per cent in the partly industrialised plains area of Jamtara (see Table 6.1).

Most Santals own some land, mostly un-irrigated uplands. The coarse cereals and rain-fed paddy that is cultivated is insufficient to sustain livelihoods, and this is supplemented by income from forest produce or wage labour. A survey of eight villages in 1992 in Gopikandar block by Adithi, a women's organisation working in the region, showed head-loading firewood as the primary occupation of 44 per cent workers (56 per cent women and 36 per cent men) in these villages, as agriculture was not remunerative. Of the total workforce 45 per cent women and 27 per cent men identified this as their secondary occupation.

My research in 1997 however found that only 7 to 10 per cent of the population identified head-loading firewood and collecting forest

Table 6.2 Changing Occupational Status in Gopikandar Block, Dumka

Occupation	Primary (1992)		Primary (1997)		Secondary (1992)		Secondary (1997)	
	Women	Men	Women	Men	Women	Men	Women	Men
Head-loading and MFP	56	35.7	9.6	7.4	45.6	27.6	28	17.5
Agriculture	20	37.6	42	48	26.3	38.4	40	40.5
Wage labour	18.5	17.8	40	39	26.3	21.3	32	42
Service	2	4.3	8.4	5.5	1	2	—	—
Business	0.5	0.5	—	—	—	2	—	—
Others	3.0	3.7	—	—	0.5	0.5	—	—

* all figures in percentages
Source: Rao (1999).

produce as their primary occupation, but 25 per cent women identified it as their secondary occupation. The figures were similar in 2000, with forest produce being seen to contribute 26 per cent to their livelihood basket and wage work accounting for 25 per cent and the family farm 35 per cent. Table 6.2 presents the change in occupational status, both primary and secondary, for women and men in Gopikandar block during the period 1992–97.

The example of Sona Hansdak, a woman head loader from Gopikandar block illustrates this. Walking eight miles to and from the forest every-day carrying heavy loads of firewood is exhausting. In addition, with new forest protection norms based on community management, the villagers from whose forests they were bringing the loads caught her and a group of women and confiscated their implements. They had to beg them to return these—the basis of their livelihood—and promised to go to a different forest henceforth.[10] Two members of her family go for wage work, at least for 15 days a month. Her husband and daughter migrate to Bengal seasonally. The income earned there helps them purchase clothes for the entire family for the year. Sona cannot afford to educate her children. They have a little land on which they grow maize, but the produce barely suffices for two months in the year. Their livelihood is a fine balance between cultivation, head-loading, making leaf plates, wage-work and migration.

An important issue arising from the life of Sona and others like her is the seasonality characterising their livelihood options. During the lean seasons the household may often depend on women's enterprise and men's wage-work, if available, but in the peak cultivating seasons, it is often women who migrate for agricultural labour, leaving men behind to take care of their own fields and assets. Regular seasonal migration of both men and women from the Santal Parganas to West Bengal for paddy cultivation is widespread. Having planted paddy at home, women, preferred for transplanting paddy, move to Bengal to earn some rice and cash, to tide over the difficult time until their own crop is harvested, while the men stay behind to tend the land. As the output is not sufficient to see them through the year, they continue to migrate even after the harvest. Where there is no second crop and the household is clearly facing survival difficulties, the men go too.

Apart from the gender segregation of labour markets that prefer women for transplanting paddy, there is a strong ideological dimension to this pattern. Given a choice, men prefer to stay back in the village and tend whatever little land they have to preserve their identity as 'chasa hor', or cultivators. They see migrant work as a loss of status and attempt to project their migration decisions as an adventure to see new places or a strategy to build capital for investing in their own land.[11] They prefer long-term migration to distant locations, usually leaving after ploughing the land for the monsoon paddy and returning before the next planting season. Even though the women undertake all other operations, through the act of ploughing men assert their control over the land and their identity as cultivators.

Women's identity as 'ora hor' or homemakers permit them to undertake a diverse range of activities to fulfil their roles and contribute to household subsistence—to its food supply, clothes, and perhaps for an unmarried girl to build up her dowry. Unlike the Hindu castes that tend to withdraw female labour as a sign of status, among the Santals men prefer to stay away from wage-work and let women engage in it.[12] This is clearly visible in Panni's household. They cultivate their own lands, but with many mouths to feed, this is not sufficient. Hence her daughter-in-law, daughter and granddaughter migrate, while her sons stay behind.

Thus apart from the resources available for making a livelihood locally, particularly access to land and forests, household composition as well as gendered notions of appropriate work do play a key role in migration decisions. In the next section I explore in greater depth the changes in patterns of land ownership and tenancy, how these are gendered and thereafter I attempt to relate this to the process and experience of migration.

Changing Control Over Land: Ownership, Tenancy and Alienation

Land alienation in the region has a long history, persisting despite legislation, as is revealed through an analysis of the various land settlement reports and records. Several people who had migrated to the tea gardens of Assam in the late 19th century, ostensibly for a short period, found they had lost their land to the headman or his kin in their own village, or to the moneylender. They had no option but to migrate permanently.[13] It is interesting to note that over 50 per cent of the lowlands were in the names of non-Santals, who had settled here as traders and 'writers' (clerks) after the establishment of British rule in 1856.[14]

The Santal Pargana Tenancy Act (SPTA) passed soon after Independence in 1949, prohibited all land transfers (Section 20), yet the decade after Independence saw an increase in exploitation by the *mahajans* (moneylenders), in collusion with the official machinery. Kunjiram Tudu, one of the leaders of the protest that followed, said:

> The *Mahajans* controlled almost all the land of the Santals. If a person borrowed Rs 100, he would record it as Rs 300. As the Santal had nothing in the house, he got an order from the civil court and confiscated the crop. People started losing their land. Many people ran away to Bengal during this period. The police and the courts supported the *mahajan* (Bagnol village, 21 December 2000).

The parents of Hari Rajwar, a poor scheduled caste peasant, were among those who fled. Migration at this instance was of entire families. Some Santals whom I met settled in a village in Bardhaman district mentioned that they too had lost their land and migrated. They felt that their living conditions were worse; they missed their home village and tried to return during the annual harvest festival *Sohrai*, though this was not always possible.

In 1966, a movement evocatively titled the *hul* Jharkhand (Jharkhand rebellion) began in Dumka district. It aimed at releasing land as well as securing debt relief. Apart from *dhan katai* (forcible harvesting), other direct action strategies included the non-repayment of loans, theft of grain from *mahajans'* fields and court cases. Mass meetings were held; the word spread through the district and so did the resistance.[15] Several households, as of Hari Rajwar, were brought back to the village and made to reoccupy their land.

The widespread agrarian and anti-*mahajani* movements in the Santal Parganas and other parts of Jharkhand during the late 1960s and early 1970s led to a spate of state actions and legislation. In 1969, the Bihar Scheduled Areas Regulation sought to control more strictly the illegal transfers of land, amending the provisions of Section 20 (v) of the SPTA. Soon after, the Bihar Moneylenders Act, 1974[16] and the Bihar Debt Relief Act, 1976 were also passed.

In the late 1970s the current settlement process was launched in the district. Many people suddenly realised that plots of land that had been mortgaged for several years were actually still owned by them. A Santal from Jama block in Dumka district narrated his story. His land had been mortgaged to one Upen Mandal over 20 years ago in lieu of a small loan. This was repaid many times over, yet when he tried to cultivate the land, he was threatened. The revenue *karamchari* asked him to file a case in the court of the Circle Officer (CO). He did so. It ran there for four years, then at the court of the Sub-Divisional Officer (SDO) for another two years. At that time, there was a settlement camp in this block and the SDO sent him there. He secured a decree in his favour. He was able to cultivate for a year, but was again threatened so he fled to Assam, and Mandal started cultivating his land again. The Santal then returned to his village and started fighting the case again. He must have been to the CO's court more than twenty times and to the SDO's court a dozen times, spending anything between Rs 30 and Rs 300 on each trip, yet there was no settlement. The dates for hearing were constantly extended. He still does not have possession of his land.

This is not an unusual case. Even Adivasi men, who are educated and not really the poorest, are unable to use legal processes and institutions in their favour. Clearly it is next to impossible for the poorest and resourceless, more so for women.[17] While the first step forward has been made in terms of awareness, as the numerous objections and appeals reveal, the persistent structural inequalities hamper implementation, as the opposing party is usually the economically stronger one.

In fact, as land transfers are legally prohibited, the major insight into alienation is found through looking into the range of tenancy arrangements in the district. Interestingly, as Table 6.3 shows, it is the Santals who seem to be primarily leasing out land, though a few—the better off—also lease in land. This seems to suggest an extent of inequality in the relationship, usually based on debt.[18] A case in point is that of

Table 6.3 Extent of Tenancy Arrangements

Block	No. Leasing in*			No. Leasing out		
	ST	Others	Total	ST	Others	Total
Jarmundi	3	2	5	45	3	48
Gopikandar	9	—	9	26	—	26
Dumka	4	16	20	39	38	77
Total	16	18	34	110	41	151

Source: Rao (1999).

* The figures for the number of people leasing in land do not tally with those for leasing out, as many of the former are moneylenders residing in a larger village or market centre, rather than the villages selected for the study. Further, in each village a sample was surveyed, with a focus on small and marginal farmers, hence many of the more prosperous households were left out.

Bittan Kisku of Jarmundi block. On the records a large farmer with 14 acres of land, Bittan doesn't cultivate even a single acre. While a part of his land has been mortgaged to a moneylender, another sharecrops the rest. The household survives by borrowing both for consumption and emergencies, and adjusting these amounts with the rent or share of produce. During the monsoons, they work as wage labourers on their own land, or migrate to Bengal to bring back a lump sum that can be used to repay the loan and perhaps reclaim a part of the land.

A majority of women-headed households, particularly widows, too end up giving out at least a part of their land, due to lack of resources, but also under pressure from their male kin. In the next section, I discuss briefly the issues around women's property rights and the use of kinship ideologies to thwart their claims.

Women's Property Rights

The first recorded statement of women's inheritance comes from McPherson, the then Settlement Officer, reproducing the note prepared by the Divisional Commissioner (DC) Bompas on this matter (1909: 123). He noted that daughters got no share of land, and beneficiaries of land titling were the male kin. While the practice of women cultivating was widespread, titling began leading to the creation of exclusionary land systems.[19] Formalisation of rights meant the shrinkage in a range of flexible and informal rights in land,[20] contributing in turn to a renegotiation of land use and inheritance practices as well as power relations within the 'community'—between individuals, households and kin groups as well as the state. Women tended to lose out in this process.

The record of a meeting of the *Parganaits, Desmanjhis, Sardars* and other leaders in Dumka on 15 February 1916 reveals that the issue of inheritance by women had become a subject of discussion. The leaders felt that if a man had only daughters, they would be his heirs when they married. When a man had sons and daughters, and the sons died without having children, the girls would become the heirs. For a widow, they argued for a life interest in her husband's property, as long as she did not remarry (Bodding et al. [1942] 1994: 198). In a context where individual titling seemed to be reinforcing patriarchal principles to exclude women, at least from the official discourse, the public reassertion of principles of community support to women was an important counterpoint. In light of the erosion of their formal authority (through the establishment of Settlement Courts), this move by local male leadership to support women's land claims can also be seen as an assertion of their moral authority as protectors of all members of the community—men and women.

In the land settlement that followed, Gantzer states, 'according to Santal Adivasi law of inheritance, only males can inherit land' (Gantzer 1936: 22). Yet, he also indicates daughters being recorded as cultivators, where not doing so would have involved real hardship to them (ibid.: 23). Archer ([1946] 1984) in his survey of 1945–46[21] found in practice a much more flexible system of inheritance, and one that was more supportive of women than recorded by Gantzer.

The SPTA, however, repeated the provisions of inheritance recorded by Gantzer, rather than the more liberal systems documented by Archer. It does however provide legal sanction to women's rights to inherit land as *gharjawae*s (literally a house son-in-law). Archer ([1946] 1984) gives several reasons why a *gharjawae* is brought—the need for an extra man to look after the land, to fill the house with children and guard against the loneliness of old age, love for particular daughters, where the daughter is disabled or has an illegitimate child, and the desire to keep the land in the family rather than letting it pass on to the kin. Goody (1976) has pointed out that in contexts of intensive plough cultivation as well as individual titling linked to the commoditisation of property, the desire to transmit one's property to one's direct descendants becomes strong. In the case of a failure to produce a son, alternate strategies can be used depending on the particular point in the man's life-cycle, including allowing the daughter to inherit by gift (*taben jom*), appointing her as a social male through the formal adoption of a son-in-law (*gharjawae*) or adding more wives. Through a *gharjawae* marriage, as far as her father's lands are concerned, the daughter becomes a son.

A case in point is that of Baha Marandi of a remote village in Gopikandar block. The only child to her parents, Baha was married as a *gharjawae* in 1981 at the age of eleven. Her father died in 1984. She and her husband lived and cultivated their land of almost nine bighas, had three children and were well settled. In August 1995 Baha's mother died. That year they completed their cultivation and collected the output. Then her male kin started threatening to kill them, so they moved to her husband's village. There is little land there, and they have to depend on wage labour or migration for survival.

In 1996, she came to her natal village to ask for her share. Charan, her father's brother's son said, 'Nothing has been cultivated on the land, so what share can I give?' In June 1997, she again tried to cultivate, asking her brother-in-law to plough her fields, but Charan obstructed this. A village meeting was held, yet no consensus could be reached. On 9 January 1998, there was a second village hearing on this dispute and she was to receive her share. She has been paying the rent since 1996–97, yet is unable to live in the village and cultivate the land. The village elders advised her to file a case in the court. Following the *hul* Jharkhand, in which women were actively involved both in the process of planting and harvesting of the fields, and in providing food and shelter to their men, who were often on the run, the leadership—though largely male—has been unanimous in supporting women's claims to land, particularly that of *gharjawae*. One sees here a historical continuity from 1916 in terms of the reassertion of women's property rights in a context of growing challenge to them.

It has been expensive to fight the case, travelling all the way to Dumka several times a year and paying the lawyer's fees. The case is still ongoing and though likely to go in Baha's favour, her male kin continue to threaten her. They justify their resistance on grounds that if she inherited the land, it would then go to her sons. In line with patrilineal kinship systems, they would take the name of their father; hence the land would be transferred to another kin group. The key issue at play here is the question of land scarcity and the struggle for survival. Baha's male kin are amongst the poorest in the village and desperately seeking to survive, apart from enhancing their social and wealth status. Where there is scarcity of land, clearly everybody cannot have enough, and over the generations a selection has to be made between claimants. In a patrilineal society, where women move between kin groups at marriage, their claims are thus the first to be excluded. Rather than Archer's explanation that offers a much broader view based on emotional and social bonds, Goody's emphasis on descent and the separation of inheritance of property from inheritance of lineage name has in fact become the major justification for challenging, rather than supporting, *gharjawae*.

A second category of women, whose claims cannot be openly challenged, but in fact are often unable to operationalise their property claims, are widowed women, especially those without sons. By refusing support, especially for ploughing, male kin create a situation that leads to the leasing out of their land and migration. A telling case in the same village is that of Mukhi Tudu. She was widowed when her children were still young. She was unable to find support to cultivate her husband's land, so started migrating to Bengal with her children. She couldn't save any money to restart cultivation, however, while migrant; she came in contact with missionaries who promised her support. When her son entered his teens, she asked them for financial help to rebuild her house in the village and start cultivation. Though it took her several years to do so, the presence of a male heir helped protect her claims to the land. Migration served the purpose of building contact with her patrons—the missionaries—rather than contributing directly to capital formation. In this sense, it provided an opportunity.

There is one more category of women I would like to briefly mention and these are separated women. In the event of separation, the husband is expected to give them sufficient land for their maintenance. Often however separation occurs when the husband brings another wife, so even if he is prepared to give land, the first wife, feeling insulted and hurt, does not want to continue living there, and returns to her parents' village. According to Santal custom, a common practice was to gift a married woman some land in her natal village as *taben jom*, or maintenance by her father, brothers, or other male agnates. Not more than ten bighas, this gift was generally made out of affection or obligation to a daughter or sister, a kind of insurance against a bad marriage (Archer [1946] 1984). This right is however even more tenuous than *gharjawae* rights and rarely observed in the present context of not just land scarcity, but more importantly, the marginalisation of Adivasis vis-à-vis other social groups.

Maku is one such woman, accustomed to migrating with her parents from when she was a little child. Her marriage didn't work and she and her six-year-old daughter stay now with her parents. Her three brothers are unwilling to give her a share of the family land. While her father's household is secure due to his investment in cattle and in moneylending, he does not own much land. To support herself and her daughter, Maku migrates four times annually to West Bengal.

While Maku is away, her brothers perform the household tasks, as their mother is bed-ridden. As soon as she returns, however, all these responsibilities are once again hers. While Rogaly and Coppard (2003) have argued that migration can lead to a renegotiation of identities and relationships, my own work suggests that these shifts are often of a temporary rather than permanent nature.[22] Despite her earnings and economic independence, Maku's bargaining position is weak, as she is staying in her brother's home. The only long-term solution to improving her position she sees is remarriage, which would provide her access to land. Maku is by no means the only one, and in a context of high marital mobility,[23] this is an issue that requires serious attention.

Clearly then, access to land, mediated by gender, seniority and kinship relations, has much to do with who migrates and who does not, as well as the position from which they migrate. Similar in many ways to the findings of Mosse et al. (2002) in western India, amongst the Santals too, those with some resources—material and social—are better able to benefit from the process of migration than those without.

I now turn to the experience of migration itself, with a view to analysing the different levels of decision-making involved and its implications for men and women as gendered subjects in a context of poverty.

Extent, Conditions and Experience of Migration

Short-term seasonal migration to Bardhaman district of West Bengal appears to be a major livelihood strategy for both men and women.[24] Observations at the bus-stand in Dumka over a period of four years revealed almost 100,000 workers going to Bardhaman, Birbhum and Hooghly within a period of 15 days in the months of January and February.[25] This excludes workers travelling directly from other blocks of the district, adjacent to West Bengal.

Data from the 1997 study reveals that while women and men migrate in almost equal numbers seasonally, long-term migration appears to be

Table 6.4 Ethnic Distribution of Migrant Population (By Block)

Block	Caste	Sex	Long-term migration	Short-term migration	Total population	% of total in long-term migration	% of total in short-term migration
Jarmundi	Santal/Paharias	F	0	23	76	0	30.2
		M	3	23	79	3.8	29
	SC/Other	F	1	11	90	1	12.2
		M	4	13	89	4.5	14.6
Sub-total			8	70	334	2.4	21
Gopikandar	Santal	F	1	7	196	0.5	3.6
		M	2	13	185	1	7
	Others	F	0	0	2	0	0
		M	0	0	2	0	0
Sub-total			3	20	385	0.8	5.2
Dumka	Santal	F	0	6	82	0	7.3
		M	7	6	91	7.6	6.5
	SC/Other	F	0	0	90	0	0
		M	2	2	95	2	2
Sub-total			9	14	358	2.5	4

Source: Rao (1999: 149).

a male preserve (see Table 6.4). This is both on account of the nature of work to be performed and also the gender roles and gender division of tasks in society. Seasonal work is mainly paddy transplanting and harvesting, both backbreaking jobs. Transplanting is viewed as a woman's task and fetches lower payments compared to ploughing and other male jobs. Further, with primary responsibility for household maintenance tasks, women cannot afford to be away from their homes for long periods of time, unless the entire family migrates.

Often men transplant paddy as migrant labourers in West Bengal, something they would not do in their own fields. This is rationalised by the need to accompany their women to protect them from sexual abuse. There seems to be a 'tacit acceptance by men of the fact that women would be exploited by outsiders', says Mitra (1987) in a case study of Santal women's lives. The women therefore never move alone, but always in the company of at least one man from their group, yet often the landowners, their sons and other relatives threaten these men, force them to keep quiet and exploit the women. Despite the futility of male presence in many cases, joint migration with men, for the purpose of physical security, has now become the rule. Even if it is not possible for all couples to migrate together, they ensure that there are at least a few men in each group migrating from a particular village or kin group. And once there, men claim that it is better for them too to work and earn.

Two sisters, Bahamani Marandi and Sajhli Marandi, live with their parents, and another sister and a brother. The family owns less than an acre of land, and the output does not last for more than three months. The cycle of indebtedness to the moneylenders at high interest rates starts anew. These two sisters migrate to Bengal four times a year, to earn money for the repayment of debts, and purchase of other essentials and clothes.

Migrant workers, particularly women, face many difficulties. Setting out from their homes with clothes and utensils on their heads, they have to walk to the road several kilometres (km) away. The bus is over-crowded and there are no seats or space to keep the luggage.[26] Often the non-Adivasi men harass them. Standing for several hours, and without any food, they reach Bardhaman and then the village, some 15 km away. The farmer gives them accommodation in the cowshed. They clean the place a bit and put their things there. They are given *muri* (puffed rice) for breakfast, and rice, potatoes and oil, along with firewood, to cook their other meals. The day after they arrive, they start work in the fields at six in the morning. While they receive their provisions everyday, their wage is accumulated with the employer and given to them just before they leave for home. They eat leftovers from the previous day at noon in the fields. The evening meal is cooked after completing the day's work. In their team of workers, they have divided the task amongst themselves, so that two of them take turns to cook the evening meal.

Drinking water is a major problem. It has to be collected from the open ponds located some distance away. Toilet facilities are non-existent. The farmer further insists on having a sexual relationship with Bahamani. All this increases risks to their health. Yet, if they fall sick and can't go for work on a particular day, they are not paid wages or given rations for that day. They have to buy the necessary medicines from their own money. In times of illness, they therefore often decide to leave the work and return home.

Though the employers are supposed to meet the transport costs of the workers as per the provisions of the Inter-State Migrant Workers Act, 1979, the workers travel at their own expense. Even if the agent purchases the ticket for them, the money spent on this is deducted from their wages. At the end of about 25 days of work, they hope to take back a sum of Rs 300 to 400 per person, and some grain saved during the period from their daily rations.

Hoponmai Hansdak, a 25-year-old, had two young children, aged four and six. She had nowhere to leave them at home. A big worry for her was the lack of childcare facilities. Moving between Dumka and Bardhaman four times a year, the chances of education for these children are remote. Though in this group the women themselves took turns to keep an eye on the children, it is not uncommon to find young girls accompanying groups of men and women labourers with the specific purpose of taking care of the young children.

Despite these difficulties, every evening they sit and sing together for a while, and this helps them relax and forget their tiredness. On their return home, they hand over the money they have earned to their parents. It is immediately used for the repayment of debts and purchase of foodgrains. The only benefit they personally get out of their hard work and earnings is perhaps a set of clothes. They stay at home as long as the food lasts, then move again for the next crop season.

Migration may yield incomes in the short run, but it does not necessarily lead to economic independence or an improvement in the status of migrant women. The Khandeshi women migrants from Maharashtra, for instance, who accompany their husbands for planting and harvesting of sugarcane in south Gujarat, have no control over the income or means of production, as the contract is with the family (Teerink 1995). This raises important issues in terms of the process of recruitment—whether as individual labour or household units—and the relationship with the recruiter. Further, my own research suggests that the impact of migration on women, particularly poor women, is not positive—the work environment is harsh, living conditions are poor and the need to perform domestic chores in the camp after working in the fields doubles their workload. Problems of sexual harassment, lack of childcare and healthcare persist.[27]

A second issue emerging from the data is the preference among men for long-term migration to construction projects in the border areas. In Jamabaihar village of Jarmundi block, the majority of men migrated for road construction work to Mizoram, Nagaland, Kashmir and Punjab for almost six to eight months of the year. As much of this long-distance migration is state sponsored, meant to support the work of the Army and the Border Security Force in remote parts of the country, the workers are registered. The contractors come to Dumka to enrol workers during the month of March. The men are paid between Rs 1,200 and Rs 1,500 per month, given subsidised rations, warm clothes and reimbursed medical costs. They can also claim compensation if injured at work, and their families can do the same if they are killed while at work. Transportation costs are however borne by them.

Though this also involves hard work (migrants are expected to work harder than their local counterparts), and not necessarily higher wages, there is security of the returns they get every month. This money is either sent home by money order, or brought home by them at the end of the period of work, and used to meet major expenditure such as house construction, debt repayment, purchase of clothes and other assets, giving them a higher status, prestige and power within the community. It also maintains their identity as 'providers'.

The impact of male migration on women who stay put, however, is not always positive. In the Santal Parganas, characterised as it is by irregular remittances, male migration tends to enhance the physical, financial and emotional burdens on women. Rather than empowering women, this has led to food shortages, indebtedness, overwork and illness, and hence their further subjugation.[28]

Conclusion

What I have argued in this paper is that while migration has for long been a part of the livelihood strategies of the Santals, the results are not always beneficial. Contrary to conventional analysis, migration is neither a result of individual choice, nor is it merely a response to deforestation and insufficient agricultural production. Just as other relations of production, migration decisions, experiences and outcomes too are mediated by ideologies of ethnicity and gender, of power, status and relative valuations of work in society. Of course, the access to resources—both material and social—do reflect the types of choices available to individuals and groups for making a living, the types of everyday and structural forms of discrimination that they have to overcome, and consequently the nature of labour flows.

Migrant labour markets are highly segmented, as also gendered. Engagements in these have different implications for men and women of different groups, in terms of the capacity to earn as well as the conditions of work. The negative consequences of migration, in terms of the impacts on schooling and health care, poorer living and working conditions, and for women the constant fear of sexual abuse by strangers, are clear. In a context of extreme deprivation, short-term seasonal migration does contribute towards the accumulation of some savings, both in cash and as paddy, and helps tide over the lean months. In a few cases, it contributes to the acquisition of land and purchase of assets for their own cultivation. Such an outcome however is strongly influenced by control over resources, particularly of land, as well as gendered notions of identity.

Over the years there has been a gradual alienation of land to both non-Adivasi traders and moneylenders in lieu of unpaid debts, and to the better off amongst the Adivasis who have adequate capital and resources for cultivation. In many cases, the original owners themselves cultivate the lands either as mere labour or as sharecroppers. Women particularly either do not have land in their own name, and even if they do, it is not very secure. They are often obliged to lease out their land to their male relatives and migrate for a living.

As the data and analysis presented reveal, there are considerable variations between the Santals living in different parts of the district as well as amongst different types of households. Yet what is striking is the shift in the nature of migration—from long-term to seasonal and from male to female. In a general context of deprivation, this appears to reflect a growing challenge to women's property-based rights: land is seen as an essential part of male identity, but not female identity. In such a context of subsistence and gendered ideologies of inheritance and work, survival rather than choice seems to be the main motivating factor for a majority of migrant women.

Notes

1 Schenk-Sandbergen (1995), Rogaly (1999), Breman (1996), and the collection of essays in de Haan and Rogaly (2002).
2 See also de Haan (2000) on differences in migration experience by gender, caste and wealth.
3 Recruiting agents from Bengal, in my own study area, often stayed with the better off, somewhat educated Santal households—those with the potential for mobilising labour in the village, hence a degree of social standing and authority.
4 He has now stopped migrating completely and focuses on cultivation.
5 Their vulnerability is exacerbated by deforestation, which denies them the opportunity to earn a little extra income by sale of forest produce. See also Menon (1995) on this point. Teerink (1995) makes the link between land alienation, deforestation and

restrictions on the use of forests, leading to debt bondage, mortgage of land and then migration.

6 See also Chant (1992) on this point, what she calls household structuration.

7 Though most definitions of 'workers' undervalue women's work, it is accepted that 46 per cent of agricultural labour in India is female (Karlekar 1995).

8 The first round of fieldwork was conducted in three blocks of Dumka district, namely, Jarmundi, Dumka and Gopikandar, with a local group Ayoaidari, literally meaning women's collective empowerment. In the second phase, in-depth ethnographic research was conducted in two villages located in Dumka and Gopikandar blocks as part of my Ph.D. research. More recently, in 2003, research was conducted in the context of government policies as part of a Ministry of Rural Development–UNDP–Pradan project.

9 The *Food Insecurity Atlas of Rural India* (MSSRF/WFP 2001) classifies Bihar and Jharkhand as the two most food insecure states in the country.

10 Sarin (1997) discusses the conversion of women head loaders into 'thieves' by JFM (joint forest management) practices.

11 Interviews with several men during the course of my fieldwork.

12 See also Sjoblom (1999) on this point, namely, the loss of reputation, status and social position through long absence from the village and dependence on distant patrons, amongst Bhil men in Dungarpur district of Rajasthan.

13 According to the records, their land was leased out for a period of five years, but they were given the impression that they had lost their land, so persuaded to stay on in Assam.

14 Based on a survey of 20 villages in Dumka district in 1997 (Rao 1999).

15 In the Damin region, people had meetings, but in the absence of other options, decided not to oppose the *mahajans*. While the *hul* of 1855 had started in the Damin region, in 1996 the movement was more intensive in the plains near Dumka.

16 The government ordered all moneylenders to be registered and provide a report of their transactions within 30 days. No reports were received. In fact most *mahajans* in the village destroyed their records.

17 One needs however to mention that during the *hul* Jharkhand, several lawyers supported the cause and tried to use the legal process to secure the rights of the Santals to their own land.

18 Mosse et al. (2002) highlight the links between debt and migration among the Bhils in western India.

19 He says when the Santal courts became acquainted with the Santal law, they ceased to record women as successors to *jotes*. Before that time, the Settlement Officers following the ordinary settlement rules had recorded whatever cultivators were found in possession and in so doing had noted Santal women for a number of holdings (Archer [1946] 1984: 683).

20 Prominent among these is women's rights to homestead or *bari* plots. Loss of such rights carries on today and is compounded in the contexts of rehabilitation and resettlement (Rao 2003).

21 W.G Archer, a civil servant, was appointed by the British State to enquire into and record Santal law as a reference point for the civil courts. He submitted his report in 1946. It was however filed and never published till 1984, when the Anthropological Survey of India and Indian Council of Social Science Research published it jointly as a rich anthropological documentation of the Santals rather than as a legal text.

22 See also Jolly et al. (2003) on this point.

23 My research in two villages of Gopikandar and Dumka blocks during 1999–2000 revealed that 27 and 20 per cent of all women and men respectively in the villages had remarried at least once.

24 During my in-depth study in 1999–2000, I found that one to two members of 50 per cent of Santal households in the village in Dumka block migrated seasonally. Income from migration contributed roughly one-fourth of their family budget. None of the Hindu or scheduled caste households migrated from the village.

25 With a cultivated area of about 464,000 hectares in 2,570 villages, and 75 per cent of this under paddy cultivation, it is estimated that about 450,000 workers are required for a period of 30 days to complete transplantation work. Migrant workers make up an estimated 75 per cent, a third or half of them from Dumka. Personal communication from Kumar Rana, 24 November 2003.

26 Field observation revealed that during the peak season almost 120–150 persons were packed into buses that had a capacity of 60 or 70 persons.

27 Mitra (1987) reports wage discrimination and sexual harassment of women, while Ray (1989) focuses on the vulnerability of the migrant child, particularly the girl child. See also Mosse et al. (2002), Breman (1996), Rao and Rana (1997) and Teerink (1995).

28 Menon (1995) notes a similar experience amongst the Saoras of Orissa.

References and Further Readings

Abril, A.R. and B. Rogaly. 2001. 'Migration and Social Relations: An Annotated Bibliography on Temporary Migration for Rural Manual Work', Working paper, CLARA (Changing Labour Relations in Asia), International Institute for Asian Studies, Amsterdam.

Archer, W.G. (1946) 1984. *Tribal Law And Justice*. New Delhi: Concept Publishing Company.

Banerjee, N. 1987. 'Women's Work and Family Strategies: A Case Study from Bankura, West Bengal', unpublished Report, Centre for Women's Development Studies: New Delhi.

Bernstein, H. 1996. 'Agrarian Questions Then and Now', *The Journal of Peasant Studies*, special issue, 24(1&2): 22–59.

Bodding, P.O., L.O. Skresfrud and S. Konow. (1942) 1994. *Traditions and Institutions of the Santals*. New Delhi: Bahumukhi Prakashan.

Breman, J. 1985. *Of Peasants, Migrants and Paupers: Rural Labour Circulation and Capitalist Production In West India*. New Delhi: Oxford University Press.

———. 1996. *Footloose Labour*. Cambridge: Cambridge University Press.

Chant, S. 1992. *Gender and Migration in Developing Countries*. London/New York: Belhaven Press.

da Corta, L. and D. Venkateshwarlu. 1999. 'Unfree Relations and the Feminisation of Agricultural Labour in Andhra Pradesh, 1970–95', in T. J. Byres, K. Kapadia and J. Lerche (eds), *Rural Labour Relations in India*, pp. 71–139. London: Frank Cass.

Fernandes, W. and Thukral, E.G. (eds). 1989. *Development, Displacement and Rehabilitation*. Indian Social Institute: New Delhi.

Fernandes, W. (ed.). 1992. *National Development and Tribal Deprivation*. New Delhi: Indian Social Institute.

Gantzer, J.F. 1936. *Final Report on the Revision Survey and Settlement Operations in the District of Santal Parganas, 1922–35*. Government Printing: Patna, Bihar.

Goody, J. 1976. *Production and Reproduction: A Comparative Study of the Domestic Domain*. Cambridge: Cambridge University Press.

Government of India. 1991. Census of India. Directorate of Census: New Delhi.

de Haan, A. 2000. 'Migrants, Livelihoods, and Rights: The Relevance of Migration in Development Policies'. Social Development Working Paper No. 4. DFID: UK.

de Haan, A. and B. Rogaly (eds). 2002. *Labour Mobility and Rural Society*. London: Frank Cass.

Heyer, J. 1989. 'Landless Agricultural Labourers' Asset Strategies', *IDS Bulletin* 20(2): 33–40.

Jolly, S., E. Bell and L. Narayanaswamy. 2003. *Gender and Migration in Asia: Overview and Annotated Bibliography*. BRIDGE: IDS, Sussex, UK.

Karlekar, M. 1995. 'Gender Dimensions in Labour Migration: An Overview', in L. Schenk-Sandbergen (ed.), *Women and Seasonal Labour Migration*. New Delhi: Sage Publications.

Kelkar, G. and D. Nathan. 1992. *Gender and Tribe*. New Delhi: Kali for Women.

Kothari, U. 2002. 'Migration and Chronic Poverty', Working paper 16, Chronic Poverty Research Centre: University of Manchester.

Lipton, M. 1983. *Labour and Poverty*. Washington D.C.: The World Bank.

McPherson, H. 1909. *Final Report on The Survey and Settlement Operations in the District of Santal Parganas, 1898–1907*. Bengal Secretariat Book Depot: Calcutta.

Menon, G. 1995. 'The Impact of Migration on the Work and Status of Tribal Women in Orissa', in L. Schenk-Sandbergen (ed.), *Women and Seasonal Labour Migration*. New Delhi: Sage Publications.

Mitra, M. 1987. *Women's Work and Household Survival Strategies: A Case Study of Santal Women's Lives and Work*. Centre for Women's Development Studies: New Delhi.

Mosse, D., S. Gupta, M. Mehta, V. Shah and J. Rees. 2002. 'Brokered Livelihoods: Debt, Labour Migration and Development in Tribal Western India', in de Haan, A. and B. Rogaly (eds), *Labour Mobility and Rural Society*, pp. 59–88. London: Frank Cass.

MSSRF/WFP. 2001. *Food Insecurity Atlas of Rural India*. M.S. Swaminathan Research Foundation/World Food Programme, India: Chennai.

Rao, N. and K. Rana. 1997. 'Women's Labour and Migration: The Case of the Santals', *Economic and Political Weekly*, 32(50): 3187–189.

Rao, N. (ed.) 1999. *Owning Their Land: The Life Rights of Santali Women*. New Delhi: Friedrich Ebert Stiftung.

Rao, N. 2002. 'Standing One's Ground: Gender, Land and Livelihoods in the Santal Parganas, Jharkhand, India'. Ph.D. thesis, School of Development Studies: University of East Anglia, UK.

Rao, N. 2003. Study on land rights in the Santal Parganas, conducted as part of the GOI/UNDP/CBPPI (Community Based Pro-Poor Initiatives Programme)/Pradan study on pro-poor policies in Jharkhand, draft, New Delhi.

Ray, L. 1989. *The History of Hunger*. Centre for Women's Development Studies: New Delhi.

Rogaly, B. 1996. 'Agricultural Growth and the Structure of Casual Labour-Hiring In Rural West Bengal', *The Journal of Peasant Studies*, 23(4): 141–73.

Rogaly, B. 1999. 'Dangerous Liaisons? Seasonal Labour Migration and Agrarian Change in West Bengal', in Rogaly, B., B. Harriss-White and S. Bose (eds), *Sonar Bangla? Agricultural Growth and Agrarian Change in West Bengal and Bangladesh*. New Delhi: Sage Publications.

Rogaly, B. and D. Coppard. 2003. 'They Used to Go to Eat, Now They Go to Earn: The Changing Meanings of Seasonal Migration from Purulia District in West Bengal, India', *Journal of Agrarian Change* 3(3): 395–433.

Roy Chaudhary, P.C. 1965. *Santal Parganas District Gazetteer*. Secretariat Press: Patna, Bihar.

Sarin, M. 1997. 'Gender and Equity Concerns in Joint Forest Management', in Rao, N. and L. Rurup (eds), *A Just Right: Women's Ownership of Natural Resources and Livelihood Security*. New Delhi: Friedrich Ebert Stiftung, 267–336.

Schenk-Sandbergen, L. (eds). 1995. *Women and Seasonal Labour Migration*. New Delhi: Sage Publications.

Sjoblom, D. 1999. 'Land Matters: Social Relations and Livelihoods in a Bhil Community in Rajasthan, India'. Ph.D. thesis, School of Development Studies: University of East Anglia, UK.

Standing, G. 1985. *Labour Circulation and the Labour Process*. London: Croom Helm.

Teerink, R. 1995. 'Migration And Its Impact on *Khandeshi* Women in the Sugarcane Market', in Schenk-Sandbergen, L. (ed.), *Women And Seasonal Labour Migration*. New Delhi: Sage Publications.

Thadani, V.M. and M.P. Todaro. 1984. 'Female Migration in Developing Countries: A Conceptual Framework', in Fawcett, J.F. et al. (eds), *Women in the Cities of Asia: Migration and Urban Adaptation*. Westview Press: Boulder, USA.

Todaro, M.P. 1969. 'A Model of Labour Migration and Urban Unemployment in Less Developed Countries', *The American Economic Review*, 59: 138–48.

Wood, C. 1981. 'Structural Change and Household Strategies: A Conceptual Framework for the Study of Rural Migration', *Human Organisation*, 40(4): 338–44.

7

ADIVASIS, GENDER AND MIGRATIONS: RE-SITUATING WOMEN OF JHARKHAND

Shashank Shekhar Sinha

Gender studies have long been employed for the study of caste and class societies. This paper attempts to locate and contextualise the changing contours of gender relationships and identities in largely the 20th century tribal Chotanagpur. The crux of the problem lies in the fact that the region has simultaneously been the heartland of a large Adivasi population, and India's mineral base, known as the 'Ruhr of India'. This rich resource base has broadly encouraged two types of migrations. First, the colonial land and forest legislations together with the subsequent development of mines, industries, dams and multipurpose projects brought large migrant (non-tribal, or *diku*) populations to this region, including various caste and religious groups. Second, the dispossessed Adivasis were migrating to new industrial and plantation opportunities opening up either in Bihar itself, or in Bengal and Assam. In either case, the interaction between Adivasi cultures and the new patterns of livelihood produced unprecedented contradictions in the tribal social fabric. While the Adivasis were generally affected in the process, the consequences were particularly deleterious for the women. While dovetailing the experiences of women migrating outside their villages or Chotanagpur, this paper also discusses the social ramifications of in-migration into the region.

Out-migrations from the region had started very early during the colonial period. Cuthbert points to regular seasonal migration during the winters of the *dhangars* (hill coolies) of Chotanagpur, with some of their family members, to the Bengal districts as early as 1827. They were employed in indigo factories and conservancy work in Calcutta. Some of them also worked as agricultural labourers and were hired for winter harvesting of paddy (Cuthbert 1846: 413). What characterised the emigration in the late 19th and early 20th centuries (more precisely 1880–1920) was not only a massive increase in the volume of migration but also a shift in the destinations. Emigrations were now directed more towards the tea plantations of Assam and the Dooars in north Bengal (but also sometimes to the sites of early industries and mines coming up in Bengal and its neighbouring areas), and after 1900, with the opening of mines at Jharia and Hazaribagh, to the coalfields (Mohapatra 1985: 252). While migrations to Assam were more of a permanent nature, those to Bengal plantations and industries, thanks to relative proximity to their native lands, generally, though not exclusively, happened to be temporary affairs.

The post-colonial migrations, on the other hand, had both an intra- and inter-state dimension, and some distinctive features as well: first, they were relatively temporary or seasonal in character; second, the route followed by them was mainly of two types—from rural areas to urban/industrial areas to cater to the huge demands of unskilled labour (migrants had more of a male component) or, at times, also inter-state to cater to the demands of the ever-expanding construction industry (a substantial female component); and third, when men migrated to urban areas, they maintained contact with their agricultural villages, generally leaving their women and children behind to look after the agricultural operations while they would themselves visit their fields at the time of sowing and harvesting. This type of migration has a significant internal dimension which has generally been overlooked by scholars working on gender. One of the significant consequences of these rural-urban migrations was the removal of a large section of the male labour force from the primary sector, and therefore greater dependence on women in maintaining agriculture. Women were left alone to deal with exploitative elements like moneylenders, landlords and businessmen. Adivasi women in areas with low female literacy were particularly susceptible to these elements, leading to land alienation, cheating in weighing and pricing, and sexual exploitation. In addition, increased workloads left them with little time to look after their households and their own health.

Out-migrations: Beyond Meta-narratives

Meta-narratives citing a single decisive reason for migration have now become increasingly untenable. Migrations are seen as emanating from many factors and the emerging scholarship on the subject argues for the need to move even beyond pure economic determinism. The colonial land, forest and judicial legislations, while impoverishing the Adivasis as a whole, laid down 'legally' defined institutional parameters leading to the diminution of women's economic role in the 'traditional' division of labour (Sinha, forthcoming). The development of capitalism, with the aid of both 'native' and foreign capital, during and after the colonial rule and the consequent marginalisation further added to the 'push' factors. But on many occasions the patriarchal structure of Adivasi households also contributed to the migrations. It is argued that women migrated not only on account of developments in the area of production, but also because their position in the patriarchal family was crumbling; many female migrants were single women, either widows or abandoned by their husbands because they were barren or because their husbands had left in search of livelihood elsewhere (Engels 1999: 228).

The socioeconomic dislocation caused by the colonial-capitalist-patriarchy combine together with the availability of 'remunerative' employment prospects opened up migrations, first seasonally (to temporary opportunities opened up by the expansion of roads and railways), and then of longer, even permanent, nature as the tea gardens were opened up by the British towards the middle of the 19th century, mainly in Assam and Bengal. Successive Census reports from 1891 to 1921 show that family migration was the dominant mode of migration, and the available figures on sex distribution indicate that on an average 45 per cent of the total adult migrants were female (Mohapatra 1985: 259). Single women migrants were settled either on the plantations with relatives if they had any, or as 'family units' with single male migrants. Women's reproductive role meant that such migrants shouldered the double burden of working both inside and outside the household (Engels 1999: 226–28).

The tea planters were keen to employ women and children who were available as cheap labour for the labour intensive task of tea plucking. Between 1890 and 1920, more than half the workers in the Darjeeling and Jalpaiguri tea gardens were Adivasi women; in the Raniganj coalfields in West Bengal, though, their proportion was slightly lesser (ibid.: 225). Life in the tea gardens was extremely harsh and demanding. The plantation estates were located in the vicinity of jungles that were unhealthy and disease-prone, and the labour regimes governed by the infamous Workman's Breach of Contract Act. There were cases of mistreatment and abduction of married women (Guha 1977: 16–18). Women's recruitment to the tea plantations was doubly negative; not only were they subjected to exploitative contract regimes in common with male workers, but also suffered sexual abuse at the hands of managers, supervisors and fellow male workers (Sen 2003).

Towards the end of the 19th century, migrant Adivasis were also recruited in the industries coming up in Bengal and in coal mines in Raniganj, Jharia and Dhanbad. The Burdwan District Gazetteer points to the prevalence of a large number of Mundas, Santhals, Oraon, Kols and Bauris among the labourers migrating from the neighbouring districts of Bankura, Manbhum and Santhal Parganas to cater to the demands of labour in the mines and factories of Asansol and Raniganj (Peterson 1910: 134–35). In the early 1920s more than 15,000 women worked in the mines. Over 9,000 of them carried coal in the pits and together they accounted for 34.5 per cent of the underground workforce (Engels 1999: 231). The common parlance of the mines was imbued with gender—women coolies were called *rezas*, and in their capacity as loaders attached to male hewers (coal cutters) were known as *kamins*—a term signifying the performance of service (Simeon 1988: 23). Buchanan was struck by the 'somewhat strange relic of the old days whereby the loading of iron was from the baskets on women's heads rather than by steam shovels'. But the American mine manager explained the situation, saying 'rice to feed women costs less than coal to feed the steam shovel' (Corbridge 1982: 48).

The living conditions for workers in the mines and factories and mills were particularly bad. Added to the squalor, poverty, poor diet, malnutrition and waterborne diseases were the problems of drunkenness. To cope up with their miserable conditions, Santhal women increasingly started taking jobs loading coal onto trucks while others allegedly started living as concubines to non-tribal workers. The latter could be particularly associated with the Bauris (Banerjee 1978: 187–91). Dagmar Curzel wrote that 'respectable Bengal women do not undertake industrial work and practically all such Bengalis found in the mills are degraded women or prostitutes'. She informs that in the mill areas none of the women lived in regular families but under the protection of men they were not married to (Curzel 1923: 12). Similar revelations are brought out in evidences presented to the Royal Commission of Labour in 1930: 'There is practically open prostitution near the workers' homes and most of the workers do not bring their womenfolk—no privacy is possible under present conditions of housing.

Among female workers, one out of four admits to being a prostitute'
(Royal Commission on Labour 1932: 5E 55). The ban on women's
work in the underground mines in the 1920s however created bigger
problems of survival, and many women started taking up work loading
coal onto trucks. The tea industry also underwent a recession in the
Depression years of the 1930s while the lac industry also slowed down
because of a decline in European demand during the two World Wars.
Women labourers however continued to be employed, though in drastically reduced numbers, in the mines[1] (surface work, particularly
mineral extraction), but more comprehensively as unskilled labourers
in the growing construction industry within and outside Bihar.

Work conditions did not improve much for women in the post-
colonial period. Studies conducted at some of the industrial regions
in Chotanagpur in the 1960s reveal disturbing trends. Many Adivasi
labourers had migrated to Noamundi (64 kilometres from Chaibasa in
the district of Singbhum) in search of wage work. Besides problems of
low wages and bad working conditions, there were reports of secret
trafficking in the flesh trade in which many tribal girls were being sold
in other states. Many labourers, both men and women, working in the
mines were also found to be suffering from venereal diseases. They
would not go to hospitals for the fear of this becoming publicly known
and also losing their jobs (Prasad and Sahay 1961). The evidence of
prostitution at Noamundi and its surrounding areas of Jhinkpani and
Gua is corroborated by other similar examples. At Jamshedpur, the
Research Programme Committee Survey (Government of India)
underlined a heavy disparity in the sex ratio consequent to a huge
influx of single male labourers into the city—only 84.4 females for
every 100 males. Rapid industrialisation had not only upset the sex
ratio of the city but the Singbhum district as a whole. In 1911, there
were 1,035 females to 1,000 males, as against 968 women to every 1,000
males in 1951. The simultaneous presence of a large number of unattached poor women labourers and single male workers having greater
disposable incomes to 'seek pleasures' was not found to be 'helpful for
the maintenance of a certain moral standard' (Roy Chaudhury 1958:
319–20). The big industries attracted mostly unattached males.
Mohapatra also informs us that, according to the post 1891 Census
figures, the migrations to Manbhum coalfields had a predominantly male
component (Mohapatra 1985: 252). Similarly, prostitution among the
Bauris in the Bokaro industrial region was occasioned by the presence
of the British Army during World War II, but more specifically by the

development of the Chas and Bokaro iron and steel factories (Sengupta 1982: 84). The migrants did not bring their wives along because it involved expenditure and housing difficulties.[2] There was a fundamental economic dimension in such sexual liaisons. The workers were decently paid and hence could afford this 'luxury', while the uprooted, displaced and poverty-stricken women found in the profession an alternative source of income.

In the post-industrialisation period at Hatia,[3] impact studies reveal a functional change in the structure of family, which had begun to shed many of its functions: educational, religious, recreational and protective. Along with individualisation of the family, the traditional occupations and division of labour were also getting affected. Women were increasingly withdrawing from agriculture and the fields and working independently in industrial units (Vidyarthi 1968). In many cases, like in the Chaibasa–Jhikpani industrial region (Das Gupta 1978: 300),[4] however, in maintaining the agro-industrial economy, even the nuclear Ho family was breaking into two households; the husband, an industrial worker, living in the town with school-going sons, and the wife, with minor and unmarried daughters, staying back in the villages to take care of the fields. On many occasions, the husband had taken a second wife to manage his household in the township while his first wife struggled with the pressures of agricultural economy in the countryside. In protecting the dual interests in agriculture as well as in the factory job, polygamy was an adoptive measure within the limits of social sanction (ibid.).

A study on migrant women labourers conducted under the auspices of the Bihar Tribal Welfare Research Institute, Ranchi makes for useful reading in this context. The study was based on a survey in the districts of Palamau, Giridih, Ranchi and Dhanbad in the pre-1980–81 years. While most women migrated to nearby districts within the same state or to neighbouring states like West Bengal, Uttar Pradesh and Madhya Pradesh, some women from Ranchi migrated to areas as far as Assam, Gujarat, Punjab, Haryana, Tripura, Rajasthan, Orissa, Karnataka and Punjab. The study divulges that women's stay at the construction sites was nightmarish. Absence of proper accommodation and sanitary facilities, discriminatory work allotment, lengthy and strenuous work hours, restrictions on mobility (for the fear that they might join another contractor) only added to improper treatment. Many of them confessed that, at nights, either the contractors, work supervisors, the *munsifs* (people who make payments) or their male counterparts would sneak inside their tents and on many occasions they had to be 'obliged'. These women could not and did not protest for the fear of losing their jobs. Further, they alone had to bear the trauma for they could not share such incidents with their men. Equally demeaning was the underpayment or irregularity in the payment of wages. Most women labourers were recruited at the rate of six to seven per day but ended up getting something between three to seven rupees. Many returned home without receiving their full pay. This kind of exploitation continues even after the enactment of the Inter-State Migrant (Regulation of Employment and Conditions of Service) Act, 1979 which calls for better service conditions, accommodation and wage structure for migrants (Ray 1982).

Though these studies are confined only to some industrial areas of Chotanagpur, it can be safely stated that similar trends were observable elsewhere. Adivasi women were exposed most ruthlessly to the operation of the market and other commercial forces, and to unscrupulous elements that flocked into the tribal areas in the wave of exploitation of mines and establishment of industries (Singh 1988: 8). Breakdown of the joint family, disintegration in the nuclear family, increasing cases of prostitution and industry-induced disparity in the sex ratio became increasingly common in many urban industrial centres.

In-migrations: Emergent Contradictions and Structures of Oppression

The social composition of the tribal heartland had started changing much before the establishment of colonial rule. A crucial precondition for the formation of state in the region was the reclamation of land and introduction of agricultural technology by the peasantry from the plains. Some peasant castes were therefore encouraged by the Mughals and the *zamindars* to colonise and establish *bhums* (settlements) in Chotanagpur. In the process, many non-tribal peasants like the Kurmis, Kunbis and Keoris started settling in the region. State formation in Chotanagpur took place either within the tribal matrix, as in the case of Gonds or Cheros, or as a result of imposition of the authority of Rajputs and other castes, which established power in the highlands of Orissa, central India, Gujarat and Rajasthan. In either case, it stimulated commercial activities and development of trade routes encouraged small-scale urbanism. Very soon various castes including Brahmans (tempted by the generous grants of land) and artisan communities also started inhabiting these regions (Singh 1987: 1225).

The changing demographic configuration of the tribal heartland received a boost during the colonial period, when on account of introduction of new agrarian, industrial and capitalist relations a huge number of non-tribals started immigrating into the region. In 1872 the total resident population of Chotanagpur accounted for only 14 per cent of Bihar's population; by 1951, the average density of population of the region had become half of Bihar as a whole (Corbridge 1988: 19). The post-colonial emphasis on 'development' of the region through setting up of industries, mines and other capitalist enterprises was accompanied by the displacement of huge chunks of the native population.

Thus while a large number of people were immigrating into the region in search of livelihoods, the displaced natives were out-migrating to adjacent states. The incidence of in-migration could be borne out by the fact that in 1961, 8 per cent of Bihar's population had been born in India, but outside the state (for district-wise details see Table 7.2). The Adivasis of Chotanagpur were excluded from prime jobs in mining and manufacturing. Whereas the Anglo-Europeans, Madrasis, Punjabis and others cornered the managerial ranks of industrial enterprises, the face-workers and drillers in the mines were often recruited on contract from among the caste Hindu population of north Bihar, and Gorakhpur in Uttar Pradesh (Corbridge 1999: 134). Speaking on accommodation of the tribals in the industrialisation process, Alam says:

> They gained entry into the working class as lowly paid unskilled workers on a hire and fire basis. Every technologically sophisticated country has a core of highly skilled workers. In the case of Jharkhand, this core was drawn from other regions. The local inhabitants, both tribals and non-tribals, have been relegated to a very special section of the proletariat: *khalasi*s (assistants to drivers), peons and scavengers (Alam 1989: 158).

Simeon echoes similar sentiments:

> The gigantic industrialisation process in Chotanagpur has operated in a vicious circle for the Adivasis—on the one hand, it has rendered ever increasing numbers of them destitute through evictions, destruction of their sources of livelihood, etc. On the other hand, it has

Table 7.1 Trend of In-migration (1881–1951): Percentage Share of Total Immigrants from Different Regions

Year	Total no. of in-migrants	Proportion to total population	North Bihar	Adjacent provinces	Other provinces	Outside India and Europe
1881	143,759	4.56	65.02	28.7	6.15	0.10
1891	132,358	3.33	60	32.1	7.60	0.26
1901	133,441	2.72	53.2	42.9	03.6	0.36
1911	191,279	3.41	45.6	51.4	2.6	0.41
1921	235,286	4.16	44.4	48.4	7.07	0.97
1931	235,286	4.96	35.6	54.9	7.9	1.5
1951	506,757	5.93	37.7	39.05	10.56	12.7

Source: Compiled from place of birth data, censuses of Bengal, Bihar and Orissa, 1901–51 (Bandyopadhyay 1999).

Table 7.2 Population Born in India but Outside the State of Bihar by Districts in Absolute Numbers and in Percentage of Total Population (1961) for Chotanagpur

District	Total population	Born outside state	% of total
Ranchi	2,138,565	195,332	9
Hazaribag	2,396,411	182,299	8
Palamau	1,187,789	54,476	5
Dhanbad	1,158,610	264,176	19
Singhbhum	2,049,911	406,185	22
Santhal Parganas	2,675,203	149,786	6

Source: Ivern 1969.

utilised their destitute condition to employ them for a very specific role in this industrialisation. And that is the role of sweat labour, or sub-proletariat (Simeon 1982: 230).

In due course of time, the Adivasis began to be evicted from even unskilled jobs. According to the 1921 Census, tribals accounted for only 10 per cent in the total number of unskilled labourers in the coal mines of Hazaribag and Manbhum districts (Bandyopadhyay 1999: 39–40). Madhumita Bandyopadhyay[5] (see Table 7.1) gives an idea of the trends and source regions of immigration in Chotanagpur between 1881–1951.

The regions important from the point of view of industries and mines were generally the largest recipients of in-migrating population and thus experienced a massive increase in Hindu population. The in-migration certainly did not provide the first exposure of the Adivasis to caste societies for, since very old times, the former had been living in a symbiotic relationship with various artisan and service castes (sadans) settled in the region. Though the sadans were often of the same castes as found in the adjoining plains, yet there was little contact, as also little in common, between them and their counterparts living in the neighbouring areas. The sadans had also participated alongside the tribes of the region in many earlier revolts and shared some kind of a common worldview and a composite culture (Nathan and Kelkar 1991: 21–24).

The settlement of in-migrating Hindus and Christians[6] in the Adivasi heartland led to intermingling and interaction between different cultures. The immigrants brought along with them new social systems, beliefs, customs and value systems. The interactions between the 'old' Adivasi traditions and 'new' social systems not only exposed the latent contradictions in the tribal societies but also created new structures of oppression and control. The impact of Hinduism has been studied through concepts like 'Hinduisation', 'Sanskritisation' (Srinivas 1966: 5–7),[7] 'Tribe-Caste Continuum', 'Revitalisation' and 'Bhagat Movements'.[8]

A major factor, however, behind the socioeconomic dislocation in the tribal heartland was also the introduction of monetary and market relations in the wake of the development of a colonial-capitalist set-up. Inter-tribal haats traditionally had not only been places for economic transactions but, as Archer says 'the visit (to market) is important less for what the family buys than for whom it meets. Relatives mix at a market, weddings are often arranged, brides and grooms are subjected to scrutiny and occasionally boys secure new girls. The market is a (Santhal) 'Club' and its very essence is the opportunity it provides for intermingling' (Archer 1974: 137–38). With the entry of new forces and the creation of demand for new commodities triggered by the presence of outsiders, the traditional adivasi haats started disintegrating or getting transformed into places of formal economic exchanges and activities. With the consequent erosion of elements of reciprocity, redistribution and cooperation (and greater exposure to caste societies), the Adivasis were heading towards the peasant/caste-stratified system. Markets were thus strengthening the role of Sanskritisation

(Hasnain 2001: 317). The consequences included repression of an important social space for women. Among the tribes trying to sanskritise themselves, women thus started withdrawing from the markets as a place for social interaction. As a part of control over women's sexuality, orthodox Hinduism prescribes restricted presence of women in places of public gathering. This was true of the Kherwars. The Kherwars had long been under the influence of Hinduism. Writing in the late 19th century, Hunter observed that the Kherwars (and Cheros) were using Hindu forms of oath, employing Brahmanas as spiritual guides and domestic priests in marriages and spending lavishly on occasions like marriages (Hunter 1976: 315–17).

In fact, long and continuous contact with caste societies led to many other changes in tribal social structure. Among the Kherwars, the free mixing of youth of both sexes was coming to an end and parents were arranging marriages without any consideration for the consent of the girls. Girls were also being married much before they reached puberty. Pre-puberty marriages were becoming common among the Santhals and Kurmis of Dhanbad region as well. The Dhanbad District Gazetteer (Roy Chaudhury 1964: 125) reports:

> The Santhals and Kurmis generally got their daughters married after the girls had attained puberty but in the recent times, they have begun to marry their girls young probably under the idea that this is more honourable, being followed by a large number of Hindu castes ...

Widespread prevalence of pre-puberty marriages in the region is borne out by other evidence as well. Among the Manki-cum-Munda clan in Singhbhum district, the tendency was to lower the age of marriage for girls in imitation of their Hindu neighbours (Roy Chaudhury 1958: 247). In the case of Oraons, D.H.E. Sunder had similarly observed that following the example of caste Hindus, tribal girls were also being married between the ages of seven to nine years (Sunder 1898). Risley also gestures to the prevalence of child marriage among the Oraons (1981, Vol. II: 147):

> When Colonel Dalton published his account 16 years ago, infant marriage is said to have been entirely unknown among the tribe. A few of the wealthier men, who affect to Hindu customs have now taken to this practice and marry their daughters before they have attained puberty.

The influence of Hinduism was perceptible in the transformation of many long-standing traditions. The earlier prevalence of different forms of marriage: marriage by exchange, capture, purchase, service, probation and by trial shows that tribal girls and boys had enjoyed a considerable say in the choice of their life partners (Chauhan 1990: 25). But writing in the first decade of the 20th century, S.C. Roy (1995: 275) observed:

> ... in earlier times, it is said, Munda young folk of both sexes had a freer hand than now in the choice of their partners in life from amongst members of marriageable *kilis* or septs. But, in modern days, the selection is ordinarily made for the boy as well as for the girl by the father or other guardian ... the ultimate selection, however, rests not in human hands, but on certain omens.

Widespread use of rituals and ceremonies had also started making inroads into tribal societies; traditional marriage ceremonies were increasingly being blended with Hindu rituals. A research study in the 1950s found the prevalence of two forms of marriage in some Munda villages in Ranchi district; *arandi* and *diku arandi*. The first marriage was held in the traditional form and the second was borrowed from the Hindus. In the *diku* form, a Brahmin was called in to officiate at the marriage (Sachchidananda 1960: 54).[9] The marriage ceremonies were not only becoming ritualised but also very expensive. The expenses incurred on such marriages fell on the family of the bride, which, together with dowry, was a heavy burden for the girl's father and family. Emergence of dowry among the tribes reflects how caste identities were fast changing the position of women. In fact it was observed that dowry was an important factor in raising the marriageable age of girls among the Kharias and Mundas (Ivern 1969: 17). The Jharkhand Mukti Morcha in the early 1970s thus launched a sustained campaign to limit the marriage ceremony expenses to 12 rupees. The Morcha also proposed group marriages and cutting down of the marriage celebrations (which normally lasted over several days) to one day (Tirkey 2002: 100).

Dowry was in fact replacing the traditional bride price. According to the Hindu religious texts, bride price was regarded as an '*asuric* custom' (demonic custom) (Talwar 1978: 10). Bride price was also giving way to dowry among agricultural tribes like the Oraons and Kherwars, especially in the case of boys having jobs in government and industry (Nathan and Kelkar 1991: 148). Wherever bride price survived, as among the Hos, the once 'customary payments' were swelling up massively under the impact of a monetary economy, resulting in late marriages (Majumdar 1950: 42–43). Another perceptible reflection of changing gender identities among the Adivasis could also be seen in the increasing desire for male offspring. Unlike Hindu society, the birth of a daughter was seldom regarded as a curse in tribal societies, but under the impact of 'outside' patriarchal influences, the preference for sons started gaining ground. Consider this Santhal prayer noted by Hunter: the birth of the daughter is placed in the same league as many grave problems haunting the Santhals (1965: 100).

> May the storm snare my thatch,
> May the black not pass by my rice fields,
> Let my wife not bear a daughter,
> May the usurer be eaten by wild beasts.

The preference for a son could however also be attributed to the fact that under the traditional systems of inheritance, only sons were entitled to inherit land. With the disintegration of the communal mode of land-holdings under colonial rule and the subsequent emphasis on defined proprietary rights, the yearning for sons started gaining new ground. Increasing discrimination between boys and girls was however easily discernible in the sector of education. Female literacy, which had made an early start under the Christian missionaries, could not keep pace with the changing times. According to the 1961 Census, literacy rates in Chotanagpur (17.8 per cent) were much lower than in the state of Bihar (18.4 per cent) and the India average (23.7 per cent) (Singh 1990: 661). But while keeping their women secluded from 'external exposure', the Adivasi patriarchies were, in the past, conveniently borrowing elements from outside their culture to keep the former 'in place'. Under the influence of caste neighbours, uninhibited dressing of women was paving way for covered clothing for women. This is attested by the Singhbhum District Gazetteer (Roy Chaudhury 1958: 244–45).

> For women, the upper garment is considered essential particularly in the presence of dikhus or foreigners. The handloom lehanga has largely given way to mill made sari. One end of the sari covers the breasts. Formerly the lower end of the sari did not hang far below the knees but today it often stretches to meet the ankles in imitation of the Hindu neighbours. The Hinduised Bhumij women have gone a little further having adopted the custom of covering the head with a veil.

Like caste, religious forces also contributed to the disintegration or, in some cases, the decline in institutions of women's sexual and cultural autonomy. The institution of youth dormitories (*dhumkuria* as it was called among the Oraons, or *giti ora* among the Mundas) and community dances earlier formed an important part of the tribal cultural milieu. Roy points out (1995: 241–42).

> All unmarried girls of a village or a hamlet sleep together in the night in a house. … When young bachelors and maidens are assembled in their respective *giti oras* after their evening meals, riddles (*nutum kahani*) are propounded and solved, folk tales (*kaji kahani*) and traditions and fables are narrated and memorised and songs sung and learnt until bedtime.

There were also numerous instances of sexual liaisons between the inmates of youth dormitories. Dalton points to this saying that 'it is well known that they (girls) often find their way to the bachelors hall and, in some villages, actually sleep there' (Risley 1981, Vol. I: 140). Under the onslaught of organised religion, however, the youth dormitories and *akhra* (dancing grounds) started disappearing. Roy (1995: 353–54) talks about the disappearance of the *dhumkuria* as early as 1910–15.

> Thanks chiefly to the refining influences of education, Christianity and Hinduism, [the youth dormitory and the accompanying sexual liberty] is now on the wane. But in villages where the people have not been Hinduised or nor has the voice of the Christian missionary been heard, traces of premarital communism may still be met with. It no longer exists, however, as a regular thing nor indeed as what has been called 'group communism'.

The opposition to the existence of youth dormitories is not difficult to locate. Looked upon as 'place(s) promoting corruption among Christian boys and girls', they were declared illegal by the village councils and heavy fines were imposed on the offenders (Sahay 1976: 482). For Hinduism, disapproval of the dormitory was a part of larger attempt to discourage premarital sexual relations (Gupta 1976: 96).[10]

Like *dhumkuria*, traditional dances were physical manifestations of women's sociocultural space, a place of extended social interaction where there was an uninhibited and socially sanctified intermingling of the sexes. The dancing grounds were also known for a greater presence of women; a place where they participated as equals in an otherwise asymmetric social order and where many of the established (exploitative) social norms would be symbolically and ritually inverted or subverted through the idiom of songs, dances and recitations of folklore. But dancing girls were looked upon with disfavour in orthodox Hinduism. In ancient India, music and dance were held in high esteem and many Hindu girls from well-to-do families were taught the art of singing and dancing. From the medieval time onwards however, music and dancing started being looked upon as quite unfit for 'respectable' girls and were increasingly associated with only low caste women or prostitutes (Basham 1992: 180). The Lutheran and Anglican churches abolished community dances on the grounds that they encouraged moral degradation leading to illicit sexual relations, while other Catholic missions allowed them under strict supervision and restrictions (Sachchidananda 1979: 321–22). It is interesting to see how religion can have mutually contradictory impacts; on the one hand, Christian missionaries were the earliest proponents of female education, on the other, they circumvented the very institutions that formed the basis of tribal women's cultural autonomy. At a parallel, and at a more implicit, level, what such instances of cultural repression also go on to show is that how religion, like caste, can be used as a strategic instrument of social control and domination.

Changing situations of social existence have also had manifestations in women's access to property and resources. An observable indication is the decline in the position of divorced women and widows whose presence on many occasions is considered 'inauspicious'.[11] As outside values infiltrate the relatively closely-knit tribal societies, traditional social safeguards against widows and single women tend to break down, rendering them even more vulnerable. In addition, the breakdown in Adivasi land systems under the impact of colonialism and capitalism has also led to a destruction of women's limited land rights.[12] From life interest in land to right to maintenance and from that to living at the mercy of male relatives has been the route traversed by these women. The destruction of all residual rights of women is the point where a full-fledged patriarchy is established, one that goes along with the establishment of full-fledged forms of private property. Some tribals like the Kherwars of Palamau have actually travelled this route to the point of complete destruction of women's residual rights; a situation not very different from the mainstream caste society (Nathan and

Kelkar 1991: 103). Desire to possess women's land can at times take heinous forms like witch-hunts. Taking into account the fact that under the traditional systems of land inheritance, land accrues to the male agnates of the deceased, incidents of women being labelled as witches and hounded out, occasionally even being killed, are not without motive. Over the years there has been a marked increase in cases of 'witch-hunting', which has become popular as an extra-legal method to deprive women of control over land and resources.

Conclusion

The introduction of new agrarian and land relations under colonial rule and the concurrent and subsequent development of mines and industries gave a new spurt to migration both in and out of Chotanagpur. The emerging economic and demographic configurations while disrupting customary lifestyles and livelihood patterns created serious problems of survival for the native population. As Adivasi patriarchies negotiated with the forces and agents unleashed by the growth of colonialism and capitalism, tribal collectivism and traditional social safeguards were fast giving way to individual gains and competition. Women were either pushed to the margins of the resultant political economies or were accommodated, albeit in limited capacities, at the lowest levels. The introduction of alien capitalist relations and unequal wage regimes in the tribal heartland led to a substantial restructuring of the traditional division of labour, and relocation in women's economic roles from self-supporting agricultural workers to migrant wage-workers and casual labourers. On the other hand, prolonged and sustained interface with the immigrating caste and religious groups went a long way in re-arranging social and gender relations in Adivasi societies, with disastrous consequences for the women.

Notes

1   During the Second World War, labour shortages caused the government to lift the ban in 1943 leading to the employment of some 19,000 women in the coal pits in 1944. In 1946 the ban was reimposed.
2   The reason for a huge percentage of unmarried Adivasi rejas could also be explained by the high incidence of bride price among the Hos of Singbhum.

3 The study was conducted after the installation of the Heavy Engineering Corporation (HEC).

4 The cement plant at Jhikpani was built during the Second World War and started production from 1947. The factory with its ancillary township was located in a rural setting surrounded by tribal villages. The bulk of the labour force for the factory came from the Ho tribes who were either unskilled or had no prior experience of wage work. The study revealed that most of the tribals occupied some amount of land in the surrounding villages.

5 Bandyopadhyay's study focuses only on the Chotanagpur administrative divisions and does not include the Santhal Parganas.

6 Many Christian Missions were functional in Chotanagpur, like the Lutheran Church, the Roman Catholic Mission, the Scottish Mission, the Dublin University Mission, The Methodist Church of South Asia, The United Church of North India, The American Baptist Bengal-Orissa Mission, the Seventh Day Adventists, etc. The various Christian missions were working hand in glove with the government for the spread of Christianity and the simultaneous dissemination of the colonial ideology. The initial conversions aimed at individuals and families proved to be an uphill task for the missionaries and the subsequent shift in emphasis to humanitarian services did find a fertile ground for propagation of the ideology among the poverty stricken tribals.

7 M.N. Srinivas described 'Sanskritisation' as a process by which a 'low' Hindu caste or tribal or other group changes its customs, ritual, ideology and way of life in the direction of a high and frequently 'twice born' caste. Among the tribes, Sanskritisation results in the tribe claiming to be a caste, and therefore Hindu. In the traditional system, the only way to become a Hindu was to belong to a caste, and the unit of mobility was usually a group, not an individual or a family.

8 Though Sanskritisation and within that the Kshatriyaisation continues to form the dominant mode of analysis, scholars have proposed other models as well. N.K. Bose talks about the 'Hindu Model of Tribal Absorption'. An interesting analysis however is provided by Martin Orans who explains the phenomenon of emulation in terms of the 'Rank Concession Syndrome'. Adivasis coming in contact with caste societies not only learnt the art of cultivation but also adopted Hindu customs, traditions, beliefs, gods and goddesses, festivals and rituals, and new taboos. D.D. Kosambi has talked about the Brahmanical influence to caste societies. According to him plough agriculture was an essential contribution of the Hindu agrarian society.

9 Sachchidananda's paper forms a part of the larger research project sponsored by the Planning Commission. Similarly among the Christian Oraons, the girls' parents had to wait for the approach of the boys' parents. Some girls therefore remained unmarried even in their late 20s. Further, even though actual marriages were performed in the Church, negotiations between the prospective in-laws were completely in accordance with the traditional system of Oraon marriage. Also, certain omens continued to be observed while the negotiation process was on. Christianity in fact upheld many of the traditions for it condemned marriages within the same clan.

10 The concept of virginity enjoined upon the girls an absolute prohibition of sexual relations before marriage, and a girl deviating from the rule exposed herself to social contempt leading to a loss of chance of marrying.

11 Earlier their position was slightly better; they could be married again for they could be married within the tribes, though again in the context of some patriarchal traditions, for example among the Santhals, it was believed that since the deceased husband

continued to retain hold over his wife and could wreck vengeance, so the would-be groom was first married to a *mahua* tree and then with the widowed woman.

12 Under customary Adivasi laws, the only females entitled to land rights are widows and single women, and they enjoy two kinds of land rights: first, a life interest in land, a right to manage the land and its produce, and second, the right to a share of the produce of the land (but not to manage or use the land as per one's own discretion). The second right, to a share of the produce, is again of two types: the first is a maintenance (*khorposh*) and the second is to a share of the produce which may be a little over and above such maintenance needs, generally a small portion of any crop. In cases of families having only daughters, sons-in-law could inherit their parental property only if they agreed to settle in their wife's paternal village.

References and Further Readings

Alam, Javed. 1989. 'The Category of "non-historic nations" and Tribal Identity in Jharkhand', in P.C. Chatterjee (ed.), *Self Images, Identity and Nationality*. Indian Institute of Advanced Studies: Shimla.

Archer, W.G. 1974. *Hill of Flutes, Life, Love and Poetry in Tribal India; A Portrait of the Santals*. London: Allen and Unwin.

Bandyopadhyay, Madhumita. 1999. 'Demographic Consequences of Non-tribal Incursion in Chotanagpur Region during Colonial Period (1850–1950)', *Social Change*, 29(3&4).

Banerjee, Sukumar. 1978. 'Tribal Women in Coalfield Area', in *Tribal Women in India*. Calcutta: Indian Anthropological Society.

Basham, A.L. 1992. *The Wonder that was India*. Calcutta: Rupa.

Chauhan, Abha. 1990. *Tribal Women and Social Change in India*. New Delhi: AC Brothers.

Corbridge, Stuart. 1982. 'Industrial Development in Tribal India: The Case of Iron Ore Mining Industry in Singhbhum District, 1900–1960', in Nirmal Sengupta (ed.), *Fourth World Dynamics: Jharkhand*. Delhi: Authors Guild Publications.

———. 1988. 'The Ideology of Tribal Economy and Society: Politics in Jharkhand, 1950–1980', *Modern Asian Studies*, 22(1).

———. 1999. 'Ousting Singbonga: The Struggle for India's Jharkhand', in Peter Robb (ed.), *Dalit Movements and the Meanings of Labour in India*. New Delhi: Oxford University Press.

Coupland, H. 1911. *Bengal District Gazetteer: Manbhum*. Calcutta: Bengal Secretariat Book Depot.

Curzel, Dagmar. 1923. 'Women's Medical Service of India: Report of an Enquiry into the Conditions of Employment of Women Before and After Child Birth in Bengal Industries', File No. 2R-20/1923. Government of Bengal: Department of Commerce.

Cuthbert, S.T. 1846. 'Report about the People and Lands of Chotanagpur', *Journal of the Royal Asiatic Society*, VIII.

Das Gupta, Pranab Kumar. 1978. *Impact of Industrialisation on a Tribe in South Bihar*. Calcutta: Anthropological Survey of India.

Engels, Dagmar. 1999. 'The Myth of Family Unit: *Adivasi* Women in Coalmines and Tea Plantations in Early Twentieth Century Bengal', in Peter Robb (ed.), *Dalit Movements and the Meanings of Labour in India*. New Delhi: Oxford University Press.

Guha, A. 1977. *Planter Raj to Swaraj: Freedom Struggle and Electoral Politics in Assam 1826–1947.* New Delhi: People's Publishing House.

Gupta, A.R. 1976. *Women in Hindu Society.* New Delhi: Jyotsna Prakashan.

Hasnain, Nadeem. 2001. *Tribal India, 1991.* New Delhi: Palaka Prakashan.

Hunter, W.W. 1965 (originally published 1883). *The Annals of Rural Bengal.* Calcutta: Indian Studies, Past and Present.

Hunter, W.W. 1976 (originally published 1877). *Statistical Accounts of Bengal,* Vol. XVI, *Districts of Hazaribagh and Lohardagga.* Delhi: Concept Publishing Company.

Imperial Gazetteer of India: Provincial Series Bengal, Vol. I. 1984 (originally published 1909). New Delhi: Usha Publications.

Ivern, Father. 1969. *The Chotanagpur Survey: A Study of Socio-Economic and Health Development.* New Delhi: Indian Social Institute.

Majumdar, D.N. 1950. *Affairs of a Tribe.* Lucknow: Universal Publishers.

Mohapatra, Prabhu Prasad. 1985. 'Coolies and Colliers: A Study of the Agrarian Context of Labour Migration from Chotanagpur, 1880–1920', *Studies in History* 1(2).

Nathan, Dev and Govind Kelkar. 1991. *Gender and Tribe: Women, Land and Forests in Jharkhand.* New Delhi: Kali for Women.

Peterson, J.C.K. 1910. *Bengal District Gazetteer: Burdwan.* Calcutta: Bengal Secretariat Book Depot.

Prasad, Narmadeshwar and Arun Sahay. 1961. *Impact of Industrialisation on Bihar Tribes, A Report.* Ranchi: Bihar Tribal Research Institute.

Ray, S.N. 1982. *Migrant Women Workers.* Ranchi: Bihar Tribal Research Institute.

Risley, H.H. 1981 (originally published 1891). *The Tribes and Castes of Bengal: Ethnographic Glossary, Vol. I & II.* Calcutta: Firman Mukhopadhyay.

Roy, S.C. 1995 (originally published 1912). *The Mundas and Their Country.* Calcutta/Ranchi: Catholic Press.

Roy Chaudhury, P.C. 1958. *Bihar District Gazetteer: Singbhum.* Patna: Secretariat Press.

———. 1964. *Gazetteer of India Bihar: Dhanbad.* Patna: Secretariat Press.

Sachchidananda. 1960. 'Cultural Change in Tribal Bihar', *Bulletin of the Bihar Tribal Research Institute,* 2(1).

———. 1979. *The Changing Munda.* New Delhi: Concept Publishing Company.

Sahay, K.N. 1976. *Under the Shadow of the Cross.* Calcutta: Institute of Social Research and Applied Anthropology.

Sen, Samita. 2003. 'Migration and Marriage: Labouring Women in Bengal in late Nineteenth and Early Twentieth Centuries', paper presented at the international conference on 'Gender, Society and Development', Teen Murti Bhawan, New Delhi, 16–18 October (unpublished).

Sengupta, Nirmal. 1982. 'Three Women of Chas', in Nirmal Sengupta (ed.), *Fourth World Dynamics: Jharkhand.* New Delhi: Authors Guild Publications.

Simeon, Dilip. 1982. 'Jharkhand: Community or Proletariat', in Nirmal Sengupta (ed.), *Fourth World Dynamics: Jharkhand.* New Delhi: Authors Guild Publications.

———. 1988. 'Coal and Colonialism: An Exploratory Essay on the History of Indian Coal', *Research-in-Progress Papers, History and Society,* Third Series, XXXIII, New Delhi: Nehru Memorial Museum and Library.

Singh, K.S. 1987. 'Colonial Transformation of Tribal Society in Middle India', *Economic and Political Weekly,* 13(30).

———. 1988. 'Tribal Women: An Anthropological Perspective', in J.P. Singh, N.N. Vyas and R.S. Mann (eds), *Tribal Women in Development.* Jaipur: Rawat Publications.

Singh, R.L. 1990. *India: A Regional Geography*. Varanasi: National Geographical Society of India.

Sinha, Shashank Shekhar. Forthcoming. *Restless Mothers and Turbulent Daughters: Situating Tribes in Gender Studies*. Kolkata: Stree.

Srinivas, M.N. 1966. *Social Change in Modern India*. California: University of California Press.

Sunder, D.H.E. 1898. *Final Report on the Survey and Settlement Operations of the Palamau Government Estate*. Calcutta: na.

Talwar, V.B. 1978. 'Brahmanbad Aur Jharkhandi Sanskriti', *Shalpatra* (Hindi monthly) 5.

Royal Commission on Labour in India 1929–31, The Report of the 1932. Evidence Vol. 5, pt 2, Oral Evidence–Bengal, 3 February 1930, Delhi, 5E 55.

Tirkey, Agapit. 2002. *Jharkhand Movement: A Study of its Dynamics*. New Delhi: All India Indigenous People's Forum.

Vidyarthi, L.P. 1968. *Social Implication of Industrialisation in Tribal Bihar*. Delhi: Planning Commission.

8

JUST SURVIVING OR FINDING SPACE TO THRIVE? THE COMPLEXITY OF INTERNAL MIGRATION OF WOMEN IN BANGLADESH

Janet Seeley, Sheila Ryan, Iqbal Alam Khan and Munshi Israil Hossain[1]

Recent studies on women's migration in Bangladesh show that social factors such as the need to earn a dowry or to escape trying family circumstances are as much a cause of women's migration as economic factors. This paper reviews the existing literature on women's migration in Bangladesh, before describing the case study findings of a study of sixteen villages over eight different ecological zones, and two urban *bustees* (slums), in Bangladesh. These studies suggest that many women have mobile livelihoods out of necessity rather than choice, in order to survive, and that these are people who are not reached by government social protection schemes or NGO development programmes. Some are old women without family to care for them and who become itinerant beggars, others are divorced women refused refuge and support by natal kin and who labour in the houses and fields of others. Others find an opportunity through migration to escape conservative family settings or oppressive relationships. Some do better their lot by migrating alone or in small groups to work as garment workers, food processors and housemaids. Others, often forced by drought, flood or religious/ethnic tensions, move from place to place in family groups working as agricultural labourers or on construction sites. These are people missing from official village lists and from NGO 'baseline surveys of the poor', and whose varied lives and livelihoods do not suit the static programmes of development interventions and thus remain dependent on their own ability to move on and survive. This paper argues that the contribution of these women to the household not only needs to be recognised and documented in official statistics, but that their rights as women and as workers be upheld and protected.

One can see that a quiet revolution has taken place in Bangladesh, one which has resulted in the increased mobility of women and the rural-to-urban migration of women, not as spouses, but as independent migrants' (Siddiqui 2003a: 158). This paper is about some of these women. We ask whether this 'quiet revolution' is giving those women a chance to improve their lives or whether it is only a survival strategy, and if that is so, whether their individual rights enshrined in the Constitution of the People's Republic of Bangladesh are being upheld. We seek the answer to this question by looking at recent studies on migration in Bangladesh, and then focus on case studies of migrant women who have moved either from one rural area to another or from rural to urban areas.[2]

Women's Status in Bangladesh

Eighty per cent of the total population of approximately 130 million people in Bangladesh live in rural areas or in small rural towns (GoB 2001).[3] Seventy per cent of the total rural population is landless (GoB 1997), and 53 per cent of the total population lives below the poverty line (World Bank 1999), with about 20 per cent living in extreme poverty (Siddiqui 2003a). Women make up 49 per cent of the total population with a disproportionate number of them living below the poverty line.

Under the 1972 Constitution, women are guaranteed fundamental rights, and any form of discrimination on the basis of sex is forbidden. For example, Article 19(1) states that 'the State shall endeavour to ensure equality of opportunity to all citizens' and shall 'adopt effective measures to remove social and economic inequality' between men and women and 'to ensure the equitable distribution of wealth among citizens and of opportunities, in order to attain a uniform level of economic development throughout the Republic' (cited in Sultana 2003: 16–17).

Various acts have been passed to protect women's rights: for example, the Muslim Family Law 1961, Child Marriage Restraint Act 1929, Dowry Prohibition Act 1980 (amended 1982), Cruelty to Women (Deterrent Punishment) Act 1983, Family Court Ordinance 1985 and Women and Children Repression Prevention Act 1995. The more recent legislation draws on and supports international treaties and conventions to which Bangladesh is a signatory. The legal framework aims to protect women's rights in marriage by outlawing early marriage, dowry and verbal divorce. Provision is made for the maintenance of women within marriage and for a certain period of time following separation and divorce. But such laws while they exist on paper are meaningless unless they are enforced, and as we will recount below, this legal framework is often disregarded.

While recognising that any summary of women's status in Bangladesh will be liable to gross generalisation and oversimplification, we attempt in the following paragraphs to provide an overview of women's position in Bangladeshi society as a background to the social context of women who migrate.[4]

About 80 per cent of Bangladesh is Muslim, and social and cultural practices are influenced by Islamic law and custom. A patriarchal, patrilineal and patrilocal social system exists in Bangladesh. Men and women's lives are dominated by this system that upholds a rigid division of labour that controls women's mobility, roles, responsibilities and sexuality. The status of a woman comes from her family and while her role includes the maintenance of her family as a social institution and as an economic entity, the decision-making powers and economic control are almost always in the hands of men.

Women's participation in the economic arena in rural Bangladesh has traditionally been confined to home and homestead land due to the practice of *purdah* (Islamic female seclusion, *purdah* literally means veil or curtain). Inside the home a woman is involved in different kinds of work and subsistence activities such as crafts, horticulture, livestock and poultry rearing along with post-harvest activities. Women's behaviour is controlled through the practice of *purdah*. At the core of *purdah* is the notion that family 'honour' *(izzat)* resides in the virtue and modesty of its women; constant surveillance is necessary to ensure that women do nothing to bring 'shame' *(sharam)* on their kin. The seclusion of women from public forms of economic activity or their withdrawal from such activity once a household can afford it, is an important means of signalling social status. However, for many poor households the observation of *purdah* is something they cannot afford because women's income-earning ability outside the home is important for the family's livelihood.

Given the structure of their society, Bangladeshi women are not only supposed to be dependent on men to provide for them materially but also to depend on male protection. Throughout her life it is expected that a woman will be under the protection of a male guardian: a father, a brother, a husband, or a son. A woman without male protection is open to various forms of male harassment as well as disapproval from other women. If they are young then fear for their sexual security and virtue is an additional element in their feeling of general insecurity (UNICEF 2001). It is therefore perceived to be in most women's interest to retain intact their familial networks, but most of all, to retain some form of male guardianship. The need for male guardianship therefore gives them a strong stake in maintaining a co-operative rather than a conflictual relationship within the household (Kabeer 2000).

According to Hamid (1995: 147), 'the life of an average Bangladeshi woman in rural areas (…) provokes anything but envy'. Although at birth a girl has at least an equal chance of survival as a boy, by the time she is four years old the probability of her dying is 0.059 as compared to 0.047 for a boy. A woman is on average married before she is twenty, often to a man at least ten years older (Hamid 1995; ADB 2001). She is likely to have had four pregnancies by the time she is 30 years old. The birth of a son is important for a woman's status and the consolidation of her place in the marital home. This woman will be participating in the labour force in the home, or, particularly if she belongs to a poor family that resides in an urban area, she may be working outside the home and be poorly paid (Kabir 1999). One woman in four is divorced or widowed by the time she is 50 and 'abandoned women are yet another category, constituting the majority of the hard-core poor[5] who enter the labour market for survival' (ADB 2001: 4).

However, there are signs of change, some of which may be attributed to state and NGOs' interventions (Mahmud 2003). Since the mid-1980's various types of rural development programmes have flourished and these offer an array of services for the poor, and mainly for women, although not exclusively so.

While rural development programmes were being and continue to be implemented, the economy has been restructured over the past ten to fifteen years using the structural adjustment programme approach proffered by the IMF and the World Bank. One of the main objectives of these economic reforms was to put in place a stable liberalised macroeconomic environment free from policy-induced biases which would foster a market-led export-oriented growth (Muqtada et al. 2002). The main success story as a result of these reforms has been the readymade garments industry. In the early 1980s this industry's export earnings were US$ 0.65 million; in less than twenty years these earnings had soared to US$ 4,340 million (Karim 2000; Muqtada et al. 2002). There are conflicting figures as to how much this industry contributes to the total export earnings of Bangladesh, but it is thought to be between 70 to 75 per cent (Huq-Hussain 1996a; Karim 2000; Muqtada et al. 2002). The vast majority of the garment factories are located in Dhaka, the capital city, and some in the port city of Chittagong.

Apart from its phenomenal growth in export earnings the industry has also been credited with bringing about changes in some women's lives. The majority of the industry's employees, between 70 to 90 per cent (Karim 2000) are young mostly unmarried women who have usually migrated from the rural areas either specifically to work in the garment industry or because they have migrated with families and/or husbands and then found work (Huq-Hussain 1996a; Quddus and Rashid 2000; Muqtada et al. 2002).

Women in Migration: From Passivity to Visibility?

Women's migration has led to the increased visibility of women, at least in Dhaka and other urban areas like Chittagong. This new and increased visibility of women is often a result of poverty, destitution and the gradual erosion of the familial support system (ADB 2001). This last point requires some explanation because changes in family structure have varying impacts on different women. Some women are compelled to stay at home to carry out domestic work. For others the breakdown of joint families means that they have to work outside the home, and visit shops and offices because there is no one else available to do such tasks. These women in the rural area have to become visible in order to support their families. However, it is the urban areas which offer the most work opportunities for women and where attitudes towards women working outside the home are more flexible than in rural Bangladesh, often because parents and husbands see the financial benefits of women's work (Dannecker 2002; Nokrek et al. 2003).

There are as many definitions of the word 'migrant'. For the purpose of this paper we take the definition of a migrant to be a person who either temporarily or permanently transfers from one socioeconomic sector to another with a definite goal in mind that the new location will provide him or her with better opportunities to enhance his/her own well-being and that of their family (Hugo 2000). Given the position of women in Bangladesh, we do however recognise that the 'better opportunities to enhance well-being' may include the migration that a woman undertakes in the hope of protecting herself (and her children) from harm (at the hands of an abusive husband, for example).

Migration is generally viewed from a structural perspective as a product of income differentials and the perceived or potential earning opportunities between urban and rural areas. These are the so-called urban *pull* factors such as greater job opportunities, and rural *push* factors such as land erosion or increasing landlessness, and hence poverty. This approach further presupposes that individuals make rational choices on the basis of evidence available to them. The rational choice approach to migration focuses primarily on individuals and asks who moves and why (Brydon and Chant 1989). The underlying assumption here is that individuals calculate social and economic benefits before they decide to migrate. But individuals are not always in a position to use such reason because the decision to migrate is often made as part of a larger household livelihood assessment (Kabeer 2000). In addition, it is important to recognise that the 'push' and 'pull' factors for migration cannot just be reduced to the quest for money. People may also respond to the 'lure of the bright lights of the city' (Bilsborrow et al. 1984: 14) and the 'curiosity to live in the city' (Rosa 1989: 205) as well as turning to the city as a place of refuge or escape from oppressive social situations (Shah 2003; Khan 2000: 160).

Women account for 46 per cent of the migration in developing countries (IOM 2000: 7), but these women in the migration process have been largely invisible because gender dis-aggregated data have seldom been collected (Lingam 1998). As Morokvasic-Muller et al. (2003: 9) observe, women are not viewed as equal actors with men in migration so women's migration has been seen mainly as secondary, non-autonomous and non-economically motivated, so these women are seldom counted. Women migrants are often said to be 'passive movers' migrating in response to marriage or as dependants following the male household head (Thadani and Todaro 1979). According to Smith et al. (1984), women in Asia have long been associated with marriage migration, and women migrants have not been thought to have much social or economic impact on either their place of origin or their place of destination. This is mainly because it is assumed that they are not economically active.

The destination of migrants are often urban areas, but rural to rural migration takes place connected to seasonal agricultural labour and other rural livelihood opportunities, which is less well documented (Chant 1992; Rogaly and Rafique 2003; Deshingkar and Smart 2003; Hossain et al. 2003).

The main employment opportunities for the vast majority of migrant women in Bangladesh are in domestic service, the construction industry (brick breaking, brickfields and earth carrying), the garment industry (as noted above, this is the largest employer of migrant women), petty trading and in commercial sex work.[6] However, women are still excluded from working in the transport sector, most skilled craft works and the majority of the service industry or retail sector jobs (Salway et al. 1998).

As far as living arrangements for women migrants are concerned, these depend on whether they migrate with their families as households or as individuals. The literature suggests that when women migrate with their families they tend to retain conventional living arrangements such as those in their villages (Newby 1998). However, when women migrate alone the vast majority of them—73 per cent (Zohir and Majumder 1996)—live with relatives or siblings already in the city. There is a large variation in the figures given in existing research regarding the percentage of women who live in messes[7] or hostels. Naved et al. (2001) and Zohir and Majumder (1996) found that only five and eight per cent respectively live in messes or hostels while some studies give a larger percentage (for e.g., Afsar 1998). However, despite these discrepancies in statistics, an interesting finding from the studies is that new household living arrangements are emerging that do not involve living with the traditional male guardian figures of fathers or husbands, with single women now living with sisters or female relatives. These new types of living arrangements not only have the potential to bring about changes in the lives of the individual, but also to bring about changes in gender relations within both destination and sending households.

Perhaps because there has been only a limited amount of research on women's migration in Bangladesh, there are a number of gaps in information available in recently undertaken small-scale studies (Rosa 1989; Hossain 1990; Majumder 1995; Ahsan 1997; Huq-Hussain 1996a; Dannecker 2002). Dannecker (2002), for example, comments that most studies done on women's migration have tended to focus on the economic significance of the new labour force and not on the workers themselves.

On some information the available studies disagree. For example, there seems to be a considerable discrepancy on the education levels of women migrants. Huq-Hussain's study in 1995–96 showed that almost 90 per cent of women migrants had no education or proper skill, while Karim (2000: 5) citing the Government of Bangladesh's Bureau of Statistics (1986), Zohir and Majumder (1996), Afsar (1998) and Huq-Hussain (1996b), states:

> (A)ll surveys suggest that the majority of them (women migrant workers) are primary and secondary school graduates ... better educated compared to the rural population in general ... their education level is low, but it is significantly higher than the average rural female literacy rate of 33 per cent.

Perhaps it is not surprising that such discrepancies should exist when studies are carried out in different parts of Bangladesh, a country with a vast population currently estimated at 144 million.

In addition, it is not always clear from the literature what is meant by 'single' or 'independent' migration. When the literature talks about this, it could mean a once married woman who is now either divorced, widowed or destitute and migrating alone, or it could mean a woman who has never married and is migrating alone. Given the strong patriarchal traditions in Bangladesh, it would be fair to assume that it is highly unlikely that large numbers of young, unmarried (never married) women would decide to migrate alone to Dhaka to try and find work and shelter without some contacts in the city. This is not to deny that young, single and never married women can and do leave their natal homes without support from others due to abuse/violence or poverty or family disagreements, but from the existing studies it is not clear to what extent this type of migration contributes to the number of women migrants. Huq-Hussain (1996a: 86) states that:

> (...) it has been asserted recently by various government surveys and researchers in South Asia and Bangladesh that more and more unmarried women are joining the migration flow. Although many of them moved to the city as dependents of their families and are termed as associational migrants, a significant number of these women are autonomous movers. The data from this study (of female migrants in Dhaka) indicates that such women took their own decision to migrate to the city in order to ease their family burden and to become self-reliant.

This statement, which talks of easing the burden on the family, hints at the push for migration as an aid to household livelihoods, but the mention of self-reliance paints a positive picture of the benefits of such migration. We argue below that there are women migrants who find the space to thrive and become self-reliant, but for some life is difficult, and sometimes dangerous. The difficulties they experience go largely unseen because of the old assumptions that women are living with families, protected by fathers, brothers or husbands.

From the information in the literature available, we can identify different types of woman migrants:

Single Educated Young Women Migrants

These are women who, ostensibly, come to the city to visit family and/or relatives, mainly married sisters or brothers, and who belong to the more affluent landowning class. Once in the city, they then look for employment mainly in the private sector in office work, or with NGOs. They are generally well educated, often up to the third level of education, and they do not need to work for economic reasons. However they want to work 'to stand on my own two feet' or to 'do something with my education' (Dannecker 2002). Self-fulfilment and a desire to be independent from their parents seem to play an important role in the decision of these women to migrate to Dhaka. They do not look for work in their villages, partly because waged opportunities are even scarcer for educated women than in the city, but also because given their higher status in society they may be expected to strictly observe the practice of *purdah* in their villages.

Single Young Women Migrants from Poor Families

There are single women who migrate because of the poverty of their families, and who may not have close family they can join in the urban areas. Some may have started off as housemaids in the homes of family associates or they may have moved to the urban areas to work in the garments industry. They may have been sent by their families to earn cash for the family or to earn their dowry (Hossain et al. 2003). Their continued presence at home in the rural areas may be seen as a burden, an extra mouth to feed, particularly in households where there are a number of daughters. Migration for them is a necessity for the family. They may be able to live with family members at their destination, but given the cramped conditions in many urban *bustee*s where their family members may live, such accommodation will be temporary while they find space in a mess or hostel, or with other women in a similar situation with whom they can share.

Migration to Join Family Members

One group of women who migrate to join family in another place are those who migrate independently of the natal family for work. This migrant usually joins with friends or other family members already in Dhaka or other urban centres, such as a married sister or brother. It is important to note the value of the role that extended networks of family, friends and acquaintances play in these migration movements. These networks not only extend shelter and food on arrival but also give information about job opportunities (Khan 2000). This group of women migrants live with their siblings and tend to adapt relatively quickly to urban life and work, as they are comfortable living with their kin and do not have to experience social changes alone. They are able to fit in with the existing networks already built up by their family members, and in addition their sisters or sisters-in-law are happy to have female company in the house, someone with whom to share housework and childcare. The added income they bring to the household is often a necessity for the daily expenditure of the family and therefore creates interdependency between siblings (Dannecker 2002).

Another group of women migrants are young girls migrating to the city to work in the household of a richer family member. In-depth research into this type of women's migration is scarce, however, according to Blanchet (1996), it is quite common for poor rural families to entrust a child to richer relatives when 'help' is required by the latter. Dannecker (2002) shows that most of these girls do not receive any money for their work nor an opportunity to go to school. Working conditions are less than perfect and it is quite common for these girls to be abused physically, verbally or sexually in their relative's house. As soon as they can they try to get employment outside of the house, generally in the garments industry (Afsar 1992).

Migration with the Family When the Woman is the Main Migrant Worker

There are women who migrate with their entire family, with the objective of looking for waged employment. In this case it is usually the nuclear family that is migrating and not the joint or extended family.

This migration is mainly as a result of poverty brought about by land erosion or a lack of employment opportunities in the rural areas. Empirical evidence shows that in almost all cases the family moved with the assistance of kinship networks (Huq-Hussain 1996a; Khan 2000). The family had a place to stay in after arrival and a job opportunity was available for at least one woman in the family. The waged employment opportunities available for family members who migrate reflects the trend in economic opportunities available for women as opposed to men in the cities. It may also be the case that the husband may be unable to work due to disability or age. Thus it is the women in the family who may work outside the home to support the family (Nokrek et al. 2003). However, as Kabeer (2000) found, this is not easily acknowledged and women are more likely to admit to having migrated for economic reasons if they are living with their siblings than if they are living with their husbands and family.

Migration with Family as Dependant or Co-worker

Dannecker (2002) identifies women migrants who lived and worked in Dhaka prior to marriage and who migrated to their husband's village after marriage. However, on average, after two years of marriage and living in the village, both husband and wife migrated back to Dhaka specifically looking for waged employment for both of them. The fact that the women had already worked and lived in Dhaka prior to marriage made their re-entry into the labour force and readjustment to urban life easier for them. Social networks had already been established in the city and could be called upon again should the need arise.

There is of course another category of married woman migrant: the woman who migrates as a dependant of her husband. She does not migrate specifically for waged employment, as do the two other categories of married woman migrants, although she may take up employment in the city to help augment family income.

Single (often older) Women Migrants

There are women, often older (which in the context of Bangladesh means in their 40s and 50s) who migrate. These women may be widowed, divorced or abandoned by their husband and lack support in their marital or natal home. They make use of kin or other social networks to move to another place to get waged employment (perhaps as a domestic worker where accommodation is supplied) or to beg (Hossain 2003; Hossain et al. 2003).

This section has provided some information on women's position in Bangladesh and has described some of the complexity of women's migration, which is apparent from the literature. We now turn to the case study material to provide examples of the broad types of women's migration we have listed above. This information adds to the recent studies of women's migration by showing that social factors such as the need to earn a dowry or to escape from difficult family circumstances are as much a cause of women's migration as purely economic factors.

Case Studies of Women's Migration

In the LEP (Livelihoods of the Extreme Poor) study, 65 detailed case studies and about 230 short cases were collected through interviews during visits to the 16 villages in 2002. Background information on the villages was collected using different rapid appraisal techniques, observation and through secondary sources (like village population records). Out of a total of 294 people the team spoke to, 110 respondents gave some information on migration. Out of the 110, 26 were women migrants, of whom 13 had taken the decision to migrate themselves, although this was often a decision forced on them by circumstance, as will be explained. The other 13 had either migrated with their husbands or with their natal family. In the 'livelihoods of adolescent girls' study, out of 60 people interviewed, four provided detailed information on women's migration.[8] This gives a total of 30 cases studies from which we draw on in the following section to describe the varied circumstances of women migrants.

Eight of the women had been forced to migrate because of the death of their husband or the breakdown of their marriage. To talk of these women as being 'independent' migrants is a misnomer since it implies freedom to make a choice, and these women had little choice in the decision to move; as Ellis (2003: 6) observes, 'the term "voluntary" needs to be thought about advisedly since a great number of people live so close to livelihood failure that the actions they take to prevent such failure can hardly be described as free choices'. Usha Rani[9], for example, a 60-year-old widow, was evicted from the land on which she and her husband had been living by someone she described as a 'powerful person from the village' just two months after her husband was killed in a fishing accident (LEP team 2003: 35). Usha went to her natal village with her children. The natal home was the place such women commonly returned to get support.[10] Such a move was not always successful because of poverty in that home, which made supporting another family difficult. Amina Begum, who was abandoned by her husband, moved back to her natal village, but was unable to stay because one of her brother's two wives 'disliked her' and did not want Amina's brother to use their household resources to help his sister. Amina returned to her husband's village where she was eventually able to seek refuge with her mother-in-law.

The marriage of Shakila, a young woman living in a *bustee* in Dhaka, broke down because of her own family's 'failure' to complete her dowry payments. She was 12 years old when her marriage was arranged with a 26-year-old man. At the time no fixed sum for dowry was agreed between the two families, although her family agreed to give the couple some furniture. But within six months her husband and his family started demanding money from her family as dowry. Shakila says this is because they knew that her mother, whose marriage to her father had broken down, was working in Kuwait as a domestic worker and her husband's family assumed that she could afford a good dowry. When Shakila was beaten so hard by her husband that some of her teeth were broken she ran back to her natal home (Nokrek et al. 2003).

There were some cases of both male and female migration where the decision to migrate was linked directly to the need to pay dowry. Fathers may migrate for a time to earn cash for a daughter's dowry or the daughter herself may move. Many respondents mentioned the burden of dowry as a cost that forced people who were on the margins of poverty into poverty or deeper poverty. Moni, for example, who comes from Patgram, is an 11-year-old girl working in Dhaka as a domestic worker to earn her dowry (Hossain et al. 2003: 15). The team in the adolescent girls' study were told a similar story by Israil, also from Patgram. He is the father of six daughters. The cost of the dowry of his eldest daughter, 12,000 taka,[11] has already used up all his resources but he is yet to complete the dowry payments (he has 5,000 taka left to pay, as well as loans to repay a year after the marriage) and is under pressure from his daughter's in-laws who have beaten her and sent her back to him because of non-completion of the payment. As a direct consequence of this experience, Israil's next three daughters, aged 12, 10 and 8 years, have been sent to Dhaka and Jamalpur to work as domestic helpers. They are able to come home once a year, bringing with them

500–1,000 taka that they hand over to their father. Israil is hopeful that their employers will help with their dowries when the time comes. He told the team that he had asked these employers to help him with a loan to solve the problem of his eldest daughter's dowry. Israil believed that payment of the dowry would solve the present discord in his daughter's marriage, but the experience of others suggests that this is not always the case. Amina Begum, for example, continued to be beaten by her husband even after her dowry was settled. Her in-laws convinced her to stay saying the situation would be resolved if she gave birth to a son. Eventually her third child was a son, but the beatings did not stop and she was forced to leave (LEP team 2003: 107).

Dowry demands can also force couples to migrate together. Nasrin, for example, moved to Dhaka with her husband because his family objected to their love marriage (his family had planned an arranged marriage which would have involved a substantial dowry) and were making life very difficult for her in their home village (Nokrek et al. 2003).

However, young women do not just migrate to earn their dowries; they also seek work to support themselves and their natal families. For example Halima Begum, a 15-year-old girl, works as a maidservant. Her mother died six years ago of typhoid fever and when her father remarried she and her brothers found it difficult to survive alone when he moved to another place. Her elder brother is a day labourer, and the younger one is currently a primary school student in the fifth standard. Halima moved to Chittagong to work as a maidservant with a family; they provide her with food and accommodation, but pay her only 200 taka per month as a salary (Hossain et al. 2003: 13).

Some women, following the loss of their husband through death or separation and divorce, move to urban areas to get paid employment in order to make a living for themselves and their children. Aleya Banu, for example, is a 48-year-old divorcee who after attempting to earn some money in her native village making and selling mats, left for Rangamati, to stay at her sister's house. After a few months there, she went to Ranirhat in Chittagong in search of work. She lived there for 12 years and worked as a day labourer on farmland and as a house cleaner before returning to her husband's village at the request of her youngest son who had acquired some land and built a house in which she could stay (LEP team 2003: 50–51). Another woman, a widow, went to Chittagong for a few months to work in a garment factory and earn some money before returning to her husband's village to secure her children's right to their father's property (fortunately a local leader supported her claim and she was allowed to stay on her husband's land) (ibid.: 33–34). Farida, who was abandoned by her husband, worked in Chittagong for five years as a domestic worker before moving back to her husband's village (where her sons lived) to eke out a living selling stones collected from rivers and doing house cleaning.

Mahmuda came to Dhaka from Nalitabari a decade ago in order to support her family when her husband became too sick to work. She worked in a garment factory for several years. Now her daughter, whose marriage has broken down, works in the garment factory while Mahmuda takes care of her grandchild while selling food on the road-side (Nokrek et al. 2003). Saleha Begum also has a sick husband who she has to support (Hossain et al. 2003: 12). She was forced to look for work in different places; in Gopalgonj for example, her brother who is a rick-shaw puller helped her to find work processing rice and as a maidser-vant. Nasima, who moved from Sylhet to Rangamati with her husband, supports her family by fishing and selling her catch following an attack on her husband which left him unable to work (LEP team 2003: 147).

It is important to note that not all migrant women succeed in finding work, as some of the cases recounted above show. Those women who, following the breakdown of their marriage or the death of their hus-bands, cannot find work or who obtain support from kin have to adopt other strategies to survive. Sabiha, for example, after being abandoned by her husband moved to her natal home but her family could not sup-port her so she had to leave their home and now makes a living by tak-ing care of empty houses for migrant workers. She is not paid by the home owners, but she gets a place to stay and some food (ibid.: 149). Korimon Begum, a 50-year-old widow, now begs. When her husband died she moved from Rangamati to Subalong to do fish processing and earned enough for her daughter's dowry. Unfortunately recently both her daughter and her daughter's husband died leaving a grandson, so Korimon moved to where they had been living to care for her year-old grandson. She cannot find work so she begs for food (ibid.: 152).

The literature on migration and social protection (Mosse 2002; Kothari 2002; Biswas and Khan 2003) records how the varied lives and livelihoods of migrants do not suit the static programmes of develop-ment interventions and government relief schemes. Because these women lead mobile lives they are often not listed as household heads, or even members of the households in which they temporarily reside, and are missing from official lists and from NGO 'baseline surveys of the poor'. Indeed, the LEP team began the study by updating the lists provided by local officials and the PROSHIKA baseline survey team because their initial house-to-house visits yielded information on these 'missing persons'. The LEP study provided an illustration of this through the experiences of Khadija, who returned to her natal village after being abandoned by her husband. But on arrival she was told by a local government official 'you have no household here, so no card for you' when she applied for a government scheme that helps poor women, the 'Vulnerable Group Development' card scheme (LEP team 2003: 60). Such women who do not make the criteria for assistance from the government or NGOs depend on their own ability to make a living, which quite often may involve them in continuing to move from place to place, scraping together a livelihood. This existence may make them 'self-reliant', but it is not their free choice that they move. They have to do so in order to survive.

As we can see from the above cases, most of the women interviewed had found some way to make a living. Some who had never worked outside the home because they had observed *purdah*, had to cope with being in the public eye as well as rapidly learning how to make a living. Golapi Rani, for example, had never worked outside the home until her husband died. She recounted how soon after her husband's death her father-in-law came to her with some fish and told her to sell them in the market place. 'It was a traumatic experience; she cried and would not touch food for two days (…) but her brother-in-laws warned her that they would not provide for her and her four children' (ibid.: 33). Golapi learned to cope, as do many other women. Some, like Shakila's mother (mentioned above), who escaped a difficult marriage by migrating and moving to Kuwait, do well and serve as an example to others.

We have also described in this paper the abuse many women suffer at the hands of husbands and their families. Others suffer abuse from employers who overwork and underpay migrant women (and sometimes physically harm them) who may have little choice but to stay in the abusive situation in order to enable their family to survive. These women make a contribution to their households and the local economy that goes unrecognised and undocumented in official statistics. These women are the 'invisible' workforce and therefore in a much more vulnerable situation not only with regards to their rights as workers, but, they are also vulnerable to abuse by their employers. Not only do they need to be informed about their existing rights as workers, but also about their rights as citizens which are already enshrined in legislation.

We have told these women's stories in some detail to provide an overview of the varied lives of migrant women, a variety that the simple figure of '30 migrant women' fails to convey. These are the faces behind the different 'types of woman migrant' listed earlier in this paper. These stories not only illustrate the variety of women who migrate, but also the complicated migration history some women have. Some women do 'simply' move from one place to another and settle, but others move many times and try different forms of work in order to earn a living. And to suggest that these women either 'survive' or 'thrive' is also too simplistic. It is sometimes the same women who both survive and thrive. For some there is ambivalence—both thriving and surviving at the same time. For others it might be a movement from suffering to thriving, or vice versa over a period of time as a migrant.

Conclusion

As we have seen from this paper, there are many different forms of women's migration and, while women migrate for different reasons and under different conditions, there are many who migrate due to poverty, both social and economic. In a society that does not hold women in high regard, many of these women are in an even more vulnerable position due to age and poverty. They miss out on almost all government and NGO poverty alleviation initiatives, as they do not make the criteria for such assistance. Some women migrants do thrive; they find a space to live less constrained by tradition and find the opportunity to earn and gain some independence. But sometimes these same women barely survive and for others, often poor and lacking a supportive family, migration brings misery as they find themselves locked into difficult work and home situations that rob them of their dignity and rights. The 'quiet revolution' in Bangladesh, of increasing numbers of independent women migrants, may mean more opportunities, but hidden within it is much silent suffering.

Notes

1 We are grateful to all our colleagues for their contributions to this paper: Nasrin Sultana, Akmal Kabir, Hasneara Begum, Prokriti Nokrek, Shakila Sultana, Moniruzzaman, Mizanur Rahman, Dilara Jaman, Nazmun Nahar Lipi, S.M. Zubair Ali Khan, Nasrin Sultana, Salim Ahmed Purvez, Mohammed Kamruzzaman, Sinora Chakma, Mayee, Ahmed Borhan, Shamsun Nahar, Mohammed Shazzad Hossain,

Atiquer Rahman and Anila Pervin. We are grateful to Ben Rogaly for his comments on the first draft of this paper. We indebted to DFID, and the NGO PROSHIKA, for supporting the research on which this paper is based and to the people of the study communities for the time they spent with the study teams and the invaluable information they shared. This paper was presented at the International Conference on Women and Migration in Asia, in New Delhi during 10–13 December 2003, and we are grateful for the comments we received there, which have been incorporated into this version.

2   These case studies were collected during the 'Livelihoods of the Extreme Poor' study conducted by PROSHIKA, an NGO in Bangladesh, in collaboration with the UK Government's Department For International Development (DFID) during 2001–03. The case studies presented in this paper come from the second phase of that study where the PROSHIKA team collected information from poor people living in 16 villages in various parts of Bangladesh and from a follow-up study on the livelihoods of adolescent girls. The study of the livelihoods of adolescent girls was carried out in two villages in Patgram in the north of Bangladesh, and two urban *bustees* in Dhaka city. The detailed findings on migration from this study can be found in Hossain (2003).

3   Given the density of population in Bangladesh, many rural areas may be termed 'peri-urban', given that people's livelihoods, while often dependent in part on agricultural activity, are also reliant on incomes from urban-based employment.

4   Ryan (2003) provides a more complete picture of women's position in Bangladesh.

5   Terms such as 'absolute poor', 'extreme poor', 'hard core poor', 'poorest of the poor' and 'ultra poor' are used interchangeably by a variety of organisations and studies to categorise this group.

6   We recognise that commercial sex work is a significant area of employment for migrant women. We do not attempt to cover this area in this paper largely because this was not an area of work mentioned in any of the Livelihoods of the Extreme Poor (LEP) or 'adolescent girls study' case studies. This does not, of course, mean that it does not exist in those households; it may have been a livelihood option thought to be too sensitive to mention to the PROSHIKA team.

7   Messes are forms of accommodation shared by unrelated workers who share rent, food and other expenses.

8   This does not mean that the other 56 had not been involved in migration, since the focus of this study was on early marriage and dowry, the migration history of respondents was not probed unless it was in connection with these two topics.

9   All names have been changed to protect the identity of the respondents.

10 In all eight cases these women had moved to a different village or town after marriage, so their move was not simply a shift of location within the same village or local area.

11 One UK pound was equivalent to about 90 taka in mid-2003.

References and Further Readings

Afsar, Rita. 1992. 'Gender Based Urban Poverty Alleviation Strategies' in *Grassroots*, 1(4): 7–17.

———. 1998. 'A Case Study of the Gender Dimensions of Labour Migration in the Formal Manufacturing Sector of Bangladesh', Geneva: UNRISD.

Afsar, Rita. 2003. 'Internal Migration and the Development Nexus: The Case of Bangladesh', paper prepared for a DFID/RMRRU regional conference on 'Migration Development and Pro-Poor Choices in Asia', Dhaka, 22–24 June.

Ahsan, R.N. 1997. 'Migration of Female Construction Labourers to Dhaka City, Bangladesh', *International Journal of Population Geography*, 3: 49–61.

Asian Development Bank (ADB). 2001. 'Country Briefing Paper: Women in Bangladesh', a study initiated by the Programmes Department (West) Division 2 of the Asian Development Bank, Manila.

Bilsborrow, R.E., A.S. Oberai and G. Standing. 1984. *Migration Surveys in Low Income Countries: Guidelines for Survey and Questionnaire Design*. London/Sydney: Croom Helm.

Biswas, Gautam Shuvra and S.M. Zubair Ali Khan. 2003. 'Inclusion of the Extreme Poor in PROSHIKA Activities', thematic paper, Livelihoods of the Extreme Poor Study, IMEC (Impact Monitoring and Evaluation Cell), PROSHIKA, Bangladesh.

Blanchet, T. 1996. *Lost Innocence, Stolen Childhoods*. Dhaka, Bangladesh: University Press Limited.

Brydon, L. and S. Chant. 1989. *Women in the Third World—Gender Issues in Rural and Urban Areas*. Aldershot: Edward Elgar.

Chant, Sylvia (ed.). 1992. *Gender and Migration in Developing Countries*. London: Belhaven Press.

Dannecker, P. 2002. *Between Conformity and Resistance: Women Garment Workers in Bangladesh*. Dhaka, Bangladesh: University Press Limited.

Deshingkar, Priya and Daniel Smart. 2003. 'Seasonal Migration for Livelihoods in India: Coping, Accumulation and Exclusion', working paper 220, London, ODI (Overseas Development Institute).

Ellis, Frank. 2003. 'A Livelihoods Approach to Migration and Poverty Reduction', paper commissioned by the Department for International Development (DFID), September.

Government of Bangladesh (GoB). 1986. *Statistical Year Book*. Bangladesh Bureau of Statistics, Government of Bangladesh.

———. 1997. 'Combined Third and Fourth Periodic Report in Accordance with Article of the Convention on the Elimination of All Forms of Discrimination Against Women', Ministry of Women and Children Affairs, Bangladesh.

———. 2001. *Statistical Year Book*. Bangladesh Bureau of Statistics: Government of Bangladesh.

Hamid, S. 1995. 'Gender Dimensions of Poverty, in Rethinking Rural Poverty: Bangladesh as a Case Study', in Hossain Zillur Rahman and Mahabub Hossain (eds), *Rethinking Rural Poverty: Bangladesh as a Case Study*. Dhaka, Bangladesh: University Press Limited.

Hossain, M. 1990. Briefing paper, London, ODI.

Hossain, Munishi Israil. 2003. 'Moving Forward Looking Behind: Creation of Livelihoods Option through Migration' thematic paper, Livelihoods of the Extreme Poor Study, IMEC, PROSHIKA, Bangladesh.

Hossain, Munishi Israil, Iqbal Alam Khan and Janet Seeley. 2003. 'Surviving on their feet: charting the mobile livelihoods of the poor in rural Bangladesh', paper presented at the conference 'Staying Poor: Chronic Poverty and Development Policy' held at the University of Manchester, 7–9 April (www.chronicpoverty.org)

Hugo, G. 2000. 'Migration and Women's Empowerment' in H.B. Presser and G. Sen (eds), *Women's Empowerment and Demographic Processes*. New York: Oxford University Press.

Huq-Hussain, S. 1996a. 'Female Migrant's Adaptation in Dhaka: A Case of the Processes of Urban Socio-Economic Change', Urban Studies Programme, Department of Geography, University of Dhaka, Bangladesh.

———. 1996b. 'Female Migrants in an Urban Setting—the Dimensions of Spatial/Physical Adaptation. The Case of Dhaka', *Habitat International*, 20(1): 93–107.

International Organisation for Migration (IOM). 2000. *World Migration Report 2000*. IOM: Geneva.

Jolly, S., E. Bell and L. Narayanaswamy. 2003. *Gender and Migration in Asia, Overview and Annotated Bibliography*. BRIDGE: IDS, Sussex, UK.

Kabeer, N. 2000. *The Power to Choose: Bangladeshi Women and Labour Market Decisions in London and Dhaka*. Verso: London/New York.

Kabir, Rachel. 1999. *Adolescent Girls in Bangladesh*. UNICEF: Dhaka.

Karim, M.I. 2000. 'Female Migration and Changes in Urban Social Dynamics of Bangladesh', paper presented at the 'Urban Futures 2000 International Conference', Johannesburg, South Africa, 10–14 July.

Khan, Iqbal Alam. 2000. 'Struggle for Survival: Networks and Relationships in a Bangladesh Slum', Ph.D. thesis, University of Bath, UK.

Kothari, Uma. 2002. 'Migration and Chronic Poverty', working paper 16, Chronic Poverty Research Centre, Institute for Development, Policy and Management, University of Manchester.

LEP (Livelihoods of the Extreme Poor) team. 2003. 'Case Studies of Poor People', Livelihoods of the Extreme Poor Study, IMEC, PROSHIKA, Bangladesh.

Lingam, Lakshmi. 1998. 'Taking stock. Women's Movements and the State', republished in Ghanshyam Shah (ed.), 2002, *Social Movements and the State*. New Delhi: Sage Publications.

Mahmud, Simeen. 2003. 'Actually How Empowering is Microcredit?', *Development and Change*, 34(4): 577–605.

Majumder, P.P. 1995. 'Empowering Women: Wage Employment in the Garment Industry', *Empowerment*, 2: 83–112.

Morokvasic-Muller, Mirjana, Erel Umut and Shinozaki Kyoko (eds). 2003. *Crossing Borders and Shifting Boundaries*, Vol. 1: *Gender on the Move*. Opalden: Leske and Budrich.

Mosse, David. 2002. 'Adivasi Migrant Labour Support. A Collaborative Programme', consultant's report for the West India Rainfed Farming Project, Phase II, Gramin Vikas Trust, DFID, India.

Muqtada, M., A.M. Singh and M. Rashid. 2002. *Bangladesh: Economic and Social Challenges of Globalisation*. Dhaka, Bangladesh: UPL.

Naved, R.T., M. Newby and S. Amin. 2001. 'The Effects of Migration on Work and Marriage of Female Garment Workers in Bangladesh', *International Journal of Population Geography*, 7: 91–104.

Newby, M.H. 1998. 'Women in Bangladesh: a study of the effects of garment factory work on control over income and autonomy', Ph.D. thesis, Department of Social Sciences, University of Southampton.

Nokrek, Prokriti, Shakila Sultana, Moniruzzaman, Mizanur Rahman, Dilara Jaman and Nazmun Nahar Lipi. 2003. *Stories of the Lives of Adolescent Girls in Bangladesh*, mimeo, IMEC/GRCC (Gender Research Coordination Cell), PROSHIKA, Dhaka.

Quddus, M. and S. Rashid. 2000. *Entrepreneurs and Economic Development: The Remarkable Story of Garment Exports from Bangladesh*. Dhaka, Bangladesh: UPL.

Rogaly, B. 1998. 'Workers on the Move: Seasonal Migration and Changing Social Relations in Rural India', *Gender and Development*, 6(1): 21.

Rogaly, B. and Abdur Rafique. 2003. 'Struggling to Save Cash: Seasonal Migration and Vulnerability in West Bengal, India', *Development and Change*, 34(4): 659–81.

Rosa, K. 1989. 'Export Oriented Industries and Women Workers in Sri Lanka', in Haleh Afshar and Bina Agarwal (eds), *Women, Poverty and Ideology*. London: Macmillan.

Ryan, Sheila. 2003. 'Empowerment through Internal Migration of Women in Bangladesh?' M.A. dissertation, School of Development Studies, University of East Anglia.

Salway, S., S. Rahman and S. Jesmin. 1998. 'Women's Employment and Gender Identity among the Urban Poor of Dhaka', *Discourse* 2(1): 75–111.

Shah, Alpa. 2003. 'The Love of Labour: Seasonal Migration from a Jharkhandi Village to Brick Kilns in West Bengal', paper presented at a School of Development Studies seminar, University of East Anglia, 28 May.

Siddiqui, Tasneem. 2003a. 'An Anatomy of Forced and Voluntary Migration from Bangladesh: a gendered perspective', in Mirjana Morokvasic-Muller, Erel Umut and Shinozaki Kyoko (eds), *Crossing Borders and Shifting Boundaries*. Opalden: Leske and Budrich.

———. 2003b. 'Migration as a Livelihood Strategy of the Poor: the Bangladesh case', paper prepared for a DFID/RMRRU (Refugee and Migratory Movements Research Unit) regional conference on 'Migration Development and Pro-Poor Choices in Asia', 22–24 June, Dhaka.

Smith, P., S. Khoo and S. Go. 1984. 'The Migration of Women to Cities: A Comparative Perspective', in J. Fawcett, S. Khoo and P. Smith (eds), *Women in the Cities of Asia: Migration and Urban Adaptation*. Boulder, Colorado: Westview Press.

Sultana, Nasrin. 2003. 'Does Legislation on Marriage and Divorce in Rural Bangladesh Realise the Rights of the Poorest Women?' M.A. dissertation, School of Development Studies, University of East Anglia.

Thadani, V.N. and M.P. Todaro. 1979. *A Framework for the Analysis of the Determinants of Female Migration*. New York: The Population Council.

Zohir, S.C. and P.P. Majumder. 1996. 'Garment Workers in Bangladesh: Economic, Social and Health Conditions', Bangladesh Institute of Development Studies, research mimeo 18, Dhaka.

UNICEF. 2001. *Rural Adolescent Girls in Bangladesh*. Dhaka: UNICEF.

World Bank. 1999. 'Consultation with the Poor', Mimeo. World Bank.

9

MIGRATING FOR WORK:
REWRITING GENDER RELATIONS

Ravinder Kaur

The scope for understanding migration as a process has broadened considerably in recent years. Migration studies are no longer restricted to simply understanding 'push' and 'pull' factors. The canvas of exploration is now much larger, encompassing the understanding of the migration experience in its various sociocultural, political and economic dimensions (see Chopra 1995; Gardner and Osella 2003; Jolly, Bell and Narayanswamy 2003; Kaur 2001a). The outcomes of migration are varied and determined by the specific forms of migration and the conditions under which they take place. Further, migration is now recognised as a social process that involves not only individuals but also households (de Haan 1999, 2000; Pessar 1999). Most importantly, the gendered aspect of migration finally appears to be getting the attention that it deserves (see Karlekar 1995; Schenk-Sandbergen 1995; Sharpe 2001; Momsen 1999). This paper, in two parts, deals with the experience of poor female migrants to the metropolitan city of Delhi and explores two main areas of change in the status of female migrants employed as domestic labour. The first part analyses the continuing shift from the earlier predominantly male domestic servants to female domestic labour. NSS (National Sample Survey) data for the domestic service employment category in India shows an increasing feminisation, with an increase from 1.2 million female domestic workers in 1983 to 2 million in 1999; during this same period, the number of males working as domestic help stayed stagnant at 0.3 million. Today, 9 out of every 10 domestic workers are female. This has meant increasing work opportunities for poor women in this sector of the informal economy.

An important reason for this shift is the growing number of urban women entering part-time or full-time employment; their success in balancing their careers and homes is in large part due to female domestic workers who shoulder the tasks that women in professions and business necessarily have to delegate.

The second part focuses on the consequences of the opening up of this avenue of employment for women who get incorporated into the work world. The paper explores whether the relative economic independence gained by women through paid work is able to challenge, as Naila Kabeer phrases it, 'the seamless patriarchal discipline of family, community and capitalist work relations' (Kabeer 2000). Mukhopadhyay and Sudarshan (2003) have similarly tracked changes in gender equity on the basis of studies of working women in the countries of South Asia. They show a varied and complex picture with significant changes occurring in male attitudes in Sri Lanka and Bangladesh. It is, however, obvious that far-reaching changes are beginning to occur with greater numbers of women entering the work world.

Locating Female Migration

Studies on Asian urbanisation have highlighted the large services sector and pointed to a high percentage of the youthful labour force being employed in service activities. Most of this employment is in the informal sector and a disproportionate share is the preserve of women (Fawcett et al. 1984). Although South Asian countries as opposed to South East Asian countries have been less known for female migration, several new studies point to the increasing presence of women, especially migrant women, in the informal economies of these countries. This underlines an increasing trend of independent migration of females.

A significant number of single women migrating on their own for purposes of both social and economic improvement bring an added importance to questions of agency and mobility. Poverty is not the only push factor, and women from several classes and social backgrounds are beginning to migrate independently. Meera, for instance, a 22-year-old high school graduate, left her home in Nainital in Uttar Pradesh, and came to Delhi where she started working in a beauty parlour. She lives with her married sister in Delhi, but her decision to migrate for better employment prospects was her own. Her widowed mother did not object. Meera sends some of her earnings home to help her family.

Instances of married women migrating on their own in response to a demand for their labour is provided by women working in the tea gardens of Assam. The issues of personal and social risk are much greater in the case of such women who migrate alone leaving their households behind. The household's participation is implicated in the decision to allow the women to migrate; economic necessity and the demand for female labour in the tea industry being the compelling reasons in this case. Studies from India and China also reveal an increase in what Thadani and Todaro (in Fawcett et al. 1984) call 'marital migration'— migration for better marital prospects. Examples of women from the poorer states of Bengal and Assam moving for marriage to the prosperous areas of Haryana and Punjab reveal a linkage between poverty, marriage migration and the low sex ratio in the north Indian states. In such cases, sending daughters to far away marital homes is a household strategy to escape demands for dowry and smooth consumption for the remaining members of the household (Kaur 2004).

Earlier studies of migration treated female migration in India as a secondary phenomenon, one that was entirely dependent upon the migration of men. A great deal of evidence from case studies suggests, however, that women's migration, earlier attributed merely to mobility after marriage, is now increasingly for employment purposes. Singh (1984) and Ursula Sharma (1986), in the context of India, were the first to critique the manner in which male migration is considered as 'economic' while female migration, consequent on marriage or family moves, is considered to be 'social'. In a very perceptive argument, Sharma pointed out that even if the immediate and obvious reason for women to move was domestic, it did not mean that the move did not have important 'economic' consequences. *Many women join their migrant husbands only if there are significant opportunities for their own employment.* The earnings of migrant women, even if they are accompanied by their male relatives, cannot be regarded as marginal or supplementary—in the case of many poor households they are in fact the household's mainstay. This conclusion is reiterated by Kasturi's work (1990) among Tamil migrants to Delhi which shows that female workforce participation rates, in comparison to those of males, increased after migration.

Singh (1984) noted important differences in female migration trends between the north and the south—migration in the north was dominated by males, while there was a comparatively larger share of female economic migrants from the southern states. These regional differences were attributed to the differential social position of women in the two regions. However, such differences may be less significant with greater participation in migration by women of all regions. In the present context, one finds interesting regional and ethnic variations among female migrants to the major cities. Thus nursing is dominated by women from Kerala; construction labour by Rajasthanis; the services sector (especially the hospitality industry and sectors such as tourism, airlines, beauty and health parlours) is increasingly employing girls from the north-east, who are better educated and generally speak English; tribal girls from Bihar, Orissa, Jharkhand and Chhattisgarh work as live-in maids, while poorer and less skilled migrants from Bihar, Bengal and Orissa are to be found in factories, domestic work and other home-based work. The poorest, who do not find a place in any kind of employment, end up in occupations like ragpicking.

Several complex factors account for greater female migration—besides the usual factors of pull and push, poverty being important among these; new factors such as newly developing markets for women's work, improving levels of education and skill development, a greater desire for improving one's own and one's children's lot, and the loosening of parental and societal control over women are becoming equally important. Social capital, in the form of community and family networks, however, remains important in facilitating such movement.

Kasturi's study of female Tamil migrants engaged in domestic service in Delhi reveals the importance of sociocultural factors in influencing migration. The two caste groups she studied—the Pallans and the Devangas—explained why they had moved all the way to Delhi for domestic service instead of moving to an urban area in their own state where such opportunities would also have been available. The Pallans revealed that since they were untouchables they would not have been hired for domestic work in Tamil Nadu; the Devangas said that they were not willing to lose status in their own region. Thus the social barriers to the labour market are circumvented by moving away a long distance and escaping one's own cultural context. Another recent study on domestic workers, which corroborates several of the findings of this study, states that the majority of domestic workers from Tamil Nadu belong to the scheduled castes (Neetha 2004). In her sample, 80.7 per cent of the live-out workers belonged to the scheduled castes and 14.4 per cent to the other backward classes (OBC) category. The urgent necessity for household workers thus appears to have broken down the 'pollution' barrier, allowing scheduled caste women to take on tasks in other peoples' kitchens.

Gendered Labour Markets:
The Changing Scenario

Singh (1984) states that migrant women in urban India have significantly higher workforce participation rates than non-migrant women.
This is especially true of the domestic labour sector of the informal
economy, which is essentially populated by migrant labour. An important shift in demand from male to female labour has taken place in this
sector. A study by the Institute of Social Sciences in 1991 indicates that
20 per cent of the total women migrants to Delhi are employed as
domestic maids. In a recent overview of migration trends in India,
Srivastava (2003) points out a newer trend in which girls from the tribal
areas of Madhya Pradesh, Bihar, Chhattisgarh, Jharkhand and Orissa
are being brought by private recruiting agencies and Christian voluntary organisations to be employed as maids in Delhi households. This
underlines an increasing trend of independent migration of females.

The figure of 20 per cent of female migrants being employed in the
domestic work sector is an indicator of the high demand for household
help (Srivastava and Sasikumar 2003). Interestingly, this demand is
increasingly for female rather than male workers. In urban areas, only
1.4 per cent of male workers are in domestic work as against 15 per
cent for female workers. In rural areas, 1.8 per cent of female workers
are in domestic work. Between 1983 and 1999, the percentage of
female domestic servants in India has gone up from 80 to 87 per cent.
There are important reasons for this on the demand as well as the supply
side. On the supply side, the reasons are:

- The unskilled nature of most household work; i.e., it requires no
  particular training to do household work.
- The lower educational attainment of most female rural migrants.
- A readiness to work for lower wages.
- Willingness to trade lower wages for stability and a roof over their
  heads, especially if they have children to support.
- Readiness to work in lower status jobs.
- The preference of male domestic workers to graduate to semi-
  skilled or skilled jobs such as driving.

As men vacate various categories of unskilled work, women and other
poorer migrants move to occupy these spaces and jobs. There is also the

security aspect—an increase in violent incidents involving male household employees is another reason female domestic employees are preferred.

On the demand side, the main reasons are:

- A major reason for a gender shift in the demand for household labour is the increase in FLPR (female labour force participation rate) in urban areas. This increase leads to a greater demand for outside hired help, both full and part time, as women from all classes join productive work outside the household.

- Many more urban women are working both 'outside the house' and working 'out of the house' (own account workers).

- Jobs which entail office hours (full or even part time) keep women away from the homes for a large part of the day. As more women go to work, their need for someone else to tend to some or all of the domestic chores goes up.

- Household help is needed for chores such as cooking, cleaning, washing, looking after children.

- Sufficient numbers of old parents and dependents continue to stay with their grown children until their death, and household help is often hired specifically to look after old parents or in-laws when the woman of the house is working—this too was traditionally considered to be her role and duty.

- Single working men, and women, also depend on domestic help for household chores.

- The cultural framing of gender roles—most household chores are considered to be a woman's domain and responsibility.

- Security of female and younger male children is another reason why more women than men are being preferred for domestic work especially where the worker is needed to stay in or spend the major portion of the day at the employer's residence in the latter's absence.

- The limited emancipation of women in India has not led husbands to share household chores with working wives. Nor have technological improvements curtailed household work to the same extent as in the West. Hence domestic chores remain timebound and time consuming and are framed by cultural demands.

- Due to the availability of cheap labour, the labour of wives and mothers is not shared by men but replaced with that of other women.

Although both poor male and female migrants would ideally be available for domestic work, the above reasons are increasingly resulting in a greater demand for female rather than male labour. As more urban women of the middle classes and above join the work world, the regular absence of a woman from her home necessitates a 'replacement', somebody who can be a substitute for her. Generally, a male worker is unable to perform all the tasks that a woman takes care of in the home. Hence she has to be replaced by another woman for all the 'female chores', *especially childcare.*

Traditionally, household help (cooks, drivers) in a northern city like Delhi used to be male, the proverbial 'Ramu' (a popular name for male household servants) drawn from the hills areas of Uttar Pradesh and Himachal Pradesh. The family of the migrant, if they accompanied him to the city, would play subsidiary roles in the same household. The wife and children would not 'work' for the household on a formal basis but would help out with chores as and when needed. Generally given quarters at the employer's place, the couple would generally educate their children in a nearby government school. Many such migrants spent their entire working lives in the household of the employer. This scenario of the male domestic worker is now rare; few are willing to be lifelong family retainers.

Definitions of Work in the Domestic Labour Sector

The four main domestic chores that need to be taken care of are childcare, cooking, house cleaning and washing clothes. Several combinations and permutations of how this is attained are possible. A variety of strategies are adopted by households to fulfil the need for performing these tasks that a stay-at-home woman would have been shouldering. Part-time maids are hired in both joint and nuclear families. In nuclear families, since older relatives are absent, working women with children need full-time help. Middle class women with older, school-going children do without full-time help, hiring help only for specific chores. Frequently, non-working women with various levels of disposable income hire part-time help for chores other than cooking. Having household help, even when it is not a necessity, is an important status symbol for an urban household. Having and keeping good help is a marker of status and wise management on the part of the householder. The importance of domestic help is underlined by the fact that it is one of the most frequent topics of discussion among women in urban households!

The expanding need for domestic labour in the contemporary urban economy takes the form of basically two categories of domestic work: full time and part time. This distinction is, however, from the employer's end—those who employ full-time help and those who employ part-time help. The workers in both categories are actually working full time. Full-time (live-in) workers reside with the family or spend their whole day at the residence of a single employer while part-time (live-out) workers live in their own quarters, either self-owned or on rent. Part-timers take on jobs in several households. While male workers may still be employed as full-time domestic workers and have other female workers helping them in their tasks, part-time workers are exclusively female. Men generally do not work in several homes at a time and prefer the status of a 'cook' as opposed to an all-purpose household help. If a household employs a full-time male cook, the other chores, including the washing of dishes, are generally performed by a woman. Besides a gender hierarchy, a skill-based hierarchy also operates. Women with some education, better cooking or childcare skills are able to get well-paid jobs while those whose work is considered purely unskilled and substitutable get the lower end jobs. Unskilled workers performing the tasks of sweeping, swabbing, washing of utensils and clothes fall into the latter category. Live-in workers today tend to be single and better educated than live-out workers. However, while better conditions govern the employment of the live-ins, the live-outs treasure their independence and ability to earn a more flexible income.

Ethnographic Location of the Research

Several of the issues discussed above are explicated through field data gathered in two locations: (1) a small slum, Lal Gumbad, which adjoins the affluent colonies of Panchshila Park and Sadhana Enclave in south Delhi, and (2) an urban village, Katwaria Sarai, near the Indian Institute of Technology (IIT), and also in south Delhi. The two locations are different in that the slum was originally set up as a camp for construction labour for the Panchshila Park colony. It is over 40 years old and has been regularised. Over the years the number of households within the settlement has greatly expanded. The original inhabitants were migrant labourers from Rajasthan, Uttar Pradesh (UP) and Bihar. There are a few migrant households from Haryana, and some homes are owned by the original holders of the village land before it was bought by the colony association. At present, the population of the slum has become more heterogeneous both in terms of class and community, with migrants from various other states renting space from the original migrants. The slum is broadly organised along ethnic lines, with migrants from Rajasthan, Bihar and UP occupying distinct but contiguous sections of the inhabited area. The slum is bound on one side by a protected monument called the Lal Gumbad, and on the other side by the colonies of Panchshila Park and Sadhana Enclave, and is open to a neighbourhood park of the Panchshila Park and another Archaeological Society of India-protected monument, a Baradari (a Mughal monument), on the fourth side. Except for the Rajasthani women, most migrant women resident here are domestic workers in the adjoining colonies. Most of them own their own *jhuggi* (dwelling) in the settlement. Newcomers rent space from the older residents until they manage to buy a *jhuggi* from someone who might be moving out. The slum has a flourishing rental market, with residents adding rooms above their own and renting them out.

The urban village of Katwaria Sarai is one of three such villages bordering the IIT-Delhi (the other two are Ber Sarai and Jia Sarai). Residential land in these villages is mainly owned by the original residents who, having been divested of their agricultural lands, have taken to various other occupations, with real estate being the most lucrative one. The prime location next to the premier engineering institute has pushed up the value of land enormously. Many of the original owners have turned their single storied homes into multistoried 'rooming' houses. Each floor has several rooms with a common toilet and bathroom. Most of these rooms are occupied by migrants working in the city. The occupants range from salaried employees to those working in the informal sector. Like most other villages, the section occupied by the Harijans is set apart from the main village. The village has several commercial enterprises including those catering to the daily needs of its residents. Several migrant women residing here work as domestic labour in Katwaria Sarai and in the IIT campus households.

Domestic Workers and the Experience of Migration

This section elucidates the migration experiences of several domestic workers in the city of Delhi. It focuses mainly on the experiences of live-out workers who are mostly married women. It does not focus on unmarried migrant women in domestic work who are mostly live-in workers. Their experience of migration, their responsibilities, their aspirations, relationships with their families, their personal lives and relationships with their employers are somewhat different.

Women give various reasons for their move to the city; some of the most common reasons are—not being able to make ends meet in their village, the desire for upward mobility, positive experience of other migrants (like relatives, friends, co-villagers), indebtedness, an existing tradition of migration of at least one son in landowning families (with small land holdings), scandals, etc. Gulab, for instance, left her village in Darbhanga district of Bihar because the little land that they had was inundated in floods. Her husband had already migrated to Delhi; there wasn't much money to feed the children and as a Brahmin (high caste) she was not allowed to seek employment.

Sushma, Namita, Shakuntala, Gulab and Meera are domestic workers. Sushma and Namita, originally from Hooghly district in West Bengal, migrated to Etah district in eastern UP through marriage. Shakuntala migrated from UP while Gulab and Meera came from Bihar. Most have thus migrated from the poorer states of India to a bustling metropolis. Although they have spent a sufficient period of time in the city, mainly in one location, they see themselves as having migrated from, and still 'belonging' to, their places of origin. They retain ties with their marital as well as natal villages. For some, the move to Delhi has involved a double migration—from their rural natal homes to their rural conjugal homes and then to the city of Delhi.

These and other women of the Lal Gumbad slum and Katwaria Sarai, have migrated with their husbands or followed them once the husbands gained a foothold in the city, especially in terms of a place to stay. Like most other slums and urban villages in India these too have a concentration of unskilled and semi-skilled labour. The men work as masons, electricians, carpenters, drivers, load carriers, hawkers, shop assistants and in the hotel and entertainment industry while the women are mostly domestic labourers. Their employment can be casual daily wage employment or on a monthly basis. However, rarely is there any security in informal sector employment. The insecure nature of men's work and a strong desire to 'earn money' creates a need for women to work, most of whom enter domestic work.

Educating children, acquiring more consumption goods or simply making ends meet, in the case of the very poor, are other important imperatives. Migrants in urban areas are not necessarily among the poorest, even though those employed in the lowest echelons of the urban economy—like garbage and rag pickers, construction labourers, load carriers—may indeed lead very poor and insecure lives. As most literature on migrants reveal, it is not necessarily the poorest who migrate. Migration (whether seasonal or long-term) is often a livelihood diversification strategy practiced by several sections of rural society. Singh (1984: 101) states that between 20–35 per cent of working women among low income urban groups are the sole providers for their families—either because they are alone or because their husbands or other male adults in the household are unemployed, ill, handicapped or simply irresponsible with their incomes.

Leaving Home: Migration Trajectories

Whether migration to the city is a positive or negative experience for the migrant depends on his/her success in finding employment, establishing a residence and gaining a foothold in the city. For women who are able to find steady employment, the move to the city is a positive one. Moving away from their village frees them from the constraints of the local social structure. Paid employment, especially, is an avenue that is not always open to all women in villages. In the village even the men may have been constrained to not allow women to work, even if the need was there. In the city, women are able to take on jobs/occupations that would not have been acceptable in their villages due to both caste and status considerations. The anonymity of the city frees women in several other ways; the hold of caste and village hierarchies and norms weakens; patriarchy too can be challenged. Sushma, for example, felt cloistered in a village atmosphere. Being a Bengali married to a UP-ite, the *purdah* (veil) custom and strict patriarchal norms of behaviour were confining for her. The in-laws controlled the expenditure and her mother-in-law barely allowed her to have a decent meal. She had spent time in Delhi earlier since her mother-in-law worked in several homes as domestic help. The mother-in-law did not allow her to take on similar work and instead she and her husband earned a living as vegetable vendors. The family moved back to the village once the mother-in-law became old and fell sick. After she died, Sushma moved back to the city. The decision to move back to the city was largely hers. She felt that in the village the children would not be educated and would become idlers. No paid work was available to her in the village. Although they owned a small piece of land, they could only eke out a subsistence living. Sushma's reputation as a good worker has got her steady employment and allowed her to create an economically comfortable life for herself and her children. She earns more than her husband, and her income flow is steadier. Her expenditure is focused on taking care of the family's basic needs with a goal of getting her three children educated.

Gulab, a poor Brahmin woman from Bihar, works as a domestic help in several houses in an affluent neighbourhood. In her own village she was prohibited from seeking paid work because of her high caste. Poverty and indebtedness drove her away from the village. For a Brahmin, washing dishes, sweeping and cleaning in others' houses is considered demeaning, unclean and polluting. Yet, due to her circumstances, and the easy availability of domestic work in the city, Gulab has chosen this as her means to relieve her poverty and take care of debts incurred during her daughter's marriage. She has to arrange for the *gauna* (when the married girl returns to her marital home for consummation of the marriage) for which she needs a lakh (a hundred thousand) of rupees. Back in her village she has told people that she works in a *bindi* factory. Making *bindi*s (a decorative stick-on adornment worn on the forehead, and traditionally a sign of a married woman) is auspicious and not demeaning, work that will not compromise the reputation and purity of even a poor Brahmin. In the city her sons study in school and work part-time to earn an extra income. She is rumoured to be living with a pandit (a Brahmin priest) while her own husband, who is mentally imbalanced, appears and disappears.

Gulab's experience of migration and life in the city lends itself to complex and interesting interpretations. Gulab came to Delhi 12 years ago, after not being able to make ends meet in the village. She was accompanied by a fellow villager who was also travelling to Delhi. She took along her 7-year-old son, while another son and daughter were left behind in the village. Her husband, who was already in Delhi, had been mentally imbalanced ever since a major flood in the village inundated his land. He was no longer earning and would disappear for long periods of time. Gulab's home in Darbhanga district was constantly under threat from floods. She said that most people had left the village because there was no work and no food. There was not even fuel to keep the home fires going. During floods, the government would drop food packets from a helicopter. If it was cooked food that was supplied as aid, as Brahmins their family couldn't avail of it; caste restrictions prohibited them from consuming food prepared by cooks of unknown caste. She mentioned that only 'small' (low) castes consumed such food.

For the past 10 years Gulab has been living in the Lal Gumbad slum adjoining an upmarket Delhi neighbourhood. Over the years she has put down roots in the slum. With her savings and with a loan from Mathura (in the state of Uttar Pradesh—loans being cheaper there) and another loan from an employer she purchased one floor of a *jhuggi* for Rs 25,000, while the pandit with whom she has a relationship bought the other floor for Rs 20,000, the total cost being Rs 45,000. At present, she has her two sons, her daughter and her son-in-law, plus their child, living with her. The pandit eats with them. According to Gulab, she makes just enough money to subsist.

She cannot go back to her village home because there is neither a house nor land to go back to. In fact, the care of her mother-in-law who is back in the village is becoming a problem. She went to the village recently with plans to build a new house but could not do so because of floods. Her children want her to sell the land and buy a house in Delhi and settle down. A generational change in attitude can be observed here. While for her the village is still very much part of her world, it is not so for her children who see Delhi as their only home.

Gulab started her working life in Delhi doing household work and looking after children for a Marwari family. Soon she moved out and began to do part-time work as a domestic in several homes. She prefers to work as a part-time maid because it means earning more and having her independence. The slum also affords a community life. She is able to keep her family with her, something that would have been difficult if she was in a 'quarter' (a room at an employer's home).

What Gulab has been able to achieve in the city would not have been possible in her village. The anonymity of the city allows her to work (to take up work that is considered polluting by her caste but brings her a decent income), and the availability of work and good relationships with employers have allowed her to stabilise her household financially and put down roots in the city. Finally, the city has allowed her to have a relationship with a man who is not her husband, which would not have been possible in the village. Her husband, though around, appears and disappears from their lives, so the sense of emotional and strategic support has come from the pandit with whom she pooled in money to buy the ground floor of a *jhuggi*.

While migration for Gulab and Sushma can be considered a net positive experience that keeps them in the city, Namita and her husband have had frequent problems ever since they migrated. Their children are out of school, and with no work prospects Namita ran the household for a year by progressively selling off her gold ornaments. Some extra income she earned as a 'go-between', arranging marriages of men from her husband's village with women of her own and neighbouring villages in West Bengal, was finished quickly. She and her husband are now contemplating returning to his village in UP where they have some land and a *kachcha* (mud) house. Their financial situation was aggravated by the illnesses of the husband and one of their sons. The migration of couples like Namita and her husband can be viewed as long duration cycles, where they return to the village only to come back to the city once again.

Women's Labour and the Survival of the Migrant Family

Living in nuclear households (Sushma) or female-headed households (Gulab) in the city, the women decide how finances are to be allocated, at least the portion of the income they earn. Sushma proudly announces that her children are always well fed—they often get treats from her and she maintains an account at the local grocer who supplies the children with small items in her absence. With the money she has saved and the help of a loan, she has built a small *pukka* (brick) house in the village in UP at a cost of Rs 20,000. The family does not feel that they have left their village home for good, hence the investment in the village home which results in an improved social status in the village. In Delhi, she is proud of the few gold ornaments and a box bed that she has acquired through her own savings. Although her parents and siblings in her natal village in Bengal are extremely poor, with her father being a daily wage labourer, none of her earnings go to them. With three children to support she feels she is unable to help her natal family. Sushma's control over her own earnings has given her a certain degree of autonomy vis-à-vis her husband and his family, an issue discussed later.

Part-time domestic labourers work for several households during the course of a day. Depending on the nature of the agreement, they make one or two rounds a day per house. The working day of women employed in the domestic sector is long and arduous. They set out on their rounds very early in the day—the timetable being dictated by the work routines and needs of their employers. Most women work all seven days, with no fixed working hours, designated holidays or guaranteed vacation time. Vacation time is negotiated with the employers, generally to attend family functions or to go home. Too many sick days or un-negotiated leave can affect income and even result in loss of work. Most women enter into mutually acceptable relationships with their employers, arriving at a consensus over terms and conditions of the work. When the consensus breaks down, the relationship is terminated. Sometimes, the loss of work in even one household can set back the woman's income substantially, impacting an already tight budget.

Yet, employers can provide a cushion when needed. They are a source of small and large loans, especially for women who have had a steady and long-term work relationship with particular households. Help is especially crucial during illness or accident of a family member or when large expenditures such as on marriages and funerals are mandated. Gifts during festivals, hand-me-down clothes and presents of other consumer items ease the pressure on finances. Employers are the source of jobs for new migrants, and sometimes for the children of employees.

Cooperation and Competition for Work

Aspects of the traditional jajmani (patron-client) system are replicated in domestic work too by both patrons and by clients. Women enter into what can be called 'vertical' relationships with their patrons and 'horizontal' ones with other domestic workers. Besides the cash payment they receive for their work, workers also receive gifts on auspicious occasions in the employer's household and annually at Diwali and at some other festivals. Reciprocally, they may be required to put in extra effort on some occasions at the patron's home. As in jajmani, women zealously guard 'their households' and do not allow other workers to infringe on their turf. For the patron too, terminating a worker is not easy. When Shakuntala was replaced by her employer with Sushma who was a better worker, the former harassed the latter for days, accusing her of 'stealing her children's bread' and of 'cutting Shakuntala's stomach to fill her own'. Sushma, being a good worker, had built up a steady clientele and was in a position to help others find work. This she did for those related to her and new migrants from her own marital village. Women who lived and worked in the same neighbourhood while helping one another in times of necessity also evaluated each others' standards of living and behaviour. Expenditure that is unaffordable or outside one's means is commented upon negatively. For example, Namita's buying a colour TV when her husband was out of work and their children out of school, was considered inexcusable. Borrowing from neighbours and relatives is extremely common and almost everyone needs to borrow often. The loans, however, must be paid back, to ensure that one is able to borrow again.

If women take up work that takes them away from the house and their children, who takes care of their children? They fit their own housework, domestic lives (family duties), childcare, socialising, leisure and their children's schooling into their work routines. For childcare, women enter into several reciprocal arrangements with friends and neighbours. A parallel solution is to bring a younger female from the village to look after one's own children. Group childminding is organised in the neighbourhood for a small fee. The fact that slums and urban villages are face-to-face societies makes it easier to organise such care. The social organisation of slums and urban villages are somewhat similar to village sections or lanes—people connected with each other through links of kinship/friendship/village/region inhabit adjoining spaces. Thus doors are often left unlocked and children tend to themselves; neighbours baby-sit children whose mothers are at work; local grocers give goods on credit. There are many parallels to be seen here with international migrants who create communities in their migration destination.

The slums and urban villages where most female migrants work as domestic labour display a large element of the rural way of life. Residents of these habitations are mostly rural in origin (Bihar, one of the poorest states, sends the largest number of migrants to urban metropolises such as Delhi, Mumbai and Kolkata). Migration takes place through networks of family and friends who have migrated earlier from rural areas. Hence, parts of entire localised social networks are often transported to the urban habitat. Celebration of local festivals serves to reinforce the sense of community.

Additionally, given the low level of physical and infrastructural development in the slums and urban areas, the poor find it more economical to replicate a rural lifestyle than to switch instantly to an urban one. Thus, the homes of village neighbours can still be next to each other in the new urban location, the fuel used for cooking can be biomass and cowdung cakes, and rural modes of celebrating life-cycle rituals can be replicated accurately. Yet, unlike the village, the modes of the city intrude much more forcefully into the lives of the people. This is so especially in relation to accessing infrastructural services. The need to prove legality as residents drives the poor to acquire signs of citizenship such as ration cards, voter identity cards, water and electricity bills; these 'signs' of an urban legality can only be obtained through the mediation of the local political machine, politicising the everyday existence of the poor. Accessing services, in fact, involves activating democracy at its most local and basic level because it is only through the conduit of local representatives that poor rural migrants obtain access to basic services such as electricity, water and sanitation.

Transformation of Gender Relations and Female Identities in the Context of Migration: Ambiguities of 'Habitus'

The 'habitus' of the woman migrant is composed of a complex mental map that encompasses the imperatives of her rural as well as urban life. She has not disengaged herself completely from the values and responsibilities of her rural life, and at the same time is deeply influenced by the structure of urban life in which her present is embedded. The move to the city is thus an ambiguous experience for most female migrants. That the urban social structure allows for greater exercise of women's agency, and entering into paid work especially, and opens up choices of consumption, values and behaviour, is something undeniable. Despite the considerable control that many of these women have gained over their material lives, deeply embedded patriarchal values often remain unchallenged. The lack of opportunities for occupational mobility for women and the need to conform to norms of both the village and the city keeps women in a subordinate position to men.

Gender relations and roles are frequently transformed in the context of migration. In domestic work, a major issue that women face is protecting their sexual integrity. Women face suspicion from husbands and may face harassment from male employers. Namita, for example, quit work for a whole year because her husband kept constantly accused her of having relations with her employers. To 'show him' she decided to stay at home; eventually she had to go back to work because the husband fell ill and was not making enough money to support her and her three children. With her sister-in-law's help she managed to 'catch' (get work in) a few houses and is now better off. Her not going to work can be seen as an act of assertion, a challenge she would have been unable to mount in the context of the village where she was dependent on her husband for basic sustenance. Sushma's husband too taunts her and suspects her fidelity, but does not dare to ask her to quit work knowing that she brings in an equal or greater contribution to the household. Both Namita and Sushma pay attention to their personal grooming and believe in being well groomed when they leave for work. They spend money at festivals and look forward to festive occasions that give them a break from the monotony of an uninterrupted working life.

Although Gulab has not undergone a personal transformation in putting herself and her needs first (she hardly spends any money on herself—her clothes are given to her by the families she works for, and she does not venture out to markets or to visit relatives in the city by herself), and is totally occupied with taking care of her extended family, she has become empowered enough to be the breadwinner of the family, put her sons through school, marry off her daughter and a son; in short, accomplish her life's responsibilities as she perceives them.

As Naila Kabeer (2000) argues in her book on Bangladeshi garment workers, paid employment is a necessary condition for challenging intra-household hierarchies; however it is not sufficient to tilt the balance of power—newfound independence too is filtered through values that women have already been socialised into. Control over women's fertility is another way in which men attempt to retain control over them. Sushma's clash with her husband occurred over the adoption of birth control measures. She has two sons and a daughter. She wants to undergo a tubectomy rather than constantly worry about getting pregnant in case she forgets to take birth control pills. Her husband refuses to let her do so for two reasons. He argues that if his brothers' wives back in the village can bear five or six children each then why does she have a problem in doing the same? His frame of reference remains the village society and his family backhome. Second, he fears that if she undergoes a tubectomy she will have to be absent from work and not be able to take care of work at home for several weeks. A deeper reason is that in the village, Sushma's physical mobility and social interaction with others was easily controlled by village social norms. In the city, her husband is unable to keep her confined indoors. Sushma also poses a threat to his self-esteem. Being a hard worker, she is well liked and earns a decent monthly income. Her husband's insecurity is manifested in his drinking bouts and his subsequent ill-treatment of Sushma. Fed up with the abuse, she is often ready to leave him and lead a life on her own. Sushma sees her husband as a liability and not as an asset.

Women often become the primary earners in the household. Many studies have documented the unequal burden borne in the household by poor women (see Beneria and Feldman 1992; Kabeer 1996). Kasturi's (1990) study of Tamil domestic workers in Delhi showed that 'women were equal if not the primary earners and men often remained unemployed, depending on the income of their womenfolk'. She argues that in fact it was the men who were 'associational' migrants and not the women. Her research revealed that the women had in fact migrated in response to female economic opportunities in domestic service. Similarly, women in the two fieldwork locations feel assured that they would have work even if they returned after an absence of several months, while the men found the going harder to get work consistently. Yet, women's wages remain comparatively lower than those of men.

Although life in the city has its ups and downs, few if any return to the village permanently. Men are more likely to go back and also more likely to pay frequent visits, especially if they have property or a home in the village. Thus men frequently return during harvests and for land-related litigation. Women who have working lives in the city and in a sense have 'tasted' independence, do not wish to return to the village permanently. Although social ties to the village are kept alive and often strengthened by marrying children, especially daughters, back in the rural area, the women do not wish to return to a life in the village. Even though their work lives are hard in the city, working on the land is seen as worse drudgery and the lack of freedom is a serious deterrent.

A significant difference in perception of village and city life is made by the consumption styles possible in the city. For many of these women, upward mobility for their children is a distinct possibility. The better education facilities available in cities are a major draw; several women in the Lal Gumbad and Katwaria Sarai areas have engaged private tutors to supplement the education provided by the government school. The variety in food, entertainment and expenditure on consumption goods such as LPG for cooking, air coolers, radio and television sets, etc., also play their part in the attractiveness of the city package. With their own earnings in hand, women are also able to spend money on themselves.

Poverty and Insecurity

The insecurity in the lives of migrant women in domestic labour comes from the non-formal nature of their work and their poverty (see Kaur 2001b; Kundu 1993; Kundu and Gupta 1996; Unni and Rani 2003). Work conditions are arduous, especially for those who take up jobs in numerous households. There are no rules as to vacation, overtime or bonuses. Each employee negotiates these with the employer. The market value of the work varies depending on the income levels of the neighbourhood. However, within a neighbourhood most workers are well acquainted with prevailing rates and attempt their best to negotiate an acceptable deal for themselves. Work can be terminated by the employer or employee if either feels a cause for dissatisfaction.

A perpetual source of risk is illness in the family. A major illness can set the household back in various ways. The woman may lose her employment if she absents herself for too many days; more often than not, money is borrowed from family, friends and employers. A family operating at subsistence can sink into further poverty as a result of a major illness, especially if it inflicts one of the breadwinners. Given the poor condition of sanitation in most slums and urban villages, poor women and their families are exposed to frequent illnesses, which cut into their tight budgets. Social obligations, in one's place of residence and in the native village, also require substantial financial expenditure. Expenses incurred during the marriage of daughters, and the need to accumulate a dowry for daughters, often leads to a state of indebtedness.

Conclusion

This paper has explored the reasons for the space created for migrant women in the domestic work sector in the city of Delhi. It shows that internal migration by women is no longer male-dependent and that women are migrating in response to economic and social imperatives. Paid employment, especially if it is steady, does not only have economic consequences allowing the woman to stabilise her household financially, but also has far reaching sociological consequences. The perspective of the migrant woman includes her own and her children's future within the rural-urban 'habitus' comprising of institutions and values pertaining to both locations. The autonomy in intra-household decision-making that results from paid income allows women to challenge several patriarchal structures and relationships, both belonging to her rural and urban 'presents'. However, as revealed by the trajectories of several women rural migrants to Delhi, migration and its effects, as mediated by the city, remain complex, and migration outcomes are uneven, both in terms of changing power equations and material success.

References and Further Readings

Beneria, Lourdes and Shelley Feldman (ed.). 1992. *Unequal Burden: Economic Crisis, Persistent Poverty and Women's Work*. Boulder, Colorado: Westview Press.

Chopra, Radhika. 1995. 'Maps of Experience: Narratives of Migration in an Indian Village', *Economic and Political Weekly*, 9 December: 3156–162.

Fawcett, J.T., S-E Khoo and P.C. Smith. 1984. *Women in the Cities of Asia: Migration and Urban Adaptation*. Boulder, Colorado: Westview Press.

Gardner, K. and F. Osella. 2003. 'Migration, Modernity and Social Transformation in South Asia: An Overview', *Contributions to Indian Sociology*, New series, 37(1&2).

de Haan, Arjan. 1999. 'Livelihoods and Poverty: The Role of Migration—A Critical Review of the Migration Literature', *The Journal of Development Studies*, 36(2): December: 1–47.

de Haan, Arjan. 2000. 'Migrants, Livelihoods, and Rights: the Relevance of Migration in Development Policies', working paper, Social Development Department, DFID.

de Haan, Arjan and Ben Rogaly. 2002. 'Introduction: Migrant Workers and their Role in Rural Change', *Journal of Development Studies*, 37(5): 1–14.

Jolly, S., E. Bell and L. Narayanaswamy. 2003. *Gender and Migration in Asia: Overview and Annotated Bibliography*, Institute of Development Studies, Sussex.

Kabeer, Naila. 2000. *Bangladeshi Women Workers and Labour Market Decisions: The Power to Choose*. New Delhi: Vistaar Publications.

———. 1996. *Reversed Realities: Gender Hierarchies in Development Thought*. New Delhi: Kali for Women.

Karlekar, M. 1995. 'Gender Dimensions in Labour Migration: An Overview', in Loes Schenk-Sandbergen (ed.), *Women and Seasonal Labour Migration*. New Delhi: Sage Publications.

Kasturi, Leela. 1990. 'Poverty, Migration and Women's Status', in Vina Mazumdar (ed.), *Women Workers in India: Studies on Employment and Status*. New Delhi: Chanakya Publications.

Kaur, Ravinder. 2001a. 'Contested Spaces: Environmental Agendas and the Urban Poor', paper presented at the UGC National Seminar on 'Globalisation and India's Environment', S.N.D.T. University, Mumbai, 15–16 February.

Kaur, Ravinder. 2001b. 'Aspects of Poverty in a Metropolis: A Case Study of an Affluent Slum' in R.S. Sandhu et al. (eds), *Sustainable Human Settlements: The Asian Experience*. Jaipur: Rawat Publications.

———. 2004. 'Across-region Marriages: Poverty, Female Migration and the Sex Ratio', *Economic and Political Weekly*, XXXIX(25): 19–25 June.

Kundu, A. 1993. *In the Name of the Urban Poor*. New Delhi: Sage Publications.

Kundu, A. and S. Gupta. 1996. 'Migration, Urbanisation and Regional Inequality', *Economic and Political Weekly*, 28 December.

Momsen, J.H. (ed.). 1999. *Gender, Migration and Domestic Service*. New York: Routledge.

Mukhopadhyay, S. and R. Sudarshan. 2003. *Tracking Gender Equity Under Economic Reforms*. New Delhi: Kali for Women, and International Development Research Centre, Canada.

Neetha, N. 2004. 'Making of Female Breadwinners: Migration and Social Networking of Women Domestics in Delhi' *Economic and Political Weekly*, XXXIX(17): 24–30 April.

Pessar, Patricia. 1999. 'The Role of Gender, Households, and Social Networks in the Migration Process: A Review and Appraisal' in C. Hirschman, P. Kaisnitz and J. DeWind (eds), *The Handbook of International Migration*. New York: Russell Sage Foundation.

Schenk-Sandbergen, L. 1995. *Women and Seasonal Labour Migration*, Indo-Dutch Series on Development Alternatives 16, New Delhi: Sage Publications.

Sharma, Ursula. 1986. *Women's Work, Class and the Urban Household: A Study of Shimla, North India*. London and New York: Tavistock Publications.

Sharpe, Pamela. 2001. *Women, Gender and Labour Migration: Historical and Global Perspectives*. New York: Routledge.

Singh, A.M. 1984. 'Rural to Urban Migration of Women in India: Patterns and Implications' in J.T. Fawcett et al. (eds), *Women in the Cities of South Asia: Migration and Urban Adaptation*. Boulder, Colorado: Westview Press.

Srivastava, Ravi. 2003. 'An Overview of migration in India, its impacts and key issues', DFID.

Srivastava, Ravi and S.K. Sasikumar. 2003. 'An Overview of Migration in India, Its Impacts and Key Issues', DFID, UK, available at www.livelihoods.org.

Thadani, V.N. and M.P. Todaro. 1984. 'Female Migration: A Conceptual Framework' in J.T. Fawcett et al. (eds), *Women in the Cities of Asia: Migration and Urban Adaptation*. Boulder, Colorado: Westview Press.

Townsend, J. 2000. *Women and Power: Fighting Patriarchies and Poverty*. Zed Books: London.

Unni, J. and U. Rani. 2003. 'Gender, Informality and Poverty', in *Seminar*, 531, November.

10

Sex Work, Poverty and Migration in Eastern India

Geetanjali Gangoli

There are close connections between migration, poverty and women who enter into sex work. Migration into sex work, often understood in the public discourse as trafficking, takes place in different contexts and in different locations. International studies on migration reveal the gendered nature of migration—while one in every two migrants in the world is a woman, the economic and social choices available to migrant women and men differ (Gulchar and Ilkkarachan 2002). This paper looks at the status of migrant sex workers in different contexts and in different discourses—primarily state discourses and NGO perspectives. Are the varying discourses based on the experiences of women in the sex trade, or on inherent legal, moral and social agendas?

The paper is divided into two sections. The first section looks at the organisation of the sex trade in two states in India—West Bengal and Orissa. Why do women enter the sex trade? What are the links between sex work and migration; what links, if any, do women in the sex trade have with their families. What impact does migration into sex work have on the productive and reproductive roles of women? The second section looks at how NGOs and the state look at the issue of migration and sex work, and legislative initiatives to regulate and systematise sex work. Will the legalisation of sex work enable better working conditions, and monitor and regulate migration, or will it legalise a social evil?

Organisation of Sex Work

It has been suggested that the livelihood of women in the sex trade can be adequately gauged through a study of three stages in their lives—prior to joining the trade, during the period of work and after leaving the trade.[1] I now look at the organisation of the sex trade in Kolkata, Bhubaneshwar and Tikarapada.

Entry

Women have been known to join the sex trade for a variety of reasons. As Table 10.1 demonstrates, there is no single reason why women enter prostitution.

Table 10.1 Entry into Sex Trade

Reasons for joining	Total number	Total percentage
Acute poverty	221	49.10
Willingness	39	8.67
Family disputes	97	21.56
Misguidance	70	15.56
Tradition	21	4.67
Kidnapping	2	0.44

Source: (DMSC 1997a).

Poverty

Acute poverty is the single most important reason for women joining sex work in Kolkata. Studies in Orissa similarly suggest that economic survival, lack of employment opportunities and poverty are the central reasons for entering prostitution, with over 30 per cent women entering sex work due to poverty (Pandey et al. 2003). In addition, social and economic deprivation caused by natural calamities in the state, such as the 1999 cyclone, led to an increase in migration and sex work.[2] In tribal Orissa, women start sex work due to social and economic exploitation. They may enter contract labour, and are often raped. Then they enter prostitution. In some villages in Balasore, families sell their daughters into prostitution due to poverty. In some areas the network of traffickers is so powerful that families sometimes send their daughters into the trade under compulsion. Other reasons are dowry demands. In western Orissa (bordering Andhra Pradesh), dowry demands are very high, and women frequently enter into sex work to earn money for their dowry.[3]

Coercion and Force

Some media and academic discourse underscores the role of coercion and force in the entry of women into sex work (HRW 1995; Sinha and Sleightholme 1996). During the course of my fieldwork however, I found that while many women started off by narrating stories of coercion and violence, once a relationship had been established, their stories often changed. As a paper (Campbell 2000) on sex workers in a South African mine points out, people's stories of being tricked into sex work were remarkably similar, almost part of a script. However:

> ... the objective veracity of people's accounts is not the most important or interesting feature of the life histories. What is more important is how people reconstruct and account for their life choices, given that these accounts reflect the social identities that play a key role in shaping people's sexual behaviour. In this context, the main interest of these stories of origin lies in the role that they play as a strategy for coping with a spoiled identity ... (ibid.).

In India, as in South Africa, social stigma may be a powerful factor pushing women in sex work to cast themselves as 'innocent victims'. Once the researcher spends time and energy in the field, the stories often change. Women who started in the first instance recounting uncomplicated stories of 'innocent victimhood', later trusted me enough to recast themselves as agents. The following excerpts from my interviews make this clearer:

> I've been in India for the past 12-and-a-half years. I was brought here by my fate; nobody has kept me here by force ... I am in touch with my family. I send money and letters home regularly.[4]

> I started working because I fought with my mother-in-law. She abused me and harassed me. My husband is an alcoholic. He pushed

me to enter sex work, and I realised that it was the only way I could earn some money and feed my family. I go to Bowbazar in the morning and have rented a house there.[5]

Someone from my village who belongs to this line brought me here. I came because our family is too poor to look after me.[6]

Migration

Sex work and migration are often linked. This can be attributed to a number of causal factors: the relative anonymity of the new destination, limited options for employment and the need to survive in a new location without family support. International research has revealed that sex work is one of the most lucrative options available to women (Gulchar and Ilkkarachan 2002). For migrant women the act of migration is seen as going against the 'traditional' female role of staying at home and being looked after by the men in their families; they are therefore pushed into sex work as they are already seen as being transgressive (Chew 1999). Having stepped out of the normative 'female role', they are more amenable to opportunities that may not be acceptable in their place of origin.

How women enter the sex trade is therefore an extremely complex phenomenon. It is important to look at the multiple ways in which women and minors enter and negotiate entry into prostitution, and to look at the compulsions pushing women into arranging their lives into simplified stories of force and coercion for the consumption of researchers and journalists.

Organisation of Sex Trade

Brothel-based Sex Work in Kolkata

There are about 80,000 sex workers in Kolkata.[7] Brothel-based sex work in Sonagachi, Kolkata follows a fairly regulated system. Sex workers can start work by the time they are 9 or 10 and many continue till their mid-30s. At the lowest of the hierarchy are the *chokris* (young girls), who are mostly bound to the *maashi* (literally 'aunt', a generic term for a brothel owner) who purchases them from agents or from their relatives. The *chokris* work under highly regulated conditions and stay with their *maashi* until they can pay off the advance amount. Next are the *adhiyas* (literally 'halves'), who operate semi-independently, and pay half the amount earned to the room provider. Some sex workers operate through the *dalal-bari* system—they contract clients through a *dalal* (middleman). This allows them to escape the legal ban on soliciting clients. At the top of the hierarchy is the *swadhin* (independent) sex worker, who takes a room, pays an advance or rent, bears all the expenses and keeps all the earnings (DMSC 1997b). The average age at which girls become *swadhin* is 18. After working as sex workers till their 30s, women retire from active sex work and take up other related professions.

'Flying' Sex Workers

Another aspect of the sex trade in Kolkata is that of informal or 'flying' sex workers. Some are based in nearby villages or suburbs of the city and come to the red light area in the evening or the day. Most of them are single women; some are married with children. With factories and alternative means of employment decreasing in the city, middle-class housewives and students act as 'flying' sex workers. They are more vulnerable than brothel-based women in Kolkata. Not being a part of the protective brothel system means they have less negotiating powers.[8]

Full-time sex workers express hostility towards freelancers, seeing them as poachers on their territory. They are also resented for combining a socially respectable life with prostitution.[9] Both categories of sex workers experience the red light area and sex work differently. Part-time prostitutes see the red light area as a space where they can practice their professions and sex work as a way to supplement their personal or family income. There is some degree of shame and secrecy associated with their work, but they have the persona of respectability to fall back on, once outside the area. Full-time sex workers see the red light area as a space they 'own' and have partial rights over.

Informalisation of the sex trade has also led to decentralisation of the trade and a move away from the red light areas. It is suggested that the expansion due to NGO interventions in Kolkata (especially by the influential Durbar Mahila Samanwaya Committee, or DMSC) has given sex workers confidence to expand the scope of their workspace.[10]

Other Forms of Sex Trade Organisation

Sex work in Bhubaneswar also takes the form of street-based, family-based and brothel-based sex work. Some sex workers in Bhubaneswar are located in the red light slum of Malishahi, near the railway station. The red light area was, 11 years ago, located in an area close to the city centre. They were then relocated to a distant suburb. Faced with the decline of their trade, individual sex workers came to Malishahi, an urban slum, near the city centre.[11] Sex workers in the city of Bhubaneshwar have faced repeated fears of dislocation, stopped by legal action by the Orissa Patita Udhar Samiti (OPUS).

The trade itself is small—with only 80–100 women. They come mainly from Cuttack, Keonjhar and Kolkata. Some are from Bangladesh. The women often live with their families, or with partners. They work for 'owners', women who rent out houses to them for a percentage of their earnings, that can go up to half of their income.[12]

Family-based sex work takes place in the village of Tikarapada in Angul district of Orissa. Tikarapada has four hamlets; made up of fisherfolk, cultivators, Harijans and the *ghatashahi*s (river bank residents). The sex workers are either *ghatashahi*s or temporary migrants from Malishahi, Angul and Phulbani. Both are socially excluded within the village. Prostitution began here in the 1940s to meet the demands of the labourers of a paper mill. After the mill closed down in 1982, prostitution was given a boost by the tourist trade centring around the nearby crocodile sanctuary. Tourism takes place mostly between October and February. The sex trade is controlled by middlemen or *dalal*s who contact customers and keep 20 per cent of the earnings of the women. The income varies seasonably. The income earned during the 4–5 months is used for the entire year. Three or four sex workers can earn between Rs 5,000–10,000 a day in the tourist season. Most of the women earn about Rs 500–1,000 a day.[13]

Issues of Financial Access and Aging

Women in the sex industry experience sex work as a survival strategy; however, the issue gets complicated by the human rights violations within the trade, linked to issues of access to the resources generated. There are essentially two points of view here. One is that the sex trade should be abolished as it is discriminatory, and women in the trade rehabilitated; another that women in the sex trade have differential access to resources through their working lives.

Propagandists of the first point of view believe that while the money generated in the sex trade is linked to sexual exploitation and is 'enjoyed' by pimps and brothel owners, not the sex workers themselves (Sanlaap 1998). In the case of family-based sex work in places such as Tikarapada and Garai, activists argue that the income generated by women is used by the men in the family.[14] While there are no established statistics on the earnings of sex-workers, NGOs have tried to make some informed assertions.

Assuming there are 20,000 sex workers in Kolkata, each with a gross average earning of Rs 100 a day, the total turnover is Rs 2 million per day and Rs 60 million per month, with an average annual turnover of Rs 720 million. Only a small part of this goes to sex workers; the rest goes to recruiters, middlemen, agents, pimps, brothel keepers, live-in partners, liquor sellers, the underworld and the police (Sanlaap 1998).

However, the percentage of her income that a sex worker controls depends on a variety of factors, including the stage of sex work that she is in and the degree of NGO organisation in the area she is working in. In the earlier stages of her work, a brothel-based sex worker may have little or no access to the income that she has generated. Deductions are made from the amount earned by the sex worker to pay off the interest for the amount paid by the brothel owner to 'purchase' the woman, and for the charges made for her rent and lodging. All of these are often inflated. Even if she manages to get independent, she still has to pay rent and bribes to the police and local goons for protection. Sex workers belonging to the DMSC and OPUS however point out that unionisation has meant a reduction in the amount of corruption and extra legal payments to the police.

Women in the sex trade in Kolkata often support their families. Many send up to 50 per cent of their income home.[15] As an activist points out:

> They have a continuing link with their families. Some even send money to their former husbands regularly, even if they (the husbands) have remarried. They continue to have some allegiance with the husband, even if they have been abandoned by him. Most send money home regularly to their parents and brothers, they arrange the education of their brothers, marry off their sisters. The amount that they send varies ... But most send something home.[16]

Sex workers point out that the sex trade provides employment and income to a range of people in and around the red light area:

... our family members aren't the only people that are being supported by us. We provide livelihood to so many people: because we practice our trade, the local hotels and *paan*-cigarette wallahs do so well, they earn more money than others outside the red light area. Taxiwallahs charge more money from clients if they want to come to the red light area. But even these people, who depend on us, look at us with loathing.[17]

NGOs often express a bias against family members dependent on sex workers. This could be based on patriarchal notions of morality, masculinity and income generation. It both denies women agency—in supporting their families through sex work—and stigmatises men economically dependent on women.

Most older women are unable to eke out a living through sex work, and move on to other or related professions. If they have managed to save enough money to buy some property, they rent out rooms to practicing sex workers or run a brothel. Others sell liquor, *paan* and cigarettes in the area. There are a sizeable number of cases where older women marry their partners, but continue to live in the red light area.[18] There are, of course, exceptions to this trend, and older women in the profession sometimes continue to have a clientele. A 40-year-old sex worker in Kolkata told me that while she doesn't work regularly, she still entertains the occasional client. She spoke about a young, attractive college boy who had been coming to her for the past six months: 'I ask him why he comes to me. I am twice his age. He says that he comes here because I have such beautiful eyes. He doesn't care about my age'.[19]

In areas like Tikarapada, however, where there is no organised red light area, the economic opportunities for older women in the profession are fewer and many older sex workers end up destitute (NSS n.d.). Similarly, interviews with sex workers in Bhubaneshwar suggest that they do not have any contact with their families. None of them see leaving the sex trade as being viable due to the social stigma attached.

NGO and State Interventions

This section will explore NGO and state perceptions and interventions into migration/trafficking and prostitution. There are essentially at least three ways in which Indian NGOs and the state have addressed the issue of prostitution—silence, as hurt and violence, and as potential choice and liberation. Each of these stands has potential policy implications ranging from tolerance and zoning to legalisation and decriminalisation. I suggest that all these perspectives are limited, in that they do not necessarily take in the wide range of experiences that women in prostitution encounter. And in different ways, they may well feed into mainstream patriarchal views on prostitution—'silencing' leads to women in sex work becoming invisible, seeing sex work in terms of 'hurt and violence' portrays women as eternal victims, and understanding sex work in terms of 'choice and liberation' denies the harm and violence inherent in that activity (Gangoli 1998).

Coercion and the Sex Trade

Some NGOs and government representatives believe that prostitution cannot be seen as 'work', because it involves large-scale violence against women and children at the point of entry and because migration into prostitution is inherently involuntary and coercive (NCW 1997; Sanlaap 1999).

The term 'childhood' generally signifies easy living, easy nutrition, love, warmth, support and an overall affectionate environment. But 15 per cent of India's estimated two million prostitutes who are believed to be children have a different story to tell (NCW 1997). As trafficking and prostitution among children assumes alarming proportions (in India nearly 200 girls and women are either inducted into or enter the trade everyday), we as a nation are confronted with a grim reality that is hard to ignore (NCW 1997).

This analysis blurs the distinction between violence and degradation. While violence is experiential, degradation is socially constructed. A lot of 'legitimate' work is violent and can be degrading. Besides, by isolating prostitution as an important if not primary site of violence ignores violence against women and girl children within the family, including child marriage. The mean age of marriage and entry into sex work in India is 12.5 years (UN 1998). Early marriages can perhaps be compared in their mental and physical effects to child prostitution, since both involve premature sexual activity causing trauma for the child (Mikhail 2002). More to the point, the Sanlaap position focuses on children within prostitution and extends the analysis to adult women. Prostitution of children is certainly violative of their rights as it exposes them to sexual activity when they lack the physical and mental maturity to cope with it. Like other forms of sexual activity involving children—as in incest and child marriage—the issue of consent is irrelevant. By extending this understanding to all prostitutes, women and children are equated, leading to a certain infantilisation of women.

It has also been argued that the distinction drawn between free and forced prostitution fits into the agenda of the sex industry, since it gives the industry stability and security and makes it difficult for women to 'prove' that they have been coerced into prostitution. Further, that the move by prostitute's rights organisations to legalise prostitution is a Western influence, and unwise given the composition of the sex industry in India and the consent of the women is irrelevant as a rationale for sex work (HRW 1995; Pal 1999). These perspectives can be critiqued on the following grounds. One, like the Sanlaap position, that it infantilises adult women in prostitution. Second, it denies women agency, preferring to see them as undifferentiated and permanent victims. Finally, it draws an artificial and forced distinction between the East and the West. The West is projected as immoral, a geographical entity where women enter prostitution voluntarily. In contrast, the East—represented by India—is a space where women give up their 'honour' reluctantly if at all. Efforts to 'prevent' prostitution, thus, stems from a belief that women within the profession are uniformly oppressed and hence need to be rescued from their situation, thus taking the form of 'feminist social work' (Guha-Bhuvaneswar 1998). The issue of choice within prostitution is not even dignified with a debate on the issue. On the contrary, there is a complete silence on the issue, thus marginalising those women whose experiences do not fit into the saga of kidnapping, suffering and coercion. This rhetoric homogenises women, and lacks understanding of how cultural contexts, class and caste may play a role in trafficking. Age, caste, class and marital status are variables that affect women's control over their lives. My fieldwork reveals that among the sex workers in Kolkata, some belonged to upper caste families in Uttar Pradesh or Bihar, and had come to Kolkata after being widowed and being deserted by their natal and parental families. The widow is seen as belonging to no man, so her natal and marital families abandon her.[20] However, not all widowed women deserted by their families take to prostitution. One can suggest that those who do make a clear choice in favour of prostitution over options like destitution, begging or badly paid informal work.

Connected to the concept of forced migration and trafficking is the concept of rehabilitation, based on the presumption that 'anything'—even starvation—is better than prostitution. Conceptually, rehabilitation does not examine what it is that makes prostitution seem more degraded than any other form of labour. As one view has it:

> When people use phrases such as 'the inherent harm in prostitution' I hear alarm bells and the hairs on the back of my neck stand on end. Are they, I wonder, referring to the work itself, i.e., the literal marketing of sex and sexuality or to the inherent harm and consequent damage located in the moral judgement of the work and the current laws and effective criminalisation of the work? (Wilcock 1999).

State Policies: The Legal Position

Existing laws look at the issue of migration into prostitution with some ambivalence. Framed in the late 1980s, the Prevention of Immoral Traffic in Women and Children Act (PITA) is ambivalent in its stated purpose of preventing prostitution. Prostitution is seen as a necessary evil, and the concern is to keep women in prostitution away from the public eye. The policies framed in the 1990s are far more draconian in their scope, seeking to control prostitutes as they are now identified as a threat not only to public order and morality, but also to public health, interpreted as the sexual health of men and their families.

While debating the Illegal Traffic in Women and Girls (Prevention) Bill in 1986 in the Lok Sabha, a combination of feminist and traditionalist arguments were used. The advocacy of women's groups was a major plank. Member of Parliament Margaret Alva who introduced the bill, said:

> The exploitation of women and girls for the purposes of prostitution is an obnoxious feature of crime against them ... prostitution has ... has ... been considered an evil that wrecks the foundations of the family and the community, as basic units of human society.... A number of individuals, advocacy groups and women's and voluntary organisations ... have been urging upon the government to enlarge the scope of the Act.[21]

Alva speaks with remarkable ease of prostitution as violence against women in the same breath as she considers it to be an evil against the family, romanticised as the basic unit of society. There seems a partial assimilation of feminist understanding of prostitution as violence against women. But Alva goes on to suggest that prostitution wreck families, ignoring some trenchant feminist critiques of the family. I would argue that this is not a deliberate oversight or a misunderstanding. Feminist analysis of prostitution as violence—and that women in prostitution are victims—can feed in as easily into a mainstream understanding that does not accept the family as *another* important site of oppression. Contrary to sex work destroying the family, women in prostitution have continuing economic and social links with their families. Thus prostitution can be seen not in opposition to the family, but as an inversion of patriarchal values where the natal family supports the daughter; initially as an unmarried daughter, and later through dowry. The social acceptance of this arrangement ignores the role of single women in the family in supporting the family through their labour.

Proposals for Change: The Central Authority

Proposals for changes to the law were made in the early 1990s by the Law Reform Project, headed by a lawyer and sponsored by the Department of Women and Child Development, Government of India. The report drafted two bills: The Prevention of Immoral Traffic and The Rehabilitation of Prostituted Persons Bill, 1993, and The Prohibition of Immoral Traffic and Empowerment of Sexual Workers Bill, 1993 (Menon 1994). As the titles reveal, the proposed bills continued to operate from the parameters of socially defined morality, within which prostitution—even if seen as work—is designated as immoral, even as prostitutes are seen in gender-neutral terms as workers and persons. However, as the rationale of the former bill brings out, a panic about the spread of HIV-AIDS was behind the creation of the bills:

> Immoral traffic … is continuing unabated … it has led to the spread of dreaded diseases including AIDS threatening public health generally and the life of prostituted persons in particular.… While voluntary sexual relations are the right of every adult citizen, it cannot be commercialised to the detriment of innocent victims, immature children, destitute women, and at the cost of social hygiene and public health (ibid.).

There were however some aspects of the bill that could potentially benefit sex workers. Under the bill, sex workers can file for compensation in cases of violence, coercion or refusal of the client to use 'medically advised hygienic procedures'. In addition, prostitution involving children is punishable with imprisonment and a fine. However, all those seen as abetting prostitution, including clients, are liable to fines and correctional or compensatory work. The names of clients are liable to be circulated by the government (ibid.).

The latter clause, while acting on conservative and moralist (and some feminist) notions that men going to prostitutes should be publicly humiliated, could well work against the interests of women in the profession. It could potentially reduce the number of men who would visit prostitutes. The moral outrage seemingly shifts from the woman in prostitution to her client. Isolating and humiliating clients may serve the interests of some patriarchies that seek to preserve marriage and the conventional family. The very knowledge that men use the services of prostitutes is shameful within this discourse. The division between the prostitute and the wife/mother stands preserved (West and Austrin 2002). Ultimately, however, the shame and humiliation is vested with the prostitute, as she is considered so stigmatised that by association the client is also stigmatised and degraded.

The bill allowed scope for mandatory testing for HIV-AIDS not only on women in prostitution, but also on their children and spouses. The rights violations so far restricted to sex workers were extended to their children and husbands. In a similar vein is the second bill, The Prohibition of Immoral Traffic and Empowerment of Sexual Workers Bill, 1993. The statements of objects and reasons of the bill discuss the issue of decriminalisation and the pros and cons of treating prostitution as work. The ambivalence of the drafters is captured in this statement:

While law should severely punish people involved with immoral trafficking and those indulging in child prostitution, it should decriminalise totally the voluntary sexual work of prostitutes ... equating it with any other manual labour. This view, though apparently obnoxious to contemporary public morals, is said to be the only sensible position that law can adopt if it intends to empower the women involved and to effectively regulate the health risks of prostitutes, the customers and the public at large (Menon 1994).

The statement attempts to display a concern for prostitutes and a respect for their choices, but what comes through strongly, in the author's opinion, is an implicit moralism and concern for public health, i.e., the sexual health of male clients and their marital families.

The bill provided for sex workers to be extended the right to safe conditions of work from the client and the brothel keeper. In addition, they are entitled to refuse a client on grounds of health, safety and hygiene. The brothel keeper is expected to provide medical treatment and a monthly medical check up from a registered medical practitioner. Since the nature of the check up is not explicated, it is not unreasonable to fear that it could well include mandatory testing for HIV-AIDS (Sections 3, 4, 7 and 10).

The implicit moral agenda of the bill is revealed in its definition of 'immoral trafficking' in Section 2A:

Immoral Trafficking means and includes buying, selling or procuring women and children for sexual abuse, prostitution or such forms of sexual exploitation.

Explanation:
Causing a child or woman to be so abused prostituted or exploited by force, fraud, deceit, undue influence, or misrepresentation is trafficking within the meaning of this section.

Fake marriages and dedication of girls which compel them to give up their dignity even if done ostensibly for religious purposes would amount to trafficking under this section.

Little distinction is made between adult women and children in this Section. Besides, the words 'immoral' and 'dignity' bring to the fore the agenda of the law that sees prostitution in terms of loss of morality and dignity. Sex workers are not economic migrants, but are victims. Given this, the following definition of 'sex worker' is not as innocent or well meaning as it seems: 'Sex worker means a woman who has taken to prostitution voluntarily and is doing the activity as an occupation' (Section 2B).

If indeed immorality and loss of dignity is attached to prostitution, defining it as work or accepting that some women may choose it voluntarily and see it as an occupation, does not lend prostitution any additional value. Rather it may stigmatise such women further, as they are seen to be voluntarily giving up their dignity and morality. The real contradiction in these bills is that they attempted to reconcile the conflicting claims of identity politics, a certain kind of conventional moralism which sees prostitution as promiscuity, and a concern for public health, a euphemism for the sexual health of male clients and their families. Any concern for women in prostitution is therefore spurious. That the bills were not implemented in the 1990s reveals that the state was not serious about the rights of sex workers.

A plan of action by the Central government in 1998 recommends steps to improve the health status of women in prostitution. It also supports the rationale of the Juvenile Justice Act, 1986 that defines children of prostitutes as being 'neglected juveniles' and recommends their separation from their mothers. Regarding strategies to separate children from their mothers, the plan states:

> Coercion to remove the child and mother, wherever possible, would be more relevant in the context of the type of environment she lives in, for instance, in areas where brothels are located. Considering the fact that taking away a child by coercion would only add to the trauma of the child and the mother, and keeping in view the inadequacy of institutional facilities for sheltering children, as far as possible, persuasion and motivation would be used to remove the child to a healthy environment (WCD/HRD 1998).

The section on rescue and rehabilitation states the concerns of the plan more blandly:

> All efforts will be made to persuade and motivate women and child victims of commercial sexual exploitation to recover and reintegrate them in society to lead a dignified life. Efforts would be made through awareness programmes, counselling, cajoling, and if necessary, by coercion to remove all children above six years of age, especially teenage boys and girl children of women victims to institutional care in boarding homes/hostels/foster homes/residential schools, etc. (ibid.).

The plan recommends coercion in case persuasion fails. Even as the paucity of institutional support is admitted, the plan continues to recommend separation of children to a 'healthy' environment. As in the

Juvenile Justice Act, the actual relationship between the parent and the child is not relevant when it comes to prostitutes and their children.

Significantly, the fear expressed by the authors of the plan is that children of prostitutes will end up as prostitutes themselves. There seems little evidence to support this fear or that children of prostitutes are neglected juveniles as the law suggests. Interviews with women in prostitution reveal that most of them are in the profession for the sake of their children and take steps to ensure that their children do not enter prostitution. Even if the fear were indeed justified, there would be little rationale for separating the children from their mothers. The criminal code allows for convicted criminals to keep their children with them in prison. Given that prostitution is not a criminal activity, separating the children against their will violates the rights of both women and the children.

Feminist Responses: 'Sex Work is Work'

In contrast to the view that migration into prostitution is inherently exploitative or violent is the view that a distinction needs to be legally made between different ways of entry into the sex trade. The Delhi-based Centre for Feminist Legal Research (CFLR) has brought out an extensive memorandum on laws relating to prostitution in India, and recommends the repeal of existing laws on prostitution on the grounds that the provisions regarding trafficking and procuring are vague and concerned with policing morality. Instead, it proposes that the definition of trafficking put forward by GAATW (Global Action Against Trafficking in Women) be adopted, i.e.:

> All acts involved in the recruitment and/or transportation of a woman within and across national borders for work or services by means of violence or threat of violence, abuse of authority or dominant position, debt bondage, deception or other forms of coercion (Centre for Feminist Legal Research 1999).

A three-pronged law reform strategy is proposed: decriminalisation of voluntary sex work and criminalisation of coercive sex work and child sex work, extension of rights to sex workers and setting up of a redressal machinery. Decriminalisation would include activities such as running brothels, living off the earnings of prostitution and soliciting. However, the CFLR feels that a mere repeal of criminal provisions will not help women in prostitution access other legal rights and that there needs to be special laws 'to recognise and redress the historical disadvantage women in sex work have suffered as a result of social stigma as well as a denial of legal rights' (ibid.).

These proposed rights include: the right to work, right to safe conditions of work, right to worker status; right to health; right to education for the sex worker and her children, right to association, right to freedom of movement and residence, and the right to privacy.

These comprehensive and detailed proposals nevertheless do not address issues of citizenship and access of rights to non-citizens who form the most vulnerable section of women in prostitution.[22] A sizeable proportion of women in prostitution belong to other South Asian countries. Asserting citizenship rights therefore may be completely irrelevant to them, especially if their status in their country of residence is quasi-legal.

A meeting in Sanghli organised by the Sanghli-based Sangram, a union of sex workers, GAATW and AWHRC (Asian Women's Human Rights Commission) in March 1999 brought out a statement of concerns. Here, some suggestions were made that offer an alternative to existing anti-prostitution laws in South Asia. These include repealing all laws that victimise women in prostitution and that do not recognise voluntary prostitution, a legal recognition of the families of prostitutes as a legitimate unit, and criminal law intervention in the case of rape, sexual abuse and coercion as for mainstream women. In addition, suggestions were made that child prostitution be criminalised, but that the definition of 'child' be made community- and country-specific (Sangram/GAATW/AWHRC 1999). The Sanghli statement goes beyond a simple assertion of citizenship rights. It recommends, at a policy level, a total de-linking of trafficking and prostitution, suggesting that the purpose of the final destination for trafficking is irrelevant. What are more important are issues of coercion, abuse and deception. To quote from the statement:

The concerns and interests of trafficked women and the need to provide them support and security must take precedence over the citizenship concerns of member states regarding the legal identity of the woman. Eventual repatriation cannot be the primary goal.

The Sanghli statement therefore, exposes the limitations of the citizenship discourse that has been an important part of feminist analysis.

Alternative Perceptions of Law: Sex Workers

Women and men in the profession suggest that the existing legal and judicial system is biased against sex workers. A study conducted by the Central Social Welfare Board (CSWB) quotes the opinions of prostitutes about the judiciary: 'They do not consider us as human beings.... They add to our harassment and humiliation.... They fail to understand the human aspects of the problem. They perceive it as a law and order problem' (CSWB 1996, cited in Gangoli 2003).

The Calcutta Sex Workers Union points out that the existing laws are ineffective and useless, and that further they do little to tackle the irregularities within the trade. Hence, they should be scrapped. It makes a demand for self-regulation, not legalisation:

> We do not want any legalisation—we want our right to regulate our own lives, both within the profession and outside. This right should not be taken as 'immoral' and 'inhuman'. As the first step towards self-regulation, we would like to form a board which will make rules and regulate the entry of new girls and also deliberate on the issues that may achieve the allround development of the sex workers and control all relevant activities (DMSC 1997b).[23]

Sex workers suggest that rehabilitation is neither desirable, nor possible. What is necessary is that sex work be decriminalised, and that women and men in the profession be allowed to practice their trade without harassment.[24] Women in the profession have a critique of the law and see a link between the lawmakers and the clients in very direct ways. As a Bombay-based sex worker and activist puts it:

> The law doesn't help. PITA is a useless law. Everyone knows about us, men come to use us, then they pass a law that says that prostitution should be stopped. Most men may use condoms, but there are times they don't. So, even if a law is passed (forcing men to use condoms), they may not. And it is unreasonable to expect women in the profession to take them to the police and lose their livelihood.[25]

The voices of women quoted above bring out the limitations of legal interventions that do not take into account the reality of the lives and experiences of women in prostitution. Women in prostitution have a complex relationship with the police and the judiciary. On the one hand, there is recognition of the role that these institutions play in their lives. On the other, there is some degree of familiarity with them and the stigma that is attached in the popular imagination to arrests and association with the police seems to be missing here. The following excerpt from one of my interviews bring this out to some extent:

> I have been arrested by the police. During *puja*, at about 7 p.m., the police arrested me when I went out to get a customer. I was just standing on the road when they came and arrested four other girls and me. The food in the jail was horrible—on *sal* leaves we were served fish that was not cleaned and watery *dal* that slipped off the leaf. We couldn't eat the food. The next day, we were produced before the magistrate and I was bailed out by my friend.[26]

Conclusion

As this paper has attempted to bring out, there is a complex relationship between sex work, migration and poverty. The law cannot be effective in 'preventing' sex work and/or trafficking unless it looks carefully at this relationship. Laws and policies identify prostitution as immoral and prostitutes as victims. Simultaneously, prostituted women are constructed as immoral, as they are following an immoral profession. The corollary is that since prostitution and prostitutes are immoral, they have limited rights. Rights such as the right to have children and bring them up, the right to practice their profession without hindrance and harassment, the right to mobility and to reside in an area of their choice, and the right to support their families and friends are denied to women in prostitution. Many of these rights are available to convicted criminals. No other profession prohibits the worker to support anyone with his or her earnings. In addition, prostitutes are subjected to exploitation and harassment by the police, for which they have no recourse. Women in prostitution, due to the nature of their work, have fewer rights than the limited ones given to other women, whether as citizens or as non-citizens.

It might be fitting to end this paper with a quote from the sex workers' manifesto:

The sex workers' movement is going on—it has to go on. We believe that the questions about sexuality that we are raising are relevant not only to us sex workers, but to every man and woman who questions subordination of all kinds—within the society at large and also within themselves. This movement is for everyone who strives for a equal, just, equitable, oppression-free and, above all, happy world.

Notes

1 Interview with Aloka Mitra, Women's Interlink Foundation, Calcutta on 20.09.2001.

2 Interview with Shaheen Nilofer, Coordinator, OXFAM India Trust, Orissa. 7 September 2001.

3 Interview with Manisha Majumdar, Coordinator, Task Force on Women and Violence. 7 September 2001.

4 Interview with Rekha Lamba, sex-worker in Calcutta of Nepalese origin. 27 September 1998.

5 Interview with 'Aloka, flying' sex-worker from Garai, Calcutta, 20.09.2001.

6 Interview with Joyati, sex-worker in Malishahi, Bhubaneswar on 6.09.2001.

7 Interview with Mrinal Kanta Dutta, Director of DMSC, 27 August 2001.

8 Interview with Sandip Bandopadhyay, worked with DMSC between 1996 and 1998, currently a freelance consultant, 29 August 2001.

9 Interview with Veena, brothel owner in Sonagachi, Calcutta. 27 September 1998.

10 Interview with Shekhar Chatterjee, worked with CINI and now works for a sponsorship programme run by Sahay in 400 villages in West Bengal on 1.09.2001.

11 I owe this insight to Mr S.A. Khan.

12 Interview with Samima Khatoon, Ruchika, A Street Children Organisation. Malishahi. 3rd September 2001 and Madan Bahra, OPUS, 5 September 2001.

13 Interview with Smita Pattanaik, Nari Surakhya Samiti, Angul on 16 September 2001.

14 Interview with Smita Pattanaik, Nari Surakhya Samiti, Angul on 16 September 2001.

15 Interview with Aloka Mitra, Women's Interlink Foundation, Calcutta on 20.09.2001.

16 Interview with Sandip Bandopadhyay, worked with DMSC between 1996 and 1998, currently a freelance consultant, 29 August 2001.

17 Interview with Malati, sex-worker in Sonagachi on 27 August 2001.

18 Interview with Sandip Bandopadhyay, worked with DMSC between 1996 and 1998, currently a freelance consultant, 29 August 2001.

19 Interview with Radha, Sonagachi on 14 September 1998.

20   Interestingly, the word 'rand' in Hindi is used interchangeably for widow and prostitutes.

21   Lok Sabha Debates. 22.08.1986. Smt Margaret Alva: 140–41.

22   A number of Indian feminists have argued that Indian women have a right to equality, as they are citizens of the country. These include statements made by feminist organisations such as Forum Against Oppression of Women, Bombay and Working Group for Women's Rights, New Delhi.

23   Such a demand for self-determination has also been made by Sangram, based in Sanghli—sister organisation of VAMPS. They demand legal status, recognition and active support for Self-Regulatory Boards within communities of prostitutes to check violence from within and to evolve social support structures. While Self-Regulatory Boards exist in some parts of the country, they lack any legal status that curbs their actual powers.

24   Interview with Dr. Smarajit Jana, HIV-AIDS Intervention Unit. 16 September 1998.

25   Interview with health worker from BMC-HIV Cell, Bombay on 22 August 1998.

26   Interview with Srijona, sex worker at Khidirpur, Calcutta on 17 September 1998.

References

Campbell, C. 2000. 'Selling Sex in the Time of AIDS: Identity, Sexuality and Commercial Sex-work on a South African Mine', *Social Science and Medicine*, 50(2).

Chew, L. 1999. 'Prostitution and Migration: Issues and Approaches: Summary of Network Presentation, Kolkata, March 1998', APSNET, Bulletin of the Asia-Pacific Network of Sex-workers, 1(1): 13–16.

Centre for Feminist Legal Research. 1999. Memorandum on Reform Laws Relating to Prostitution in India. CFLR: New Delhi.

DMSC (Durbar Mahila Samanwaya Committee). 1997a. 'Sex Workers' Right to Self Determination', Calcutta, on file with Sanlaap, File no. FF12.

———. 1997b. 'The Fallen Learn to Rise. The Social Impact of STD-HIV Intervention Programme'. DMSC: Calcutta.

Gangoli, G. 1998. 'Prostitution, Legalisation and Decriminalisation. Recent debates', *Economic and Political Weekly*, 7 March: 504–5.

———. 2003. 'Sex Work and Livelihood in Eastern India', available online at www.anthrobase.com.

Guha-Bhuvaneswar, C. 1998. 'Kannagi's Daughters: HIV/AIDS Prevention for Indian Women', available online at www.http://re/productions.com (accessed on 24 June 2003).

Gulchar, L. and P. Ilkkarachan. 2002. 'The "Natasha" Experience: Migrant Sex Workers from the former Soviet Union and Eastern Europe in Turkey', *Women's Studies International Forum*, 25(4): 411–21.

Human Rights Watch (HRW). 1995. 'Rape for Profit. Trafficking of Nepali Girls and Women to India's Brothels', Human Rights Watch.

Menon, N.R.M. 1994. 'The Problem, The Concerns and The Background. Report on the Law Reform Project, 1992–1994', New Delhi, Department of Women and Child Development, Government of India.

Mikhail, S.B.L. 2002. 'Child Marriage and Child Prostitution: Two Forms of Sexual Exploitation', *Gender and Development*, 10(1): 43–49.

National Commission for Women (NCW). 1997. *The Velvet Blouse. Sexual Exploitation of Children*. New Delhi: National Commission for Women.

Pal, B. 1999. 'Against Legalisation. Women's Activists in Pune are Strongly Opposed to the Legalisation of Prostitution', *Humanscape*: 28–31.

Pandey, B., D. Jena and S. Samal. 2003. 'Trafficking in Women in Orissa', Bhubaneswar: ISED/UNIFEM/USAID.

Sangram/GAATW/AWHRC. 1999. A Statement of Concerns. Mumbai: Sangram/GAATW/AWHRC.

Sanlaap.1998. 'Yet Another Right', a report on a seminar on 'Legalisation of Prostitution'. Calcutta, Sanlaap: 20.

———. 1999. *Child Prostitution in Calcutta*. Calcutta: Sanlaap.

Sinha, I. and C. Sleightholme. 1996. *Guilty Without Trial. Women in the Sex Trade in Calcutta*. Calcutta: Stree.

UN. 1998. Women and HIV/AIDS Concerns—a focus on Thailand, Philippines, India and Nepal. Accessed online at www.un.org/aids on 24 January 2005.

WCD/HRD (Women and Child Department/Human Resource Department). 1998. 'Child Prostitutes and Children of Prostitutes and Plan of Action to Combat Trafficking and Commercial Sexual Exploitation of Women and Children'. New Delhi: WCD/HRD.

West, J. and T. Austrin. 2002. 'From Work as Sex to Sex as Work: Networks, "Others" and Occupations in the Analysis of Work', *Gender Work & Org*, 9(5): 482–503.

Wilcock, S. 1999. 'Sex Work: Choice and Liberation or Abuse and Exploitation?', *Lifeline 2000*.

11

Solicitation, Migration and Day Wage Labour: Gender, Sexuality and Negotiating Work in the City

Svati P. Shah[1]

In this paper, I offer a schematic discussion of day wage labour markets in the city of Mumbai. This discussion is framed by the urbanisation and transformation of cities in the global South, both of which have gained prominence in academic research, and in activist and international rights discourses on 'poverty alleviation', as macroeconomic and political contexts continue to be shaped significantly by the phenomenon known loosely as 'globalisation.' I say 'loosely' because the discourse on globalisation itself is a broad one, being produced in many different contexts, with many different referents, critiques and interventions, such that the term itself has been used to indicate economic and political processes occurring in many different registers. Academics, activists and advocates have used the term 'globalisation' to mean decreasing barriers in trade between some countries. The term has also been used to mean the consolidation of wealth and resources among a few rich nations and corporations. I use 'globalisation' here to flag the phenomenon of decreasing regulations on transnational migration of capital, while greater restrictions have come into effect on the migration of labour. While none of these uses are necessarily mutually exclusive, each usage is fairly specific, and requires a clear understanding of the context in which that usage is produced, and the political and economic impacts of each particular process of 'globalisation'. For the purposes of the research that I present here, I emphasise the latter usage to elicit some questions and concerns that emerge under the aegis of *labour migration*, a phenomenon which, by all accounts, is significantly impacted by the changing economic and political contexts represented by the multiple manifestations of globalisation within the global South, generally, and specifically within India.

The question of migration for researchers and activists concerned with the phenomenon of globalisation itself is a complicated one. Beyond the longstanding criticism of, for example, uneven tariffs and trade barriers and their relationship to bilateral debt incurred by poor countries, the question of migration within the context of economic globalisation is one that is still being identified and defined. A key element that impacts and complicates the theoretical framing of migration is the growing number of female migrants moving to take up employment opportunities, both in other countries and within their countries of origin. This trend, dubbed the 'feminisation of migration'[2], complicates the theoretical map of migration by the change it represents from the virtually iconic phenomenon of individual men migrating for work far from home, or of entire families migrating in search of a more sustainable collective livelihood elsewhere.

The feminisation of migration is of particular interest here for the theoretical framework it provides for producing analyses at the intersections of gender and labour in India. Unlike the majority of 'migration studies' which have tended to focus on migrants who cross international borders (legally or illegally) in order to gain access to other, potentially more sustainable or lucrative labour markets, the communities at the centre of this ethnographic research are intra-national migrants from rural areas near the city of Mumbai. As legal means of crossing borders become more regulated and restricted, and as cities like Mumbai continue to grow, intra-national migration to this city becomes an important site for research on the ways in which migrants negotiate the new, urban labour markets in which they solicit paid work.

This paper explores the connections between migration and poverty in the bodies of women, who represent 'feminised' migration and poverty, through a discussion of an ethnographic inquiry of women from several migrated, lower caste communities who are living and working in the outskirts of Mumbai. The details presented here of the community's life in the city are the result of 16 months of research with first and second generation migrant Dalit day wage workers who had been landless agricultural labourers in rural Maharashtra and Karnataka. In the city, they generated income as day wage workers, primarily in the construction industry.

The main theoretical point of inquiry in this research revolves around the question of women's solicitation for paid work in an urban public space, and is figured in the context of an increasingly globalised economy in which the 'urban street' is a site of income generation and commerce for greater numbers of men and women. The workers in this study described themselves as 'unskilled,' meaning that they had not been educated or trained in any particular trade, nor had they acquired a skill set that could be used to garner more than the most basic wage rate given to manual labourers. Some workers, usually men, described themselves as 'skilled' or 'semi-skilled,' having learned trades like plumbing, plastering or painting through apprenticing with other 'skilled' workers. For these workers, needing to solicit day wage labour contracts as their primary livelihood indicated the lack of a source of more reliable, salaried income. In this context, the spaces from which day wage labour is solicited serve as a sort of barometer for rates of employment—specifically, for the ability of the city to absorb and sustain unskilled migrants within its workforce.

This paper specifically deals with women who work as day wage labourers in the urban context because of two important factors. First, although cities are not unique in including public spaces for the solicitation of day wage work by labourers (and of labourers by contractors), the use of public spaces for this purpose is by far the most widespread in cities. Second, post-colonial, industrial and post-industrial development has facilitated, and even necessitated, the rapid expansion of cities. This expansion has been predicated on people of all castes, classes and regional origins migrating to cities in large numbers. Mumbai has been the target of large-scale migration since its inception as a centre for export and manufacturing, and has significantly contributed to the definition of urban and global prosperity in South Asia for over a century now.

The 'migrants' of interest here first came to Mumbai in the 1980s and 1990s. They were originally from rural communities of lower caste agricultural labourers who were part of caste-based conversion to Buddhism inspired by Babasaheb Ambedkar (Rajshekhar 1983; Viswanathan 1998). They were attracted to the city in the 1980s by its then booming textile, and later housing development, industries, and by the generalised notion that there was an improved chance for a better livelihood in this urban centre. These communities of migrants were from areas where rural land had become more drought-prone as more land had been used for growing water-intensive cash crops like sugar. Both the textile and real estate development industries that attracted so many migrants from these areas experienced significant downturns in the mid-1990s, leaving migrated workers to try and secure livelihoods through the more unpredictable day wage labour market. Although day wage labour was certainly prevalent before the economic downturn in these industries, the importance of day wage work for rural, unskilled migrants increased considerably afterwards.

Day wage labour is currently bought and sold from any number of urban public spaces, or 'nakas', throughout Mumbai. These spaces constitute the most visible aspect of the city's vast 'informal economies' (Hart 1973: 61–89) and, as such, are not strictly bounded in the kind of economic activity that they facilitate. In other words, although labour nakas are ostensibly sanctioned by city authorities for the solicitation and purchase of manual labour services, these nakas may facilitate a whole range of economically 'informal' buying and selling transactions. The term naka actually has a variety of vernacular meanings that follow three basic forms: i) a crossroads, corner or intersection where traffic and people meet and are regulated; ii) a toll station, or a place to collect or pay money for passage or services; and iii) a police station. The term naka in this research context adheres most closely to the first two forms, but its sense extends beyond that of a physical space where money is collected for services, but must also be described as a temporary labour market that enhances the visibility of large numbers of poor lower-caste labourers, and is subject to consistent police and municipal regulation.

This kind of naka occurs at a crossroads, corner, intersection, commuter railway station, or any other visible, easily accessible public urban space. Labour market nakas in Mumbai include three other distinguishing elements: i) they are used by individuals who use the space to sell their labour episodically, meaning that labour is sold in discrete units, and is not salaried, as an on-going job would be; ii) the space of the naka is not 'designated,' as street corners or shops or commodity markets might be, through zoning or other state-sponsored mechanisms—rather, the labour market naka is formed through spoken and, possibly, purchased agreements from local police and shopkeepers, as well as workers, building contractors and anyone else who may have a service to buy or sell from the space; and iii) these kinds of labour market nakas are demarcated by space *and* by time. Labour market nakas exist only as long as workers and contractors use the space to buy and sell services, and this usage is sanctioned for a fixed time period, usually during the first half of the day. This means that the labour market *naka* has a set of fairly fixed superficial parameters, to which all participants in the space adhere, or risk losing the privilege of using the *naka*, or even risk jeopardising the existence of the *naka* itself. This last point is critical, as the *naka* provides a key income generating space for low wage and unskilled workers in the city. This means that, overtly at least, a labour market *naka* is less a place of lingering than a place where transactions constantly occur. At the same time, this kind of *naka* is a flexible space, where sociality and multiple transactions are negotiated within a fairly unambiguous set of ideas about the appropriate use of public urban space, ideas that are enforced, through both the state-sponsored regulation of the space, and through local and community norms regarding gendered sense of propriety. The state-sponsored regulation of these spaces may take more or less literal forms, with the most literal being the presence of a police officer, a police van, or a police *naka* in the space of the labour market *naka* itself. The regulation of *naka*s, through the time-bounded nature of their existence, places the paradoxes of the relationships between police, contractors, labourers, local shopkeepers and passers-by into relief. For example, while migrant workers are required for the cheap labour they provide in both building and maintaining the infrastructure of the city, their visible presence within that infrastructure triggers regulatory mechanisms that limit their access to these spaces en masse.

Literally, the workers' *naka* is a time-bound *use* of a public space for transacting services, and becomes so through a complex set of discourses about the rightful inhabitants of the city's public spaces. Although most of the people in these communities of workers are not recently migrated to Mumbai, their transient status in the city is maintained through repeated housing resettlement and displacement within the city itself, and exclusion from access to one or more basic amenities such as education, shelter or regular access to potable water. The transition from 'migrant' to 'resident', or even 'citizen', remains undone due to the exclusions that most migrants in these communities experience from permanent housing, employment, education, and regular access to potable water.

Currently, between 500 and 10,000 people gather each day at *naka*s throughout the city; one trade union estimates that some 300,000 people seek work from Mumbai's *naka*s every day. A fraction of these people are hired, mainly for small-scale construction or building repair work. It is important to note that this day wage economy is populated by both men and women, often sitting in groups at the *naka*. The gendered geographies of these urban public spaces become inflected by multiple notions of solicitation, work, gender and sexuality, within the context of community identifications, and the rural impacts of economic globalisation. The following section discusses some of these dynamics over the course of fieldwork at a day wage labourers' *naka* in the Mumbai suburbs.

I

Around 10 women were left at the *naka* at 11 in the morning, the majority having either found jobs or gone home an hour before. There were still around 30 men left, sitting a little further down the block. While it is not uncommon for women to sit and talk in the men's space, and vice versa, it is noticeable when it happens. I walked over to sit with Subha, my main contact at the *naka*. Subha (all names of contacts have been changed) was known by everyone, and had been extremely generous with me when it came to conversation and her time. She would say with pride, 'No one will even look at you wrongly, because they know I'm here right behind you. They're all afraid of me'. When I would ask why they were afraid, she would smile and say simply, 'They just are'. After going to the *naka* for a few weeks, various men had begun to ask me, 'So, has Subha told you yet that she's a prostitute?'. When I would ask these men why this was said about Subha, a typical reply would involve a discussion of how 'freely' Subha interacted with men at the *naka*, and that she was seen 'going with' men away from her home or the space of the *naka*, to a place of privacy.

I had been talking that day with Subha about other areas in the city where women use the public spaces of the city, usually a city street, to find clients for sex. Almost all of those women had said that they go looking for construction work from their local *naka* in the morning, but 'if we don't find work there, we come here', adding, '*Pet ki liye karna pad ta hai*' ('It has to be done for the stomach'). I asked Subha what she thought about this '*pet ki liye*' ('for the stomach') argument for doing sex work. She replied, '*Hahn, izzat le kar ghar ka undar bayt sakte hai, laykin ...*' ('Yes, a woman could sit inside her house and keep her honour intact, but ... '), and trailed off and would not speak about it further.

This extremely rich and emblematic moment offers up many insights, and many more questions. I would like to draw out what we may fathom about solicitation in this context, given that, for some, Subha's identification as a sex worker was a foregone conclusion due to the fact that she interacted 'freely' with men at the *naka*. Subha both denied and maintained this image by her refusal to discuss it further. To be sure, all the women at this construction workers' *naka* were not necessarily 'sex workers'. However, all of the women at the *naka* were subject to what Gail Pheterson calls the 'whore stigma' (Pheterson 1996) by virtue of community and class-enhanced markers of gender 'appropriate' behaviour that putatively distinguishes different forms of 'respectable' and 'illicit' forms of solicitation. Women who solicited work from this space managed these distinctions through the strategic practice of signifying different kinds of solicitation.

The *naka* at the centre of this study is located in a Mumbai suburb and had a stable population of roughly 150–200 labourers who passed through the space each day. The *naka* is located at the edge of the city where municipal planners are locating large industrial and residential development projects, and where some of the largest tracts of slum developments exist in the city. The *naka* is therefore placed in an urban zone that has seen some of the city's fiercest battles over land ownership and use. Workers at this *naka* claimed that the numbers of people soliciting work from the space varied; during 'the season', some 2,000 people were said to use this *naka* to find work, although the space could scarcely accommodate the 150 that used it regularly throughout the year.

This particular *naka* formed at a street corner in front of a chemist's shop from roughly eight a.m. to noon every day. The superficial chaos of traffic, pedestrians, shops, and *naka* workers rested on an underlying spatial order where social groups, demarcated by caste and gender, sat together in distinct clusters. The social geography of most day wage *naka*s is organised by people sitting together with their own kin groups and friends, these social groupings often reflecting the subjectivities of caste and gender. The spatial order is nominally hierarchical, such that more and less dominant groups vie for position at the *naka* based on where there is space to sit over a potentially long wait for a contractor, and where one can be seen most clearly. Members of the same social group advocate for one another's right to sit or stand in a given space, to the exclusion of members of other networks at the *naka*. For example, at the *naka* in question, the Maharashtrian 'Nav Buddho'[3] women sat over a large waste-water drainage ditch at the intersection itself. These women were thus able to take advantage of one of the most visible and comfortable positions in the space, where it is possible to both be seen by potential contractors, and sit for the full three to four hours that one might spend waiting for that day's job. These non-tribal Maharashtrians at the *naka* referred to themselves as 'Nav Buddho' belonging to the 'Ambedkar jāt' (Ambedkar caste); further along the street stood the 'Nav Buddho' Maharashtrian men, who outnumbered the women as a whole roughly three to one. Throngs of men vied for positions to rest, and were generally standing and waiting for contractors alongside a community of Marathi-speaking Banjara tribal women. In the middle of the men's space sat a community of Lambadi tribal women from northern Karnataka.

For all of the women, the space of the *naka* was significant in many different ways that included, but was not limited to, the *naka* being an important potential income-generating space. The *naka* was also a space for socialising, which was critical considering that the range of public spaces that women had access to in general were few, and were clearly defined by whether or not it was 'appropriate' for a woman to inhabit a given space at a given time of day. According to the social rules of the community, the most appropriate space for a woman to be in was the home, or in public spaces that facilitated the smooth operation of the home, such as the food and commodity markets that supplied the home. For some time, both the male and female workers at this *naka* had also had access to an adjoining office space in which people could hold meetings, socialise or rest. This was the second such space these *naka* workers had used. The first one had been nearby as well, but on the second floor of a building in the neighbourhood, and away from the main road. According to several men who used the office, because the previous space had not been visible from the main road, women had been barred from going there 'because people would think they are doing some "bad work" (*bura kam*) there. Now that the office is on the street and everyone can see it, they can come and go from there freely'. This was the first instance during field research, but not the last, in which the phrase '*bura kam*' was used in this context, and helped to clarify that sexuality was the register through which the propriety of women in the public space was being defined. The significance of the use of the term '*bura kam*' in relation to women in a space that is not visible from the busy, public space of the heavily trafficked *naka* was only clear in the context of the regulation and perceptions of women's sexuality. While heavily coded, 'bad work' referenced women in private, being paid for illegitimate activities that could only take place away from the space of the public street, which by virtue of its publicness could be subject to moral regulation. The repeated use of the phrase 'bad work' in relation to women became linked more clearly with the actual and perceived practice of sex work and sex trade negotiated from the space of the *naka*'s labour market through anecdotes in which the women said that 'those contractors, sometimes they take young girls and "go with them"; they make them to do some *bura kam*'.

All women at the *naka* managed the reality of sex work and sex for work being conducted from the *naka*, whether or not they themselves participated, due, in part, to the larger economic context of the scarcity of steady, paid work at the *naka* for all workers. In addition, the signifiers of solicitation for respectable construction work and un-respectable sex work both include having proximity to large groups of men, being un-chaperoned by a family member in public areas, and visibly using a public space to seek out paid work. All of these are also signs of transgression of gendered norms of propriety for these communities, and fulfil the legal definition of solicitation for sex[4] under Section 8 of the Immoral Traffic Prevention Act (ITPA).[5] ITPA is being used less and less to police public solicitation, mainly due to a great deal of criticism for the seemingly limitless powers it grants the state, in practice, for policing women in public. However, it bears mentioning as an important site of contestation for the policing of public space, in general, and as one of the few places in which the Indian state articulates its ideal of the kind of prostitution and, therefore, the kind of social impropriety it seeks to prevent. In practice, each state (and some municipalities) continues to rely heavily on the 'police acts', which serve as localised laws designed to control public space, particularly in urban areas, and include many different kinds of public nuisance laws. Like public nuisance laws the world over, these are equally subjective, and directed toward various socially and economically disenfranchised people, including those who engage in street-based solicitation.

II

Shanti had come to Mumbai from rural Maharashtra after getting married as a teenager. Her husband had left her and her children several years ago. She lived in a slum area in a nearby suburb. To support herself and her family, she would go to a construction workers' *naka* in the morning. If she did not find work with a contractor for the day, she went to another, more commercial part of the city to solicit clients for sex. She was identified by a local NGO as a 'street-based sex worker,' a different category from the brothel-based sex workers who comprise the more visible sector of prostitution in the city. Once during a conversation at a local tea shop, Shanti said, laughing ironically, 'All we have is *majboori* (a compulsion, or necessity), and we say "50 rupees" (to a potential client), and maybe he'll wear a condom, maybe he won't'.

Recalling the other conversations I had had with street-based sex workers who also did construction work, I asked her, 'I've heard you say "*if* we don't get work in the *naka*, *then* we come here for this work". Why is that? Do you like that (construction work) better than this?' '*Hahn*,' ('Yes') she replied, as though it were obvious. She raised her arms at right angles on either side of her body, mimicking the motion that women do repeatedly as they lift pans of wet cement and rocks onto their heads at construction sites. 'That's *mehenat* (physical labour). This?' she asked, motioning at the street behind her, 'What's this? Sometimes you get a good man, sometimes a bad man, sometimes there's no work here at all, sometimes they refuse to wear a condom …'. She began speaking again about the police, about an officer who was transferred to the area where she solicited clients for sex some three months before. His harassment of street-based sex workers at his previous posting was, apparently, well known. 'Once he chased us down the road with his scooter and nearly ran me over. Another time, we ran so much, I thought that *budhi aurat* (old woman) was going to die for sure, she was breathing so hard.' She went on to describe a woman whom the officer had beaten with his *lathi* (stick) so badly that she couldn't get out of bed for two days. '*Usko puchh:na chahiye, humne kya galti kiya hai? Pet ki liye karte hai.*' ('Someone should ask him what wrong have we done? We're doing it for the stomach.')

When the chief inspector at the local police station was asked about reason for the beatings and the chasings, he replied, 'Who can tell who is a good woman and who is a bad one? This is a family area. There's a movie theatre on that street that families like to come to. We have to keep it safe for them.'

I highlight this example for several reasons, most significantly because it offers a clear insight into the relationship between two seemingly disparate economic activities—day wage construction labour, and paid sex—in the daily process of seeking out a sustainable livelihood. This example also offers a rare insight into the axes on which an evaluation is made between these distinct paid activities. Shanti's reflection reveals a complex process of negotiation in performing different kinds of solicitation. While her expressed preference is for doing construction work rather than paid sex, the way in which this preference is articulated resists compliance with the idea of prostitution as a loss of dignity or as inherently violent. Rather, it is important to see that Shanti locates the main source of brutality in police harassment, and the greatest hazard as clients who refuse to wear condoms, making '*mehenat*' (hard labour) better than paid sex, which, she implies, is something other than hard labour.

Solicitation

These ethnographic examples reflect moments in which the solicitation of two different kinds of day wage labour is being negotiated. In these moments, the similarities in the ways in which both construction work and sex work are solicited by women constitute an extremely thin boundary between legitimated and non-legitimated reasons for using the street to generate income. In the first example of Subha's solicitation of construction work, her reputation as a sex worker is a secret that is disseminated through rumours, which are sustained by a re-interpretation of her behaviour at the *naka* itself (for example moving 'freely' with the men there) as being conducted for the purpose of selling sex, rather than selling manual labour. To be sure, soliciting either form of paid labour by women involved the use of proximity to men who were clearly not related by any kin networks, or simply the fact of being women on the street unaccompanied, waiting. For women doing street-based sex work, these kinds of social behaviour constituted an active use of the 'impropriety' of single women in public to signify the sale of sexual services. The need to read the exchanged glances, smiles and whispered negotiations, all beg the question about the context-inflected meanings and uses of 'solicitation' in public. Within the context of increasing numbers of rural migrants in cities throughout the global South, these ethnographic insights raise the question of whether the parameters of solicitation itself are being extended by migrant communities seeking work from the public spaces of the city. Given this context, the intersection of public solicitation and migrancy is used here to begin the process of building a productive analysis of the forms and uses of solicitation by economically and politically marginalised women in the city.

Solicitation and Migrancy

There is much movement between cities, as well as from rural areas to urban centres; the lowest paid workers in urban centres clearly have many, fairly recent relationships with rural communities. Migration for the purpose of doing construction work, selling or trading sexual services, piece work, factory work, or any other day wage labour must be understood within the context of the growing links between migration and economic sustainability for people without access to education, land or a steady income, and is occurring against the backdrop of depleted water tables, more arable land becoming subject to increasingly frequent droughts and earthquakes, and some rural development schemes that have resulted in thousands of people being displaced. At the same time, it cannot be denied that migration is a complex process, and that the compulsion to leave a bad situation does not fully explain it. When I asked a *naka* organiser how he would describe the changes in why people migrated to Mumbai from the sugar- and labour-supplying villages in Maharashtra, he replied, 'Before, it was because people couldn't get proper food in the villages. Now, they hear that you can make money in the city, so even though they have land and water in the *gaon* (village) they leave'. Both in the decision to move, either as family units or as individuals, and in the assessment of income generating options, it is helpful to return to the idea of contingency in these kinds of context-specific decisions to move, and to work. I use 'contingency' as inflected by a Foucaultian sense of power which is everywhere and nowhere at the same time, and in which compulsion and choice are produced dialectical.

The Problem with Migration

Many rural areas in the global South have received few of the benefits of industrial growth and, instead, have been subject to large-scale infrastructure development projects like dams and highways which result in massive forced displacement of rural communities. These areas now supply the lion's share of migrant labourers to the world's urban economies. These kinds of structural conditions for labour migration are elaborated upon considerably in the literature, especially within the context of economic globalisation. The double standard of easing barriers to the migration of capital through international agreements like NAFTA (North American Free Trade Agreement), and the imminent SAFTA (South Asian Free Trade Agreement), while increasing the barriers to cross-border migration, especially for landless economic migrants, is well known. Aspects of this literature that have focused on gender in particular have also included important work on the expansion of informal and notably under-organised economic sectors, and of the increased feminisation of migration and poverty on a global scale. Research and writing in this area has included work on poor women migrants, both from India and other countries, and discusses their locations within, for example, domestic work and other home-based work, and the vulnerabilities of these women in the city, especially as those vulnerabilities are heightened by a lack of access to public spaces.

Women's negotiations for seeking work at the construction workers' *naka* and the street-based sex workers' *naka* were governed by similar sets of structural factors of caste, class and migration, and the regulation of public space through anti-trafficking legislation that govern the public solicitation by women of male clients for sexual services.

Examples from this field research demonstrate multiple negotiations of public space and of work by poor migrant women that complicate the narrative of sex work in which these assumptions are imbedded. Taking these examples together also proposes a certain utility in using migrancy and informal sector economic activity as a framework for understanding strategies for income generation that are often held apart from one another.

Conclusion

The almost centripetal pull of the debate on agency and compulsion vis-à-vis solicitation in cities is evident in the questions that emerge at the intersection of discourses on migration and public solicitation conducted by poor women in urban areas. This intersection has a broader context in that, amidst the particularities of the experience of migrants in urban settings, there is a powerfully teleological sense of development for the city as a space that should be safe for its legitimate inhabitants. The discursive relationship between migrancy and danger supports the notion that migrated communities from under-developed rural areas can and should be subject to internal and external regulation, regulation that potentially elides the city's need for a reliable supply of cheap, unskilled workers to build and maintain its rapidly growing infrastructure and service sectors. Given this critique, we may ask what the consequences of these kinds of epistemologies of urbanisation are for the regulation of intra-national borders, as well as international ones.

Ultimately, by discussing the multiplicities of solicitation, migration and sex trade in Mumbai city, this paper outlines a critique that must be situated among the connections between the practices of public urban space, and the significant changes manifested in urban Indian within the context of contemporary economic liberalisation.

This is not to imply that the idea of 'the rural' should not be subject to similar contextualisation and political critique as 'the urban', nor that a historical ideal of sustainable rural development should be the goal of any intervention that attempts to address the concerns of liberalisation. Rather, this suggests that, within these contexts, the process of movement from rural to urban areas means an exchange of vulnerabilities vis-à-vis the state, as rural landless agricultural labourers become urban landless workers participating in urban informal economies. For example, whereas most of the people in the two areas discussed here were subject to caste-related harassment and housing discrimination in their villages, almost all have been subject to slum demolitions throughout the city several times over. These phenomena inform the ways in which the intersections of migration and sex work provide a unique set of perspectives on flexible notions of work in India's urban informal economies.

Notes

1 I gratefully acknowledge the assistance of Nirman throughout this research project. Any shortcomings of the project, and of this paper, remain entirely my own.
2 There are a great many examples of this literature, which is part of a discourse that is being produced in both academic and non-academic contexts. For one example that deals with migration, poverty, gender and sex work, please refer to http://www.ilo.org/public/english/dialogue/actrav/publ/129/7.pdf.

3   Wherever possible, I attempt to use categories that were identified by people in relation to themselves. 'Nav Buddho' literally means 'New Buddhist', and refers to lower caste or 'Dalit' communities that, following the lead of Babasaheb Ambedkar, aimed to 'opt out' of the caste system by converting, as he advocated, to Buddhism.

4   This phenomenon has been addressed by feminist researchers who have engaged with questions of state regulation of public space. Two examples are Phadke (2002) and Sunder Rajan (2003).

5   'Whoever, in any public place or within sight of, and in such manner as to be seen or heard from, any public place, whether from within any building or house or not:

(a)   by words, gestures, wilful exposure of her person (whether by sitting by a window or on the balcony of a building or house or in any other way), or otherwise tempts or endeavours to tempt, or attracts or endeavours to attract the attention of, any person for the purpose of prostitution; or

(b)   solicits or molests any person, or loiters or acts in such manner as to cause obstruction or annoyance to persons residing nearby or passing by such public place or to offend against public decency, for the purpose of prostitution ...' (Immoral Traffic [Prevention] Act 1956: 9).

References

Hart, Keith. 1973. 'Informal Income Opportunities and Urban Employment in Ghana', *Journal of Modern African Studies*, 11(1): 61–89.

Immoral Traffic (Prevention) Act. 1956. Government of India.

Phadke, Shilpa. 2002. 'Women in Public in Mumbai', presentation of the Mumbai Studies Group.

Pheterson, Gail. 1996. *The Prostitution Prism*. Amsterdam: Amsterdam University Press.

Rajshekhar, V.T. 1983. *Ambedkar and His Conversion*. Bangalore: Dalit Sahitya Akademy.

Sunder Rajan, Rajeswari. 2003. *The Scandal of the State: Women, Law, and Citizenship in Postcolonial India*. Durham, N.C./London: Duke University Press.

Viswanathan, Gauri. 1998. *Outside the Fold: Conversion, Modernity, and Belief*. Princeton, N.J.: Princeton University Press.

About the Editors and Contributors

The Editors

Sadhna Arya is Reader in the Department of Political Science, Satyawati College (E), University of Delhi. She was a Senior Fellow (on deputation) with the Centre for Women's Development Studies, New Delhi, during 2004–2005. Dr Arya is actively involved with issues concerning women's rights and has written and presented several papers in this area. She is the author of *Women, Gender Equality and the State* (2001) and has co-edited *Narivadi Rajniti—Sangharsh avam Mudday* (2000). She is presently working on *The National Commission for Women—Goals and Performance in the South Asian Perspective*.

Anupama Roy is a Senior Fellow at the Centre for Women's Development Studies, New Delhi. She was earlier a Lecturer in the Department of Political Science at Punjab University, Chandigarh (1999–2004) and a Sir Ratan Tata (Post Doctoral) Fellow at the Institute of Economic Growth, University Enclave, Delhi (2002–2003). Dr Roy was elected Agatha Harisson Memorial Fellow at St. Antony's College, Oxford University for the year 2004–2005. She received the Nehru Centenary British Fellowship for research at the School of Oriental and African Studies, University of London (1990–1991). Anupama Roy has a master's degree in Political Science from Allahabad University, an M.Phil. from Delhi University, and a Ph.D. from the State University of New York, Binghamton, USA. Her research has focused on debates concerning citizenship, particularly issues of gender and citizenship. Dr Roy has previously published *Gendered Citizenship: Historical and Conceptual Explorations* (2005). Her research articles have appeared in various journals including *Contributions to Indian Sociology, Economic and Political Weekly, Indian Social Science Review,* and *Contemporary India*. She is currently working on the theme 'Crafting Democratic Citizenship: Gender Dimensions of Electoral Governance'.

The Contributors

Jagannath Adhikari is an independent researcher and development consultant in Nepal. He obtained his Ph.D. from the Australian National University in 1996. He has carried out several research projects on labour migration and the remittance economy, food security, conflict, poverty, and social issues in natural resources management. He is the author of *Beginnings of Agrarian Change: A Case Study in Central Nepal* (1996), *Decisions for Survival: Farm Management Strategies in Middle Hills, Nepal* (2001), and the co-author of several books including *Conflict and Food Security: A Preliminary Analysis* (2004) and *Debate on Poverty in Nepal* (2004). At present, he is also the convener of Martin Chautari, a discussion forum in Kathmandu.

Geetanjali Gangoli is Co-ordinating Officer of the Violence Against Women Research Group, School for Policy Studies, University of Bristol. She has worked on violence against women, feminism and law, prostitution, trafficking and social policy in India, China and the UK. She has taught modern Indian history at the University of Delhi, and is a recipient of the Panos Reproductive Health Fellowship. Geetanjali Gangoli was awarded the Sir Ratan Tata Visiting Research Fellowship at the Asia Research Centre, London School of Economics and Political Science, and has worked as a Research Fellow at the International Centre for the Study of Violence and Abuse, University of Sunderland, UK.

Arjan de Haan is a Visiting Professor at the University of Guelph, Canada, during the period 2005–2006. His work on labour migration in eastern India earned him his Ph.D. from Erasmus University, the Netherlands, in 1994. After that he worked at the Poverty Research Unit, University of Sussex. Since 1998 he has worked as social development adviser at the UK Department for International Development.

Munshi Israil Hossain has recently completed his master's degree in Research from the University of Bath, UK. His dissertation focused on migration and remittance. He is currently engaged in the research programme of the Well-being and Development Research Centre of the University of Bath.

Ravinder Kaur is Associate Professor of Sociology in the Department of Humanities and Social Sciences, Indian Institute of Technology, New Delhi. Her research interests and publications are in sociological theory and in the sociology of poverty, gender and the environment. She is currently involved in the study of demographic changes related to the low sex ratio and its impact on marriage practices.

Iqbal Alam Khan is currently engaged in research in Bangladesh with the Well-being and Development Research Centre of the University of Bath, UK. He also lectures at the University of Dhaka, Bangladesh. His Ph.D. research looked at social organisation and social control, particularly the role of gang leaders (mastaans), in the slums of Dhaka.

Sepali Kottegoda has been working with the Women and Media Collective in Sri Lanka since completing her D.Phil. at the Institute of Development Studies, University of Sussex. She also teaches Women's Studies at the Faculty of Graduate Studies, University of Colombo, and her research interests are in the areas of women and poverty, gender, households, family and reproductive health. Her most recent publication is *Negotiating Household Politics: Women's Strategies in Urban Sri Lanka*. She is a member of the National Committee on Women in Sri Lanka. She is a member of Steering Committee, Asia-Pacific Women's Watch.

Maureen C. Pagaduan has taught at the University of the Philippines. She is currently Associate Professor in the Department of Community Development, Institute of Social Sciences, The Hague, in the Netherlands. Her areas of specialisation include gender and development, women's organisation and training and research in community development.

Nitya Rao teaches gender and development at the School of Development Studies, University of East Anglia, UK. She has worked extensively in the field of women's organisation, livelihoods and literacy in South Asia for close to two decades, as a practitioner and trainer at the grassroots level in India, as well as a researcher and policy advocate. Her current research interests include gendered changes in land and agrarian relations, food security and livelihood strategies, equity issues in education policies, gendered access and mobility and social relations within people's movements. Her articles have been published in several international and national journals.

Sheila Ryan is a freelance consultant and researcher living in Dhaka, Bangladesh. She has a master's degree in development studies from the University of East Anglia, UK. She has worked with a number of different development organisations in Bangladesh over the last 20 years including the Bangladesh Rural Advancement Committee (BRAC), ICDDR, B and Concern.

Janet Seeley is a Senior Lecturer in Gender and Development at the School of Development Studies, University of East Anglia, UK. Her research interests focus on internal migration, social protection and livelihoods and health. She has carried out research in Bangladesh, India, Nepal and Pakistan as well as East and Central Africa.

Svati P. Shah is Associate Professor at the Centre for the Study of Gender and Sexuality, Faculty of Arts and Science, New York University, USA. Her research focuses on migrant labour and sex work in Mumbai, in a larger context of liberalisation, nationalism and a rapidly changing political economy. She has been a part of feminist and LGBT (lesbian, gay, bisexual and transgendered) struggles in the US and in India.

Shashank Shekhar Sinha is the author of *Restless Mothers and Turbulent Daughters: Situating Tribes in Gender Studies* (2005). He has taught history at PGDAV and Deshbandhu College in the University of Delhi and his current research interests include social and environmental history and the social history of witchcraft.

INDEX

Adivasis of Jharkhand, as tea plantation
    labour, 153–54; gender-migration
    linkages, 152–57; impact of
    social-gender relations on women
    among, 157–66; in-migrations
    impact on, 157–66; in mines and
    factories, 154–55; inter-tribal
    haats, 160; marriages, 161–63;
    out-migration, 152–57; prostitution
    among, 155–56; re-situating
    women in, 151–66; rural-urban
    migration, 152; seasonal migration,
    151, 153; youth dormitories, 164
Alam, Javeed, 158
Alliance of Migrant Workers and
    Advocates, 84
Alva, Margaret, 224–25
anti-*mahajani* movements, 136
Archer, W.G., 138, 140, 160
Asian Women's Human Rights
    Commission (AWHRC), 230
autonomous migration, 33

Bandyopadhyay, Madhumita, 159
Banerjee, Narayan, 34
Bangladesh, case studies of women's
    migration in, 182–87; circumstances
    of women migrants, 182–87; female
    migrants, 179–82; internal
    migration of women in, 171–87;
    migration to join family members,
    180; migration with family as
    dependant/co-worker, 181;
    migration with family when
    women are the main migrant
    workers, 180–81; single educated
    young women migrants, 179; single
    older women migrants, 181–82;
    single young women migrants from
    poor families, 179–80; women in

migration in, 175–82; women's
    status in, 172–75
Bhagat Movement, 160
Bhubaneswar, sex work/trade in, 214–33
Bihar Debt Relief Act, 1976, 136
Bihar Moneylenders Act, 1974, 136
Bihar Scheduled Areas Regulation, 136
Bihar Tribal Welfare Research Institute,
    Ranchi, 156
brothel-based sex work, in Kolkata,
    217–18

Calcutta Sex Workers Union 231
Central Social Welfare Board
    (CSWB), 231
Centre for Feminist Legal Research
    (CFLR), 229–30
Child Marriage Restraint Act 1929,
    Bangladesh, 172
citizenship, crisis in, 21–27
Cox, David, 79
Cruelty to Women (Deterrent
    Punishment) Act 1983, 172
Curzel, Dagmar, 154
Cuthbert, S.T., 151

Dalit women of Nepal, migration of,
    88, 96
day wage labour markets in, Mumbai,
    236–49; solicitation of, 246–48;
Department of Foreign Affairs,
    Philippine, 83
domestic labour sector, work in, 198–99
domestic workers, demand for, 196–98
Dowry Prohibition Act 1980,
    Bangladesh, 172
Draft National Employment Policy for
    Sri Lanka, 63
Dumka district of Santal Parganas,
    ethnic distribution of migrant

population, 142; gender segregation of labour markets, 134; land ownership, tenancy and alienation in, 135–37; livelihood contexts and choices of Santals of, 131–34; occupational status, 133; population characteristics, 131–32; tenancy arrangement, 136–37; women's property rights, 137–41. *See also*, Santal Parganas

Durbar Mahila Samanwaya Committee (DMSC), 218, 220

Electoral Reforms Committee, Sri Lanka, 68

Export Processing Zones (EPZs), 14, 23, 44

Family Court Ordinance 1985, Bangladesh, 172

family dynamics, of migration , 107–22

female domestic workers, demand for, 196–98

female labour importing countries, 54–55

female migration in Delhi, as domestic workers, 198, 201–5; cooperation and competition for work, 206–8; ethnographic status of, 199–200; experience of, 192–212; gendered labour markets and, 196–98; identities in context of migration, 208–11; poverty and insecurities, 211; reasons for, 193–95; survival of migrant family, 205–6; transformation of gender relations, 208–11; women's labour, 205–6

Filipino culture, kinship system in, 80

Filipino women, domestic work, 79–82; gendered dimension of migration, 77–82; government and non-government action to problems of migration of, 82–85; international convention ratified for, 83; migration strategy, 73–77; remittances from overseas, 72, 75

'flying' sex workers, 218

Foreign Employment Act 1985, Nepal, 26, 90–91

Free Trade Zones (FTZs), Sri Lanka; women employed, 51–52

Gamburd, M.R., 57

Gantzer, J.F., 138

gender, racialisation of, 20–27

gendered labour markets, 54, 196–98

gharjawaes marriage, 138–40

Global Action Against Trafficking in Women (GAATW), 229–30

globalisation, and gendered labour migration in Nepal, 87–105

Goonesekere, S.W.E., 63

Gunaratne, C., 60, 63

Gunatilleke, G., 61

Hamid, S., 174

Hinduism, 160–62, 164–65

HIV–AIDS, 225–27

hul Jharkhand, 135

Hunter, W.W., 161, 163

Huq-Hussain, S., 178

Illegal Traffic in Women and Girls (Prevention) Bill 1986, 224

Institute of Development Studies (IDS), Sussex, 117

INSTRAW (United Nations International Research and Training Institute for the Advancement of Women), 54, 56, 57, 58, 65

Integrated Child Development Scheme, 43

internal migration, feminisation of, 35, 41; from rural marginalisation to urban vulnerabilities, 27–33; in Bangladesh, 38

internally displaced persons (IDPs), 14

International Labour Organisation (ILO), 22, 24, 43

International Monetary Fund (IMF), 50, 174

Inter-State Migrant Workers Act, 1979, 143

Inter-State Migrant Workmen (Regulation of Employment and Conditions of Service) Act 1979, 42, 157

Janasaviya Poverty Alleviation Programme, 50
Jharkhand, in-migrations, 157–66; out-migrations, 152–57; re-situating women in, 151–66
Jharkhand Mukti Morcha, 162
Juvenile Justice Act, 1986, 228–29

Kabeer, Naila, 193, 209
Kasturi, Leela, 195, 210
Kolkata, female migration practices and ideologies, 109–10; labour migrants in, 108–9; migration processes, 113; sex work/trade in, 214–33

labour, racial division of, 23
Labour Act 1992, Nepal, 26, 90
labour force, feminisation of, 14
labour market *nakas* in Mumbai, 239–48; sex work negotiation at, 241–46; solicitation of day wage labour in, 246–48
labour migration, globalisation and, 236–37

Magna Carta for Migrant Workers, 84
Marcos, Ferdinand, 74
marriage migration, 194
Migrant Services Centre, Sri Lanka, 68
migrant sex workers, 214–33; coercion, 216–17, 222–24; feminist responses, 229–31; legal position, 224–29; NGO and state interventions, 221–24; organisation of sex work, 215–21; perceptions of law, 231–32; state policies, 224–25
migrant work, male identities of, 81
Migrant Workers and Overseas Filipinos Act of 1995, 83
Migrant Workers and Overseas Filipinos Resource Centres, 83
Migrante, 84
migrants, transgression and community policing image, 37
migration, adivasis of Jharkhand, 151–66; autonomous, 34; circumstances of, 182–87; citizens outsider, 19–27; citizenship right

and identity issue, 42–43; complexity of, 171–87; conditions of, 141–45; conflict, gender and, 13–14; diversity patterns in, 112; employment brokers and, 16; experiences of, 141–45, 201–5; extent of, 141–45; family dynamics of, 33–39, 107–22; female identities in context of migration, 208–11; female migrants as percentage of total international migrants by region, 9; female migration, 193–95, 237; feminisation in, 75, 111, 237, 248; Filipino women for survival, 72–85; for overseas employment, 51–68; for work, 192–212, 237; from rural marginalisation to urban vulnerabilities, 27–33; from Santal Parganas, 129–47; gender politics in Sri Lanka and, 49–68; gender racialisation and, 20–27, 36; gendered dimensions of, 49–68, 77–82, 192–212; geographic patterns of, 113; globalisation and, 87–105, 236–37; in Asia, 9–10; in eastern India, 214–33; internal migration in Bangladesh, 171–87; internal migration, 13, 27–33, 38, 41–42, 171–87; issues and concerns, 19–44; livelihood choices and access relationship with, 29–30, livelihood strategies of poor, 129, 145, 176–77; marriage migration, 15, 194; missing link in literature on, in South Asia, 107–22; motivations and decisions, 97–99; movement and, 7–8; policy implications, 15–17, 39–44; policy of identity and, 12–13, 42; poverty and, 9, 13, 31–32, 36, 87–105, 107–22, 214–33, 237; poverty-gender politics and, 49–68, 87–105; poverty linkage in South Asia, 107–22; problem with, 247–48; process, 97–99, 176; protection and inclusion, 39–44; push and pull factors for, 176, 192; rural-urban migration, 30, 34, 152; search for employment as propellants of, 10; seasonal, 30, 34–35, 88, 114, 129–47; migrant sex workers; sex work and, 214–33, 241–48; sex work in Mumbai and, 241–48; single educated young women, 179; single older women, 181; single young women from poor family, 179–80; social processes and relations in, 113–15; solicitation and, 247; state policy and, 13, 40–43; survival compulsions and, 33–39; themes, 10–15; to joint family members, 180; transnational, 12–13, 23–27; value of reproductive work–capitalism relationship, 41; voluntariness of , 33–34; with family as dependant/co-worker, 181; with family when women are the main workers, 180–81; women, work and, 14; women's experience, 9–17. *See also*, female migrants in Delhi

Ministry of Labour, Sri Lanka, 63
Ministry of Samurdhi, Sri Lanka, 50
Ministry of Women's Affairs, Sri Lanka, 63
movement process, and migration, 7–8
Mumbai, day wage labour markets in, 236–49; gender and sexuality at *nakas*, 241–46; labour market *nakas*, 239–46; sex work negotiation at public space, 241–46; solicitation of day wage labour, 246–48
Muslim Family Law 1961, Bangladesh, 172

National Committee on Women (NCW), Sri Lanka, 63
National Housing Development Authority, 61
Nepal, disadvantages and discrimination to women in migration, 90–91; foreign labour migration in, 87, 103; gendered labour migration in, 87–105; government attitude towards women migration, 92; government perspective towards migration of women, 92–94; poverty reduction, 92–93; seasonal migration of Dalit women, 88; women in migration in, 90–91

Nepali women, difficulties and discrimination at workplace, 99–100; disadvantages and discrimination, 90–91; ethnicity and class, 96–97; foreign labour migration, 94–95; gender and methodological problems, 94; government attitude and perspectives towards, 92–94; income and empowerment from migration, 100–102; magnitude of migration, 92; migration process, 97–99; poverty and migration, 92–94; reintegration into society, 102–103; remittances, 92; seasonal migration, 88; society and, 96–97

Network Opposed to Violence Against Migrant Women (NOVA), 84
new migratory flows, racialisation of gender and, 20–27; women in, 22

Orissa, sex work/trade in 214–33
Orissa Patita Udhar Samiti (OPUS), 219–20
overseas contact workers (OCWs), 74–75
overseas Filipino workers (OFWs), deployment of, 76, 82; remittances of, 72, 75
overseas labour markets, gender profile of migrants, 54; institutional mechanisms for, 52–54; migrant workers to, 52–54
Overseas Workers Welfare Administration (OWWA), 83

Philippine Overseas Employment Administration (POEA), 75, 77, 83
Philippines, deployment of OFWs, 76–77; gendered dimensions of migration, 77–79; government

action to problems of female migration, 82–85; international conventions ratified in, 83; land-based workers, 76; non-government action to problems of female migration, 82–85; occupational specification of migrants from, 75–76; overseas remittances, 72, 75; stereotypes in labour and gender constructs of domestic work in, 79–82; strategy for migration in, 73–77; unemployment rate, 77; women surviving migration, 72–85

Pingol, A.T., 81

poverty, alleviation, 236; gender politics and migration in Sri Lanka, 49–68; government's perspective on, 92–94; in eastern India, 214–33; in Sri Lanka, 50–51; migration and, 9, 13, 31–32, 36, 92–94, 107–22, 214–33; sex work and, 215–16

Prevention of Domestic Violence Bill 2005, Sri Lanka, 68

Prevention of Immoral Traffic in Women and Children Act (PITA), 224–25, 231, 244

Prohibition of Immoral Traffic and Empowerment of Sexual Workers Bill, 1993, 225–27

Rehabilitation of Prostituted Persons Bill, 1993, 225

Revitalisation Movement, 160

Rogaly, Ben, 44

Roy, S.C., 162, 164

Royal Commission of Labour, 154

Sainath, P., 28

Samurdhi Poverty Alleviation Programme, 50, 60

Sanghli statement, 230–31

Sangram (union of sex workers), 230

Sanlaap, 222–23

Sanskritisation, 160

Santal Parganas, control over land in, 135–37; extent, conditions and

experience of migration of women from, 141–45; gendered seasonal migration from, 129–47; land ownership, tenancy and alienation, 135–37; livelihood contexts and choices, 131–34, 145; women's property rights, 137–41

Santal Pargana Tenancy Act (SPTA), 135–36, 138

seasonal migration, 30, 34–35

Seeley, Janet, 38

servants, nation of, 23

sex work/trade, brothel-based in Kolkata, 217–18; *dalal-bari* system, 218; entry into, 215–17; family-based, 218–20; feminist responses, 229–31; financial access and aging issues, 219–21; 'flying' sex workers, 218; legal position, 224–29; migration link, 217; NGO and state interventions, 221–24; organisation of, 215, 217–21; perceptions of law, 231–32; plan of action by government for improvement of health status of, 228–29; poverty, 215–16; reasons for joining, 215–17; role of coercion and force in, 216–17, 222–24; Sanghli statement on, 230–31; state policies, 224–25; street-based, 245, 248

Shah, Svati, 31

Sharma, Ursula, 194

Simeon, Dilip, 158–59

Singh, A.M., 194

Sohrai harvest festival, 135

solicitation, of day wage labour in Mumbai, 246–48

South Asia, extended households in, 117; family dynamics and processes of migration in, 107–22; female migration and employment practices and ideologies, 109; fluid family, 116; gendered migration perspective, 108–10; migration-family linkages, 118–21; migration-gender, family linkages, 115–18; migration-poverty linkages in, 107–22; nuclear family, 116; social processes and relations in migration, 113–15

Sri Lanka, female labour force participation rate in, 51; female labour importing countries from, 54–55; foreign exchange earnings from remittances, 55–56; gender politics in, 49–68; household responsibility, 64–65; housewives, 61–62; institutional mechanisms for recognition of women as workers in, 63–64; law, policy and reality about head of household in, 58–61; migrant workers to overseas labour markets, 52–54; migration and poverty in gender politics in, 49–68; occupational specifications of migrant from, 55; poverty in, 50–51; women as primary income earners, 65–68; women workers, 61–64; women's employment and unemployment in, 51–52

Sri Lankan Bureau of Foreign Employment (SLBFE), 22, 24, 27, 50–55

structural adjustment programmes, Nepal, 23

survival migration, 33–39

tribal women, seasonal migration among, 35

Tribe-Caste Continuum, concept of, 160

UN International Convention on the Protection of the Rights of All Migrant Workers and Members of Their Families (1990), 43, 52, 83

West Bengal, extent conditions and experience of migration, 141–42; family dynamic of migration in, 107–22, 141–42; gendered migration linkages, 108–10; migration-family linkages, 118–21; migration-gender-family linkages, 115–18; seasonal

migration in, 114, 141; sex trade/work in, 214–33; social processes and relations in migration in, 113–15

women, and migration, 9–10; as absentee income earner for family-based household, 56–61; changing roles of, within family, 62; Dalit women migration, 88; day wage labourers, 238; difficulties and discrimination at workplace, 99–100; disadvantages and discrimination at workplace, 90–92, 99–100; domestic work, 79–82; domestic workers, 198, 201–205; employment and unemployment in Sri Lanka, 51–52; empowerment from migration, 100–102; experiences of migration, 141–45, 201–205, 208–11; extent, conditions and experience of migration, 141–45; factors in decision to migrate, 56; foreign exchange earnings from remittances, 55–56; government and non-government action in Philippines to problems of migration of, 82–85; habitus ambiguities, 208–11; head of household, 58–61; household responsibility, 64–65; housewives, 61–62; identities in context of migration, 208–11; income from migration, 100–102; insecurity in lives of migrants, 211; institutional mechanisms for recognition as workers, 63–64; internal migration in Bangladesh, 171–87; labour, 205–206, 238; labour importing countries, 54–55; migrant workers to overseas labour market, 52–54, 76; migration in Nepal, 87–105; occupational specifications of migrants, 55, 75; primary income earners, 65–68; property rights, 137–41; re-situating in Jharkhand, 151–66; sex work, poverty and migration, 214–33; solicitation for paid work, 238; status in

Bangladesh, 172–75; stereotypes in labour and gender constructs in domestic work of, 79–82; surviving migration, 72–85; transnational migration of, 23–27; workers, 61–64
Women and Children Repression Prevention Act 1995, Bangladesh, 172
Women in the Cities of Asia, 120

women migrant workers, demand for, 22
Women's Bureau, Sri Lanka, 63
Women's Charter, Sri Lanka, 63
Women's *samithi*, 60
Workman's Breach of Contract Act, 153
World Bank, 24, 50, 174

Yapa, L.A., 56–58
Year of Overseas Filipino Workers, 80
Year of Service Providers, 80

STAKING A CLAIM

Current Books in Women's Studies

Basis of the Bargain: Gender, Schooling & Jobs Carol O'Donnell

Caring for Australia's Children: Political & Industrial Issues in Child Care Deborah Brennan & Carol O'Donnell

Contemporary Feminist Thought Hester Eisenstein

Crossing Boundaries: Feminisms & Critique of Knowledges Edited by Barbara Caine, E.A. Grosz, Marie de Lepervanche

Ethnicity, Class & Gender in Australia Edited by Gill Bottomley & Marie de Lepervanche

Female Crime: The Construction of Women in Criminology Ngaire Naffine

Feminist Challenges: Social & Political Theory Edited by Carole Pateman & Elizabeth Gross

Gender & Power R.W. Connell

Gender Agenda Terry Evans

Gender At Work Ann Game & Rosemary Pringle

Getting Equal: Labour Market Regulation and Women's Work Carol O'Donnell & Philippa Hall

Good & Mad Women: The Historical Construction of Femininity in Twentieth Century Australia Jill Julius Matthews

Program for Change Edited by Marian Sawer

Secretaries Talk: Sexuality, Power and Work Rosemary Pringle

Sexual Subversions: Three French Feminists Elizabeth Grosz

Short-Changed: Women and Economic Policies Rhonda Sharp & Ray Broomhill

Subordination: Feminism & Social Theory Clare Burton

Teaching Gender? Sex Education & Sexual Stereotypes Tricia Szirom

Which Way Is Up? Essays on Class, Sex & Culture R.W. Connell

A Woman's Place: Women & Politics in Australia Marian Sawer & Marian Simms

Women, Social Science & Public Policy Edited by Jacqueline Goodnow & Carole Pateman

Women Working: Economics and Reality Karen Mumford

STAKING A CLAIM

Feminism, bureaucracy
and the state

*Suzanne Franzway, Dianne Court
and R.W. Connell*

Allen & Unwin
Sydney Wellington London Boston

First published in 1989
Allen & Unwin Australia Pty Ltd
An Unwin Hyman company
8 Napier Street, North Sydney, NSW 2059 Australia

Allen & Unwin New Zealand Limited
60 Cambridge Terrace, Wellington, New Zealand

Unwin Hyman Limited
15-17 Broadwick Street, London WIV IFP England

Unwin Hyman Inc.
8 Winchester Place, Winchester, Mass 01890 USA

National Library of Australia
Cataloguing-in-Publication entry:

Franzway, S.
Staking a claim: feminism, bureaucracy and the state.
Bibliography.
Includes index.
ISBN 0 04 820044 1.
ISBN 0 04 352239 4 (pbk.).

1. Women — Government policy. 2. Feminism. 3. Women —
Social conditions. 4. State, The. I. Court, Dianne,
1945–1986. II. Connell, R.W. (Robert William),
1944–   . III. Title.

323.3'4

Library of Congress Catalog Card Number: 88-83144

Set in 10/11pt Bembo by SRM Production Services Sdn Bhd, Malaysia
Printed in Hong Kong by Dah Hua Printing Press Co. Ltd

Contents

Tables   ·   vii

Introduction   ix

Biographical note   xiii

Part I: The state in sexual politics

1   *The problem: seeing sexual politics and seeing the state*   3

    Traditional views of the state   3
    Some facts about the state and gender   6
    From policy to theory   10

2   *Current theories*   14

    Liberal feminism and imperfect citizenship   14
    Regulation   17
    The class state   19
    Class and patriarchy   23
    The patriarchal state   27
    Patriarchy as procedure   29

3   *A framework*   33

    Criteria for a theory of the state   33
    The place of the state   37
    State structure   41
    The state's people   47
    State-society dynamics   52

Part II: Case studies

4   *Child care*   59

    What is child care?   60
    Feminism and mothering   61

Child care and the state 70
Femocrats in the 1980s 83

5 *Equal opportunity* 87

Development of the strategy 88
Debate about the strategy 95
The reform workforce and the feminist agenda 100

6 *Sexual violence* 104

The state and sexual violence 105
Feminists and sexual violence 106
Rape law reform: the New South Wales Act 108
Child sexual abuse: the Furler Report 114
The strategic problem 128

Part III: Feminism and bureaucracy

7 *The 'femocrat' strategy* 133

Early days 134
Electoral politics 136
From influence to entrism 137
Tensions and connections 140
The 'bureaucratisation of feminism' 143
Bureaucratisation as process 146
The state's problems 149
Femocrats act 151

8 *Gains and losses* or *Where will it all end?* 156

Resources 157
Changing conditions 161

Appendix: Di Court's project 169

Bibliography 176

Index 188

Tables

		Page
1.1	Sex and occupation among New South Wales state employees	8
1.2	Sex and salary among New South Wales state employees	9
3.1	A taxonomy of state apparatuses derived from class analysis	43
4.1	Main types of child care provision	61

Introduction

In 1983 the American feminist Catharine MacKinnon, at the start of an influential article on law, bluntly stated that 'Feminism has no theory of the state'. Five years later this is still true. Indeed, the point can be made more broadly. Gay liberation has no theory of the state and sexuality. Social science has no theory of the state as an institution of gender relations. The whole area of sexual politics and the state is a theoretical dust bowl.

Why should this matter? Principally because there is a great deal of practice in the area. Though neither its rhetoric nor its theory generally acknowledges it, modern feminism has developed in very close relation to the state. The movement has developed only under certain kinds of state structure—broadly, liberal capitalist states. There is no substantial feminist movement in the USSR, in China, in Indonesia, in Saudi Arabia. Many feminist activists, perhaps a majority, are state employees, often being teachers, researchers, health or welfare workers. A significant part of feminist political agendas has consisted of demands on the state: to decriminalise abortion, to criminalise pornography, to fund women's refuges, to introduce anti-discrimination laws, to replace sexist school curricula. Part of feminist politics has attempted to change the structure or personnel of the state itself, as witness the American Equal Rights Amendment, the Canadian Charter of Rights and Freedoms, and Equal Employment Opportunity machinery in Australian government agencies. Much of the resistance to feminism has attempted to capture the state for reactionary purposes, for instance the 1970s attempts to make abortion illegal or difficult, or the recent attack on 'gender studies' at Griffith University in Queensland.

The point holds for other progressive movements in sexual politics. Gay Liberation, for instance, first emerged in response to state repression: specifically, police attacks on gay men in New York City. Its early focus in many countries was on persuading the state to decriminalise homosexuality. The homophobic 'backlash' of the late 1970s similarly chose the state as battleground. The flagship campaign, led by Anita Bryant in Florida, targeted local government and overturned an ordinance giving equal employment rights to homosexual people. Gay men's politics has been reshaped around the AIDS epidemic, and again the state has been central, especially public health measures to control the spread of the disease.

For practical politics the state is not just important, it is unavoidable. It matters a great deal to have a clear understanding of what it is, how it works, and how it can be influenced. A great many arguments about strategy embody differences in theoretical assumptions. Is the state inherently patriarchal? Is it inherently homophobic? Is it capable of change from within or does it corrupt those who try? These are practical questions but they are also questions of general theory. Until we get them clear as theory it is likely we will remain confused about the practice.

The late 1980s poses a different and more complex agenda than the early 1970s, when the ideas of modern sexual politics were framed. On the one hand are the trends summed up in the idea of a 'post-feminist' age. They include the decline of feminist street politics, the religious/ conservative backlash, and the political ascendancy of the New Right; the fashion for deconstructionist scepticism among radical intellectuals; the reaffirmation of femininity in fashion and media. Balancing this are the effects of radical successes, including the growing presence of women in trade unions, in male-dominated professions such as law and medicine, in state bureaucracies, and in academic life. This has led to a new kind of institutional feminism with a strong streak of pragmatism and a highly ambivalent relationship to its own radical heritage.

The project of this book is in some sense counter to both these trends, though it is very much influenced by the experience of the second. Against the 'post-feminist' rhetoric we would emphasise that the key insights of 1970s radical sexual politics were correct. Gender inequalities are widespread and systematic, they are deep and damaging in their effects, and they have not yet been redressed. These insights need to be extended and clarified rather than discarded. The growth of a pragmatic feminism, and the strikingly similar growth of a pragmatic gay politics which is even more complete in its displacement of 'liberation' politics, tends to substitute organisational know-how for social critique. While we can accept many of the criticisms of radical rhetoric and moralism made by those who have to survive in a bureaucracy, we would argue that holding even a small part of state power increases, rather than decreases, the need for theoretical and strategic clarity.

This book aims to bring feminist experience and social theory together to produce a systematic view of the state as an agent in sexual politics. We would emphasise that *this places in question the nature of the state itself*. Most analyses so far, as suggested by titles such as 'Women and the welfare state' or 'The state and working women', have taken for granted a conventional socialist or liberal understanding of the state and have asked how women, or sexual politics, fit into the picture. A much more drastic theoretical shift is called for. We must examine how the state is itself constituted by gender relations and shaped by the vicissitudes of sexual politics. This is a difficult and complex project. We approach it at two levels: an argument about the general theory of the state and the social analysis of gender; and a set of case studies on the interplay between feminism and state structures in Australia during the

last fifteen years. Moving back and forth between these levels will, we hope, keep the general theory honest and give the detail of events a wider meaning.

Di Court died in 1986 leaving drafts of her unfinished PhD thesis on the feminist movement and the state. Her friends, relations and colleagues considered that these manuscripts embodied an original contribution to feminism and to social science which should not be lost. The scale of her work suggested a book, but the texts were far from complete and could not be published as they stood, nor 'edited' into a book without extensive rewriting. Since Di was addressing key issues, other people were working on closely related questions, and this provided a solution. It proved possible to combine parts of her manuscript with texts recently written by the other two authors, and thus publish the core of her work in book form.

The text has three main sources. First are drafts from Di Court's papers, which included, in different stages of completeness: four essays or thesis outlines dealing with methodological and theoretical questions; four draft chapters on issue areas (housing policy; trade unions and socialist feminism; rape law reform; feminism, bureaucracy, and equal employment opportunity); and a detailed chronology of the Australian women's movement's interactions with the state (in New South Wales and at the federal level) 1969–79. The arguments of her theoretical essays form a substantial element of Part I of this book, especially Chapters 1 and 2; the case studies on rape law reform and EEO are the basis of the relevant sections of Part II; the material on bureaucracy has been incorporated into Part III. Since little of Di's text had progressed beyond a first draft, little could be published as it stood. Rather than take a pious attitude to her text, we have treated it as she treated her own drafts, freely reworking both expression and argument to build old material into newer and more comprehensive analyses. Nevertheless we think readers will be interested in her own writing, and include at the end of the book one of Di's latest drafts which describes the theoretical position and research plan she had finally arrived at.

Second is Suzanne Franzway's MA thesis 'Australian Feminism and the State: The Case of Child Care,' completed in the Department of Sociology at the University of Essex in 1985. This included discussions of the welfare state and feminism, here incorporated into Part I; feminism and the ideology of motherhood; child-care policy, the basis of the case study in Part II; and a discussion of 'femocrats' (feminist bureaucrats) which is the basis of Part III. This last grew into the paper 'With problems of their own: femocrats and the welfare state' given at a conference of the Sociological Association of Australia and New Zealand in 1986, and later published in *Australian Feminist Studies* (no. 3, 1986). These pieces stressed that femocrats act within a mesh of feminist politics and the contradictory interests of 'the state'.

The third source is a paper by Bob Connell called 'The State in Sexual

Politics', versions of which were given at conferences of the Australasian Political Studies Association and the Sociological Association of Australia and New Zealand in 1985 and 1986. This expanded the brief discussion of the state in *Gender and Power,* arguing the need for a general theory of the state as an actor in sexual politics and as constituted by the history of gender relations. It provided the framework for Part I, especially Chapter 3, and some material for Part III.

Those are the sources—but only the sources. We have tried to write a book, rather than a compilation, to provide an argument that will hang together across a wide range of issues. Though the three authors have different backgrounds and experiences, there was enough common ground in the three sets of arguments to make the attempt at synthesis worthwhile. The process involved some initial talks to establish a framework for the book and for the use of Di's texts; exchange of drafts and comments on drafts; some nervous long-distance telephoning; and several interstate (Adelaide–Sydney) visits to work intensively on manuscripts and plans.

Di's commitment to a thoughtful feminist activism underlies our collective emphasis on the interaction of theory and sexual politics. We have aimed at analysis which is equally sensitive to political dilemmas and to political consequences. In the play between argument about the state in sexual politics and the specific case study examples, we are as much concerned with the whys and wherefores of feminist strategy as we are with making out a particular case. We have gained from those who struggle to bridge the widening gap between abstract principle and pragmatism. In turn we hope that what follows will be of use in the difficult practical business of challenging sexual politics, especially where it must be 'on the run'.

The following people have given labour, source materials, reflections on political experience, very useful suggestions, technical support, comfort and unprintable anecdotes: Julienne Vennard, Susan Sheridan, Christa Schlosstein, Anne Scheppers, Penny Ryan, Rosemary Pringle, Louise Portway, Murphy Sisters, Frances Meredith, Pip Martin, Susan Magarey, Rosie McDonell, Bronwen Levy, Virginia Lee, John Lee (with special thanks for timely assistance), Wendy Heath, Elizabeth Furler, Neil Franzway, Helen Easson.

Biographical note

Dianne Joyce Court

Di Court was born in Sydney in 1945, the youngest of four children, and grew up in the city's northern suburbs, finishing her schooling at North Sydney Girls' High. She trained in physiotherapy and practised in Australia and several countries overseas, including the United Kingdom, Canada and Norway. Returning to Australia she specialised in respiratory physiotherapy, holding a senior position at St Vincent's Hospital. At the age of 30 she went back to university and in 1979 graduated from the University of New South Wales with first-class honours in political science.

Di's interests included international affairs and she co-authored a monograph on Soviet involvement in South-East Asia. She won a postgraduate scholarship and enrolled for higher degree work in sociology at Macquarie University, launching a project on feminist theory, the state, and the history of the women's movement. This grew out of her practical involvement in both feminism and the labour movement, and her passionate concern that they should meet, on equal terms. In 1983 she published a theoretical paper on the concept of patriarchy, arguing its importance for the adequate understanding of society, class and the state. She taught social science at the University of New South Wales and the New South Wales Institute of Technology; and maintained an interest in the health sector and its workers through teaching, conferences and practice as a physiotherapist. She continued an active unionist and served as president of her union branch. She became increasingly critical of both the Labor Party, which she eventually left, and of an elitist feminism which ignored the everyday experience of working women.

Despite outstanding talents and achievement Di was troubled by an unjustified but nonetheless enormous sense of failure. Sadly, she chose to end her life on 4 May 1986.

Publications:

'The Centrality of Patriarchy' *Arena* 1983, no. 65, pp. 162 – 171.

The Soviet Union in Southeast Aisa, Canberra Papers on Strategy and Defence No. 29, 1984: Research School of Pacific Studies, Australian National University.

'Women's Studies: Ghetto or Goer?' *Australian Feminist Studies* 1986, no. 2, pp.55–57.

Part I

The state in sexual politics

1

The problem: seeing sexual politics and seeing the state

Traditional views of the state

Classic accounts of the nature of the state had little to say about gender. To liberal and marxist, conservative and radical alike, questions of sexuality and gender were outside the public realm. Pierre Trudeau once quipped that 'the State has no business in the nation's bedrooms'. It seems that two centuries of political theorists agreed. Recent reviews of the history of theories of the state by Held (1985) and Knuttila (1987) show how slight was their attention to sexual politics and to the social position of women.

This exclusion has been achieved in different ways. Many theories of the state are built around the relationship between the state and the individual. In such a framework 'the individual' is abstracted from all social relationships other than the one with the state. Concepts of 'rights', 'liberties' or 'obligations' are thus attached to an abstract—sexless, classless, colourless—person.

The political consequences of this doctrine are complex. On the one hand it becomes a mechanism for the exclusion of women because the formally sexless 'individual' is always discussed as if he were a man. So interesting and important a text as Rawls' *A Theory of Justice* makes the representative individual a 'head of family'—implicitly a man, thus naturalising the family and its internal inequalities (see Kearns, 1984). Social contract theories, which picture the state as the agent of an agreement among individuals, usually have hidden gender assumptions. Pateman (1988) speaks of the 'fraternal social contract' as the real substance of this theory of the state.

On the other hand an abstract formulation of rights allows anyone at all to claim those rights. J.S. Mill's famous argument for the enfranchisement of women is constructed exactly along these lines: there is nothing, he argues, that should exclude women specifically from general rights and obligations of citizenship. Liberal theory has accordingly been

3

a basis on which women and gay men have at times made successful claims for political access. In later sections of this book we will be very much concerned with the political strategies that flow from these claims. At this point, however, we must emphasise that they follow only from what is implicit in liberal political theory. Explicitly, gender is not part of the liberal concept of the state at all. Mill thought the subjection of women an anomaly, not a basic feature of the state.

The position is not very different in marxist and anarchist accounts of the state. Certainly socialist theory has moved beyond the abstracted individual and sees a connection between the state and social structure. But it sees only one kind of structure. People are linked to the state by being members of a class and by the way the state hooks up with class interests. In Lenin's *State and Revolution* for instance the state is seen straightforwardly as the bearer of the class interests of the bourgeoisie, therefore must be smashed by the insurgent workers. The shift towards social analysis of the state is an important advance on liberalism, but is still severely limited. For in mainstream socialist thought and action, class issues come to define a new kind of 'public' realm, an arena of political legitimacy. Other aspects of social relations, such as gender, are thought marginal: at best secondary contradictions, at worst a distraction from the class struggle. Accordingly the mainstream of socialist thought about the state, from Bakunin and Lenin through Gramsci and Trotsky to Poulantzas and Offe, ignores sexual politics as comprehensively as liberalism does.

As in liberalism, there was another voice to be heard. From early in the industrial revolution, some socialists had been arguing for equality of the sexes, a theme of the 'utopian' socialist colonies and of certain theorists such as Bebel and Engels. Engels had even connected the subordination of women, in a speculative way, to the origin of the state. In the 1890s women in the socialist movement began to organise and theorise in ways that connected the 'social question' (i.e. class) with the 'woman question'. For a fascinating few years Russian socialist feminists led by Kollontai even brought Lenin's government to introduce a program for the emancipation of women, thus swinging the post-revolutionary state to a radical position in sexual politics. This experience, however, left no impression on the main body of socialist theory. How resistant that tradition has been is shown by the fact that in the mid-1980s—after fifteen years of renewed public debate about feminist ideas—most books of socialist theory about the state were still virtually silent about sexual politics (e.g. Clark and Deer, 1984; Offe, 1984; Giddens, 1985; Frankel, 1983—this last registers feminism as a movement but not the issues feminists are raising).

Neither liberalism nor socialism has held the high ground in recent public discussion of the state in advanced capitalist countries. This lead has been taken by the New Right, which in most areas has been concerned to roll back the state. Monetarist and 'deregulating' attacks on

Keynesian views of the state as an economic regulator have been conducted without reference to sexual politics, like the broader New Right attack on taxation and the welfare state as an imposition on the free individual and a constraint on free enterprise. The economic aggregates discussed in the policy debates (money supply, Gross Domestic Product, levels of investment, rates of return, etc.) are unspecified as to gender. Like 'the individual', such concepts as 'the economic actor' and 'the entrepreneur' are abstracted from the social relations of gender.

Once again, as feminists have forcibly pointed out, there is an implicit discourse about gender. 'The entrepreneur' is really a man, and it is blandly assumed by economists that he has a wife to cook and clean for him and raise his children while he battles it out in the grim deregulated marketplace. When the New Right 'trims the fat' from the welfare state and returns welfare functions to 'the community', what it actually means is a lot more unpaid work for women: care of the old, care of the sick, care of children (see Wilson, 1982; Finch and Grove, 1983; Mowbray and Bryson, 1984). Even the aggregates of economic statistics are gendered. As Stretton (1976) pointed out a good while back, orthodox economic concepts select certain kinds of production for counting and ignore others. The work not counted is typically women's work. Similarly, many women workers are not counted in 'the workforce' simply because they do domestic work in family homes. (Deacon, 1985, notes that statisticians of an earlier era defined the workforce more generously.)

Even in rhetoric the New Right has been unable to keep the state and sexual politics entirely apart. In the area of sexual morality New Right politicians have presented themselves as champions of 'traditional family values'. In the United States especially, but to some extent everywhere, the economic program of rolling back the state is mixed with a program of state action to enforce a repressive sexual morality. The claim that this represents 'traditional values' is specious. Traditional sexual morality in Western societies includes a good measure of practical tolerance which the New Right desires to abolish. Partly for that reason, the moral program of the New Right requires *expanded* state intervention in areas like censorship, sexual behaviour, the surveillance of medical practitioners, and even the surveillance of (whisper it) families.

This brief review of the leading Western traditions of thought about the state shows two things clearly. First, gender and sexuality are rarely major concerns of the theorists. These issues are not formally included as components of theories of the state. Second, no tradition of thought about the state can actually avoid issues of sex and gender. They are always present, at least as unspoken assumptions or limits to argument, and sometimes more visibly. It seems that sexual politics is unavoidable in analysis of the state. Some of the practical reasons for this will be shown in the next section.

Before leaving conventional theory, however, we should note two

recent developments in it. In some socialist writing, such as the German 'capital logic' school and the work of Frankel, there has been a reaction against seeing the state as an object, an institution or 'apparatus', in the much-used term of the Althusserian school. Rather, the state tends to be seen as a kind of social process, or as a particular moment in a larger social process. And in some radical and some conservative writing (e.g. Bahro, 1978 and de Jasay, 1985) there has been increased emphasis on the state as a social actor in its own right, not just a vehicle for other social interests. The state has its own interests and its own dynamic of growth. Both points can be exaggerated; but they have some relevance for the analysis of gender, as will be seen in Chapter 3 below.

Some facts about the state and gender

The reason *theories* of the state must deal with gender, at least implicitly, is simply that gender is *as a matter of fact* a major feature of the state and sexual politics is *in fact* a major sphere of its operations. The evidence for this is massive and would take a book to expound in detail. In this section we will simply sketch some of the highlights. Another view of the evidence can be found in a useful article by Burstyn (1983).

The connection appears at a very basic level in the concept of the 'public realm' itself. The state is quintessentially of the public realm. It even defines the public realm in contexts like the Thatcher government's policy towards the British telecommunications system, where the sale of a state enterprise to capitalists is called 'privatisation'. Generally, however, the public realm is defined more broadly, and in this sense a distinction between public and private can be found in most societies.

As the cross-cultural researches of feminist anthropologists in the 1970s found, this distinction is everywhere connected to gender (Rosaldo and Lamphere, 1974; Burton, 1985). Women's work tends to be specialised in the domestic realm, men's in the public. A symbolic equation of women with domesticity and men with the world 'outside' the home is a widespread feature of popular culture. In Anglo-American culture, this can be seen in matters as diverse as the joke conventions of situation comedies, children's toys, and employment practices. Though the attempt to found the whole analysis of women's subordination on the public/private dichotomy failed, the distinction still has a great deal of force. It is, for instance, the main cultural presupposition behind the exclusion of domestic work and child care from economic statistics, and the exclusion of housewives from 'the workforce', mentioned above.

Thus there is an elemental connection between the pattern of gender relations and the way the state is constituted as a specific institution in social life. The state is constituted within a specialised 'public' realm marked out by sexual ideology and the sexual division of labour. In this sense the connection of the state with gender relations is *more* intimate

and fundamental than is the state's connection with class relations in traditional socialist theory. For here the state appears as an intervention in a class dynamic already constituted. It is, for instance, a stabiliser of class relations: 'the factor of cohesion' in a social formation, to cite Poulantzas' (1973:44) famous definition of the state. It is not constituted from fundamental categories of class structure itself.

The state is constituted in a realm culturally marked as masculine. Masculinisation of the state is a practical reality as well as an implication in basic structures. The top personnel of the state, in every country around the world without exception, are overwhelmingly men. For instance men make up 96 per cent of the US Congress, 91 per cent of the Indian parliament, 97 per cent of the superior court judges in Britain, 95 per cent of the federal court judges in Australia, 99 per cent of the generals in the US military, 100 per cent of the generals in Japan, 96 per cent of the Central Committee of the Communist Party of the Soviet Union. Figures like Margaret Thatcher and Indira Gandhi are genuinely rare exceptions.

This is not just a matter of statistics, but also of the atmosphere, style and functioning of the top levels of the state. Fasteau (1974) observed some time ago the role of a cult of masculine toughness in the shaping of US foreign policy. Feminists in Australian government have given vivid pictures of the masculine culture of the upper levels of the bureaucracy and the difficulties women consequently face there (Dowse, 1983; Lynch, 1984; Eisenstein, 1987).

A similar disproportion between the sexes appears in the personnel of particular parts of the state such as the military and the police. Ninety-two per cent of the United States military are men, 99.9 per cent of the West German military; 93 per cent of the Australian military and 94 per cent of police in Australia are men. Again this is not just a matter of the statistics but also of the ethos and functioning of the institutions. This is vividly shown in discussion of the small minorities in those branches of the state who are women, such as Chapkis' *Loaded Questions: Women in the Military*. Even more poignantly it is seen in Ollif's *Women in Khaki* about femininity and soldiering in World War II. Over 35 000 women were enlisted in the Australian army, but they were carefully held back from the battle zones. The nearest they came to combat was in the second-line coastal artillery, where they were allowed to plot the targets but not to fire the guns.

This degree of dominance by men is not found in other parts of the state such as the teaching service, social welfare and health services. Most social workers, nurses and primary teachers are women. Nor is general administration wholly done by men. Departments such as Treasury and External Affairs include a good many women as clerks, typists and secretaries.

The point is not that the state is completely 'male' in its personnel. Many women are state employees, and the modern state depends on

women workers. The Commonwealth Public Service in Australia, despite a history of massive discrimination (Deacon, 1984), was 35 per cent women in 1980; the percentage had grown as the service itself expanded. The point is rather that there is a systematic gender patterning *within* the state in the distribution of its personnel.

Systematic evidence of this has piled up as 'equal opportunity' programs have been introduced and have researched both the problems of discrimination and the impact of affirmative action. A good example is the survey of state employees in New South Wales done in 1985 by the Office of the Director of Equal Opportunity in Public Employment. It found a marked gender pattern in major occupational categories (Table 1.1). Men dominate professions and trades and predominate in administration; women dominate clerical work. The connection of gender with organisational power suggested here is more clearly shown in the findings on imcomes (Table 1.2). The dominance of men at the top is overwhelming; and the percentage of women increases, with mechanical regularity, at each step down the salary scale.

Table 1.1 Sex and occupation among New South Wales state employees

Occupation	Men %	Women %	Total no. surveyed
Clerical administrative (included management)	64	36	13 105
Clerical support (includes typists)	14	86	9 164
Professional	74	26	9 398
Professional support	62	38	9 083
Supervisor (e.g. foreman)	96	4	2 029
Skilled trade	95	5	2 898
Non-skilled trade	92	8	3 011
Unskilled	79	21	6 697

Source: Recalculated from *Equal Employment Opportunity Management Plan Resurvey 1985, Preliminary Report* Office of Director of Equal Opportunity in Public Employment, Sydney, 1985, Table 4.

The details of these statistics are, of course, specific to one time and place, and are changing (if slowly) even as they are recorded. But the overall patterns revealed here are typical of modern state structures in all parts of the world. There are concentrations of men in top management, in the apparatuses of coercion (military, police, judiciary, prisons) and in quasi-industrial activities such as transport and construction. There are concentrations of women in secretarial work, in certain professional areas, and in certain kinds of unskilled work (e.g. cleaners). A systematic sexual division of labour is a major feature of the internal organisation of the state. And this division is closely connected with power. Both the

Table 1.2 Sex and salary among New South Wales state employees

Salary	Men %	Women %	Total no. surveyed
$44 601 and above	94	6	740
$35 201–$44 600	92	8	1 829
$27 000–$35 200	86	14	6 460
$21 101–$27 000	82	18	10 140
$18 601–$21 100	70	30	8 135
$13 701–$18 600	58	42	18 174
Up to $13 700	32	68	11 218

Source: as for Table 1.1; recalculated from the report's Table 7.

making of state decisions and the enforcement of those decisions is substantially in the hands of men.

Thus what the state *is,* is gender-structured; and so is a great deal of what the state *does.* Consider the legal system, the police, courts and prisons. Though the concept of 'crime' does not formally refer to gender, in practice the process of criminalising people is markedly gendered. Ninity-six percent of the Australian prison population are men, as are 93 percent of the United States prison population. Though women's rates of conviction for a range of offences have been rising, they are still far below men's.

By contrast, the clientele of the state's welfare services is mainly women, and children being cared for by women. Women are the majority of age pensioners, and the vast majority of lone parents. The so-called 'feminisation of poverty' in recent decades has perhaps intensified this connection (Cass, 1986). It must also be said that women's vulnerability to poverty is also, in signficant part, an outcome of state policies. These include education policies, which in the past have directed technical training almost exclusively to boys; taxation policies, which have created incentives to keep married women out of the workforce; and wage policies such as those administered through the Australian arbitration courts which, until 1969, legally enshrined the principle of lower wages for women and still refuse to adopt the principle of 'comparable worth' (O'Donnell and Hall, 1988).

Low wages in regular employment makes prostitution attractive to some women, and there they meet the state again. The courts and police, supposedly concerned to punish prostitution as a crime, in effect regulate and tax it as an industry. (For a superb historical analysis of this, see Golder and Allen, 1979.) The interviews with a sample of Sydney prostitutes done by Perkins and Bennett (1985) show both the scale of this intervention and something of its character: 68 per cent had been arrested at least once; there was routine corruption and incidental violence by police; and the intensity of control fluctuated according to the political needs of the time.

Particular hostility was directed by the police at gay male prostitutes, and this too is part of a gender pattern. The state is deeply implicated in the construction of 'homosexuality' as a social category and in the oppression of homosexual people. Adam (1988) surveying the situation in the United States, describes discriminatory laws and administrative actions, police harassment and entrapment, and victimisation in public employment. The United States, it should be noted, is one of the most liberal states in the world in relation to sexuality.

Some state activities which were once gender-segregated have become much less so: education is an important case. Most public schools are now co-educational and formal barriers to women's entry into universities and technical courses have been abolished. Public education has become an important vehicle for feminism and increasing numbers of women have indeed moved through the education system into professions. Yet it would be a rash politician who declared that sex equality in education has now been achieved. Working-class girls have not benefited in the way middle-class girls have. Blackburn (1984) points to the legacy of sexism in curriculum, and to the disempowering experiences of education common among girls. The advent of New Right governments makes it possible that gains of the recent past can still be reversed. The new policy of the Australian federal government, outlined in 1987, is to direct higher education funding strongly into management, science and technology—all areas where the majority of both students and staff are men.

Once again we emphasise that the details just recited are only a fraction of the evidence that can be assembled on the connections between the state and the gender order. These connections appear in the basic constitution of the realm of the state; in the composition of the controllers of the state apparatus; in the staffing of the state machinery and in its internal organisation; in what the state does, who it impinges upon and how. Clearly, the state is deeply implicated in the overall social advantaging of men and subordination of women. The evidence reveals not just a sexual division of labour but, more decisive, men's greater access to power in and through the state. This is the central issue on which the argument in this book turns, the issue that has been persistently excluded from mainstream theories of the state and which cannot be evaded any more.

From policy to theory

Facts of the kind recited in the previous section have been brought to light largely through the efforts of feminists and gay activists. As soon as the question of sexual oppression and sex inequality came into focus in the late 1960s, the state's role in producing them became of interest. In books like Morgan's *Sisterhood is Powerful*, Firestone's *Dialectic of Sex*,

and Altman's *Homosexual: Oppression and Liberation,* the state is a somewhat shadowy beast but its activities are much in evidence. As the sexual
liberation campaigns crystallised into political movements, the state
became a matter of practical concern. There were legislators to be lobbied, police to be confronted, bureaucrats to be persuaded, in order to
accomplish even the earliest of movement goals. Since 'sexual liberation'
ideas sprang directly from the New Left milieu of the 1960s with its virtually anarchist antagonism to governments, there was from the start a
tendency to see the state as the enemy and to be at best ambivalent about
calling on its powers to accomplish reforms.

It is therefore a tribute to the practical unavoidability of the state in
sexual politics that all varieties of feminism and all strands in gay politics
rapidly found themselves dealing with the state. Not only dealing with
it at arm's length but often joining committees, receiving funds, writing
policies, and sometimes taking jobs. By the mid-1970s the roll call of
movement interactions with the state included courses in the elite public
educational institutions, the universities (the first women's studies course
in Australian higher education opened in 1973 and by 1974 there were
fifteen: Garrett, 1987); funding for welfare projects such as women's
refuges and women's health centres (the first Sydney centres opened in
1974 after discussions in 1973); women's advisers in the bureaucracy
(Elizabeth Reid was appointed as adviser to the Prime Minister in 1973);
consultative machinery (even the conservative government of New
South Wales established a Women's Advisory Board in International
Women's Year, 1975); research and policy inquiries (the Schools
Commission published *Girls, School and Society* in 1975).

This was not accomplished smoothly. There was tension among
feminists about each of these steps, such as the sharp dispute about the
appointment of the women's adviser to the prime minister. There was
wide criticism of the control of this decision by men in the bureaucracy
and the lack of consultation with women's groups. Some radical
feminists rejected the very idea of a representative for women in the state
elite, and remained hostile to the adviser throughout her stormy tenure
of the post from 1973 to 1975. Nevertheless, the tendency through the
1970s and early 1980s was for the scope of interaction between the state
and feminism to grow. It gradually included the legal system, through
rape law reform and anti-discrimination legislation; personnel matters in
the bureaucracy, through equal opportunity legislation; welfare and
policing in relation to violence against women and child sexual abuse;
labour market and economic policy in relation to the employment of
women and the scale of welfare expenditure. By the mid-1980s this
engagement was so extensive and so accepted that the New South Wales
government, through its Women's Co-ordination Unit (1987), could
publish a celebratory book which not only listed the reforms but also
included portraits and biographies of a number of the leading feminists
in the State.

Liberationist ambivalence about the state perhaps contributed to the absence of feminist theorising of the state as such. But this practical engagement with the state fuelled a great deal of research and thinking about particular policy areas. Accordingly, the bulk of feminist writing about the state has taken the form of *policy studies*. There is now a formidable body of North American and British writing in this genre, ranging from general surveys of women and public policy (e.g. Lipman-Blumen and Bernard, 1979; Bonepath, 1982; Grelb and Palley, 1982) to studies of particular areas such as women and the law (Atkins and Hoggett, 1984; Heverner, 1983; Brophy and Smart, 1985); women's employment (Ruggie, 1984; OECD, 1980); sexuality and abortion (Petchesky, 1984); and education (Deem, 1984). In Australia the anthology of policy studies was virtually the leading genre of feminist publishing in the mid-1980s, as witness *Women, Social Welfare and the State* (Baldock and Cass, 1983), *Unfinished Business: Social Justice for Women* (Broom, 1984), *Australian Women and the Political System* (Simms, 1984), *Women, Social Science and Public Policy* (Goodnow and Pateman, 1985). To a certain extent gay movement intellectuals followed the same path, producing studies of homosexuality and the law, the treatment of homosexuality in education, and now of course politics and policies around the AIDS epidemic (e.g. Altman, 1986).

Taking these policy studies as a group, a strong case is established both for the scale and the complexity of the state's involvement in sexual politics. Much of this involvement is organised around the family, specifically around the efforts of state agencies to construct, impose and sustain a particular patriarchal family form, and to provide an ideological defence of this form. There are nevertheless cross-currents which contradict or undermine family policy; from population policy (e.g. attempts to control fertility), labour force policy (e.g. attempts to get married women into 'the workforce') and education policy (moves towards equal access, widening the 'pool of talent'). While law, police, state employment practices, school curricula, and housing policy have all been direct agents of the oppression of women, they have also been vehicles for reform. (This is true even of the police, in areas like domestic violence.) The liberation movements' ambivalences about the state seem to have been well founded.

This somewhat confusing outcome is no doubt one reason why the impressive output of analysis and commentary on particular policies has not been matched by an equal volume of *strategic* argument about what reforms are required, in what order, and just how to get them. But in a larger sense this absence is characteristic of policy research as a genre. There is nothing in a study of policy itself that drives a synthesis, even a cumulation. Indeed, a good deal of the writing about 'women and X' is formulaic and repetitive. It tends to *presuppose* a set of feminist priorities, and a view of the state, rather than build towards them. It does not seek to become theory.

Baldock and Cass, the editors of an excellent policy anthology, are quite explicit about their distance from theory:

> The basic question addressed in each chapter is: to what extent do various state interventions reinforce, challenge or transform some elements of the enduring but changing pattern of women's unequal access to economic security and social autonomy? One of the clear conclusions of the book as a whole is that this question cannot be addressed, let alone answered, by abstract theory at the level of 'the advanced capitalist state'. (1983:xi)

Why can't it? we may ask. Does the state *as a whole* have nothing to do with 'the enduring but changing pattern' of women's subordination?

The problems of strategy are, we would argue, among the strongest reasons for developing theories of the state and sexual politics. Without the framework and perspective such theories (however imperfect) can provide, practical action on any one set of issues is vulnerable in two major ways. First, it is vulnerable to the effects of isolation, from other issues and other groups of activists. Unintended consequences may be serious: as witness the tendency of much equal opportunity practice to widen class divisions among women; the tendency of anti-pornography and child sexual abuse campaigns to widen state powers of moral surveillance; or the failure of those non-feminist initiatives about domestic violence which treat it as a specific form of 'deviance' and fail to connect it with the economic inequalities between husbands and wives and the lack of housing for women.

Second, policy work without theory is vulnerable to ideology. Accounts of the experience of Australian 'femocrats' are eloquent about the force with which a patriarchal bureaucratic culture affects new recruits, however strong their personal commitments to feminism. 'Ideology' includes the policy workers' own implicit and unexamined theory. Implicit theories of the state abound in sexual politics (as will be seen in the case studies in Part II below), just as implicit views of gender abound in classical theories of the state. They need examining, criticising and developing.

Thus the problems of practical politics, like the silences and hidden messages of classical theories of the state, point to the need for an explicit theorisation of the state in relation to sexual politics. There are several starting points for this; the record is thin but not blank. As already shown, both liberal and socialist traditions have generated debate about sexual politics. Both frameworks have been taken up by feminists in discussions of the state. Modern feminism has itself generated an important organising concept, the idea of the 'patriarchal state'. In the next chapter we turn to these beginnings to see how they can be developed.

2

Current theories

Liberal feminism and imperfect citizenship

Liberal feminism adopted from the general framework of progressive liberalism a view of the state as a social arbiter: in principle 'above the battle' but able to step in to redress injustice. Access to the state, in the sense of the right to participate in shaping state policy, is given by citizenship. Liberal thought accordingly was central to the spread of the suffrage in the nineteenth century and the spread of social security, as an aspect of citizenship rights, in the twentieth.

Liberalism does not assume that the state is in fact a neutral arbiter, simply that it should be. Liberal feminism acknowledges that the state is not neutral in its treatment of women. It sees the state, in effect, as having been captured by men. It treats sexism and patriarchy as a case of imperfect citizenship, requiring redress.

Liberal feminism is often regarded by radicals as weak-kneed and its ideas as muddy, but we would stress that in its own territory this is a powerful and sharp-edged analysis. A document like Ziller's *Affirmative Action Handbook,* the EEO 'Bible' for the New South Wales public service, is a model of clarity, consistency and political tough-mindedness. There are many parts of the state where liberal-feminist principles have been fought for with persistence and determination in the face of great resistance, mainly from men.

Further, liberal sexual politics have had considerable political impact. Liberal ideas of citizenship were the cutting edge of the struggle for the suffrage—and it is worth saying that the suffrage is still not established as a political right of women everywhere in the world. Liberal ideas about equal access to public decisionmaking are central to the modest but detectable increase in the number of women legislators and judges in the last two decades. The liberal idea of equal citizenship has been central to the expansion of women's access to welfare services in the advanced capitalist countries. Liberalism provides the arguments about unequal treatment and unequal access which have validated 'women's studies' and counter-sexist programs in education, and funding for women's services in the welfare sector. Similarly, liberal arguments about personal

14

freedom and equality before the law have been central to political gains made by gay men in the decriminalisation of homosexuality. The notion of 'anti-discrimination' legislation arises directly from liberal concepts of citizenship. 'Equal opportunity' machinery embodies both the liberal endorsement of equal citizenship and the liberal concept of individual competition as its expression.

That said, it also has to be said that the liberal–feminist conception of the state is theoretically rootless to a striking degree. In a basic sense it treats patriarchy as an accident, an imperfection that needs to be ironed out. So far as there is a social theory here, it is some version of 'sex role' theory. In this framework the unequal treatment of one sex is basically derived from the stereotyped attitudes or expectations that both sexes have in their heads. Reform proceeds by changing those attitudes and the practices that reinforce or embody them. When prejudice against women is eliminated, for instance by affirmative action campaigns and the removal of sex role stereotypes in education, the reasons for unequal citizenship will likewise be eliminated. Then the state can be properly neutral towards men and women.

The liberal–feminist analysis of citizenship accordingly suffers from the well-documented shortcomings of sex role theory as an analysis of gender (see Franzway and Lowe, 1978; Edwards, 1983; Connell, 1987). Most pertinently it suffers from sex role theory's inability to account for the sexual division of labour and its evasion of the issue of power as a feature of social structure. The idea of 'imperfect citizenship' has been politically effective, not because it has developed out of a powerful analysis of gender, but because it resonates with key problems in modern state structures. 'Citizenship' is central to the legitimation of modern states and thus to the power of the groups that control them, yet claims for citizenship are a fruitful source of political turbulence (an extreme example being South Africa). Habermas (1976) has argued convincingly that the state in advanced capitalist countries has severe structural problems of legitimation. (The recent history of Poland with Solidarity, and the Soviet Union with *glasnost,* suggests this may also be true of communist states.) At least at the level of political tactics, state elites are highly sensitive to shifts in popular attitude. A serious claim of unequal access or discriminatory treatment, backed by electoral pressure, has a good deal of force.

This was exactly the formula followed by the Women's Electoral Lobby, the main Australian representative of liberal feminism, in its notable intervention in the 1972 federal election. It has been equally notale how cautious the major parties have been since then about issues of discrimination against women, how careful not to risk and electoral sanction. The pursuit of the Equal Rights Amendment in 1972–79 by American liberal feminism seems to tell on the other side, since the amendment was eventually defeated. But this was more a matter of the constitutional peculiarities of the US system than a lack of political

response. Both the federal legislature and a majority of State legislatures did in fact ratify the amendment before its deadline expired (Bowles, 1979).

Liberal feminism runs into trouble at the points where sex role analysis becomes inadequate and the politics of legitimacy runs out. The argument of imperfect citizenship is forceful in validating women's access to bureaucratic promotion ladders under 'equal opportunity', as the *Affirmative Action Handbook* illustrates:

> Equal employment opportunity refers to the right to be considered for a job for which one is skilled and qualified. It is the chance to compete with others and not to be denied fair appraisal or be excluded during this process by laws, rules or attitudes. Equal employment opportunity is the operation of the principle of recruitment and promotion by merit... The test for equal employment opportunity is the outcome of selection and promotion procedures. Only the successful passage of qualified women and migrants through these procedures...is convincing evidence that equality of opportunity in employment exists. (Ziller, 1980:13)

But such a framework gives no purchase on jobs for which there are no relevant 'qualifications', or jobs where there is no promotion. It gives no help to groups of workers who cannot compete as individuals because their labour-power is economically interchangeable, nor groups who are qualified only for jobs which happen to have low pay. In short, it does not cover the situations of most working-class women. It gives no grip on the labour market issues which the labour movement has traditionally addressed, and it is no accident that liberal feminism has made little headway in the unions.

Similarly, the liberal-feminist framework gives no grip on problems of violence. The importance of this issue to an understanding of the state is suggested by Weber's famous definition: 'a state is a human community that (successfully) claims the monopoly of legitimate use of physical force within a given territory' (Knuttila 1987:47). Feminism has reason to contest this definition, for instance pointing to the legitimation of domestic violence against women, but it certainly cannot miss the issue. Some strands of feminism emphasise the state's connection with force, for instance Daly's (1978) comments on the 'sado-state', and the arguments of the women's peace movement of the 1980s that the nuclear-armed state embodies masculine violence (e.g. Kelly, 1984). But liberal feminism has great difficulty grasping the issue. A telling illustration is the chapter in Friedan's book *The Second Stage* which describes a visit to West Point, the elite military academy in the United States. Friedan's viewpoint is a celebration of women's entry into military command, with some spectacular ambivalences:

I am relieved and proud that those first women cadets did not suc-

cumb to the machismo role model; they mastered the skills of military defense, in service still to the values of life.

And even more wonderfully:

> I leave West Point, as the first female cadets are about to graduate, feeling safer somehow because these powerful nuclear weapons that can destroy the world and the new human strategies therefore needed to defend this nation will henceforward be in the hands of women and men who are, with agony, breaking through to a new strength, strong enough to be sensitive and tender to the evolving needs and values of human life. (Friedan, 1981:195,204)

That a viewpoint centring on women's citizenship has problems with the issue of violence is not accidental. Historically citizenship has meant not only the right to vote but also the right and duty to bear arms. This is markedly in conflict with sexual ideologies that prescribe women must remain disarmed. The historian Jill Roe has suggested that the nineteenth-century drive for equal citizenship was confounded by World War I, which saw mass conscription on an unprecedented scale and provoked a crisis in feminism as it did in socialism. It is certainly striking that this war was followed simultaneously by the enfranchisement of women (e.g. in the USA, UK and Russia) and by the most drastic reassertion of masculine hegemony and disenfranchisement of women in modern history (in European fascism). The continuing refusal of most states to conscript women into the military (Israel being a notable exception) suggests that the gender contradiction within citizenship persists.

Liberal feminism has perhaps reached its conceptual limit and can go no further in its own terms (cf.Z. Eisenstein, 1981). Certainly its implicit theory of the state limits its strategies, and a full-scale assault on gender inequalities must go beyond them. For a more comprehensive picture of sexual politics and a more sophisticated understanding of the state we must turn to other sources. Nevertheless we would emphasise that the problems of legitimation have not been solved. Even in terms of citizenship rights the modern state is, as some of the statistics cited in Chapter 1 show, highly unequal. Therefore the political strategies that are based on the politics of citizenship are still important. The language of 'rights' remains one of the key practical tools of sexual politics.

Regulation

The most effective modern critiques of liberalism have shown the impossibility of 'neutrality', by demonstrating that interests or relations of power are embedded in the way the state works. Most arguments of this kind have been indifferent to gender, but there is a recent body of research which has been centrally concerned with issues of gender and sexuality. Donzelot's *The Policing of Families* and Foucault's *History of*

Sexuality are the classics of this approach. It has been taken up by some theorists of gay liberation (e.g. Weeks, 1986) and one school of feminism (e.g. Pateman and Gross, 1986).

In this research the state is seen as an apparatus of social 'regulation'. The word in French has overtones both of 'domination' and of 'reducing things to rules', making things orderly. The state is seen as part of a dispersed apparatus of social control which works as much through the production of dominant 'discourses'—i.e. ways of symbolising and talking about the world—as it does through naked force. Accordingly the state is seen in close association with the rise of professions such as medicine, social work and psychiatry, which become part of the apparatus of surveillance that identifies deviance for segregation and treatment. Donzelot's research in particular traces the growth of an apparatus of state control over family life in France, an apparatus embracing a range of welfare 'services' as well as police and courts.

This approach is helpful in getting beyond the notion of 'the state' as a preconstituted object, as an organisation and nothing else. It directs attention both to the way state organisations work in handling issues of sexuality and social life, and to the connections between the state and processes in 'private' life such as marital relations and psychotherapy.

In sharp contrast to the monolithic idea of the state in traditional socialist rhetoric, this research points to the multiple, overlapping and sometimes contradictory apparatuses at work. For instance, in handling issues of sexuality the criminal justice system may be at odds with psychiatry. In handling changes in the family the courts may be at odds with social work. Donzelot and Foucault have wonderful accounts of the rhetoric of normalisation, the stigmatisation of the deviant and the self-justifications of the regulators.

Yet in emphasising the importance of discourses about the family and sexuality, have we not lost our grip on what is being regulated? The material reality of family life, the practices of sexuality, the experience of femininity and masculinity, the sexual division of labour, are largely absent from Donzelot's and Foucault's texts. It is difficult to see how they could be got back into an analysis which has such a strong focus on the strategies of the powerful.

Most important, the lack of an account of the practices being regulated means that theories of regulation do not account for the constitution of *interests* in sexual politics. Foucault explicitly avoids this question, perhaps because he is so concerned to avoid any hint of economic determinism. It might be possible to develop an account of interests from his analysis of the sexual 'types' produced by the process of regulation (the hysterical woman, the perverse man, etc), but the trend of his analysis is against this. Donzelot consistently ignores the matter. A consequence, as Barrett and McIntosh (1982:104) point out, is that Donzelot tends to see women in alliance with state agencies, and implicitly mourns the

passing of the independent patriarchal family. Weeks does not avoid the issue but has great trouble with it, falling back on concepts from the libertarian marxist tradition that was Foucault's bugbear.

In feminist discourse theory there is a similar tendency to play down the idea of 'structure' through a concentration on 'text' (e.g. Weedon, 1987). In the process of deconstructing the ideological constructs of femininity and women's place, the practical bases of these constructs get marginalised. In the result the state gets lost from view—an ironical outcome for a line of thought that began with close attention to the state.

Because theories of regulation have no theory of interests, they ultimately have no explanation of why the state bothers to regulate families and sexuality. 'Policing' seems to grow in scale and efficiency without reason, and also without the possibility of resistance. There is perhaps an echo of Weber's conception of the irresistible triumph of bureaucracy. If the patriarchal state appears to liberal feminism as a kind of mistake, it appears to theorists of regulation as an embodiment of prurience run riot. One does not have to be committed to a doctrine of economic determinism to feel that something more is needed here, even within the very 'field of practice' (Donzelot, 1979:6) the theorists of regulation are concerned with, the state's attempts to manage private life. This research has identified important mechanisms of state action in sexual politics; we still need an account of its dynamics.

The class state

An argument about underlying dynamics is the centrepiece of the socialist approach to the state which was taken up both in women's liberation and in gay liberation, though in somewhat different forms. Broadly, in this framework the state is treated as the bearer of the class interests of the bourgeoisie, having effects on sex and gender in the pursuit of this interest. Gay liberation tended to pick up the variant of this argument developed by the 'Freudian left', from Reich to Marcuse. Sexuality is seen to be repressed in accordance with capitalism's needs for personal and social discipline, or is carefully ventilated in accordance with capitalism's need to stimulate consumption and pacify the working class. The state represses homosexuality in pursuit of a general goal of social order and conformity; nuclear families are factories of obedience.

Socialist feminism focused on the social subordination of women and how that might be seen as functional for capital: guaranteeing the reproduction of the workforce, or subsidising the wage via unpaid housework, or providing a pool of cheap labour. In a number of debates on these topics through the 1970s (usefully summarised by Barrett, 1980), the state figured as the agent of a general capitalist interest. It was the

state that did most of the dirty work, undereducating women, regulating family life, and organising the welfare system so as to support the patriarchal family form; but it was capitalists as a class who benefited.

In all arguments of this kind there is an obvious gap between the state's motive, gain for a class, and its effect, the subordination of women. The gap can be bridged abstractly by an argument about function, claiming that the control of sexuality or the subordination of women is functional for capital and that the state as the agent of capital must achieve these ends. But something much more specific than this is wanted. A participant at the 'Women and Politics' conference in 1975, sponsored by the Australian government for International Women's Year, exclaimed:

> What worries me is that if you identify with some kind of class analysis, based on the capitalist class, then what is this bloody change which has to be brought about? I want to know because one has to identify the missing theoretical link and it seems to me in this conference we have not identified it and I want to know what it is. It's not socialism, it's not class, it's not capitalism; what the hell is it? (Women and Politics Conference, 1977:168–69.)

The 'domestic labour' debate of the 1970s sought the link in the productive contribution of the family to capitalism. This was valuable in exploring the nature of domestic labour and in shifting the focus from the family as an isolated institution. However its construction of the problem as one of 'locating' domestic labour in relation to the dominant mode of production was a blind alley. While it promised to relate patterns of domination in the domestic sphere to those in the public sphere, it bogged down in the theoretical maze about 'surplus value'. In any case it could not explain how notions of femininity and masculinity derived from the sexual division of labour relate to the class relations of production. Further, it did not explain the sexual division of labour *in* those relations of production which has now emerged as a major issue (cf. Game and Pringle, 1983).

The crucial problem in this family of arguments is the privileging of production (and in practical terms, the conflict of feminist strategy with established left strategies premised on that priority) within a conventional marxist analysis of production. The 'mode of production' in most of this literature means the *class* categories of production, and the mode of production remains the key to the dynamics of history in all marxist thought. Attempts to overcome this problem without diminishing the significance of class, such as the 'domestic labour' debate, and the reproduction theory and analysis of ideology that began to replace it in marxist feminism in the late 1970s (cf. Barrett, 1980; Burton, 1985), moved things forward a little. They underscored, if only implicitly, the need for rethinking 'work' itself.

But these efforts stalled for several reasons. At a practical level the

economic and political changes of the late 1970s put marxist feminism into a reactive position which tended to rigidify thinking. The dichotomy of 'class' and 'gender' which underpinned this theorising led to a conception of state power which was posed in dichotomous terms (class/gender choices, reform/revolution). Perhaps most important, though marxist-feminist theorising came from a dialectical tradition it was not dialectical enough in its own methods. It held to an understanding of production and of class formation that was insufficiently transformed by gender analysis. The effect of this was to reproduce in its own theory—especially in discussions of the state and the family—the ideological division of the public from the domestic sphere, and an implicit ideological view of the family as normative.

This is serious, because it is these ideological constructs which produce the socially accepted view of 'women's work' and its proper place in the home. Reproducing the static entities and the dichotomies of ideology robs the theory of any power to grasp the way in which the state historically *constitutes* gender ordering. The state, in this body of theorising, is essentially reactive.

Even referring to the family as 'the site of women's oppression' frustrates the attempt to escape its ideological confines. To question that seems like questioning a feminist shibboleth. But there is an impasse if we do not. Barrett (1980:211) illustrates this in describing the family as 'the site of the oppression of women...an important organising principle of the relations of production of the social formation as a whole'. The family and the construction of sexuality tend then to become isolated from production. This fails to grasp the complexity of state practices (for instance in education, housing, taxation and income support) which shape the options within which people *live* households and their work. Walby (1986) has recently argued more or less the reverse: that the position of women in the economy determines their position in the nuclear family. We need to move towards a more comprehensive concept of the sexual division of labour as a whole, before the action of the state in regulating some part of it will make much sense. But that tends to break up the functional logic of the argument from the needs of capitalism.

Another line of thought tended to see the state structure itself, especially its welfare apparatus, as the 'missing link'. Wilson's pioneering study of *Women and the Welfare State* illustrates the problems. The focus here is on the ideological premises of social policy, and its targeting of women from the Victorian era through Beveridge to the age of Bowlby. 'Social policy is simply one aspect of the capitalist State, an acceptable face of capitalism, and social welfare policies amount to no less than the *state organization of domestic life*. Women encounter State repression within the very bosom of the family' (Wilson, 1977:9). This affords the state a dubious rationality, within the logic of capital. But it compounds the separation of a 'social' sphere, where women are oppressed, from an 'economic' sphere where that oppression is determined.

This separation underpins even McIntosh's (1978) analysis of the role of the state in the oppression of women, which remains perhaps the most sophisticated version of the argument from a class state. McIntosh pictures a triangular relationship between the state, the capitalist labour process, and the family. The pattern of state intervention and non-intervention in the family (e.g. not restraining the assertion of husbands' authority over wives), and in the economy (e.g. sustaining differential wage rates for men and women) is determined by a balancing of needs and demands which are not always consistent with each other. Overall, however, the function of the state is to guarantee the general social conditions which allow capitalist production to continue; and it does this mainly by propping up the patriarchal family and providing minimal services where the family and wage system between them are manifestly inadequate.

McIntosh's argument is a major advance in establishing the *strategic complexity* of state action in sexual politics, the contradictory pressures and demands under which state agencies act and which are reflected in ambivalent policies. But as a theoretical framework this is much less satisfactory. It accepts the conventional distinction of the spheres of family, workplace and state, and tends to fix or reify the triangular relationship among them. Despite McIntosh's concern with feminist strategy, this framework leaves little room for a political practice.

McIntosh emphasises that the state's role in the oppression of women is generally indirect—it plays a part in establishing 'systems' (the family, wage labour) in which women are oppressed. Sophisticated socialist analyses also point to the indirect character of the link with class, emphasising that the state is not directly controlled by capitalists but that the state's role in capitalism depends on its *form*. The 'capital logic' school of marxist analysis that emerged in the 1970s emphasises this. To Hirsch (1978) it is the form of the bourgeois state which gives it the possibility of performing its functions. The state functions to secure the general conditions of the reproduction of capital because it can only maintain its form by doing so. This is a highly dynamic process, a 'result of often contradictory and short-sighted struggles and conflicts'. Such a perception of the state as a product of change, as a constant process—and as often short-sighted—is pertinent to the issue of gender. Rather than seeing the state as either a class instrument or as a fixed function of securing the reproduction of capitalist relationships, this suggests a process of struggle with limitations or inadequacies in guaranteeing those conditions. The argument here about the *form* of the state raises crucial questions, for instance about bureaucracy, which are now coming into focus in feminism and will be discussed shortly. Yet it is difficult to see the 'capital logic' approach as providing a broad enough account of the motives of state action (as Gerstenberger, 1978, observes) to account for the politics of the family, education and welfare.

These lines of thought produce a more sophisticated view of the state

but they cannot overcome the basic limitations of the concept of the class state. The concept leads to functionalism or indeterminacy, sometimes both. The general limitations of functionalism as a form of social theory are familiar. In this case functionalism also defeats the purpose of understanding the nature of domestic labour. It blurs the distinction between preconditions for capitalist production and byproducts of it. If one denies the logical primacy of class analysis, which is simply presupposed in most marxism, the arguments about function melt away. Even if one accepts this, some uncomfortable questions are left hanging. Put crudely, does the state or the accumulation process care *who* does the washing and cooking, with the laundromat and a Colonel Sanders on the corner? Why is there not a full-day child-care centre on the next corner?

In the last analysis it is not established why *gender* effects are essential for the reproduction of capitalism as a social system, however convenient or comfortable they may be at a given place and time. As a theory of gender this must be transcended. But it has opened up important questions about the form of the state, about how to relate the historical dynamic of the processes constituting the family, and about the analysis of production.

Class and patriarchy

To reject the model of the 'class state' is not to say we can ignore the whole question of class. That would result in massive distortions in the analysis of the state. There is unquestionably a major class dynamic in the formation of the modern state, which constantly intersects and interacts with gender. This is convincingly shown by histories of parts of the state apparatus, from Wilson's (1977) account of the British welfare state to Miller's (1986) history of state education in South Australia.

It follows that the question often posed about the state, 'is it capitalist or is it patriarchal?', cannot be answered in those terms. Class and patriarchy are not logical alternatives. They are social structures of rather different kinds which are both present in the same situations. What is needed is not an either/or choice but a better understanding of the connections. It is clear that this requires a major reconstruction of received theories of class and of the state.

Perhaps the most common path through the problem taken by theorists in the last ten years has been the conception of 'dual systems'. For instance Baldock begins: 'Throughout this book we maintain that capitalism and patriarchy are mutual reinforcements in the production of public policies which affect the lives of women in Australia' (1983:20). Zillah Eisenstein insists that theories of class power and theories of patriarchal power cannot simply be added together as separate systems. She speaks instead of 'the mutually reinforcing dialectical relationship bet-

ween capitalist class structure and hierarchical sexual structuring' (1979:5), emphasising the 'interdependence of capitalism and patriarchy'.

'Mutually reinforcing' and 'interdependence' imply reciprocation, and it appears that is exactly what Eisenstein wants to argue. Nonetheless, having said this, her discussion slips into a separation of the two structures. When they meet, they meet in a relation of hierarchy rather than reciprocation. The hierarchy derives from a functionalism involved in Eisenstein's understanding of capitalism:

> capitalism needs patriarchy in order to operate efficiently... male supremacy, as a system of sexual hierarchy, supplies capitalism (and systems previous to it) with the necessary order and control. This patriarchal system of control is thus necessary to the smooth functioning of society and the economic system and hence should not be undermined. (1979:27–28)

Patriarchy comes to make only for smooth functioning. The argument suggests an image of the capitalist state as a smoothly running machine somehow serviced by patriarchy.

But the capitalist state is not smoothly running; it is racked by crisis and difficulty. In the mid-1970s capitalists themselves were openly doubting the 'governability' of modern democracies, the theme of a celebrated report by the Rockefeller-sponsored Trilateral Commission (Sklar, 1980). If the New Right has temporarily solved that problem, it has done so at the cost of much higher levels of social tension. Nor is patriarchy an addendum to the functional logic of capitalism. Far from 'reinforcing', patriarchy and capitalism often cut across and undermine each other, creating *difficulties* of political management and legitimacy in the state. The turbulence around the issue of women's labour force participation, employment rights and unemployment rates is an important example. State policy has chopped and changed for the last two decades as economic circumstances and the political balance of forces have shifted.

The impasse of a 'dual systems' conception was registered in Hartmann's (1979) well-known article on the 'unhappy marriage' of feminism and marxism. This marked a widespread disillusionment with the prospects of developing a coherent socialist-feminist synthesis. The 'dual systems' notion in a sense staved the problem off rather than solved it. In so doing it led to a disturbing rigidity of dichotomous thought. The stand-off between fixed categories of class (or ' capitalism' or 'mode of production') and gender (or 'patriarchy') cannot be escaped by a different privileging of one of its terms. The dichotomy is a stand-off in the sense that these conceptions do not provide any sense of social change, nor the political means for it. The tendency for dichotomies to become a politics of 'difference' is disturbing for any radical in terms of its implications for state power. It leads readily to a corporatist state strategy on the model of multiculturalism, where a range of socially differentiated

groups are drawn into a pluralist consultative structure, which delivers legitimacy while undermining any demand for structural change.

The basic conceptual problems here lie in the notion of 'systems' and of a 'link' between them. Given such a framework, the tendency is for the analytic logic of one system to establish its priority; and class analysis is accustomed to doing so. This happens even where theorists are explicitly trying *not* to give class priority. Burstyn (1983) argues eloquently against orthodox marxism and develops an important argument about the state's commitment to patriarchy. But in her analyses of the structures of class and gender it is always capitalism which is the historically dynamic force, kinship and patriarchy which are static and reactive. That view is, indeed, built into the basic understanding of the social structure of gender which modern socialist-feminist theory derived from Lévi-Strauss via Mitchell (1975) and Rubin (1975). The tendency to presuppose the class dynamic can be seen again in Ursel's (1986) interesting attempt to spell out a more detailed dual-systems model as a basis for analysis of the state. Ursel's three-stage model of the history of patriarchy (communal–family–social) is in fact derived from a class periodisation of history. Her analysis of the role of the state is strongly functionalist; the essential difference from Poulantzas is that to Ursel the state is the factor of cohesion straddling the systems of production and reproduction (i.e. class and patriarchy), not just confined to the relations of class. Most socialist-feminist discussions of the state are in fact functionalist (see the recent reconsideration of this by Shaver, 1987). Even where a 'class-first' bias is avoided, the tendency is towards dichotomy and a socially static analysis.

To get past these problems requires a more dialectical form of thought which confronts the labour process rather than presupposing it. Zillah Eisenstein's work is important in this process, for all its problems. Her suggestion that the two systems of power are interrelated through the sexual division of labour is basic to much of the argument that follows. It is necessary to think of women's work as waged, unwaged and sexed—and somehow to think that all together. Examining the *politics* of women's work demonstrates the need for such an approach. In showing the state as constitutive of women's work, we can provide an understanding of the state as both the product and the determinant of struggle.

The most important alternative to 'dual-systems' theory is the approach that has generalised the socialist-feminist idea that patriarchy provides conditions for the reproduction of capitalist relations of production. Burton's *Subordination* (1985), the most sophisticated statement of this approach, is particularly pertinent as her 'extended theory of social reproduction' treats the state as central to the dynamic. She extends the scope of the 'reproduction' analysis from class relations to social structure generally, and points to the importance of state action in spheres that marxist-feminist analysis tended to bypass, biological reproduction and education.

A good deal of Burton's argument is consistent with the analysis presented here and will be incorporated as our argument develops. At this point we would call attention to two points in particular. One is her conception of what the state is: 'The state is not a thing; it does not exist as a single, monolithic entity. It is a complex of relationships, embodying a certain form of power operating through various institutional arrangements' (1985:104–5). The parallel with the 'process' orientation in recent conventional state theory is clear.

Second is the reversal that the 'general social reproduction' framework allows Burton to make in the fundamental conception of the state's place in the social dynamic. With hardly an exception the socialist and feminist analyses presented so far have seen the state and state action as shaped by a pre-given social structure. Burton forcibly draws attention to the role of the state in constituting the categories of social structure. In particular she emphasises the ways in which masculinity and femininity (and the relation between them) are produced as effects of state policies and in state structures (e.g. in the interplay between schools and families). This is a fundamental point, with ramifications through much of what follows.

This framework does not logically privilege 'class' over 'gender' or vice versa. It is consistent with a rather different solution to the problem of the 'link'. In the previous section we asked whether the state or the reproduction process cared who does the washing and the cooking—noting the rapid commodification of some domestic labour, e.g. in the fast foods industry. Gardiner (1975) suggests examining the limits to the state's or economy's capacity to socialise these processes. These may be fiscal limits, not a trivial point in the current recession. The extraordinary difficulty of getting state provision for child-care services anywhere near the established level of need is a striking example (Brennan and O'Donnell, 1986). The limits may also be ideological. The limits to the capacity to socialise child care certainly involve the social processes that construct women as mothers. Chodorow (1978) and others have accustomed us to seeing the psychological mechanisms here; Burton's argument points to the importance of state agencies such as schools.

Rather than seeing patriarchy as functional (or even a tolerated dysfunction) for capitalism, we might see gender relations as constituting class relations, in the sense of setting (historically specific) limits to class relations, and vice versa. On the one hand there are limits to commodification and class-based accumulation which are set by sexual character, and by the domestic organisation of some part of total social labour. On the other hand there are limits to gender differentiation set by tendencies in class relations, such as the spread of abstract labour and the dynamic of deskilling. There are limits to mobilisation in sexual politics set by class difference and class antagonism. The state may well emerge, in such an analysis, as the point where many of these limits are materialised in social and economic policy and its contradictions.

The patriarchal state

MacKinnon's bald statement that 'feminism has no theory of the state' is a daunting starting point. At one level it is all too obviously true—and surprisingly true. Feminist classics from de Beauvoir's *The Second Sex* through Millett's *Sexual Politics* to the present rarely address the state. More striking, feminist work which might have been expected to tackle the state head-on does not do so. O'Brien's *The Politics of Reproduction,* a notable Canadian feminist critique and reconstruction of political theory, somehow omits the theory of the state. Eisenstein's American collection *Capitalist Patriarchy* (1979), equally concerned with politics, likewise skirts around the issue of the state. Baldock and Cass (1983), editing an Australian book which names the state in its title, eschew abstract theory as we have already noted, and follow up by not theorising the state at all.

It is almost as if there were a motivated avoidance of the problem of the state. Perhaps the state has been moving faster than we can think; certainly many patterns of state action that seemed settled in the early 1970s appear very different in the 1980s. Yet there is a theoretical *attitude* towards it, based in experience. Feminists have not hesitated to talk of 'the patriarchal state', to treat the state as being in a general sense male or masculine.

Game's statement in a discussion of the New South Wales government's report on child sexual abuse succinctly puts both this theoretical attitude and a key problem it raises:

> Feminists face a dilemma in developing strategies for state intervention: how can demands be made on the state to intervene in the interests of women when the state embodies the interests of men? If the state is not neutral and benevolent with respect to women, is a challenge to patriarchy possible through state activity? (Game, 1985:167)

There are two main inflections of this theoretical attitude, two implicit theories, so to speak, of the nature of the patriarchal state. One treats the state as an *agent* of patriarchy, as acting on behalf of an interest (men's) which is constituted outside it. Tough-minded versions of liberal feminism approach this position, as does some marxist-feminist writing. Barrett comments, apropos Wilson's and McIntosh's accounts of state support for the patriarchal family: 'Other feminists, insisting equally strongly on the centrality of the state in maintaining these patterns of dependence, have tended to interpret the same evidence in terms of its benefits for men rather than for capital' (1980:231). This is precisely the position argued in detail by Burstyn (1983). Feminist thought in the 1960s and 1970s was as much shaped by radical elite theory as it was by formal marxism, with men seen as a ruling elite and women subordinated in much the same way as workers, blacks, and third world people.

A clear example is the idea of women as the 'colonised sex' in Summers' history of Australian women, *Damned Whores and God's Police* (1975). In this vein it was easy to interpret the state in the style of 'instrumental' theory, as the expression or vehicle of men's patriarchal dominance.

On the other hand there was a current in New Left and feminist thought in which the state could appear as itself the oppressor. In this inflection the state is itself patriarchy, or at least a core part of it. It is interesting to see the drift of Zillah Eisenstein's argument in an essay on 'the patriarchal state and the defeat of the ERA' (1982). The political resistance to the Equal Rights Amendment appears to her to reflect the interests of 'those in power'; i.e. the US political elite *is* the patriarchal power structure, and the state acts directly to destroy the revolutionary threat of feminism. Scutt, reflecting on rape law reform in New South Wales, arrives at a very similar positon in her criticism of women in the bureaucracy who allowed a watering down of the new law. The state itself acts as a collective patriarch. Though there are many women in state employment they are liable to be corrupted and thus work 'on the patriarchal side'.

> Ultimately, however, women should not have an allegiance to the establishment akin to that of men: governments and laws are established for the benefit of men, and against women. Surely every woman must ultimately recognise that laws are used against her; that they are not for her benefit. Given the world as it is, perhaps we have to believe that the times of the sell outs will be fewer than those times when women inside, and the women out-side, will be able to launch a spirited attack on the true insiders—men. (Scutt, 1985a:22–23.)

Though this version of the 'patriarchal state' appears more polemical, it is also sociologically more complex. It requires a new analysis of the structure of the state to show how it functions as a patriarch, how exactly the interests of men are 'embodied' (Game) or institutionalised within it. Such an analysis has begun to be produced, and will be discussed in the next section.

Before that, however, we need to register some complications. If the state embodies the interests of men, not all states do it in the same way or to the same extent. The case study by Ruggie (1984) is very much to the point. She compared the position of employed women in Britain and Sweden, found that it was markedly better in Sweden, and that this had a great deal to do with differences in the goals and mechanisms of state intervention in economic life. Britain operated a residual welfare system at a time when Sweden was running a pro-active policy to reskill the workforce, equalise incomes and stimulate women's employment. The lesson is that we must pay attention to historical differences in state structure and action in relation to sexual politics.

It is also necessary to register the extent to which the state has been

the vehicle for advances in the position of women. Setbacks on the ERA or rape law reform suggest the state as patriarch. But it cannot be correct to see the state as always embodying a unitary male interest and always excluding a female interest. Ramirez (1981) presents a thought-provoking statistical finding. Comparing measures of the status of women (legal equality, and the extent to which marital status impedes participation in the paid workforce) with measures of the strength of state structure and the scope of state action, he finds that they tend to be positively correlated across a sample of 36 countries. That is, by and large, the stronger the state the better the position of women. (Analysis shows this is not an artifact of levels of economic development.) Such a finding does not refute the idea that the state is patriarchal—strong states may simply be more liberal patriarchs—but it does emphasise that the equations about interests are complex. We must reckon with a balance of forces rather than a unitary patriarchy.

Patriarchy as procedure

An obvious problem with the idea that the state pursues men's interests is that this approaches a conspiracy theory. One is left searching for Patriarch Headquarters to explain what goes on. In recent years an alternative conception has been emerging from research in several fields: law, employment policy, and bureaucracy. It appears that the main mechanism of the power of the state in sustaining men's interests, in resisting or limiting feminist demands, has not been the direct assertion of men's privilege—naked patriarchy so to speak—but rather the character of the state's procedures as impersonal processes. Patriarchy resides in the 'objectivity' of the state's structures.

The objectivity of law has been explored particularly by MacKinnon in her widely read study of rape cases in American courts. She argues that the oppressiveness of this part of the legal system does not come from bad laws or badly applied laws, but from the underlying legal structure itself. Rape is construed as a crime from the point of view of men, as is shown for instance in the importance of the issue of consent in rape trials. The legal system translates this interested point of view into impersonal procedural norms. Objective legal process is patriarchal in its very 'objectivity': 'When it most closely conforms to precedent, to "facts", to legislative intent, it will most closely enforce socially male norms and most thoroughly preclude questioning their content as having a point of view at all. Abstract rights will authorize the male experience of the world' (MacKinnon 1983:658).

MacKinnon's work was path-breaking in raising the issue of state procedure. It explores what might be called the 'ideology of procedure', the beliefs that justify a particular pattern of practice and persuade us to regard that pattern as just or efficient. As a general approach to analysis

of the state this is less satisfactory: a sophisticated polemic but polemic nonetheless. The argument is premised on a simple categorical opposition between men as a bloc and women as a bloc. It equates, and then slides between, 'men' and patriarchal interests. In the United States, black feminists have pointed out the very different significance of rape law for black men and white men. Rape charges have long been a means of racial oppression, and in such a context 'men' cannot be regarded as having a unitary interest supported by the state.

MacKinnon's argument treats legal norms as issuing directly from the interests of men, and this leads to two difficulties. First, it underplays the historical significance of women's struggles. They have often been directed to the state and have had some impact on law-making in a variety of fields, including divorce law, prostitution, public health, education and of course the suffrage itself. Biographies of nineteenth-century feminists such as Catherine Helen Spence (Magarey, 1985) and Elizabeth Cady Stanton (Oakley, 1972) illustrate the point. Legal procedure itself has not been immune from feminist influence, as witness the advent of women on juries and as counsel, and very recently as judges.

Second, the straightforward equation of legal objectivity with male interest creates a paradox for practice. For in areas like civil liberties, constitutional rights, industrial rights, EEO and anti-discrimination statutes, it is precisely legal objectivity and the impersonality of procedure that gives leverage for the representation of women's interests in the law. The repeated embarrassment caused to patriarchal interests by decisions of the Equal Opportunity Tribunal in New South Wales (see Burvill, 1986; Bailey, 1987) is a telling illustration of this feature of the law. An adequate theory of the state needs at least to tell us where this kind of mechanism will operate and where the mechanism described by MacKinnon will.

Feminist action in the state is, by contrast, the starting point for a second body of thought about procedure, the analysis of bureaucracy. The importance of this issue is indicated by the central role the idea of bureaucracy has played in mainstream thinking about the state since the time of Weber. Weber's concept of 'bureaucracy' was of course originally constructed without reference to gender, and most modern social-scientific and political discussions of it are equally gender-blind (as noted by Clegg and Dunkerley, 1980:400ff). But the ideas that went into Weber's ideal type of bureaucratic authority—rationality, impersonality, ordered hierarchy—now sound with a suspiciously patriarchal ring. Grant and Tancred-Sheriff (1986) state the key point concisely in calling bureaucracy a 'gendered hierarchy'.

Hester Eisenstein (1985a) addresses the question of the gendered nature of bureaucracy in terms of the embeddedness of masculinity in the structures of public life. Her argument comes from practical experience as an equal opportunity officer, and is part of an evaluation of an apparent milestone in feminism's encounter with the state, equal

employment opportunity and affirmative action programs. Eisenstein discusses interventions which point to three different aspects of the 'embeddedness' of masculinity: 'the right of men to sexual access to women against their will; the (on average) greater physical strength of men as the basis of entitlements to paid work; and the organisation of the work day to the requirements of a male breadwinner' (1985a:113). The affirmative action mechanisms, she notes, have not changed these features of male power but they have helped challenge their legitimacy.

Eisenstein defines the maleness of the state descriptively: 'until recently public power has been wielded largely by men and in the interest of men (and indeed by only a small number of them)'. At this level the idea is little different from the liberal-feminist discourse of access and citizenship discussed above. The decisive advance is in her demonstration of a range of mechanisms within the bureaucracy that *institutionalise* this unequal access to public power. These range from recruitment practices and job definitions to complaints procedures. Reform is not just a matter of changing the personnel at the top. It is a matter of unpicking a complex texture of institutional arrangements which intersect with the construction of masculinity and femininity.

The recent study of a job evaluation scheme by Burton et al. (1987) dramatically illustrates this. The strategy of improving women's wages by demonstrating the 'comparable worth' of their work relies on the existence of an objective standard of worth. Such a claim is made for job evaluation schemes which are now widely used by technocratic managements as a means of rationalising pay structures. The case study of the Hay job evaluation system as applied in an Australian public institution shows that the appearance of technical neutrality is just an appearance. The underlying rationale of the scheme embodies traditional evaluations of the different worth of men's and women's work—for instance in the weighting given to different aspects of a job. Implicit evaluations can even be found embedded in the descriptions of the jobs themselves, before the application of the evaluation scheme. In many ways the findings are reminiscent of MacKinnon's on legal procedures. Burton and her co-workers, however, spell out the steps by which this situation might be changed, given pressure from women workers through unions and anti-discrimination machinery.

Grant and Tancred-Sheriff similarly note that women have some representation within bureaucracy—but note also that it is uneven. In fact they suggest this is a key feature of the state. They speak of 'dual structures of unequal representation'. Women are unequally distributed through the hierarchy of state personnel as a whole (as shown in the statistics given in Tables 1.1 and 1.2 above). At the same time those organisational units where women's interests *are* articulated are peripheral in the internal organisation of the state. Thus women's advisory units have slight organisational power compared with, say, economic policymaking units dominated by men.

This is a key point, that patriarchal interests may be embodied quite impersonally in the hierarchy of units (as collectivities) and the hierarchy of functions within the state. It is at least the beginning of an answer to the paradox about the double function of law noted above. Criminal courts are more central, more embedded in the state structure, than are anti-discrimination tribunals. It also reinforces Hester Eisenstein's (1987) observations on the different groups covered by the notion of 'femocrat'. Feminist bureaucrats may be those operating in the units charged with representing women's interests, or they may be operating in line management and concerned with the distribution of resources in the bureaucracy as a whole. The prospects of gaining significant power or influence, and the prospects of pursuing a feminist strategy, would seem to be inversely related in the two situations.

As yet these approaches do not amount to a feminist theory of bureaucracy, but they have certainly opened up that possibility and shown what some of its components must be. Eisenstein has emphasised the possibility of change: 'up to now the state has been male', but future directions are open. We share this guarded optimism. However we need to take things further and ask how we know when the state *stops* being male. A feminist theory of the state must be able to help answer the question: how do we know when we are winning? If the state is genuinely a 'terrain of struggle', as Eisenstein puts it, then theoretical and strategic judgments are necessarily linked. We need to know the ways masculinity is embedded in state structure, because without clarifying the mechanisms of men's power, it is impossible to anticipate the ways in which potential feminist transformation may be demobilised and men's power reconstituted. At the same time we need to identify points of opportunity and the mechanisms of change that make successful strategies possible.

3

A framework

Criteria for a theory of the state

Theorising the state in relation to gender cannot be done in isolation. The argument must be integrated both with the more general analysis of the state and with the more general analysis of gender.

Chapter 2 showed that the concept of the 'patriarchal state' is more adequate to contemporary knowledge about the state and gender than are less forceful models. But this does not imply that the state is only patriarchal, that the gender dimension exhausts the social analysis of the state. The state is also a class state, and is (in many cases) imperialist or sub-imperialist.

The case of South Africa illustrates this dramatically. The state there has been unusually active, and unusually repressive, in sexual politics. Yet this cannot for a moment be divorced from the racial policies of the South African regime and the way the state is organised to enforce them. Athol Fugard's play *Statements After an Arrest under the Immorality Act* illustrates how apartheid and sexual politics have been interwoven: the Act names forbidden sex ('immorality'), but the content of what is forbidden is racial interaction and race equality (Fugard, 1974).

Analysis of the state and gender relations therefore must be done in the context of research and political practice directed to other aspects of the state (just as they must take account of sexual politics). Chapter 1 noted two developments in conventional pre-feminist state theory that need to be taken on board. One is the growing tendency to see the state as a social process, not just a legal category or set of institutions. Processes of mobilisation, institutionalisation, the negotiation of hegemony between social groups, are all central to the character of the state. The second is the renewed recognition of the state as a social force in its own right, not just the vehicle of outside interests. The state may legitimately be seen as the initiator of important dynamics and as a place where interests are constituted as well as balanced.

To these we may add two points that emerge both from the class-based theories discussed in Chapter 1 and the research on gender

reviewed in Chapters 1 and 2. First is the importance of the internal
differentiation of the state. It is no longer adequate to think of a modern
state as embodying *a* class interest, or pursuing *a* sexual politics. Even
the most sophisticated of recent treatments (e.g. Burstyn, 1983; Ursel,
1986) tend to present the state as unitary, and rational in the pursuit of
a dominant interest. Modern state structures are far more complex, and
their operations more contradictory, than that. This is not just a matter
of scale. There are systematic divisions of interest and systematic sources
of conflict within states which affect the way a particular part of the state
interacts with its environment.

Second, we must recognise how tactically complex is the interplay
between the state and its environing structures. Even to pursue a single
interest, for instance a capitalist class interest, is not necessarily easy. As
Habermas and Offe argue, unstable trade-offs—for instance between the
delivery of economic advantage and the need for legitimation—are the
best that can be done. Habermas talks of 'steering problems', and that is
all too mild a term. States and state instrumentalities can run violently
amok (Uganda, Argentina, Fiji), go bankrupt (Latin American loans,
New York City), crack up (Pakistan), shudder into massive policy
reversals (Britain at the end of the 1970s). Adding the presence of different interests within the state, and the interplay of different structures
(class, imperialism, gender) with the state, it is clear that the complexities involved in a realistic analysis of modern states are formidable.
Simple formulae will not do.

At the same time the state must be located within an adequate social
theory of gender. The lack of this undermines liberal feminism, for all
its effectiveness on particular issues. Sex role theory is too weak to yield
an account of the state as an institution. At best it offers an account—
presupposing the institution—of unequal participation in it. More radical
positions also suffer in the same way. Ferguson's *Feminist Case Against
Bureaucracy* (1984), promising in conception, lacks an overall concept of
gender relations and hence can only see feminism and state bureaucracy
as simple alternatives. Categorical theories of gender, such as those
implicit in some separatist feminisms, are too black and white to yield a
theory of the state. They characterise gender relations through an absolute dichotomy between men and women and an opposition of interests
which presents the state only and always as the agency of the dominant
sex.

A theory of gender which is fully social, which gives full weight to
the structure of power and inequality, yet which recognises complex dif-
ferentiations within gender and the uneven institutionalisation of dominance, is needed. This has gradually been emerging in feminism, gay
liberation theory, and the sociology of gender (for details see Connell,
1987, chapters 3 and 5). This is consistent with the broad tendency in
modern social theory which has sought to overcome the antinomy of
'structure' and 'agency' by treating them as constitutive of each other.

Action requires social structure as its condition; while structure is realised and reconstituted only through social practice. Practice is historically concrete, developing in time. Accordingly neither patterns of action nor structural patterns are fixed, are outside time—though their pace of change is sometimes painfully slow.

Within such a framework for the analysis of gender as a social structure and a type of social practice, the state appears as a realm of practice whose core is an institutionalisation of power relations. It follows that the state cannot be analysed in abstraction from history. It does not exist as a reflex of the functional needs of a system, whether a class system or a gender system. It is the product of specific, historically located social processes. Quite specifically, the shape of the state is the outcome of particular social struggles. What kind of state we have depends on who was mobilised in social struggle, what strategies were deployed, and who won.

Such a view is now a commonplace about the class dynamics that shaped the modern capitalist 'welfare state'. It is a little less commonplace but also true of the construction of modern bureaucratic structures and personnel policies. It is equally true of the state's connections with gender relations, though the historicity of struggle here has only recently come into view.

The point is particularly clear in discussions of the origins of state structures. Engels' (1884) famous argument connected both the creation of the state and the 'world-historical defeat of the female sex' to the emergence of private property. This was mainly taken up as a 'class-first' explanation of women's oppression, but could have been developed differently. Several recent theorists have asserted a more direct link between the history of patriarchy and the formation of the state.

Sutcliffe (1980) for instance has argued that structural explanations of state formation are inadequate and the psychodynamics of gender relations must be brought into the picture. Starting from a text on the early kings of Kashmir, she suggests that state formation revolves around kingship and that kingship itself develops with ego-defensive personality structures among men. This can be historically located in a reaction against the matrilineal social structures characteristic of early horticulture. Far from kingship growing out of patriarchal family structures, familial patriarchy derives from the early state. This course of events matters, Sutcliffe suggests, because the political exclusion of women follows from the perpetuation of these dynamics within the state as an institution:

> Women seeking political roles in the modern state are pitted against not merely the unenlightened prejudices of individual men, but against the psycho-cultural bias embedded in the origin of the excluding institutions and in the personality construction of all

those who are socialised within the cultural ambience dictated by that institution. The state, that is, may be best understood to be as inherently misogynist as the Christian churches, or other religious or social institutions whose raison d'etre is to make ego-defensive cognitions and values and behaviours available to adult men. (1980:41)

Fernbach places the key development further back and connects it with the 'masculine specialisation in violence' that was already a feature of hunter-gatherer society. 'The decisive subordination of women, together with the beginnings of social (i.e. class) hierarchy, has its immediate cause in the expansion of the masculine sphere in the division of labour from hunting to warfare, and the systematic rearing of large numbers of violent men' (1981:33). The rise of warfare was not accidental: it was connected with the emergence of agriculture, and the population explosion and pressure on land that resulted from the enormous gain in productivity with the domestication of plants and animals. To Fernbach, endemic warfare and the institutionalisation of armed force was the basis of state and class at the same time. For economic exploitation initially occurred through the state directly: property was collective not individual. The division of gender in violence was thus central to the emergence of the state and its role in class relations. The 'class state' at a very fundamental level embodies the social ascendancy of men, and the state's continuing involvement in violence reproduces the dominance of forms of masculinity specialising in violence.

There are problems in all theorising about 'origins'. An emphasis on origin can imply that nothing much has changed since the origin, that history is simply divided into a 'before' and an 'after'. Even where continuing change is allowed, it has to be said that the history of gender relations for the whole sweep of human history up to the last four hundred years is very little understood. Some bits of archaeological evidence from the earliest towns of South-West Asia suggests a more egalitarian relation between men and women than Fernbach's argument about agriculture and population density would imply (e.g. Mellaart, 1967). What holds for the transition to urban society in the Mediterranean basin, Engels' and Fernbach's focus, may not hold for India, which Sutcliffe discusses. Confucian culture in China did not honour masculine 'specialisation in violence' in the way that European culture has done. The traditional Chinese clan rules, for instance, advise young men to be scholars or farmers but put military life outside the pale: 'The rules consider that soldiers, boxers and pugilists do not have a regular vocation, and regard their activities as another form of loafing. Such members should be excluded from the ancestral hall' (Hui-Chen, 1959:164).

But these arguments are nevertheless a starting point for thinking about the historical trajectory of states in gender terms. They highlight social questions about the significance of the head of state, the place of armies, and the way the state is involved in accumulating productive

surpluses. They go part of the way towards meeting the final criterion suggested here for any theory of the state in sexual politics: that it must recognise at a fundamental level the historicity of the social processes that constitute and reconstitute the state.

The place of the state

The state is a structure of power, persisting over time; technically, an institutionalisation of power relations. This is the common ground between those conceptions of the state based on a notion of the monopoly of force and those based on a contrast between the state and 'civil society' or market. It is not, however, the only institutionalisation of power, or even of force. Feminism points to the family—the classic institution of 'civil society'—as a locus of power relations. In the early 1970s it was commonly argued that the family was the main site of the oppression of women (e.g. Comer, 1974).

The state is not even the monopoly holder of the *legitimate* use of force, as in the classic definition already quoted from Weber. The facts of sexual politics give the lie to this idea comprehensively. Force used by parents upon children—short of systematic injury—is wholly legitimate in our society, even expected. Those few parents who never hit their children are regarded as odd. Husbands' violence against wives is also widely regarded as legitimate; though it is strictly speaking illegal in contemporary Western countries, the law is rarely enforced. There is a large body of folk humour and folk sayings that express the legitimacy of marital violence ('a wife is like a carpet, all the better for a good beating') Violence against gay men is also widely regarded as legitimate— 'they deserve what they get'. As with domestic violence the laws against assault are rarely enforced in these cases.

The state, then, is only part of a wider structure of power relations that embody violence or the possibility of violence. So we cannot see it as coextensive with a sphere of force. Rather it is a node within a network of power relations.

Similarly power relations do not alone account for the social organisation of gender. There are other structures within gender, in particular gender relations of production and consumption (incorporating the 'sexual division of labour'), and relationships expressing emotional attachment and antagonism. (For a detailed explanation of these distinctions see *Gender and Power* Chapter 5.) These structures are also involved in the constitution of the state as a social organisation.

The importance of the sexual division of labour within the state has already been shown in Chapter 1. The structure of cathexis—that is, the pattern of emotional attachments and antagonisms—in and around the state has been less obvious in formal theorising. It is touched on in some of the research already mentioned (e.g. Sutcliffe, 1980, on kingship). It

is a major theme in psychoanalytic speculation about politics (e.g. Jones, 1924), political science informed by psychoanalysis (e.g. Little, 1985), and psychoanalytically influenced research on fascism especially (e.g. Macciocchi, 1979; Theweleit, 1987). Mosse's *Nationalism and Sexuality* (1985) is a path-breaking historical exploration of connections between the state and the cultural construction of masculinity and femininity. At present this remains the most obscure dimension of the gender-state, largely because the methods for researching such issues are very much underdeveloped.

Nevertheless it is clear that the state is centrally and distinctively an institutionalisation of power relations. An understanding of its 'place' in the whole organisation of gender relations involves mainly an understanding of how it is related to, and distinguished from, other institutional nodes of power, such as domestic patriarchy or the sexual hierarchy of industry.

The idea of a monopoly of force will not do, but it is worth re-examining the older concept to which that idea alluded, sovereignty. In terms of gender relations sovereignty has two aspects. First, it is constituted within a 'public' realm in societies where a public/private distinction is culturally marked. (NB the public realm is not *defined* by the state, since there are stateless societies with a public politics: see e.g. Gluckman, 1971.) Given the gendered character of this distinction, the state is culturally marked as masculine whoever happens to control it.

Second, it involves a claim to be the central, ultimate institutionalisation of power, the place of last resort. It is a very important fact that this places the state potentially in conflict with other institutionalisations of power. It is a familiar historical theme that oppressed people can call upon the state. The King protects the powerless; *fiat justitia ruat coelum,* let justice be done though the heavens fall. Since the state normally disposes of the greatest concentration of force, a familiar pattern of politics arises around the legitimacy of its intervention in other power relations. This pattern can be recognised in situations as diverse as classical Greek polemics against 'tyranny' and the murderous attacks on judges of the Family Court of Australia after contentious divorce awards. In such a conflict of powers the state may be at odds with the conventional construction of masculinity. Some researchers have suggested a changing balance, with state power increasing as that of individual patriarchs— fathers, employers—recedes (e.g. Klein, 1981; Game and Pringle, 1983; Ursel, 1986).

As this suggests, and as the theoretical argument about the historicity of structure and practice requires, the institutionalisation of power is not accomplished once and for all. The form of the state has changed through social struggle quite markedly in the last two centuries. A long and bitterly fought struggle eventually opened legal and electoral citizenship to women. The success of the woman suffrage movement was the largest single step ever accomplished in the democratisation of state structures. The inadequacies of the market as a means of distributing

social goods, and of the family as a means of compensating for the market, led to the growth of the 'welfare' machinery of the state, through the struggles discussed by Wilson, McIntosh and Shaver. Struggles are now spreading around attempts to dismantle these welfare provisions and to 'privatise' state services, with the outcomes still in doubt.

In such struggles the state becomes the focus for the mobilisation of interests. Woman suffrage was sought as an abstract right, but also in order to accomplish certain ends. It is striking that American feminism only became a mass movement through the Women's Christian Temperance Union with its package of social and religious purposes. Similarly contemporary feminism has placed a series of demands on the state, from abortion rights to child-care provision and anti-discrimination action, and has tried to organise campaigns around them.

This mobilisation of interests is very obviously lop-sided. There is no comparable counter-mobilisation of men. There have been some attempts to mobilise, such as the 'Free Men' in the USA in the late 1970s, who argued against feminist positions on issues such as custody of children in divorce. There has also been some organising of fathers in response to campaigns about child sexual abuse or incest. But all these efforts have been on a very small scale. This is a major difference from the pattern of class politics, since capitalist parties have not only emerged in response to labour mobilisations but have been highly successful. The absence of this kind of mobilisation 'from above' in gender politics raises crucial questions about the way men's power is institutionalised, and about the connections between different sites of power. The key point is that masculine domination is so firmly entrenched in existing political institutions, such as the bureaucracy, the press, and the major parties, that they can normally be expected to do the job as they stand. The 1987 dispute over diagnoses of child sexual abuse in the town of Middlesbrough in England ('the Cleveland case') illustrates the point. Regardless of the rights or wrongs of the particular diagnoses, the most striking feature of the episode was an hysterical press compaign against the women doctors and social workers who made them, a campaign which had the very obvious purpose of intimidating others who might follow suit. The case of rape law reform in New South Wales illustrates a similar process in the bureaucracy. Scutt's (1985a) narrative traces some remarkable defensive manoeuvring by which reform was pre-empted or watered down. (See the more detailed discussion in Chapter 6).

In the case of woman suffrage it might appear that the state is the focus for the mobilisation of a social group and a social interest that is already constituted. This is not necessarily the case. A social category may exist in a dispersed form, with the political mobilisation being part of what *constitutes* the category as a social group with a shared identity and a capacity for collective action. In this sense the state, as the focus and antagonist of mobilisation for the suffrage. is involved in the constitution of the sociopolitical group 'women' as protagonist.

The role of the state in the constitution of the collective actors in

sexual politics has been overlooked in almost all theoretical work in the area. Feminism has had rhetorical reasons for taking the category of 'women' to be primary or pre-social. Sex role theory has had little space theoretically for the state, while socialist feminism (as argued above) has had the state full of a class dynamic. However this aspect of state action has come into focus in gender history. Weeks (1977) traces the gradual creation of a self-conscious homosexual politics in England at the end of the nineteenth century in response to changing state strategies, notably the medicalisation of lesbianism and men's homosexuality, and the criminalisation of men's homosexuality. Walkowitz (1980) similarly analyses the way the British state constituted the category 'prostitute' through action to regulate health and sexuality, notably through the Contagious Diseases Act. In both cases we see the state as protagonist in sexual politics virtually creating an antagonist. At least state action creates the circumstances in which a collective consciousness of oppression is likely to arise.

These episodes show another complexity in the state's involvement in sexual politics. The gay politics generated by the criminalisation of homosexuality did not head off into outer space, but was directed back at the state. The axis of homosexual politics up to the advent of Gay Liberation in 1969, and still a continuing theme after that, was homosexual law reform. Thus the state was both actor and stake in sexual politics. What was at issue in the mobilisations, and in the counter-mobilisations organised by New Right homophobes like Anita Bryant in the USA in the 1970s (see Bryant, 1977 and Adam, 1987), was control of state policy and influence on those parts of the state machinery—from central courts to local government—which implement it. The fact that the state is both an actor in social struggle, and what is at stake in social struggle, appears again and again in different fields of sexual politics.

The state is constituted within a culturally defined 'public' realm. But this realm, though cross-culturally familiar, is not historically fixed. There are major changes in what are regarded as legitimate areas of state action. In sixteenth-century Europe for instance, the religious beliefs of citizens were a lively concern of state policy, even the major focus of politics, as the continent was racked by religious civil wars. In the late twentieth century in most of the Western world the religious beliefs of citizens are firmly defined as part of the 'private' realm.

This has large significance for sexual politics because religion used to be the key cultural framework of sexual ideology. The gradual expulsion of religion from the 'public' realm has removed key cultural underpinnings of traditional patriarchy. The depth of this change was illustrated in 1987-88 by a bitter dispute in the Anglican church of Australia over the ordination of women as priests. The conservative rejection of this policy, now a minority position within the church, was based on a belief in the patriarchal ordering of the family as the model for the organisation of the church. The progressive campaign used a public-

realm rhetoric of equal citizenship to attack what was and is now seen as private-realm ideology, closet prejudice, on the part of the conservatives.

The boundaries of the private and public realm can explicitly become a stake in political struggle. Certain feminist campaigns, notably those about domestic violence and child sexual abuse, have involved attempts to bring 'into the light' oppressive practices formerly treated as the private business of families. Conversely gay politics has attempted to remove some kinds of sexual behaviour from the scrutiny of the law. The classic feminist slogan 'the personal is political' defines a kind of problem rather than states an inevitable principle. It is nevertheless a very fruitful problem.

It is difficult to sum up this argument, except to say that any idea that the state occupies a clear-cut and fixed place in the structure of gender or the field of sexual politics dissolves on close inspection. The state is dynamic and sexual politics is dynamic; and that is perhaps the key point. The state is culturally marked as masculine and functions largely as an institutionalisation of the power of men, especially heterosexual men. In that sense it is patriarchal, can often be seen as the collective patriarch. Yet this institutionalisation is uneven and generates paradoxical reversals, in which the state participates in constituting antagonistic interests in sexual politics and can become a vehicle for advancing those interests. This is not, however, a case of an in-principle-neutral state apparatus that can be taken over by any social interest. The form of the state reflects the dominant interest in it, and struggle for the advancement of women or homosexuals must be a struggle to change the form of the state. To this issue we now turn.

State structure

As we noted in Chapter 1, the overall form of the state has become an issue in socialist theory. It has been suggested that state structure is itself a source of power:

> The organization of political authority differentially affects the access, political consciousness, strategy and cohesion of various interests and classes. State structure is not neutral with respect to its effects on class conflict. The structure of the state intervenes between social needs and the way these are translated into political demands, between demands and state outputs, and between specific outputs and the ability to organize and raise new demands in future. (Esping-Anderson, Friedland and Wright, 1976)

The notion of state structure as a source of power, which shapes and is shaped by social struggle, appears very relevant to a case such as child-care policy (see Chapter 4 below). The administrative maze spread the struggle. Interests organised at State (i.e. provincial) level, both political

and professional, were able to confound federal government policy intentions. Privileged classes were able to turn to their advantage federal government attempts at the restructuring of state power through the 'new federalism'.

The state structure is not neutral. At the same time it is not monolithic. In the case of abortion, federal/State responsibilities have been interpreted in such a way as to benefit the feminist cause in New South Wales. Overall, the structure of the state is of greater significance than questions of legitimation. The structure of the state becomes important in shaping the feminist movement.

An approach which highlights the constant *interplay* between state organisation and social forces fits the emerging theoretical conception of the state as process, as well as the detail of such cases. It allows also for considering certain aspects of the feminist movement's development with greater subtlety. For instance, the emergence of feminist bureaucrats in the last decade is regarded by some as co-option and depoliticisation of the movement by the state. But closer examination of the interplay between state structure, the feminist bureaucrats within it, and their connections with the movement outside, may reveal a much more complex picture. This issue is taken up in Part III below.

State structure can be studied in such familiar terms as federalism, bureaucracy, democracy; it can also be studied in terms of the categories of gender. How should we understand the gender regime of the state, its internal sexual-political ordering? Both the evidence recited in Chapter 1 about the different distribution of women and men through the bureaucracy, and Grant and Tancred-Sheriff's argument about the gender ordering of units of the state, point to powerful effects here.

In terms of staffing, clear divisions appear between (a) parts of the state with a high concentration of men—the coercive apparatus, the military, police, courts, prisons; and the central directorate, the policy-making levels of the bureaucracy and the political leadership—and (b) sectors with much higher levels of women's employment, comprising the welfare apparatuses of education, health, social security. In some parts of the welfare sector there is not only a higher concentration of women workers but a degree of hegemony by women (e.g. nursing, early childhood education, social casework).

The differentiation of these parts of the state is not only a matter of the statistics of the sexual division of labour. There is also a cultural differentiation. The coercive apparatus is 'masculinised' in its ideology and practice as well as the composition of its workforce (c.f. Patton and Poole, 1985). Accounts of life in the state directorate (e.g. Pat O'Shane in Mitchell, 1984) similarly describe a cultural milieu actively antagonistic to femininity, well supplied with 'threatened chauvinist males'. That this has practical political effects can be seen in the story of Senator Susan Ryan, a liberal feminist and the only woman in the Hawke Labor cabinet 1983–87. Stripped of her major portfolio (education) for not

being 'tough' enough in imposing the economic-rationalist line of the dominant group in the government, she was left to languish as 'Minister for Nothing' until she took the hint and left parliamentary politics. Feminists now speak of the 'misogyny' of the Hawke government, and apart from some weak anti-discrimination legislation it is increasingly difficult to distinguish its sexual politics from that of any recent conservative government.

The distinction between these two parts of the state does not cover all instrumentalities, but it already has an interesting overlap with a distinction derived from the theory of class. Clark and Deer suggest a taxonomy of state sub-apparatuses based on four main 'functions' the state performs in a capitalist order. These are shown in Table 3.1. Some of the classifications appear a little arbitrary: for instance the 'treasury' sub-apparatus might better be thought of as part of the executive of the state. Deriving a classification of parts of the state from a functional analysis of capitalism plays down the role of the internal and strategic problems of the state itself in determining state form. However this classification usefully highlights the state's involvement in the direct production of goods and services, what we might call the 'infrastructural' activity of the state: the provision of transport facilities, public housing, and the like.

Table 1.3 A taxonomy of state apparatuses derived from class analysis.

Consensus	Production	Integration	Executive
political	public	health, education and welfare	administration
legal	public provision	information	regulatory agencies
repressive	treasury	communications and media	

Source: Clark and Dear (1984:50)

In the light of these observations we suggest a preliminary classification of state instrumentalities, for the purpose of gender analysis, in the following four groups:

1 the central directorate
2 machinery of coercion and social order
3 welfare instrumentalities
4 infrastructural services.

Two further distinctions have to be added before this classification is useful. One is the distinction between 'levels of government' whose tac-

tical significance in sexual politics was noted earlier in this section. The absence of federal structures in Britain has been a tactical disadvantage for feminism, for instance making the feminist initiatives achieved through the Greater London Council vulnerable to the abolition of that body by the Thatcher government. The familiar trio of local, State and federal government does not exhaust the distinction. There are also regional instrumentalities at the intermediate level, and joint instrumentalities that cut across levels. More important is the beginnings of recognition of a fourth level, the international state. This includes the United Nations and its instrumentalities, the World Court, the EEC and its instrumentalities, and the international treaties and conventions to which national governments may adhere (e.g. ILO conventions on labour). This too has become of tactical significance in sexual politics. The UN-declared International Women's Year and the Decade for Women were occasions that provided legitimacy for feminist action. At a more mundane level the Australian government has used its 'external affairs' power to validate anti-discrimination legislation, in particular the Sex Discrimination Act of 1984 based on the International Convention of the Elimination of all forms of Discrimination Against Women. This constitutional device has come under sharp challenge from conservative parties (see the excellent review of this legislation by Ronalds, 1987:16–17, 202–3).

The second, less familiar, distinction is between mainstream government and what Shaver (1982) has called the 'non-government state'. In social security a good deal of public policy has been pursued through nominally 'private' bodies, many initially set up as vehicles of charity, and heavily subsidised by the state. They continue in a highly ambiguous relationship with the state directorate, as both agency and lobby group. The Australian Council of Social Service, for instance, was one of the key groups who defeated the federal government's attempt to win consensus for a shift to indirect taxation at the 'Tax Summit' in 1985. To Shaver's welfare agencies we must add the education sector. In 1986 there were 2496 nominally 'private' schools providing schooling for nearly 800 000 of Australia's children, and subsidised to the tune of more than \$1 billion by federal and State governments, through direct grants plus assorted privileges and tax concessions. Similar arrangements can be found in public health (subsidised semi-private hospitals) as well.

The significance of the 'non-government state' in sexual politics is considerable. This sector has been the principal means (until very recently) by which women have had any significant role in shaping state policy or controlling state instrumentalities or state funds. This has been helped by the very definition of voluntary welfare work as 'soft', even as 'women's work' for upper-class women. It has also been helped by the fact that some of these bodies operate in sex-segregated fields (e.g. girls' schools, women's hospitals). This sector was important in forming and transmitting feminist traditions earlier in the century. It is no accident that a good many feminist activists of the 1970s worked in this

sector, nor that feminist welfare initiatives such as health centres and refuges took the shape of subsidised voluntary agencies already familiar in the non-government state. At the same time the 'non-government state' can be the vehicle for sexual reaction. State-subsidised private schools are prominent in the resistance to anti-discrimination measures and many convey a heavily conservative sexual ideology (in the name of religion) to their pupils.

The more the internal complexities of the state are emphasised, the more our picture of the state seems in danger of total fragmentation. What can save theory from collapsing into a pluralism that treats the units of the state as competing baronies in a kind of modern feudalism? Functional analysis will not, once multiple functions are recognised. Rather we should see the unity of the state as a practical accomplishment, always limited but constantly being renewed. It has three key mechanisms: administrative, fiscal and ideological.

Administrative co-ordination is implicit in the idea of a 'state directorate' or executive. The existence of a directorate does not in itself guarantee successful co-ordination. On the contrary one sees in practice constant attempts to impose co-ordination. The fact that strategies of central control are needed implies a tendency to escape it. The strategies may issue from different centres. In Australian public-sector bureaucracies, for instance, there have been three main strategic centres: the personnel authority (Public Service Boards, now in decline), the political leadership's service bureaucracy (Premier's Department, Department of Prime Minister and Cabinet), and the financial authorities (Treasury, Finance). They are often in conflict with each other, and their strategies may open significant possibilities in sexual politics. The NSW state government's Equal Employment Opportunity policy, already mentioned several times, was directly a consequence of a review of the bureaucracy sponsored by the Premier and pursuing strategies of efficiency that contested the policies and power of the Public Service Board (see O'Donnell, 1984a).

The fiscal mechanism is less dramatic and until recently has been less noticed. All state activity has to find its place in a budgetary process and questions of priority are often resolved in budgetary terms. In the post-war period of buoyant state finances this involved relatively little pain. In the recession, fiscal coordination has been harsher and the visibility and power of finance departments in setting the state's agenda have grown. Feminists in the bureaucracy have to speak the language of finance; the current head of the Office of the Status of Women in Canberra is noted for her ability to analyse every issue in these terms. This shift is not gender-neutral. Finance departments are among the most conservative units within the state structure. The language of finance and 'economic rationalism' has been the vehicle for a major attack on welfare ideology and a downgrading of women's interests on a very broad front, from the introduction of fees in higher education to the gutting of child-care provision.

Ideological unity is implicit in the claim of sovereignty and in the distinction of the 'public sector' from the rest of the economy. Part of the process here is the construction of the career public servant as a category. In this process the 'career' has been defined in terms that apply particularly to men, while women as state employees have been concentrated in non-career grades.

To describe the state as an 'institutionalisation of power' is very abstract; much hangs on the form of institutionalisation. Weber's classic distinction between forms of authority (traditional, charismatic, rational-legal) points to the variation historically possible. The discussion of bureaucracy and legal objectivity in Chapter 2 emphasised the sexual politics implicit in certain institutional forms. 'Bureaucracy', the form of institutionalisation central to the modern state, is marked both by a strong sexual division of labour (for instance between administrators and secretaries) and by a cultural masculinisation of authority. The rise of bureaucratic forms of organisation is historically linked to the rise of new forms of hegemonic masculinity oriented to technical knowledge and personal competitiveness, displacing aristocratic models of masculinity.

Bureaucracy itself is not static. The techniques of control change: a modern Weber would lay less stress on formal rule-following and more on the technology, both physical and social, of surveillance. Waves of reform move through bureaucracies. Though they have by and large resisted Taylorisation—the time-and-motion study applied to factories—they have their own drives for efficiency. A current reform movement centres on the notion of 'accountability' and the development of 'performance indicators' defined around conceptions of organisational goals. Reforms initiated by the political directorate may be countered either by entrenched power-holders in the administration or by reform movements from below. Workers' control, industrial democracy, community control, representative bureaucracy, are all principles of reform that contest centrally imposed notions of efficiency and accountability. The EEO mechanism is likely to be a battlefield, being a centrally imposed reform with a democratic as well as an efficiency purpose, which reduces the autonomy of peripheral units of the state and hence the scope for local, decentralised or workers' control.

As these cases suggest, there is wide scope within the state structure for conflict around sexual politics. Can we go further and say (as with Habermas' arguments about 'steering problems' and the 'rationality deficit' of the state) that there is structured conflict within the state, of a kind which makes it difficult for the state to achieve a consistent strategy in sexual politics? The case of the criminalisation of homosexuality and the emergence of homosexual politics suggests a long-term difficulty in maintaining a policy of selective sexual repression—a policy that is however required if the state is to sustain the dominance of heterosexual masculinity. The cases of the woman suffrage movement and equal oppor-

tunity policy suggest a long-term difficulty in sustaining either de jure or de facto exclusion of women where the state's legitimacy has come to rest on principles of citizenship. The institutional masculinisation of the military and police is somewhat different from that of the state directorate, and the more the directorate comes to operate on criteria of productive efficiency the more prospect there is of a clash with the unwieldy and expensive apparatuses of coercion. Examples are Kruschev's and Gorbachev's conflicts with the Soviet military, and Congressional claims of military 'waste' in the USA. The constant friction over prison administration in New South Wales is a local case in point.

These considerations emphasise the costs and risks of state strategies in the various fields of sexual politics. We are far from an understanding of the gender interests constituted within the state which would be complete enough to allow a systematic accounting of gains and costs. But what is known about the state structure already points to a multiplicity of interests and a complex policy calculus. It is at least plausible to suggest that the state directorate will often be uncertain what strategies to pursue, and that there is often considerable scope for policy changes even in the short term.

The state's people

In a structuralist account of the state all that matters is the framework of social relations that construct certain social positions or places; who occupies them is of little concern. In post-structuralist analysis of discourses the particular 'subjects' are likewise of little interest. In a practice-based account of the state the people do matter. It even matters that the term for which one naturally reaches is 'personnel'. This is a term that came into use with the rise of bureaucracy—its use in English dates from the mid-nineteenth century—and it embodies a particular view of people as units of administration. It is important to consider the sexual division of labour through the state structure, the process of selection and the construction of career paths that affect the sexual politics of the bureaucracy, and the kinds of masculinity and femininity constructed in the very diverse milieux embraced by the state.

A key mechanism is the construction of different kinds of labour markets in and around the state. These labour markets are gender-structured. As we have noted, the 'career service' that was created along with a powerful federal bureaucracy during the first half of the century was a career service for men. Women employees of the Crown were not expected to 'progress', to have a 'career', at all. Formal bars on the appointment of women to certain grades of public employment have often existed in the past. Bars to the employment of *married* women have had the effect of excluding women from career positions in generations where almost all women did marry. Rules giving preference in employment to war veterans—very widespread in Australia since World War

I—have a similar de facto effect, since relatively few women served in the armed forces. (The usual term is 'preference to ex-servicemen'; women who were veterans rarely got a slice of this cake.) Rules requiring country service for promotion, common in the teaching services, excluded most women from promotion since few husbands would follow their wives to a country job. Distinctions between 'permanent' and 'temporary' employees have often operated in a similar way. 'Temporary' employees (who may serve many years in that status) have less chance of promotion and less access to superannuation; and they are disproportionately women. (For documentation of these points see Ollif, 1981; O'Donnell, 1984a; Deacon, 1984; Director of Equal Opportunity [NSW], 1985.)

We can distinguish two processes here. First is the direct fencing-off of the men's preserves. This strategy is now badly undermined by both efficiency arguments and equal opportunity programs. It appears both bad management and discriminatory.

Accordingly it is now largely replaced by a second group of mechanisms, the indirect ones. This includes the operation of informal networks among men from which women are quietly excluded, for instance the 'grooming' of young high-fliers for promotion to the top ranks of a department. Women have no official recourse because such networks have no official existence. Another mechanism is the construction of types of employment, through job design or the organisation of career paths, which presuppose that the occupant is a man with a dependent wife, or at worst a single man with no dependents.

This is a level at which the masculinisation of bureaucracy operates powerfully though subliminally. Think of a group of officials sitting around a table negotiating a policy, a budget or an organisational change. Some go home at the end of the day, after drinks and some informal networking, to a household which runs on wheels for their convenience: dinner is on the table, the children are bathed, the evening is clear to work on the papers and prepare a strategy for the next day. Others rush straight home to cook the dinner, get the children ready for bed, and start organising entertainment, clothes and breakfast at 6 the next morning. It is not hard to guess who will be more effective in the committee, get the reputation and earn the promotion. The head-of-household model is not obligatory but it is certainly hegemonic. The pressure is on everyone to pretend they have that amount of support and leisure, even if they do not. Anyone who complains that they have not had time to work on the papers has lost the battle from the start.

In these respects the situation within state bureaucracies is not very different from that in capitalist industry, as traced by researchers such as Cockburn (1983, 1985) on printing and other trades, and Collinson and Knights (1986) on the insurance industry. They are simply aspects of the contemporary sexual politics of work. What is distinctive about the position in the state? Two things especially, which have contradictory implications in sexual politics.

On the one hand, state employment is more susceptible to claims of equal rights, hence to affirmative action and equal opportunity programs. These are now widespread in Australian state instrumentalities, apart from local government, while they are almost nonexistent in corporate employment. Workers can bring anti-discrimination suits against companies for bias in employment, but private employers, who with hardly any exceptions are men, have been effectively exempted from the obligation to take positive action towards equal opportunity. (The Australian legislation—applicable only to a minority of companies—is backed by the devastating penalty that companies not complying may be named in parliament!) It is worth considering why. To some extent it must reflect the degree to which state legitimacy now depends on the mechanism of citizenship. By contast the legitimacy of corporate power depends on the inherently anti-democratic mechanism of private property. Corporate managers, when they are answerable to anyone at all, are answerable only to other businessmen.

On the other hand, state employees are engaged substantively in the development and implementation of policy which generally supports a patriarchal gender order in the society as a whole. The state manages gender relations (in a way most businesses do not—though media companies are also in this trade), and broadly does so in the interests of men and in defence of hegemonic heterosexuality. Women in the state are usually, whether they like it or not, involved in a masculinised policy process. To resist this means to contest issues in sexual politics within a structure immediately controlled by men (as seen in the statistics in Chapter 1) and in organisational terms permeated with patriarchal interests. It can be done—it is done—but not easily, in a context where women are anyway in a minority and where the assertion of their interests necessarily disrupts the organisational logic of the state.

These organisational dynamics bring us up against that most elusive but important of processes, the construction of masculinity and femininity. Since bureaucracies are almost never studied from this point of view we have only a few indications about how it happens. It is likely that different parts of the state structure construct gender through different mechanisms and on different patterns. The military, for instance, operates differently from the teaching service.

In the military a dominance-oriented masculinity is deliberately cultivated and the space for femininity of any kind is narrow indeed: traditionally the hospitals, more recently some secretarial work. There is fascinating evidence of this process in the reminiscences of women who were recruited into the general support services of the armed forces during World War II and who had to go through contortions to prove they were both good soldiers and real women.

Through all the controversy and difficulty, Colonel Irving was absolutely determined that women in the Army would remain women, and no matter what type of man's job they attempted,

they would not become 'male-aping' soldiers. It seemed that the solution to the whole problem was that women might attempt any job, no matter how difficult, but at no time should they ever lose their femininity. (Ollif, 1981:39).

But we cannot simply distinguish sectors of the state and assume that gender is homogeneous within them. On the contrary, what is central is the *relationship* between different sexual characters. The violent masculinity of the frontline soldier would be worse than useless in the commanding general, whose job is to run an organisation. The most successful general of World War II, Georgi Zhukov, was domineering and brutal but never fired a shot at the Germans; he was a superb organiser, not a superb fighter. A modern army is built around the *relationships* between frontline fighters, managers, and technical experts. None can function without the others. And even then, the majority of people in modern armies are supply and support personnel. Wars are won and lost by logistics, not by Rambo exercises.

In civilian bureaucracies, likewise, it is the *relationships* of gender that are crucial. A masculinised bureaucratic elite cannot function without a feminised immediate support staff. The counter-figure to the 'manager' is the 'secretary'. The two types of occupation have historically grown in tandem, though research on the 'managerial revolution' has so far been quite separate from the literature on the feminisation of 'the secretary'. In the health services the profession of nursing was deliberately constructed in relation to a masculinised medical profession (Gamarnikow, 1978).

Like military bureaucracies, civilian ones construct a range of gendered situations. Professional employees for instance have a different position from that of mainstream administrators. The kinds of sexual character that can be constructed around the possession of technical knowledge are different from those constructed around the possession of line authority. Certain professions are historically associated with women (primary teaching, nursing, social work), and to a lesser degree have provided a social niche for homosexual men (notably nursing in recent years). On the other hand, manual employment in the infrastructural sectors of the state is overwhelmingly men's employment, and its culture—workplace customs, language, songs, unionisation—is heavily masculinised. A fascinating example is the folklore of railway workers recorded by Adam-Smith (1969), full of episodes like this:

Jack Rice, Fettler, Queensland Government Railways
In the heat up here at Normanton, north of Capricorn, it's a job to keep the rails straight. They buckle all the time so you straighten them all the time: with a 28 lb hammer in my day. You swung that hammer until your tongue hung out. B'jeez I swung one for years. If they strike a bell on doomsday I'll mistake it for a ham-

mer on the rails. We got a new ganger once and he saw this 28 lb hammer.
'What's that for ?'
I picked it up and swung it.
'You don't straighten rails with that!'
'Too right we do. Even gangers have been known to swing one at times.'

The masculinisation here has a very different inflection from that of the state directorate, or even of the military, revolving around endurance, skill with tools, irreverence. The class basis of the difference is obvious.

The general framework we are proposing emphasises that all such patterns are historically constructed and are the objects of social struggle. There is always a politics of access, representation and gender construction within the bureaucracy. In a certain historical conjuncture the exclusion of women from state employment is intensified, while in another, the state actively recruits women. Thus women teachers were pushed out of the service during the 1930s, desperately sought during World War II and in the 1950s. Nor was the initiative all on the side of the state. Women teachers sought employment rights and equal pay—in South Australia splitting the union in 1937 because their male colleagues would not support an equal pay campaign or allow equitable representation within the union (Miller, 1986: 194). At one point the state criminalises homosexuality; at another it becomes possible for gay men to contest exclusion from state employment under anti-discrimination legislation or charters such as the Canadian Charter of Rights and Freedoms.

The emergence of the 'femocrats', the principal subject of Part III of this book, is part of this continuing politics, and is far from being an isolated event. It is clear that feminist bureaucrats have occupied an ambiguous position from the start. Their power has depended on gaining reasonably senior positions in the bureaucracy, but the bureaucracy has historically been constructed on gender lines which presuppose that women do not hold power. The 'brief' of the femocrats, especially from the women's movement, has been to pursue the interests of women. But, apart from the difficulties in doing so that have just been discussed, women within the state are not all in the same situation and do not all share the same interests. Typists and professionals, for instance, have different interests in having educational qualifications prioritised as criteria of 'merit'. The much satirised personal style and dress of feminist bureaucrats—beige suits, silk dresses and a slimline briefcase a few years ago (Lynch, 1984), recently smart black suits and crocodile-skin shoes—expresses some of the ambiguities of operating as powerful women in a masculinised milieu. Ferguson (1984:182–93) nicely analyses the link

between 'success' and conformity in the popular American manuals of advice for upwardly mobile women.

State – society dynamics

The state is not 'outside' society, though one often talks of 'state and society' as if it were. The question here is, more accurately, the place of the state in the macrodynamics of gender. Gender relations form a large-scale structure, embracing all social institutions in particular ways. This structure changes historically. The state participates in this dynamic on the same footing as any other institution (for instance reflecting the overall changes in women's employment in the last generation). It also has a specific place in the story, a role no other institution performs. That is the focus here.

The state is the *central* institutionalisation of social *power,* and both terms of that phrase have importance. As an institutionalisation of power relations, the state is most directly involved in that aspect of gender relations which is itself a power structure. The state sets limits to the use of violence, protects property, criminalises stigmatised sexuality, embodies masculinised hierarchy. Indeed it is difficult to think of the power structure of gender without thinking of the state.

As a *central* institution the state is involved with the overall patterning of gender relations, the 'gender order' of the society as a whole. The state has itself a particular gender regime, but this internal order is not necessarily the same as the overall ordering of gender relations in the society as a whole. For instance the state constitutes an internal sexual division of labour through paid employment, but it shapes the division of labour in families (e.g. through its labour market, taxation and welfare politics) principally as a distinction *between* paid and unpaid work.

To say that the state is concerned with the gender order as a whole is to mark the state as a regulatory, managing agency. This line of argument is familiar in class analysis and economics, and leads with fatal speed towards functionalism. It is easy to conclude that the *function* of the state in gender relations is the regulation of the gender order, in particular the maintenance of patriarchy or the repression of sexuality. Such an argument presumes that the basic structure of gender relations is pre-constituted. The trap is avoided by refusing that presupposition, by seeing the *constitutive* role of the state. The state takes a prominent part in constituting gender categories (the homosexual, the prostitute, the housewife, the family man) and regulating the relationships among them by policy and policing. Compare, for instance, the role of the police in organising prostitution; and the link between domestic science education and the creation of the housewife (cf. Reiger, 1985).

As well as 'reproducing' gender relations, the state creates historical possibilities. Through its policing of sexuality it created the possibilities of modern homosexual politics. Through its educational apparatus it

helped create the possibility of modern feminism. The growth of state bureaucracies was central in the ascendancy of new forms of masculinity. The possibilities of the state in abolishing sex inequalities have been seen repeatedly, and in many contexts during this century have been put to use.

At the same time the state obliterates possibilities. Though we will be concentrating on the more or less benevolent side of state activities, it should never be forgotten that the state is violent, is in fact the major institution of violence. Modern states kill on a horrific scale. Probably the most destructive single action in modern history was not the atomic bombing of Hiroshima but the now virtually forgotten firebombing, by the British and American air forces, of the old German city of Dresden on a clear day in February 1945. It made even less sense than the attack on Hiroshima, since the town had no military significance and as a result was undefended. About 135 000 civilians were burned to death. Irving (1974), tracing the history of this attack, shows how it followed more or less mechanically from a bureaucratic planning process. An 'area bombing' approach had become basic strategy in Bomber Command and in the Anglo-American political leadership, which lied throughout the war about what its bombers were doing. Masculine toughness in effect became institutionalised in a machinery that delivered genocide; and no process in a military bureaucracy could stop it, any more than the atomic bomb could be stopped once it was ready to use.

The pattern of state action is not simple because neither the structures nor the interests involved are simple. Further, the state as a central institutionalisation of power has its own problems. Perhaps we should say more precisely that the state directorate recognises problems that apply to the state structure as a whole. The use of state power must be balanced with the search for legitimation (the ballot-box credibility of governing parties; the willingness of the citizens to pay taxes and obey officials; the discipline or compliance of state employees), if the power is to continue.

Here the state's place in sexual politics—an unavoidable fact about the state—poses problems, sometimes severe. Feminism places demands on the state which may be difficult to avoid without putting legitimacy at risk. The liberal-feminist platform of equal citizenship, employment rights, and anti-discrimination measures is formulated in a way that maximises this leverage on the state, one reason why liberal feminism on certain issues has been very effective. At the same time, meeting these demands will produce changes in other areas of gender relations which may have a direct legitimacy cost. A telling example is the turbulence in US politics created around abortion after a 1973 Supreme Court decision effectively legalised it. 'Pro-life' mobilisations attempted to use the Congress to reverse this decision, resulting in a complex and bitter series of disputes about constitutional issues as well as the ethics and sexual politics of abortion (see Segers, 1982).

The end of the postwar boom, the 'fiscal crisis', and recession in the

1970s and 1980s have reconfigured problems of legitimation. A strategy of expanding and diversifying state services as a means of buying off diverse pressure groups is no longer possible; the state directorate is now concerned to limit costs, which leads to giving 'efficiency' priority. The state itself comes under attack in the shift from Keynesian to neo-conservative political economy, with the result that 'legitimacy' seems to depend on visibly cutting taxes and expenditure. With mass unemployment, state strategies that bring more people onto the labour market have a high legitimacy cost. They are often reconfigured around a conservative sexual politics. Thus immigration is reorganised around 'family reunion'; the government backs off long-day child-care commitments, which support full-time employment for women; unemployment benefits for youth are cut on the grounds that families should support them; and so on.

In such a context certain strategies of reform have a higher relative pay-off than they did before. The creation of a network of 'women's services' was a feature of the 1970s, and the momentum of this kind of action has died away. Those reforms that have few budgetary implications but fit in with other state strategies, such as modernising the bureaucracy, become more prominent. Equal employment opportunity and anti-discrimination legislation are highlighted. Of course reform is not all in the same direction. The ascendance of marked-oriented technocrats in central government leads to a reshaping of higher education that emphasises training for men (technology, engineering, business, physical sciences) and drains money from areas with a high proportion of women (welfare, social science other than economics, humanities).

Examples could be multiplied, but the point has perhaps been made. The state is embedded in gender relations and unavoidably involved in sexual politics. Conversely, any significant movement in sexual politics must deal with the state, if only because of its role in the regulation of the gender order and the constitution of the social categories of gender. On both sides this creates opportunities and involves risks.

For feminism, the state provides leverage for the reform of sex inequalities mainly through the citizenship–legitimacy nexus. But that strategy also involves serious risks for feminism. Most notably it leads to a form of politics organised around 'representation', and 'equal opportunity' conceived in terms of career paths. This gives priority to the interests of an educated minority of women and may create a structural split between organised feminism and working-class women, the movement's potential mass base.

For the state, dealing with feminism is unavoidable too. Though changed in form, the movement has weathered the recession and survived as a player in politics. To dismiss it out of hand is not possible: the state has had to negotiate over demands across a broad front, and grapple with legitimacy questions. Even Reagan has sought legitimacy by

appointing women cabinet ministers, women judges. Yet there are risks for the state. Too close an alignment with feminism gives offence to patriarchal ideology as mobilised in the churches, and to men's employment interests as mobilised in male-dominated unions and corporate managements. There are potential destablising effects on the gender order, such as the risks of too vigorous an intervention in the family in pursuit of domestic violence and incest offenders, or in support of women's rights in divorce. The gender order is not static and the state, as a regulatory force, has complex calculations to make about the allowable pace and directions of change. Nothing guarantees that the political arithmetic will come out right.

The result is, inevitably, a complex patchwork of strategies, and compromises and trade-offs between strategies, on both sides of the interaction. This is more obvious in feminism because different strategies have been to some extent embodied in visible factions or tendencies within the movement: socialist feminism, liberal feminism, separatism. But the same goes on within the state as well, if in more mediated and muted ways. Within the same government there is a treasury line and a welfare line, an economistic strategy and a consensus strategy. It has even been known for a minister in office to change his views on sexual politics.

The following parts of this book will bring some of these strategic dilemmas into focus. Part II takes a case-study approach to three issues where the interaction between feminism and the state has been intense: child care, equal opportunity and sexual violence. These issues have been chosen to indicate both the scope of this interaction, and the range of feminisms in action. Part III focuses on the strategy of feminists entering state employment. This is a type of action that has relevance across all issue areas. It raises general questions about the nature of bureaucracy, the nature of feminism, and the dynamics of the state.

Part II
Case studies

4

Child care

Feminist demands for the right to choose whether to have a child, and for free 24-hour child care, were on the books from the start. In May 1971, Adelaide Women's Liberation distributed a 'Mother's Day Card' calling for child care, and for abortion, maternity leave, an end to job discrimination and to the low status of mothers (Kinder, 1980:52).

Feminist demands are touchstones for feminism and provide focus for political campaigns. But demands reduce and compress complex issues into tidy packages, 'so they can say, "They want this", while you know you want vastly more but can't put a shape to it in their terms' (Rowbotham, 1983:73). The problem with the demand for child care is that the Australian women's movement took some time to undo the package again. Feminists have been slow to go beyond the slogan, to recognise its implications.

Feminists assume that the liberation of women requires that the bearing and rearing of children must cease to be inevitable in women's lives. They assume that women must have the right and the power to determine their own childbearing capacities; that women's economic independence, and thus the end of their oppression, requires freedom from full-time child-care responsibilities. Such assumptions fuelled campaigns for contraception and abortion, 'The Right to Choose', and helped to generate intense theoretical debate. But child care has failed to arouse similar passion or widespread attention. Child care is properly provided at feminist conferences but rarely features as a central topic on the agenda.

'How shall we care for and support our children, in terms of collective responsibility?' is a question we think has been too often ignored. As Sheila Rowbotham reminds us, there are 'the dilemmas of strategic focus...which arise whenever women seek not simply to describe what is wrong but to make tangible improvements' (Rowbotham, 1985:59). Struggling for social change in one area, such as paid work or contraception, may well contradict or obscure women's needs in another. This seems to have happened with child care.

What claims our attention about the feminist politics of child care in Australia is that *femocrats* agitated for it strongly during a period when

other feminists tended to overlook it. The reasons for this pattern are complex. Among them, we suggest in this chapter, are feminist approaches to mothering; and the way feminists generally saw *state* provision of child care as central, in contrast to voluntary or private provision. The chapter reviews several phases of the struggle to translate and to implement the demand. The child-care saga of the 1970s reads as a classic of 'femocrat' politics. Policy developments in the Hawke period equally suggest the fragility of these politics. The strategy now faces a very complex and difficult series of problems.

The struggle for state provision is no simple matter. State provision has led to state intervention: in the processes of the family, including parenting; and increasingly in the definitions of the form and content of child care. The issue raises in a particularly clear way the dilemmas about the role of femocrats which will be considered more closely in Part III.

What is child care?

Two points are essential as starting points for thinking about the care of Australian children: the deeply entrenched view that mother-care is the norm; and the diversity of other child-care arrangements.

As a matter of fact, preschool-aged children cared for exclusively by their mothers are in a minority, according to the 1980 Australian Bureau of Statistics Child Care Survey (Sweeney, 1983:51). In the child's home, the primary care-giver is almost always the mother, who may share to some degree with the father. Graeme Russell (1983:46) estimates that fathers are either primary caregivers or share care equally in 1–2 per cent of Australian families with young children. Mothers' labour force participation rates suggest that about one third of them are simply not available for full-time care. Overall, 44 per cent of all children not at school in 1980 were cared for part of the time by informal arrangements which included relatives, neighbours and spouse of the person mainly responsible.

Eighteen per cent of all children not at school have formal care. This is provided, as Deborah Brennan and Carol O'Donnell (1986) remark, by a 'maze' of organisations, whose complexity is barely suggested by Table 4.1.

This heterogeneous array will result in only 9.5 per cent of 0–4 year olds having access to subsidised child care by June 1988. The whole thing has the character of an elephant straining to deliver a mouse. And not a very happy little mouse at that. Workers in the child-care field feel as though they are on a treadmill of never-ending change. Endemic uncertainty and scarce resources have long required desperate measures to stay in the one spot. The pressure is now increased with federal government exhortations to be 'realistic' about economic stringency in the midst of constant and huge demands for child-care services.

Table 4.1: Main types of child care provision

Type	Service	Funding	Staff
Centre-based day care	8 hours daily (min) ages 2–6 (some baby care)	Commonwealth subsidies, income-related fees	Trained and untrained mix, variable conditions
Preschools	Half day sessions, age 3–4	State	Trained teachers
Family day care	In carer's home, negotiable hours, limited to 4–5 children	Commonwealth subsidies for supervision, parent fees	Little training
Occasional care	Short-term: emergencies, brief parent free time, children 'at risk'	State	Largely volunteers, little training
Out-of-school-hours care, vacation care	On school premises, but separate	Commonwealth subsidies, parent fees	Trained and untrained mix
Private, for profit	8 hours daily (min)	Parent fees	Trained and untrained mix

Source: After Brennan and O'Donnell, 1986

The sense of distress is widespread, but the field itself cannot be described as cohesive. Attitudes and approaches to the public care of children vary considerably, ranging from child minding to the skilful development of educational programs, from care understood as a poor substitute for 'mother' to the belief that it can add a valuable dimension to a child's life. Assumptions about mothering underlie these attitudes. Conflicts around such assumptions have their effect on the approaches taken by the state. Accordingly, the assumptions feminism makes about mothering, families and child care affects the impact it has on conflicts over the state provision of child care.

Feminism and mothering

The feminist demand for child care seeks the liberation of women. And liberation requires the transformation of women's status as wives and mothers, since it is this status which embodies women's dependence.

An account of feminism's approach to mothering and to child care encounters a great deal of diversity among feminist groups. There are mixed reactions to prevailing ideologies of child care, struggles to theorise women's experience, and inherent difficulties in developing

political strategies. But we find too that the politics of child-care provision has received relatively little feminist attention. Initially, from about 1970, motherhood was generally rejected in feminist writing, with a consequent neglect of the politics of child care. Later, during the mid-1970s, interest in motherhood burgeoned but was related to child care in confused ways.

The first phase

The social base for the renewed feminist movement of the 1970s was middle-class and skilled working-class women. This was an expanding group who were entering, or training to enter, the growing range of professional, technical, administrative and skilled occupations, and for whom 'traditional' home-bound motherhood would be a major stumbling-block. The experience of mothering was itself described by feminists as one of self-denial and guilt, eroding personal identity (e.g. Comer, 1975).

Early attempts to explain women's oppression rested on an attack on the conventional social interpretation of biology. Feminists such as Shulamith Firestone argued that biological differences between men and women were socially constructed in the interests of men. Biological differences had justified the subjugation, oppression and exploitation of women. The argument led to a rejection of women's biological difference, expressed most powerfully as their capacity to bear children. Consequently, Women's Liberation rejected the identification of women with motherhood.

Feminist work on the history of Australian women affirmed the significance of motherhood for the analysis of women's oppression. In 1975, Anne Summers' history posited the dichotomy 'damned whores/ God's police'. The latter stereotype

> describes and *prescribes* a set of functions which all Australian women are supposed to fulfil: the maintenance and reproduction of the basic authority relations of society. The prototype of these is found within 'the family' and it is here that women ideally perform their task, but the task of shoring up these authority relations requires extensive support systems, among them the education and social welfare network... [the] stereotype is posited as the apotheosis of womanhood, as that to which all women strive. (Summers, 1975:152–54)

Summers argues that motherhood was elevated to a vocation in the nineteenth century. Even suffragettes did little to challenge the notion that motherhood was woman's highest destiny and the home her only natural sphere. To escape from being a wife-and-mother meant, still means, almost inevitable poverty, and the consequences of the 'damned whore' stereotype. Although Summers' argument centres on the oppressiveness of the nuclear family for women, her final chapter, 'Prospects for Liberation' has little to offer as an alternative to it.

Concerned to develop alternative strategies, the wider movement directed attention towards women's work, waged and unwaged, indicating the influence of the labour movement and (among intellectuals) marxist theory at that point. Motherhood was not the immediate focus. Australia conducted its own 'domestic labour' debate about the economic significance of domestic unpaid work. 'At the heart of understanding what is distinctive about women's labour in modern industrialized societies is understanding the decisive part that housewifery plays in it.' (Thornton, 1975:96). The convoluted debate about theorising 'domestic labour' eventually became trapped in a maze of abstractions. Nevertheless, it had the effect of emphasising that women's unpaid work is 'work'. Ann Game and Rosemary Pringle subsequently reformulated the question in terms of consumption, where consumption is as *active* an exchange as production: 'A woman's value as housewife and *mother* is reflected in her success as a consumer, filling the cupboards and fulfilling herself. (Game and Pringle, 1979:11). The care of children received scant attention in any of this literature, slotted in as part of the work of consumption in an unproblematic way.

The experience of motherhood was analysed as work: child care. A number of studies (Gavron, 1966; Oakley, 1974) sought to shift the experience and meaning of mothering away from the realm of the emotional, the natural nurturance of women, to the experience of care as work, influenced by the organisation and conditions of the job. This was a gain for feminist analysis, at the cost of neglecting the dynamic relations between mother and child.

The way child care for feminist conferences and other activities was thought about is illustrative. Although the work of mothering was seen as a problem, the actual children of feminist mothers were sometimes rendered invisible. When planning child care feminists rarely considered details of the diverse needs and interests of children or matters of resources. The main questions debated were whether to organise men as carers, and when were boy children too old to be included. Many mothers experienced these debates as an expression of the movement's hostility to children and to themselves as mothers. In theory, motherhood was a 'political' problem; in practice it remained a 'private', domestic issue.

Yet, considered in context, the feminist rejection of motherhood is remarkable. As Sol Encel and his co-authors noted (1974:40) 'for nine out of ten Australian women adult life means marriage, and for most of them, marriage means motherhood'. Home ownership on the quarter-acre block became the dream setting for the nuclear family (Game and Pringle, 1979). While men's lives continued to revolve around work and their mates, for women motherhood gained renewed impetus in the post-war decades. The widespread notion 'maternal deprivation' stressed children's dependence on their mother's care. The social emphasis on the exclusive mother–child relationship carried well beyond the 1950s. When, in 1970, Liberal Prime Minister John Gorton promised federal

government assistance for the establishment of child–care centres, he was roundly criticised in terms of 'maternal deprivation' by child psychiatrists and church ministers (Encel, 1974:50–52). Sixteen years later, Jan Kelly reported that a majority of trainee Early Childhood teachers, educated young women, many of whom were destined to work in childcare centres, firmly espoused the traditional view that mothers and babies belong at home together (Kelly, 1986:8).

However, allegiance to a single view of motherhood was never complete. An array of conflicting perspectives coexist, indicating the diversity of family experience as well as the contradictory meaning of motherhood itself, supposed to be fulfilling for women yet demeaning to their status. The Royal Commission on Human Relationships in the mid-1970s received a great variety of oral and written submissions on the topic. The report of the commission, an important document of the ideological complexity of the issues, found that family forms and relationships were changing rapidly and hence under considerable pressure. The rising divorce rate, changing sex roles, the movement of married women into the paid workforce, new modes of sexual expression and the level of domestic violence were all cited as both evidence for, and cause of, these new pressures (Deveson, 1978).

The report's interpretation of findings represented an important critique of traditional motherhood and of women's social position. It assumed, in liberal-humanist style, the right of the individual to self-fulfilment and equality of opportunity. Conflict must be therefore the result of misunderstanding which may be smoothed away by adjusting attitudes, given a measure of good will.

Such a belief was characteristic of a particular section of the women's movement. Among those who engaged directly with the state apparatus, liberal humanism constituted a significant influence. Their approach to strategies aimed at ameliorating women's position headed away from the general feminist rejection of motherhood. But both derived impetus from the contradictions of the ideology of motherhood.

The movement's generally hostile stance was connected with the experiences of many women, including working mothers, who found aspects of motherhood oppressive. Rejection was premised on the critique of biological determinism and efforts to revalue women's work, paid and unpaid. A major strand of feminist theory argued that the separation of women from the public sphere of production through the social arrangements for rearing children within the private sphere of the family was the basis for women's dependence on men. This was the key to men's power over women. But this argument led to strategies addressed to changing women's work rather than strategies focused on reconstructing child care.

This assessment of the period has been queried recently by British feminists Sheila Rowbotham (1987) and Lynne Segal (1987). Segal says bluntly that 'it is not true that feminists then were unconcerned about

mothers and their children'. Rowbotham recalls meetings, demonstrations, piles of leaflets and articles on mothering. This does not dispute our view that the women's movement in Australia, and influenced by overseas developments, took an instrumental approach to children which saw them as obstacles to women's liberation. Rowbotham observes that it proved easier to criticise than to remedy, and we must agree. The demand for public child care was made early on but it is striking that feminist child-care centres were not established in the same way that refuges, rape crisis and women's health centres were. The politics of child care raised problems that the women's movement had yet to confront (Dowse, 1983). Meantime it was regarded as important but dull. There were sporadic suggestions that men should change their roles to include caring for children but the exploration of alternatives was left to feminists within the state, and to mothers themselves in unions or community groups.

The second phase

Both Rowbotham and Segal agree that a subtle but distinct shift in women's movement theory began during the mid-1970s. Theories emerged which emphasised and valued gender differences in contrast to rejecting them. This led to a new confrontation with the meaning of motherhood.

Two elements contributed. First, increasing numbers of women were responding to feminist politics. For those who were already mothers, feminist rejection of motherhood was less than useful. For others, the question of whether to become mothers at all began to figure as they approached the end of their optimum childbearing years. Feminist evocation of 'the personal' provided an impetus to discuss mothering, coinciding with rising interest in the control of women's bodies and the establishment of state-funded women's health centres. In addition, feminists began to explore the histories of their own mothers and so began to reconsider mother–daughter relationships.

Still, the first national discussion of the experience of motherhood did not take place until 1982, when the biennial Women and Labour Conference in Adelaide held a workshop on it (Wishart, 1982). The packed session highlighted the complexities inherent in the issue. Far more questions were raised than could be answered: around shared parenting, the primacy of the biological mother, ownership of children, reproductive technology, the depth of feeling towards one's 'own' children. The session exhibited a tendency to idealise the mother–daughter relationship; and the matter of non-familial care was not explored. The significance of motherhood for women was acknowledged, but the problem of tackling the related political issues was barely defined.

The second element contributing to the shift away from the rejection of motherhood was the publication of feminist analyses of motherhood.

Among them was the influential work of Adrienne Rich (1976), who sought to reclaim the question of motherhood for feminist theory. She distinguished between two meanings: the potential of the experience for women; and the institution of motherhood under male control (patriarchy). Motherhood itself need not be rejected but rather the oppression of the current institution needs to be destroyed. 'The repossession by women of our bodies will bring far more essential change to human society than the seizing of the means of production by workers' (Rich, 1976:285). Rich proposed a revolution of consciousness linked to the body. Her American radical feminism, duly suspicious of the state, led her to reject state provision of child care since it would be used to introduce women into the labour force. Rich highlighted but failed to resolve the dilemma about how to value women's mothering while seeking to alter institutional arrangements.

Nancy Chodorow's (1978) solution to the oppressiveness of the institution was for men to mother. It is the fact that mothering is almost universally done by women which is the primary cause of the sexual division of labour, and of the continued domination of women by men. The way to break through was for men to share in the nurturance of children. Chodorow offered a feminist analysis of the depth of the maternal and the possibility of modifying it. Although she posited a link between the organisation of gender and the organisation of production, the problem remained: how to disrupt it. How can feminism get men involved in child care? Indeed, should the attempt be made? Other feminists saw this as allowing men to move in on one of the few areas where women still had authority.

Such work, in conjunction with theoretical work on understanding constructions of gender difference, shifted 'women-centred' analyses towards the valorisation of that difference. Psychoanalytic accounts of the embeddedness of gender difference, of gendered subjectivity (e.g. Gatens, 1983; Weedon, 1987), are a decided advance on the explanatory capacity of sex role theory which underpins liberal feminism (see Chapter 2). But the political implications are less than clear. The consequences for the development of strategy tend to be left unconsidered. Tensions inherent in the politics and experience of motherhood are lost from view. For example, in the workshop discussion of motherhood at the Women and Labour conference, assumptions about gender difference obscured the political and social implications of the questions raised.

Although influential among feminists, analysis premised on gender difference by no means dominates the field. The earlier feminist challenge to motherhood as ideally and naturally constituting women's identity gained increased impetus from social changes represented by certain demographic shifts—declining birth rates, increased divorce rates, increased participation rates of married women in paid work (Burns, 1983). Perhaps of particular significance was the growing proportion of

mothers in paid work. Since conservative assumptions about mother-hood still held considerable force the reality of a substantial number of 'working mothers' raised questions about the impact of mother's work on children, about women's mothering role. Feminist researchers took up the question of how women were negotiating this relatively new ter-rain where the question of workforce participation had become a matter requiring decision even by mothers of young children. Jan Harper and Lyn Richards (1979) reported from their study *Mothers and Working Mothers* that this change in mothering experience exposed contradictory images of motherhood: the 'good' mother cares for her preschool children full-time, although the full-time housewife is lazy, boring and unattractive; the working mother is the 'bad' mother—selfish, hassled, tired and with little time for her children.

Although Harper and Richards do not suggest that confusion of norms may constitute an ideology related to gender divisions, they show that women's experience of motherhood betrays a tension be-tween the smoothness of motherhood ideals and the jagged inegalita-rianism of those same ideals. The 'good' mother is at once both nur-turant and passive. She acts, as mother, and is primary to the child, yet she is dependent.

At the same time women do not experience motherhood as uniformly oppressive. Indeed, it may be satisfying and central to their lives. Betsy Wearing investigated the puzzle of this ambiguity which she saw as the 'ideology of motherhood'—'the legitimation of male power which obfuscates the subordination of women in relation to their responsibility for child care' (Wearing, 1984:23–24). Looking for varia-tions among her broad sample of mothers, Wearing found none who had 'successfully been able to share the *primary responsibility* for the care of her child' (p.82). We recall Russell's estimate that this occurs in 1–2 per cent of families. Wearing argues that the absence of any strong chal-lenge to the ideology of motherhood implies an insufficient shift in the balance of power between men and women in the wider society.

Wearing's analysis mediates between the structure of gender divi-sions and the subjective experiences and beliefs of women as mothers. Women are active subjects of the ideology of motherhood. Individual change depends on multiple social factors. So political strategies aimed at challenging its oppressiveness must reckon with material conditions, and contradictory beliefs and ideas.

Omissions

And yet there is a missing dimension. Feminist work on motherhood shows that where the family 'presents certain advantages *within the con-text* of a particular society' (Barrett and McIntosh, 1982:131), mother-hood is privileged as a significant role for women while all other alter-natives are devalued. But in *this* society, some women, at some time,

strive hard to find others to do the work of mothering. The sainted victorian mother had her nannies; now we find in the surveys that children
cared for exclusively by their mothers are in a minority. Since 1969, surveys have shown consistently that very large numbers of mothers want
child care. In 1975 a government-sponsored survey *Mothers' Child Care
Preferences* reported that the majority wanted paid work and child care
(Cullen). Money was not their chief reason for wanting work. Ten years
later, Tania Sweeney identified similar strong responses with parent-
centred reasons given as much importance as child-centred reasons.
Child care allowed the mother time, for paid work and for other
activities (Sweeney and Jamrozik, 1984:180–81).

The wish for child care is certainly put to the test if the 'cases' cited
by Sweeney and Jamrozik are any indication. The business of locating
care, reckoning suitability and cost, juggling work, school and care
times—and then doing it all again, perhaps several times because some
part of the complicated arrangement goes awry—is evidence of the
extraordinary lengths people go to, must go to, if they want alternatives
to exclusive mother-care.

All this effort sits oddly with the pervasive ideology of motherhood.
Feminists register a certain ambivalence in women's experience of
motherhood, but few people are as cranky about it in public as Joyce
Nicholson in *The Heartache of Motherhood* with her summary of the
problem: 'In theory, everyone loves children. In practice, people dislike
them' (1983:67). Barrett and McIntosh are more circumspect:

> Usually [mothers] find their relationship with their children deeply
> rewarding; but at the same time they feel frustrated that it has
> become such an exclusive and demanding one... Gradually the
> knots linking the woman to the home and family become tigh-
> tened. If she is lucky she may find it rewarding; if she does not she
> is unlucky. Most likely though, she feels deeply ambivalent about
> it because it is her love for her children that ties her down.
> (1982:62)

Feminists aim to free women from being tied. The provision of child
care is a necessary precondition. But such a strategy requires recognition
of the ways women experience sharing the care. Although texts on child
care (e.g. Brown, 1980; Burns and Goodnow, 1985) discuss the impact
of shared care on children, they rarely consider its impact on mothers.
Kaye Hargreaves provides a rare example: 'It was clear [from her inter-
views] that many [working] women feel bad about leaving their children, even if satisfactory arrangements are available. They also feel
vulnerable to criticism and to getting into trouble if their arrangements
are inadequate'. (Hargreaves 1982:267). Hargreaves shows however that
attitudes to child care were not simply a question of being for or against
it. Much depended on the nature of the child care itself: accessibility,
cost, control of the service. And Sweeney and Jamrozik found that when

care approximates their own approach many feel relief, suggesting perhaps a place for father-care.

Feminists such as Chodorow and Curthoys have argued for shared parenting, but until recently the very idea seemed so wayward that Russell spends some time in his book demonstrating that men are capable of doing it. However English feminist Suzanne Moore believes that change is unlikely when representations of fatherhood as late as 1987 are still peculiar, ranging from the sentimental to the unrealistic: 'Ironically, images of the perfect [father] never actually show him doing anything useful either, and it is, in its slickly middle-class way, just as sentimental a view of fatherhood as any other' (Moore, 1986:7).

Diane Ehrensaft takes an acerbic view of the consequences of shared parenting since the gains and losses are not equal for men and women. Women gain freedom from the burden of a continuous responsibility, and opportunity to participate in the public world. Men caring for children are assumed often to be either 'disabled, deranged or demasculinized'. But the woman gives up power in the domestic sphere, historically her domain, with little compensation from increased power in the public sphere. She may feel guilt, anger, a reluctance to share what she 'knows' about 'mothering'. 'The underlying point is this: powerful tensions arise when the sexual divisions of labor and power in the family are altered without simultaneous sweeping restructuring of gender-related power relations outside the family' (Ehrensaft, 1981:51). We too observe 'powerful tensions' between parents where shared parenting results in blurred roles and uncertain expectations, suggesting that Ann Curthoy's notion of shared parenting as necessarily a 'mode of transitional practice' has some point (1976).

The meanings of shared care entangle the problem of strategy. For many women, sharing may mean giving up socially legitimate power to fathers or to care workers. Public child care may conflict with notions of nurturance rooted in the familial home. The problem demands strategy sensitive to such meanings while it challenges the ideologies which privilege individualised and private mother-care.

The underlying theme of our discussion of feminism and motherhood has been the conundrum of feminist approaches to child care. The demand for public provision is almost a basic tenet of feminism. But there is something rather instrumental about it. Child care allows women's participation in the paid workforce, and offers a way to breach the privacy of familial care. Child care as such has never been the focus of spirited feminist debate. Child care is simply A Good Thing. Paradoxically, to paraphrase Lynne Segal, the question of how to affirm the real value of women's mothering while seeing how it also serves to perpetuate women's oppression, can lead to a reduced emphasis on the politics of care. The connections need to be made politically between the challenge of child care to the oppressiveness of motherhood, and ways of valuing women's mothering.

Nevertheless feminists, particularly femocrats, tackled the issue of state provision. They were influenced by the shifting concerns of the women's movement, while confronted by the contradictions of the state and the dilemmas of feminist engagement with it.

Child care and the state

The relationship of the state to 'the family' is central to child care. How much responsibility the state assumes for the care, education and socialisation of young children poses the question of state intervention in the family. Not only a matter of extent but of purpose: whether the state fulfils a universal need or compensates for failings produced by departures from the 'ideal' family. Prevailing discourses of intervention are premised on notions that it is anomalous for the state to do so and that there is some clearly defined area into which the state intervenes. Much of the controversy focuses on whether responsibility for child care is social or personal. Child care thus sits squarely on the great ideological divide of the public/private spheres.

The question for the state, and for feminism, is the extent to which the state intervenes in the private sphere, or refrains from so doing. The public/private dichotomy may be a false division, an idiological construct, but it is not merely a chimera, a fanciful conception. If the feminist demand for equal employment opportunity requires state intervention in the public sphere of women's lives, and campaigns against sexual violence involve intervention in the private sphere, then the demand for child care exemplifies the peculiar permeability of the division itself. For example, the state may determine that a mother not be allowed to look after other people's children in her home as a Family Day Care Worker but it does not follow that the state intervenes to prevent her from looking after her 'own'.

Australian feminists have characteristically sought to transform the ideological divide by focusing on the state in seeking child care, in contrast to the Americans who rely on self-help voluntary groups or profit-making 'professional day care'. Femocrats were early advocates of state provision and were rapidly engaged in struggles around the ways policy conceived the care of children.

Child care in the 1970s

Femocrats took up the issue of child care on the following grounds:

> Women are construed as taking the major, if not total responsibility for the care and nurture of the dependent child. The consequent assumptions of gender roles are arguably the most poweful determinants of women's access to social and economic power... The possibilities women have of sharing the responsibilities for child care outside the immediate biologically-bonded

group depends on acts of omission or commission *by the state* in providing certain types of services... This makes the issue of child care a crucial one. (Cox, 1983a:186)

Eva Cox, herself involved in the femocrat campaign from the Whitlam era, conceives the state as patriarchal and capitalist but also thinks it has the capacity to intervene and substantially ameliorate women's oppression. It is in short a site of contest. Cox questions the state's reluctance to provide services for the preschool-age child given its considerable intervention in families overall. She argues that the patriarchal state acts consistently to legitimate women's dependence by treating early child care as the untouchable private domain of women. If the state were to provide public child care such an intervention would contradict its patriarchal nature and alleviate women's dependence.

On this basis femocrats advocate long-day care, particularly community, centre-based child care. 'Choice' is deemed to be good, but centre-based care is regarded as more likely to meet women's needs; and also to meet the needs of children who, contrary to the maternal deprivation thesis, risk social deprivation when confined to maternal care alone (Brennan, 1983:18).

The state was at first not favourably disposed towards this argument. However, other pressures began to have effect. As the state is implicated in the organisation of the labour force, it was obliged to recognise that the economy had been developing an unprecedented demand for female labour. As already noted, a Liberal prime minister responded with promises to provide child care. The Child Care Act of 1972 allowed federal funding of child care for the first time. We note that this was not the initiative of a social reform government nor a response to feminist pressure, but derived from the demands of the economy. The government argued defensively that it was not encouraging women to enter the workforce, simply facing a reality of 'modern industrial society'. Its concern was the welfare of children. Funding was based on a submission model, aimed to include the professional and voluntary child-care sectors.

The Whitlam Labor government had a commitment to universal access to preschool education. Women in the Labor Party and WEL successfully campaigned for the adoption of a policy on child care at the party's Federal Conference in 1973. But politicians (almost all men) did not see much difference between preschool and child care. 'Unhappily, this confusion was to become a serious impediment to the development and implementation of the Whitlam government's children's services policy' (Dowse, 1983:205).

The government's 'confusion' was intensified by conflicts between preschool interests and the femocrat proposal. The preschool lobby was well established, especially at State levels, having its roots in the long-lived kindergarten movement. Two assumptions characterised its approach to children: that families deemed 'inadequate' needed a certain

public assistance, and that children need maximum maternal contact. Thus preschool programs were limited to half-day sessions, with the mother expected to care for the child the other half of the day.

The Whitlam government responded to what it saw as an undifferentiated demand by calling for a report on measures necessary to provide universal preschool access. After reading the resulting Fry Report (1973) one cannot help observing its orientation towards the professional interests of preschool educators. The report was concerned to dispel the myth that the needs of young children can be adequately met by 'merely warm-hearted people who are fond of children'. Contradictorily the report proposed that only 10 per cent of children be catered for by professionals, the remainder to have access to family day care. Thus the main form of child-care provision would remain privatised, simply transferred from one domestic sphere to another. Such carers may be warm-hearted, but a survey conducted by Di Court in 1976 in Surry Hills, Sydney, found they were also working-class. They were often migrant women with few marketable skills who preferred the (small) wage labour of child care to participation in the labour force. In all, the Fry Report saw child care as an extension of the domestic sphere.

The report was challenged by an alliance of women in and outside the bureaucracy, although success depended on Elizabeth Reid who 'was able to convince cabinet' (Dowse, 1983:207) that the report was biased. In a typical bureaucratic move, further reports were called—from the new Social Welfare Commission chaired by Marie Coleman. This report, *Project Care* (1974), strongly countered the previous case, arguing that traditional preschool programs did not serve broad community needs. It emphasised the need for community participation in the planning and the provision of services.

At stake in the disputes over responsibility for children's services were a large budget—$75 million announced by the treasurer in Septimber 1974 following much political conflict (Brennan and O'Donnell, 1986:33)—and the opportunity to determine the manner of its allocation. The result was a bureaucratic compromise (Graycar, 1979:41). A structurally separate Children's Commission was proposed which did not get beyond the interim stage before the Whitlam government was thrown out. Designed to circumvent conflict between child-care interests and preschool lobbies, it served to disguise that conflict rather than open it up to public debate.

Feminists and femocrats had successfully challenged the Fry Report although they did not, according to Lyndall Ryan (forthcoming) and to Sara Dowse, 'win the war'. The feminist child-care lobby was weak and uncoordinated perhaps because many activists became absorbed in writing submissions for the $2.2 million International Women's Year allocation.

Political difficulties for child care were exacerbated by the model of submission-based funding. The social democratic Whitlam government favoured user submissions as a devolutionary mode of budget allocation.

This had, as femocrats found, unfortunate consequences. The already established organisation of preschool groups facilitated submission work, while the relatively unorganised child-care sector had little time to set up new services. Working women were generally in no position to develop complex submissions for alternative care arrangements. One of our children attended such a child-care centre, the result of a small group of middle-class mothers who combined to write a submission. This was no small undertaking since the document had to demonstrate extent and kind of need, identify a site and recognise legal requirements for staff and buildings. All costs had to be met at first by the group and were not recoverable if the submission were unsuccessful. Not only this, but submission writing requires the translation of needs, hopes and plans into language amenable to bureaucratic interpretation. It is little wonder that so few were able to achieve success.

In sum, the short Whitlam period saw feminists and femocrats gain a toehold for public child-care provision. The Labor Party had adopted a policy of universal provision, but with characteristic ambivalence supported both child-care and preschool positions. Femocrats made some gains but they remained marginal to bureaucratic structures, a marginality aggravated by their own inexperience and frequent relocation.

Although femocrat gains were linked to feminist activities outside the state, the women's movement at this time had not gone beyond the basic demand for universal, free child care. State provision of child care was sought as a reform, yet this relatively moderate position was strongly contested. The ideology of motherhood continued to be articulated by groups such as the preschool lobby, male bureaucrats, politicians, churchmen and some welfare professionals. Nor was the issue one of clear-cut gender conflict. The contradictions of motherhood as a source of oppression and of identity for women, and the risks that state provision of child care opened up a space for state control of mothers' lives, tended to obfuscate the politics of child care.

Child-care gains scarcely disrupted the welfare state's continued maintenance of women's dependence. But the struggle for child care presented a real and direct challenge to this imperative. The child-care case sought the unacknowledged interests of women, especially working women, from a state whose legitimacy depended on representing the interests of all citizens. The problem for the state was one of accommodation. The Interim Children's Commission was one solution, but so too was the submission-based funding model, construed as more democratic than top-down budget decisions. 'Let people speak their own needs.' However, some people were in a better position to speak than others, and in the end the state could 'hear' only certain speech forms.

The Fraser period

In the short space of three years the Whitlam government's enthusiasm for social reform apparently turned into a full-scale legitimation crisis for

the state. The constitutional coup of November 1975 was a moment of considerable tension for the women's movement as its engagement with the state had involved implicit support for the male-dominated Labor Party. Should an autonomous movement become further implicated with the state and with party politics? Splits occurred between those committed to working for change through the state and those who were either antagonistic to the patriarchal/capitalist state or simply pessimistic about the new conservative government. Indeed demoralisation and dismay affected the whole movement.

Fraser's landslide election victory in December 1975 signalled a strengthened conservatism. Of particular concern were the monetarist attack on social welfare, and the moral conservative focus on the family. Drawing on a rhetoric of individual freedom and the free market, the attack on welfare construed state intervention as costly, inefficient and oppressive. Second, the New Right argued that state intervention, rather than supporting the family, the site of morality and cohesive social reproduction, contributed to its decline, replacing voluntary caring relations and responsibilities with impersonal bureaucratic transactions. State welfare undermines the authority of the father and the caring role of the mother. State intervention must contract in order to restore the family's integrity. Women must return to the role of carers of the family (Poole, 1983).

Such rhetoric directly attacked the femocrat position that the state could intervene to ameliorate the dependence of women. Further, it threatened the very existence of femocrats.

The state apparatus itself faced severe internal problems as monetarism demanded that the state contract and alter its direction. Staff cuts were imposed, budgets reduced and policies reviewed. All involved considerable internal conflict. The already vulnerable situation of femocrats was susceptible; positions were downgraded and funding was reduced (Dowse, 1983:215).

However, the consequences were not straightforward. The state did not contract so much as undergo a restructuring and a recasting of its ideology. The meaning of resistance necessarily altered as the question became not how to oppose cuts, which did occur, but how to maintain a foothold on the shifting terrain. Paradoxically, the femocracy's perception of a liberal state contested a revamped ideal of a state facilitating individual freedom.

The Fraser government was against maintaining previous child-care commitments. Although social welfare expenditures are difficult to eliminate completely, child-care policy was restructured. New legislation, intended to replace the inadequate Child Care Act of 1972, was not proclaimed even though it had proceeded through the upper house when dominated by the Liberals in opposition. The Interim Commission was abolished and children's services shifted to the Department of Social Security, which established on Office of Child Care headed by

Marie Coleman. The move symbolised the government's view of child care as a residual welfare service rather than a universal right. In addition, the government sought to withdraw by shifting responsibility from the federal level to the States. Overall resources are thereby reduced since the States' capacity to generate funds is limited.

Actual child-care expenditure was reduced during the Fraser period, but not equally. Preschool funding was substantially withdrawn, although the States increased their contributions. The proportion of other funding increased, but was diversified with a significant shift away from child-care centres towards family day care. Tania Sweeney estimates that between 1976 and 1981, 1500 centre-based places were established in contrast to 10 000 family day care places. Family day care has two attractions for the New Right: it requires minimal state support; and it does not challenge directly mother-care at home (Freeman, 1982:137).

Such policy changes suggest that both femocrats and feminists had difficulty maintaining their position. The federal femocrats faced severe internal problems. The abolition of the Interim Commission and the relocation of the prime minister's women's adviser to a low-level department of Home Affairs reduced opportunities to have substantial impact on policy. The Fraser government was also sensitive to attacks by New Right women's groups opposed to femocrats.

The state directorate manifested increasing antagonism to femocrat commitment to social reform. Yet even the restrictive provision of child care maintained some federal funding. The possibility that the state might deliver at least a modicum of assistance remained. Thus, rather than reject involvement outright, femocrats and other feminists sought to reset their course. Their arguments began to take a different tack.

The 1983 report on child-care policy in South Australia by Marie Coleman illustrates the kinds of shifts which began during the Fraser period. What happened to the report also advances our story of the public provision of child care.

The Coleman report

By the 1980s, South Australia like the rest of the country had an array of inadequately funded children's services developed in piecemeal fashion. The major agencies were the Kindergarten Union, the Education Department and the Department for Community Welfare. The DCW, uniquely, ran the family day care program. Local government, unlike the position in other States, sponsored very little. Encouraged by the Hawke government's new child-care funding formula, the new State Labor government undertook to tackle this 'administrative confusion'. At the suggestion of Rosemary Wighton, the women's adviser to the premier, Marie Coleman was commissioned to review early childhood services. A similar inquiry in Victoria at this time approached it as an 'exer-

cise in public participation' in contrast to the South Australian 'social planning' model (Healey, 1987:30).

Coleman sees South Australian child-care provision in 1983 as thoroughly inadequate and inefficient. But she refuses the ideal that mothers at home should and could meet all child-care needs. Basing her case for improved provision on the validity of feminist claims and on Labor policy, Coleman advocated child care as a 'normal public utility rather than a service provided for the disadvantaged' (1983:2). But it still must be implemented:

> Comparatively, the government child care field is new, while the demands of the feminist movement for personal autonomy are still being addressed. Hence the likely cost of policy (and public demand) is such that the development of a child care system is an urgent matter upon which government and the field must find common ground. (Report, 1983:64)

Where demand and political policy coincide, the state will/must respond. The problem as Coleman sees it is to ensure that response is efficient and cost-effective.

The state provision of services requires a diversity sensitive to the plurality of needs of a heterogeneous community and a centralised administration. Administration needs to be rational and rationality means bureaucratic centralism. Coleman justifies centralism on two specific grounds. First, resource allocation is uneven where it depends in the first instance on user-submissions. A central administration can ensure appropriate resource allocation to children with special needs, e.g. Aboriginal and ethnic minority children, or the physically disabled. Second, the low priority of childhood services within the bureaucracy is exacerbated by their dispersal across several departments with the result that resources tend to be leeched from these sections for the department's mainstream functions. The primary perspectives of departments also have their effect; the DCW adopts a residual welfare approach while the Department of Education favours education at the expense of care. Coleman proposes centralism as a bureaucratic counter: a separate department with ministerial status and its own budget line.

This strategy allows Coleman to shift the balance between child care and preschools. Her report opposes the Kindergarten Union, sponsor of preschools, on three grounds. First, the KU's philosophy of childhood services assumes that at-home mother-care is best. Its services are designed to enhance child development and compensate those children for whom mother-care is deemed inadequate. Coleman opposes the privileging of mother-care and endorses those alternatives provided by public, universal care. Second, the KU received a greater proportion of government resources (at both State and federal levels) than the child-care sector. For example in 1982–83 total recurrent expenditures were 82 per cent and 18 per cent respectively. (Coleman herself was involved in

disputes over funding ratios at the federal level during the 1970s.) Third, Coleman saw the KU as an obstacle to centralism, to the 'harmonising of bureaucratic activity' with government policies since it was not subject to ministerial direction. She was disturbed that the Management Board of the KU did not feel an obligation to implement government policies if, in its judgment, such policies were 'not in the best interests of children'.

> An organisation may feel justified in taking a different view from that of the government. However, if the Government is the source of its funds, then such a view is not conducive to the co-ordination of effort with government policy. It also raises the question of accountablity to the Parliament for expenditure of public monies. (p.61)

The KU, established in 1905, had been accorded the status of a statutory authority in 1975 by the Kindergarten Union Act 1975–76. Coleman recommends the repeal of that Act, to be replaced by legislation designed to establish a new State department.

The language and assumptions of Coleman's report illustrate shifts in femocrat argument. On the one hand, child care was emphasised as a need of all women, not only working mothers—an important move in the face of rising unemployment. Child-care services should 'provide community support for mothers to participate more fully in society'. Coleman shows an acute awareness of the pliability of the concept of 'need'. She marshals evidence to demonstrate the diversity of 'need' but comments pragmatically: 'the definition of "need" is often dependent upon the resources available, hence children who were not previously given special attention may now have the access to once restricted opportunities' (p.48). On the other hand, terms such as 'efficiency' and 'cost-effective' begin to surface. The straightforward point that more child care costs more money is underplayed. Instead Coleman directs attention to criteria for an 'effective administrative structure'. This requires 'provision of effective machinery for planning and co-operation in achieving policy goals...and performance accountability through the Minister to the Parliament. Ability of the administrative structure to re-direct existing resources promptly and efficiently in response to changing circumstances' (p.78). Reform is proposed as a restructuring of administration rather than of policy or budgets.

Similarly, 'choice' as in 'parental choice of child care services' aligns itself with notions of individual freedom, although this blurred the chance to distinguish politically between family day care and centre-based child care, both of which could be deemed to serve equally the needs of women and children. For Coleman at least such pluralism contested the KU's prior claims.

Not surprisingly, the report created a political tumult in South Australia. Under the auspices of an administrative review Coleman

managed to weigh the balance in favour of a femocrat approach to child-hood services. The Labor government was sympathetic and keen to adopt a policy which promised rational, efficient and, most important, cost-effective services.

But the adoption of the report was not plain sailing. A number of interests were at stake, from budget lines to ideologies of welfare and family relations. The KU mounted a campaign to retain its autonomy. When this failed it bid to have its own chief executive appointed to head the mooted new department. This also failed. Yet Coleman's proposals did not entirely succeed. Out of the political shuffle, the Education Department retained its preschool sector, and instead of a department, an Office, a bureaucratic beast with less status, was set up to administer the rest.

Until legislation was finally passed in February 1985, debates were quite public, and often 'confused and bitter'. Accusations in parliament that the bill was the result of '...the female Mafia in action...' and/or '...the feminist Marxist left...' (*South Australian Parliamentary Debates* 5 December 1984) seem a touch shrill. Curiously, the Liberal opposition anticipated a Hawke government theme when it argued that the bill would 'extend child minding for the greedy in the Metropolitan area...'—the greedy being grasping working mothers who only want a second Volvo. But in so doing, as Judith Healey points out, the opposition ignored its own Liberal women's associations who are commited to expanded child care (Healey, 1987:32).

The report gave some purchase to feminist demands for universal child care. However the significance of the feminist case was obscured by conflicting groups in and outside the bureaucracy striving to take advantage of opportunities to renegotiate their relations of power. Although the report favoured certain positions, it became the springboard for contest rather than its arbiter. Those approaches opposed to the report were well established. A feminist politics of child care was not. Although feminist claims were seen as disruptive to dominant ideologies of the welfare state, we cannot read the apparent spectre of a greedy feminist Marxist Mafia as indicative of actual power. Rather feminist claims including those made in the report took on the character of merely another interest competing within a plurality of contending interests.

Marie Coleman attempted to accommodate a feminist politics of child care with the politics of the state. The report sought to improve rather than to change, offering efficiency without increased resources. Nevertheless it initiated substantial conflict within the state apparatus. Her argument was designed to align with certain aspects of welfare policy such as the universal right to state support for 'need', but perforce quarrelled with other aspects of welfare ideology, such as the commitment to mother-care. Although the latter has lost some ground, there can be no suggestion that South Australia will soon attain universal child care.

The new Children's Services Office was established in July 1985, with a central office and six regional offices. The majority of its managerial staff was relatively new to the field, perhaps to avoid 'bias' towards any particular service. This model coincides with widespread moves towards a 'rational' management throughout the public service, based on the assumption that good managers can manage anything.

South Australian child care has gained a centralised infrastructure, an advantage when the Commonwealth modifies (reduces) funding formulae. Tensions, not unlike those between femocrats and other feminists, exist between managers and service deliverers. Which is to say, there are conflicts between the way problems are understood by those who work within the state apparatus, and by those who work outside the state or with clients.

The Hawke government: quality versus cost

Child care has not had an easy ride during the Hawke government's tenure of federal office since 1983. Rather, the demand for child care has been submerged beneath a welter of complex and contradictory issues. Deborah Brennan and Carol O'Donnell characterise the period 1975–85 as a 'decade of turbulence'. The five years of the Hawke government can only be described as one of even greater turmoil. Things began rather well with Labor policy committed to child care as a right for all families; a new system provided more generous subsidies to low and middle-income families; a rapid expansion of services was initiated. Even the money was increased. It was the biggest spending item promised during the 1984 election campaign, and the Hawke government made a commitment to provide an extra 20 000 places by June 1988. In the wake of the gloom and low morale induced by Fraser's cuts, it seemed child care would achieve, finally, social and political priority. Enormous complications have since arisen from the imposition of complex changes to funding formulae chiefly aimed at cutting funds.

Initially, child-care lobby groups gained renewed enthusiasm. The National Association of Community Based Children's Services (NACBCS) was formed and was able to hold a national conference in 1983. Bringing together workers, union organisers, parents and bureaucrats, the Conference aimed to politicise care and canvassed the plethora of problems. It reflected the contention by Eva Cox that women had kept the issue bubbling.

> It is women in the union movement that have raised child care as an industrial issue, and women in political parties who have raised it as a policy issue...The issue of child care has the power to unite women across political boundaries within parties and between them. And it is concern for women's votes which made both parties put some child care funding into their election promises. (Cox, 1983b:3)

Perhaps most exciting was the increased attention to the industrial conditions of child-care workers, which included abysmally low wages and poor work conditions.

The rot set in far too soon. Before the problems of ways and means could be properly tackled the Hawke government began to change the rules. In the 1985 mini-budget it withdrew completely from funding early childhood education. M.A. Jones commented that 'the aim of integrating early childhood care and education has been put to rest, at least as far as the Commonwealth is concerned' (Jones, 1985:24). Lest the child-care lobby saw this as a victory in the long-running dispute over funding ratios, a substantial reduction to child-care funding was also announced.

Twelve months earlier, the government had signalled a shift away from the goal of universal access towards selective access priorities. By April 1986 these were, in order: children of parents working, training for work or seeking work; children with a disability; children at risk of abuse or neglect; and children of single parents or parents with more than one child at home (Hurford,1987:6). Given the scarcity of places, this priority list, which recognises mothers' workforce participation, appears to warrant a round of applause from feminists.

However, government fee tables reveal that working mothers' incomes are subsumed by 'family' incomes. Public child care charges fees which are subsidised by the Commonwealth according to family income, with a cut-off point for fee relief. Recollecting itself as a Labor Party, the government began to worry about 'equity'. The minister, Senator Grimes, frequently complained that families earning $100 000 received the same fee subsidy as those earning $31 000. But this is 'family' income. Such a sum can be made up by one parent earning it all, or by both earning a proportion. The family income limit would be less than the combined incomes of two cleaners or two factory hands—workers not usually in the market for Volvos. The Labor government has an unrealistic view of working-class incomes and none at all of the necessary and established labour force participation of working-class women (Brennan and O'Donnell, 1986:57). It is even further from recognising that families do not simply pool their incomes, although the fact is well demonstrated by Meredith Edwards (1985). And it is women who typically pay for child care. The result is that groups who will be able to use subsidised child care will be those on the $100 000 incomes, together with those who can limit their costs by part-time arrangements, or who can manage the minimum fee on the lowest incomes.

Still, child care is scarce, and the government claims it a progressive virtue to shift the emphasis to working parents (mothers) away from care as welfare. Yet this claim is contested by those who argue that it buttresses class divisions. Tania Sweeney contends that the priority to children of employed mothers, in conjunction with the fee policies, results in child care becoming part of the social wage for middle-class

families. By contrast, poor families, 'without parents in the workforce or under the surveillance of welfare authorities have no, or limited, access to stigma-free child care but have access or are forced to use clearly defined residual welfare services' (Sweeney, 1987:123).

Equally disturbing are those changes by the Hawke government which affect care workers. Their wages and conditions are both poor and highly varied; this relatively new industry is covered by up to 38 awards and 22 unions (Forbath, 1983:40). The government's alterations neither improve the conditions of individual workers nor recognise the claims of the industry overall. At the moment when care workers, overwhelmingly female, had begun to challenge their isolation and low status the government demolished the national minimum staffing standard incorporated in legislation by cutting the nexus between operational subsidies and award wages. The 1985 Child Care Amendment Act replaced the subsidy formula calculated on 75 per cent of funding for staff required by legislation with a formula based on approved child-care places. The new formula puts pressure on staff–child ratios and on the employment of more expensive trained staff. Although centres must still comply with State licensing requirements (where they exist), the management committees, who are formally the employers, are compelled to employ fewer and cheaper staff. Care workers are placed in the invidious position where any award improvements must be borne by increased parents' fees or by the loss of jobs. Deborah Brennan believes this is a severe blow to career opportunities in the industry. 'Affirmative action apparently does not extend as far as workers in government child care centres' (Brennan, 1986:40). Nor does it extend to other care workers, such as those in the commercial centres where improved awards and conditions are even more difficult to achieve.

The low wages of centre-based workers are further undermined by the lower costs to the government, of family day care. Organised into regional schemes, caregivers may charge a maximum of $1.63 per hour per child for parents to receive government Fee Relief; some may be paid as little as $1.10. They provide almost everything within their own homes, with the government-funded support structures providing advice, supervision, toy libraries, and playgroups.

Family day care continues to be a very inexpensive form of public child care, for the state. In 1987, the government 'saved' $9 million from the Big Promise of 20 000 places by increasing the proportion of family day care places within the total. Although the government increasingly uses the family day care option it appears determined that carers' poor wages and conditions will remain unchanged. A recent minister responsible for the area, Chris Hurford, said there are 'plenty of "ladies" willing to take on the work, and warned that although he was ready to hear submissions from caregivers, they should be careful not to price themselves out of the market' (Powell, 1987:21). Not surprisingly, caregivers are becoming harder to recruit. These isolated workers have begun to

seek collective solutions to their poor conditions. They face as many obstacles as centre-based workers, if not more.

Cost has become the central theme in child care. The costs are too high for everyone: parents, workers, children, and as the minister for finance keeps saying, for the government too.

Senator Walsh's remarks may be traced to the general problem of legitimation for the state. The terms are stark, now construed as conflict between social welfare and economic pragmatism. The response to child care typifies the Labor government's solution: to gain credit for expanded service while visibly reducing costs. (A similar strategy is now proposed for tertiary education.)

The terms of the child-care debate are limited to quality versus cost with the Government apparently favouring the latter. Thus Senator Grimes:

> The Government is acutely aware of the need for funded centres to ensure that their costs do not put child care out of the reach of ordinary parents... I am appealing to high cost services to act responsibly and reduce their costs so that child care can remain affordable. They must realise that there is a limit to the level of subsidy which the Commonwealth can afford to put into child care. (Press Release, 18 July 1986)

The government also searches for cheap solutions. In 1986, the Office of Child Care commissioned private consultants, Touche Ross Services, to determine what causes high costs in subsidised long day care centres, and to recommend on how costs might be reduced.

No doubt centres would benefit if their extraordinarily complex funding arrangements could be streamlined. The Touche Ross Report itself observed: 'Management committees are reluctant to plan because of perceived unfairness of having made long term commitments only for funding guidelines to change, impacting on short term viability' (1986:7). However, its focus on cost allowed the report little scope to comprehend public child-care philosophies or needs. Its recommendations threaten 'quality' (the nature of the service) by proposing reductions to the proportions of qualified staff, and to ratios of staff to children (e.g. 1:25 for over-threes), and four-week annual closures (for working parents?). It favoured a form of privatisation with a system for contracting child-care services to be delivered at negotiated prices, but did not spell out how this might work.

The report, and the government, have drawn strong criticism across the childhood services field. Senator Grimes 'acknowledges' that certain costs have to be met 'in order to provide the quality child care which parents want and children deserve'. But it is simply not clear what costs the government believes are essential to 'quality child care'. Everything is up for question—capital costs, training, wages, resources, administration.

Quite simply, the government betrays no more than a vague notion of what the nurturance of young children involves. After all, any 'good' mother can do it—and male politicians know little enough of that. Even so, the skills required are different where more than one family of children are involved (Clough, 1987:13), demanding something more than warm and wise responses to responsive children. At best, it is seen as emotional work, stereotypically women's work, which supposedly does not require organised effort, considerable energy, thought or planning. These assumptions are greatly at odds with the reality of what Penny Ryan calls 'the texture of work in a child care centre'. In addition to working directly with the idosyncracies of young children, it involves tasks ranging from managerial, to counselling, clerical and onwards (Ryan, forthcoming).

The government has laid claim to the goal of 'equity of access'. It has initiated plenty of activity with some attempt at long-term planning for strategic responses to high demand. Still, access to subsidised child care remains below 10 per cent and equity for care workers has been pushed aside.

Such 'pragmatism' has been contested by struggles for quantity as well as for quality. A notable example was the national campaign against the cuts during 1985–86. when parents, workers, union organisers, and child-care bureaucrats united with sufficient force to reduce the proposed $30 million cut to $10 million, and ensured that preschool funding would be picked up by the States. Given the nature of the work and the isolation of the workplaces, this was a significant achievement.

The campaign showed that alliances could be built across the diverse field which is children's services. Difficulties arise from differences over priorities between regions and sectors, and resources are severely stretched. This is countered somewhat because some unions have begun to add their weight to the demand for child care and for improved conditions for care workers.

Femocrats in the 1980s

Femocrats have featured very little in our account of the Hawke period. We find it difficult to discern what their approach has been , in sharp contrast to the visibility of femocrat involvement in the 1970s. There appear to be some differences between femocrats at the federal and at the State levels where, for example in New South Wales and South Australia, femocrats associated with child care are rather more visible. We note that the current women's adviser to the prime minister periodically underlines the importance of child care to working women, but public statements by femocrats to the press, at conferences, in the child care or feminist literature are rare. We find in informal discussions with child-care bureaucrats a mix of perceptions similar to those of femocrats

in other areas. Some are concerned about the directions of government policies while others are irritated by criticisms from the field which they believe undervalues the practical gains.

Some appear to have a strong commitment to a pragmatism which emphasises the question of cost since child care is a 'very expensive' community service. A consultant on child care to the minister for community services puts the argument this way: the problem is that in the past no-one has been game to say 'no' to the goal of universal access.

> ... even within the Department ... most discussion has focussed around the expansion of the [Children's Services] Programme and the remedying of existing defects. On that basis, the Federal Government and the Office of Child Care cannot win because it is impossible financially to provide universal access and to remedy existing problems. What is needed is for the people with the knowledge of child care, both in the Department and in the field, to face the hard questions and to come up with some workable solutions. (Hunter, 1985:20)

Margaret Hunter does refer to other problems such as poor pay, the possibility that family day care will become a cheap, unacceptable alternative to centre-based care, and conflicts between care and welfare. However, her 'hard' questions already propose the solution: replace the vision of universal access with a planned limited service. Anything else is either 'unrealistic' or 'unfair'. The argument becomes one of strict and specific management of scarce resources, leaving no room for the possibility of reforms as leverage for even gradualist social and political gains.

Others assume that nothing more need be done once the 20 000 places are realised. Certainly their establishment requires considerable organisation, but what then? We may expect some experimentation with 'multifunctional centres', more family day care and occasional care, more encouragement of commercial care. The possibility of achieving socialised care appears overwhelmed.

Ironically, Margaret Hunter sees the 'feminist lobby' as particularly influential, and no doubt feminist politics have had their effect. Feminists agree on its central importance. Still child care is not a central political issue in feminism. Partly this reflects ambivalence about children, about sharing care with men, and about sharing with other women. The English feminist Ruth Wallsgrove, reflecting on her own experiences of non-biological parenting and conflicts with feminist mothers, ponders the divisions between feminist mothers and non-mothers. Facilities to support mothers should be 'a major priority of the women's liberation movement'. Divisiveness arises out of the issue of control, which however restricted is granted to women as mothers. While recognising the attractions, she asks:

> Is the only way to survive such a woman-hating, child-excluding culture to take the small power and status the label 'mother' gives

us in return for the isolation? In which case, how can we prevent endless tension between mothers who feel unsupported—and non-mothers who feel betrayed? (Wallsgrove, 1985:28)

An example closer to home of political tensions around the issue may be found in the report of the National Women's Refuge Conference in 1986. Refuges typically shelter as many children as adult women. Funding usually includes one wage for a designated child-care worker. The conference devoted a block of time to discussion of children's issues which included the needs of Aboriginal children, of migrant children, and problems of incest, abuse and neglect. Considerable tensions emerged between those who worked with children and those who did not:

'Many women don't want to work with children and I think that's fine.'

'The low status of child care as I see it proves to me that children in refuges are put up with because we assist their mothers.' (Report 1986:9)

A long series of recommendations from the conference addressed other issues, for example the problem of incest; but there were none on child care.

Feminist ambivalence to the politics of child care perhaps derives from the association of children with women's dependence, such that the baby has been thrown out with the muddied ideological water of motherhood. Any challenge to women's primary responsibility for child care must entail the objective of sharing care with men. This involves a considerable strategic obstacle—men's cooperation. Such strategy questions the relationship between child care and the sexual divison of labour and the construction of sexual identity, including female dependency, male fears of intimacy and men's social power. Further, the replacement of an isolated mother with an equally isolated father is hardly an advance. And what happens when there is no parenting couple? Denise Riley cautions against the political goal of shared parenting: 'The redistributive justice of "shared parenting" does not do away with the stifling couple, the dead hand of the parent: instead all stays firmly within the family, in a way severely at odds with women's liberation aspirations ...' (Riley, 1983:152) Moreover, it is feminism which argues that the couple engaged in this private matter of domestic reorganisation do not start on an equal footing.

These are not problems created by feminists, but it is the task of feminism to find ways through them. The straightforward demand for universal child care must open out to encompass the complex of contradictory issues which child care has become. How do we reconcile critiques of ideologies of motherhood with family day care, where mothers are poorly paid to look after another mother's children? Public

child care enables mothers to work, but how does that low status, low paid form of 'women's work', child care itself, challenge the sexual division of labour?

Child care is still caught in the public/private dichotomy. Other components of women's domestic labour such as food preparation, cooking, laundry have moved readily into the public sphere of takeaways and laundromats. Child care as an extension of reproductive potential is that aspect of women's domestic labour most closely related to sexuality. Why has it been cornered so squarely?

The Australian feminist strategy of demanding state provision of child care must be re-evaluated politically. The initial campaign for state provision of centre-based child care resulted from a strategy seeking women's equality and the necessity to contest the terrain occupied by the pro-family preschool lobby. Implementation of such policy has tended to benefit middle-class English-speaking mothers. However, this bias was consequent on the way the policy was implemented, via submission-based funding, and recent funding formulas, rather than deriving from the child-care strategy itself.

We suggest that two lines of possibility are opened up. First, femocrat activity achieved sufficient child-care provision to provide the basis for broad political demands of the kind being made by the child-care movement. Second, centre-based care, managed by users and staff, is potentially progressive in contrast to other forms such as family day care which tends to affirm familial ideologies, privileging mother-care. A democratic centre-based management committee blunts the impact of state intervention, and the form of care incorporates a social component. The ambiguities mothers experience in relation to shared care would benefit from the increased visibility of such socialised care.

However, we must ask whether the limits of state reform have been reached. Clearly, the state's interests in the patriarchal gender order sustains its commitment to child care by women within the private sphere of the family. Should feminist child-care campaigns be directed more strongly at employers? Since child care is a crucial cost in the reproduction of labour why should not employers contribute instead of being subsidised as they are presently? But as unionists warn, there are difficulties in a proposition which allows employers even greater control of workers' lives.

Although the liberation of women demands fundamental change, including change in the state, feminist achievement of state-funded child care, albeit severely limited, provides an important beginning. To achieve feminism's goals Sheila Rowbotham's question—how shall we care for our children?—must become central to our political agenda.

5

Equal opportunity

'Equal opportunity' programs are probably the best known, the most
politically visible, product of feminism's interaction with the state. And
they deal for the most part with an equally visible issue. As Cynthia
Cockburn (1985:15) remarks, 'It is a fact known to the youngest school
child that women and men "do different jobs". A sexual division of
labour is one of the most marked and persistent of the patterns that
characterize human societies everywhere'.

A challenge to the discrimination inherent in the sexual division of
labour is intrinsic to the feminist project. The ways and means are
diverse and have certainly not been limited to the recent period.
Attempts to expose the poor conditions of women's paid work and to
counter them through unionisation, legislation, education or cooperatives, were all begun during the nineteenth century. As these challenges
continue to be mounted, so do the dilemmas over appropriate strategy.
So do theoretical questions, 'the problem in explanation' (Curthoys,
1986:320) about the continuous reproduction of job segregation by sex.
For it is not just a question of inheriting a 'traditional' division of
labour. As new technologies are introduced and new industries grow,
fresh sexual divisions of labour are created in them. The gender hierarchy in computing is a spectacular example (see Game and Pringle, 1983).

Our aim in this chapter is to ponder the challenge to job segregation
developed in the 1970s and 1980s under the rubrics of 'affirmative
action', 'equal opportunity' and 'anti-discrimination'. Much of this has
involved feminist pressure for legislation, and has thus highlighted the
sexual politics of the state. We will not present a detailed inventory of
programs; that is now available in a number of recent and useful sources.
(A general review of affirmative action can be found in Sawer, 1985; a
handbook on federal and State legislation is Ronalds, 1987; a summary
of New South Wales public and private sector programs is in Women's
Co-ordination Unit, 1987:74–82; an update on national programs is in
O'Donnell and Hall, 1988, chapter 5). Rather we will be concerned here
with the strategic shape of the issue. We will focus on what it tells us
about the interaction between the sexual politics of the state and the
character of paid work for women, and on the consequences, both

theoretical and practical, of the 'equal opportunity' strategy for feminism.

Since the terminology is overlapping and can be confusing, we define our terms as follows:

Anti-discrimination legislation applies to individual cases and forbids such actions as refusing to hire a woman for a job because of a preference for men in such jobs. Action under such legislation is case by case, and each case must be established retrospectively.

This is not sufficient to achieve equal employment opportunities for women. *Equal opportunity* (sometimes 'equal employment opportunity') is a broader term covering strategies to improve women's position in the labour market. (Like 'anti-discrimination' it can also apply to other disadvantaged groups). The idea is pro-active measures to open up a greater range of jobs to women as a group, and to ensure that women can compete on equal terms with men for promotion.

Anti-discrimination legislation is one means towards equal opportunity, but the principal means for achieving this policy is *affirmative action*. This is defined in the federal government's policy paper *Affirmative Action for Women* as a 'systematic means, determined by the employer in consultation with senior management, employees and unions, of achieving equal employment opportunities (EEO) for women. Affirmative Action is compatible with appointment and promotion on the basis of the principle of merit, skills and qualifications' (Department of Prime Minister and Cabinet, 1984:3).

Development of the strategy

Historically the most contentious aspect of the sexual segregation of labour in Australia has been unequal pay for women and men. Campaigns for equal pay after the Second World War eventually resulted in the 1969 Equal Pay Case, where women doing the same work as men were granted equal pay. As few women were doing the same work, about 15 per cent, the demands were not stilled. In December 1972, following a change of government, the Commonwealth Arbitration Commission adopted the concept of equal pay for work of equal value. Althouth women working under federal awards benefited from this decision, turning the concept into practice for all women workers has proved very troublesome. Part of the trouble lies in working out what 'work of equal value' means.

For the feminist movement the idea of the oppression of women in terms of their work did not rest entirely on the industrial concept of unequal pay. Familial ideologies, the constraints embedded in the motherhood 'role', constructions of sexuality, socialisation into a narrow band of expectations, and the division between public and domestic spheres, were reckoned to play their part. Thus, while campaigns seek-

ing to have unions and employers implement the 1972 decision continued, feminists began to make demands in other terms as well.

Equality of opportunity and an end to discrimination were early and consistent terms used by this wave of the feminist movement. One of the earliest Women's Liberation demonstrations protested against sexist job advertising. Equal opportunities for work and education was one of the major demands of a broadsheet in 1972. At the 1974 WEL Conference resolutions were passed to direct lobbying activity towards anti-discrimination legislation. In 1975 the South Australian parliament passed a Sex Discrimination Act and this was taken up as a model for lobbying in other States. Thus at WEL's National Conference the following year the New South Wales branch reported that it had presented a draft bill, based on the South Australian draft legislation, to the government and opposition of their own state.

Anti-discrimination legislation was achieved relatively quickly in South Australia (1975), New South Wales (1977) and Victoria (1977), making discrimination in employment on the grounds of sex unlawful. Similar demands made at the federal level were refused by the conservative Fraser government. In spite of the difficulties, demands that the state act to institute such change were increasingly made. The National Women's Advisory Council, established by the Fraser government, sponsored a conference on sex discrimination legislation in 1979. Two years later Senator Susan Ryan, of the Labor opposition, introduced a private member's bill which included provisions for mandatory affirmative action in the public sector. Commonwealth legislation was finally achieved under the Hawke government, with Susan Ryan as the sponsoring minister, with the Sex Discrimination Act 1984. Western Australia enacted anti-discrimination provisions in 1985. The conservative-controlled parliaments of Queensland and Tasmania (and the Northern Territory) hold out in favour of discrimination.

It seems that a broad spectrum of feminist women were, by the late 1970s, convinced that anti-discrimination legislation was essential—and that they had developed the political power to force the state to act. However, both lobbyists and those working within the state observed that anti-discrimination legislation was at best, a prerequisite for economic equality. Margaret Wallace (1985:20) points out the difficulty women have in proving that demotion, dismissal and retrenchment may be discriminatory under such policies as retrenching or demoting part-time workers first, the lack of job security for those in lower-paid jobs, and lack of economic benefits that accompany them. Recognition of discrimination against women in employment did not extend to the seemingly neutral practices of job segregation.

When discrimination is proved, the causes and therefore the locus of blame are difficult to sheet home. The findings of the first inquiry held by the New South Wales Anti-Discrimination Board drew attention to the unwitting nature of discrimination by finding *for* discrimination,

without intent being established. The case involved a woman teacher who claimed discrimination by the Department of Technical and Further Education (TAFE) in listing for promotion.

> In its decision the Board drew attention to the fact that the findings against TAFE did not involve findings that there was discrimination proceeding from what might be called high-handed, malicious motives but rather that it proceeded from sub-conscious assumptions and attitudes which when translated into behaviour, became unlawful. (Anti-Discrimination Board, 1978:11)

Findings of discrimination thus did not imply a conspiracy of conscious exclusion. In that sense, discrimination arose from a *world-view which was exclusive*. These assumptions became incorporated into the administrative practices and rules of the organisation and thus became systemic.

This analysis suggested that the problem was how to tackle *systemic* discrimination. But this is an interesting term. Feminist theorists of patriarchy (and capitalism) would claim that discrimination was already understood, in some part at least, in structural terms, i.e. beyond individual and conspiratorial attitudes. However the legal concept of 'systemic discrimination' does not necessarily imply an invidious patriarchy. Rather it is used to mean discrimination which is the unintentioned consequence of administrative rules and practices based on outdated assumptions about women's role in the workforce. In other words, it may imply no more than the well-worn notion of the 'centuries-old script' which is nobody's fault, consciously.

More importantly, the term suggests an attempt to grapple with the problem of the connection between individuals, their attitudes and behaviours, and social structures. While it is individuals who act, they do so within the context of existing sets of meaning. Perhaps none are more conscious of this paradox than those who work in bureaucracies. For those seeking to combat consistent discriminatory outcomes, the problem is particularly sharp. Umbrella concepts of 'patriarchy' which may name the connection between structure and outcome offer little help at this level. The question becomes one of finding the most effective strategic leverage.

If the focus is on individual actions, as in anti-discrimination legislation, social justice is obstructed by social structures. Yet tackling social structures is no small task, may allow individuals to escape, and *may*, depending on how the process is conceived, obscure gender difference. The idea of 'systemic discrimination' attempts to escape this dilemma by identifying and seeking to remove unintentional barriers to women's employment, be they attitudinal or structural. Any recognition of the relation between individual fate and social structure implies a need for means of action that go beyond the individual case. There is an inherent limit in the 'anti-discrimination' approach, which became well recognised. Much feminist lobbying energy was therefore exerted to broaden the perspective and emphasise the goal of 'equal opportunity'.

It was not enough for feminists to argue that equal pay and anti-discrimination legislation had failed—or more exactly, that so far resistance to the implementation of these principles had been largely successful. Some feminist groups, particularly those in unions, battled to overcome that resistance through, for example, the Working Women's Charter campaign. Others began to argue for additional measures to challenge systemic discrimination based on notions of efficiency, representation of interests and equity.

The argument in favour of equal opportunity based on efficiency seemed most persuasive, and was readily taken up by men engaged in modernising the state structure. Peter Wilenski, head of the inquiry into New South Wales government administration, wrote:

> The State can ill afford not to utilize to the full the energies and talents of the men and women who have been denied and are often still denied the opportunity to carry out jobs commensurate with their ability. The overall result of such discrimination has been that the quality and efficiency of government administration has been less than it otherwise might have been. (Wilenski, 1977:179)

The efficiency argument is designed to appeal both to the rationality of bureaucracy and to the productivity of the private sector. An *Australian Financial Review* article of 1979, observing the Australian reluctance to follow the North American example in implementing EEO programs, noted that the North Americans had done so on the grounds of productivity and profit: 'These programs, which operate compulsorily in the United States and voluntarily in Canada, are based on the premise that employing women is compatible with the need to improve productivity and profitability' (28 August 1979). Although the efficiency argument was taken up both by the Wran Labor government in New South Wales and by the Hawke Labor government in their endorsement of EEO, the North American precedent proved a political liability. It was perceived that the American model involved 'quotas' and compulsory positive discrimination for women—which is translated by conservatives as discrimination against men. Marion Sawer (1985) notes that proponents of equal opportunity have been anxious to disavow the American experience in order to distance themselves from the political problems now besetting those programs. This is unfortunate as it has cut Australian practice off from a rich source of experience. It has conceded from the start the argument against quotas—yet quotas of some kind are almost inevitable in an affirmative action program with teeth.

The argument from 'representation of interests' also has some force, especially with the Labor Party, which historically has got a lower proportion of women's votes than the conservative parties have. Involving more women in the party and in the government could improve its appeal to women voters. The argument even had some appeal to reformers of bureaucracy. Research has shown how socially selective in various ways the upper levels of bureaucracies are, and ideas of 'rep-

resentative bureaucracy' have some currency. 'Representation' is a familiar part of the language of democracy and hence of the legitimation
rhetoric of the liberal state.

However this democratic notion has limited effect. On the one hand,
it comes up against the view that in a liberal democracy everyone is
equally an individual and their various interests should be mediated only
by a neutral state. While this principle of the 'objectivity' of the state in
relation to its citizens is constantly being challenged in class and race
terms, and as we saw in Chapter 2 can equally be challenged in terms of
gender, the assertion of the specific and different interests of women is
both tricky and demanding in the face of the sexual politics of the state.
The state is not gender-blind, but rather, contributes to particular constructions of gender. Therefore gender interests cannot be simply 'added
on'.

Further, women may share the experience of gender-based oppression, yet such experiences are differentiated by class, race and sexuality
(at least). Yet 'representation of interests' came to mean simply that
women as a category were entitled to a fair proportion of the state's
jobs. An underlying assumption was that, since those who got state jobs
were women, they would automatically represent the interests of other
women. Differences among women were obscured, and major difficulties in the practice of representation glossed over. How, for instance,
were the specific interests of lesbian women (e.g. in housing, or in
divorce and custody) to be represented by heterosexual women whose
heterosexuality might be a criterion (however implicit) for having any
political power? Even homosexual men have had great difficulty getting
recognition in this context, and it is only the AIDS crisis that has finally
forced Australian governments to begin incorporating them into
representative/consultative structures.

The notion of a 'fair share' of the jobs is also the basis of the equity
argument, as seen in *Affirmative Action for Women*: 'The notion of equity
implies that everyone should have equal access, limited only by their
availability, to the opportunities and rewards available in society. In
terms of employment this means consideration of individuals on their
merits' (Department of Prime Minister and Cabinet, 1984:10). The idea
of 'merit' was the answer to fears of imposed quotas, and we will return
to it later. The equity argument sought to appeal to the principles of the
liberal democratic state—even perhaps to an Australian rhetoric of 'fair
go'. However, equity implies that if women do not have equal access
then something must be done in order for them to achieve it. And where
the availability of 'opportunities and rewards' is diminishing, the balance
may be evened up only if some men lose their access. The potential for
resistance by men, and organisations controlled by men, is very close to
the surface here.

In these three ways, the equal opportunity strategy promised the state
both rationality and legitimacy. It promised Labor governments a poli-

tical pay-off in terms of equity and popular support, at a certain risk. We do not suggest that it was simply the effectiveness and logic of these arguments which resulted in the adoption of equal opportunity policies and affirmative action programs. Nevertheless they began to materialise.

There is a certain confusion about targets. Although the terminology of 'equal opportunity' refers to all employment, in practice the target employer has been the state itself. Even more specifically the target has been the public service, and some aspects of education employment. Health work employment, especially nursing, has received relatively little attention compared with the education sector. Perhaps the relations between the state as employer and nurses as workers are more complex than with teachers. But we must look to the organisation and over-whelming meaning of nursing work as feminine, and to the long advo-cacy of equality of opportunity by feminist teachers and students for the beginning of an explanation.

The equal opportunity strategy importunes the state both as employer and as legislative apparatus. Underlying equal opportunity advocacy is the demand that it be buttressed by law. The absence of appropriate legislation in South Australia persuades Denise Bradley and Deborah McCulloch that equal opportunity policy alone can have little effect: 'Without legislation [EEO units] have to depend on the under-standing and goodwill of key people in the department concerned, who may give the matter priority if they decide to or who may push it to the bottom of the in-tray' (Bradley and McCulloch, 1985:99).

Legislation means both a requirement to act and a public commit-ment by the state. The paucity of argument directed at legislation for private sector employers is striking. Facts and figures on women's employment generally cover both private and public sectors, but action proposals usually focus on the latter. There is Australian legislation con-cerned with the private sector, but extremely cautious. The federal government's Affirmative Action (Equal Employment Opportunity for Women) Bill, 1986, described by one senator as a very gentle piece of legislation, invites private sector employers to establish affirmative action programs but does not oblige them to do so. When the Women's Co-ordination Unit in New South Wales was collecting material for its *A Decade of Change* (1987), it obviously had to scratch very hard to fill two pages on 'EEO initiatives in the private sector' (as compared with six pages on the public sector); and most of what it found was about the Commonwealth government's initiative.

Challenging the state's employment practices is no simple task as we shall see; but taking on the private sector through legislation involves even more difficult 'political factors'. As the *Age* reported on 2 October 1985: 'Senator Ryan concedes that the strategy was influenced by poli-tical considerations. "We wanted to keep business on side, yes ... I cer-tainly think it's a politically intelligent decision to go at a pace that will keep business locked in in a positive way".'

We could interpret this as faint-heartedness by a government committed to retaining power. Women's Electoral Lobby, for example, has criticised the phasing in and the weak sanctions as unnecessary concessions to the male controllers of the private sector. However, we suggest that the 'political considerations' indicate the state's lack of autonomy, or to put it another way, this shows how it is enmeshed with the relations of capital. The government is under pressure to sustain 'business confidence' and keep the controllers of capital contented. At the same time, as the contemporary socialist analysis of the state mentioned in Chapter 1 shows, the state is far from being a mere agent of capital. WEL is correct to criticise, since the issue is one of how far the state can assert its own interest (or indeed the long-term interests of capital) in the face of resistance by particular capitalists. The timidity of the Labor government refuses to make the test.

We have focused on the arguments around equal opportunity; let us now turn to the process of implementation. The mechanisms of implementation comprise an explicit program, variously called 'Action Plans' or 'EEO Management Plans', and one or more staff with specific responsibility for the program, known as 'EEO coordinators' or practitioners. The programs generally seek to be seen as rational and logical within the terms of corporate management science. Thus the typical program, based on 'problem solving models' and 'corporate planning models', would distinguish several stages, for instance:

1 *Preliminary* gaining commitment from the staff, appointing EEO staff, consultation
2 *Research* employment statistics of women, identification of barriers, discriminatory practices
3 *Development* of remedial programs and strategies
4 *Implementation*
5 *Evaluation*

'Implementation' stated so baldly seems rather breathtaking. Undaunted, the rational approach breaks it up into objective, specific target, specific action, responsibility, evaluation, timing, and so on. What is to be done—and what can be done—appears under 'specific action'. The possibilities range from producing and circulating information, stepping up training programs, eliminating practices in selection which assume a male work pattern, treating women and men in the same way in both selection and wage conditions, seeking equal representation of women on committees.

The plan is sponsored by the EEO practitioners, although the rhetoric is that everyone in the organisation becomes a practitioner. The various manuals we have consulted emphasise that EEO is a management initiative and therefore EEO practitioners must be appointed at management levels. Their job descriptions refer to an understanding of

EEO, negotiation skills, knowledge of the organisation's structure and functions, and credibility. Here the possibility of conflict over implementation begins to surface. Rationality alone will not win the day. A South Australian manual says pointedly: 'The success of the EEO management planning program will depend on the choice of [the senior] executive officer' (Equal Opportunities Branch, 1985:7).

Still, appointment of any EEO officer constitutes an appropriate 'action', a signal of compliance, if not commitment. The women (mainly) who take up these appointments are commonly located in 'units', a term which disguises the small numbers of staff in them. They themselves carry out many of the tasks designated in affirmative action programs, while endeavouring to obtain cooperation from other staff. At a minimum, they seek to sidestep resistance and to gain enough resources to achieve something.

One experienced observer notes: 'For most EEO co-ordinators the workload continues to be overwhelming. In part this resulted from the under-resourcing of EEO offices, sometimes because the size of the undertaking has been underestimated' (Eisenstein, 1985b:82). Although commitment by 'top' management is deemed vital, low cost was an important selling poing. Coordinators are left with small budgets and, with some exceptions, an abstract commitment. (A significant exception was Neville Wran as premier of New South Wales, who was known to override bureaucratic obstruction to equal opportunity from time to time. Few other ministers have done this).

These circumstances encourage EEO officers to attempt to move their programs into the mainstream and themselves into 'top' management. Or at least, themselves. This causes trouble with other feminists, an issue that will be explored in Chapter 7 below. EEO officers characteristically face the dilemma of being marginal to the bureaucracy or being suspected, even ostracised, by the women's movement.

Debate about the strategy

Hester Eisenstein (1986) has nicely called affirmative action 'feminist judo'—'throwing with the weight of the state'. Given the major organising and legitimating role the state plays in the economy, plus its significance as a direct employer, it offers powerful leverage on the sexual division of labour—if that leverage can be used.

There is disagreement on what the record so far reveals, whether the game has proved to be worth the candle. Most proponents argue it is too soon to tell, although they believe equal opportunity work has large potential to challenge discriminatory employment practices and to achieve equal access to paid work for women. They can point to a substantial record of EEO research and action, perhaps most notably (in Australia) in the New South Wales bureaucracy under the aegis of the

New South Wales Director of Equal Opportunity in Public Employment, Alison Ziller. Research done by her office (cited by Chapter 1) documents gradual changes in employment patterns in the 1980s which are moving in the desired direction.

Feminist critics range from those expressing caution to those expressing complete rejection. Verbal debates we have heard tend to confuse programs and people. Where there is hostility it is frequently focused on the EEO practitioners. The issue becomes 'Are they feminists?' For present purposes we will distinguish between equal opportunity as a strategy and EEO practitioners (affirmative action officers) as people.

The most damning criticism of equal opportunity as a strategy is directed at the notion of 'equality'. Feminists have couched many of their demands in terms of equality yet they have long made stringent criticisms of its meaning. Quite simply, equality has a relativity problem: equal with what , or whom?

The liberal-feminist answer was 'other individuals'. In this framework, equality of individuals is possible within the liberal democratic state which represents and protects the rights of free and equal individuals as citizens. However, we can easily notice that the 'other individuals' are men (although not all men are free and equal). Feminists are often bemused that liberal political theory fails to make this observation. Feminism has put much energy, historically, into strategies that enable women to become equal individuals. As a result, women can now act as citizens in many ways. They can vote, incur debts, have custody of their children and so on. Proponents of equal opportunity argue that they should also be able, as men are, to act as equal individuals in employment. There is a kind of citizenship right in economic life also.

And this is the problem. Equalness denies difference. Specifically, the equal opportunity strategy appears to deny *women's* difference, since the goal is to become equal with the normative male individual. As Carole Pateman points out (1986:8) this can 'all too frequently result in absurdities, or work against women'. She cites the US example of a decision that the exclusion of maternity benefits from insurance was constitutional because it depended on 'disability' (i.e. pregnancy) and not on sex—as if men could suffer from this 'disability'. 'Equality' then fails to challenge the model by which the male individual is taken as the universal case.

This is a central point in feminist theory, over the last decade, and it is clear that simple conceptions of 'equality' cannot gain general feminist support. Can a repair job be done on the concept, adding a recognition of difference on to the principle of equality—a kind of 'equal but different' approach? One danger here is that this has been the legitimating rhetoric of patriarchy in the past—for instance the ideology of 'companionate marriage' and 'togetherness' in the 1950s. Perhaps more importantly, it runs into the problem raised earlier in the book, how do we know when we are winning? How could progress be tested? As Merle Thornton asks,

What performance among women shall we compare to senior public service performance, say, among men, in order to make a judgement whether women are rising towards equal freedom with men in their self-development? Alternatively, we might see that certain changes in the structure of the public service would favour women's development through the public service ... How much change, which changes, would count as having made the structures equally hospitable to the genders' divergent developments through the public service? (Thornton 1986:96)

Although state institutions assume men's interests as normative, they do not currently enable the development of all men, or even most. Here the socialist-feminist emphasis on the interplay of class with gender is essential. The main beneficiaries of the current system are a privileged minority among men. Large numbers of working–class men, in state employment as in the private sector, are confined to monotonous jobs with little creativity or responsibility.

For the institutions to become 'hospitable' to women's development, change would have to be fundamental enough to shift this structure of dominance which delivers authority to bourgeois, white, heterosexual men and institutionalises it in a hierarchy among men. We suspect that we would recognise change then. In such a process of change, the relational terms of 'equality' would shift. It would be impossible to sustain a 'universal male individual' as a norm—indeed it would become clear that that norm has always been fraudulent. Diversity of social character, within a framework of shared access to the collective resources of society, would be the norm.

It is clear that the 'equal opportunity' strategy in itself does not intend such a change. Paradoxically, however, the strategy does bring the 'universal male individual' into question through its practice. Sue Wills, an equal opportunity practitioner, points out how the strategy assumes that the employment problems of an extraordinary diversity of groups can all be solved by the same mechanism (Wills, 1986). When they are not, the notion of a single standard of reference comes into question.

The issue of 'equal pay' was, clearly enough, framed around the concept of a male norm. The 'equal opportunity' strategy inherited from it a focus on ensuring equal access to jobs as they are presently structured. Affirmative action modifies existing training, recruitment and selection procedures in order to remove any practices which discriminate against women. This is the point of the 'equity' argument. Workers have a right to be treated fairly, without bias based on sex difference. Equity challenges the presumed objectivity of these procedures. It does not address the way jobs themselves are valued.

Affirmative action does not propose that clerical work, for example, be paid an increased wage. Nor does the hierarchical organisation of jobs, in terms of pay and autonomy, come into its purview. Rather affirmative action seeks to lift some women from the typing pool into the decisionmaking and management sections of the hierarchy. The

emphasis, perhaps the most visible priority of affirmative action, is on promotion: promotion in the refurbished terms of the organisation. The possibility of demanding equal pay for work of equal value is sidelined and fundamental challenge to conventionally defined work is severely limited.

Two qualifications must be made to this criticism. First, the quickest glance at the distribution of women through employment hierarchies, be they public or private, reveals an appalling skew to women's participation. In November 1987, 30.6 per cent of full-time paid workers were women, but they made up 78 per cent of part-time paid workers. The full-time workers averaged 79 per cent of male earnings (Australian Bureau of Statistics, 1987). In June 1985, some 78 women made up 5 per cent of the Senior Executive Service of the federal public service (the management level), despite women being 39.5 per cent of federal government public servants as a whole. The pattern of few or no women in senior positions is depressingly familiar whether we examine government bureaucracies, private industry, educational institutions or unions and political parties.

On this evidence, if equal opportunity has focused on promotion and access to seniority, it has not been without reason. Seniority means greater power. As Eva Cox remarks: 'Women may have the illusion of power or autonomy because they "manage" services and resources in households and community, even the workplace. However, as long as women are not in decision making positions they will still be objects not subjects in control of the situation' (1982:31). We will return to the dilemmas inherent in this approach but here will remark that in their own terms the statistics encourage the stress on promotion.

Our second qualification is that while 'equal opportunity' in general does not question existing occupational structures, in practice it can lead to their being challenged. An example is attempts to develop career structures for some occupations that have not had them in the past. Thus the *Affirmative Action Handbook* suggests the following action:

> The identification of career structures with limited opportunity, e.g. key-board operation and nursing, and, where appropriate, their consolidation with related career structures which provide more scope for advancement, or the creation of greater opportunities for lateral transfer to related career structures. (Ziller, 1980:60–61)

Removal of barriers, or at least monitoring their impact, additional training and changes of titles constitute the specific actions of this strategy. The value of the occupations and the division of labour are not changed; here affirmative action seeks to remove impediments to the upward flow of workers into the rest of the structure.

Value and the division of labour can nevertheless come into question. The former is likely to require large-scale industrial action, such as

occurred in nursing in South Australia and Victoria in 1986. Employer resistance (and indeed that of some unions) to that endeavour provides an indicator of how embedded ideas of the value of occupations are. Part of the reason for the new industrial politics of nurses is a changing division of labour in their industry. The issue can arise in equal opportunity work. Sue Wills gives a nice example:

> I've spent time over the last six months following the job evaluation officers at Macquarie University around while they interviewed members of the general staff about whether of not the work they're doing warrants the position they occupy being upgraded. The job evaluation system does not allow for any element of personal merit and the major criterion for upgrading is whether the responsibilities and duties of the job—not the volume of work done—have increased over time.
>
> The job evaluation officers can't actually articulate how they determine whether responsibilities have increased. One of the criteria being applied is that of supervision of others within a fairly strict hierarchical notion of supervision: and supervision of others is rewarded by upgrading.
>
> One of the sections under review consisted of several women. When two of the more highly graded of them were interviewed, they were asked whether they supervised the others in the day-to-day sense of work allocation, approval of leave and flexitime, and so on. Good heavens, no, we all work it out together, we do the work that has to be done and we just make sure that we're not all away at the same time. No supervision, no upgrading. (Wills, 1986:24)

A possible response to that, Wills argues, 'would be to try to change the system of values at work which penalises co-operative work relations rather than rewards them'.

How far that potential in equal opportunity work will be realised has yet to be seen. The fact that it emerges in practice gives some support to the arguments of those proponents who emphasise the potentials in the strategy. It must still be said that for the most part the strategy has limited reach. Within specific boundaries, it has considerable leverage. The resistance to equal employment opportunity measures that keeps emerging inside bureaucracies as well as in the media is an index of its practical impact.

The 'equal opportunity' strategy makes extensive use of a claim to objectivity. Appointments and promotions should be based on objectively assessed skills, more broadly on 'merit', uninfluenced by attributes such as sex or race. The notion of merit is a keystone of affirmative action.

Yet as we have seen, in several discussions of patriarchy as procedure (Chapter 2 above) the basic idea of objectivity is called into question by feminism. So it is to be expected that the definition of 'merit' comes into question in equal opportunity work. It tends to be used in ideological

ways. We recall, for instance, two promotion rounds in a college of advanced education. The first saw one woman among the nine people promoted; the second saw six women among the eleven promoted. Some men objected that obviously the second round was not based on merit. They were shocked at the suggestion that in that event perhaps the first was not either. When men are promoted it is merit, when women are it is news.

The meaning of 'merit' can no longer be taken for granted. Indeed a national conference was organised in 1985 called 'Defining Merit'. Here Clare Burton proposed a definition which referred 'not to a stable quality of an individual but a range of qualities, many of which are the product of relationships with other people and of responses to opportunities offered' (Burton, 1985:1). She argued that as those relationships are constructed in terms of gender, and as definitions depend on the power of groups to define them, the attribution of merit is not neutral. This is the sticking point for criticism of affirmative action's emphasis on merit. The dominant liberal view of the individual is confronted by social conceptions of merit. Already the neutrality of the term is assailed by conflict over meaning. And yet, while affirmative action has provoked this debate, it must retain the objectivity, the neutrality of merit. Equity or fair treatment requires a transcendent marker, fixed beyond the reach of particular interests.

Here both the potency and the limits of liberal thinking are visible. The equal opportunity strategy argues that were merit to be truly objective, if it could be drained of gender, the meritorious qualities of women as individuals would be recognised. This argument is impossible to refute within bureaucratic terms of reference. Its consequences may be evaded, but as argument, equal opportunity has carried the day. However, the liberal understanding of individuals qua individuals fails to comprehend the historical processes by which 'individuals' are socially constructed. It gives no grip on the texture of sexual, racial and class experiences that shape both situations and responses to them.

In consequence the equal opportunity strategy abstracts from the social context in a radical way, and tends to miss much of the potential (e.g. for solidarity and collective action) in the lives of the disadvantaged groups with whom it deals. This leaves it in a relatively weak position to deal with the political conundrum created when, in challenging the gendered distribution of 'merit', it engages in the politicisation of the concept whose objectivity is its own tactical base. Opponents of affirmative action well recognise this conundrum.

The reform workforce and the feminist agenda

The equal opportunity strategy has become highly visible in the 1980s among women in various public service bureaucracies, in education

especially at the tertiary level, and in some white-collar unions. The people responsible for the programs, affirmative action officers, likewise have come in for an unusual degree of attention. Discussions of equal opportunity, including those among feminists, focus readily on their actions and attitudes. Debates give way to complaints directed at their behaviour. This is understandable but inadequate. To grasp their political significance requires analysis, getting some grip on the perennial problem of how to comprehend the individual and the social together.

The role of affirmative action officer seems designed to attract criticism. Formally it is supposed to initiate change within the organisation of which it is part. The location of affirmative action officers intrudes upon mainstream bureaucratic structures. Their presence challenges procedures and taken-for-granted assumptions about issues of promotion, merit and skill. And they require resources. Given all this, it is not surprising to find resistance. But it is the content of the change, the goals of affirmative action, which generate the real resistance.

Criticism of affirmative action officers comes from two sides, conservative and feminist. Conservative criticism, usually but not exclusively from men, regards affirmative action officers as disruptive and threatening. They are likely to be seem as 'radical feminists' promoting sectional interests. They are thought to have found short cuts through the organisation.

Such antagonism was foreseen by the proponents of equal opportunity. Alison Ziller's *Affirmative Action Handbook* for example devotes a whole section to ways of 'forestalling and withstanding negative and hostile responses'. As 'figurehead of the programmes' the affirmative action officer represents the easiest target for sexist attacks and fears of the programs (Ziller, 1980:77,79). Clare Burton (1986:295) suggests that such antagonism arises from the fear that affirmative action challenges the masculine meaning of work. The maleness of power, bound up with the sexual construction of the value of work, is put on the line by the presence of affirmative action officers. There is a level of symbolic politics which is powerfully stirred by the equal opportunity strategy.

Although the *Affirmative Action Handbook* is imaginative about the difficulties that officers are likely to encounter, it stresses the role of the individual officer. She should seek advice, gain support, adopt a fair but firm demeanour; but, by and large, she stands alone. It is understandable then that, confronted by men's resistance and the coils of bureaucratic politics, affirmative action officers tend to advocate 'beating them at their own game'. As the man said, 'if you want a man's job, then you have to drive a man's car'. Isolation is overcome by an emphasis on 'networking' (to counter the 'old boy's network'). Bureaucratic weakness is overcome by a search for promotion, and in Adelaide perhaps peculiarly, by personal skills workshops. The intention is to gain the kind of power that men have.

In bureaucracies this means the individual achievement of senior

management positions. As Lesley Lynch points out: 'EEO co-ordinators are increasingly stressing [their] role as EEO managers ... or even, in terms of current management school jargon, as Human Resource Managers' (Lynch, 1984:43). We suggested earlier that to construe affirmative action as a management initiative encourages this tendency. It coincides with the liberal-feminist argument that women must seek decisionmaking positions to gain control and thereby overcome or overwhelm conservative male resistance. Paradoxically the position of affirmative action officer, which is designed to advocate equality of opportunity for women, has taken on board the admonition to 'drive a man's car'.

In neat counterpoint, feminist critics of affirmative action officers see this tendency as confirmation of their original suspicions. Charges of elitism, co-option, management style, poor management, self-interest, anti-unionism, even criticisms of their dress (the silk shirt syndrome) have all been levelled. In their turn affirmative action officers believe themselves misunderstood and rejected, and think non-bureaucratic feminists naive. Anne Summers (1986:64) sees such critics as betraying an 'ignorance of the power of bureaucratic structures and the ability of governments to marshall these to their political ends'. If feminists only knew the inside story of the twists and turns of state power they would understand, their suspicions would be allayed.

These criticisms and tensions are well known. The femocrats who have gone into print on their experiences readily admit to them. Very often, what they boil down to is the question: 'Are affirmative action officers feminist?' Better, we might ask how to comprehend the relation of affirmative action officers to feminism.

Our starting point on this question is that whether affirmative action officers claim to be feminist or not, they have taken up appointments formally designed to implement and promote equal opportunity in their organisations. They are therefore involved in woman-oriented programs which assume, broadly, that women are disadvantaged in employment. There is an inextricable connection with the feminist project. Thus affirmative action officers are inescapably part of the women's movement. More: they are a major part of the women's movement's *power,* its outreach (so to speak), its ability to influence the world.

This gives a particular edge to debates about the interplay. The responsibility cuts both ways. Affirmative action officers cannot deny accountability to the movement by pointing to the rules of bureaucracy which may demand secrecy. But neither can feminists outside the bureaucracy escape the import of the equal opportunity strategy through the rejection of affirmative action officers.

So we argue that 'Are they feminists?' is the wrong question. However, we do think it appropriate, indeed essential, to ask about practices and objectives. For example, we would question the lack of progress in having child care considered as an essential component of affirmative

action. Affirmative action officers seek to ensure that women may not be asked at job interviews about their child-care responsibilities, this being a familiar move in discrimination against women. But without access to adequate facilities, job opportunity *is* restricted by the material reality of child-care obligations. We are also concerned by failures to recognise the significance to the goals of equal opportunity of the political struggles of feminists in trade unions. Here the orientation of affirmative action officers towards management, and their tendency to absorb management perspectives as they rise into the upper echelons, may be seriously damaging to the relevance of the equal opportunity strategy to working-class women.

Our questions must be addressed to the politics of equal opportunity, not only to the practices of the affirmative action officers. Since the strategy is premised on liberal feminism it is subject to the general criticisms of that perspective made earlier. The formal agenda of affirmative action officers is construed in liberal-feminist terms and therein lies the limit to their potential to mount a fundamental challenge to the state and to the sexual division of labour. The political practices of affirmative action officers are limited by the theory of liberal feminism, even if they represent a distinctive version of it.

There is a danger that bureaucratic liberal feminism, materialised in the equal opportunity strategy, limits the agenda of the broad women's movement which affirmative action officers are widely held to represent. The outcome will depend on the actions of both the officers and other feminists. We have argued that affirmative action officers and their programs are in important ways disruptive of the conventional practices of bureaucracy. We agree with Zillah Eisenstein (1981) that liberal feminism is potentially subversive, but realising that potential depends on pushing at the contradictions of liberal feminism and of the state's relationship to it. Eisenstein is not alone in claiming that the struggle must be joined by feminists outside the state. This issue has not been resolved within the Australian women's movement. Struggle there will continue to be, since the impact of the equal opportunity strategy on the women's movement, and its effect on the state's relationship to women's employment, cannot be ignored.

6

Sexual violence

Nothing betrays the awful ambiguities of the state's part in the construction of the patriarchal gender order as sharply as sexual violence. Nothing reveals the dilemmas of feminism's relation to the state as intensely as struggles to challenge sexual violence. A dramatic statement perhaps, but the threat and the fact of sexual violence is unremitting and pervasive. Sometimes flaring into a cryptic headline which solicits shock and horror, sexual violence more commonly grinds on with a numbing banality: a wife's constant fear; the lurking threat of no promotion, no pass grade, if you don't 'come across'; gay men bashed in a main street; 'it's just our little secret'; no means yes; a few acres of video porn; a woman and child escaping from 'home' with nowhere to go. The apparent endlessness of sexual violence grows into a fatiguing monotony for the refuge workers, counsellors, medical workers, police, social workers who get very tired from dealing with it. But the victims too get tired, from the pain of physical and emotional damage, from deciding what to do, repeating the story to helpers, to interrogators, to the courts—and living with the results.

This is the paradox of sexual violence: horrifying yet dull; we don't want to know but become fascinated by sensational detail. The issues are enormously complicated and at the same time obviously simple.

In this chapter, we discuss two instances of feminists' challenge to sexual violence: the campaign to reform rape law, and the development and implementation of social policy on child sexual abuse. Both of these feminist campaigns are distillations of immensely complex historical, political and social issues. But as we shall see these campaigns are not the pure essence of the issues. How could they be when they exemplify politics in process; the interplay of theory and practice?

In each of the case studies, our focus is that interplay in so far as it bears on the politics of feminist engagement with the state. We will concentrate on those arguments on sexual violence which emerge in the campaigns rather than consider the whole gamut of ideas on the subject.

Not the least of the problems involved are those to do with terms, and we shall consider specific debates in the relevant sections. On

'sexuality' we adopt an approach along the lines developed by writers like Jeffrey Weeks who sees sexuality as relational: '[it] is shaped in social interaction, and can only be understood in its historical context, in terms of the cultural meanings assigned to it, and in terms of the internal, subjective meanings of the sexed individuals that emerge' (Weeks, 1981:12). The conjoint term 'sexual violence' is useful, although we are wary of the tendency for 'violence' to suggest only physical force. Physical force is usually mingled with other forms of coercion and it is the whole spectrum of aggression and abuse that is in question. The major difficulty however, lies in the link between 'violence' and 'sexual'. Is it possible to separate them, for example in an analysis of rape? This question in particular has great bearing on feminist campaigns.

We suggest that feminism's challenge to sexual violence is fraught with dilemmas; the association of sex and violence is one. Equally difficult, we argue, is the role of the state. Feminist campaigns on sexual violence cannot ignore it.

The state and sexual violence

A central characteristic of the state is its capacity to exercise power: to claim a monopoly of physical force to protect citizens and to set limits and establish constraints on behaviour. The state exercises legitimate violence and defines what is illegitimate. But it does not have a monopoly of violence. Rather it aims to act as the agency of regulation, as the recent attempts at gun law reform illustrate. The state seeks to maintain a 'particular configuration of power relationships'—including force and violence—among citizens, and among the institutions of society (Hall, 1984:22). The state seeks to arbitrate social order through the law, the courts, the police, welfare bureaucracies. State power is exercised through a set of practices in the apparatuses of the modern state machine. But state apparatuses are not unitary, as we demonstrated in Chapter 3.

When women and children are raped, sexually and physically assaulted, and they turn to the state seeking protection and retribution, the response at best is ambiguous. The situation for gay men is at least as punitive and as complex; gay men almost never report assault for fear of being criminalised themselves.

The state monopolises the control of violence among its citizens but it distinguishes sexual violence from other forms. This distinction may be understood as based on the premise that sexual relations, and thus sexual violence between men and women, are usually private, familial and therefore beyond state intervention, if not state control. But the state does intervene. It devises stringent legal sanctions against sexual violence, especially certain types of rape. As the Crown it takes the part of

prosecutor against the perpetrator. The problem for women and children is not the absence of intervention but the underlying assumptions of intervention and their effects.

The assumptions made are patriarchal in that the state relates to women and children through their familial connections with husbands and fathers. Both rape law and social policy on child sexual abuse are shaped by the state's commitment to patriarchal familial relations. The citizenship rights of women and children are mediated by the family, and in this sense the state recognises the privacy of sexual relations. But it is a privacy dominated by men as husbands and fathers. So the state exercises its power to protect its citizens from the sexual violence of men ambiguously and, at times, reluctantly.

Sexual relations are not only defined as private but are also imbued with patriarchal ideologies of sexuality. Women are passive and seductive, don't know what they want, yet somehow are manipulative. Men are active and sexually excitable, dominated by sexual desire, yet responsible. The connections between the state and ideologies of sexuality are a minefield of contradictions. When the Crown prosecutes on behalf of the victim the woman is the witness. But she becomes the subject of interrogation. The procedures of the law focus on the question of her capacity as a witness. This question emerges as central because patriarchal assumptions about women as citizens, as sexual beings, preclude natural honour. It is not enough for the woman to say: I have been violated and I demand the retribution of the law.

Feminists and sexual violence

How have feminists tackled the problem of sexual violence? Elizabeth Wilson (1983:59) says that one of the main tasks for feminists has been to get the world at large to take crimes of sexual violence against women seriously. This task involves making clear what sexual violence means, to 'the world at large' and to women specifically; and developing political strategies for change. As always, the dynamics of theory and politics are not simple, but one point is clear: the inescapable presence of the state. The state's monopoly of the control of force ensures that feminism must deal with the state in relation to sexual violence. Vengeance is mine; I will repay, saith the state.

To be taken seriously first requires that sexual violence be seen to be a problem, and this feminists have achieved. But not all at once. Although men's violence against women was recognised in early second-wave feminist writings, its effect and meanings were not emphasised. Thus *Sisterhood is Powerful* (1970) included no articles on rape nor on the broader problem of sexual violence. One writer notes that 'the other crude and often open weapon that a man uses to control his wife is the threat of force itself' (Jones, 1970:47). Germaine Greer's

The Female Eunuch, published in the same year, canvasses the problem in powerful terms of male loathing and disgust, the implications of which 'have got to be understood by any movement for female liberation' (Greer, 1970:258).

Five years later, Anne Summers produced a detailed discussion of rape as the male colonisation of women's bodies. She goes beyond the legal definition of rape to include marital rape, petty rape (*sic*) and rape by fraud. Although 'everyone is against rape, even rapists' Summers reaches the dismal conclusion that rape can occur any time, anywhere. There is virtually nothing women can do to prevent it (Summers, 1975:209). In addition to the discussion on rape, she makes brief reference to other dimensions of sexual violence. The setting up of the first Sydney Women's Shelter, Elsie, in 1974, is recorded but Summers does not elaborate on the problems for women forced to share houses with 'brutal and violent men' (1975:132).

By force Summers means women's lack of alternatives to their economic dependence on men within the family—and this has become an important element in explanations of women's responses to most forms of sexual violence. Feminists consider that state policies on taxation, welfare services, work conditions (e.g. pay and child care), police practices, etc. tend to buttress the family rather than provide opportunities for women's independence. The consequence is that domestic violence remains hidden within the family.

During the 1970s, feminists, drawing on their own experiences and those of women who had come to shelters, information from telephone counselling and so on, began to dispute the view that sexual violence occurred as isolated, deviant acts. Susan Brownmiller's influential book *Against Our Will* made the striking claim that '[rape] is nothing more or less than a conscious process of intimidation by which *all* men keep *all* women in a state of fear' (Brownmiller, 1976:107). Acts of sexual violence are not aberrations but rather, consistent with a whole culture's antagonism towards women. The state's policies and practices are not exempt, as Catharine MacKinnon (1982:83) subsequently argued.

We are struck by the degree of consensus in the feminist literature on sexual violence. The general premise is that sexual violence represents assertions of patriarchal power by men against women. Differences arise over questions of emphasis (Is rape central to women's oppression?) and of strategy. The latter is not derived solely from analysis of the sexually violent event but is necessarily shaped by legal and social policy definitions which vary according to the several 'forms' of sexual violence. Thus the various feminist tendencies focus political strategies on different aspects of the problem.

Radical feminism holds that rape is the fundamental instrument of the system of male domination. 'Rape is the ultimate outward and physical act of coercion and depersonalization practised on women by men ... When you strike the chord of sexuality in the patriarchal psyche, the

chord of violence is likely to vibrate in response; and vice versa' (Rich, 1979;110–15). Men, male sexuality, heterosexuality are the problem. Separatism is an obvious response although of itself cannot stop rape. Solutions are difficult. Susan Griffin says 'no simple reforms can eliminate rape' (Griffin, 1971:168). But Brownmiller recommends that women take over the police and seek harsh legal punishments. In effect, women must become part of the state apparatus of coercion.

Australian radical feminists, like their sisters elsewhere, sought solutions through the self-help of direct action—self-defence and the support service of rape crisis centres. They offered a challenge both to ideologies of rape and to women's acceptance of their own complicity. Such strategies rapidly came up against the state through necessary contact with the police, the courts, and welfare agencies; and through the need for funds to provide feminist services. Women victims of sexual violence reported that the subsequent legal, medical and welfare proceedings frequently exacerbated the trauma of the event itself. Feminists were dismayed, although perhaps not surprised, that the state agencies caused such ordeals. Direct action in support of women had to include close attention to the workings of those agencies. Radical feminists began to demand reforms to agencies, demands which coincide with those being made by liberal feminists.

Liberal feminists agreed with the emphasis on the oppressiveness of rape for all women, but saw reforms to rape laws as the key strategy. Changes to the law would achieve social justice for rape victims, and would alter community perceptions of rape and of the victims. And women must be involved in that process of change.

Rape law reform: the New South Wales Act

During the last ten years, reforms to rape laws have been achieved in most State jurisdictions. This appears a notable victory for feminist politics. The question is, reforms to what effect? Do such reforms represent a successful challenge to the state's patriarchal assumptions about sexual violence? We shall consider the New South Wales Crimes (Sexual Assault) Amendment Act 1981 and the feminist campaign around it as our main focus.

The feminist push for law reform gained some ground when the newly elected New South Wales Labor government established, in 1976, the Criminal Law Review Division in the Department of the Attorney-General and of Justice. The Attorney-General directed that priority be given to the review of the law of rape, since the government had received 'many submissions calling for reform'. A review committee was constituted, its members including lawyers, and representatives of the Police Department, of Women's Electoral Lobby and of the New South Wales Women's Advisory Council. Its report in 1977 proposed

reforms compatible with the climate of the New South Wales Anti-Discrimination legislation.

The report saw the common-law definition of rape—that rape consists in having unlawful vaginal intercourse with a woman without her consent—as sexist. The 1981 legislation arising from the report amended the definition so that the victim could be male, the crime sex-neutral. It extended the meaning of rape to include 'sodomy' (anal penetration) and 'penetration per os' (through the mouth). And the legislation recognised that rape could occur within marriage.

The last caused little controversy in New South Wales in striking contrast to the conservative outrage aroused by the South Australian reform five years earlier. Then, as one politician complained, the criminalisation of rape in marriage was 'minority legislation designed to protect the few, yet putting at risk an institution revered and respected by the majority of Australians'. Anne Summers quipped: 'it was not clear whether he was referring to rape or to marriage' (Summers, 1977: quoted in Russell, 1982:335). In New South Wales this particular reform allowed the government to claim it was addressing 'the entire area of violence against women' since recognition of rape in marriage implied cognisance of domestic violence generally. Nevertheless, the prosecution of rape in marriage remains more a stated principle than a procedural reality in both States.

The most controversial recommendation of the New South Wales committee was to rename the crime of rape 'sexual assault'. The committee agreed that the definition of rape and hence the law and its procedures were sex-specific: rape was a crime against a woman involving penetration of the vagina. The recommendation drew on a US precedent in the Michigan Sexual Assault Act of 1975 which replaced 'rape' with graded offences of 'sexual assault'.

Feminists split on the issue. The WEL submission to the committee (WEL Draft Bill) strongly advocated 'sexual assault' with its associated possibilities of graded offences. Although WEL consulted the Sydney Rape Crisis Centre, the centre later published its unequivocal opposition to renaming. Changing the words would further disguise who rapes (men) and who is raped (women); it would contribute to the ideological denial of the 'all-pervasive and persistent threat' of rape. The radical feminist position of the Rape Crisis Centre saw renaming as *not* naming rape. Those in favour of renaming sought to separate the violence inherent in rape from sexual desire, i.e. to take the sex out of rape. But this is not simply done.

The meanings of rape and sex are complex. The complexities are commonly discussed in terms of myths, and most writing on rape refers to the 'mythologies' of rape. They are generally described either as instances of unwarranted sexism or of male oppressiveness. In a rare study of the conceptual background, Lesley Stern attempts to get

beyond this by analysing rape myths as ideology, drawing on marxist concepts of ideology and on psychoanalytic concepts of sexuality. This approach allows her to make connections between rape and bourgeois ideologies of masculinity and femininity, of romantic love and of the family. The meaning of rape is 'situated within the ideology of masculinity, and functions to perpetuate patriarchal structures' (Stern, 1977:9). The question of cause is shifted away from the either/or choice of sexism or men. The problem is not one of learned sex roles nor men as such, but is located in the reproduction of patriarchal ideologies. Women's guilt and confusion about rape arises because women as well as men are implicated in these ideologies. Change for Stern therefore demands collective political struggle against ideologies of rape. What this may mean in terms of specific strategies—for example, the divisions over renaming—is less clear.

Whether or not rape myths are understood as ideology in this sense, feminist accounts do seek to cut into patriarchal connections between sexual desire and enforced sexual activity, which is rape. In the New South Wales feminist debate, radical feminists emphasised that it is men who are the enforcers; liberal feminists aimed to sever the connection, to remove assumptions about the complicitness of women's sexual desire. In seeking to take the sex out of rape, liberal feminists intended that 'sexual assault' would minimise the legal focus on the question of the woman's consent. This is the difficult one.

The question of consent is very difficult to resolve because it becomes a matter of the woman's word against the man's. Neutral witnesses and indisputable evidence are seldom available. The Islamic-influenced law in Pakistan resolves the problem by requiring that the rape must be witnessed by four adult Moslem men of upstanding character (Morgan, 1984:530).

Consent gained a particular meaning following the Morgan case which came before the House of Lords in 1975. The Law Lords decided that a man should not be found guilty of rape if he honestly believed that the woman consented, no matter how unreasonable his belief might be (Naffine, 1984:13). Many feminists saw this decision as a rapist's charter since the man would simply have to tell the court that he believed the woman consented. Melissa Benn and her associates in a British pamphlet *The Rape Controversy* (1986) point out that it is still the jury which decides whether or not the defendant is telling the truth.

The role of the jury is fundamental to our system of criminal law. However, Suzanne Callinan's (1984) account of her experience of jury service in a rape case in South Australia raises disturbing questions about this bulwark of justice. The accused was acquitted although he agreed that intercourse had occurred, and the jury agreed that he and the woman were virtual strangers, and that he had broken into her flat in the middle of the night. Callinan observes that community prejudice about rape victims and general ignorance of the technical meaning of legal process practices combine to undermine the possibility of justice.

Benn and associates also argue that the 'Morgan' decision upholds an important legal principle: that no person should be convicted of a crime which he or she did not intend to commit. However, feminists in Britain were angry at the renewed emphasis the 'Morgan' decision gave to consent. While the man had to prove his honest belief, the woman's claim that she did not consent could be tested by the rules of evidence as to whether she was a credible witness. Her credibility became the central issue for the court—and this led inexorably to the question of her womanliness. Which kind of woman is she: virgin or whore? There are two dimensions to this issue. First, her behaviour during and following the event, as well as her previous sexual experiences, were subject to detailed question. In addition to the obvious evidence such as bruises (by no means conclusive in practice), what evidence do her circumstances provide about her alleged refusal of consent? Does she live alone, go into places not-for-women, maintain a monogamous relationship? In effect, how closely does she approach white, bourgeois ideals of femininity?

Second, the woman is not assumed to be an honourable citizen. Judges were bound to warn the jury to be careful of a woman victim's evidence because 'a charge of rape is easily made'—and, it was implied, women are more than likely to do so.

The court adopted this view even though it might safely have assumed that deceitful and spiteful women were already filtered out by a vigilant police. Police are implicated in the ideologies of rape, exacerbated in their case because the onus is on them to prove in court the absence of consent. Paul Wilson (1978:72) found that two-thirds of police had the possible falsity of complaint uppermost in mind at the time of the initial report. (Oddly, Wilson, 1986, later warned about false complaints of child sexual abuse, although his research on rape showed that false complaints were rare.) Feminists contest ideological assumptions about false complaints, drawing on a considerable research which shows that women often do not report instances of rape at all, let alone make them up. For example, the 1983 large-scale survey on victims of various crimes by the Australian Bureau of Statistics suggests that only one in seven rapes are reported

For liberal feminists, especially the members of WEL involved with this reform, these legal consequences flowed from the legal definition of rape. The 1981 New South Wales legislation changed the meaning of rape somewhat by specifying that the victim no longer had to struggle. The assumption that rape had to be an act of overt physical violence was removed. Yet assumptions about the woman remained largely intact. For example judges were allowed to decide that the victim's sexual history could be admitted as evidence in court. And the legislation did not escape from the question of consent.

On this critical point, Ngaire Naffine concludes that the issue of consent cannot be avoided. 'The only thing which distinguishes the crime from the lawful act of sexual intercourse is the wishes of the victim [*sic*]. The act only becomes unlawful when consent is absent and the accused

is made to realize this' (Naffine, 1984:21). If lack of consent is an 'inevitable ingredient of rape' then law reform can seek only to exclude sexist interpretation of its meaning. This the 1981 legislation failed to do. For those feminists who doubted the value of law reform, this was not surprising. But for WEL and those involved in the campaign, it was a matter of great concern. The details of their demand for effective rape reform had been carefully designed to fit within the parameters of the law.

So what went wrong? Feminists had run a comprehensive, careful campaign. The government of the day seemed sympathetic. Yet the situation of rape victims was little improved by reformed legislation. Writing a bitter evaluation of the campaign, Jocelynne Scutt lays most of the blame at the feet of 'women bureaucrats'. In the patriarchal bureaucracy where reforms must be fought out the position of such women was crucial. But they 'subverted' feminist demands and sold out.

> Was their failure to be supportive, and worse, their active subversion of feminist demands, the result of genuine inability to sum up the position correctly, so that for the sake of what reforms were possible (in their view) they tailored the demands to suit? Or were the bureaucratic games that were played the result of intoxication with the 'power' they thought they wielded in advisory and governmental positions? Was there a desire to see the reform of the rape law as theirs alone, rather than the result of a massive movement, of co-operation between thousands of women?' (Scutt, 1985a:21).

Or were they manipulated by and in the interests of male bureaucrats? Scutt does not finally answer these questions. Her dilemma is that her framework limits her to the hope that women bureaucrats individually will choose feminism—despite the 'sell-out' so far.

The problems here are twofold. First, this oversimplifies and unifies the position of women bureaucrats, casting them as simply for or against feminism—an issue we will explore in the final section of this book. Second, the process of law reform is inextricably bound up with the bureaucratic state, which has its own strategic concerns. We must analyse the process in terms which recognise the necessary but risky business of contesting the bureaucracy's approach to law reform. Scutt and WEL were dismayed by the outcome of the reform campaign, but was nothing gained? In Lesley Stern's terms, the campaign was a political struggle against the ideologies of rape. It helped to expose the ways male dominance benefits from the confusion of sex with sexual violence. The German feminist Barbara Sichtermann suggests that the implications of ideologies of rape run deep, well beyond their permeation of definitions of rape: '[The] fact that the patriarchy feels so damn sure of itself in this confusion is a severe indictment of the quality of the erotic culture which it has created' (Sichtermann, 1986:40). The challenge of reform campaigns to sexual violence extends beyond changes to legal

terminology, but campaigns aimed at undermining the 'confidence' of patriarchy confront the manifold consequences of confusion.

Where ideologies of sexuality portray women as passive, men as forceful initiators, sex and violence converge—for women, men, and the law. Catharine MacKinnon, like Lesley Stern, argues that while men apparently have difficulty in telling the difference between sex and rape so too do women, 'under conditions of male dominance' (MacKinnon, 1983:647). The dividing line for women between consent and coercion can be so tenuous that they feel implicated. They feel guilt or they blame themselves for not taking proper precautions. Meanwhile, the law's demand that the question of consent be absolutely clear assumes an equality between the man and the woman which simply mystifies the facts of patriarchal sexual relations. The 1981 Act did not address rape as a manifestation of inequality but sought to preserve the appearance of objectivity of the law through the apparent objectivity of 'consent'. The law maintained a patriarchal interpretation of sexual relationships and of male and female citizenship.

The reform legislation cleaned up the law to the extent that rape was less narrowly defined and women were less overtly harassed by procedures. Although feminists continue to agitate about rape, attention has shifted away from law reform. Other strategies are developed to demonstrate links between the patriarchal interests of the state and sexuality. Anzac Day marches claiming the right to mourn all women raped in war expose connections between militarism and ideologies of masculinity. Police arrests of women marchers signals the state's recognition of the point. For women such campaigns aim at building collectivity as much as at attacking the problem of rape (Pringle, 1983:33).

In addition to strategies directed specifically at the problem of rape, feminists are tackling other dimensions of sexual violence. Campaigns against rape based on the view that male violence against women is a particular form of domination dependent on social relationships of unequal power helped to develop and popularise that perspective. As women began to speak of those relationships in the context of the women's movement the extent of violence in personal relationships began to emerge (Ward, 1985). The existence of such violence is not new; what is new is the recognition that it is not confined to isolated instances of perversity. Most perpetrators are known to their victims. Indeed sexual violence most frequently occurs within the 'family'—in striking contrast to the long-held view that attackers are crazed strangers. For feminists, the problem of the oppressive nature of familial relationships became a fundamental issue of sexual violence.

Making connections between sexual violence and familial ralationships disturbs the foundations of the 'good family' and causes havoc to deeply held values of love, nurturance, protection and sexual harmony. Feminists too have to deal with these consequences. Such connections inevitably lead to the part played by the state in the maintenance of pat-

riarchal familial relationships and its interest in the containment of sexual violence within the privacy of the family. Challenging sexual violence means challenging the sexual politics of the state. Feminists have besieged the law with limited effect. But also they have bought into the arena of the state's social policies and practices. We consider the risks and pay-offs of this approach through the example of the recent development and implementation of a policy on child sexual abuse in South Australia.

Child sexual abuse: the Furler Report

The terms include 'child molestation', 'incest', 'Father–Daughter Rape', 'child rape'. We shall use 'child sexual abuse' as presently being the most widely used term.

Whatever the label, its most striking feature is its rapid emergence as a public issue. Although public discussion of the 'battered baby syndrome'—child abuse—has increased gradually during the last twenty years, there has been a sudden proliferation of press articles, editorials, children's colouring books, television programs (fiction and 'documentary'), government reports, and curriculum packages on child sexual abuse. In 1986 an international conference on child abuse, including sexual abuse, was held at a prestigious hotel in Sydney. Australian media carried accounts, detailed if somewhat difficult to interpret, of the English 'Cleveland scandal' where there was a significant increase in 1987 in the number of children diagnosed as sexually abused. In South Australia, 'children at risk of specified harm, such as physical or sexual abuse' currently tops the list of official priorities for the Department for Community Welfare.

Suddenly everyone is aware of child sexual abuse. But, to paraphrase Judith Allen (1982) on domestic violence, it is a practice without a history. Indeed, the whole area of familial sexual violence has a timeless quality about it. In the literature, especially in policy documents, such violence seems to float as a problem unconnected to anything. Tied neither to history nor to social structures, the recognition of familial sexual violence, and in particular child sexual abuse, is imbued with assumptions of essentialism and moralism. The cause of such violence appears to be a kind of randomly distributed essential evilness. Children are construed as essentially innocent, or amoral (so they lie readily), or sometimes both.

This appearance, except in some feminist writing, has much to do with attempts by journalists and political authorities to defuse the political complexities and dangers which public recognition of the issue involves. What is at stake is the sexual politics of the state and the patriarchal family. Recognition by the state of child sexual abuse represents a potential challenge to patriarchal relations. The problem for the state is

to balance its concern to maintain families, to control and arbitrate violence, with its interest in deflecting the challenge of gender politics. And yet, child sexual abuse elicits strong concern from many, not only feminists, within the state apparatus. It is not just a matter of ducking and weaving; the issue has been taken up rigorously by 'mainstream' bureaucrats. Considerable conflict between groups within as well as outside the state arise as interest groups struggle to define the state's strategies.

Feminist activity has had much to do with the emergence of the issue, the 'discovery' of the hidden problem of child sexual abuse. Feminism has helped create an environment in which private troubles could break through the bonds of familial privacy. Cathy Waldby (1985), a member of the New South Wales Women Against Incest Collective, suggests that two developments contributed: first, the establishment of women's services as alternatives to health and welfare agencies; second, the permeation of feminist ideas into tertiary institutions where professionals such as social workers trained. Nevertheless, compared to other aspects of violence such as rape, child sexual abuse was taken up rather slowly by feminists.

Waldby believes this was because it constitutes a dilemma for feminists.

> In the women's refuges it was common to discover that the husband who had been violent towards his wife had also been sexually molesting his daughters, a discovery usually as much a revelation to the mother as to the refuge workers... The intricate and intense family dynamics, particularly the hostility between mother and daughter, presented difficult problems for workers trying to deal with the incest in a way that was sympathetic to the feminist position. (Waldby, 1985:9)

Feminism's fundamental aim to support women in general means support for both mother and daughter. However, the mother–daughter relationship is not necessarily harmonious under such painful conditions. The abusive father's betrayal of them both may put their relationship with each other under serious pressure. In practice, feminists must deal with less than ideal mother–daughter relations, and with differences between young children and adult 'survivors'.

In spite of these difficulties feminist analysis starts from the fact that the overwhelming majority of offenders are men. Carol O'Donnell and Jan Craney summarise the general position as follows:

> Incest is one expression of the power relations to be found in the patriarchal nuclear family where the power of men is expressed through sexual domination and control, and women are seen and see themselves as subordinate sex objects. Sexuality within the nuclear family is seen as an expression of male domination over women and control of them. Incest is described in terms of an

extension of these 'natural' family relations of domination and subordination. (O'Donnell and Craney, 1982a:159)

The ideology of the family as a private place of love, mutual care and
trust helps conceal incest, child sexual abuse, within the patriarchal
family.

Feminist explanations reject notions of 'deviant' individuals, and of
dysfunctional families, and are not stuck with legalistic definitions. The
focus on the effect of patriarchal power rather than the technical specificity of behaviours allows feminists to make connections between
ideologies of masculinity and femininity, patriarchal relations within
families and the contribution of the state to the maintenance of such relations. Not all feminists agree with the view of some radical feminists
that men per se are the problem, but the argument that abusers are
deviant pathological individuals is generally rejected. (See MacLeod and
Saraga, 1988; Rush, 1980, Schechter, 1982).

Feminists firmly reject the idea that those subjected to abuse are culpable. The difficulty in this approach is that women may be defined as
passive victims. This is particularly so in the case of children. Thus
feminists object to the argument that young girls seduce their fathers, or
fantasise about it as some versions of Freud would have it, but they also
seek to validate children's sexuality. '[It] is important to recognise that
children have emotional needs, and sensual and sexual desires and fantasies, including about their parents' (MacLeod and Saraga, 1987:24).
But strategically, these arguments are difficult to maintain in an adversarial legal system where any admission of a child's sexual desires may
be readily construed as contrary to childish innocence, therefore abnormal, and therefore seductive. Recognition of the child's own active
sexuality slips away. Still the notion of the 'seductive child' does give
one pause; how serious is the idea of a grown man so in thrall to a young
child that he must sexually force himself upon her?

Feminist perspectives and activism have provided some opportunity
to break the silence. However, the 'child protection lobby' outside
feminism has also contributed to the current visibility of the issue of
child abuse. In its modern form, the lobby was initiated by public discussion of the 'battered child syndrome' in the early 1960s. Defined as
maltreatment of children, the syndrome involves physical injury and/or
deprivation of nutrition, care and affection in circumstances which
showed that such injury was not accidental (O'Donnell and
Craney 1982b:177).

Documentation of the nature and extent of abuse began to appear. In
1978, Ann Deveson reported that the Commission on Human Relationships found that as many as 14 000 children were deliberately injured—
burned, battered, sexually abused and starved—every year by their
parents. Other reports from hospitals, welfare organisations and researchers began to surface, based on an approach which saw sexual abuse as

part of a more general abuse of children. For the child protection lobby, sexual abuse is but another facet of the child-battering problem with which it is already familiar (D. Finkelhor in the Furler Report:15).

Such an approach has important consequences, especially when allied to the notion that the family is an inseparable unit comprised of two parts: parents and children. This model of the family does not distinguish between parents or among children. Where any kind of child abuse occurs, the whole family is deemed 'at risk'. Survival of the particular family as a unit may well be at risk but that is a different matter (to which we will turn later). Research based on this approach shows little interest in the sex of the parents (Justice and Justice, 1979; Scott, 1983); we understand some welfare departments have refused to collect statistics according to sex. What evidence is available suggests that mothers are just as likely to abuse as fathers, even though the number of children living in fatherless homes tends to skew the figures. Commentaries usually refer to the abuser as 'the mother'. But research specifically on child sexual abuse shows that the proportion of male abusers ranges between 90 and 98 per cent, and approximately 75 per cent of abusers are known to the child as family or friends (Report:19).

We must be wary of these figures. Feminist analysis of child sexual abuse concentrates on the predominance of male abusers. Do the statistics on female abusers undermine feminist argument about 'the problem of masculinity'? And what of current suggestions in the popular press that the incidence of female abusers has been seriously underestimated? A detailed review of the research by Russell and Finkelhor (1984) found that many studies included women in the figures for perpetrators, not only when they abused a child but when they 'allowed' sexual abuse to occur. Their findings raise questions about the relationship of the woman to her male partner in abuse.

Women are capable of abusing their power in relation to children. But if sexual violence, in general, were primarily to do with unequal power alone we would expect that many more women would sexually abuse their children. Russell and Finkelhor found that where women are abusers their behaviour differed in that it was more likely to constitute emotional abuse. This does not get us far since distinctions between emotional abuse and sexual abuse must be premised on a narrow definition of the sexual. What is clear, however, is that women rarely abuse children in the same sexual ways that men do. All this suggests that in analyses of sexual violence, gender must be central to conceptualising interactions between sexuality and power.

When the definition of 'abuse' includes all forms, the gendered nature of sexual abuse is submerged. Sexual politics is obscured. It is this which divides the child protection lobby from feminism and causes conflict between them.

Now, what of the state? First, we reiterate that the politics of sexual violence necessarily encompasses the state; and the state is neither unitary

nor immovable. As the state seeks to gain and regain legitimation it must respond to conflicting interests. Due recognition of all types of familial and sexual violence has been slow and reluctant. It has depended very much on political demands; laws on rape in marriage are a notable example. At the same time, responses are contested within and between the apparatuses of the state, clearly shown by the different strategies of the several Australian States. South Australia instituted mandatory reporting of child abuse in 1969, but Victoria was still debating the question in 1987. Among other things the divergent interests of welfare and criminal justice departments have led to conflicts over the direction and extent of reforms.

Such conflicts, and the state's general reluctance to intervene, derive in part from struggles over the political meanings of child sexual abuse. D.H. Lightfoot noted in 1980 that the dominance of the medical model of families as deviant, created problems in social policy development in New South Wales. The model served to deny the widespread extent of familial violence. Since then, sufficient ground has been won that most States at least formally acknowledge the social dimensions of the problem. Western Australia has established a task force on child sexual assault; Victoria has employed a consultant, attached to the Premier's Department, to report on the nature of the problem; Queensland commissioned a barrister to report on legal reforms; New South Wales has developed a Child Sexual Assault Programme to which feminists from a variety of women's services contributed, including those from women's refuges, the Women Against Incest Collective, and health centres.

As child abuse slowly emerged through the family's front door, state agencies such as the courts had necessarily to deal with it. Their practices, based on concepts of adult citizen rights and responsibilities, had considerable difficulties with concepts of the child. Available definitions of the child's rights and responsibilities were of little assistance where, for example, the young child may be the chief witness. Children were treated as adults by adversarial legal procedures, obliged to face the accused as though they were peers in the court; yet they were considered non-adults, with uncertain capacity to swear an oath. With the growing assertion that children's rights must be reconceptualised, that the child was not simply a non-adult, some commentators began to argue that concepts, methods and procedures should be modified. The complexities of child abuse and the demands that state agencies respond directly to them added weight to these arguments.

'Children's rights' emerged as a problem; their absence was regarded as a severe inadequacy. In South Australia, Ian Bidmeade, an experienced bureaucrat in the field of child protection and the state, and consultant on relevant procedures, took this line in his report to the minister for community welfare.

It seems to me to be a system designed for lawyers and social workers, but not necessarily for children, and it is arguable that [the] Child Protection (and Young Offenders Act) in this State may work not because of the legislation and the structures and procedures established by the legislation, but despite them. I would particularly urge the Government to implement changes which will more clearly delineate the roles of the Department [for Community Welfare] and the Court, and enable the Court, through a different composition and powers of inquiry, to play a proper and effective role in child protection. If ever there is a need for a creative and imaginative approach to the way in which decisions in our community are made, then this is it. (Bidmeade, 1986:3)

Even in terms of mainstream reform, there is still a long way to go.

However, the denial of child sexual abuse—through silence, medical models, or familial ideologies—has been challenged during the last decade. Child sexual abuse became politicised as an issue which required that something must be seen to be done. In South Australia, as elsewhere, there was and continues to be considerable conflict about what that might be. In this context, the 1986 *Final Report of the S.A. Government Task Force on Child Sexual Abuse* (Furler Report) is a remarkable document. Its considerable interest lies first in what the report and its reception suggest about the outcomes of conflict, and thus where the issue is going, and second in the light it throws on what part feminist politics can play in the matter of the state and sexual violence.

The brief of the task force, which emerged after some political debate in 1984, reveals the way the state directorate understood its role in relation to the issue. State practices which impinged on the issue needed to be modified. The task force was to identify problems associated with the existing law and current methods of service delivery, and to recommend on ways of integrating and coordinating policies and services (and thus reduce both conflict and costs). It undertook no comprehensive research, although it recognised the general lack of systematic information. Rather the task force relied on a practice common to such inquiries, namely public meetings, submissions, some individual interviews and literature surveys.

The task force described itself as responding to 'increasing professional and public concern about the plight of children who have been or are being sexually abused'. Its membership appears to reflect a careful attention to the diversity of interests in this field, interests as diverse within the state apparatus as they were among groups outside the state. Chaired by Elizabeth Furler, then women's adviser in the Health Commission, the membership included officials from government departments spanning a variety of perspectives—law, welfare, social health, education—some femocrats and several feminists from women's services. Child sexual abuse was understood as an issue where feminist

perspectives must at least be heard. Finally, as is usual with public inquiries, a strategic role was played by the executive officer, Rennie Gay, in the complex process of achieving a series of recommendations for state policy.

The task force faced three problems: how to respond to the situation of the child victim; how to deal with alleged and convicted abusers; and what would contribute to prevention.

The report defined child sexual abuse broadly as 'the imposition of explicit sexual activity on a child who lacks the power and authority to prevent being coerced into compliance'. This defines the child as the aggrieved party and holds the adult legally culpable. Thus the key premise of the report focuses on the child and on the rights of the child. It refused the argument that the child bears any responsibility or is an agent in the events. The child is defined as asexual, not sexually seductive, on the grounds of the child's relative powerlessness.

At this point, the report proposes two main concerns: the child and its rights, and the problem of power. However, the following 350 pages read as an uneasy balance between conflicting perspectives on both. On power, the report asserts that 'only by addressing the issue of male power and authority both within and without the family will we truly be engaging in preventive action' (p.28). A strong statement of principle. However, nowhere does the report directly address this issue. For example, we find a welcome discussion of the needs of 'non-offending parents ... in almost all cases the mother'. But as response to these needs the report relies on making information more available, and on encouraging self-help groups within existing women's and community health service networks. Feminists also think information 'empowering', but it is not clear how, in isolation, 'male power and authority' is challenged thereby.

The report reveals a considerable conflict on the question of the state's response to offenders, conflict which continued during the subsequent period of implementation of the report's recommendations. The question may be described as a legal problem of balancing the interests of the accused with the rights of the child, and the connected problem of punishment and/or rehabilitation. The underlying conflict however has to do with the state's part in the sexual politics of child sexual abuse. Feminists argue that offenders should, where necessary, be removed from the home, but observe at the same time that this implies a need for the provision (by the state) of economic support to the family. What happens to offenders next, in the feminist literature, is much less clear. Although the reasons are different the problem is common. As MacLeod and Saraga note, any 'work with abusers is pitifully inadequate and unimaginative'.

The task force recommended that the offence remain criminal but contemplated ways to diversify sentencing options. What is interesting here is the shift from penal punishment to a highly controlled therapy.

Oddly, punishment and rehabilitation become muddled. The dilemmas about offenders are exacerbated because in sexual abuse cases they rarely admit to the charge. Therapists are generally agreed that an admission is a necessary prerequisite for successful therapeutic treatment. Since offenders also apparently refuse voluntary therapy, forced therapy becomes a kind of punishment. Thus, for the task force it followed that therapy was not a 'soft option'.

Therapy represents a different kind of state intervention from a gaol sentence. But it is not clear just what that difference meant to the task force. It recognised that 'the extent of intervention in the offender's life, made a treatment programme and the conditions imposed by being admitted to such a programme, would in most cases be perceived as a harsher penalty than those resulting from at least some conventional sentences' (sic) (Report:p.227). Does the task force assume that treatment would demand such a radical modification of behaviour that it would be harsh to offenders? Or does it assume that offenders would be habituated to prison sentences and thus less affected by them? If the latter, then we must suspect that the task force assumed that the majority of offenders would belong to that group which is most likely to be gaoled, namely young working-class men.

The report itself notes the stringent criticisms of therapeutic treatment, observing that it is an 'individualistic solution'. Further, few services are available and little seems to be known about the effectiveness of treatment. One submission from a prison psychologist illustrates the problem. It seems that for five years the Department of Correctional Services has offered two separate treatment programs for sex offenders: one for unmarried rapists and paedophiles and a second for married rapists and paedophiles. The task force tartly observes that it has 'problems with the conceptual distinction between married and unmarried offenders' (p.156).

Feminist writers are suspicious of treatment programs. 'Teaching him to use 'other behaviours' will not necessarily end abusive acts towards his wife (or children): rather, he may resort to or expand psychological methods of indulging his violence against her' (Scutt, 1983:280). Elizabeth Ward proposes that punishment should be clear. Therapy is all very well for those 'who wish to deliver such services'. But offenders must not be forgiven; 'what they have done is unforgiveable' (Ward, 1985:212). Feminist solutions to the immediate problem of offenders aim at direct punishment, although they argue that changing the ways masculinity is constructed is essential to the real prevention of men's sexual abuse of children. Their chief concern is the child and her mother oppressed by a father-dominated family system. The significant political point of such concern is that it represents a counter to those forces which begin with the integrity of the family system. But at present, and in the task force, this concern weighs only lightly in the balance.

Faced with the complex array of argument, the task force drew back

from recommending therapy as an alternative to a criminal trial. Pre-trial 'diversionary programs' where the accused may enter a program of therapy before, perhaps instead of a trial, have been established in New South Wales, but the South Australian report was cautious about this option. On the one hand, diversion assumes guilt before it has been established at law, thus provoking concern for the rights of the offender. On the other hand, pre-trial diversion may undermine the criminality of child sexual abuse.

Such debates overwhelm arguments about the oppressiveness of the patriarchal family, and how it might be changed. The task force favours both rehabilitation and the symbolic value of criminal prosecution. But its argument, and the public debate in general, is cast in terms which assume that the family system should continue untouched. In spite of its assertions about unequal power, the task force does not question the position of the father within the united family, and so does not question the ways masculinity is constructed. Child sexual abuse remains an aber-ration rather than something integrally connected to oppressive sexu-ality.

The consequences of a commitment to maintaining the patriarchal family, and to a therapeutic model of state intervention into the family, which the task force did not discount, are most disturbing in the approach to the child. Its report's granting of significance to the rights of the child is consistent with a growing public advocacy of children's rights. Such advocacy is generally acclaimed as progressive. However, interpretation is highly political.

The issue of services for victims of child sexual abuse illustrates the point. Submissions to the task force from women's services endorsed provision of services for all child sexual abuse survivors, both adults and children. Based on a feminist perspective, the submissions sought to argue that child sexual abuse is a matter of sexual politics, that the essen-tial point is that men sexually abuse women, whatever age they may be. The task force dealt with the argument by labelling it 'specialist', i.e. one which neglected the specific needs of children and which 'over-emphasized the sexual aspect of abuse'. Taking a strong line against the stress on the sexual, the task force mounts a similar argument to that by the New South Wales Women's Electoral Lobby on the question of the naming of rape. Here too the intention is to emphasise the issue of power, in this case the powerlessness of children in abuse situations.

We have noted earlier some political difficulties in the conception of children's sexuality. Here we observe that taking the sex out of child sexual abuse leads to an assumption that the child is asexual. To recog-nise children's sexuality does not imply that the child connives in abuse; nor should it imply that children's sexuality is the same as adult sexu-ality. Judith Ennew argues: 'Children's sexuality should be regarded as different from adult sexuality not only because of physical differences, but also because of differences in knowledge and understanding of

sexual activities and their consequences' (Ennew, 1986:61). Thus we return to the question of power. We argue that the recognition of children's sexuality need not eliminate the problem of power. Since children do not have equal knowledge, nor the political and economic power of adults, they are unlikely to be able to give informed consent to sexual activity. The inequalities of gender, which are usual in child sexual abuse, unbalance the position between adult and child further.

Ennew argues that the 'rights of the child' must involve recognition of these inequalities and must extend to protection from exploitation by the more powerful. She proposes that the feminist recognition of power relations shaped by class and race needs to be extended to include age. Although adult women and children do have the experience of male abuse in common, a girl child stands in a different position to a male abuser from that of her mother or of her adult sister, and presumably from the adult survivor of abuse in childhood. The task force maintained that the significant difference was that between the needs of children and those of adults.

However, the question of differences between adults and children is not the main point at issue in the report. Something else is at stake. At its heart lies the problem of sexual politics and the ways it is contested. The report records the following exchange on strategies for children:

> Preventative programmes should therefore examine the power relations involved, and combat sexist attitudes, particularly those which argue that men have the 'right' to exercise sexual and proprietorial power and authority over women and children in a family or quasi-family situation. (Adelaide Women's Community Health Centre Submission, Report, p.280)

And the reply:

> The Task Force stands by its original proposal that programmes which help children and young people to be safe, which give them accurate information about their bodies and their right to respect and equality in relationships, be an established part of the school curriculum. (p.280)

We recall the report's early statement about the need to address male power, but here we find an explicit refusal to do so. It may be read as provision for a right to equal knowledge, but it is knowledge designed to avoid the question of power relations.

In the report thus far the 'rights of the child' has meant the need to be treated differently from adults, the provision of neutral information and the right to equality—in effect, the right to say no. But MacLeod and Saraga argue that 'learning to say no' is a weak solution. 'Many children do say no; but this is ignored. To see prevention in terms of children learning to protect themselves is to implicitly accept the way men are' (MacLeod and Saraga:26). And it is fairly well known that the assertion of one's right to equality does not always guarantee its achievement.

Although everyone agrees that the rights of the child should be paramount, the way such rights are defined, particularly by the state, requires critical scrutiny.

First, rights are understood in terms of the individual child, undistinguished by class, race or gender. Child sexual abuse has become a visible problem but generally is not understood as a problem which extends beyond particular individual behaviours. It may be a public issue but it is seen in terms of individual, private troubles, and its solutions likewise tend to be individualised.

Furthermore, while there is plenty of formal and informal concern about the incidence of child sexual abuse, and of horror that individuals should do such things, where is the equivalent concern about the social abuse of particular groups of children? Where is the public rhetoric at the social treatment of Aboriginal children who suffer high infant mortality, malnutrition, chronic ill-health and poverty? As O'Donnell and Craney suggest (1982b), it is difficult for this issue to register because such effects are clearly related to the economic and cultural oppression of a whole social group rather than the actions of a series of unconnected individuals.

Second, the state claims a primary right to be advocate for the child and thereby gains a mandate to intervene in the child's relationships. As the rights of the child are allegedly upheld, the rights of the non-abusing parent (usually the mother) become secondary. Even where neither parent has been abusive the state may replace them as guardians or remove the child from their care.

Such state intervention is not new to working-class or to Aboriginal families. For example, in New South Wales the Aborigines Protection Board (later renamed) which operated from 1909 until 1969 had sufficiently wide powers that it could forcibly remove Aboriginal children from their families and place them with white families—and often did (Brennan and O'Donnell, 1986:13). Nor is it new for the state to set aside the mother's rights. Mary McIntosh has made the case that the state relates to women mainly through their husbands, a kind of non-interference which leaves women vulnerable to familial violence and abuse (McIntosh, 1982:306). In the matter of child sexual abuse the state bypasses the husband and in a sense takes the role of patriarch for itself. It asserts the right to make decisions about the child and relates to the mother through her child. As the state determines the rights as well as the needs of the child the mother's parental rights are eroded. She becomes vulnerable to the state's requirements for appropriate mothering behaviour. The argument made by English social historian John Eekelaar (1986:174) underlines this point: 'The statutory enshrinement of the paramountcy of the child's welfare was a result not so much of a desire to elevate the children's interests above those of the parents, but to stave off feminist demands for equality of parental rights' (Eekelaar, 1986:174).

This leads to a third feature of the construction of the 'rights of the child': the renewed emphasis on the 'good' family. For the state apparatus of welfare, the good family represents a solution to the problem of the sexual politics of patriarchal family relations raised by child sexual abuse. The family is understood as the basic unit of society, 'the natural environment for the growth and well-being of children'—a phrase used in a South Australian Department for Community Welfare discussion paper of 1987 and echoed in numerous other documents. The child has the right, it is argued, to live in a family defined as one which offers 'continuity of relationships with nurturing parents or caretakers'. The role of the state is to ensure that right by supporting a particular kind of family care of children.

The problem for the state becomes one of balancing the rights of the child with the integrity of the family and the father's status within in. The 'rights of the child' has become bound up with the politics of child sexual abuse which demands direct action by the state; thus that action must be construed in terms of those rights. What these terms mean, and what they mean in relation to 'the parents' and 'the family' becomes of central importance in the construction of the state's response.

A common strategy now emerging can be seen in the discussion paper just mentioned. The paper emanates from the Department for Community Welfare, the department in South Australia which is presently charged with a substantial responsibility for handling the state's interests in the family and the child. It argues that the way round *its* problem is to see parents as having responsibilities and duties towards the care of their children. Where the parents' failure puts the child in danger, then the state may intervene. In the case of child sexual abuse within families, the child is at risk from both parents because one parent failed to protect the child from the other. 'Where the protection of the child cannot be guaranteed within the home, the Department will remove that child from parental care' (Discussion Paper, 1987:14). No distinction is made between parents. Both are culpable. Such a view is supported by the perception of child sexual abuse as a part of the general abuse of children. The specific nature of father–daughter abuse is thereby disguised.

However, the state's responses are not all of a piece. We have noted that the task force does distinguish between the abuser and the non-offending parent. It refers to the need to foster the mother's sense of control, to restore the mother–daughter relationship, and recognises the difficulties mothers experience when abuse occurs (Report:133). The task force believes that it is preferable for the child to stay in the home and for the offender to leave. The child should only be removed when she wishes to go or when the mother cannot or will not provide adequate support (Report:165). The task force thus gives some credence to the wishes and needs expressed by the child and the mother.

But the position of the Department for Community Welfare, which

has major responsibility for dealing with child sexual abuse in South Australia, tends to separate the mother out into a kind of limbo. First, it takes the view that the child is best protected by living in good families. By definition, families in which child sexual abuse occurs are not good and that comes to mean all members of those families. Family problems become problem families. Problems do not have to do with particular family members, with differences between the parents. Rather families are seen as made up of parents and children, undistinguished by gender. And certainly not divided by gender—at this level of the argument. Thus the fact that a high proportion of sexual abusers are male family members is submerged within the 'problem family'. The child is protected by relocation to a good family. So the department's solution to its problem about its conflict between maintaining the family and protecting the rights of the child escapes the underlying problem in child sexual abuse of patriarchal relations within the family.

This leads to a second element of the department's position which does distinguish between parents—to the mother's disadvantage. This is the principle that first of all one should 'believe the child'. Departmental policy is that in any case of child abuse, this must be the starting point. But the consequence is that the mother remains suspect: of collusion in the abuse, of maternal inadequacy, or of making a false complaint. It allows case workers to claim a greater competency to represent the child's interests. The effect is to marginalise the mother.

However, the difficulty for feminist politics is that 'belief in the child' has other political consequences. Thus the principle proposes to alter the unequal position of the child in the investigative and court procedures of the legal system. Its adversarial structure assumes a fundamental equality between the parties. The child must be subject to the same legal tests as the adult which leads to the situation where a young child must stand alone, literally, in the court and face her alleged abuser, in the name of the 'rights of the accused'. If the child breaks down and is unable to do it, the whole procedure is made void. 'Belief in the child' argues that the rights of the child must be understood as different from those of the adult, become equal with them, and that the procedures should accommodate such rights. It cuts across widespread and muddled conceptions of the child, assumed to be at once innocent but seductive, less than adult yet available to adult legal tests of evidence. It is a strategy which aims to challenge the heavier weighting granted to the rights of the accused by conventional legal procedures.

Feminists engaged in advocating reforms to child sexual abuse policies are ambivalent about opposing 'the child' to 'the adult' in this way since both become gender-neutral. The problem is compounded by opposition to belief in the child which argues that children (like women) readily lie, or at best cannot tell the difference between truth and fantasy, and are susceptible to manipulation, easily led by mothers of welfare workers to allege abuse.

The tactical necessity for feminists to defend the rights of the child is

sharpened by conflicts between the role of the state welfare apparatus and that of the law. In South Australia, allegations of child sexual abuse incur intervention by welfare into the family, and into the relations between parents and child. Conservative arguments about the damaging extent of such intervention are strengthened by opposition to it from within the legal apparatus itself. The law advocates the citizenship rights of individuals, including protection from violation by the state. In the area of child sexual abuse it turns out that the 'individuals' are adult men who must be protected from allegations by children led astray, or supported in their fantasies, by welfare workers. Far less attention is paid to the child. Thus the law is resistant or at best tentative about quite modest proposals to alter court procedures, for example, to allow a supportive adult to sit beside a child giving evidence in court.

The sexual politics inherent in such conflict is rarely far below the surface. The public charge that welfare workers are 'biased zealots' in a case in point. In February 1988 a South Australian member of parliament, speaking in debate on amendments arising from the task force recommendations, raised the question of motivation 'behind the pursuit of child sexual abuse zeal'. He identified the cause as 'the feminist origins of some of the theories' about child sexual abuse, and in particular 'the theory that all sexual activity is an attempt by the male to dominate the female and that there is a great feminist reaction to that which gives an ideological base to some of the zeal' (Ritson, *SAPD,* II February 1988). The real causes of the problem were then explained by the same politician—a doctor—in a wonderful mixture of professional arrogance and blaming the victim:

> I suppose one of the difficult things to accept if you are a short course diploma social worker is that in most cases of inappropriate sex within a family—and in most cases of abused children—there is at least subconscious maternal condonement and family pathology involving every member of the family.

Feminists must support social workers who reject such conclusions. But they cannot regard the role of welfare with equanimity.

Nor must the part played by the legal apparatus be allowed to remain on the sidelines. Feminists have catalogued the damaging effect of child sexual abuse which may extend far beyond childhood. Putting a stop to individual incidents requires the subjection of the child to both welfare and legal procedures. At present this is necessary if the child is to be protected from further abuse and given some opportunity to overcome the trauma. The dilemma is that such procedures may be themselves very damaging.

The task force showed awareness of the problem as it bears on criminal proceedings.

> One of the major obstacles to the successful prosecutions of child sexual abuse has been the difficulties in getting the evidence of

child victims before the Court. These problems have arisen
because of the unwillingness of some parents to allow their children to undergo the trauma of appearing in the Court, the
approach taken by courts in not accepting the sworn evidence of
children under ten years and the requirement that, for a successful
prosecution corroboration is required of unsworn evidence.
(Report:218)

Their concerns echoed those expressed by Bidmeade in his review of
child protection procedures. We are struck by the fact that procedures
which isolated the child within a combative arena needed to be modified, that the law hitherto had done little to accommodate the specific
needs of the child. The strength of entrenched legal practices and principles which make change difficult obliged the task force to weigh the
chance of success for any reforms to legal procedures it might recommend. Its choice among a variety of reform options depended not only
on what research might suggest as the best solution to obstacles to successful prosecutions, but also on calculations about the likelihood of
achieving a particular option politically.

At the time of writing, the amendments to the several related parliamentary acts lie on the table for debate. The recommendations of the
report, already negotiated within the task force, continue to be contested. The 'rights of the child' have gained some footing; the conflicting
roles of the welfare department as both child advocate and investigative
agency (in the first instance) may be clarified; the practices of the law
have been challenged to some extent.

We have sketched a picture of the politics of child sexual abuse which
emphasises conflict. This means conflict within the state as much as
around the state. The 'discovery' of the hidden problem of child sexual
abuse raises questions of sexuality, familial relations and power. The
heavily contested strategies developed by the state deflect the risk these
questions pose to the existing gender order, by asserting the rights of the
child within the family. The ways those rights are constructed serve to
neutralise the sexual politics of the problem. Our reading of the South
Australian report and the associated policy documents and public
debates suggests that the insistence on denying sexuality, in conjunction
with a focus on the child at the expense of the mother, are important
moves in evading the issue of the oppressive nature of gendered power
relations.

The strategic problem

Where does the feminist challenge to the state's part in the politics of
sexual violence now stand? First, we argue that challenging the state is
a crucial move. Women have little choice but to demand state intervention in sexual and familial violence. When we consider the individual
isolation of each experience of sexual violence, whether it occurs in pub-

lic places or within the family home; the economic and social disadvantages of women and children; and the state's claims to control violence and its actual control of the human services, there is no practical alternative to making demands on the state.

Feminism has broken through public silences to make such demands. Increased reporting rates bear witness to an improved public sensitivity towards abused women. Feminist arguments that sexual violence is not confined to an aberrant minority now jostle with deviancy models. Similarly, feminist constructions of sexuality contest concepts of woman as the sexually devious female.

However, responses by the state to feminist demands are ambiguous at best. Feminist influence can be discerned in the reformed laws and the published policy documents. But the predominant state strategies are designed to manage conflicting interests and to defuse challenges to patriarchal relations. Faced with ambivalent or mutilated outcomes of reform campaigns, the prominent legal reform advocate Jocelynne Scutt has recently argued that feminist demands for reforms may be ill-conceived: 'Confronted with a legal system that refuses to recognise all women as equal to all men, a battle has been fought to change laws rather than to acknowledge that the problem lies in the very nature of law and in the dominant ideology of those who interpret it' (Scutt, 1985:137). The argument may indeed be extended to cover the entire problem of the connections between the state and sexual violence.

It is imperative to recognise fundamental patriarchal assumptions in state strategies. But it does not follow that the state is omnipotent, that those strategies will necessarily *work*. We have stressed the ways the state's strategies are developed through conflict. The articulation of patriarchal interests is not pre-given; it must be worked out in a complex process of struggle. At the same time, our analysis of the state also proposes that those who advocate feminist demands within the state are implicated in a complex of contested interests. They act to translate demands strategically; they do not simply betray, or keep, the feminist faith.

Our analysis points to the necessity and significance of political struggle. Reasoned argument, even embedded in the most careful legal terms, will not win the day. Nevertheless, the feminist politics of sexual violence has obliged the state to make certain shifts. Practices have been changed and internal as well as external conflicts have to be managed with all the attendant risks to the maintenance of the state's part in patriarchal relations.

But the feminist challenge to the politics of sexual violence has a considerable distance to go. Australian feminists can ill afford to bail out of engagements with the state. Nor do we believe it possible to avoid the state. Debate among feminists must concern the ways and means of the battle since the terrain is given: the politics of sexual violence must largely be fought out on the territory of the state.

Part III

Feminism and bureaucracy

Part III

Pluralism and Bureaucracy

7

The 'femocrat' strategy

'Femocrat?' exclaims the overseas visitor. 'I've never heard the term.' 'It's an Australian phenomenon,' we answer with uneasy pride. Uneasy because uncertain whether we are being politically creative or merely foolhardy. For the visitor from the United States 'femocrat' may be simply an example of Australian linguistic creativity. She will recognise the strategies, from affirmative action programs to dress-for-success workshops, since the reform strand of US feminism has considerable influence in Australia. The visitor from Britain may be more equivocal. Equally influential on Australian feminism, British feminism tends to see working for reforms within state structures as a betrayal of feminist ideals. At best, this strategy tinkers with the details of administration (Barrett, 1980; Phillips, 1987). British feminists do work within the state, but their most visible encounter has been with progressive local councils. In the event, Australians may be pleased to note, the British report difficulties in resolving complex dilemmas of conflicting and competing interests: among groups of women and between the goals of feminist ideals and the tedious bureaucratic work of funding and supplying regular services.

Australian feminists are by no means alone in seeking to represent 'women's interests' within the state. For example, Canada established a Women's Bureau in the Federal Department of Labour in 1954, to which have been added a variety of bureaux and agencies, such as a central Office for Equal Opportunities, and Advisory Councils on the Status of Women. Sweden appointed an Advisory Council to the Prime Minister on Equality Between Men and Women in 1972. Five out of fifteen ministers were women in 1983. More surprisingly, India established a National Commission on the Status of Women in 1971. Representation now includes a Women's Welfare and Development Bureau under the Central Ministry of Social Welfare. Indonesia gestures with an Associate Minister on the Role of Women.

The term 'femocrat' is unique to Australia and New Zealand. Sometimes spoken pejoratively, it refers to those women appointed to work in 'women's affairs' and women's units in the state apparatus, the bureaucracies. (Its currency is now expanding to include feminist

bureaucrats who seek to work on behalf of women whatever their position.) The invention of a specific term denotes the importance of the group to the Australian women's movement, if not its size. Femocrats signify the Australian movement's approach to the state, carrying feminist demands to extend women's rights and opportunities into a direct engagement with the state. This does not mean that Australian feminism has resolved in favour of participation, in contrast to the British rejection of it. On the contrary, debate has continued since the appointment of the first femocrat in 1973.

The significance of the feminist political strategy warrants evaluation. How do we reckon the gains and losses in terms which recognise the risks and dilemmas faced by femocrats and by the wider movement? Appraisal demands that our theory of the state be up to the task. We need the kind of analysis which the first section of this book provides. We need room to recognise the internal dynamics of the state; lost neither in descriptive detail of policy development nor in reified concepts of the state.

In this final section, we wish to take such an approach to the femocrat phenomenon. We propose to consider the emergence of feminist bureaucrats and state responses; the issue of the 'bureaucratisation' of feminism; relations between femocrats and other feminists, the femocrat strategy and the women's movement.

Early days

The women's movement has long questioned whether the appointment of feminists to public policy positions in the bureaucracies of the state represents the 'bureaucratisation' of feminism, its co-option and depoliticisation, or the creation of a feminist bureaucracy capable of effecting social change. Underlying the issue, the nature of the power of the state focuses our attention on the strategic responses of the state during the femocrat period. Why did the state respond to feminist demands, develop positions and policies designed to deal with them? Why appoint women's advisers, equal opportunity officers, make room for women's units? Why this particular strategy? We believe the answers have as much to do with a specific moment of the history of the state as it does with the politics of the Australian women's movement.

Before this period, the exclusion of women from public policy and decisionmaking was evident in their scarce numbers in parliament, and legally explicit in the upper levels of bureaucracy through the operation of the marriage bar. 'Women's issues' lacked bureaucratic structures for their specific representation. Their absence was noted occasionally, as when Mr Enderby commented during a 1973 parliamentary debate on abortion (the McKenzie-Lamb Medical Practice

Clarification Bill): 'We sit here making decisions for women when there is not a woman amongst us.'

The exclusion of women is not new; nor indeed the awareness of it. With skilful irony Virginia Woolf pondered the conundrum of women's small presence in public life twenty years after they had won the right to enter it. She saw that 'nature, law and property were all ready to excuse and conceal [the cause]' (1938:244). What was new in the 1970s was that exclusion came to be seen as challenging the legitimacy of the state in liberal terms.

Such change resulted from the substantial inroads women made into the public sphere, the legitimate domain of the state. Their numbers in the labour market increased rapidly during the 1950s and 1960s. A renewed political women's movement began to make its presence felt—Mr Enderby made his remark after referring to the women protesting outside Parliament House. And the election of the Whitlam Labor government in December 1972, highlighted the absence of women as this government promised to renew the welfare state and to extend representation to all citizens.

However, exclusion of women and of 'women's issues' was not simply a matter of the lack of women representatives within the state. Rather, the gendered nature of the bureaucratic apparatus of the state is at issue. As argued in Chapters 2 and 3 above, not only does the state function to sustain partriarchal relations, but state structures are themselves patriarchal in form.

Feminists agreed that the oppressive configuration of the gendered state should change. They differed over means. In Australia feminists, particularly liberal feminists, focused on the state bureaucracies. Educational institutions, and to a lesser extent the Labor Party, received attention; work in the unions built up more slowly until the 1980s. Optimism about the potential for social change through the bureaucracies sprang from the energy of a burgeoning women's movement and from the election of an enthusiastic social democratic federal government.

The opportunity for changing 'the rules of the game' seemed clear: 'If we change the norms of political behaviour it could help overthrow the system; if we play with the boys but refuse to play by their rules the game may suffer a severe change' (Cox, 1974:30). The argument assumes that this was the only game in town. Many feminists were not so certain. Some wished to consider other possibilities: some felt that the whole game should be given away in order to start somewhere else.

For the 'players', involvement meant far more than broadening the political agenda.

Feminists had become reconciled to a need to work within existing institutions, not only to increase the community's resources

directed to women, but to change the institutions themselves. We understood the root of discrimination against all disadvantaged groups to be systemic, integral to the structures of social, economic and political institutions, and that radical change in these institutions was required if any significant social change was to be effected.(Dowse, 1981:10)

Crucial to evaluation of feminist engagement with the state is the extent to which the 'rules of the game' have changed. Put another way, was the emergence of the femocrat a contradiction for the women's movement, or for bureaucracy and the state, or a contradiction for both?

The commitment to work within state structures brought difficult political questions in its train. How could political representation work in a feminist movement organised on non-hierarchical principles? What form of bureaucratic machinery could deal with the way feminist issues cut across all policymaking fields? How could femocrats maintain credibility both within the bureaucracy and with the movement? If femocrats sought to influence legislative processes, how significant was legislation itself for social change? And more problematically, how predictable were the consequences of specific policy changes?

Answers emerge out of feminist political origins and from feminist experiences within the state. In the early days, a discrete feminist organisation, the Women's Electoral Lobby, led the push for the representation of women's affairs in decisionmaking. Its approach subsequently influenced the femocrats.

Electoral politics

In 1972, the newly formed Women's Electoral Lobby succeeded in making the representation of women's affairs an electoral issue. WEL aimed to gain access to policymaking power structures indirectly by a skilful use of the media at the same time as the Labor opposition was winning the high ground on social change and equality of opportunity.

An important tactic, borrowed from the reform-oriented strand of the US women's movement, NOW and *Ms* magazine, was the evaluation of candidates for the federal elections. Candidates were surveyed, interviewed and graded according to their knowledge of and attitudes towards feminist concerns, such as family planning, abortion, child care, social welfare, divorce, women in education and the workforce. WEL sought politicians' commitment as part of the strategy to establish a feminist political influence.

Divisions over such strategies arose within the women's movement as other feminists were wary of taking on the 'boys' in mainstream politics. (Left politics presented another set of problems.) Helen Glezer and Jan Mercer replied:

WEL grew out of the Women's Liberation movement but its sub-

sequent development and concern with reforms has led to its establishment as an autonomous organisation. Lack of revolutionary tactics has broadened its membership appeal to many women. Ironically, therefore, it may be more influential in changing the balance of power between men and women than the Women's Liberation Movement. (1975:403)

The success of WEL in achieving visibility for feminist issues gave an early credibility to its claims.

WEL saw feminist politics as not necessarily corresponding with any one party ideology. Its campaign was premised on a certain recognition of gender difference. WEL challenged male definitions of politics and of the norms of political behaviour in two ways: by asserting its autonomy from male party politics; and by its inclusion of issues which had hitherto been ruled out of party policy. Abortion, for example, had been designated a 'matter of conscience', an instance of the kind of gendered assumptions underlying public/private dichotomies.

WEL regarded the confinement of women's issues to the private sphere as itself a matter of politics. Seeking to haul 'private' issues into the legitimate public arena, WEL began to broach 'the barrier of dominant values':

> The barrier serves to suppress grievances reflecting values that conflict fundamentally with prevailing norms, and rejects from serious public consideration the demands which are publically articulated, but which are radically at odds with the dominant view of what constitutes a publically legitimate issue. (Bachrach and Baratz, 1970:58)

At odds with the dominant view, WEL asserted the public legitimacy of private-sphere concerns.

WEL tackled political legitimacy via legitimate public means, assuming that, with a sufficiently powerful electoral base, the 'barrier of dominant values' could be opened up to influence and to persuasion. Its strategy was based on a liberal assumption that the exclusion of feminist issues from public decisionmaking was mainly a result of ignorance. Even powerful men could be persuaded to alter their values.

The WEL campaign was a precursor of feminism's entry into the state bureaucracies. In particular, its assumption that the exclusion of women could be transformed by education and consciousness-raising informed the femocrat project. But this assumption likewise curtailed its potential.

From influence to entrism

The impact of women's political activity registered immediately the Whitlam government came to power. The Equal Pay case was reopened; legislation for supporting mothers benefit was introduced as

well as maternity leave for Australian government employees. So much parliamentary talk followed that 'women' became an indexed subject in Hansard! Most interesting was the appointment of Elizabeth Reid as women's adviser to the prime minister in April 1973. This was not a wholehearted response by the new reform government since she was expected to advocate all women's issues, and initially with no support staff. A year later, the establishment of the Women's Affairs Section in the Department of the Prime Minister remedied this small difficulty.

Elizabeth Reid was appointed as a feminist. Not surprisingly, she became the focus of women's movement demands on the government. The appointment represented the first tangible step towards the direct involvement of feminists within the state. But it struck at a touchstone of feminist organisational principles: the deliberate structurelessness of collectivity. Placed high in the bureaucratic hierarchy the women's adviser was meant to represent women in their generality and in their diversity. A high-flying kite, but how good was the view, and who could send messages up the string?

Labor State governments followed Whitlam's example. In South Australia, Deborah McCulloch was appointed women's adviser to the premier in late 1974, and subsequently an equal opportunities commissioner, Mary Beasley was appointed to implement the Sex Discrimination Act 1975. Individual departments also appointed women's advisers, for example the appointment of Denise Bradley to the Education Department in 1976. By December 1977 there were twelve women's units throughout the country (Clarke and White, 1983:147), and the numbers have more than doubled since then. All appointments were lateral recruitments from outside the public service, an important characteristic of femocrats, whose previous work experience was chiefly in tertiary education. As a group they are generally of Anglo origin, middle-class, tertiary-educated. Their feminism was largely informed by that represented by the Women's Electoral Lobby although other feminisms have been influential.

They faced a number of problems. First, they had to find their way within an overwhelmingly male bureaucracy. They were lateral appointments, in part because the Australian Public Service is a complex hierarchical system dominated by men. The marriage barrier for women was not lifted in the federal system until 1966, with equal pay introduced in the late 1960s. The top layer, the First division, which consists of the permanent heads of departments, is almost entirely male (Boreham et al., 1979). In the federal system, few women have ever been members: Marie Coleman, the first, who undertook the review of Childhood Services discussed in Chapter 4, was a member from 1973 to 1976 when she chaired the Social Welfare Commission. In the State systems there have been a few more, notably Pat O'Shane, an Aboriginal lawyer, appointed as the first woman department head in the country by the New South Wales government in 1981 (Clarke and White 1983:142).

Femocrats not only enter a male-dominated organisation but they enter it as outsiders. Knowledge of internal structures and politics is hard won in a context which is at best indifferent, if not overtly hostile, to their presence as feminist policymakers. Clarke and White, who interviewed female public servants in 1983, found that femocrats experienced 'some difficulties in adapting to the male culture of the workplace, and some difficulties in being accepted in positions of authority' (1983:143). These problems were at least as sharp for the first femocrats.

A second major problem is that, in contrast to most public servants at policy levels, femocrats were highly visible. We have noted the attention the women's movement paid to Elizabeth Reid, but so too were she and other women's advisers the focus of anti-feminists. The first women's adviser in Victoria, Penny Ryan, was forced to resign by an 'embarrassed' government, the result of a campaign by right-wing women who publicised her membership of the Communist Party. The federal women's adviser received such adverse publicity that Whitlam declared his intention to abolish the position and Elizabeth Reid resigned in October 1975 (Dowse, 1983:211).

The third revolves around the issue of marginality. Central to neither bureaucratic structure nor to policy, women's units are specifically charged with the unwelcome task of initiating change to policy and more recently, under affirmative action legislation, to structures as well. Located outside the bureaucratic mainstream, femocrats have to work out what a more central involvement would imply, if it could be achieved. Dilemmas implicit in this kind of engagement with the state materialise as issues that appear to be bureaucratic trivia.

For example, Sara Dowse resigned as head of the Office of Women's Affairs when the Fraser government proposed to relocate the unit to the Department of Home Affairs. This represented a further marginalisation; according to Marion Sawer such a structural move from the Department of Prime Minister and Cabinet severely limited the working potential of the Office.

> The relocation of the Office in a low-ranking ministry [Home Affairs then ranked 26th out of 27 ministries] made it very difficult to gain automatic access to Cabinet submissions. It also meant that the co-ordinating role of the Office became dependent on personal relationships established between the Head of the Office and key decision-makers in functional Departments. Once moved away from a central co-ordinating Department to a peripheral one the Office was no longer able to play such an effective role as the hub of the women's affairs wheel and the IDWG [Interdepartmental Working Group, chaired by the Office to coordinate women's units] gradually became moribund. (Sawer, 1986:9)

Marion Sawer and Sara Dowse both conclude that tangential positions can have little impact on mainstream policy.

Yet, if femocrats could achieve a more central location, their capacity

to advocate clear feminist policy might be blunted by close involvement in the state directorate's own strategies. Femocrats cannot escape this dilemma. Later in the chapter we argue that they necessarily develop their own strategies to meet internal problems. Recognising the need for such strategies is an important factor in our evaluation of the femocrat project.

Fourth, the complex relationship with the women's movement variously affects femocrats and the femocrat project. Drawing largely on the WEL position, femocrats are concerned chiefly with women's rights. Such a position has an immediate utility because it represents an alignment between the advocacy brief of femocrats and a liberal-pluralist view of the state, assuming that 'it is an arena within which interest groups can compete' (Simms, 1981:229). Women are understood to constitute such a potentially unitary group whose interests therefore can be extended through the state. Such assumptions conflict with other feminist positions, notably marxist and radical-feminist, both of which in principle see the state as part of the problem rather than part of the solution. In practice, neither of these latter positions are clear-cut. Some femocrats are sympathetic to the arguments, and many feminists of whatever persuasion have engaged with the state, for example in direct negotiation for the funding of feminist services.

The four problems outlined here were largely problems for femocrats. If we widen our lens we may capture the play between femocrats and the women's movement.

Tensions and connections

When Elizabeth Reid was appointed, both the appointment itself and protests against it, such as that by the Women's Liberation *Mejane* group, who opposed it publicly on the grounds that the appointment violated the organisational principles of the feminist movement, caused dissension within the movement. Since 1973, tensions between and among feminists within a social movement, and feminists designated by the state to be representative, not only of feminists but of all women, have been endemic. They produced an embattled resistance among femocrats of the kind we observed in Chapter 5; and a frustration, sometimes anger, among other feminists, as we saw in Chapter 6.

The New Zealand writer Jesvier Singh reported that during her research on that country's 'bureaucratic feminism' she 'encountered resistance, defensiveness and even hostility'. Femocrats felt that

> they work their guts out, endure the enormity of 'White male power' to gain reforms for the benefit of all women, only to be maligned by their 'sisters'...Critics are rejected as ignorant and ungrateful—critique has been synonymous with 'trashing' where dissent is dismissed as personal attack (1987:13).

Yet criticism of femocrats has been ambivalent, muddled by confusions about the significance of personal style, tactical priorities, conflicting feminist analyses of power and the difficulties of theorising about the state. And of course, as for any political movement, the difficulties of working out the politics on the run.

Femocrats are criticised as 'tall poppies' because they do occupy, relative to most women, high-status, well-paid positions. They do experience the seductions of success, authority, career opportunities, the elitism of influence and invitations into informal networks. Yet their contributions to the practical gains of policy reforms under enormous pressure cannot be denied. They in turn, while affected by such criticism, rely on the women's movement for personal support and, more decisively, for their political *raison d'être*.

But there are disjunctions. Some years ago, Rosemary Pringle expressed some of the anger and concern about the implications for feminism of the gaps which, by then, had developed—gaps within the movement that the femocrat presence itself appeared to be creating. She observed that many feminists feel too mystified and unconfident to apply for positions within the now sprawling women's bureaucracy. Those outside need to rethink their approach to the state.

> There is nothing more insidious than the paranoia and caution that sets in on anyone who has been there more than a year or so. This can only be halted by the infusion of new people, and perhaps some willing to accept short-term appointments who will not thereby be overwhelmed by the general elitism, chauvinism, authoritarianism and secretiveness of the Public Service. (Pringle, 1979:60)

Otherwise femocrats will be lost, beyond recovery.

The gaps remain, in spite of the explosion of femocrat positions associated with the Hawke government's affirmative action legislation, and the increased visibility of certain 'women's issues' on social policy agendas. The public talk about the femocrat strategy increases. Witness the packed sessions at the 1982 and 1984 Women and Labour conferences on legislative reforms, working in bureaucracies and women's work conditions, and the series of sessions on 'women working in and around the state' at the 1987 Socialist Feminist conference in Sydney. Still it is rare for a femocrat to say:

> I am a bureaucrat. The community regards me as a bureaucrat and so I'm distrusted, and rightly so. I'd feel the same way. I have loyalties, obligations and duties to the department. I take them lightly but I can't take them too lightly. I also have an obligation to the taxpayer and the community that I work effectively and responsibly. We're caught in the middle. (Singh, 1987:14)

Although we agree with Singh that the 'personal motivations, the aspirations and definitions are not beyond criticism', at least in the context of

their political consequences, such a focus does not get us very far. We end with an explanation cast in terms of individual attitudes, and of individual feminist sincerity. As in Jocelyn Scutt's account of what went wrong with the New South Wales rape law reform (see p.127) we are left with the hope that their commitment to the feminist cause will unite them with other feminists against the patriarch. Blaming femocrats for lack of success fails to recognise that alliances, even those among sisters, are not achieved simply. Moreover, it leaves out the part played by the state. Unity is not a matter of everyone recognising their common interests as women. A key presupposition of liberal feminism, and of some strands of radical feminism, is that the category 'woman' includes a commonality sufficient to transcend the differences of age, race, culture and class. Although feminism has always striven towards a common vision, based on the shared concerns of women oppressed as women, those same concerns are frequently disrupted.

Anne Phillips' study of British feminism illustrates the historical dilemmas feminists have faced, and still face, because of the lack of fit between the oppressions of sex, race and class.

> We organise a reclaim the night demonstration through an area where women are sexually harassed—but it is an area where many Afro-Caribbean people live, and our activities fuel racist stereotypes of marauding blacks. We challenge an apprenticeship scheme that has excluded girls from training—and we find ourselves linked with employers in an attack on union power ... At the end of the day, the real issues about class in the women's movement relate not to a hierarchy of oppression but to the problems of unity, of alliance across what is difference, of troubled choices between competing demands. (1987:11–14)

This is one side of the coin. On the other lie those dilemmas arising out of the contradictions of the state itself. At present, these look especially sharp as the New Right weighs in against legitimation of the liberal state. Rosemary Pringle worried about femocrats during what seemed the pits of Fraser government conservatism. But now we are confronted by a right-wing Labor government committed to being *really* pragmatic about social justice. Its approach to child care, education and training, and welfare, whether through policies, legislation or service provision, is governed by a 'pragmatism' which itself reflects a narrow band of social interests.

It follows that the task of comprehending and evaluating the strategic value of feminist engagement with the state requires that we look more closely at the workings of that state. The task has an important bearing on the issue of feminist unity. The personal attitudes of femocrats are not sufficient to explain or to predict the possibilities of alliance. Our attention must turn to structural considerations.

We may posit that the workings of the state will prove to be disruptive of women's shared concerns. The anonymous bureaucrat quoted by

Singh makes the point that it is her location as a bureaucrat which both arouses suspicion and places her in the difficult position of 'divided loyalties'. This is to raise the issue of the 'bureaucratisation of feminism'.

Direct engagement with the state appears to endanger feminist politics through 'bureaucratisation'. A problem for femocrats, the question whether or not they have been tainted with bureaucracy puts the debate in terms of a moralistic role theory. We argue, rather, that the workings of the state constitute very real structures which shape femocrat actions.

The 'bureaucratisation of feminism'

The term 'bureaucratisation of feminism' has several angles to it. First, it implies notions of bureaucracy as an organisational form and assumes that feminism's entry into bureaucracy involved feminism's adaption to that form. Second, bureaucratisation can be regarded as a mechanism of state power with implications for the object of the exercise of that power. As an organisational form, bureaucratisation suggests adaptation to Weberian principles of hierarchical authority, functional rationality, objective expertise and regulated impersonal structures. These appear contradictory to feminism's own organisational ideals which are antipathetical to hierarchy, rules and authority, and problematic for the multifaceted and subjective nature of feminist issues. As we noted in Chapter 3, for some feminists the two are completely opposed. By contrast, the femocrat project wades in and, not without difficulty, seeks to use the bureaucratic form.

In Weberian terms, objective expertise, a fundamental precept of bureaucracy, was a characteristic of the modern state which distinguished it from a system of personal patronage. Objectivity provided bureaucracy with its predictable outcomes, 'calculability of results'. The state benefits from objectivity in the bureaucracy, achieved through the removal of personal relationships:

> Its specific nature, which is welcomed by capitalism, develops the more perfectly the more the bureaucracy is 'dehumanized', the more completely it succeeds in eliminating from official business love, hatred, and all purely personal, irrational, and emotional elements which escape calculation. This is the specific nature of the bureaucracy and it is appraised as its special virtue.
> The more complicated and specialized modern culture becomes, the more its external supporting apparatus demands the personally detached and strictly 'objective' *expert,* in lieu of the master of older social structures, who was moved by personal sympathy and favor, by grace and gratitude. (Gerth and Mills, 1948:216)

Weber praises objectivity, the removal of the emotional and the irrational, and envisages a process of increasing expertise and an increasing concomitant objectivity.

The principle of objectivity offers some leverage for reform. For example, feminists justified anti-discrimination legislation on the grounds that it would remove outdated, demonstrably ideological and hence irrational assumptions. Such argument uses conventional definitions of objectivity. But the principle of bureaucratic objectivity takes the high ground as free of values. Any challenge to it may be readily construed as value-laden, as political, not objective. The contest then becomes a struggle over the power to define what is 'value-free'. The struggle itself brings the definitions into question. As we observed in Chapter 5 on equal opportunity, the definition of merit as an objective principle, once challenged by feminists, loses its objectivity as it becomes tainted with politics, although that was not their intention. We may suppose that if feminists had sufficient power, merit could be rescued, as a signifier of agreed standards.

Objectivity, synonymous with rationality and the value-free, also excludes the personal. Since women are associated historically and ideologically with the domestic, the sphere of emotion and desire, this criterion of what is appropriate to the public sphere suggests a principle which excludes women. The 'emotional' stereotype insinuates that women in the public domain are 'unstable, unpredictable, and generally too soft for top jobs' (Wells, 1987:115). If they are not emotional, they are 'tough bitches'. Senator Janine Haines is not alone in her observation that:

> A man is expected to be assertive, determined, persuasive, to achieve his goals and he's allowed to get angry at something not going his way. If a woman does the same thing, she's aggressive, she's pushy, she nags and she can't control her temper and is emotional. So we're damned if we do and damned if we don't. (Wells, 1987:117)

A minor industry has grown up in response to the problems femininity poses in the public sphere. Glossy magazines offer 'role model' stories and 'how to' articles. Private consultancies offer day and weekend sessions on leadership and self-esteem (unfortunately our research budget did not extend to the $100+ enrolment fee which is typical). Affirmative action programs incorporate workshops for those who implement the programs, as well as for those who are supposed to benefit from them. Arguably, the approach improves on the 'business' manuals for secretaries which recommend that 'she' must remind the boss of his wife's birthday. For Kathy Ferguson the industry merely provides recipes for conformity. She remarks that advice manuals 'argue that women are oppressed collectively simply because they are women; but they tie this insight to a set of values and assumptions that leads to virtually total acceptance of the status quo' (Ferguson, 1984:183). By contrast, Hester Eisenstein has called for a close study of the femocrats, since she believes that too little is known about the ethnography of how femocrats respond to the pressures of masculine bureaucracy (Eisenstein,

1987). In the meantime, we observe that the Survival-and-Success industry bears witness to the pressures on women both to learn the 'language' and loosen the links between femininity and the personal.

In spite of all the effort, women still fail to 'pass' as impersonal, objective bureaucrats. Why so? Fifty years ago, Virginia Woolf's answer was: 'The cat is out of the bag; and it is a Tom' (1938:94). Clare Burton uses different words, but argues similarly when she says that while masculinity remains dominant in the workplace, homosociability, the preference for the same sex, will continue to provide a powerful basis for resistance to the presence of women. Women as equals threaten the status and satisfaction men gain from the workplace, and threaten the definitions of work itself as they blur the distinction between the workplace and the private sphere.

> [This] is clearly exacerbated when women—the nurturers of small children—hold positions of authority over men at the workplace. Cultural blasphemy indeed, when our cultural traditions have emphasized not only the connection of women with dependence and subservience but the necessity for them to take the private, domestic load so that men could be free to engage in more important, public affairs. (Burton, 1986:297)

The femocrat push to achieve positions of authority does challenge masculine homosociability in the workplace. It challenges the divisions between the public and the private, a premise of the sexual division of labour. It does not challenge the overall social division of labour. The cat is not completely out of the bag.

The objectivity of the bureaucrat is defined in gendered terms, but we should be aware that the ideal bureaucrat is very narrowly defined. Characteristics other than the feminine are also deemed peculiar. Colour, class, religion and language are restricted; homosexuality and physical disabilities are generally ruled out. Resisting these pressures for conformity and their associated definitions of 'deviance' can be more or less risky, to both protagonists and to the bureaucracies. It should be no surprise that femocrats rarely personify differences other that gender.

Whether femocrats successfully pass as objective bureaucrats raises political problems about the strategy of trying to do so. Bureaucrats ideally engage in impersonal relationships and so provide the anonymity regarded as a prerequisite of non-political administration. The appointment of femocrats as specialist women's advisers to highly politicised policy areas creates tensions for bureaucracy's anonymity. However, anonymity preserves non-accountability. Thus the women's movement questions how and to whom women's advisers, representatives of women, are accountable. The objectivity of the femocrat leads to a wariness about representation.

These issues coincide with the objective organisational principle of functional specialisation which provides a legitimate basis for efficient organisation. Efficiency itself is a fundamental tenet of bureaucracy since

it is efficiency which provides bureaucratic organisation with its authority. Femocrats promoted equal employment opportunity as the efficient maximisation of talent within the bureaucracy's own terms. Functional specialisation results in policy areas which are not only divided into departments but tend to be confined by them. Thus 'women's affairs' is defined as a social welfare policy area concerned with the disadvantaged, rather than as something integral to general social and economic policy. Specialisation fragments the universal warrant of feminism. Yet specialisation has the tactical capacity to preserve insight and to protect policy definition. (This may be seen in the case of equal opportunity practitioners discussed in Chapter 5.) Functional specialisation has served to gain a place for women's issues. Femocrats function as specialists of that place. They *are,* in bureaucratic terms, 'experts'.

Paradoxically, femocrats achieve specialist expertise but never objectivity. Functional specialisation, an apparently objective principle, provides the means of preserving a subjective definition of reality. The logic of functional specialisation for femocrats conflicts with the principle of objective expertise. In Weber's terms, any neutral individual might specialise to function as an expert. Against this, femocrats assert that their expertise inheres in the particularity of their experience as women. They specialise in representing those women's issues. But ultimately, the liberal feminist resolution of women's issues demands the integration of women. So we have conflicting pressure on femocrats to move out of the specialist structures such as women's units, to transform the definition of the objective bureaucrat as masculine to the truly neutral.

Bureaucratisation as process

The second notion of 'bureaucratisation' as a process of power with political intent, points to the question of outcomes. Where bureaucracy as an organisational form draws attention to the actual mechanisms which feminism confronted as an acknowledged area of public policy, bureaucratisation as a process implies political outcomes. In this sense bureaucratisation is equated with institutionalisation, and thus political co-option.

Weber recognised the significance of bureaucracy as process and described it as formidably powerful:

> Once it is fully established, bureaucracy is among those social structures which is the hardest to destroy. Bureaucracy is *the* means of carrying 'community action' over into rationally ordered 'societal action'. Therefore, as an instrument for 'societalizing' relations of power, bureaucracy has been and is a power instrument of the first order—*for the one who controls the bureaucratic apparatus.*

Under otherwise equal conditions, a 'societal action' which is methodically ordered and led, is superior to every resistance of 'mass' or even of 'communal action'. And where the bureaucratization of administration has been completely carried through, a form of power relation is established that is practically unshatterable. (Gerth and Mills, 1984:228 emphasis added)

Weber proposes that bureaucracy's translation of 'community action' into rational order implies potential for bureaucratic control.

The process of bureaucratisation begins with the political effect of the bureaucratic selection of 'community actions' deemed worthy of attention. Critics of pluralist notions of competitive interest group representation point to the lack of equitable access to the bureaucratic decision-making process. Matthews (1976) described the process as biased towards 'institutionalised' groups. This means that groups required certain forms of organisation to be acknowledged in the first place. He included organisational resources such as a secretariat, a stable membership and concrete negotiable objectives. 'Limited organisational continuity and cohesion' was, in Matthews' terms, a distinguishing characteristic of groups which were not institutionalised (Matthews, 1976:337).

The implications for the feminist movement are that institutionalisation demands particular organisational structures within the movement, and creates divisions if such structuring were resisted. Interestingly both were experienced with the establishment of WEL which has influenced the selection of certain 'women's issues' for attention, as well as the form and approach of the bureaucratic response—the ways in which community actions have been translated. Divisions and tensions have arisen around the question of organisation, and not only between feminists inside and outside the bureaucracy.

The feminist form of organisation, collectivity, is exhilarating and effective when it 'works' but is very difficult to sustain. The long-term feminist problem of 'tyranny of structurelessness' has not been resolved and is under considerable pressure when the group undertakes 'community action'. Those involved in women's refuges, rape crisis centres, women's health centres, resource centres, abortion counselling services and so on, may begin with the gloss of letterheads and management committees but find themselves increasingly caught up in bureaucratic procedures. Susan Schechter's observation on the US situation could equally be made here:

Activists learned the problems inherent in simultaneously trying to run oppositional organisations, often based on principles of collectivity and consensus decision making, and keeping services funded through government grants that stipulated hierarchies and professionally trained staff. Moreover, when conflicts arose, the movement was sometimes too weak—because of underfunding, too few paid staff or volunteers, and exhaustion—to respond effectively. (Schechter, 1982:42)

Schechter believes that the women's movement has not resolved the dichotomy between services and political movement. In Australia, the femocrat phenomenon has blurred the distinction between the two.

We observe the effects in the tactics consequent on the demand for representation. Where representation demands institutionalisation, the process becomes potentially divisive when it involves the formation of an elite removed from the members. The requirement that representatives gain 'recognition', albeit for the issue or group, through conforming in behaviour and outlook to prevailing 'norms', compounds the difficulty. In this sense, dressing-for-success and a collective's carefully crafted grant submission are not unrelated. Submissions take time and skill to write, and the intention to share the process is often blighted by the kinds of obstacles Susan Schechter describes. In addition, resources and access are subject to political priorities. We note, for example, that child care frequently falls to the bottom of the agenda.

So far, the argument suggests that the bureaucracy is determinant. It draws the boundaries of representation, defining the issues and their mode of representation, and thus designates what will be the legitimate objects of its consideration. The result: conflict with the state is depoliticised, and the protagonists co-opted.

Two points demand attention. First, notions of simple co-option and incorporation assume that the process is unproblematic for the state. The argument grants such omnipotence to the state that everything is grist to its mill. Second, to treat state processes as Weber's 'unshatterable' control is to assume passivity on the part of the 'co-opted'. Struggles in and around feminist engagement are denied.

The consequence is a heavily weighted choice: either engage with the state, becoming assimilated, with political goals corrupted; or reject the state entirely. Set in these terms, who would choose corruption? But can the state be ignored? Is such political purity possible? Rebecca West once wrote an enormous exploration of this theme and concluded that the rejection of power for the sake of purity is itself a betrayal. 'They want to be right, not to do right.' As she peeled back the layers of the Slavic story of the 'black lamb and the grey falcon' she identifies the metaphor of the sacrifice of the black lamb as representing the 'friends of liberty'.

> We had regarded ourselves as far holier than our tory opponents because we had exchanged the role of priest for the role of lamb, and therefore we forgot that we were not performing the chief moral obligation of humanity, which is to protect the works of love. We have done nothing to save our people, who have some little freedom and therefore some power to make their souls, from the trampling hate of the other peoples that are without the faculty for freedom and desire to root out the soul like weed. (West, 1940:915)

Political events in the Europe of the 1930s gave West's despair a dramatic urgency.

Her terms were no more dramatic, however, than the outright rejection of an impervious patriarchal state and society by American feminists such as Mary Daly, Andrea Dworkin and Catharine MacKinnon. Consider Mary Daly for whom political engagement means to be assimilated as a token. 'Spinsters are spooked by fear of the Ultimate Irony, which would be to become a martyr/scapegoat for feminism, whose purpose is to release women from the role of martyr and scapegoat' (1978:318). Ironically, Andrea Dworkin and Catharine MacKinnon are prepared to lobby the American state for legislation to ban pornography (Rich, 1987:340).

So spinning and sparking are not enough. Perhaps they would argue a question of ways and means; that campaigns directed *at* the state are a different matter from bureaucratic entrism. Nevertheless the decision to seek legislative reform undermines the case for pure rejection. Although each of these writers develops vigorous arguments against the baleful intransigence of patriarchy, still the state cannot be ignored. The central part it plays in the construction and maintenance of the gender order cannot be sidestepped, as the issue of sexual violence well shows.

Are we still left with the diametrically opposed moral imperatives of engagement and corruption, or rejection and betrayal? We do not propose to rule this paradox out of court. The risks are great; there is no simple formula. But we need to challenge the view that the state is omnipotent and co-option inevitable.

The state's problems

What follows is an adaption of two writers on the welfare state, Ian Gough (1979) and Claus Offe (1984), whose accounts of the workings of the state offer some way through our dilemma. The 'welfare state' here refers to that form of the state which has dominated Western societies for the last 40 years.

Gough and Offe argue that the state is contradictory; it has both to guarantee the survival of capitalist economic processes over which it has no ultimate control *and* simultaneously make the social system appear to be fair, just and reasonable. They stress the contradictory, crisis-prone, inegalitarian and often oppressive aspects of capitalist economies, which since the early 1970s have again lurched into a prolonged crisis.

For Gough, the welfare state is specific to advanced capitalist countries and denotes 'the use of state power to modify the reproduction of labour power and to maintain the non-working population in capitalist societies' (1979:45). He argues, with reference to Elizabeth Wilson (1977), that this represents a new relationship between the state and the family. The dynamic of capital accumulation continually alters both the requirements of capital, particularly with regard to the state, and the capacity of the family to meet these requirements.

Offe's stress on the way the state is enmeshed in the contradictions of

capitalism argues that it has contradictory tasks. The state must sustain the process of accumulation and the private appropriation of resources; and it must preserve belief in itself as an impartial arbiter of class interests, thereby legitimating its power. The state is riven with contradictory functions; accumulation and legitimation. But this formulation 'tells us nothing about whether or not the state meets these requirements or the manner in which it responds to them' (Gough, 1979:51).

Recent writers such as the British marxists David Held (1984) and Stuart Hall (1984) suggest that the state's response depends on the outcome of contested interests. The state becomes the *site* of conflict. The problem with this metaphor is that it suggests the state is simply a battleground across which contests are fought. To picture the state as 'site' helps to escape the determinism of Weber's 'unshatterable' control, but assumes that the state as such is quiescent—and we have every reason to doubt that.

Offe argues rather that state responses are neither wholly determined by the state nor should be conceived simply as 'answers' to already contested demands. The state has its own, contradictory interests at stake. It suffers the problem that its own institutions and interests are only precariously compatible. In Offe's terms,

> the explanation of innovations in social policy is therefore the problem of the *internal rationalization* of the system of performance of social policy; in this view, the corresponding *pressure* for rationalization results from the fact that conflicting 'demands' and requirements faced by the politico–administrative system continually call into question the compatibility and practicability of the existing institutions of social policy. (Offe, 1984:104)

Social policy innovations, state responses, are not designed to meet specific 'demands' but instead incorporate reactions to dilemmas posed by those demands. Offe calls the state's resolution of its internal problems 'solution strategies', strategic solutions for continuing dilemmas.

We suggest that the state directorate attempted to resolve the demand for the representation of women's issues by the appointment of a single bureaucrat: a visible women's adviser who would be seen to be an advocate. Women's increasingly public participation in the labour market, combined with the political campaigns of Women's Liberation, challenged the legitimacy of a state which constructed women's issues as external to the public domain. The kind of solution devised was influenced by the newly elected government for which issues of equitable representation were central.

Feminist demands were not simply that women be included, although the absence of women from decisionmaking areas of the state apparatus gave impetus to that case. Rather, feminists demanded that the way the state approached women's interests be transformed (even as feminist conflict about it continued). The position which carried

feminism into direct engagement assumed a liberal state. Transformation required the recognition of the legitimacy of women in the plurality of competing interests.

However, the state can never successfully control the consequences of policy implementation, the effects of its own strategies. The outcomes are open and ambivalent precisely because strategies are developed through conflict within the state, and the state is itself implicated in conflict. It is neither a neutral nor determining mediator of contested needs. This is not the liberal-pluralist site of competing interests since the state has its own vested interests in the outcomes.

Feminist demands for representation called into question the compatibility of existing patriarchal institutions with representative democracy. The problem for the state became how to appear to include women without undermining patriarchal interests. Judith Grant and Peta Tancred-Sheriff make a similar point in their reflections on the Canadian state's responses discussed in Chapter 2 above. They argue that 'the representation of male interests is built into the bureaucratic apparatus generally', and can afford a subordinate and specific representation of women. The representation of 'women's issues' is suitable to the state because it 'has selected out those "potentially dissident" women who may need to be "regulated", and accorded them relevant representation' (1986:12).

We agree this describes the state directorate's strategy, but not the inevitable outcome. Gains made through severely limited representation led the state further into the mire. For the job to be seen to be done, a certain tangibility in the way of resources and a visible impact on policy was required. One femocrat was not enough. Increased and conflicting demands followed. The struggle over the representation of women's interests within the state was on.

We have argued for a dynamic view of the state, a state which is implicated in unpredictable conflict. But what of the state workers, specifically the femocrats? Are they the bearers of feminist demands? Do they become, inexorably, agents of the state? Interestingly, the early appointments of women's advisers were understood in these terms by everyone, particularly where they were members of WEL. Their critics tend to endorse the narrative that, individually and collectively, they have *become* agents of the state. We think there is a different story to be told.

Femocrats act

If the state is riven with contradiction, then the workers are faced with that contradiction. If we see the process of the conversion of 'demands' into 'policies' refracted and mediated through the internal structures of the state's contradictory tasks, a different light is cast on the actors

within the state apparatus. Those who are responsible for social policy responses constantly confront the predicament that demands cannot be reconciled neatly with the state's own needs. If social policies incorporate reactions to dilemmas posed by those demands, it follows that the actors who design the policies must act. They are not passive functionaries who simply implement already contested demands. Our reading of the Report on Child Sexual Abuse in Chapter 6 illustrates the dilemmas involved in translating demands into policy.

It is here that Offe's analysis of the state apparatus offers a useful point of departure. His focus on the state's own interests makes room for the recognition of the particular kinds of exigencies workers confront within the state apparatus. We bear in mind that the state apparatus is limited by the contradictory location of the welfare state, but Offe also recognises the strategic intelligence which government and state agencies often display.

Bureaucrats have their own problems. Since the state is implicated in conflict, in determining need through the development of solution strategies, so, necessarily, are state workers. Not only are they faced with multiple tasks and well-defined conflicts of interest among social classes or interest groups, but they also confront the logic of policy production 'based on bureaucratic rules, purposive action and consensus formation' (Held and Krieger, 1983:489). At the same time, the requirements for continual maintenance of the state must constantly seek to rationalise and to 'de-activate problems of internal state organisation'.

Bureaucrats are unable to avoid the logical imperatives of policy production. Or as Weber has it: 'The individual bureaucrat cannot squirm out of the apparatus in which he (*sic*) is harnessed'. But neither is the bureaucrat a 'mere cog in an ever-moving mechanism' (Gerth and Mills, 1948:228). As state workers, bureaucrats have their own basis for action, their own interests which shape and are shaped by internal problems. The organisation and the industrial strategies of the public sector unions evidence the specific interests and concerns of bureaucrats.

But the contradictory nature of the state constructs their interests and constrains their options for manoeuvre. Thus among bureaucrats interests may conflict and may deter the coherent development of solution strategies. By contrast, Weber's ideal bureaucracy shows the attraction of narrowly defined, 'normal' bureaucrats, operating with clear but rigid rules. They act in concert since the interests of each bureaucrat will more likely coincide. The actual modern state's solution strategies to legitimation difficulties, resulting in expanded personnel definitions and structural changes, have thrown these bureaucratic ideals out of gear. Oh, for the good old days!

Femocrats as bureaucrats are not simply the bearers of feminist demands within the state. They must act to translate those demands. Their appointment constitutes a kind of recognition of women's issues, but the matter of selection and interpretation of issues remains. Bureau-

cratic procedures and politics limit the means available to them. For example, as noted in Chapter 5, structural marginality presents the problem of whether to remain tangential to the bureaucratic structure in order to advocate a critical feminist policy, or to seek a more central location to engage directly in the development of policy. Should femocrats target the top or hassle on the margins? Risk bedevils both strategies.

We argue femocrats do have a choice, but one limited by the peculiarities of the state. Throughout the femocrat period, the choice has inclined towards reducing marginality through aiming for the top ranks. We note, in Chapter 1, that in terms of numbers there is plenty of room up there. The affirmative action program is designed to achieve the promotion of women into senior and decisionmaking positions.

Such a choice argues for pathfinders, a strategic vanguard, in contrast to the potential of a mass movement. These may be influenced by the notion of 'role-models' which has considerable currency. Appropriate role models are presumed to encourage a gradual rise of women. In addition, femocrats aim to intervene at decisionmaking levels directly in order to represent other feminists and women as 'clients' of the state. In consequence, until quite recently, they have not been recruited from, nor have they represented, the sizeable group of women workers within the state at the lowest hierarchical levels (see Chapter 1). We consider the conflicts which arise over this point in the next chapter.

But femocrat choice, shaped by a particular feminist politics, is also limited by structure. Although we have proposed that bureaucrats have their own basis for action, we must observe that the femocrat base is small; their numbers are few and their political interests are oppositional. Such circumstances weigh heavily in compelling decisions to aim for individual power. The risk is that everything depends on getting to the top.

Women's issues are in danger of being lost to the mainstream unless they are championed by femocrats in senior positions. For example, federal affirmative action programs are under threat. Until shortly after the 1987 federal elections, the programs were fostered by centrally located EEO units. Observers such as Lois Bryson fear that the devolution of affirmative action responsibilities to individual departments endangers the programs. 'Given the embryonic nature of EEO policy and programs it is doubtful that it will survive without centralised leadership' (Bryson, 1987:30).

The choice also risks undermining connections with the women's movement since feminism is as much about practices as it is about 'issues'; targeting the top poses questions about how femocrats act. Do they seek to negate bureaucratic hierarchies or adapt to them? Do femocrats adopt the 'rules of the game' or negotiate new ones? We agree with Hester Eisenstein that femocrats' 'lived experience' should be taken on board, and recognise the difficulties of going 'public' about the problems

of conflict and of alliances. No doubt, our understanding and analysis would be the better for having details of ways and means of femocrat practices. For the time being, we pore over the tea leaves of the anecdotal for signs. We attend conference workshops, scan feminist journals and newsletters, participate in informal discussions, and try to discern patterns and what underlies them.

We need, in any case, to know a good deal more about the culture of work: the texture of day-to-day work must be woven into our feminist analysis of women. But what is new about femocrats is that they are women workers with an unusual degree of power: power within the state to translate and to implement feminist demands. We find, underlying the interest in femocrats, the important question: what is a woman with public power? How does she think, feel, behave? Such questions challenge constructions of feminity, and feminists as much as do the issues around the representation of women. We will return to this question of 'power' in the next chapter.

Meantime, we are not entirely happy with an emphasis on femocrats' work, since bates about femocrat strategies too often focus on style. 'It's not what she does, but the way she does it.' But this leads to political evaluations based on individuals. We believe we must pay attention to structure in the terms we have suggested. It is important to recognise that femocrats are located within the structures of the state and thus working within the state demands the development of solution strategies specific to the internal problems of the state. Factors which constitute that environment must be taken into account. They include the contradictory location of the state, internal struggles for internal power, the dominance of hierarchical modes peopled with white, middle-class men, and shifts in language, in the discourse of policy development.

Evaluation of the femocrat project must recognise that femocrats constitute a challenge to the state's interest in the gender order and to the masculine dominance of public power. The notions of an omnipotent state and of the inevitability of co-option must be scrapped. In their place, we argue for recognising a state which has its own concerns. The state interprets demands in terms of its own solution strategies aimed at reconciling its internal mode of operation with conflicting constellations of interests. The state apparatus does not simply reflect whichever demands are successful in the contest, but is implicated in the determination of success.

State workers, and thus femocrats, are actors implicated in the strategic concerns of the state. The specific outcomes of action cannot be predicted, but we may identify the limitations of structural relationships of power and the internal requirements of the state apparatus. Femocrats are incorporated into a substantial agency of oppression where issues are contested and transformed within as well as in relation to it. They are

implicated in the transformation of demands into policies, but the consequences are uncertain because the process is the subject of political struggle within, as well as outside, the state apparatus.

We propose two further points in our concluding chapter: that neither the state nor the femocrat strategy/phenomenon is static; and that links between femocrats and the political women's movement are crucial.

8

Gains and losses
OR
Where will it all end?

Who knows where? But to understand where we are going we need to know where we are coming from and where we want to go. Where the women's movement is coming from, in Australia, has been shaped very substantially by feminist interactions with the state.

This book has sought to offer an analysis of that engagement. The argument has shown that theorising the state must involve the part it plays in constituting and maintaining the gender order. The discussion has covered several examples of feminist political practices which aim at challenging and/or renovating state processes. This inspection has shown something of the nuances, contradictions and resistances which feminist politics encounters. The Australian feminist experience of engagement has exposed an intricate texture of connections between the state and the gender order, and the complex ways in which the state has to be understood as gendered.

This may be harvested to useful theoretical and political effect. We must ask what have been the political gains for feminism, what have been the costs. At first glance, Australian feminism looks overwhelmingly committed to directing its political energies towards the state. However we have been struck by a pervasive ambivalence among feminists. We have several times noted the criticisms, even hostility, feminists frequently express towards feminist state strategies. This is often informal but no less vehement for that. Moreover femocrats, their actions and their attitudes are commonly the focus. That is to say, the overall strategy of engagement is often questioned in terms of individual behaviour, rather than in terms of political assumptions or theoretical issues.

To get a clearer sense of where we are now, we need to untangle this paradox, that a vigorous interventionist strategy meshes with a substantial doubt about, even suspicion of, the approach. Where we go next depends very much on what emerges from this paradox in terms of

156

feminist political priorities. To unravel it requires integrating the history of the last fifteen years into current theory and politics. Yet current political strategy can no longer rely on the framework of the 1970s. For example, there is no point debating whether or not we should engage with the state, since it has been going on for quite a while and has already changed the landscape. What we must continue to debate is ways and means, strategies and political assumptions. The debate must move forward. What follows is our reading of what is to hand for the task.

Resources

First, the state is inescapable for feminism. The accumulated experience of the women's movement demonstrates this. The feminist project to transform gender relations, to end the oppression of women, requires that the state be challenged, subverted, revolutionised. This does not imply that the state is the only or even the primary focus of feminist strategy. It does imply that in pursuing existing goals the state cannot be avoided or circumvented. The case studies in Part II illustrate how closely the state is implicated in the organisation of work, in the constitution of sexualities and of the family: in the shaping of both material and ideological conditions of life.

Although this is understood, at least implicitly, by feminism in many parts of the world, Australian feminism has perhaps taken farthest a strategy of carrying the challenge into the machinery of the state. But, as we argue in the previous chapter, the resulting femocrat phenomenon was not created entirely by feminist strategy. The emergence of femocrats is equally the result of solution strategies developed by the Australian state directorate in a particular configuration of party politics, a particular balance of class as well as gender forces. Our consideration of ways and means must bear in mind the continuous reciprocity implied in the phrase 'interaction with the state'. The process has been interactive, even if it often feels as if feminists have been chipping away at a wall of solid granite.

Third, the consequences of interaction, as femocrats are well aware, have as much to do with the state's interests and responses as they do with the attitudes and actions of femocrats themselves.

Now to return to the issue of feminist ambivalence about interaction with the state. What underlines these tensions, and why does argument focus on the femocrats? We attend to these tensions because they signal some unresolved political dilemmas. Like icebergs, and with the same dangerous properties, they are hazardous. The mostly submerged and in some ways very traditional conception of 'politics' looms up, politics seen as a boys' game connected to a destructive anti-human system which women should avoid; yet in the same image it is women who

have the capacity to clean it up. And the latter view gains credence through the long-term interaction of feminism with the state. In consequence, a substantial political space is occupied by a particular set of assumptions which are called into play by the nature of this interaction.

These assumptions belong for the most part to liberal feminism. Women's rights, the redistribution of existing social and economic rewards, the balancing or convergence of male and female roles, and the capacity of the present social system to deliver sex equality, constitute the liberal-feminist perspective. There are strong political and theoretical criticisms to be made of liberal feminism, some set out in earlier chapters; but its strength must be acknowledged also. Feminists' political interaction with the Australian state has largely been constructed in liberal-feminist terms with some radical-feminist influence but very little socialist-feminist.

How did this come about since feminist structures do not allow for clear-cut decisions. We cannot say that Australian feminists deliberately chose liberal feminism. Nor was it simply a consequence of the greater energy or political nous of liberal feminists. Rather, liberal feminism proposed a political program based on achieving reforms through the state, and to which the state could respond on its own terms. There is a correspondence between the rhetoric of the democratic state serving the citizens and the liberal-feminist approach to equal rights for women. The state gains legitimacy from showing itself willing to remove obstacles which prevent the inclusion of women in the democratic process. Women can be added on: to senior management in the public service, to science education, to non-traditional occupations, even (temporarily) to cabinet. Legislation can guarantee that women are included in the arithmetic. Liberal feminism goes further than this however. It wants the state to assist the process actively. As well as wanting discrimination excised from existing policies, it calls for new policies and new budget lines. It wants the state to clean up its act, to be pro-active in reforming its approach to women.

The reforms that have been achieved are not trivial. In contrast to the situation in 1970, Australia in 1988 has new legislation such as Sex Discrimination and Equal Opportunity Acts, reformed legislation such as new provisions on sexual assault, subsidised child care, non-sexist curriculum policies, publicly funded women's shelters. These gains are valued by the whole women's movement. But they are part of the problem for feminists. They are gains which many fought hard to achieve. Feminists have a vested interest in retaining them. So where is the space to raise political questions about the limits of such reforms? Or to challenge femocrat strategies which contributed to their achievement?

Disputes occur, but rarely in public forums. Consider for example the political difficulties that would be involved in holding a public debate on the assumptions inherent in an affirmative action program within an institution where many of the men are hostile to the program's gender-

inclusive intentions. Feminists end up defending a program like affirmative action because it represents some advance for women's claims for equity, and some moderation of oppressive institutional practices.

In these ways, the agenda for feminist political action is formed. It is not the only political agenda for the women's movement but it certainly holds considerable sway. The difficulty is that it cannot succeed, even on its own terms.

Quite simply, the state is unable to deliver the liberal-feminist program. Equality for women cannot be achieved without a substantial modification of the gender order, and this would necessarily involve transformation of the state. Even if we assume a narrow definition of equality to mean a crude numerical distribution of women throughout the bureaucracy, its achievement would require enormous changes. As feminists have already discovered, the business of adding on a few women here and there reverberates through a multitude of practices within and outside the state. The recent study of job evaluation procedures by Clare Burton and associates, discussed in Chapter 2 demonstrates that including women is no simple matter. The complex of gendered language, hierarchical job status (with 'female' jobs predictably low), and contradictory attitudes about gender difference, do not add up to explicit conspiracy or simple ignorance, readily resolved by well-argued policy documents against sexism. And job evaluation is merely one element, one of the array of practices, around employment. For women to achieve equity in employment, *all* these practices must change.

The problem is, how can such change be brought about? Showing the details of how sexist practices work is an important first stage, but what next? At this point feminists fall out. For some, the evidence from the first stage shows once again that the system is intractable and must be overturned or circumvented. Liberal feminists and femocrats assume that something can be done from within the system and resort to a combination of policy directives and mechanisms to alter attitudes.

This suggests a fundamental problem in the project: its lack of a coherent political theory of social change. To develop such a theory requires that debate be opened out. To date, it has been constrained within the limits outlined above. Limited to either/or choices of gradualism or revolution, the argument has curbed exploration of the dynamic consequences of change strategies.

As our case studies suggest, the implications of a change program always go beyond the level of simple arithmetic. Feminist strategy pushes up against the state's solution strategies aimed at balancing demands for equality with the patriarchal gender order. The liberal-feminist program cannot begin to be put in place without disruption. Femocrats have much experience of resistance to what appear to be the most modest of demands. Yet the state also has a varying interest in accommodating at least elements of the program. It follows that the

battle becomes one about where in a process of change to draw the line. Both 'sides' perform a balancing act between accommodation and disruption.

This too becomes a point of tension between femocrats and other feminists. Femocrats are seen to draw the line, or at least to calculate where it could be; to determine the strategies. And in one sense, as we suggested in the previous chapter, they must, in terms of their own survival—and do, in terms of the movement. Let us bear in mind that femocrats do not always agree, nor is their situation static: the kinds of consideration they take into account have varied during the period. Disquiet arises from femocrat interpretations of strategic requirements especially where femocrats are seen to devise strategies in isolation from the movement: why didn't they push harder? why didn't they ask us? (Why didn't femocrats argue for tougher sexual assault legislation? Why didn't they take account of feminist activists around rape law reform?)

These tensions have much to do with power and how feminists deal with it. Where feminism assumes that women are oppressed, the fact that sometimes in some places some women exercise power is difficult to integrate. Femocrats do have some degree of power. They are able to make decisions about final drafts of legislation or policy, they can mobilise information and resources, they choose between options. Because they do all this in hostile contexts, because of the ambivalence about powerful women, not only among feminists but throughout society, femocrats and other feminists have difficulties in comprehending that power. Among the difficulties is the question of where the power comes from, on what does it depend? Other feminists want femocrats to exercise power on behalf of the movement. But they may also consider that access to power, especially within the state, signals a taint, a corrosion of feminist ideals. The women's movement suffers all the difficulties that a determinedly democratic, even anarchistic, political movement could be expected to have.

Everyone is fascinated with powerful women; witness the huge sales of Suzie Mitchell's book *Tall Poppies*. One problem with the fascination about powerful women is that notions of collective power pale in comparison. So femocrats are liable to be perceived as the powerful individuals within the women's movement, not 'stars' perhaps, but certainly leaders. The sting is that their individual power is derived from their location within the state but their access to that location depends on the collective power of the women's movement.

So, 'Why didn't she fight harder?' is not an unreasonable question, but only if we are prepared to ask 'What is the women's movement doing?' and 'What is being fought for?' Too often the answers to the last question have been supplied by femocrats themselves: they interpret the question, make the calculations, draw the line, write the answer. Yes, femocrats have 'problems of their own' (Franzway, 1986) but both they,

collectively, and the rest of the women's movement can ill afford to leave them alone to get on with it.

Changing conditions

So far our discussion has proceeded as though in some timeless moment. We began by asking 'where are we coming from?' We need to notice that although the movement has been coming along this road for quite a while, it is not the same kind of road as it was ten or fifteen years ago. How to characterise these changes is a difficult matter.

We have already observed the kinds of changes which distinguish the state now from what it was like at the beginning of the femocrat period. During the 'fiscal crisis' and the recession, notions of social reform to meet or dampen the demands of the 'disadvantaged' have been overwhelmed by the spine-stiffening rhetoric of efficiency and accountability. 'The poor things' must be made to stand on their own two feet, unless of course one is a struggling property developer or media magnate. In the last couple of years the electoral dangers of this have become more obvious, and several Labor governments have begun to add to their economic program a 'social justice' strategy. This is at present largely rhetorical; it remains to be seen if it will develop any power in the bureaucracy comparable to that of the push for economic efficiency.

Over the period corporatist relations between government, unions and representatives of capital have become more visible as part of the state's planning and legitimising processes. Issues deemed to be 'social' rather than 'economic' should, in this rhetoric, wait at the side of the pool for the beneficent ripples generated by corporatism and economic recovery to reach them. Still the state's legitimation problems continue. The government must appear neutral towards its corporate partners; it must maintain its sovereignty at least in appearance; and with a Labor Party wishing to retain power, it must balance these requirements with electoral pressures from the demands of other interest groups. Women now see the state netted into a corporate structure dominated by men and by the interests of specific groups of men. But also they see a state which manages some legislation, provides some resources, and employs some feminist advocates, directed towards the interests of women.

What this means is that the kind of state that feminists engage with now differs somewhat from the state that second-wave feminists set out to tackle. So too there are new uncertainties. Will the state be captured by the New Right and transformed into a monetarists' heaven with devastating consequences for feminism including the femocrats? (The new conservative government in New South Wales has already begun to dismantle equal opportunity programs in its departments.) Can recent reforms be used to more thoroughly undermine the ways the state constitutes the gender order?

Our argument suggests that we cannot rely on recent strategies and assumptions since they were premised on the way the state was rather than the way it is now. Welfare ideologies, the need to accommodate more women in the labour market, the newly articulated demands for the women's movement—even the idea that the simple addition of a few women would be counted an achievement—all this has now changed.

As for changes to the women's movement, their scale is suggested by the changes in terminology, from women's liberation to women's movement. For some the latter term implies a coherence, a collectivity, which no longer exists, or of which it is now impossible to speak. We hear umbrella words like 'feminists', 'feminist activists', 'feminisms'; or sectional words such as cultural feminism, peace women (cf. Greenham women), academic feminists, socialist feminists, Woman-spirit Movement, union women (but no common label to specify 'feminist unionism') and of course femocrats, yet we think the term 'women's movement' may still be used to encompass all these, to mark out a political boundary, to refer to a collective perspective on the oppression of women. The movement is, however divided, a tangible social fact. It represents a collective resource created from the allegiance of thousands of women with a shared political experience, a network of feminist institutions and enterprises, and some credibility (however contested) as a representative of women's interests. Part of this resource is Australian feminism's accumulated experience in and around the state. Something feminist has been growing, and for the present we continue to call it the women's movement.

Part of the process of change is that it becomes increasingly difficult in practice to characterise the politics of the women's movement into identifiable strands, such as the familiar trio of radical feminism, liberal feminism and socialist feminism. In part, they do not quite fit the story. In part, the strands shred or spin into new shapes, or weave raggedly together. This does not mean, however, that they have become completely tangled nor that feminism has a unitary voice. Thus, we argue, liberal feminism dominates feminist strategies in and around the state, and since the state is so central to the oppression of women, liberal feminism tends to dominate the women's movement.

But this project is not wholly liberal-feminist. In practice, other feminist assumptions get woven in, especially those derived from radical feminism. The notion that the category 'woman' can and always does transcend all others derives from early radical feminism. It is mobilised, for its tactical utility, in liberal-feminist campaigns such as those around law reform. The celebration of 'woman', speaking as 'we', can provide liberal feminists with sustenance in conflict with 'the boys'—not a small point, given the pressures and hostilities femocrats often face. The passion of radical feminism combined with the realism of liberal feminism has fuelled numerous feminist actions. The problems appear when some women seem to have more to celebrate than others, and solidarity is disrupted by class, race, familial, and sexual divisions.

In this context, conflict between women somehow seems shocking, especially given the potential exhilaration of the collective. Yet feminism has grown through its theoretical and political exploration of these divisions. We do not argue that disputes for their own sake are a good thing but there is a delicate question at stake here. Without collective action, feminism can achieve little. But in the matter of interaction with the state, too often the imperative to get the job done forces a papering over of cracks or the submergence of contradictory factors. For the submission to be written, the policy drafted, the funding obtained, complications must get smoothed out, the issues inscribed in terms which can be read by the state. And this is the rub, a political dilemma which must be resolved again and again.

Of the various strands in feminist thought it is socialist feminism which has faced the issues of divisions among women most consistently, because of its concern with the question of class. It is also socialist feminism which inherited, as we saw in Chapters 1 and 2, the most sophisticated theories of the state. Its ideas have been woven into feminist campaigns in and around the state from time to time, but not as consistently as those of liberal and radical feminism. We think it is time for a re-examination of the resource that socialist feminism provides and for a wider awareness of significant developments in this approach in the 1980s.

The crucial intellectual problem for socialist feminism, at the start, was the privileging of 'production' in socialist theory, especially in marxism. At the level of practice, this meant conflict with established left strategies premised on that priority. Attempts to overcome the problem without diminishing the significance of class, such as the theoretical enterprises of the 1970s—the domestic labour debate, reproduction theory, and the re-examination of ideological processes—moved things forward in underscoring, if only implicitly, the need for rethinking 'work'. The theoretical and political task was not made easier by the historical context of a rapidly changing political economy and, as part of that, a changing form of the state.

These efforts stalled for several reasons. First, the historical context of the late 1970s put socialist feminism into a reactive and often defensive position which tended to rigidify thinking and confuse practices. Second, ambivalence about the class–gender relationship, compounded by a belated awareness of race, provided an inadequate conception of the dynamic of social power. Understanding the power of the state was limited by either a pluralist or a reductionist logic. Although Pringle and Game (1976) challenged the feminist conception of state power, significantly from an analysis of a social reform (Whitlam) government, they remained within the logic of ambivalence by posing the problem as one of dichotomies: class/gender, reform/revolution. Third, socialist feminism lacked a thoroughly dialectical approach; it held to an understanding of production and of class formation which were insufficiently transformed by gender analysis. The effect was to reproduce the

ideological divisions of public/domestic spheres and an implicit ideological view of the normative family as a basis for social analysis. In turn, reproduction of dichotomous divisions and static entities reduces the ability to grasp the way in which the state is historically constitutive of gender ordering.

By the early 1980s socialist feminism had begun to change in two ways. First, some feminists began to look beyond the traditional domain of socialist feminism for ways to break through the rigidity of dualisms. They met up with other feminists who were mining the field of French philosophy and of psychoanalysis for new modes of conceptualising gender and power. Although the politics of state power were side-stepped for a period the Sydney Socialist Feminist Conference in 1987 devoted sessions to analysis and to discussions of problems of working in and around the state.

Second was the emergence of a feminist unionism. Links between union activists and other socialist feminists have strengthened gradually, illustrated by the agendas of the 1982-84 Women and Labour Conferences, the 1984 Melbourne Socialist Feminist Conferences and the Sydney Conference. Feminist unionism itself gained impetus from the political and economic crisis of the late 1970s. This movement connects with femocrat interactions with the state but comes at it from a different base. Although women's liberation had early criticised unionism's gender blindness and hierarchical organisation (for example at the 1971 Melbourne 'Women and Work' conference) unionism was not a priority issue with the movement in its early days. However by 1976 the Working Women's Charter campaign was established, focusing debate on socialist-feminist strategy and the connections between feminist organisation and union organisation.

The dynamic is illustrated by the Wollongong 'Jobs for Women' campaign which began from a seminar on sexual harassment organised in 1980 by the Working Women's Charter Committee—a nice illustration in itself of the ways actions can be generative. The campaign involved migrant women and women claiming the right to work in a non-traditional area. The employer's use of legislation—the provisions barring women from lifting heavy weights—is a good example of the means provided by the state to constitute 'women's work' in the economy. But the campaign too could use the state, in particular the New South Wales government's women's unit and anti-discrimination legislation, to win its case. The significant point is that political struggle involving working-class women could take advantage (not without difficulty) of reforms made within the state and realise their potential.

Other kinds of links have been made between feminist unionism and the state, not only because Australian unionism is bound up with the state through the Conciliation and Arbitration legislation. For example, services such as work-related child-care centres and working women's centres are joint enterprises managed by state and union representatives.

The South Australian Working Women's Centre in central Adelaide, as well as providing services to individual women, lobbies governments and unions on issues such as repetition strain injury, migrant women's working conditions, and sex discrimination in existing industrial awards. Union women have been delegates on National Women's Consultative Councils; Jan Marsh, an ACTU advocate, was the first. Union women have acted on their interest in the appointment of women's advisers in some government departments, making submissions about the nature of the positions such as the 1987–88 submission by the Women's Standing Committee of the South Austalian Trades and Labour Council to the Department of Labour.

There are similarities between union activists and femocrats. Some unions, such as the white-collar Administrative and Clerical Officers' Association and several teachers' unions as well as Trades and Labor Councils (e.g. in Victoria, New South Wales and Western Australia) have appointed officers to represent the interests of women. Both groups are faced with organisational structures dominated by men and conceived in terms of men's interests. The goal of gaining inclusion of women into these structures is much the same. But until recently the union movement remained highly resistant to arguments for equal representation although much of the growth in postwar union membership has resulted from increased unionisation of women. Thirty-nine per cent of women workers are union members, and 50 per cent of men workers (ACTU, 1988). The combination of increased and longer-term participation of women in the workforce, the growth of white-collar unionism, the slow decline of the traditional union base in the manufacturing sector, and the accumulation of feminist campaigns around women's work, are beginning to have some effect.

The union movement, like the state directorate, seeks ways to accommodate women's interests without disruption. Thus the ACTU Congress in 1987 agreed to make some space specifically available for women on the executive, in addition to the lone position won by Jenny George of the Teachers' Federation through traditional procedures. In a typical deal, the factional balance on the executive was to be maintained by increasing the overall size of the executive and each faction was allocated a position. Nevertheless some union women took the opportunity to argue their right to control the procedures of selection and of representation.

Similarities, but there are major differences too. Meredith Burgmann's description of the historic election of Jenny George to the ACTU executive captured the distinction when she said 'We may be feminists but women who work within unions can never be separatists' (1984:13). Feminist unionists struggle with the predicament of how to integrate their commitment to unionism with their commitment to feminism. Politically and theoretically construed in terms of the class/gender dichotomy, the problem has implications for ways of organising

as much as for decisions about political priorities. How far can the structures of the union movement be challenged without undermining the collective principles of unionism? How viable or useful are autonomous women's organisations during a period of corporatism, where the top-level connection of union organisation with the state puts enormous pressures on the whole movement? Yet how can the impetus to tackle the oppression of women in and around work be sustained and amplified without the collective activity of women unionists supported by organisations of their own?

As the position of women unionists becomes more politically significant, it also becomes more complex. The relation to the femocrat project is equivocal. We have noted the possibilities provided by reforms: they may be utilised, but they may also be contested. An historical case study of the New South Wales public service by Carol O' Donnell (1984) makes the point that where EEO provisions were used to pursue *managerial* aims 'to free up operation of the market principle', it had to be opposed by unionists. However, the argument always has to be seen in its practical context. For example, O'Donnell saw the 1980 dispute between the New South Wales Public Service Association (the main union) and the Public Service Board as a dilemma for women unionists.

> They [the women] recognised the importance of appeals procedures for employees and the importance of supporting the union; however, they also recognised that open advertisement of positions, lateral transfer and promotion by merit rather than seniority worked in favour of women employees in a service where males had reached positions of seniority because of overt and systemic discrimination against women, particularly at the point of recruitment (1984b:28).

But Diane Hague, writing in the same issue of *Refractory Girl,* argued that the issue was 'academic' for the majority of women members, whose temporary status barred them from promotion positions. Although critical of the union leadership she says that the New South Wales femocrats 'failed to realise the limited application' of the reform. She further expresses a common view that 'EEO officers' show a lack of understanding of the role of the union movement, and have different objectives from union women. Although EEO is a desirable reform, 'when all is said and done, women bosses are still bosses and their relationship to women workers is not qualitatively much different to the relationship between men bosses and workers' (1984:21). The whole issue is made more difficult because unions do not consistently support and represent the interests of women workers; often indeed they provide very little support to women members.

Finally, in reviewing changing conditions, we must note that femocrats too are changing. The situation is qualitatively different from the days when Elizabeth Reid took up office as the first women's adviser.

Femocrats in the federal and State bureaucracies are now numbered in the hundreds, albeit unevenly distributed. A certain level of institutionalisation has occurred in the sense that a routine set of practices and mores is now established. There are handbooks of procedure, training courses, a body of advice as well as of experience. In addition to the state, some other organisations such as unions and a few private sector employers appoint women's advocates. The issues have gained a degree of visibility and of legitimacy.

But Elizabeth Reid sallied forth during a period of public sector expansion, in contrast to the loud demands for reduction of the public sector which have accumulated almost into a new political 'common-sense' by the late 1980s. Now the public sector must be efficient, effective, lean, athletic. Equity is seen as a cost more than as a goal. This has at least two consequences for femocrats. First, the recruitment of feminists from outside the bureaucracy becomes less likely. Replacements must be found from within the service, and any increase in staff must be fought for against the general hostility, patriarchal interests *and* against other equally desperate demands for staff and resources in equity programs.

Lois Bryson spells out the second consequence, which is that the public sector response to the new situation is to undertake continuous massive structural reorganisation of itself. The focus shifts inwards. 'Management is at centre stage, not service to the public' (1987:30). To retain any sort of foothold femocrats likewise become preoccupied with administrative issues. In the shuffle to rationalise they may be marginalised (as in the federal system), submerged or subverted.

In this context of hyperactivity 'pragmatism' takes on new force and becomes a kind of expediency. In the sense of a commitment to getting on with the job of achieving tangible objectives, pragmatism has long been a femocrat trait. But there has been a change. It is illustrated by the view held by some femocrats that once the Hawke government's goal of 20 000 child-care places is achieved, claims for more, and for improved subsidies and conditions, are unreasonable. The issue is expected to be closed off. The feminist demand for universal child care is simple utopian. We see a distinct change in approach from that taken by femocrats ten years ago, when the battle for child-care funding was regarded as being at the start of the campaign, not at the end.

Pragmatism is relational, resulting from specific assessments of what will 'work'. If expediency now appears a major determinant of femocrat solution strategies, questions about why these kinds of assessments are made must address their political environment. We have argued throughout that femocrat actions cannot be explained as individual idiosyncrasies. Rather femocrat response attests to the political state of play between the state and feminism. Thus femocrat pragmatism signals changes in the state's interpretation of its requirements, and the limits of feminist intervention. Is this where it all ends?

We think not. Neither of these outcomes is fixed. What must have

full play in any conclusion is the import of 'politics' as open-ended practice. The femocrat program and state responses are themselves the result of conflict. To date, the femocrat phenomenon has derived from the centrality of the state to the gender order, and Australian feminism's particular response to it. Changes to the political environment are now such that the women's movement needs to reconsider the focus of this strategy. The emergence and growth of feminist unionism must be taken into account; and the regrouping of socialist feminists suggests some shifts are occurring. As new political questions are constructed, the initiative and the reforms achieved by femocrat strategies need to be transformed. If femocrats are to continue to have a part to play, if they are to continue to be at the cutting edge of feminist interaction with the state, the politically active women's movement must sharpen the knife.

Appendix

Di Court's project

Through the impasses

I seem to have emerged from the impasses! I feel now that the impasse and general flounderings derived in large part from imposing the wrong methodological framework onto political practice. Doing so, however, was a necessary part of the process, since in working through the 'wrongness' I was forced to clarify my thinking. In itself, that process makes the initial proposition of the woman's movement/state interaction as a means of conceptualising the state, an important part of the main argument. It also makes for an argument for praxis, which is compatible with my political/intellectual disposition.

The major problem with the framework, as I recognised earlier this year, was the attempt to divide the politics of the women's movement into predetermined ideological strands and into its issues from that. A few people questioned the wisdom of doing so but one learns. The approach was wrong for several reasons: to begin with, it didn't fit the story, nor did it allow for breaking through (some) of the conceptual problems of the respective positions.

The thesis now

The thesis is placed clearly within a socialist-feminist framework, the state and its conceptualisation as a problem of and for socialist feminists. *Women's work and the politics of work* is its central organising theme. This entails a rigorous rethinking of work which the radical critique of sexuality and of the family demanded. The radical critique, and the attempts to develop a viable socialist feminism from that, made Women's Liberation an historic disjuncture with the socialism and feminism of the past.

The crucial problem for socialist feminism has been the privileging of production and, at the level of practice, conflict with established left strategies premised on that priority. Attempts to overcome the problem without diminishing the significance of class, such as the domestic labour debate, reproduction theory and the re-examination of ideologi-

cal processes, moved things forward in underscoring, if only implicitly, the need for rethinking work. The theoretical and political task was not made easier by the historical context of a rapidly changing political economy and, as part of that, arguably a rapidly changing form of the state.

The efforts stalled for several reasons. First, the historical context I have just referred to put a socialist feminism into a reactive and often defensive position which tended to rigidify thinking and confuse practices. The intensity of the debates and divisions and the fragmentation of the movement bear evidence of this. I hope to demonstrate the way in which the political and economic crisis of the mid to late seventies impinged on the politics of the women's movement and, in particular, the politics of women's work. I will be arguing that the emergence of a feminist unionism grew out of the exigencies of the crisis and was dependent for its impact on changes within the state established in more favourable times—'reforms' which allowed for moving the struggle to a more transformative level.

Second, the ambivalence of the class–gender relationship, compounded by a belated awareness of race, provided an inadequate conception of the dynamic of social power. When it came to an understanding of the power of the state, this necessarily had either a pluralist or reductionist logic. Here, I think Pringle and Game (1976) were spot-on in challenging the feminist conception of state power and, significantly, did so from an analysis of a social reform government. However, they remained then within the logic of ambivalence by posing the problem of state power as class/gender choices and the reform/revolutionary dichotomy. The notion of state power which I hope to present may appear as some sort of marxist-pluralist hybrid (Foucaultian with Weberian remnants??!). In presenting the state as constitutive of gender ordering and of women's work, I see the interventionist state not as an intervention into 'the economy' or into 'the family' but as constitutive of those constructs. I understand 'the economy' as being fuelled not by disembodied labour power but by sexed work.

Third, there was a lack of a thoroughly dialectical approach which held to an understanding of production and of class formation insufficiently transformed by gender analysis. The effect of this was to reproduce the ideological divisions of public/domestic spheres and an implicit ideological view of the family as a normative entity. This is serious, because it is those very constructs which produce a notion of 'women's work'. Further, reproducing the seemingly dichotomous divisions and static entities robs any potential of grasping the way in which the state is historically constitutive of gender ordering.

For example, I think even referring to the family as the site of women's oppression frustrates the attempt to escape its ideological confines. Questioning that seems like questioning a feminist shibboleth. However, Barrett (1980) is exemplary of the impasse involved in the

thinking, in describing the family as 'the site of the oppression of women ... an important organising principle of the relations of production of the social formation as a whole' (1980:211). The family and the construction of sexuality tends then to become isolated from production. To me, it is insufficiently material in not grasping the complexity of state practices which shape the options within which people live households and their work. I would apply the same critique to the Wilson-type (1977) approach to the welfare state where the focus on the ideological premises of social policy affords the state a dubious rationality and compounds the separation of the social from the economic. I prefer to view the family as an axis of social relationships, its forms the outcome of complex material processes within which the state has regulative power.

I referred above to the persistence of a public-domestic sphere division in thought even when the division was challenged. For example, I found Beechey (1978) suggestive in her criticism of a location of the dynamic of sexual division *either* in the labour process *or* the family. However, in her reproduction of labour power and reserve army solution, the fixed separate spheres resurfaced. The separation becomes particularly fixed when the state comes into the picture as in McIntosh (1978), presented as fixed, structured relationships between the state, the labour process and the family. That fixity leaves no room for a political practice.

In passing, I wonder whether the historical context of crisis I referred to above made McIntosh (1978) the last serious socialist-feminist attempt to theorise the state—the state moving faster than we can think. From there, the problems were sidestepped by a requestioning of liberal feminism's transformative potential (Eisenstein, 1981) or by turning into a not altogether helpful polemic such as MacKinnon's (1983), a sophisticated polemic but polemic nonetheless. In the Australian literature, Baldock and Cass (1983:xi) notably eschewed any pretence of addressing the state as, in their words, 'abstract theory at the level of the advanced capitalist state'. I agree with eschewing abstract theory; nonetheless many of the contributions in that collection assume the abstract theory and assume its problems to be settled. For example Baldock begins: 'Throughout the book we maintain that capitalism and patriarchy are mutual reinforcements in the production of public policies which affect the lives of women in Australia' (1983:20). That framework, patriarchy and capitalism as mutual reinforcements, ignores the impasse reached with Hartmann's (1981) approach.

Hartmann is important because the disillusionment with the prospects of developing a coherent socialist-feminist analysis, which the dual-system notion in part elicited, led on to disturbing rigidity of dichotomous thought, fixed stand-offs which a different privileging does not escape. They are fixed stand-offs is the sense that they do not provide any sense of social change nor the political means for it. The tendency

for dichotomies to become a politics of difference is disturbing in terms of state power for any radical for its corporatist implications.

In all, I am arguing for a resuscitation of dialectical thought which *confronts* the labour process, a 'triple vision' which can think women's work as waged, unwaged and sexed—and somehow think that all together. Examining the *politics* of women's work demonstrates the need for that and in showing the state as constitutive of women's work provides an understanding of the state as both the *product* and the *determinant* of struggle.

Thesis plan

The aim is to develop an analysis of the patriarchal nature of the state which I understand as the regulatory processes of social power. I will present this along the lines discussed above, that is, as a problem of and for socialist-feminist analysis and practice. The method is to examine the interaction of the women's movement with the state. Since the approach becomes an important part of the argument, I may include a short discussion of the lessons learned from adopting the earlier framework.

The historical period is something of a problem, since to demonstrate my argument I must include material extending beyond the period originally intended. This makes it not as 'neat' as a defined ten-year period or a period determined by governments' terms of office. I feel this can be got around by arguing that social change does not periodise neatly!

Part 1

A   A discussion of the literature—an extended version of the above.
B   Nature of the Sydney women's movement:

The socialist-feminist framework makes this section far less formidable. It will still cover the women's movement as a whole. The task will be easier in that I can discuss the liberal reform approach as a contrast with W.L. politics and strategies—the reform/revolution dilemma. That dilemma was interpreted differently at different times: inside/outside the state, issue politics/consciousness-raising, class/gender priorities. The different politics within W.L. can be discussed, in the process of showing how a socialist feminism, or the perceived need for a politics identifiable as that, emerged. I see the National Women's Conference on Feminism and Socialism, 1974, as a landmark in that emergence.

In terms of making an argument for the need to rethink work, I will be stressing that a politics of women's work involves not only different strategies, but engages in different issues to those generally seen to be within the ambit of work, for example, women's services, abortion action. Those actions developed from the radical politicisation of the personal. I shall be showing how that shaped a developing feminist unionism.

Part II: Politics within the state

This section includes women's units, child care, anti-discrimination legislation, EEO, rape law reform, as already written up. The addition to this section is equal pay. In my discussion of that, I show the way in which the state was both constitutive of women's work and impinged on its politics. I see the family wage/child allowance saga as a demonstration of state activity in several respects: those already well covered in the literature, the wage injustice and the gender segmentation of the workforce. I give a greater emphasis to the state's structuring of the politics of work, both in terms of making a male unionism reluctant to support women's politics and also making issues of women's work appear to be social rather than industrial, i.e. central to the economy.

Part III: The struggle outside the state

This is largely a discussion of feminist unionism and its development. That begins with the W.L. critique of unionism's gender-blindness and its hierarchical nature—the 1971 Melbourne Women and Work conference is a valuable source here. Actions included ACTU lobbying, Alternative Conferences and groups, culminating in the WTUC Conference (1976). It is clear that although there was W.L. activity in this direction, it was not a priority until the mid-seventies. W.L. action, and socialist feminism less identifiable within that, was then directed more to the development of women's services. This is important given the later debate about the direction of socialist feminism as either workplace- or community-based, which I see as a false dichotomy. From the mid-seventies, after the political crisis and with the deepening recession, a feminist unionism begins to emerge along with a perceived urgency to clarify a socialist feminism in terms of analysis, strategy and even as an identifiable group within W.L.

The discussion of the emergence of a feminist unionism takes the Working Women's Charter campaign as its starting point. Part of the debate around that was the question of feminist activity as lobby or job action. As a means of discussing the issue involved in that, I make a brief comparison of feminist activity within the PSA (Public Service Association) and New South Wales Teachers' Federation. The comparison is valuable in illustrating the way in which the gender-segmented workforce shapes the strategies of feminist unionism, that is, impinges on the politics of women's work. The Teachers' Federation, as a single industry union, presented far less problems for developing feminist structures within the union than did the PSA. In the latter, the gender-segmented structure of the occupations covered makes difficult the links between Women's Caucus and workplace action. The discussion of the Teachers' Federation allows for some discussion of feminist action re education also.

From there, I take the story on to the Wollongong Jobs for Women

Campaign, a story too good to miss for my argument for several reasons. The campaign began from a seminar organised by the Working Women's Charter Committee on sexual harassment, a nice illustration of the way in which action on an outcome of a sexed labour gets placed into its broader context of women's work. The campaign involved migrant women and women claiming the right to work in a non-traditional area. The saga also brings in the women's units and anti-discrimination legislation, making the point of the way in which struggle could take advantage of reforms made earlier within state structures but those being dependent for their authority and transformative potential on the struggle outside. In all, a nice story about state power and its historically changing nature demonstrable from the saga of a political struggle.

Part IV: Feminist politics as work

This section has as its theme feminist politics as work focused on the unionisation of women's services or the attempt at it. Discussion centres on the Australian Social Welfare Union (ASWU), whose coverage includes women's health centres, abortion clinics, refuges, rape-crisis and child-care workers.

The problems the union has faced in unionising those workers are illustrative of women's work and the state's impact on that. It is illustrative also of the way in which feminist politics can aid or confound that. The union has confronted several problems in unionising workers. First, the issue of voluntarism, less so since the recession has deepened. Voluntarism has its limits in a time of high unemployment. Second the apparent clash of unionism and collective organisation. This makes for a reluctance to unionise. However, conflicts within collectives can be individualised and political sackings made possible by the collective situation where the collective is both boss and worker. Ironically, the numbers game is no less operative here, perhaps worse because concealed. With respect to this, feminists have become somewhat less hostile to unionisation since being under threat from the anti-feminist Christian and welfarist elements of the industry. That makes for a different case for the role of women's organisation, or at least points to its contradictory nature. It also throws very much into question notions of 'women' as an uncomplicated social category.

The union has fought also the professionalism problem, arguing for job experience/certification parity. This is significant for underscoring notions of 'skill' along with the middle-class bias of certification. Unionisation potentially also alters the politics of funding, moving it out of the realm of welfare and political expediency into the more sticky— for the state—industrial arena.

Not surprisingly, because of all of the above, the union has not had a happy time with the state, most clearly evident in the absence of an award. There is something of a vicious circle here in that the union needs

to be able to demonstrate coverage to secure an award but cannot get the membership because of the problems discussed above. The union refers to itself as pink-collar unionsm to make a nice point about the way in which blue- and white-collar classification has dubious relevance for women, i.e. regarded as 'respectable' work but with lousy pay and work conditions. It is 'pink' also in the sense that its radicalism deters conservative workers.

The New South Wales government has done amazing footwork to limit the ambit of the union, action aimed at absorbing its coverage into the more politically controllable Pulic Service Association (PSA), tactics enhanced by the misguided feminist reticence about unionism.

In all, the saga of the ASWU provides a good example of women's work and its politics. It is a less optiministic story than that of the previous section, since the union is in a highly vulnerable position for being, if not knocked off, very restricted, by the right-wing attack against feminism, moves which some of the complexities of feminist politics fall in with. To me this says something of the political role of feminism as having either a revolutionary or reactionary potential.

Conclusion

I feel the discussion clearly shows that the state plays a constitutive role in 'women's work' and the signficance of that for an unequal gender ordering. It also shows the state as both product and determinant of struggle.

P.S. At the moment, the already written section on housing and urban policy doesn't fit. It does so in terms of the overall argument as an example of the way in which state practices materially shape households and 'the family'. I'm reluctant to discard any already written words but I'm not sure where to fit it in.

Bibliography

Adam, Barry (1987) *The Rise of a Gay and Lesbian Movement* Boston: G.K. Hall

Adam-Smith, Patsy (1969) *Folklore of the Australian Railwaymen* Adelaide: Rigby

Allen, Judith (1982) 'The invention of the pathological family: a historical study of family violence is NSW' in Carol O'Donnell and Jan Craney (eds) *Family Violence in Australia* Melbourne: Longman Cheshire

Altman, D. (1972) *Homosexual: Oppression and Liberation* Sydney: Angus and Robertson

—— (1986) *AIDS and the New Puritanism* London: Pluto Press

Anti-Discrimination Board of NSW (1978) *First Annual Report* Sydney: NSW Government Printer

Atkins, Susan and Brenda Hoggett (1984) *Women and the Law* Oxford: Basil Blackwell

Australian Bureau of Statistics (1984) *Crime Victims Survey, Australia, 1983, Preliminary, Cat. No. 4505.0* Canberra: Australian Government Printing Service

Australian Bureau of Statistics (1987) *The Labour Force, Australia, November 1987, Cat. No. 6203.0* Canberra: Australian Government Printing Service

Australian Council of Trade Unions (1988) *National Directory and Union Officials' Manual 1987–88* Melbourne: ACTU

Australian Government Social Welfare Commission (1974) *Project Care: Children, Parents, Community* Canberra: Australian Government Printing Service

Australian Schools Commission (1975) *Girls, School and Society* Canberra: Australian Government Publishing Service

Bachrach, Peter and Morton Baratz (1970) *Power and Poverty: Theory and Practice* New York: Oxford University Press

Bahro, Rudolf (1978) *The Alternative in Eastern Europe* London: New Left Books.

Bailey, Margaret (1987) 'The Melinda Leves case: educational discrimination confronted' *Refractory Girl*, 30, pp. 21–29

Baldock, Cora V. (1983) 'Public policies and the paid work of women' in Baldock and Cass *Women, Social Welfare and the State*

Baldock, Cora V. and Bettina Cass eds (1983) *Women, Social Welfare, and the State* Sydney: Allen and Unwin

Barrett, Michele (1980) *Women's Oppression Today* London: Verso

Barrett, Michele and Mary McIntosh (1982) *The Anti-social Family* London: Verso

Beauvoir, Simone de (1972 [1949]) *The Second Sex* Harmondsworth: Penguin

Benn, Melissa et al. (1986) *The Rape Controversy* London: National Council for Civil Liberties

Bidmeade, Ian (1986) *Review of Procedures for Children in Need of Care* South Australia: Commissioned by Minister for Community Welfare

Blackburn, Jean (1984) 'Schooling and injustice for girls' in *Unfinished Business: Social Justice for Women in Australia*

Boneparth, Ellen ed. (1982) *Women, Power and Policy* New York, Pergamon

Boreham, P. et al. (1979) 'The Australian bureaucratic elite' *Australian and New Zealand Journal of Sociology* 15, 2, pp. 45–55

Bowles, Janet (1979) *The Politics of the Equal Rights Amendment: Conflict and the Decision Process* New York: Longman

Bradley, Denise and Deborah McCulloch (1985) South Australia: a question of commitment in Sawer *Program for Change*

Brennan, Deborah (1983) *Towards a National Child Care Policy* Melbourne: Institute of Family Studies

—— (1986) 'Rights—at a price' *Australian Society* 5, 6, pp. 38–40

Brennan, Deborah and Carol O'Donnell (1986) *Caring for Australia's Children: Political and Industrial Issues in Child Care* Sydney: Allen and Unwin

Broom, Dorothy H. ed. (1984) *Unfinished Business: Social Justice for Women in Australia* Sydney: Allen and Unwin

Brophy, Julia and Carol Smart eds (1985) *Women in Law: Explorations in Law, Family and Sexuality* London: Routledge and Kegan Paul

Brown, R.G. ed. (1980) *Children Australia* Sydney: Allen and Unwin

Brownmiller, Susan (1976) *Against Our Will* Melbourne: Penguin

Bryant, Anita (1977) *The Anita Bryant Story: The Survival of our Nation's Families and the Threat of Militant Homosexuality* Old Tappan (NJ): Revell

Bryson, Lois (1987) 'A game of strategies' *Australian Society*, 6, 11, pp. 29–31

Burgmann, Meredith (1984) 'Women at the 1983 ACTU Congress' *Refractory Girl*, 27, pp. 13–15

Burns, Ailsa (1983) 'Population structure and the family' in Burns et al. (eds) *The Family in the Modern World* Sydney: Allen and Unwin

Burns, A. and J. Goodnow (1985) *Children and Families in Australia* Sydney: Allen and Unwin

Burstyn, Varda (1983) 'Masculine dominance and the state' *Socialist Register* London: Merlin, pp. 45–89

Burton, Clare (1985a) *Subordination: Feminism and Social Theory* Sydney: Allen and Unwin

—— (1985b) Merit and gender: organisation and the 'mobilisation of masculine bias', paper presented to the conference 'Defining Merit', Macquarie University

—— (1986) 'Equal employment opportunity programmes: Issues in implementation' in Norma Grieve and Ailsa Burns (eds) *Australian Women: New Feminist Perspectives* Melbourne: Oxford University Press

Burton, Clare et al. (1987) *Women's Worth: Pay Equity and Job Evaluation in Australia* Canberra: Australian Government Printing Service

Burvill, Chris (1986) 'Women beat the Big Australian' *Refractory Girl*, 29, pp. 7–8

Callenan, Suzanne (1984) 'Jury of her peers' *Legal Service Bulletin* 9, 4, pp. 166–168

Cass, Bettina (1986) 'Women's income distribution and housing policy' *Australian Journal of Social Work* 39, 2, pp. 5–14

Chapkis, W. ed. (1981) *Loaded Questions: Women in the Military* Amsterdam, Transnational Institute

Chodorow, Nancy (1978) *The Reproduction of Mothering: Psychoanalysis and the Sociology of Gender* Berkeley: University of California Press

Clark, Gordon M. and Michael Dear (1984) *State Apparatus: Structures and Language of Legitimacy* Boston: Allen and Unwin

Clarke, Jocelyn and Kate White (1983) *Women in Australian Politics* Sydney: Fontana

Clegg, Stewart and David Dunkerley (1980) *Organization, Class and Control* London: Routledge and Kegan Paul

Clough, Jim (1987) 'Deregulation and children's services' *Australian Journal of Early Childhood* 12, 2, pp. 13–14

Cockburn, Cynthia (1983) *Brothers: Male Dominance and Technological Change* London: Pluto Press

—— (1985) *Machinery of Dominance* London: Pluto Press

Coleman, Marie (1983) *Review of Early Childhood Services in South Australia* Adelaide: South Australian Government

Collinson, David and David Knights (1986) '"Men Only": Theories and practices of job segregation in insurance' in David Knights and Hugh Willmott *Gender and the Labour Process* Hampshire, UK: Gower

Comer, Lee (1974) *Wedlocked Women* Leeds: Feminist Books

—— (1975) 'The motherhood myth' in Jan Mercer (ed.) *The Other Half: Women in Australian Society* Melbourne: Penguin

Connell, R.W. (1987) *Gender and Power: Society, the Person and Sexual Politics* Sydney: Allen and Unwin

Court, Dianne (1986) 'Women's studies: ghetto or goer' *Australian Feminist Studies* 2, Autumn, pp. 55–57

—— (1983a) 'The centrality of patriarchy' *Arena* 65, pp. 162–71

—— (1983b) 'Feminism throws down the gautlet' *Tharunka*, 29, 3

Cox, Eva (1974) 'Politics aren't nice' *Refractory Girl* 7, pp. 29–30

—— (1982) 'Women and the state' *Refractory Girl* 23, pp. 28–31

—— (1983a) 'Pater-patria: child-rearing and the state' in Baldock and Cass *Women, Social Welfare and the State*

—— (1983b) 'Child care is a political issue' Sydney: National Association of Community Based Child Care, Conference Papers

Cullen, James et al. (1975) *Mothers' Child Care Preferences: A Report to the Australian Government Advisory Committee on Child Care* Sydney: Australian Government Printing Service

Curthoys, Ann (1976) 'Men and childcare in the feminist Utopia' *Refractory Girl* 10, pp. 3–5

—— (1986) 'The sexual division of labour: theoretical arguments' in Norma Grieve and Ailsa Burns (eds) *Australian Women: New Feminist Perspectives* Melbourne: Oxford University Press

Daly, Mary (1978) *Gyn/Ecology: The Metaethics of Radical Feminism* Boston: Beacon Press

Deacon, Desley (1984) 'The employment of women in the Commonwealth Public Service: The creation and reproduction of a dual labour market' in Simms *Australian Women and the Political System*

—— (1985) 'Political arithmetic: the nineteenth century Australian census and the construction of the dependent woman' *Signs* 11, 1, pp. 27–47

Deem, Rosemary (1984) *Co-education Reconsidered* Milton Keynes: Open University Press

Department of the Prime Minister and Cabinet (1984) *Affirmative Action for Women. A Policy Discussion Paper, Vol. I, May,* Canberra: Australian Government Printing Service

Deveson, Anne (1978) *Australians at Risk* Melbourne: Cassell Australia

Director of Equal Opportunity in Public Employment, Office of Equal Employment Opportunity Management Plan Resurvey (1985) *Preliminary Report* Sydney: New South Wales Government

Donzelot, J. (1979) *The Policing of Families* New York: Pantheon

Dowse, Sara (1981) 'The transfer of the office of Women's Affairs' in Sol Encel et al. *Decisions. Case Studies in Australian Public Policy* Melbourne: Longman Cheshire

—— (1983) 'The women's movements' fandango with the state: the movement's role in public policy since 1972' in Baldock and Cass *Women, Social Welfare and the State*

Edwards, Anne (1983) 'Sex roles: A problem for sociology and for women' *Australian and New Zealand Journal of Sociology* 19, 3, pp. 385–412

Edwards, Meredith (1985) 'Individual equity and social policy' in Goodnow and Pateman *Women, Social Science and Public Policy*

Eekelaar, John (1986) 'The emergence of children's rights' *Oxford Journal of Legal Studies* 6, 2, pp. 161–183

Ehrensaft, Diane (1981) 'When women and men mother', *Politics and Power* 3, London: Routledge and Kegan Paul

Eisenstein, Hester (1985a) 'The gender of bureaucracy: Reflections on feminism and the state' in Goodnow and Pateman *Women, Social Science and Public Policy*

—— (1985b) 'Affirmative action at work in NSW' in Sawer *Program for Change*

—— (1986) 'Feminist judo: throwing with the weight of the state' *Australian Left Review* 96, 20–22

—— (1987) Women, the state and your complexion: towards an analysis of femocracy. Paper presented to Sociological Association of Australia and New Zealand Conference, Sydney

Eisenstein, Zillah, R. (1979) *Capitalist Patriarchy and the Case for Socialist Feminism* New York: Monthly Review Press

—— (1981) *The Radical Future of Liberal Feminism* New York: Longman

—— (1982) 'Some thoughts on the patriarchal state and the defeat of ERA' *Journal of Sociology and Social Welfare* 9, 3, pp. 388–390

Encel, Sol et al. (1974) *Women and Society: An Australian Study* Melbourne: Cheshire

Engels, F. (1970 [1884]) 'The origin of the family, private property and the state' in K. Marx and F. Engels *Selected Works* 3, Moscow: Progress Publishers

Ennew, Judith (1986) *The Sexual Exploitation of Children* Cambridge: Polity Press

Esping-Anderson, Grosta, Roger Freidland and Erik Olin Wright (1976) 'Modes of class struggle and the capitalist state *Kapitalistate* 4–5, pp. 186–220

Equal Opportunities Branch, Department of the Public Service Board South Australia (1985) *An Approach to Equal Employment Opportunity Management Planning Working Papers* 1 and 2, August

Fasteau, Marc Feigen (1974) *The Male Machine* New York: McGraw Hill

Ferguson, Kathy E. (1984) *The Feminist Case Against Bureaucracy* Philadelphia: Temple University Press

Fernbach, David (1981) *The Spiral Path* London: Gay Men's Press
Finch, Janet and Dulcie Grove eds (1983) *A Labour of Love: Women, Work and Caring* London: Routledge and Kegan Paul
Firestone, S. (1971) *The Dialectic of Sex* London: Paladin
Forbath, Brenda (1983) 'National perspectives' Sydney: National Association of Community Based Child Care, Conference Papers
Foucault, Michel (1980) *History of Sexuality* New York: Vintage
Frankel, Boris (1983) *Beyond the State? Dominant Theories and Socialist Strategies* London: Macmillan
Franzway, Suzanne (1985) Australian Feminism and the State: the Case of Child Care, MA thesis in Sociology, University of Essex, UK
—— (1986) 'With problems of their own: femocrats and the welfare state' *Australian Feminist Studies* 3, pp. 45–57
Franzway, Suzanne and Jan Lowe (1978) 'Sex role theory: political cul-de-sac?' *Refractory Girl* 16, pp. 14–16
Freeman, Caroline (1982) 'The 'understanding' employer' in Jackie West (ed.) *Work, Women and the Labour Market* London: Routledge and Kegan Paul
Friedan, Betty (1981) *The Second Stage* London: Michael Joseph
Fry, Joan (1973) *Care and Education of Young Children* Report of Australian Pre-schools Committee Canberra: Australian Government Printing Service
Fugard, Athol (1974) 'Statements after an arrest under the Immorality Act' in A. Fugard, J. Kani and W. Ntshona *Statements: Three Plays* London: Oxford University Press
Gamarnikow, Eve (1978) 'Sexual division of labour: the case of nursing' in Annette Kuhn and Anne Marie Wolpe (eds) *Feminism and Materialism* London: Routledge and Kegan Paul
Game, Ann (1985) 'Child sexual assault: the liberal state's response' *Legal Service Bulletin* pp. 167–170
Game, Ann and Rosemary Pringle, (1979) 'Sexuality and the suburban dream' *Australian and New Zealand Journal of Sociology* 15, 2, pp. 4–15
—— (1983) *Gender at Work* Sydney: Allen and Unwin
Gardiner, Jean (1975) 'Women's domestic labour' *New Left Review* 89, pp. 47–58
Garrett, Catherine (1987) Women's Studies in Australian Universities and CAEs, BA Honours Research Essay, Sociology, Macquarie University
Gatens, Moira (1983) 'A critique of the sex/gender distinction' in Judith Allen and Paul Patton (eds) *Beyond Marxism? Interventions after Marx* Sydney: Intervention Publications
Gavron, Hanna (1966) *The Captive Wife* London: Routledge and Kegan Paul
Gerstenberger, Heide (1978) 'Class conflict, competition and state functions' in J. Holloway and S. Picciotto (eds) *State and Capital* London: Edwin Arnold
Gerth, H. H. and C. Wright Mills eds (1948) *From Max Weber: Essays in Sociology* London: Routledge and Kegan Paul
Giddens, Anthony (1985) *The Nation-State and Violence* Cambridge: Polity Press
Glezer, Helen and Jan Mercer, (1975) 'The history of WEL' in Jan Mercer (ed.) *The Other Half: Women in Australian Society* Melbourne: Penguin
Gluckman, Max (1971) *Politics Law and Ritual in Tribal Society* Oxford: Basil Blackwell
Golder, Hilary and Judith Allen (1979) 'Prostitution in New South Wales 1870–1937: Re-structuring an industry' *Refractory Girl* 18/19, pp. 17–24

Goodnow, J. and C. Pateman eds (1985) *Women, Social Science and Public Policy* Sydney: Allen and Unwin

Gough, Ian (1979) *The Political Economy of the Welfare State* London: Macmillan

Grant, Judith and Peta Tancred-Sheriff (1986) A feminist perspective on state bureaucracy, paper presented to conference on L'Etat Contemporain, Lennoxville, Canada

Graycar, Adam (1979) *Welfare Politics in Australia* Melbourne: Macmillan

Greer, Germaine (1970) *The Female Eunuch* London: Paladin

Grelb, Joyce and Marian Palley (1982) *Women and Public Policies* New Jersey: Princeton University Press

Griffin, Susan (1983 [1971]) 'Rape: The all-American crime' in Laurel Richardson and Verta Taylor *Feminist Frontiers: Rethinking Sex, Gender and Society* Sydney: Addison-Wesley

Habermas, J. (1976) *Legitimation Crisis* London: Heinemann

Hague, Diane (1984) 'The State and reformism: One step forward two steps back—a Public Service union response' *Refractory Girl* 27, pp. 16–22

Hall, Stuart (1984) 'The state in question' in Gregor McLennan et al. *The Idea of the Modern State* Milton Keynes: Open University Press

Hargreaves, Kaye (1982) *Women at Work* Melbourne: Penguin

Harper, Jan and Lyn Richards (1979) *Mothers and Working Mothers* Melbourne: Penguin

Hartmann, Heidi (1979) 'The unhappy marriage of marxism and feminism: Towards a more progressive union' *Capital and Class* 8, pp. 1–33

Healy, Judith (1987) *Children's Services in South Australia* Flinders Studies in Policy and Administration, 2

Held, David (1984) 'Power and legitimacy in contemporary Britain' in Gregor McLennan et al. (eds) *State and Society in Contemporary Britain* Oxford: Basil Blackwell

—— (1985) 'Central perspectives on the modern state' in David Held et al. (eds) *States and Societies* Oxford: Basil Blackwell

Held, D. and J. Krieger (1983) 'Accumulation, legitimation and the state: the ideas of Claus Offe and Jurgen Habermas' in D. Held et al. (eds) *States and Societies* Oxford: Martin Robertson

Hevener, Natalie Kaufman (1983) *International Law and the Status of Women* Boulder Colorado: Westview Press

Hirsch, Joachim (1979) 'The state apparatus and social reproduction: elements of a theory of the bourgeois state' in J. Holloway and S. Picciotto (eds) *State and Capital,* London: Edward Arnold

Hui-Chen, Wang Liu (1959) *The Traditional Chinese Clan Rules* New York: Association for Asian Studies and J. J. Augustia

Hunter, Margaret (1985) 'The cost of child care for all' *Community Child Care Newsletter* 25, pp. 19–20

Hurford, C. (1987) 'Child care since 1983—priorities and achievements' *Australian Journal of Early Childhood* 12, 2, pp. 3–8

Irving, David (1974 [1963]) *The Destruction of Dresden* Elmfield: Morley

Jasay, Anthony de (1985) *The State* Oxford: Basil Blackwell

Jones, A. (1985) The child care policies of the Hawke Labor Government, 1983–1985. Paper presented to the Annual Conference of the Australian Political Studies Association, Adelaide

Jones, Beverley (1970) 'The dynamics of marriage and motherhood' in Robin Morgan *Sisterhood is Powerful*

Jones, E. ed. (1924) *Social Aspects of Psycho-Analysis* London: Williams and Norgate

Justice, B. and R. Justice (1979) *The Broken Taboo: Sex in the Family* New York: Herman Sciences Press

Kearns, Deborah (1984) 'A Theory of Justice—and love: Rawls on the family' in Simms *Australian Women and the Political System*

Kelly, Jan (1986) 'Day care—an unfortunate necessity of a desirable community resource' *Australian Journal of Early Childhood* 11, 1, pp. 3–9

Kelly, Petra (1984) *Fighting for Hope* London: Chatto and Windus

Kinder, Sylvia (1980) *Herstory of Adelaide Women's Liberation Movement 1969–1974* Adelaide: published by the author

Klein, Dorie 'Violence against women: some considerations regarding its causes and its elimination' *Crime and Delinquency* 27, 1, 1981, pp. 64–80

Knuttila, Murray (1987) *State Theories: From Liberation to the Challenge of Feminism'* Toronto: Garamond Press

Lightfoot, D.H. (1980) 'Specialist units in the identification and management of child abuse—a social policy approach' in Jocelynne Scutt (ed.) *Violence in the Family* A Collection of Conference Papers, Canberra: Australian Institute of Criminology

Lipman-Blumen, Jean and Jessie Bernard eds (1970) *Sex Roles and Social Policy: A Complex Social Science Equation* Beverley Hills: Sage

Little, Graham (1985) *Political Ensembles: A Psychosocial Approach to Politics and Leadership* Melbourne: Oxford University Press

Lynch, Lesley (1984) 'Bureaucratic feminisms: bossism and beige suits' *Refractory Girl* 27 pp. 38–44

Macciocchi, M.A. (1979) 'Female sexuality in fascist ideology' *Feminist Review* 1, pp. 67–82

McIntosh, Mary (1978) 'The state and the oppression of women' in Annette Kuhn and Anne Marie Wolpe (eds) *Feminism and Materialism* London: Routledge and Kegan Paul

MacKinnon, Catharine, A. (1982) 'Feminism, Marxism, method, and the state: an agenda for theory' *Signs* 7, 3, pp. 515–44

—— (1983) 'Feminism, marxism, method, and the state: Toward feminist jurisprudence' *Signs* 8, 4, pp. 635–58

MacLeod, Mary and Esther Saraga (1987) 'Child sexual abuse: a feminist approach' *Spare Rib* 181, pp. 22–26

—— (1988) 'Challenging the orthodoxy: towards a feminist theory and practice' *Feminist Review* 28, pp. 16–55

Magarey, Susan (1985) *Unbridling the Tongues of Women: A Biography of Catherine Helen Spence* Sydney: Hale and Iremonger

Matthews, Trevor (1976) 'Interest group access to the Australian government bureaucracy' in *Royal Commission on Australian Government Administration, Appendixes to Report, Vol. 2.* Canberra: Australian Government Publishing Service pp. 332–65

Mellaart, J. (1967) *Catal Huyuk* London: Thames and Hudson

Miller, Pavla (1986) *Long Division* Adelaide: Wakefield Press

Millett, Kate (1972) *Sexual Politics* London: Abacus

Mitchell, Juliet (1975) *Psychoanalysis and Feminism* New York: Vintage

Mitchell, Susan (1984) *Tall Poppies—Nine Successful Women Talk to Susan Mitchell* Melbourne: Penguin
Moore, Suzanne (1986) 'Fathers '86: Playboys or mother care men? *Women's Review*, 12, pp. 6–7
Morgan, Robin ed. (1970) *Sisterhood is Powerful* New York: Vintage Books
—— ed. (1984) *Sisterhood is Global* Melbourne: Penguin
Mosse, George L. (1985) *Nationalism and Sexuality—respectability and abnormal sexuality in Modern Europe* New York: Howard Fertiz
Mowbray, Martin and Lois Bryson (1984) 'Women really care' *Australian Journal of Social Issues*, 19, 4, November, pp. 261–72
Naffine, Ngaire (1984) *An Inquiry into the Substantive Law of Rape* South Australia: Women's Adviser's Office, Department of Premier and Cabinet
National Women's Refuge Conference (1986) *Report* Conference Proceedings, Sydney
Nicholson, Joyce (1983) *The Heartache of Motherhood* Melbourne: Penguin
Oakley, Ann (1974) *The Sociology of Housework* Oxford: Martin Robertson.
Oakley, Mary Ann B. (1972) *Elizabeth Cady Stanton* New York: Feminist Press
O'Brien, Mary (1981) *The Politics of Reproduction* Boston: Routledge and Kegan Paul
O'Donnell, Carol (1984a) *The Basis of the Bargain* Sydney: Allen and Unwin.
—— (1984b) 'Gender division in the NSW public service: An historical perspective' *Refractory Girl* 27, pp. 23–29
O'Donnell, Carol and Jan Craney (1982a) 'Incest and the reproduction of the patriarchal family' in Carol O'Donnell and Jan Craney (eds) *Family Violence in Australia* Melbourne: Longman Cheshire
—— (1982b) 'The social construction of child abuse' in Carol O'Donnell and Jan Craney (eds) *Family Violence in Australia* Melbourne: Longman Cheshire
O'Donnell, Carol and Philippa Hall (1988) *Getting Equal: Labour Market Regulation and Women's Work* Sydney: Allen and Unwin
Offe, Claus (1984) *Contradictions of the Welfare State* Melbourne: Hutchinson
Ollif, Lorna (1981) *Women in Khaki* Sydney: AWS Association of NSW
Organisation for Economic Cooperation and Development (1980) *Women and Employment: Policies for Equal Opportunities* Paris: OECD
Pateman, Carole (1986) 'Introduction: the theoretical subversiveness of feminism' in Pateman and Gross *Feminist Challenges*
—— (forthcoming; 'The fraternal social contract' in J. Keane (ed.) *The Rediscovery of Civil Society* London: Virago
Pateman, Carole and Elizabeth Gross eds (1986) *Feminist Challenges: Social and Political Theory* Sydney: Allen and Unwin
Patton, Paul and Ross Poole, eds (1985) *War/Masculinity* Sydney: Intervention Publications
Perkins, Roberta and Garry Bennett (1985) *Being a Prostitute: Prostitute Women and Prostitute Men* Sydney: Allen and Unwin
Petchesky, Rosalind (1984) *Abortion and Women's Choice: The State, Sexuality and Reproductive Freedom* New York: Longman
Phillips, Anne (1987) *Divided Loyalties* London: Virago
Poole, Ross (1983) 'Markets and motherhood: the advent of the new right' in A. Burns et al. (eds) *The Family in the Modern World* Sydney: Allen and Unwin
Poulantzas, Nicos (1973) *Political Power and Social Classes* London: New Left Books and Sheed and Ward

Pringle, Rosemary (1979) 'Feminists and bureaucrats—the last four years' *Refractory Girl* 18/19, pp. 58–60

—— (1983) 'Rape: the other side of Anzac Day' *Refractory Girl* 26, pp. 31–35

Pringle, Rosemary and Ann Game (1976) 'Labor in power. The feminist response' *Arena* 41, pp. 71–78

Ramirez, Francisco (1981) 'Statism, equality and housewifery: a cross-national analysis' *Pacific Sociological Review* 24, 2, pp. 175–95

Reiger, K. M. (1985) *The Disenchantment of the Home: Modernizing the Australian Family 1880–1940* Melbourne: Oxford University Press

Rich, Adrienne (1976) *Of Woman Born: Motherhood as Experience and Institution* New York: Norton

—— (1980) *On Lies, Secrets and Silences* London: Virago

Rich, Ruby B. (1987) 'Anti-porn: soft issue, hard world' in Feminist Review (ed.) *Sexuality: A Reader* London: Virago, pp. 340–54

Riley, Denise (1983) 'The serious burdens of love?' Some questions on childcare, feminism and socialism' in Lynne Segal (ed.) *What is to be Done About the Family?* Harmondsworth: Penguin

Roe, Jill (1987) 'Chivalry and social policy in the Antipodes' *Historical Studies* 88, pp. 395–410

Ronalds, Chris (1987) *Affirmative Action and Sex Discrimination: A Handbook on Legal Rights for Women* Sydney: Pluto Press

Rosaldo, Michelle and Louise Lamphere (1974) *Woman, Culture and Society* Stanford: Stanford University Press

Rowbotham, Sheila (1983) *Dreams and Dilemmas* London: Virago

—— (1985) 'What do women want? Woman-centred values and the world as it is' *Feminist Review* 20, pp. 49–69

—— (1987) 'Listen to mother' *New Society* 23, January, p. 21

Rubin, Gayle (1975) 'The traffic in women: Notes on the "political economy" of sex' in R. R. Reiter (ed.) *Toward an Anthropology of Women* New York: Monthly Review

Ruggie, Mary (1984) *The State and Working Women: A Comparative Study of Britain and Sweden* Princeton: Princeton University Press

Rush, Florence (1980) *The Best Kept Secret: Sexual Abuse of Children* New York: McGraw-Hill

Russell, Diana (1982) *Rape in Marriage* New York: Macmillan

—— (1984) *Sexual Exploitation* London: Sage

Russell, Graeme (1983) *The Changing Role of Fathers?* St Lucia: University of Queensland Press

Ryan, Lyndall (forthcoming) 'Feminism and the federal bureaucracy 1972–83' in Sophie Watson (ed.) *Playing with the State* London: Verso

Ryan, Penny (forthcoming) 'The context of care: staff' in Anne Stonehouse (ed.) *Toddler and Infant Care* Canberra: Australian Early Childhood Association

Sawer, Marion ed. (1985) *Program for Change: Affirmative Action in Australia* Sydney: Allen and Unwin

—— (1986) The long march through the institutions: Womens Affairs under Fraser and Hawke. Paper to Australiasian Political Studies Association, Brisbane

Schechter, Susan (1982) *Women and Male Violence. The Visions and Struggles of the Battered Women's Movement* Boston: South End Press

Scott, D. (1983) 'Incest—a matter of models' *Australian Social Work* 36, 4, pp. 23–30

Scutt, Jocelynne (1983) *Even in the Best of Homes* Melbourne: Penguin

—— (1985a) 'United or divided? Women "inside" and women "outside" against male lawmakers in Australia' *Women's Studies International Forum* 8, 1, pp. 15–23

—— (1985b) 'In pursuit of equality : women and legal thought 1788–1984' in Goodnow and Pateman *Women, Social Science and Public Policy*

Segal, Lynne (1987) *Is the Future Female? Troubled Thoughts on Contemporary Feminism* London: Virago

Segers, Mary (1982) 'Can Congress settle the abortion issue?' *Hastings Center Report,* June, pp. 20–28

Shaver, Sheila (1982) The non-government state : the voluntary welfare sector. Paper to Social Policy in the 1980s Conference, Canberra

—— (1983) 'Sex and money in the welfare state' in Baldock and Cass *Women, Social Welfare and the State in Australia*

—— (1987) Class and gender in Australian income security. Paper presented to Sociological Association of Australia and New Zealand Conference, Sydney

Sichtermann, Barbara (1986) *Femininity: The Politics of the Personal* Cambridge: Polity Press

Simms, Marion (1981) 'The Australian feminist experience' in Norma Grieve and Pat Grimshaw (eds) *Australian Women: Feminist Perspectives* Melbourne: Oxford University Press

—— (1984) *Australian Women and the Political System* Melbourne: Longman Cheshire

Singh, Jesvier (1987) 'Targeting the top' *Broadsheet* 152 (Part One), 153 (Part Two)

Sklar, H. ed. (1980) *Trilateralism* Boston: South End Press

South Australia, Forty Fifth Parliament 1984–85 *South Australian Parliamentary Debates* Adelaide: South Australian Parliament

South Australia, Forty Sixth Parliament 1987–88 *Soutyh Australian Parliamentary Debates* Adelaide: South Australian Parliament

South Australian Department for Community Welfare (1986) *Intervention on Behalf of Families and Children Discussion Document* Philosophy Role Policy

South Australian Government Task Force on Child Sexual Abuse (1986) *Final Report* Adelaide: South Australian Health Commission

Stern, Lesley (1977) 'The language of rape' *Intervention* 8 pp. 3–15

Stretton, Hugh (1976) *Capitalism, Socialism and the Environment* Cambridge: Cambridge University Press

Summers, Anne (1975) *Damned Whores and God's Police* Melbourne: Penguin

—— (1986) 'Mandarins and missionaries: Women in the federal bureaucracy' in Norma Grieve and Ailsa Burns (eds) *Australian Women: New Feminist Perspectives* Melbourne: Oxford University Press

Sutcliffe, Glynn (1980) Fathers, kings and early state formation. Paper to Asian Studies Association of Australia Conference, Brisbane

Sweeney, Tania (1983) 'Child welfare and child care policies' in Adam Graycar (ed.) *Retreat from the Welfare State* Sydney: Allen and Unwin

—— (1985) Child care: the question of need. Paper presented at the National Conference of the Australian Early Childhood Association, Brisbane

—— (1987) 'Services for children and families: social control of part of the social wage' in Peter Saunders and Adam Jamrozik (eds) *Social Welfare in the late 1980s: reform, progress or retreat* SWRC Reports and Proceedings 65, Kensington: Social Welfare Research Centre, University of New South Wales

Sweeney, Tania and Adam Jamrozik (1984) *Perspectives in Child Care: Experiences of Parents and Service Providers* SWRC Reports and Proceedings 44, Kensington: Social Welfare Research Centre, University of New South Wales

Theweleit, Klaus (1987) *Male Fantasies* Cambridge: Polity Press

Thornton, Merle (1975) 'Women's labour' in Ann Curthoys et al. (eds) *Women at Work* Canberra: Australian Society for the Study of Labour History

—— (1986) 'Sex equality is not enough for feminism' in Pateman and Gross *Feminist Challenges*

Touche Ross Services for Department of Community Service (1986) *Peer Review of High Cost Child Care Centres in Australia* Canberra: Australian Government Printing Service

Ursel, Jane (1986) 'The state and the maintenance of patriarchy—a case study of family labour and welfare legislation in Canada' in James Dickinson and Bo Russell (eds) *Family, Economy and the State—the Social Reproduction Process Under Capitalism* Beckenham, UK: Croom Helm

Walby, Sylvia (1986) *Patriarchy at Work. Patriarchal and Capitalist Relations in Employment* Cambridge: Polity Press

Walby, Cathy (1985) *Breaking the Silence: A Report Based Upon the Findings of the Women Against Incest Phone-In Survey* Sydney: Women Against Incest

Walkowitz, J. (1980) *Prostitution and Victorian Society: Women, Class and the State* Cambridge: Cambridge University Press

Wallace, Margaret (1985) 'The legal approach to sex discrimination' in Sawer *Program for Change*

Wallsgrove, Ruth (1985) 'Thicker than water?' *Trouble and Strife* 7, pp. 26–28

Ward, Elizabeth (1985) *Father–Daughter Rape* New York: Grove Press

Wearing, Betsy (1984) *The Ideology of Motherhood* Sydney: Allen and Unwin

Weedon, Chris (1987) *Feminist Practice and Poststructuralist Theory* Oxford: Basil Blackwell

Weeks, Jeffrey (1977) *Coming Out: Homosexual Politics in Britain from the Nineteenth Century to the Present* London: Quartet

—— (1981) *Sex, Politics and Society* London: Longman

—— (1986) *Sexuality* London: Horwood and Tavistock

Wells, Lana (1987) *Knowhow. 36 Australian Women Reveal Their Career Secrets* Sydney: Australasian Publishing

West, Rebecca (1982 [1940]) *Black Lamb, Grey Falcon* London: Macmillan

Wilenski, Peter (1977) *Directions for Change. An Interim Report: Review of New South Wales Government Administration* Sydney: NSW Government Printer

Wills, Sue (1986) 'Big visions and bureaucratic straitjackets' *Australian Left Review* 96, pp. 23–24

Wilson, Elizabeth (1977) *Women and the Welfare State* London: Tavistock

—— (1982) 'Women, the "community" and the family' in Alan Walker (ed.) *Community Care: The Family, the State and Social Policy* Oxford: Basil Blackwell and Martin Robertson

—— (1983) *What is to be Done About Violence Against Women?* Middlesex: Penguin

Wilson, Paul (1978) *The Other Side of Rape* St Lucia: University of Queensland Press

—— (1986) 'False complaints by children of sexual abuse' *Legal Service Bulletin* 11, 2, pp. 80–83

Wishart, Barbara (1982) Motherhood within partriarchy—a radical feminist perspective. Adelaide: Women and Labour Conference Papers

Women and Politics Conference 1975 (1977) *Report,* Canberra: Department of Prime Minister and Cabinet, 2 vols

Women's Co-ordination Unit, NSW (1987) *A Decade of Change: Women in New South Wales 1976–86* Sydney: NSW Women's Advisory Council to the Premier

Woolf, Virginia (1938) *Three Guineas* London: Hogarth

Ziller, Alison (1980) *Affirmative Action Handbook* Sydney: Review of NSW Government Administration

Index

Adam, B., 10, 40
Adam-Smith, P., 50–51
Adelaide Women's Community
    Health Centre, 123
Adelaide Women's Liberation, 59
affirmative action, 81, 87, 88, 95,
    97–8,99
Affirmative Action (Equal
    Employment Opportunity for
    Women) Bill (1986), 93
Affirmative Action for Women, 88,
    92
Affirmative Action Handbook, 14, 16,
    98, 101
affirmative action officers see EEO
    practitioners; femocrats
Allen, J., 9,114
Altman, D., 11, 12
Anti-Discrimination Board, NSW,
    89–90
anti-discrimination legislation, 88,
    89–91, 164
Atkins, S., 12
Australian Bureau of Statistics, 98, 111
Australian Council of Social Service
    (ACOSS), 44
Australian Council of Trade Unions
    (ACTU), 165
Australian Labor Party (ALP), 71,
    73,74,91
Australian School Commission, 11

Bachrach, P., 137
Bahro, R., 6
Bailey, M., 30
Bakunin, M., 4
Baldock, C., 12, 13, 23, 27
Baratz, M., 137
Barrett, M., 18–19, 20, 21, 27, 67, 68,
    133
Beasley, M., 138

Benn, M., 110–11
Bennett, G., 9
Bernard, J., 12
Bidmeade, I., 118–19
Blackburn, J., 10
Bonepath, E., 12
Bradley, D., 93, 138
Brennan, D., 26, 60–1, 71, 72, 79, 80,
    81, 124
Broom, D., 12
Brophy, J., 12
Brown, R., 68
Brownmiller, S., 107, 108
Bryant, A., ix, 40
Bryson, L., 5, 153, 167
bureaucracy, 30–2, 46, 90, 91–2
    bureaucratisation, 143–9; and
        feminists, 144–5, 147–9
    and gender, 48–51, 53, 135–6
    masculinisation, 42, 48–51, 53
Burgmann, M., 165
Burns, A., 66, 68
Burstyn, V., 6, 25, 27
Burton, C., 6, 20, 25–6, 27, 31, 100,
    101, 145, 159
Burvill, C., 30

Callenan, S., 110
Cass, B., 9, 12, 13, 23, 27
cathexis, 37–8
centre-based day care (community
    child care; long day care), 61, 71,
    75, 77, 86
Chapkis, W., 7
child care
    access priorities, 80–1, 84
    cost, 80–2, 84
    feminist perspectives on, 59–60, 63,
        78, 84–6
    and femocrats, 70–5, 83–6
    main types, 60–1

and mothering, 67–9
in and around the state, 70–83
Child Care Act (1972), 71, 74
Child Care Amendment Act (1985), 81
child care workers, 60–1, 70, 81–3, 85
child protection lobby, 116–17
children's rights, 118–19, 122–8
Children's Services Office, 79
child sexual abuse, 39, 114–29
 feminist perspectives on, 114–17, 121, 122–4, 126–7
 the Furler Report, 119–28
 the legal system, 126–8
 state responses, 117–28
Chodorow, N., 26, 66
Clark, G.M., 4,43
Clarke, J., 138, 139
class
 and partriarchy, 23–6
 and state, 19–23
 see also state, traditional theories
Clegg, S., 30
'Cleveland case', 39, 114
Clough, J., 83
Cockburn, C., 48, 87
Coleman, M., 72, 75, 138
Coleman Report (Review of Early Childhood Services in South Australia), 75–9
Collinson, D., 48
Comer, L., 37, 62
comparable worth, 31
Connell, R.W., 15, 34, 37
Court, D., 72
Cox, E., 70–1, 79, 98, 135
Craney, J., 116–17, 124
Crimes (Sexual Assault) Amendment Act (1981), 108–9, 111–13
Cullen, J., 68
Curthoys, A., 69, 87

Daly, M., 16, 149
Deacon, D., 5, 8, 48
Deem, R., 12
Deer, M., 4, 43
Department for Community Welfare, SA, (DCW), 114, 118–19, 125–7
Deveson, A., 64, 116
'domestic labour' debate, 20, 63

Donzelot, J., 17–19
Dowse, S., 7, 65, 71, 72, 74, 135–6, 139
dual systems theory, 23–5
Dunkerley, D., 30
Dworkin, A., 149

Edwards, M., 15, 80
Eekelaar, J., 124
EEO Management Plans, 94–5
EEO practitioners, 94–5, 101–3, 166; *see also* femocrats
Ehrensaft, D., 69
Eisenstein, H., 7. 30–2, 95, 144, 153
Eisenstein, Z., 17, 23–4, 25, 27, 28, 103
Encel, S., 63–4
Enderby, K., 134–5
Engels, F., 4,35
Ennew, J., 122–3
Equal Opportunities Branch, SA, 95
equal opportunity (equal employment opportunity; EEO), 15, 16, 45, 46, 87–8, 91–5, 159, 166
 criticisms, 96–100
Equal Opportunity Tribunal, NSW, 30
equal pay, 88–9, 97–8
Equal Rights Amendment, ix, 15–16, 28, 29
Esping-Anderson, G., 41

family, 21, 64–9
 income distribution in, 80
 and sexual violence, 113, 115–16, 117, 121, 122–6
 and state, 22, 70
family day care, 61, 70, 75, 77, 81
Fasteau, M.F., 7
fathers
 child care, 60, 69
 child sexual abuse, 115, 116, 122, 125–6
feminism
 ambivalence towards the state, 11–12, 157–8
 and bureaucratisation, 144–5, 147–9
 and child care, 59–60, 63–5, 78, 84–6

and child sexual abuse, 114–17, 121, 122–4, 126–7
and equal opportunity, 91–5
and mothering, 61–70, 84–5, 115
and sexual violence, 106–8, 128–9
and the state, ix–xi 54–5, 135–7, 150–51, 156–60
see also femocrats; liberal feminism; radical feminism; socialist feminism
feminist bureaucrats *see* femocrats
feminist discourse theory, 19
femocrats, xi, 32, 42, 51–2, 94–5
and child care, 70–5, 77, 83–6
criticisms, 101–3, 160
definition, 133–4
emergence, 134–8
and established bureaucracy, 138–40
and rape law reform, 112
relations with women's movement, 140–3, 153–5
and the state, 151–5
strategies, 70–2, 88–100, 128–9, 144–5, 152–3, 167
Ferguson, K., 34, 51–2, 144
Fernbach, D., 36
Finch, J., 5
Finkelhor, D., 117
Firestone, S., 10, 62
Foucault, M., 17–19
Frankel, B., 4, 6
Franzway, S., 15, 160
Fraser government, 73–5, 142
Freeman, C., 75
'Free Men', 39
Friedan, B., 16–17
Friedland, R., 41
Fry Report, 72
Fugard, A., 33
Furler, E., 119
Furler Report (Final Report of the SA Government Task Force on Child Sexual Abuse), 117, 119–28

Gamarnikow, E., 50
Game, A., 20, 27, 28, 38, 63, 87, 163
Gardiner, J., 26
Garrett, C., 11
Gatens, M., 66
Gavron, H., 63

Gay Liberation, ix, 11–12, 18, 19, 40-1; *see also* homosexuality
gender
and bureaucracy, 30–2, 48–51, 135–6, 144–5
history, 38, 40
and public/private dichotomy, 6, 38, 40–1
and state, 7–13, 35–7, 92, 117
theories, 34, 66, 163–4
gender relations and the state, 52–5, 159
Gerstenberger, H., 22
Gerth, H., 143, 147, 152
Giddens, A., 4
Glezer, H., 136–7
Gluckman, M., 38
Golder, H., 9
Goodnow, J., 12, 68
Gorton, J., 63–4
Gough, I., 149–50
Gramsci, A., 4
Grant, J., 30, 31, 42, 151
Graycar, A., 72
Greer, G., 106–7
Grelb, J., 12
Griffin, S., 108
Grimes, D., 80, 82
Gross, E., 18
Grove, D., 5

Habermas, J., 15, 34, 46
Hague, D., 166
Haines, J., 144
Hall, P., 9, 87
Hall, S., 105, 150
Hargreaves, K., 68
Harper, J., 67
Hartmann, H., 24
Hawke government, 78, 79–83, 91, 94, 141, 167
Healey, J., 76, 78
Held, D., 3, 150, 152
Heverner, N. K., 12
Hirsch, J., 22
Hogget, B., 12
homosexuality, 10, 40, 46, 51, 92
Hui-Chen, W. L., 36
Hunter, M., 84
Hurford, C., 80, 81

Interim Children's Commission, 73, 74
Irving, D., 53

Jamrozik, A., 68
de Jasay, A., 6
Jones, B., 106
Jones, E., 38
Jones, M.A., 80
Justice, B. and R., 117

Kelly, J., 64
Kelly, P., 16
Kinder, S., 59
Kindergarten Union (KU), SA, 76-8
Klein, D., 38
Knights, D., 48
Knuttila, M., 3,16
Kollantai, A., 4
Krieger, J., 152

Lamphere, L., 6
legitimation, 15, 54, 73-4, 82, 161
Lenin, I., 4
liberal feminism, 14-17, 53
    equal employment opportunity, 96, 100, 102-3
    influence on femocrat strategy, 158-60, 162
    and rape, 108, 109-13
Lightfoot, D. H., 118
Lipman-Blumen, J., 12
Little, G., 38
Lowe, J., 15
Lynch, L., 7, 51, 102

Macciocchi, M.A., 38
McCulloch, D., 93, 138
McIntosh, M., 18-19, 22, 27, 67, 68, 124
MacKinnon, C., ix, 27, 29-30, 107, 113, 149
MacLeod, M., 116, 120, 123
Magarey, S., 30
Marcuse, H., 19
Marsh, J., 165
Matthews, T., 147
Mejane, 140
Mellaart, J., 36

men, 35-6, 39
    and child care, 66, 69, 85
    and equality, 97, 101, 145
    and sexual violence, 107-8, 110, 113, 115-17, 123
Mercer, J., 136-7
merit, 92, 99-100
Mill, J. S., 3-4
Miller, P., 23, 51
Mills, C. W., 143, 147, 152
Mitchell, J., 25
Mitchell, S., 42, 160
Moore, S., 69
'Morgan' decision, 110-11
Morgan, R., 10, 110
Mosse, G. L., 38
mothering
    changing feminist ideas on, 61-70; rejection, 62; as work, 63
    and child care, 67-9
    ideologies, 67, 68, 85
mothers
    and child sexual abuse, 115, 120, 126
    participation in child care, 60
    working mothers, 67-8, 78, 80-1
    see also mothering
Mothers' Child Care Preferences, 68
Mowbray, B., 5

Naffine, N., 110, 111-12
National Association of Community Based Children's Services (NACBCS), 79
National Women's Advisory Council, 89
National Women's Refuge Conference (1986), 85
New Right, 4-5, 40, 74-5, 161
Nicholson, J., 68

Oakley, A., 63
Oakley, M., 30
O' Brien, M., 27
O' Donnell, C., 9, 26, 45, 48, 60-1, 72, 79, 80, 87, 115-16, 124, 166
Offe, C., 4, 34, 149-50, 152
Office of Child Care, 75, 82
Office of Equal Opportunity in Public Employment NSW, 8, 48, 96

Office of the Status of Women, 45
Office of Women's Affairs, 139
Ollif, L., 7, 48, 50
Organisation for Economic
  Cooperation and Development
  (OECD), 12
O'Shane, P., 42, 138

Palley, M., 12
Pateman, C., 3, 12, 18, 96
patriarchal state, 27–32, 149
patriarchy, 23–32, 90, 151
  and class, 23–26
  and family relations, 114, 122,
    125–6
  as procedure, 29–32
  and sexual violence, 106–8, 112, 129
Patton, P., 42
Perkins, R., 9
Petchesky, R., 12
Phillips, A., 133. 142
Poole, R., 42, 74
Poulantzas, N., 4, 7
Powell, S., 81
preschools (kindergartens), 61, 71–2,
  75
Pringle, R., 20, 38, 63, 87, 113, 141,
  142, 163
Project Care, 72
public/private distinction, 6, 21, 38,
  40–1, 64, 137, 164
  and child care, 70, 86
  and sexual violence, 106, 124
Public Service Association (PSA), 166

radical feminism, 34, 66, 162
  on rape, 107–8, 109–10, 116
Ramirez, F., 29
rape
  definitions, 109–12
  and feminism: liberal feminism,
    108, 109–13; radical feminism,
    107–8, 109–10, 116
  ideologies, 110, 111, 113
  law, 29–30
  law reform, 28, 108–14
Rape Crisis Centre, NSW, 109
Rawls, J., 3
Reich, W., 19
Reid, E., 11, 72, 138, 139, 140, 166–7

Reiger, K., 52
Rich, A., 66, 108
Rich, R., 149
Richards, L., 67
Riley, D., 85
Ritson, R. J., 127
Roe, J., 17
Ronalds, C., 44, 87
Rosaldo, M., 6
Rowbotham, S., 59, 64–5, 86
Royal Commission on Human
  Relationships, 64, 116
Rubin, G., 25
Ruggie, M., 12, 28
Rush, F., 116
Russell, D., 109
Russell, G., 60, 67, 69
Ryan, L., 72
Ryan, P., 83, 139
Ryan, S., 42–3, 89, 93

Saraga, E., 116, 120, 123
Sawer, M., 87, 91, 139
Schechter, S., 116, 147–8
Scott, D., 117
Scutt, J., 28, 39, 112, 121, 129, 142
Segal, L., 64–5, 69
Segers, M., 53
Sex Discrimination Act (1984), 44, 89
sex role theory, 15–16
sexual division of labour, 8, 20, 87
sexuality, 105, 110, 112–13
  of children, 116, 122–3
sexual violence
  state intervention, 105–6, 128–9
  feminist perspectives on, 106–8,
    114–16
Shaver, S., 25, 44
Sichtermann, B., 112
Simms, M., 12, 140
Singh, J., 140–1
Sklar, H., 24
Smart, C., 12
socialist feminism, 19–22, 24–6, 64,
  97, 163–4
Socialist Feminist Conference (1987),
  141, 164
Social Welfare Commission, 72, 138
Spence, C. H., 30

Stanton, E. C., 30
state
    and class, 19–23
    and the family, 22, 70
    and feminism, ix–xi, 14–17, 54–5,
        70
    feminist ambivalence towards,
        11–12, 157–8
    gender composition: personnel,
        7–8, 42, 47–52, 138, 153; policy
        studies, 12–13; subjects, 9–10
    homosexuality, 10, 19
    legitimation, 15, 54, 73–4, 82, 161
    and patriarchy, 23–32
    power relations, 37–41, 52–5
    and public/private dichotomy, 6, 21
    traditional theories: exclusion of
        gender, 3–6; social contract
        theories, 3; liberal, 3–4; socialist,
        4, 7, 22–3, 149–50
    see also child care; equal
        employment opportunity;
        femocrats; sexual violence
state structure, 21, 35, 37–8, 41–7
Stern, L., 110, 112
Stretton, H., 5
structure and agency, 34–5
Summers, A., 28, 62, 102, 107, 109
Sutcliffe, G., 35–6, 37
Sweeney, T., 60, 68, 75, 80–1
Sydney Women's Shelter (Elsie), 107

Tancred-Sheriff, P., 30, 31, 42, 151
theories of regulation, 17–19
Theweleit, K., 38
Thornton, M., 63, 96–7
Touche Ross Report, 82
trade unions, 83, 164–6
Trotsky, I., 4

Ursel, J., 25, 38

Walby, S., 21
Waldby, C., 115
Walkowitz, J., 40
Wallace, M., 89
Wallsgrove, R., 84–5

Walsh, P., 82
Ward, E., 113, 121
Wearing, B., 67
Weber, M., 16, 19, 30, 37, 46, 142,
    146–7, 148, 152
Weedon, C., 19, 66
Weeks, J., 18, 19, 40, 105
Wells, L., 144
West, R., 148
White, K., 138, 139
Whitlam government, 71–3, 135,
    137–9
Wighton, R., 75
Wilenski, P., 91
Wills, S., 97, 99
Wilson, E., 21, 23, 27, 106
Wilson, P., 111
Wishart, B., 65
woman suffrage, 38–9
Women Against Incest Collective,
    115, 118
Women and Labour Conferences, 65,
    66, 141, 164
Women and Politics Conference
    (1975), 20
Women's Advisory Board, NSW, 11
Women's Christian Temperance
    Union, 39
Women's Co-ordination Unit, NSW,
    11, 87, 93
Women's Electoral Lobby (WEL), 15,
    71, 89, 94, 109, 111–12, 122, 136–7,
    138, 147
women's movement *see* feminism
women's work, 5, 23, 24, 25
    and job evaluation, 31, 99, 159
    see also child care workers; equal
        employment opportunity;
        state, gender composition
Woolf, V., 135, 145
working women, 8, 73, 87
Working Women's Charter, 91, 164
Wran government, 91, 95, 108–9
Wright, E. O., 41

Zhukov, G., 50
Ziller, A., 14, 16, 96, 98, 101

DATE DUE			
GAYLORD			PRINTED IN U.S.A.